REVOLUTION AND EVOLUTION IN PRIVATE LAW

The development of private law across the common law world is typically portrayed as a series of incremental steps, each one delivered as a result of judges dealing with marginally different factual circumstances presented to them for determination. This is said to be the common law method. According to this process, change might be assumed to be gradual, almost imperceptible. If this were true, however, then even Darwinian-style evolution—which is subject to major change-inducing pressures, such as the death of the dinosaurs—would seem unlikely in the law, and radical and revolutionary paradigms shifts perhaps impossible. And yet the history of the common law is to the contrary. The legal landscape is littered with quite remarkable revolutionary and evolutionary changes in the shape of the common law.

The essays in this volume explore some of the highlights in this fascinating revolutionary and evolutionary development of private law. The contributors expose the nature of the changes undergone and their significance for the future direction of travel. They identify the circumstances and the contexts which might have provided an impetus for these significant changes.

The essays range across all areas of private law, including contract, tort, unjust enrichment and property. No area has been immune from development. That fact itself is unsurprising, but an extended examination of the particular circumstances and contexts which delivered some of private law's most important developments has its own special significance for what it might indicate about the shape, and the shaping, of private law regimes in the future.

Revolution and Evolution in Private Law

Edited by
Sarah Worthington
Andrew Robertson
Graham Virgo

• HART •
PUBLISHING
OXFORD AND PORTLAND, OREGON
2018

Hart Publishing
An imprint of Bloomsbury Publishing Plc

Hart Publishing Ltd
Kemp House
Chawley Park
Cumnor Hill
Oxford OX2 9PH
UK

Bloomsbury Publishing Plc
50 Bedford Square
London
WC1B 3DP
UK

www.hartpub.co.uk
www.bloomsbury.com

Published in North America (US and Canada) by
Hart Publishing
c/o International Specialized Book Services
920 NE 58th Avenue, Suite 300
Portland, OR 97213-3786
USA

www.isbs.com

HART PUBLISHING, the Hart/Stag logo, BLOOMSBURY and the Diana logo are trademarks of Bloomsbury Publishing Plc

First published 2018

British Library Cataloguing-in-Publication Data
A catalogue record for this book is available from the British Library.

ISBN: HB: 978-1-50991-324-4
ePDF: 978-1-50991-326-8
ePub: 978-1-50991-325-1

Library of Congress Cataloging-in-Publication Data

Names: Worthington, Sarah, editor. | Robertson, Andrew, 1966-, editor. | Virgo, Graham, editor.

Title: Revolution and evolution in private law / Edited by Sarah Worthington, Andrew Robertson, Graham Virgo.

Description: Portland, Oregon : Hart Publishing, 2018. | Includes bibliographical references and index.

Identifiers: LCCN 2017042043 (print) | LCCN 2017042424 (ebook) | ISBN 9781509913251 (Epub) | ISBN 9781509913244 (hardback : alk. paper)

Subjects: LCSH: Civil law. | Common law. | Comparative law. | Civil law—Great Britain. | Civil law—Australia.

Classification: LCC K623 (ebook) | LCC K623 .R48 2018 (print) | DDC 346.41—dc23

LC record available at https://lccn.loc.gov/2017042043

Typeset by Compuscript Ltd, Shannon

Preface

This volume contains a selection of essays originally presented at the Eighth Biennial Conference on the Law of Obligations, which was co-hosted by Melbourne Law School and the Cambridge Private Law Centre and held at Downing College Cambridge in July 2016. We are very grateful to Hart Publishing, Freshfields Bruckhaus Deringer, Herbert Smith Freehills and Travers Smith for their sponsorship of the conference, Imogen Dodds, Emily Gordon, Robert O'Sullivan, Rajiv Shah and Elizabeth Virgo for their assistance as student volunteers, and Daniel Bates for his very capable IT support. Thanks are also due to all of the presenters, chairs and participants in the Obligations VIII conference for their contributions to the discussion of the theme of this collection and the individual chapters. Finally, we would like to thank Caitlin O'Neil for her editorial assistance.

Sarah Worthington, Andrew Robertson and *Graham Virgo*
May 2017

Table of Contents

DOCTRINES

Table of Cases

Table of Legislation

Australia

Canada

China

European Union

France

Germany

Ireland

Switzerland

United Kingdom

Notes on Contributors

TT Arvind is Professor of Law at Newcastle Law School.

Elise Bant is Professor of Law at the University of Melbourne.

Hugh Collins is Vinerian Professor of English Law at the University of Oxford.

Paul S Davies is Professor of Commercial Law at University College London.

Sir Terence Etherton is Master of the Rolls of England and Wales and an honorary Fellow of Corpus Christi College at the University of Cambridge.

Paula Giliker is Professor of Comparative Law at the University of Bristol.

Amy Goymour is University Senior Lecturer in Land Law and Fellow of Downing College at the University of Cambridge.

Steve Hedley is Professor of Law at University College Cork.

David Ibbetson is Regius Professor of Civil Law at the University of Cambridge.

Hector MacQueen is Scottish Law Commissioner and Professor of Private Law at the University of Edinburgh.

Joanna McCunn is Lecturer in Law at the University of Bristol.

Mitchell McInnes is Professor of Law at the University of Alberta.

Pauline Ridge is an Associate Professor of Law at the Australian National University.

Andrew Robertson is Professor of Law at the University of Melbourne.

Helen Scott is Professor of Private Law at the University of Cape Town.

Jenny Steele is Professor of Law at the University of York.

Graham Virgo is Professor of English Private Law and Fellow of Downing College at the University of Cambridge.

Sarah Worthington is Downing Professor of the Laws of England and Fellow of Trinity College at the University of Cambridge and a Professorial Fellow at the University of Melbourne.

FOUNDATIONS

1

Revolution and Evolution in Private Law

SARAH WORTHINGTON

REVOLUTIONS IN THINKING are common in many disciplines. Early discoveries that the world was round, that planets rotate, that there is a space–time continuum or a genetic code are all familiar examples. Examples could also be given in philosophy or in economics, as great thinkers have advanced their own ideas and, once digested, these have forever altered our perceptions of the realities around us.

But revolutions in legal thinking, especially revolutions in private law, are of a different order. Such revolutions affect not only how we see the world around us, but also what that world around us then becomes. Legal rules do not simply describe reality; they govern it. This means that a shift in legal rules necessarily effects a shift in legal reality. Scientists joke that only in economics is it possible to say that when the facts do not fit the theory, the facts fail—or, in economic terms, when the market does not match the model, the market fails. But the joke does not work for lawyers. For lawyers, the model *does* govern the market, however imperfectly: our accepted legal rules, and any shifts in those rules and their paradigms, work to define or redefine the reality that is sought.

That makes any investigation of legal revolutions, or of gentler evolutionary shifts in legal thinking, all the more interesting. These revolutions and evolutions can profoundly affect the rules by which we live. Given this, it might seem useful to have a greater awareness and a clearer understanding of how these changes have come about in the past and who or what has driven them. We might then be more alert to their arrival in future. It is in this general sense of 'important change' that we use the terms 'revolution', 'evolution' and 'paradigm shift' throughout this book.[1]

[1] 'Paradigm shift' is defined in the OED in wide terms: 'a conceptual or methodological change in the theory or practice of a particular science or discipline; (in extended sense) a major change in technology, outlook, etc.'. Of course, whether these important changes are truly revolutionary or paradigm shifting might be endlessly debated, especially if the Kuhnian view of 'necessarily incommensurable' paradigms is taken literally: see TS Kuhn, *The Structure of Scientific Revolutions*, 4th edn (Chicago, University of Chicago Press, 2012). But a less restrictive view is more common: many scientific discoveries are widely regarded as revolutionary without meeting this test, the most obvious example being our ability to hold fast to the ideas of both Newtonian and Einsteinian mechanics, using each in different contexts.

This focus on revolutions and evolutions in private law provided the theme for the biennial obligations conference, Obligations VIII, held in Cambridge in July 2016, and the chapters in this volume represent a selection of the many compelling papers presented over those three days. The endeavour was initially inspired by a pointed question from a Cambridge scientist: what is the next big thing in law—what is the next *Goff and Jones*?[2] By perfect coincidence, the conference itself coincided with the 50th anniversary of the publication of *Goff and Jones*, and chapter 10 of this volume is a multi-authored assessment of the international impact of that body of scholarship and its descendants.

Since this volume is not styled as a murder mystery, the 'whodunnit' in delivering these revolutionary and evolutionary shifts can, and perhaps should, be revealed at the outset. Indeed, such acknowledgment may be even more necessary than in a murder mystery, since the chapter authors themselves rarely allocate credit or blame very precisely; the 'who' or 'what' that impels revolutionary or evolutionary change is typically left hanging in the air. But if these chapters reveal anything, it is that there is both radical change and long-standing continuity aplenty. That should not surprise.

If the staccato findings from these chapters can be generalised across the domain of private law, they confirm that the essential components of legal change are provided by a triple cocktail of novel aspirations from transacting parties and their lawyers pushing the boundaries, bringing novel cases on strong facts with creative pleadings and persuasive and innovative arguments to justify them. This must then be followed by sympathetically inventive responses from judges faced with their claims. Finally, the rigorous but imaginative gaze of scholars is then needed to depict clearly the bare bones of the newly conceived structural framework. Without all three—the parties and their lawyers, the judges and, finally, the scholars—there would be no revolution or evolution at all; we would still be firmly entrenched in a society with primitive social rules rather than one with a sophisticated legal infrastructure delivering the rule of law.

Once this process of change is set in motion, however, any clarified structure emerging from scholarly analysis is then itself a source of further change. Inventive parties will typically seek to use the new framework to support an ever-growing range of aspirations. These attempts will in turn require the judges to decide whether the newly conceived additions are still part of the newly renovated structure or part of some other structure, or perhaps part of an entirely new and independent structure that has yet to be created. This assessment and its clarification is invariably aided—indeed, impelled—by scholars, who will then revise, modify, streamline or qualify the earlier structures and formulate the new ones. And so the cycle continues. Recognition of structures as independent units (as with contract or tort) and the separation of new structures when the need becomes plain (as with unjust enrichment) are vital to effective development of a coherent legal system able to support the rule of law, treating like cases alike.

As noted, the most dramatic modern illustration of the emergence of a new and independent legal structure is found in the development of the law of unjust

[2] R Goff and G Jones, *The Law of Restitution* (London, Sweet & Maxwell, 1966).

enrichment. That development undoubtedly began with judges delivering particular forms of remedies in compelling cases before them, but the torch that shed light on the ideal direction of travel was undoubtedly the book by Robert Goff and Gareth Jones, *The Law of Restitution*.[3] Those remarkable lawyers, one a judge the other an academic, but both scholars of the highest order, have had a profound impact on the development of the law of unjust enrichment throughout the common law world. In chapter 10, four academics and a senior judge reflect on the impact of this early scholarship on the law of unjust enrichment in different jurisdictions, and contemplate what might lie ahead.

But new and independent structures are not the only route to evolutionary success. The reverse may also be important in developing coherent frameworks. In short, sometimes logical routes to synthesis must be identified, rather than routes to novelty and independence. This tension between the two outcomes is clearly reflected in current debates in the area of estoppel. The question raised is whether this part of the law merits its own independent structure, with its own distinctive analytical paradigms, or whether it is simply an area delivering nuanced adjustments to other more substantial structures. In chapter 9, Andrew Robertson tracks the swings in this debate and argues that equitable estoppel is best regarded as *sui generis*, meriting its own independent structure.

Alternatively, sometimes the structures may be ancient and plain for all to see, but still enormously difficult. For example, we continue to struggle with the most appropriate analysis of property, especially equitable property. Many ancient and modern scholars have tried their hand at describing its essential structural framework, aiming to provide something accurate, useful and coherent. Here we include yet another attempt. In chapter 11, Sarah Worthington revisits the very different development followed by the common law when compared with its civilian counterparts, and suggests that a great deal turns on the common law's willingness to ignore the *numerus clausus* principle and instead to track a boldly innovative route in allowing for different forms of sharing of assets, with those shared interests including not only interests by way of possession, but also interests under a trust, a charge or an equity of redemption. She suggests that the creation of these *shared* interests and their protection is the real job—and the real genius—of the common law's rules on property, and might best describe the essential structural framework of English property law.

The process of drawing out accurate legal structures is never simply a depiction of the past, seeing that landscape with greater clarity and thus being able to provide better mechanisms for future work in the field. It is instead its own process of development. This was the point made earlier about the special nature of legal paradigm shifts. That reality and its impact are discussed to great effect in chapter 4 by TT Arvind. He contrasts 'revolution' by radical rupturing and 'revolution' by turning full circle and revisiting the past. He considers which approach the law can and should adopt, concluding that the rupturing model is inherently disruptive and destructive, and the cyclical one impossible and undesirable. Instead, he suggests, we ought to confine ourselves to a more modest local and practical focus, one designed

[3] ibid.

simply to deliver a better adaptation of law to the needs of a particular society at a particular point of time.

But that cannot be all. This process of seeing structures more clearly, whether old or new, and whether reconfigured or simply stripped bare, and doing so precisely as all the great textbook writers did, is surely not the only generator of paradigm shifts. Roman law and the Napoleonic Code were equally paradigm shifting. In chapter 3, Hector MacQueen considers the input from authors, codifiers and merchants, and paints a fascinating picture of their contributions to revolutions. He hangs his storyline for these different actors on a discussion of the potential implications of Harold Berman's two volumes on *Law and Revolution*.[4] MacQueen's chapter questions Berman's exclusion of classical Roman law from the story of the emerging Western legal tradition, and warms to the possibility of internal legal revolutions generated by authors of law books, starting with the second-century Roman jurist, Gaius, and moving more recently to codifiers of law. Many of these modern developments still deploy the same structures first set out by Gaius, notably the analysis of all private law as being about persons, things and actions (although with obligations lying within things[5]). The conclusion reveals a lively mix of revolutionary forces in which Berman may have played a part, but in which Roman law, canon law, juristic thought, mercantile practice and codification all played a possibly more significant role.

Indeed, the influence of merchants and other users of these legal structures, combined with the effect of the social climate in which they operated, can have a profound impact on the pace and direction of the law's development. Notable instances are highlighted in several chapters in this volume. For example, in chapter 5, Jenny Steele presents an extended and illuminating discussion exploring the 'revolution' meted out by the particular mix of social change which effectively reconfigured society's approach to security and risk over the late nineteenth and early twentieth centuries. With the benefit of hindsight, this 'risk revolution' might have provided a battleground for contests over the cost of achieving security and who should bear the responsibility for it. By contrast, the modern and growing rhetorical emphasis is on responsibility, with a diminishing emphasis on security in many areas. These pendulum swings may have profound ramifications for the legal rules which are required to support any change in structure.

In similar vein, in chapter 6, Steve Hedley notices that the wide availability of modern insurance makes a nonsense of most of tort's traditional justifications. It follows that tort no longer punishes or deters wrongs, or deals even-handedly between claimant and defendant. Instead, the defendant simply drops out of the picture in favour of the employer or insurer. The current legal structure, however, simply refuses to acknowledge the new reality. Responsibility for this state of play would seem to fall squarely on the theorists, who continue to emphasise deterrence, personal responsibility and corrective justice, none of which has much to do with

[4] HJ Berman, *Law and Revolution: The Formation of the Western Legal Tradition* (Cambridge, MA, Harvard University Press, 1983).

[5] A point which might bear reflection in the context of Worthington's chapter 11.

tort's bureaucratic reality. The lesson for scholars is plain, but still we seem unable to respond appropriately.

This is not the only failing portrayed in the developing structure of modern tort law. In chapter 7, Paula Giliker assesses the dramatic modern movements in the doctrine of vicarious liability. She examines why these changes occurred, noting in particular the impact of a series of child sexual abuse scandals which came before the courts from the 1990s onwards. However heinous the underlying intentional torts, vicarious liability remains deeply controversial in many contexts. It imposes strict liability on innocent defendants for the torts of others, typically on an employer for an employee's wrongs, and so conflicts with notions of corrective justice and fault-based reasoning. On the other hand, it fits rather neatly with the growing pragmatism of an insurance culture and its focus on risk-based liability. Judged from that perspective, justice and fairness might demand remedies from the employers. Notably, and rather oddly, this is regardless of the absence of any failure to take reasonable care on the employer's part. This leads Giliker to wonder whether the relevant tort doctrines have escaped their initially limited contexts and evolved so rampantly that they may undermine the certainty and structure of the common law of torts.

These policy-motivated areas of tort law are not the sole contexts where such pressures can be seen. Even in the interpretation of contracts, Joanna McCunn shows in chapter 8 that the path of development has been a sustained and slow evolution in better formulating the rules of interpretation so as to deliver what has been a consistent and long-standing focus on more precise identification of the parties' real intentions. Viewed from this perspective, some of the recent ructions in doctrine appear to be nothing of the sort, reminding us that the long view matters.

Although we may be able to see that merchants and private users of the legal system play their own very significant part in impelling the legal regime towards particular conclusions, can we say anything predictive about the likely direction of travel? It is noticeable that across the developed world, whether in common law or civilian jurisdictions, the law of obligations delivers much the same ends regardless of the route taken to reach the destination. Somehow, we all have some unerring compass directing efforts towards a particular equilibrium point which seems to represent a fair outcome on a given set of problematic facts. David Ibbetson, in chapter 2, tracks this development in obligations through the ages. He reminds us that, viewed from close range, even small changes may appear revolutionary. By contrast, however, his chapter takes the broad sweep of private law history from 2000 BC, and from that perspective he demonstrates that only very few instances of change may be seen as truly revolutionary, and even those typically attract a measure of scepticism. Amongst the perhaps doubtful possibilities, Ibbetson includes land registration, possibly the formulation of a law of unjust enrichment, the statutory introduction of limited liability companies and the even earlier invention of equitable interests as a series of secondary property rights, although he notes that even these have their parallels with ideas of double ownership in the context of feudal relationships.

This vision of continuity across time and geography in the law of obligations is not so apparent in the law of property. There the legal rules are traditionally seen as pursuing distinctive paths: not only has the common law struck its own radical and distinctive course when compared with civilian jurisdictions, but the common law has also done the same when compared with equity. The truth of this vision is assessed by Pauline Ridge in chapter 12. She contrasts two strands of thinking which dominate modern debates: first, the revolutionary narrative initiated by Birks, which seeks integration of common law and equity, and adopts the language of simplicity, order, fixed categories, predictability of outcome, certainty and clarity; and secondly, the counter-narrative, originating in the courts rather than the academy, which seeks to maintain the difference between common law and equity, and adopts the language of nuance, complexity, metaphor, gradations and spectrums in which the haphazard evolution of the law is acknowledged. The question, then, is which prevails, or which should prevail. This is difficult. As Ridge notes, both sets of characteristics are present to different degrees in every aspect of both sets of legal rules, so how are preferences to be assessed? Moreover, even if such preferences are identified, what then follows?

Whatever the difficulties just aired, each one of these distinct structures, if they have been properly identified as distinct, will have certain unique features which compel a degree of analytical segregation one from the other—as in contract, tort and unjust enrichment. Yet unless we wish to descend into a complete muddle of incoherent obligations and remedies, we must not lose sight of the fact that, taken together, these structures must also form a unity, providing a coherent legal regime which works productively for society. This means that issues such as concurrent liability across each of the independent structures must be addressed, and mechanisms adopted to ensure that outcomes are rational, with explanations that can be clearly articulated. In chapter 13, Paul Davies addresses the problem of concurrent liability, tracing its evolution across different strands of private law.

Equally, this complex legal edifice cannot be seen simply as providing rights and imposing obligations on parties. It also gives them access to a legal system that will support and enforce their rights. Deciding when that access might be barred is crucial. The consequences for individuals may be profound. One area that has troubled judges and scholars for some time is the area of illegality. In many common law jurisdictions, courts and legal scholars have had several attempts at describing a workable system. In chapter 14, Graham Virgo examines the latest efforts from the UK Supreme Court. He assesses the Court's judgment on its own terms and also according to its wider significance. The latter is important, since it reveals a great deal about the nature of judging in the twenty-first century. Virgo suggests that it is this which might prove to be the most revolutionary aspect of the case: its stated preference for discretion over rule may have significant implications for the development of other parts of the law of obligations.

Finally, and by way of closing the loop and revisiting the idea that revolutionary and evolutionary ideas emerge by virtue of the force of the social environment, mediated by legislators and judges and analysed and depicted by scholars, the final chapter in the book is by Hugh Collins. It takes us outside the zone of domestic law to look at a number of EU Directives which have been described as constituting EU contract law. Collins suggests that these 'techno-laws' adopt a novel, highly instrumental paradigm or conception of law-making which national private law systems find hard to accommodate and integrate. Collins argues that ensuing revisions to the sources of EU contract law necessarily entail what in Hart's terminology amounts to a change in the Rule of Recognition, or a revolution. The result, argues Collins, has been a profound reorientation of the legal system towards both a rights-based and a post-national conception of the sources of contract law.

Lawyers should perhaps be more keenly aware of some of the phenomena explored in this book. Society operates within a legal framework. That is in part what we mean by the rule of law. How our legal structure develops and changes is worth examining. This volume suggests that users, codifiers, judges and scholars all have an essential role to play. Those amongst them who take on responsibility for defining the shape of the legal structure need to pay close attention to what each is doing and work in tandem to deliver the best possible societal outcome. A strong rule of law depends upon it.

2

Revolutions in Private Law?

DAVID IBBETSON

I. INTRODUCTION

IT IS ALL too easy when looking at legal changes in close-up to reach a conclusion that some change or other is a revolutionary change. Every chapter in this volume has the word revolution or revolutionary in the title, so we might be forgiven for thinking that private law was at a time of almost unprecedented radical change. Yet looked at in a rather longer perspective, things can look rather different. An apparently revolutionary change seen from that standpoint may be no more than a relatively minor change of direction or a clarification of what had been happening for some time.

Looking at English private law over the last few decades, the one change that might genuinely deserve the description of revolutionary is probably that of land registration, though even there one cannot be sure. Tenure and estates are still there, though the former may have lost its relevance once the practical effects of escheat disappeared, and the effective disappearance of the estate tail may have reduced that latter almost to vanishing point. It may be that the changes we see are really just consequences of changes in the ways in which one can prove title. It may be that the formulation of a law of restitution or unjust enrichment—whatever one's preferred name—was revolutionary, but time alone will tell.[1] Somewhat earlier, we get the statutory introduction of limited liability companies; this has had an enormous effect on the legal landscape since the middle of the nineteenth century, though it is noteworthy just how much of the law is still formulated in language more appropriate to morally responsible individuals than to large corporations without souls. But is there much else that can truly be called revolutionary since the middle of the nineteenth century? Even going back a lot further, we might argue that the one truly revolutionary introduction into English law was the development of a secondary series of property rights as equitable interests, whether under a trust or otherwise, coming to be treated as having effects *in rem* and not simply *in personam*. Yet even there the more scholarly medieval and early-modern lawyers were perfectly familiar with ideas of double ownership, *duplex dominium*, in the context of feudal relationships.

[1] See section IV below.

Even if we turn our attention across the English Channel, where the codifications of the nineteenth century might truly claim to have constituted revolutionary breaks with the past, we need to be a little sceptical. True, they brought about some changes in the law, though I think not many in private law, but in general their aim was to codify the law that was in force and not to change it. They may have been revolutionary in terms of legal method, but not significantly so in terms of the law itself. Even where some earlier law had not been embodied in the code it might nonetheless continue to exercise its influence: the availability of the Roman *actio de in rem verso* in French law, though not in the Code Civil, is just one example among very many.[2] Continuity is a much more potent feature in the law than revolution. This is especially so when dealing with high-level general principles, and it is only at this level that we can realistically think of revolutions.

If we look simply at the main features of the law of tort and contract in the last couple of centuries, I see nothing but a more or less gradual evolution, even if their sphere and mode of application have shifted enormously. Unjust enrichment may be different, though even there the story has some odd twists. This is not to deny that there have been changes which might be regarded as revolutionary in the creation of these features of our modern law, but the major steps may have been taken a very, very long time ago.

I will begin by framing my assumptions. I will start in Mesopotamia some 4000 years ago, then move on through Greece, Rome and medieval Europe to the modern world.[3] There are very clear commonalities between the legal texts of the Sumerians, the Babylonians and the Hittites in Anatolia.[4] That these peoples were ethnically distinct was of no matter. It is therefore highly unlikely that we are looking at different versions of customary law so much as a legal cultural unity in the territories to the east of the Mediterranean. There is a gap of many hundreds of years before we have any legal inscriptions in Greece, but they too seem to fit into the same cultural unity.[5] So too, I think, do the theorising works of Aristotle, once we make allowance for the fact that he is not just giving us formulations of legal rules. Continuity between Greece and Rome may be controversial, but I think that anyone who approaches the evidence with an open mind, rather than with the assumption that the Romans had an inherent genius for law which was different from every other people's, will see the connections. And I hope it goes without demonstration that there is at least some continuity between Roman law and modern European law—and England is part of Europe for these purposes—as well as between Aristotle and modern legal thinking.

[2] Section IV below.

[3] Note that in any paper aiming to cover a large subject area over four millennia it is impossible to give full references for every detail. Where possible, I have instead referred to my own publications, wherein fuller references can be found. In particular, for English law I have made heavy use of one of my own works: D Ibbetson, *Historical Introduction to the Law of Obligations* (Oxford, Oxford University Press, 1999).

[4] These are most conveniently collected in MT Roth, *Law Collections from Mesopotamia and Asia Minor* (Atlanta, Scholars Press, 1995).

[5] The epigraphic texts are conveniently accessible in I Arnaoutoglou, *Ancient Greek Laws* (London, Routledge, 1998).

Already in Sumeria at the start of the second millennium BC there are features in the early texts which look eerily familiar. Just one example will suffice. I neglect my land adjacent to yours and you make a formal demand that I fortify it, which I ignore; a thief gets through the land, enters your house and steals from it. I am liable to you.[6] The result may perhaps be different from the one we would reach today, and we cannot see the reasoning process that went into it in Sumeria, but the rule may well be a generalisation from a real case. That the question could have been asked at all and given an answer in these terms cannot fail to suggest that the Sumerians' legal world might not have been all that different from today's.[7]

I want to focus on the three principal strands of the law of obligations as we think of it today: tort, contract and unjust enrichment. All of these have roots going back long into the past, and in each of them we can trace particular moments at which fundamentally important steps have been taken, steps which with hindsight we can regard as revolutionary in the formation of our modern map of the law. But even the map itself is not all that modern. The same tripartite division is found in Hugo Grotius' introduction to Dutch law, published almost 400 years ago,[8] which should perhaps be seen as one of the most influential books in our legal history.

II. THE LAW OF TORT

We should begin with the heartland of the law of tort: compensation for injuries to the person or damage to property.[9] We might guess that any legal system would have to deal with this sort of wrongdoing, though they might do so in different ways, and the underlying fact patterns will be more or less identical. If we go back to the earliest bodies of law where there is enough evidence to reach anything like a conclusion, those of Babylon in the eighteenth century BC, we can make out something astonishingly like our idea of negligence: the causation of injury as a result of a failure to take reasonable care.[10] However, it is not articulated as such. There is no suggestion that anybody would have generalised a rule or stated it at any abstract level. Indeed, it is only when dealing with more complex situations, such as where the alleged wrongdoer was acting under a mistaken belief,[11] that we can see the idea of negligence at work. Most Babylonian provisions which we would regard as dealing with torts simply refer to payments to be made by a person bringing about a particular

[6] *Laws of Lipit-Ishtar* 11.
[7] cf *Smith v Littlewoods Organisation Ltd* [1987] AC 241.
[8] H Grotius, *Inleidinge tot de Hollandsche Rechts-Geleerdheid*, F Dovring, HFWD Fischer and EM Meijers eds (Leiden, Leiden University Press, 1963), 3.1.9, 3.1.14–16.
[9] I have essayed some remarks on this topic from a comparative perspective in the following works: 'Harmonisation of the Law of Tort and Delict' in R Zimmermann (ed), *Grundstrukturen des Europäisched Deliktsrechts* (Baden-Baden, Nomos, 2003) 83; 'How the Romans Did For Us: Ancient Roots of the Tort of Negligence' (2003) 26 *University of New South Wales Law Review* 25; 'Wrongs and Responsibility in Pre-Roman Law (2004) 25 *Journal of Legal History* 99; 'Historical Reflections on the Compensation Culture' (2005) 1 *Journal of Law* 100. What follows is largely derived from these.
[10] Ibbetson, 'Wrongs and Responsibility', ibid 100–13.
[11] *Laws of Hammurabi* 226, 227.

injury: breaking a limb, knocking out a tooth or putting out an eye, for example.[12] Here, there is no reference to any fault standard, but it would be wildly anachronistic to treat these as examples of strict liability. No doubt the paradigm case was an intentional act, but liability might stretch wider than this; just how much wider it is quite impossible to say.[13] It may be that the payments specified were fixed penalties, but it is more likely that they should be treated as indications of appropriate payments and reflect the relative seriousness of harms to the body; that said, there is no hint in most of these texts that there was expected to be any assessment of actual loss, though one provision in the *Laws of Hammurabi* clearly points to the duty of an aggressor to pay the victim's medical expenses.[14]

A thousand years later, Hellenistic legal inscriptions reveal the same approach: a certain type of injury is associated with a certain penalty—no fault criteria are specified, and there is no way of telling whether the penalty should be seen as a fixed sum or as a guideline. Aristotle provides relatively sophisticated thinking about responsibility for wrongdoing, out of which our ideas of criminal responsibility have grown; but that is another story. When we come to his analysis of corrective justice, however, I can see no requirement of fault or blame at all, but it is clear within this framework that the person who causes loss is required to compensate up to the level of the loss, to redress the inequality which has been brought about, to put the victim in the position that he or she would have been in had the loss not been caused. The language is unmistakably that of what we should think of as unjust enrichment, and Aristotle says as much: 'We talk in such cases, even if perhaps inappropriately in some, about the "gain" accruing to the assailant and the "loss" suffered by the victim.'[15]

Whether the difference between the legislated texts and Aristotle's ethical discourse was any more than a reflection of the two very different genres need not concern us, but we see the same shifts of ideas in Rome, and there it was undoubtedly a development in the law. The Twelve Tables, of the middle of the fifth century BC, retained the traditional approach of identifying a fixed penalty for specific types of harm,[16] whereas the *lex Aquilia*, probably of the third century, was focused on giving compensation for the loss caused.[17] Moreover, it specified that the loss must have been caused wrongfully, though what was meant by this was left undefined. Scholars have puzzled over the name of the delict created by the *lex Aquilia*, apparently *damnum iniuria*, which Peter Birks passionately (and in my view correctly)

[12] Ibbetson, 'Wrongs and Responsibility', above n 9, 101–108.

[13] 'There may be an instructive parallel with the contemporaneous Hittite law of homicide, where we find a penalty for killing [*sic*], but then reduced penalties for killing by accident and killing in hot blood': *Hittite Laws* 1–4, *Edict of Telepinu* 49. Some modern commentators treat this as constituting a division into murder and manslaughter, but this completely misrepresents the nuances of the Hittite.

[14] *Laws of Hammurabi* 206.

[15] Aristotle, *Nicomachean Ethics*, C Rowe trans (Oxford, Oxford University Press, 2002) V.4 1132a11–12.

[16] M Crawford (ed), *Roman Statutes* (London, Institute of Classical Studies, 1996) 604–608, Table 1.13–15.

[17] ibid 727.

translated as loss wrong.[18] We have in the name the crystallisation of nearly all of our modern understanding of the law, the bringing together of the two fundamental features of wrongful conduct and the causation of loss.

We should not underestimate the importance of this explicit focus on wrongfulness, but the really significant shift came about a little later; we see it most clearly in the Institutes of Gaius in the middle of the second century AD. The concept of wrongfulness is clarified; it means, we are told, deliberately or blameworthily, *dolo* or *culpa*;[19] a few decades later, exactly the same clarification is attributed to Ulpian.[20] We need to pause on this for a few moments. This grafting of blameworthiness onto the notion of wrongfulness looks to have come about in the first century BC, and it seems to have had two dimensions. For some, perhaps, it was already the appropriate standard to trigger liability,[21] but its main function was almost certainly to cut through problems of causal responsibility. One particular text, read by many generations of law students, brings this out well.[22] A slave goes to a barber to be shaved. Some boys are playing ball nearby. One of them kicks it, it hits the barber and jolts his hand, and the slave's throat is cut. The earliest jurist mentioned in the text says that liability is imputed to whichever of them was to blame. This is obvious, the modern lawyer might think; but it might not have been so obvious in the first century BC. Later, jurists referred to in the text discussed *who* was to blame, not *whether* someone was to blame, but in this oldest stratum of the text it was enough to say that whoever was to blame was liable.

We see the same in another very well-known text.[23] Young men are practising with javelins, a javelin hits a slave and the slave dies. As we have it, the text is concerned with identifying whether the thrower was at fault and therefore liable, but we can penetrate behind the legal text. The situation looks to have been a standard discussion point in schools of rhetoric,[24] and if we go back into the writings of the Greek orators where almost exactly the same case was discussed we see that the original question was not whether the thrower was guilty of any wrongdoing, but *who* it was that had killed.[25] And this depends on blameworthiness, which determines who the death ought to be imputed to, just as in the barber case.

Whatever the origins of the focus on blameworthiness, its status in the developed Roman law of the Empire was clear: those who had caused harm would be liable if and only if they had been at fault. What was meant by fault was not defined, but was treated on a case-by-case basis.[26] It included overenthusiastic chastisement by a teacher, doing a job without the necessary skill or strength and, in a text with a long

[18] cf A Rodger, 'What Did *Damnum Iniuria* Actually Mean?' in A Rodger and A Burrows (eds), *Mapping the Law* (Oxford, Oxford University Press, 2006) 421.
[19] G.3.211.
[20] D.9.2.5.1.
[21] D.9.2.31, referring to the late-Republican Quintus Mucius.
[22] D.9.2.11.pr.
[23] D.9.2.9.4.
[24] Plutarch, *Pericles*, 36.3.
[25] Antiphon, *Second Tetralogy*, 3.
[26] G MacCormack, 'Culpa' (1972) 38 *Studia et Documenta Historiae et Iuris* 123.

history ahead of it, failing to foresee or guard against what a reasonable man would foresee or guard against.[27] A Byzantine commentator on Roman law essentially said that it was a matter of policy.[28] By the reign of the Emperor Justinian, as the ancient world was creeping into the medieval, the formal law in much of Europe could be stated very simply: you were liable if you caused loss by your fault, and should compensate the victim to the extent of the loss.

Roman law was, of course, built upon and developed by the medieval church and by the scholars in the universities, but this core of the law of delict was largely untouched, apart from scouring away some technical, largely procedural, rules of Roman law and generalising what counted as loss.[29] Liability depended on fault, though what fault was was ill-defined. In places in continental Europe, especially around northern Italy, Spain and southern France, much Roman law was substantially integrated into legal practice, though legal practice in the law of delict seems to have been largely independent of Roman law. There was a far greater concern with the victim's loss than with the other party's wrong, with clear traces of group liability where the perpetrator of an injury could not be identified, and more generally a sense that it was the causation of loss that generated the duty to compensate without any explicit requirement of fault.[30]

We may see this in two ways, both of which may be right. On the one hand, it may simply be that the legal texts are formulated in causal terms, since it was the fact of injury that was the primary trigger for liability, though fault of some sort might have been relevant (for example, through allowing a defence of accident). On the other, it may reveal that there was a tension between the Roman model of the *lex Aquilia* and the Aristotelian idea that the person who suffered harm at the hand of another should be compensated, the former dominating in scholarly law, the latter in practice.

The tension between the two models of liability came to a head explicitly in sixteenth-century Spain, more particularly in the University of Salamanca. Here, scholars wrestled to reconcile Roman law with Aristotle's ethical philosophy, as interpreted by Saint Thomas Aquinas, whose *Summa Theologica* was the subject of renewed attention at the time and the object of prolonged and careful analysis.[31] The tension between the two models was transparent. Moreover, it could be seen as a conflict between law and ethics, not just between Justinian and Aquinas. The Spanish writers set about trying to resolve this conflict, and, in the best scholastic tradition, the arguments of the individual scholars are not always easy to follow. But the solution appears to have been to shift the focus of the Aristotelian theory away

[27] D.9.2.6, 8.1, 31.

[28] Schol ad Bas 60.3.11, in FH Lawson, *Negligence in the Civil Law* (Oxford, Clarendon Press, 1950) 180.

[29] R Zimmermann, *The Law of Obligations* (Cape Town, Juta, 1990) 1017–30.

[30] See, eg, the French customs of Beauvais, 841: P de Beaumanoir, *The Coutumes de Beauvaisis of Philippe de Beaumanoir*, FRP Akehurst trans (Philadelphia, University of Pennsylvania Press, 1992) 305.

[31] H Thieme, 'Qu'est-ce que nous, les Juristes, doivent à la Seconde Scolastique Espanole' in P Grossi (ed), *La Seconda Scolastica nella Formazione del Diritto Privato Moderno* (Milan, Giuffrè, 1973) 7; D Ibbetson, 'Historical Reflections', above n 9, 114–17.

from redressing the loss towards redressing the wrong. The final step was apparently taken not by a Spaniard but by a Belgian working in the Thomistic tradition, Leonard Lessius, better known today as someone who was able to demonstrate the consistency of modern business practices with orthodox Roman Catholic theology.[32]

What might have been a slightly obscure byway of theology came into the legal mainstream when Lessius' ideas were taken up by Hugo Grotius, in his *Law of War and Peace*. For Grotius, wrongdoing was defined as 'any fault whatsoever',[33] locking in place the role of blameworthy conduct at the heart of thinking about what we would call tort. Crucially, *The Law of War and Peace* became the classic source of natural law thinking in the early-modern period, hence forming the interface between law and moral philosophy. Only one more step needs to be noted here, taken by Grotius' successor as the intellectual leader of the Natural Law movement, Samuel Pufendorf. His concern was with what we ought to do rather than when we ought to be liable for doing what we ought not to do, and he formulated this in terms of a duty to take reasonable care not to injure others by our acts,[34] picking up on the Roman text that treated the failure to guard against what a reasonable man would guard against as a form of blameworthiness. In Pufendorf's work, it was given far greater force as the very definition of blameworthiness.[35]

English law was to pick up on Pufendorf's thinking in the eighteenth century, but before this the situation was very similar to what we see elsewhere in Europe.[36] What we think of as tortious liability was concentrated in the action of trespass; unsurprisingly so, since both 'tort' and 'trespass' just mean 'wrong'. We can almost summarise trespass in one sentence from a fifteenth-century case: 'If a man suffers damage it is right that he be compensated.'[37] One can only *almost* summarise, since there were defences, which went a long way to define the scope of liability. Some of these defences touched on fault, but it was always the *plaintiff's* fault: I did hit you as alleged, for example, but I am an innkeeper who was ejecting you from my bar when you were being disruptively drunk, so it was your own fault.[38] Practically nowhere in trespass do we see any concern with the *defendant's* fault.

The emergence of an alternative way of framing the action of trespass, known as trespass on the case, did bring the defendant's fault to the surface, but this was largely concerned with situations where injury had been done in the course of carrying out a contract.[39] Here, the defendant's fault was the element that made the conduct actionable; it could hardly have been wrongful if he had done no more

[32] L Lessius, *De Justitia et Jure* 2.7.6.

[33] H Grotius, *De Jure Belli ac Pacis*, BJA De Kanter-Van Hettinga Tromp ed (Aalen, Scientia Verlag, 1993) 2.17.1.

[34] S Pufendorf, *De Jure Naturae et Gentium* 3.1.6; D.9.2.31.

[35] B Kupisch, 'La Responsibilità da Atto Illecito nel Diritto Naturale', in L Vacca (ed), *La Responsibilità Civile da Atto Illecito nella Prospettiva Storico-comparatistica* (Turin, G. Giappichelli, 1995) 123.

[36] See n 31 above.

[37] '*Hulle v Orynge (The Case of Thorns)* (1466)' in Sir John Baker, *Baker and Milsom, Sources of English Legal History*, 2nd edn (Oxford, Oxford University Press, 2010) 369.

[38] Ibbetson, above n 3, 59–60.

[39] SFC Milsom, 'Trespass from Henry III to Edward III' (1958) 74 *LQR* 407; Ibbetson, above n 3, 48–56.

than what he had agreed with the victim that he would do. It might also have been appropriate where the defendant was only indirectly responsible for some damage or injury, as where a man's servants who were guarding a fire were caused to flee, as a result of which the fire got out of control.[40] However, we do not find many examples of the use of trespass on the case in this latter context until the end of the seventeenth century, and they become common only in the eighteenth.

By the 1760s, this fault-based pleading was being aligned with Pufendorf's moral philosophy, and we find it stated as a rule in an introductory law book, Francis Buller's *Introduction to the Law Relative to Trials at Nisi Prius*, that there is a duty to take reasonable care not to injure one's neighbour.[41] The borrowing of this idea from Pufendorf, either directly or indirectly, is abundantly clear. For Buller, it was a general principle of tortious liability, though technically it applied only to trespass on the case and not to trespass, which was still formulated in straightforwardly causal terms subject to defences. However, for procedural reasons, in the eighteenth and nineteenth centuries tortious litigation was increasingly channeled into trespass on the case,[42] so that trespass itself became just one minor tort alongside others. The duty to take the care that would be taken by a reasonable man had, by the middle of the nineteenth century, become a near-canonical statement of the content of the law of tort, and it is still trotted out as such by examination candidates today.

Yet, we still see undercurrents of earlier ideas at work. Do we really, in the tort of negligence today, assess the defendant's conduct against that of a reasonable person, or do we in truth not just ask whether the defendant was to blame in the same way as a classical Roman lawyer would? Do we not bring policy factors into play in assessing fault, as our Byzantine commentator on the Roman law suggested? And in the light of the Aristotelian and Thomistic approach to corrective justice, not to mention the medieval action of trespass, we can hardly see today's so-called compensation culture as especially modern.

Where are the revolutions in all of this? In our more sceptical moments, we might sometimes think that the closest we get to a revolution is that associated with a turning wheel as we have reinvented the past. But in the story outlined above there do genuinely look to have been one or two revolutionary changes. The Romans' collocation of loss and wrong in the *lex Aquilia* of the third century BC looks to have been one such change, and their explanation of wrongfulness in terms of blameworthiness another. The bringing together of fault-based and loss-based reasoning in the decades before Grotius was another, and it may be that the equation of fault with the failure to take the care of a reasonable man was a fourth, though that might have been no more than a false step which it has taken some time to recover from. Perhaps the only revolutionary step specifically in England was the integration of the common law shaped in terms of the forms of action into the highly principled structure of Pufendorf and the seventeenth-century natural lawyers in the 1700s. The rest is

[40] *Berden v Burton* YB T 6 Ric II (Ames Foundation) 19 (1382).

[41] F Buller, *An Introduction to the Law Relative to Trials at Nisi Prius* (London, H Woodfall and W Strahan, 1767) 24.

[42] MJ Prichard, 'Trespass, Case and the Rule in Williams v Holland' [1964] *CLJ* 234; Ibbetson, above n 3, 155–63.

noise, tiny perturbations in an otherwise smooth fabric of law, or small adjustments in the law to reflect different social or economic circumstances.

Before turning to the other main institutions of the law of obligations, a more general point needs to be made. It can hardly be said that a survey beginning in Mesopotamia 4000 years ago and hopping through Greece, Rome, Italy, Spain and Holland before arriving in England in the eighteenth century is a proper approach to legal history.[43] The historian cannot leap from place to place and millennium to millennium and pretend that he or she is portraying a history of legal reality. But ideas do leap from place to place and do cross millennia, and what we have here is an overview of a part of the history of ideas; and at this level of abstraction, we are more concerned with ideas than with legal rules in any concrete sense.

III. CONTRACT

Practically all our evidence for a 'law of contract' in the Ancient Near East comes from documents written on clay tablets.[44] These provide a good deal of evidence about contracts, but tell us practically nothing about any general conception of contract. Moreover, the picture they paint is almost inevitably imperfect, since purely oral transactions will have left no trace. However, it is possible to make some general observations. First, though most (but not all) of the documents are sealed, neither the seal nor the document itself had any more than symbolic effect: other people's seals might be used; sometimes the seal was substituted by the impress of the hem of a garment or of a fingernail; and, most importantly, the document was always framed as evidence of an antecedent oral transaction taking place before witnesses.[45] Secondly, insofar as we can deduce any common feature from the acts described in these documents, it is that the parties invariably swore oaths not to resile from the transaction, and it was probably this that gave the contract its effective force.[46] If there had been some underlying feature which made the obligation binding, we might have expected that there would not always have been a reference to an oath. Thirdly, the general word for 'contract' in Akkadian, *riksātum*, is cognate with the verb 'to bind', and shows merely that there was some conception of a binding obligation without carrying any connotation of what it was that made the obligation binding.[47] Exactly the same is true of Hittite *ishiul* and the Hebrew *berith*.[48]

[43] DJ Osler, 'The Fantasy Men' (2007) 10 *Rechtsgeschichte* 169.
[44] R Westbrook (ed), *A History of Ancient Near Eastern Law* (Boston, Brill, 2003).
[45] J Renger, 'Legal Aspects of Seals in Ancient Mesopotamia' in M Gibson and RD Biggs (eds), *Seals and Sealing in the Ancient Near East*, Bibliotheca Mesopotamica vol 6 (Malibu, Undena Publications, 1977). For the symbolism, see M Malul, *Studies in Mesopotamian Legal Symbolism* (Kevelaer, Butzon & Bercker, 1988) especially 299–309.
[46] For the centrality of oaths in treaties, see in particular Westbrook, above n 44, 748.
[47] S Greengus, 'The Old Babylonian Marriage Contract' (1969) *Journal of the American Oriental Society* 505, 506–12; note the reference at 509, showing that the word was capable of encompassing a unilateral gift.
[48] GJ Botterwick and H Ringgren, *Theological Dictionary of the Old Testament* (Grand Rapids, Erdmans, 1977) 253–79, with comparisons with other ancient systems.

The Greeks may have taken a step further. Writers of the fourth century BC refer to an Athenian law that agreements (*homologiai*) were binding,[49] though the legal sources do not point to there having been any distinct remedy to enforce the agreement.[50] So far as the future was concerned, the most important source of Greek thinking was not the Athenian law but Aristotle's *Nicomachean Ethics*.[51] Aristotle has nothing like a general theory of contract, but the building blocks of what we think of as contract are here. There are three pertinent features. First is the virtue of truth-telling.[52] Nothing is said here about the keeping of promises, and Aristotle expressly excludes from his discussion of truth-telling the wrong associated with the failure to keep an agreement.[53] Nonetheless, it is easy to see how one might see keeping one's word as a form of truth-telling, and this step was taken by later thinkers such as Cicero and Thomas Aquinas. Secondly, there is the idea of justice in exchange.[54] This was an aspect of corrective justice, here involving voluntary transactions, the counterpart of the involuntary transactions lying at the root of our law of tort.[55] Both the language and the logic here point to the basis of responsibility lying in the reciprocal relationship between the parties and the equality or proportionality in the exchange, but it is expressly picking up on the earlier reference to agreement in the *Ethics*.[56] We may understand it, therefore, specifically in terms of a reciprocal agreement, such as a sale. Third in Aristotle's mix is the virtue of liberality, bringing (reasonable) gift-giving into his picture.[57]

Roman law was more forthcoming. By the end of the Republic, we find a formal mechanism for undertaking to do something in the future, known as the *stipulatio*, which was based on a formal question and answer almost certainly accompanied by some conventional gesture or act, such as a handshake or the sharing of a drink. Its gestural background is eerily similar to modern practice, though we would not today insist on the congruence of words. Alongside this, there were a number of common situations recognised by law as imposing duties: sale, partnership and the like.[58] As yet, however, there was no unified category. The first move in this direction was probably taken by the influential jurist Labeo in the early Empire. Transparently adopting a Greek idea, and using the Greek word, he identified a common thread in *synallagma*, that is, reciprocity or exchange.[59] That was enough to bring

[49] Hyperides, *Athenogenes*, 13; Demosthenes, *Evergus and Mnesibulus*, 77 (and elsewhere); DM MacDowell, *The Law in Classical Athens* (London, Thames & Hudson, 1978) 140, 152.

[50] S Todd, *The Shape of Athenian Law* (Oxford, Oxford University Press, 1993) 255; E Carawan, 'The Athenian Law of Promise and Agreement' (2006) 46 *Greek, Roman and Byzantine Studies* 339.

[51] J Gordley, *Philosophical Origins of Modern Contract Doctrine* (Oxford, Oxford University Press, 1991) ch 2. I follow the thrust of Professor Gordley's analysis, though differ from him in some points of detail.

[52] Aristotle, above n 15, IV.7, 1127a–1127b.

[53] Gordley treats breaking one's word as pertaining to another virtue 'as well', but that is not supported by the text: above n 51, 11.

[54] Aristotle, above n 15, V.4, 1131b–1132a.

[55] See n 15 above.

[56] See n 54 above.

[57] Aristotle, above n 15, IV.1, 1119b–1120a.

[58] A Watson, *The Law of Obligations in the Later Roman Republic* (Oxford, Oxford University Press, 1965) chs 3–9.

[59] See n 55 above.

together most of the informal relationships that generated liability, but it did not encompass the *stipulatio*, for the formal question and answer imposed an obligation only on the person answering, not the questioner. A different line was taken in the early second century by a rather obscure jurist, Pedius. For him, all contracts, even the *stipulatio*, were based on agreement, *consensus*.[60] A few years after this, Gaius, in his *Institutes*, was able to distinguish between the verb form of contracting an obligation and the noun form of an obligation based on contract. A person receiving money paid by mistake and a person receiving money as a loan equally contracted an obligation to repay, but only the borrower entered into a contract. Contract, the noun, was based on agreement.[61] *Synallagma* emerged as the basis of certain agreements being classified as enforceable contracts,[62] but it did not displace agreement as the essential element of the genus contract.

Cicero, almost certainly reflecting late Stoic thinking, had written of the virtue of doing what one had agreed to do, extending the Aristotelian virtue of truth-telling.[63] Hence Pedius' analysis of contract as consensus aligned with Stoic moral theory: it was not merely the law that agreement created duties, it was consonant with justice that they should do so. It should be stressed that the duty was based on the parties' agreement, their *consensus*, their joint act, rather than on the unilateral promise of the person who was becoming obliged. They agreed *with* each other, rather than one making a promise *to* the other. There was still scope for the purely unilateral promise, *pollicitatio*, but only in the context of undertakings making charitable gifts to municipalities.[64] Non-charitable *pollicitationes* only took effect on acceptance.

Aristotle's ideas were further developed in the thirteenth century by Thomas Aquinas. Like Cicero, he built on the virtue of truth-telling, but where Cicero had written of the duty to keep an agreement, Aquinas wrote of the duty to keep one's promise or vow, with the focus purely on the person obliged.[65] The lawyers' approach was the same as in Roman law, that there had to be *consensus*, agreement, except in the case of the charitable promise or *pollicitatio*; otherwise a promise, or offer, only generated an obligation when it was accepted and thereby lost its unilateral character.[66] There was, therefore, a subtle tension between the promise-based analysis of Aquinas and the lawyers' analysis of the agreement as the basis of liability. This tension came to the fore in the works of those Spanish writers of the sixteenth century who based themselves on Aristotle and Aquinas, and were hence more or less committed to the virtue of keeping promises, but who tried to reconcile this with Roman law.[67] The dominant view of the Spanish writers was that the promise was binding in itself, but in the early years of the seventeenth century—in the southern

[60] D.2.14.1.3. For Pedius, see W Kunkel, *Die Römischen Juristen* (Cologne, Böhlau, 2001) 168–69.
[61] G.3.90–91.
[62] WW Buckland, *Textbook of Roman Law*, 3rd edn, PG Stein ed (Cambridge, Cambridge University Press, 1963) 521.
[63] Cicero, *De Officiis*, 1.7; see n 53 above.
[64] D.50.12.3.
[65] Aquinas, *Summa Theologica*, II.II 110 a.3 ad 5, 88 a.3.
[66] eg *Summa Silvestrina*, sub verb *pollicitatio*.
[67] Gordley, above n 51, ch 4; W Decock, *Theologians and Contract Law* (Leiden, Nijhoff, 2013) 162–92.

Netherlands rather than in Spain, but in the same tradition—Leonard Lessius asserted that the promise only created binding obligations when it was accepted.[68] Lessius focused on the Roman *pollicitatio*,[69] which he said only became binding on acceptance. He gave two reasons. First was that this was what had been said by Antonio Gomez to be indigenous Spanish law,[70] second was the Roman rule that an obligation only arose from the mutual consent of the parties.[71] In this way, he was able to align the Thomistic enforceability of promises with the Roman rule of the enforceability of mutual agreements. Importantly, though, Lessius followed the orthodox Thomist line that a promise was the deliberate taking on of an obligation of fidelity, not simply an undertaking to do something,[72] so that the obligation stemmed from the promise itself and the acceptance merely determined the moment at which it arose. Grotius followed Lessius, like him citing Gomez.[73] The legal and ethical formulations were in practice identical; it did not matter whether they were shaped in terms of an agreement, an accepted promise, or—as Savigny, following Kant, would later have it—as giving effect to the joint wills of the parties.[74]

Conceptually, things are slightly more complex in England in the Middle Ages. The core of the idea of contract was the agreed exchange of one thing for another, with the emphasis on exchange rather than agreement.[75] This is brought out well in the inaccurate etymology of the word *contractus* as *actus contra actum*, an act against an act, rather than *contrahere*, to bring together. But there was another word, covenant, in Latin *conventio*, which was based on the parties' agreement, their coming together, from the Latin *convenire*. Already in the early fourteenth century the covenant could be described in very Roman terms as the mutual assent of two parties.[76] The sixteenth century added to the confusion, with the introduction of liability on the face of it based on the breach of a promise. But promise here was interpreted as meaning agreement, even if it rarely mattered in practice whether it was the defendant's promise or the parties' agreement that was said to be the basis of liability.[77] As early as 1600, it was said that the obligation was based on communication and acceptance, reflecting the language of the Spanish lawyers.[78] Furthermore, the only promises which generated liability were those which had been made on good consideration—generally speaking, those where something had been given broadly in exchange for the promise.[79] But all of this was really bundled up behind the forms of action, so that the theoretical basis behind liability was nearly always concealed.

[68] Lessius, above n 32, 2.18.6.
[69] See n 67 above.
[70] Gomez, *Variarum Resolutionum* (Antwerp, 1624) 2.9.1. The work first appeared in 1552.
[71] D.2.14.1.
[72] Lessius, above n 32, 2.18.1, esp ad 5.
[73] Grotius, above n 33, 335 n 4.
[74] Gordley, above n 51, ch 7.
[75] JL Barton, 'The Medieval Contract' in Barton (ed), *Towards a General Law of Contract* (Berlin, Duncker & Humblot, 1990) 15–37.
[76] *Waltham Carrier Case* (1321) in Baker and Milsom, above n 37, 319.
[77] Ibbetson, above n 3, 139–40.
[78] *Milles v Rainton* (1600) Harvard Law School MS 2076, fol 48.
[79] D Ibbetson, 'Consideration and the Theory of Contract' in Barton, *Towards a General Law of Contract*, above n 75, 67–123.

It was only in the eighteenth century that this mess began to be sorted out and only in the nineteenth that the process was completed. Thomas Hobbes's social contract theory might have had a part to play, for there the power of the sovereign was created by the mutual agreement of the citizens and no more.[80] These ideas were picked up by Jeffrey Gilbert in the first decade of the century, but his work was not printed and presumably had little influence. The first step in print towards a general notion of contractual liability was seemingly taken by an obscure lawyer called Henry Ballow in the 1730s, who wrote about contracts and subdivided his treatment under chapter headings copied from Pufendorf's big book on Natural Law, *De Jure Naturae et Gentium*, hence reflecting the promissory theory which could be traced back to Aristotle and had come through Grotius.[81] The reality of his theory was that contracts were based on agreements, and it could be said that agreements were made by an offer, or proposal, and acceptance. It was an attractive model. Marriage was based on agreement, too, and young men had been proposing to young women since time immemorial, and young women had been accepting. The one thing that did not fit was the English idea of consideration. It could hardly be ignored, so it was included in a chapter whose heading was *not* lifted from Pufendorf and was to some extent marginalised. Blackstone was able to give this a superficially respectable lineage. All contracts in Roman law, he said with consummate inaccuracy, were based on this idea of exchange, citing in a footnote an impeccable Italian work.[82] The Italian work did not say this, of course, only that *almost* all Roman contracts depended on exchange, which was true. A decade or so after Blackstone's *Commentaries* were published, English lawyers were introduced to the work of the Frenchman Robert-Joseph Pothier, written in the orthodox natural law tradition. His *Traité des Obligations* was translated into English in 1806, and thereafter, as Brian Simpson demonstrated in the 1970s, his treatment of contract came to shape the English lawyers' doctrines of contract.[83] The centrality of agreement, offer and acceptance was now fixed in place. Consideration was still an embarrassment, but where Pothier had referred to mutual agreement his translator added a lengthy note on mutual consideration. So it fitted in after all, though it was to become increasingly irrelevant as a matter of practice.[84] If the law of contract was based on agreement, or giving effect to the mutual will of the parties, it hardly mattered whether this was based on any element of exchange.

To add to the confusion, most significant undertakings up to the eighteenth century were made in writing and under seal, and these were not known as contracts at all. Rather, they were deeds, bonds or, more generally, obligations. They had their own rules, and were unaffected by this integration of natural law thought. In the nineteenth century, however, they came to be thought of as a type of contract. Chitty's Treatise on Contracts, first appearing in 1826, was on the law of contracts

[80] M Lobban, 'Thomas Hobbes and the Common Law' in D Dyzenhaus and T Poole, *Thomas Hobbes and the Law* (Cambridge, Cambridge University Press, 2012) 39, 46–53.
[81] Ibbetson, above n 3, 218. The attribution to Ballow is uncertain.
[82] Bl Comm 2.444, 445, citing GV Gravina, 'De Iure Naturali, Gentium et Duodecim Tabularum' in *Opera Omnia* (Leipzig, 1717) 153.
[83] AWB Simpson, 'Innovation in Nineteenth Century Contract Law' (1975) 91 *LQR* 247.
[84] Ibbetson, above n 3, 236–39.

not under seal. Though excluded from the book, undertakings by sealed document were clearly contracts. The next major textbook on contract, that of Charles Addison in 1847, did include contracts under seal, but at first under separate sub-headings. By 1860, these subdivisions had disappeared, leaving just contracts, though where there was a sealed document special rules of proof and the like might apply.

Where is the revolution in this? There is a good deal of attraction in James Gordley's conclusion that all we see is the Aristotelian theory being gradually stripped of its supporting theoretical framework, though the Roman heritage must not be underestimated. It is probably the case that Pedius' foregrounding of agreement as the source of contractual liability was revolutionary, though it may be that we know too little of what went before him. Bridging the divide between the unilateral promise and the bilateral agreement was important in a way, though it made little or no real difference. The reorienting of English law along the natural law path looks significant, though I suspect that most of the apparently new elements were there already, hidden behind the forms of action.

This picture is probably right, but it is probably the wrong picture. The law of contract is primarily concerned with facilitating the making of binding obligations, not with solving problems *ex post facto*. The apparent rules of contract law provide the framework within which contracts fall to be drafted, and almost any rule can be contracted around. Take privity of contract, a fairly rigid rule up to 1999. But any competent draftsman who put his mind to it could find ways round it, provided that no unborn children were involved, by 1240 at the latest. Even where there was not a contract put together by a competent draftsman, a moderately imaginative pleader could normally get around the rules, though once juries began to disappear from contractual cases in the nineteenth century it might have been a shade more difficult to pull the wool over judges' eyes. Sticking with the rules, even if they appeared superficially inconvenient, was even a positive virtue, insofar as it allowed parties a greater measure of predictability in making their arrangements. Perhaps we shouldn't expect to see revolutionary changes in real-world contract law.

IV. UNJUST ENRICHMENT

The third head of the modern law of obligations is unjust—or perhaps unjustified—enrichment. The roots of this lie clearly in the theory of corrective justice in Aristotle's *Nicomachean Ethics*; a man unjustly making a gain and causing another loss should be required to disgorge his gain.[85] The idea was picked up by Cicero, reflecting late-Republican Stoic thought: 'For a man to take something from his neighbour and profit from his neighbour's loss is more contrary to nature than death or poverty or pain or anything else that can affect our person or our property.'[86] This generated two near-identical texts of Pomponius in Justinian's Digest. The closer to Cicero was

[85] Aristotle, above n 15, V.4, 1131a1–a8.
[86] Cicero, above n 63, 3.21.

D.12.6.14: 'For it is by nature fair that nobody should enrich himself at the expense of another.' D.50.17.206, from a different book of Pomponius, was the same, but added that it was only wrongful enrichments that were unfair.[87] These were probably little more than throwaway maxims, sounding good but carrying little substantive weight. Greater importance, as a matter of legal reality, attached to the *condictio*, the remedy which can be described accurately as a claim for a debt. Some debts arose out of agreements, and once contract was expounded in terms of agreement, these claims were easily categorised as contractual. The rest were divided into several sub-forms in the Digest, most generally where property was transferred without a valid ground (the *condictio sine causa*), and here there was no contract. Probably the commonest case, claims for the repayment of money paid in the erroneous belief that it was due were brought together in Justinian's Institutes with some other non-contractual claims where the obligation was described as having arisen *quasi ex contractu*, as if from contract,[88] the most important being *negotiorum gestio*, the unrequested management of another's affairs. Formally unconnected to these, but substantively linkable, was the *actio de in rem verso*, where a master might be held liable to disgorge a benefit which had come to him under a contract made by his slave or a member of his family. The building blocks of the modern law are all here.

In the Middle Ages, there was no inevitable friction between lawyers and theologians in this area. For Aquinas, there was a wide general principle that one should not be unjustly enriched, based both on Aristotelian and Stoic thinking and on biblical texts,[89] the same principle (in narrower form) as had been found in the Digest. Canon law followed this approach, recognising a wide discretion in the judge to do justice.[90] The approach of the civil lawyers was rather different. In the twelfth century, the radical Martinus Gosia would straightforwardly apply the general principle, based on a broad notion of *aequitas*, but the dominant line was to use the principle to justify an extension or restriction of an existing remedy, not as an independent source of obligation.[91] The sixteenth-century Spanish scholastics operated within Aquinas's framework, a framework adopted by Hugo Grotius, most obviously in his *Introduction to the Law of Holland*.[92] Here, the source of obligation is twofold, promise and inequality, with the latter further subdivided in effect into inequality caused by wrongdoing and inequality caused by unjust enrichment.[93]

Cutting across this, though, was Justinian's category of obligations arising as if from contract, *quasi ex contractu*, for it was all too easy for the adverbial phrase to

[87] 'Jure naturae aequum est, neminem cum alterius detrimento et injuria fieri locupletiorem': the Latin is slightly ambiguous—it could mean 'to the loss *and injury* of another'.

[88] Inst 3.27.

[89] Aquinas, above n 65, II.II q 62. Other theologians put more weight on the Bible.

[90] J Hallebeek, *The Concept of Unjust Enrichment in Late Scholasticism* (Nijmegen, Gerard Noodt Instituut, 1996) ch 2.

[91] J Hallebeek, 'Developments in Mediaeval Roman Law' in EJH Schrage (ed), *Unjust Enrichment* (Berlin, Duncker & Humblot, 1995) 59.

[92] R Feenstra, 'Grotius' Doctrine of Unjust Enrichment as a Source of Obligation' in Schrage, ibid, 197, 200–207.

[93] Grotius, above n 8, 3.1.9, 3.1 14–16.

shift into a substantive *quasi-contractus*. This is already seen in France in the twelfth century and in England in the thirteenth,[94] and in glosses to Justinian's Institutes 3.27 attributed to the fifteenth-century Franciscus Aretinus.[95] More importantly, as an indication of the way in which thinking was to move, in a marginal note in his *Introduction to the Law of Holland* Grotius gives '*Obligatio ex Quasi Contractu*' as the Latin equivalent of the Dutch.[96] Although there was some discomfort in the verbal shift, it was recognised as convenient by scholars after Grotius; and, increasingly, it came to be treated as representing a type of obligation based on an implied or presumed contract.[97] Importantly from an English perspective, it was so treated by Samuel Pufendorf.[98]

So far as continental European systems were concerned, this implied contract thinking was probably restricted in its influence outside the schoolroom. The question in most countries was whether the law should follow the atomised structure of Roman law or adopt a general remedy to reverse unjust enrichment. In the Code Civil, France followed Pothier in approaching the subject through the quasi-contracts, specifically the *condictio* and *negotiorum gestio*.[99] However, by the middle of the nineteenth century there was academic pressure to achieve a generalised remedy, expressed either as unjust enrichment (*enrichissement illégitime*) or unjustified enrichment (*enrichissement sans cause*); the former was most obviously based on the general principle of Roman law, while the latter term was largely limited to studies of the Roman *condictio* until the publication of Raymond Saleilles' work on German law in 1889.[100] In 1892, in the *Affaire Boudier*, the *Cour de Cassation* succumbed to the pressure and fashioned a general remedy out of the Roman *actio de in rem verso*,[101] framing it as *enrichissement sans cause*. Only in 2016 was this incorporated into the redrafted Code Civil.[102] Italy went along the same route, codifying in 1865 in the same terms as France, the widening of the *actio de in rem verso* paving the way for the recognition of a general principle, then codification of the general principle in the redrafted Codice Civile of 1942.[103] In Holland, the general principle of Grotius was followed in the seventeenth and eighteenth centuries, but this was left behind in the Burgerlijk Wetboek of 1838, which followed the lead of the French Code Civil. The general principle, however, continued to be influential and

[94] Placentinus, *Summa Institutionum* (Mainz, 1537) 62; *Fleta* 2.60, HG Richardson and GO Sayles eds, vol 72 (Selden Society, London, 1955) 198.

[95] I have used the edition printed in Lyons, 1612.

[96] Grotius, above n 8, 3.26.2.

[97] P Birks and G McLeod, 'The Implied Contract Theory of Quasi-Contract: Civilian Opinion Current in the Century before Blackstone' (1986) 6 *OJLS* 46.

[98] Pufendorf, above n 34, III.6.2.

[99] Code Civil (1804), Arts 1371–81 (France).

[100] R Saleilles, *Étude sur les Sources de l'Obligation dans le Projet de Code Civil Allemand* (Paris, Cotillon, 1889); this is given more general currency in the same author's *Essai d'une Théorie Générale de l'Obligation d'après le Projet de Code Civil Allemand* (Paris, Cotillon, 1890).

[101] JP Dawson, *Unjust Enrichment* (Boston, Little, Brown & Co, 1951) 92–107. For *Boudier*, D.92.1.596, S.93.1.281 note Labbé (*enrichissement 'sans juste cause'*).

[102] Code Civil (2016), Art 1303 (France).

[103] Codice Civile (1865), Art 1307 (Italy); Codice Civile (1942), Arts 2028–42 (Italy); P Gallo, 'Remedies for Unjust Enrichment in the History of Italian Law' in Schrage, above n 91, 275.

was reinserted into the new code of 1992.[104] In Germany, there was disagreement as to the desirability of a general remedy, but Savigny had identified a general principle of unjustified enrichment (*ungerechtfertigte Bereicherung*), building on the Roman *condictio sine causa*,[105] and this was incorporated in the Bürgerliches Gesetzbuch; and in the 1930s scholars began to theorise its internal structures.[106]

It may be that the terminological difference between unjust and unjustified enrichment is unimportant, the former being based explicitly on Pomponius and the latter anchored by the *condictio*. The Swiss Code of Obligations of 1881 points in this direction, with the German version of the text expressed in terms of lack of justification, the French version lack of justice.[107] But the nineteenth-century trend towards a general principle is nonetheless marked, together with a trend towards lack of justification as its focus under the influence of the German model.

Spain stands a little outside the main stream of continental development. The thirteenth-century Siete Partidas had included a version of D.50.17.206, that none should be enriched wrongfully (*tortizeramente*) to the loss of another.[108] The Siete Partidas as a whole came to be treated as part of the general law of Spain, but this particular clause seems to have had little influence before the middle of the nineteenth century. It was then rediscovered, and featured in a series of cases to justify the grant of a remedy where none might otherwise have existed. In 1926, the Presidential Address to the Academy of Jurisprudence and Legislation of Barcelona tried to make sense of these cases, providing a framework of what we can only call unjust factors.[109] Then, in 1934, a monograph appeared on the topic;[110] after no more than a nod in the direction of the native Spanish analysis, it remodelled the whole remedy along French and German lines, reversing benefits conferred without a valid ground.

The English history was rather different, but the building blocks were essentially the same as in continental Europe.[111] The principal form of action at common law, from the sixteenth century, was the action of assumpsit. This dealt primarily with contractual situations, but—for wholly technical procedural reasons—had been structured largely in terms of implied promises to pay debts. It was therefore applicable to non-contractual debts too. Here, the language of implied promises could easily slide into the language of implied contracts; it is found in this form, for example, in Blackstone's *Commentaries*: 'which are such as reason and justice dictate, and which therefore the law presumes that every man has contracted to perform'.[112] This was a reflection of Pufendorf, and hence may be seen as bringing this area of law

[104] EJH Schrage, 'The Law of Restitution in the History of Dutch Legislation' in Schrage, above n 91, 323.

[105] F von Savigny, *System des Heutigen Römischen Rechts* (Berlin, Veit, 1841) 5.525–5.526 ('grundlose Bereicherung').

[106] Zimmermann, above n 29, 887–91; Bürgerliches Gesetzbuch, Arts 812–22 (Germany).

[107] Code of Obligations, Art 62 (Switzerland): 'ungerechtfertigte Bereicherung, enrichissement illégitime'.

[108] P.7.34.17.

[109] M Borrell i Soler, 27 Revista Jurídica de Catalunya 10, 12–50.

[110] R Nuñez Lagos, *Enriquecimiento sin Causa en el Derecho Español* (Madrid, Reus, 1934).

[111] I have discussed this in slightly greater detail in 'Unjust Enrichment in English Law' in EJH Schrage (ed), *Unjust Enrichment and the Law of Contract* (The Hague, Kluwer, 2001) 33.

[112] 3 Bl Comm 162.

into line with the contemporaneous developments of tort and contract. But where the implied contract analysis of quasi-contractual obligations was easily dropped from continental European thinking, the stress of the action of assumpsit on implied promises meant that it was more deeply rooted in England. It was only at the end of the nineteenth century that there was any hint that this was open to question.

Blackstone's category of implied contracts had a threefold division: judgment debts; penalties and customary dues; and 'natural reason', 'what duty or justice requires' or 'equity'. This was picked up by the legal historian James Barr Ames in an essay on the use of assumpsit in the absence of contract which appeared in the *Harvard Law Review* in 1888.[113] The majority of cases fell under the third heading, and these Ames recharacterised in unmistakably Roman terms as situations where one person had been unjustly enriched at the expense of another. From here, it passed into England through Sir William Holdsworth's *History of English Law*,[114] and in the 1930s formed a principal strut in Percy Winfield's *Province of the Law of Tort*[115] and RM Jackson's *History of Quasi-Contract*.[116] It was consolidated by the publication of the American *Restatement of the Law of Restitution* in 1937 and by a greater familiarity with the law in continental legal systems, and although it still had its detractors (seemingly mostly in Oxford),[117] it had by this time become something of a mainstay of academic opinion.

The courts clung for some time to the implied contract analysis—its high point was *Sinclair v Brougham*[118]—but in the 1940s the academics' thinking began to be taken up by the courts.[119] Nor was it only academics' thinking that was influential. Scots law had long incorporated the Roman *condictio*, recognised by the House of Lords (Scotland) in 1923,[120] and this too fed into the English decisions. It was to be another half century before the self-standing nature of liability in unjust enrichment was fully recognised,[121] but the die was cast.

Although the terminology of the 1930s was unstable—the labels 'unjust enrichment', 'unjustified enrichment', 'unjustifiable enrichment' and the more general 'restitution' are all found in the literature—it was 'unjust enrichment' that was favoured. Structurally, perhaps, this was inevitable. The (Roman) principle had been introduced by Ames to explain cases of quasi-contract where liability had been imposed without a genuine contract; this was a disparate group of situations, held together by nothing more substantial than 'justice' or 'equity', so there was little that could be done beyond listing the situations in which the principle could be seen to have

[113] JB Ames, 'The History of Assumpsit: Implied Assumpsit' (1888) 2 *Harvard Law Review* 53, reprinted with minor changes in his *Lectures on Legal History* (Cambridge, Mass, Harvard University Press, 1913) 149. See also, to the same effect, W Keener, *Treatise on the Law of Quasi-Contracts* (New York, Baker, 1893); Keener's book was dedicated to Ames.

[114] WS Holdsworth, *A History of English Law* (London, Methuen, 1925) 8.88–8.98.

[115] P Winfield, *Province of the Law of Tort* (Cambridge, 1931) 116–89.

[116] RM Jackson, *History of Quasi-Contract* (Cambridge, Cambridge University Press, 1936).

[117] D Logan, 'Restatement on Restitution' (1938) 2 *MLR* 153, 59.

[118] [1914] AC 398.

[119] *United Australia Ltd v Barclays Bank Ltd* [1941] AC 1, 26–29; *Fibrosa Spolka Akcyjna v Fairbairn, Lawson, Combe Barbour Ltd* [1943] AC 32, 61–64.

[120] *Cantiare San Rocco SA v Clyde Shipbuilding and Engineering Co Ltd* [1924] AC 226.

[121] *Lipkin Gorman v Karpnale Ltd* [1991] 2 AC 548.

been engaged, hence creating a list of 'unjust factors'. The Spanish solution, the wholesale adoption of a generative rule of unjustified enrichment taken from foreign law in place of the explanatory principle of unjust enrichment found in indigenous Spanish cases, was antithetical to the common-law method, where case law could be explained or moulded but not totally swept away by academic fashion.

The English story may not yet be complete. Along the way from Blackstone's threefold division of quasi-contract to the modern principle of unjust enrichment, we have lost the enforcement of judgment debts and customary dues. The future might see the dropping of those 'unjust factors' which do not fit into a rule of unjustified enrichment.[122]

V. CONCLUDING THOUGHTS

We can hardly conclude from this that there is no room in private law for revolutions. At this level of abstraction, the law's building blocks are no more than devices used to explain sets of legal rules, to provide a morally acceptable justification for them and to provide a framework enabling us to bring a measure of order to the law's complexity. They do not provide a complete framework. If we have a threefold division of our sources of obligation into contract, tort and unjust enrichment, we also need the non-category of 'other' to mop up the things that do not fit.[123] They have enormous value as explanatory, justificatory or ordering categories, but we must be careful not to invest them with too much reality. They only exist because we choose to use them.

They cannot provide the 'skeleton of principle' which holds 'any legal subject' together,[124] except to the extent that we have already chosen to predefine the legal subject under examination by reference to that particular principle. Nor should they be seen as immanent in any set of rules, unless, again, we have predefined our set of rules by reference to that principle. As this chapter has perhaps demonstrated, abstract ideas can be borrowed from outside the law and from outside any particular legal system, and their institutionalisation may be little more than fashion coupled with inertia.

[122] P Birks, *Unjust Enrichment*, 2nd edn (Oxford, Oxford University Press, 2005) xiii.
[123] ibid 22.
[124] P Birks, *Introduction to the Law of Restitution*, 2nd edn (Oxford, Clarendon Press, 1989) 1.

3

Private Law's Revolutionaries: Authors, Codifiers and Merchants?

HECTOR L MACQUEEN

I. INTRODUCTION

HAS THERE EVER really been a revolution in private law, never mind the law of obligations? This chapter approaches that question by first considering the relationship between law and revolution in general as set out by the late Harold J Berman. In rejecting Berman's view that Roman law was not in its own right part of the Western legal tradition, I suggest rather that the Roman jurists provided many of that tradition's foundational concepts, especially in private law and obligations. These included juristic presentation of private law as a unified whole comprising three subjects: persons (the actors in law), things (put simply, their property and obligations) and actions (the means by which they could claim property and obligations from others). As Berman recognised to a limited extent, these concepts played a further role in legal development from the Middle Ages to the present, not just in juristic writings, but also in association with the ecclesiastical and political revolutions on which Berman focused most. For example, the tripartite division of private law is to be found in all post-revolutionary codifications achieved or attempted from the French Revolution on, including those in the USA. The use made of Roman concepts did, however, change over time, and it is here, if anywhere, that we may detect revolution rather than evolution inside the law itself. Within obligations, a general understanding of contract as comprising all agreements had its roots in Roman texts; but Roman law itself had never taken the idea very far as a tool for legal analysis. Instead, it was developed in juristic writing from the sixteenth century on, in part responding to the realities of contemporary commerce, which had long ceased to correspond with the Roman categorisations of particular contracts. The argument, therefore, is that if the development of private law can be characterised as revolutionary at any point, then the revolutionaries included those who wrote about law in a systematic manner, the codifiers whose work followed on from political revolutions and the merchants whose business needs otherwise left the law behind.

II. BERMAN'S LAW AND REVOLUTIONS

I first read Berman's *Law and Revolution: The Formation of the Western Legal Tradition* when it came out in 1983.[1] At the time, I was completing my PhD thesis on medieval Scots law, and thought that the book was exactly the kind of legal history I could not and would not ever write. My research mainly involved rooting around in archives in search of hitherto unknown or untapped fragments of evidence to try and build a picture about how aspects of land law developed in one small jurisdiction over a couple of centuries. In stark contrast, Berman's vision was epic, with a range of knowledge and coverage, geographical as well as chronological, that was simply vast. At the same time, his tone was elegiac: an age or an era in law was ending in Berman's view and with that backward-looking, regretful perspective he could identify not only the characteristics of that era, but also what had been good about it and what therefore ought to be preserved, if possible. This aspect of the book, too, aroused purist suspicions: history was worth studying for its own sake, not for what might be learned from it for the present.

The era ending for Berman in 1983 was that of a Western legal tradition that had begun, he said, in the eleventh century of the Christian era. Key contemporary elements in its decline were the failures of both legal theory and legal history to recognise its existence, especially analytical jurisprudence or positivism on the theory side and, on the other side, both nationalist and 'scientific' ideas of history. For the former, only national histories were important, while for the latter, history should be based upon hard evidence alone. The latter was the kind of history I thought I was trying to write myself back in 1983; although my focus was Scotland, it was set in British and European contexts. Berman argued further that in the twentieth century government control over economic life had become pervasive. Private law had been transformed by the 'radical centralization and bureaucratization of economic life, of which socialism in one form or another—including state-controlled capitalism—is an aspect or a consequence'.[2] This could be seen, for example, affecting contract, tort, family and social law, and also in criminal law. All of these had previously been components not just of the law of individual states, but of the 'basic modes of characterization' of law, forming a 'common bond among the various legal systems'.[3] Touching directly on this volume's subject area for a moment, Berman noted as one of these common bonds that in all of the Western legal systems, 'civil obligations are divided, either expressly or implicitly, into contract, delict (tort), and unjust enrichment (quasi-contract)'.[4]

Of the ten basic characteristics that Berman identified as forming the Western legal tradition,[5] law, he thought, still retained four in 1983. These were (i) its autonomy from other social institutions, such as politics and religion, and other scholarly

[1] HJ Berman, *Law and Revolution: The Formation of the Western Legal Tradition* (Cambridge, Harvard University Press, 1983).
[2] ibid 34.
[3] ibid 25 (both quotations).
[4] ibid.
[5] ibid 7–10.

disciplines; (ii) its existence as a domain of professional specialists; (iii) it being taught in specialist centres where legal institutions were conceptualised and systematised; and (iv) the existence of a meta-law of legal learning by which legal institutions were evaluated and explained.

The six other characteristics, according to Berman, 'have been severely weakened in the latter part of the twentieth century, especially in the United States'.[6] First, law had ceased to be treated as forming a coherent whole. Secondly, belief in the development of law through time by reinterpretation of the past was now portrayed as merely an ideological belief. Further, change in the law was seen not as a response to its internal logic or as resolutions of tensions between legal science and legal practice, but as responses to other, external forces. Law had come to be seen not as transcending politics, but rather as a means of effectuating the will of those holding political authority. The state increasingly monopolised the law, pushing aside additional or other sources of authority such as the church or autonomous mercantile communities, while denying individuals access to alternatives such as international law. Finally, law had become wholly subordinate to revolution, whereas, in Berman's over-arching theme, the Western legal tradition had been successively challenged by great revolutions stretching back to the eleventh century but had re-emerged each time, reshaped but also strengthened, and not fundamentally altered until the way he saw happening in the twentieth century.

Berman maintained that there were six great revolutions: (i) the Papal Revolution or Reformation of 1075–1122; (ii) the Protestant and especially the Lutheran German Reformation of the sixteenth century; (iii) what he called the Calvinist English Revolution of the seventeenth century;[7] (iv) the American Revolution of 1776; (v) the French Revolution of 1789; and (vi) the Russian Revolution of 1917. The 1983 book dealt with the first of these; in a further volume, published in 2003, he treated the second and third in detail, while also briefly discussing, in an introduction recapitulating his overall thesis about law and revolution, the American, French and Russian Revolutions.[8] Aged 85 when this second book came out, he may have sensed that there would not be enough time left for him to complete a third, although an unfinished manuscript was in existence when he died in 2007.[9]

In each of these great revolutions, Berman saw 'certain patterns or regularities'.[10] Each marked a fundamental, rapid, violent and lasting change in the social system as a whole. Each sought legitimacy in a fundamental law, a remote past and an apocalyptic future. Each took more than one generation to establish roots. Each eventually produced a new system of law, embodying some of the major purposes of the revolution and changing the Western legal tradition, but ultimately remaining

[6] ibid 38.

[7] Berman here ignored the fact that Scotland and Ireland were also wholly embroiled in these events: see also, eg, T Royle, *Civil War: The Wars of the Three Kingdoms 1638–1660* (London, Little, Brown & Co, 2004).

[8] HJ Berman, *Law and Revolution II: The Impact of the Protestant Reformations on the Western Legal Tradition* (Cambridge, Harvard University Press, 2003).

[9] See J Witte Jr and FS Alexander, 'Foreword' (2008) 57(6) *Emory Law Journal* ii. This issue of the journal consists of tributes to Berman, including one from Reinhard Zimmermann.

[10] Berman, above n 1, 19.

within that tradition. These successively renewed systems of law each arose 'in the context of what was conceived as a total social transformation'.[11] The preceding law or legal system had failed to respond in time to ongoing social change, possibly through not keeping sufficiently in balance its twin purposes: the preservation of order on the one hand, and doing justice on the other. The revolutions represented the demand for justice prevailing against the established order. Berman did not hesitate to deploy Thomas Kuhn's 'structure of scientific revolutions': shifts from an older but now demonstrably inaccurate paradigm to a new one that better fits or explains the now known facts.[12] 'In law, the old justice may have to give way to a new one.'[13]

Berman went on to argue that none of the revolutions could completely displace the old law, whether immediately or in the longer run. Frequently the revolution based its appeal, or ideology, at least partly around ideas of a return to a better past state of things. Further:

> Eventually ... each of the great revolutions made its peace with the pre-revolutionary law and restored many of its elements by including them in a new system that reflected the major goals, values, and beliefs for which the revolution had been fought.[14]

Thus, it was on the basis of the Bible and early patristic writings (perhaps especially St Augustine) that the Papal Revolution established the distinct legal spheres of church and state. The claim of the church's expansive and expanding legal system to ultimate superiority then virtually forced the state to develop its own system in response. While the Protestant Reformation re-emphasised the primacy of scripture and maintained the division of church and state, the Lutheran reformers accepted that the state prevailed over the church but the Calvinists did not. For the latter, there were two separate spheres, but the state was subject to the church. In all Protestant countries, however, papal jurisdiction was completely displaced, and in the process the law overall became more secular, with the church's claims being squeezed. Whether Lutheran or Calvinist, the Reformation gave high status to the power of the individual, who had a God-given free will regulated primarily by conscience.

The American and French Revolutions next firmly pushed aside, in issues of government, not only monarchy and aristocracy, but also all organised religion, promoting instead the general rule of enlightened, rational and secular humanity organised as the state. The emergent liberal democracies were then countered in their turn by revolutionary socialism and what in Berman's view became the religion without a God, the Communism that in 1983 was still seemingly triumphant in the Soviet Union. But in none of these great shifts, even the last, was the past wholly obliterated. Thus, in the Soviet Union, the state used law extensively, not only to

[11] ibid 20.

[12] TS Kuhn, *The Structure of Scientific Revolutions*, 3rd edn (Chicago, University of Chicago Press, 1996). The first and second editions had been published in 1962 and 1970, respectively. A fiftieth anniversary edition with an introduction by I Hacking was published in 2012 by the University of Chicago Press. Kuhn, born in 1922, died in 1996. Further on Kuhnian thinking applied to the development of law, see TT Arvind, 'Paradigms Lost or Paradigms Regained? Legal Revolutions and the Path of the Law' this volume, chapter 4; G Samuel, 'Have There Been Scientific Revolutions in Law?' (2017) 11(2) *Journal of Comparative Law* 186.

[13] Berman, above n 1, 22.

[14] ibid 29.

plan and control economic activity, but also to achieve the egalitarian goals of the revolution and to strengthen the cohesion of family, neighbourhood and workplace. Even though the revolution ultimately failed in the 1990s, Berman argued in 2003 that Soviet law had left its mark in the Western legal tradition through general acceptance of a much increased role for the state in economic and social relationships: '[n]ot just in Russia but throughout the West, the law of the state has come to play the role of parent or teacher in nurturing attitudes officially considered to be socially desirable'.[15]

In sum, the whole history of the Western legal tradition was one of interaction between revolution and evolution. But Berman emphasised the impact which revolution had upon the law—his focus was on that, and not so much on revolution from within the law itself. He conceded that one of the key elements in his Western legal tradition was law seeing its own change as a response to its internal logic or as resolutions of tensions between legal science and legal practice. But he specifically rejected the idea that the law changes incrementally or evolves gradually over time;[16] rather, it changed radically, he thought, at specific periods (although not necessarily all at once) as a result of forces external to the law. But these periods of legal change were not quite like the extinction of the dinosaurs when the Earth collided with a gigantic meteorite. In Berman's thinking, the dinosaurs got back onto the feet that remained to them post-catastrophe, dusted themselves down in a new environment, and carried on in renewed and different forms.

III. ROMAN LAW IN THE WESTERN LEGAL TRADITION

It is not my intention here to engage in a comprehensive analysis of Berman's thesis and pronounce either for or against it in whole or even in part,[17] but it is helpful in

[15] Berman, above n 8, 21.

[16] Berman, above n 1, 15. For views less inclined to revolution as the explanation of significant change in law, see, eg, P Stein, *Legal Evolution: The Story of an Idea* (Cambridge, Cambridge University Press, 1980); JW Cairns, 'Development of Comparative Law in Great Britain' in M Reimann and R Zimmermann (eds), *The Oxford Handbook of Comparative Law* (Oxford, Oxford University Press, 2006) 131, 135–38; A Watson, *The Evolution of Western Private Law* (Baltimore, John Hopkins University Press, 2001); SFC Milsom, *A Natural History of the Common Law* (New York, Columbia University Press, 2003).

[17] Elsewhere I have found Berman's argument that the growth and claims of the medieval canon law compelled a systematic response from the state supported by the expansion of royal justice in twelfth- and thirteenth-century Scotland: see HL MacQueen, 'Canon Law, Custom and Legislation: Law in the Reign of Alexander II' in RD Oram (ed), *The Reign of Alexander II, 1214–49* (Leiden, Brill, 2005) 221. It also seems to me that the Protestant Scottish Reformation of 1560, which was Calvinist rather than Lutheran, was even more of a revolution than its German counterpart and even more Calvinist than its English counterpart, with profound consequences for the law and the secular legal system: see my review of RH Helmholz (ed), *Canon Law in Protestant Lands* (Berlin, Duncker & Humblot, 1992) in (1994) 124 *Zeitschrift der Savigny-Stiftung für Rechtsgesschichte* 582. But it fits with Berman's overall thesis that the substantive and procedural pre-Reformation canon law survived in the new post-1560 dispensation in Scotland so long as consistent with scripture, the most notable and studied example being the law of marriage. Inconsistency with scripture, however, once determined, did lead to reform to ensure consistency, as in the case of the law of incest; or to abolition or virtual desuetude, as in the case of sanctuary. See also HL MacQueen, 'Girth: Society and the Law of Sanctuary in Scotland' in J Cairns and O Robinson (eds), *Critical Studies in Ancient Law, Comparative Law and Legal History: Essays in Honour of Alan Watson* (Oxford, Hart Publishing, 2001) 333.

approaching the issue of revolutions in the law of obligations at least to pose some of the questions Berman's work seems to suggest. Is there such a thing as the Western legal tradition and, if so, did Berman characterise it correctly? Does fundamental change in law follow only from revolution outside the law? Does revolution necessarily involve physical violence in the accomplishment of change? How was the paradigm shifting in Kuhn's scientific revolutions achieved, for example? Then, as this last question suggests, are the revolutions identified by Berman the only ones of significance for law? What about, for example, the print revolution of the fifteenth century, perhaps foreshadowing other communications revolutions arising later from the regularisation and widening availability of postal services, followed in fairly rapid succession by telegraphy, telephony, broadcasting and the internet? What about the Industrial Revolution and the transport revolution which arose not only from mechanisation, but also from canals, railways, the macadamisation of roads and the development of powered flight?

From the internal perspectives of the law itself, one might ask where did Roman law fit as—one might have thought—a crucial base for the Western legal tradition? Berman did address this question. In his view, Roman law's place in the Western legal tradition arose only because of its rediscovery in the late eleventh century and because thereafter both church and state adopted it for their own ends. In between the fall of Rome in 476 CE and the eleventh century, Roman law lapsed into virtual disuse—or, to renew my earlier metaphor, it was a dinosaur killed by the meteorite. It was the medieval lawyers and jurists who, in Jurassic Park style, recovered the dinosaur's DNA from its physical remains and then transformed it into a living system again, capable of deployment within both current ecclesiastical and secular law. Before then, there was no Western legal tradition in Berman's definition of the concept: it was the medieval, not the Roman, jurists who referred to Roman law as the *corpus iuris* (the body of the law) and who accordingly interpreted it as a whole.[18]

There are, however, some difficulties arising from this exclusion of Roman law in its own right from the Western legal tradition. While the classical Roman lawyers of the first to third centuries may not have specifically described their law as a body, they could certainly see it as a system or a whole, lending itself to general description and analysis as such. Ulpian, who wrote around the beginning of the third century CE, gave us this description of what a 'complete' *jus* (ie right, or law) was about: 'either of acquiring or of keeping or reducing; for the question is either how something may come to be somebody's, or how a person may keep a thing or keep his *jus* or how he may alienate or lose it'.[19]

Ulpian further detected three basic precepts or principles underlying or underpinning the law: 'to live honourably (*honeste*), not to harm any other person, to render to each his own'.[20] He also formulated the distinction between public law and private law: '[p]ublic law is that which respects the establishment of the Roman

[18] Berman, above n 1, 3, 8–9.

[19] Justinian, *Digest*, A Watson ed (Philadelphia, University of Pennsylvania Press, 1998) D.1.1.3.41.

[20] ibid D.1.1.10.1.

commonwealth; private that which respects individuals' interests; for there are some things which are useful to the public, and others which are of benefit to private persons'.[21]

Perhaps a few decades before, in the mid-second century, Gaius could say that all law related to persons, things or actions, and then structured his Institutes, most probably a student textbook or course, around this idea.[22] Within that structure, Gaius sub-divided the category of things between corporeal and incorporeal, and obligations formed part of the latter sub-division. In terms of Gaius' treatment, they also shaded off into the last of the law's divisions, actions. The characteristic feature of an obligation was that it was a claim to a performance from another person which might, but did not necessarily, also involve a claim to a corporeal thing. Obligations themselves were further divided into those arising from contract and delict, although, in his Institutes, Gaius also acknowledged that this division did not cover all the obligations known to the law, in particular that of repaying a mistaken payment.[23] In another work of which we know only through the Digest, Gaius went further: 'Obligations arise either from contract or from wrongdoing or, by some special right (*jus*), from various kinds of cause.'[24]

In Justinian's Institutes, explicitly dedicated to young law students around 400 years later, in the sixth century, a fourfold division of obligations would be given: contract, quasi-contract, delict and quasi-delict.[25] However, Justinian maintained Gaius' fourfold classification of contracts: those arising from handing things over (the real contracts), words (the verbal contracts or *stipulatio*), writing (the literal contracts) and (finally) consent.[26] Justinian's Institutes was also structured as Gaius' book had been, on the basis of persons, things and actions.

What distinguished contract from other obligations was never made clear by Gaius or, indeed, Justinian. Reinhard Zimmermann, following Tony Honoré, suggests that Gaius drew on the Aristotelian distinction between voluntary and involuntary transactions.[27] From a scattering of texts through the Digest, we can tell that by the classical period of Roman law the basic idea of contract in its different forms was as an agreement intended to be binding, with it also being possible in a few cases to make an enforceable unilateral promise.[28] Agreement (or paction) was

[21] ibid D.1.1.1.2.

[22] Gaius, *Institutes*, WM Gordon and OF Robinson eds (London, Duckworth, 1988) 1.8. L Waelkens, *Amne Adverso: Roman Legal Heritage in European Culture* (Leuven, Leuven University Press, 2015) 59 argues that the *Institutes* 'are too unsystematic, too lacunal and too difficult to have been a textbook'.

[23] ibid 3.88 and 91.

[24] Justinian, above n 19, D.44.7.1.

[25] Justinian, *Institutes*, P Birks and G MacLeod eds (London, Duckworth, 1987) 3.13.2. See also the dedication of the *Institutes* to the 'cupidae legum iuventuti' (to the young eager for law).

[26] Justinian, above n 25, 3.13.2.

[27] R Zimmermann, *The Law of Obligations: Roman Foundations of the Civilian Tradition* (Cape Town, Juta, 1990) 10–11, citing AM Honoré, *Gaius* (Oxford, Clarendon Press, 1962) 97ff. See Aristotle, *Nichomachean Ethics*, 3.1, in J Barnes (ed), *The Complete Works of Aristotle: the Revised Oxford Translation*, vol 2 (Princeton, Princeton University Press, 1984).

[28] Justinian, above n 19, D.2.14 (mainly Ulpian and Paul); D.44.7 (Gaius); D.45 (mainly Ulpian, Paul, Pomponius and Julian on *stipulatio*); D.50.16.7 (Paul), 19 (Ulpian); D.50.17.31, 34, 116 (all

defined as the consent of two or more persons to the same thing.[29] Characteristically, however, the classical jurists did not pursue the implications of this general analysis in any great depth. They threw in tantalising statements, such as there being no action arising from a *nudum pactum* (a bare or naked agreement), although it might provide a defence to a claim;[30] and that nobody could stipulate in favour of a third party.[31] The determination that the practice of barter could not be classified in law as sale triggered the development of 'innominate real contracts'. These were characterised by exchange of performances, where the first performance had to be rendered before the counter-performance became enforceable, ie potentially every voluntary exchange of performance which did not already come under one of the named contracts, like sale or hire.[32] As we shall see in due course, these statements and ideas would become critical in the medieval and later discussion of Roman law.

At least part of the explanation for the success of Roman law in the medieval period, I would suggest, is because it already provided—even if it did not fully articulate—a persuasive *system* within which to think about law. The surviving texts were not just disconnected pabulum with which the medieval jurists could begin to build a structure. The division of persons, things and actions has a long history of influence on legal writing across Europe. Berman himself recognised this in his second book. He argued that use of the division by German Protestant jurists of the sixteenth century in order to systematise the treatment of the law as a whole was the crucial final step in the shift away from the scholastic approach of the Middle Ages, through the successive sceptical and principled stages of legal humanism, and on to the idea of a general legal science.[33] This was achieved by elaboration of the division through deployment of the Aristotelian analysis of 'causes'.[34] All these jurists were teachers of law, and a notable feature of their work is the use of what we would call flow charts to provide easily memorised visual representations of their schemes.[35] Berman further argues that in the sixteenth century the focus of juristic attention shifted from the Digest to Justinian's Institutes, and began also to embrace

Ulpian). M Hogg, *Promises and Contract Law* (Cambridge University Press, 2011) 109–16, argues that a promissory concept underpinned the *stipulatio*, and was also recognised in the *pollicitatio* in favour of a municipality.

[29] Justinian, above n 19, D.2.14.1.2 (Ulpian).

[30] ibid D.2.14.7.4; D.2.14.7.5 (both Ulpian); D.19.5.15 (Ulpian). See also Zimmermann, above n 27, 508 (also citing Paul Sent II.XIV,1; C.2.3.10).

[31] ibid D.45.1.38.17 (Ulpian); Justinian, above n 25, 3.19.19.

[32] Zimmermann, above n 27, 534.

[33] Berman, above n 8, 108–29. Berman here highlights the work of four jurists: Johann Apel (1486–1536), Konrad Lagus (*c* 1499–1546), Nicolas Vigellius (1529–1600) and Johann Althusius (1557–1638). Samuel, above n 12, draws attention to the French humanist Hugues Doneau (Donellus; 1527–91), who in his *Commentarii de Jure Civile* (1596) 'set about re-arranging the order of the *Digest* using the Gaian classification scheme of persons, things and actions'. Berman notes as 'a striking fact that three of the most outstanding French jurists of the sixteenth century, Duarenus (Duaren), Donellus (Doneau), and Du Moulin, did indeed organize and analyse the enormous mass of rules found in the texts of Justinian by use of Melanchthon's topical method, and that one of them, Duarenus, was sympathetic to Protestantism, and the other two, Donellus and Du Moulin, were converts to Protestantism who fled to Lutheran universities in Germany to write and teach': above n 8, 129.

[34] Berman, above n 8, 114, 119–20.

[35] These flow-charts are illustrated in ibid 117, 121.

non-Roman positive law.[36] Certainly, the division of persons, things and actions became the basis for instructional books on national laws across continental Europe (and, indeed, in Scotland) until the end of the eighteenth century. Following the example of Justinian, these books were usually entitled *Institutes* or *Institutions*.[37]

The use of persons, things and actions as the basis for writing about the law as a whole included England. As early as the thirteenth century, Henry de Bracton explicitly deployed the division as the basis and structure of his book *Laws and Customs of England*, 'the crown and flower of English medieval jurisprudence'.[38] Despite its title, Coke's seventeenth-century *Institutes* did not follow the institutional pattern; however, John Cairns has shown it used in John Cowell's *Institutiones iuris anglicani* (1605), and also as influencing both Matthew Hale's *Analysis of the Civil Part of the Law* (published in 1713 but written before 1676, the year of Hale's death) and Thomas Wood's *Institute of the Laws of England* (first edition 1720). It was, finally, used again in Blackstone's *Commentaries* (first edition 1765–69).[39]

Gaius was thus someone who succeeded in establishing a way of presenting the law that over a very long period of time could hold good—or at least be thought useful—for teaching students, writing textbooks and, eventually, as we shall soon see, preparing systematic legislative codes.[40] This leads me to the reference in the title of this chapter, or at least part of it: authors as possible revolutionaries in law. First, we do not know of anyone who anticipated Gaius in his thinking about the overall structure of the law and how to present it. He also seems to have been the first to distinguish between property and obligations, and, within obligations, between contract, delict and other kinds of obligation. How did he manage to achieve this possibly revolutionary, and above all enduring, scheme? It did not occur in the context of a political revolution of the kind discussed by Berman. So far as we can tell, it occurred simply because an author, as a teacher, had to think about how to present the law in a way that could be understood by the reader, or student, coming to the subject without prior knowledge, or at least very little. Even the author who wanted only to present the rules had to think how to begin and how to go on, and recognise that it would not be enough to reel off a list of rules without reflecting at least a little on what connected one rule to another. And in this, perhaps, as already suggested, use could be made of the existing thinking of Greek philosophy.[41]

[36] ibid 101.

[37] The classic study is K Luig, 'The Institutes of National Law in the Seventeenth and Eighteenth Centuries' [1972] *Juridical Review* 193.

[38] The current edition of *Bracton, De Legibus et Consuetudinibus Angliae* is by GE Woodbine (ed) and SE Thorne (trans), (London, Selden Society, 1968–77). The quotation is from F Pollock and FW Maitland, *History of English Law*, vol 1, 2nd edn (Cambridge, Cambridge University Press, 1968) 206.

[39] See JW Cairns, 'Blackstone an English Institutist: Legal Literature and the Rise of the Nation State' (1984) 4 *OJLS* 318, reproduced in idem, *Law, Lawyers and Humanism: Selected Essays on the History of Scots Law*, vol 1 (Edinburgh, Edinburgh University Press, 2015) 413.

[40] Even in uncodified and devolved Scotland, the Gaian trichotomy is used in statute to define Scottish private law: see Scotland Act 1998, s 126(4).

[41] We can perhaps see a similar but slightly different process going on in the twelfth century with Gratian, the so-called 'Father of Canon Law'. As Berman fully recognises (above n 1, 143–49), Gratian was an important figure in the twelfth-century consolidation of the Papal Revolution; but it was certainly

Gaius may also have seen the division as a good descriptor of the human realities with which the law had to deal—people, their relationships and interactions with each other and the world around them, and the means of enforcing their rights and duties—a Kuhnian paradigm, perhaps? The late Peter Birks always enthused about Gaius' originality and intellect: he was 'the Darwin of the law' (in the present context, possibly an unconscious link to both revolution and evolution),[42] whose division of the law into persons, things and actions 'represents an immense intellectual achievement'.[43] The division became the basis for *English Private Law*, first published under Birks's editorship in 2000.[44] Birks's enthusiasm was shared by the also sadly late Neil MacCormick:

> Even in the twenty-first century, one can still say rather as Gaius said twenty centuries ago, that all law concerns persons, things and actions. Law imposes requirements on persons about their conduct. It does so also with a view to protecting persons from the misconduct of others. It regulates persons in their access to things that they need for survival, health and comfort. It provides systems of exchange whereby people can get from each other things that they need. When arrangements break down, or when harm is done or things unwarrantedly taken, sanctioning action may be taken either at the instance of public authorities or the instance of private persons, leading possibly to criminal penalties or to enforceable civil remedies.[45]

MacCormick might have wanted to add the point that the law actually defines what a person is: excluding the dead, the yet to be conceived (but not absolutely the yet to be born), animals and fish, vegetable life, and (for the moment at any rate) extraterrestrials and robots. And in modern law, it also includes certain collectives of living humans, such as corporations and (in Scotland, at least) partnerships, but not unincorporated associations or trusts.

in a teaching rather than an official, papally approved, context that his writing was created and mainly used in the ensuing centuries. He began by collecting the canons (ie the laws promulgated by the church over the centuries before his time), then producing what he called a 'concordance' of the seemingly 'discordant' canons. In this he was certainly a revolutionary whose work eclipsed the more chronological and/or topical approach of those collectors who had gone before him, such as Burchard of Worms and Ivo of Chartres. But again, although we know even less about Gratian than we do about Gaius, his Bolognese context makes it seem most likely that he, too, was a teacher. When Gratian began work some time before 1140, however, he did does not seem to have known much, if any, Roman law. What probably inspired him most was contemporary scholastic philosophy derived again from the rediscovered Aristotle, the *sic et non* of dialectical reasoning by which seeming contradictions in texts could be resolved by drawing distinctions between them, questions could be put and analysed via disputation, and hypothetical examples or *causae* worked through in the same way.

[42] P Birks, 'Definition and Division: A Meditation on *Institutes* 3.13' in P Birks (ed), *The Classification of Obligations* (Oxford, Clarendon Press, 1997) 1, 2. It is noteworthy here that Thomas Kuhn made almost no mention of Darwin in his *Structure of Scientific Revolutions*.

[43] P Birks, *The Roman Law of Obligations*, E Descheemaeker ed (Oxford, Oxford University Press, 2014) 5.

[44] See now A Burrows (ed), *English Private Law*, 3rd edn (Oxford, Oxford University Press, 2013).

[45] N MacCormick, *Institutions of Law: An Essay in Legal Theory* (Oxford, Oxford University Press, 2007) 77.

IV. CIVIL CODES AND REVOLUTIONS

My next observation arising from Berman's law and revolution thesis relates to the book he did not live to write, on the French and American Revolutions. In a striking contrast, one crucial consequence of the French Revolution, but not the earlier American one, was a Civil Code for the new republic. The French code was undoubtedly a deliberate departure from the *ancien régime*, albeit one drawing heavily on the European legal tradition. Berman sees it as reflective of a deist belief system in which God had provided men with powers of reason to determine their own welfare.[46] But codification was also to provide a less exalted, more nationalistic model for many other reconstructed or newly emerging states in the nineteenth century: as when Belgium[47] and the Netherlands were liberated from French hegemony in 1830 and 1838, respectively, or, even more strikingly, following the unifications of Italy and Germany later on in the nineteenth century. Greek aspirations towards a civil code, although not completely realised until after the Second World War, seem also to have begun after the country gained independence from Turkey in 1827. Even where the stimulus of nationalist fervour inspired by newly won independence or unification was lacking, nineteenth-century continental European states seem to have seen codes rather as their twentieth-century successors saw airlines, as an essential badge of contemporary statehood: hence the codification in Portugal (1867), Spain (1889) and, after decades of preparation, Switzerland (1907).

Outside Europe, there are civil codes in Louisiana and Quebec, helping to maintain each jurisdiction's distinctive legal identity and traditions within the much larger and typically non-codal federations of the USA and Canada, respectively. The first Louisiana code, of 1808, was at least partly a reaction to the USA's Louisiana Purchase of 1803, while the first Quebec code, of 1866, immediately preceded the confederation of Canada in 1867.[48] Back in Western Europe, the twentieth century saw at least three complete re-codifications, in Italy (1942), Portugal (1966) and the Netherlands (1992). I know little about the origins of the current Portuguese code, other than that it follows the German model; but the new Italian code began as a project in Mussolini's reconstitution of the country after the First World War, while the work towards a new Netherlands code (completed in 1992) commenced in the immediate aftermath of the Second World War, as part of the reconstruction of a country shattered by years of war and foreign occupation. That civil codes have not lost their symbolic standing as a signal of statehood for new, newly independent or freshly starting states is shown very clearly by the ongoing creation of codes in the former Iron Curtain countries since the fall of the Berlin Wall in 1989 and the collapse of the Soviet Union in 1991: for example, in Russia (1994–2006),

[46] Berman, above n 8, 10–13.

[47] The French Code Civil continued in force as the Belgian Civil Code after Belgian independence in 1830; the projected fundamental revision did not, however, take place. See K Zweigert and H Kötz, *Introduction to Comparative Law*, 3rd edn, T Weir trans (Oxford, Oxford University Press, 1998) 101.

[48] On these codifications see JW Cairns, *Codification, Transplants and History: Law Reform in Louisiana (1808) and Quebec (1866)* (Clark, NJ, Talbot Publishing, 2015).

Lithuania (2000), Estonia (2002), Ukraine (2004), Hungary (2014) and the Czech Republic (2014). Poland, however, has had its present Civil Code since 1964.

Like the lawbooks of the Roman, medieval and early modern eras, codes are a way of presenting the law for ease of understanding and use. Even the most recent examples in the formerly Communist world follow the ancient Gaian division of persons, things and actions (although, since at least the German Code in 1900, the last is often hived off into separate codes of procedure and remedies). The focus of the codes is the individual human being as a bearer of powers, rights and duties from conception to death, in relation to the self, other persons and objects in the surrounding world. In this, they reflect the secularisation of law identified by Berman as the legal transformation which followed the Reformation and was completed with the French and American Revolutions. Subsequent codes have often, if not invariably, arisen as part, or in the aftermath, of fundamentally significant political events—not necessarily revolutions, but also what the codifiers may have seen as liberations, reconstructions or at least declarations of identity or renewal within a larger whole.

The question is why the American Revolution did not lead to such a codification; or, perhaps, why the later French Revolution did. It may be that whereas France became a unified republic, the USA became a federal one in which private law, the classic territory of the code, remained in the hands of the constituent states. There had already been 'codes' in some of the pre-revolutionary states as early as the seventeenth century, however.[49] A codification movement developed after the Revolution, based on the idea that the new sovereignty of the people required, amongst other things, clear limitations upon judicial power to determine the law.[50] This movement gained new momentum in the early part of the nineteenth century as a response to the flow of cases and the fragmentation of law in the rapidly expanding republic.[51] In the second half of the century, codes were adopted in Georgia (1860, in force 1 January 1863), the Dakotas (1865), California (1872), Idaho (1887) and Montana (1895).[52] These codes can often be linked to each territory's recognition as a state within the federation, and a number of them were influenced by a comprehensive draft Civil Code for New York published in 1865, but in the end not adopted there. The draft, produced by commissioners led by David Dudley Field, was structured as 'persons' and 'things'. Actions had already been dealt with in a separate Code of Civil Procedure, enacted in New York in 1848.[53] Lawrence Friedman suggests that

[49] LM Friedman, *A History of American Law*, 2nd edn (New York, Simon & Schuster, 1985) 90–93.

[50] MJ Horwitz, *The Transformation of American Law 1780–1860* (Cambridge, Harvard University Press, 1977) 17–18.

[51] G Gilmore, *The Ages of American Law* (New Haven, Yale University Press, 1977) 25–27, 119–20. See also CM Cooke, *The American Codification Movement: A Study of Antebellum Legal Reform* (Westport, Greenwood Press, 1981), astringently reviewed by RW Gordon: (1983) 36 *Vanderbilt Law Review* 431.

[52] See EC Surrency, 'The Georgia Code of 1863 and Its Place in the Codification Movement' (2003) 11 *Journal of Southern Legal History* 81; ME Harrison, 'The First Half-Century of the California Civil Code' (1922) 10 *California Law Review* 185; AP Morriss, 'Debating the Field Civil Code 100 Years Late' (2000) 61 *Montana Law Review* 371.

[53] Friedman, above n 49, 391–98, 403–409. Field was also one of the commissioners in the preparation of the Code of Civil Procedure.

codification succeeded in the USA only in 'sparsely settled states in a hurry to ingest a legal system' and with 'something of a civil-law tradition', as well as a local bar without vested interests in keeping the old rules.[54] Not quite Berman's enlightened revolution in the United States, then, whether codes are seen as secular expressions of the power of human reason or as a means of making the law known to the people in general or of restricting judicial power over the law. There is, however, nonetheless a significant contrast in the legal experience of two revolutionary republics where the revolutions were driven by similar political ideals: the single code for the whole state (France) against late and scattered instances of codes in a few of the federation's constituent parts (the USA).

V. REVOLUTIONS IN THE LAW OF OBLIGATIONS: SCOTLAND AND STAIR

I return now to my initial question: has there ever been a revolution in the law of obligations? One candidate for consideration is the emergence of a general law of contract in the sixteenth and seventeenth centuries, and the displacement of the fourfold division of contracts in Roman law as the starting point of legal analysis. David Ibbetson touches on this in his contribution to the present collection, following James Gordley in attributing a crucial role to the sixteenth-century Spanish scholastics' synthesis of Roman law with Aristotelian and Thomist thinking.[55] Berman, too, noted the emergence of a general law of contract as an aspect of the overall systematisation of law in the period, in which Protestant jurists in Germany such as Mattheus Wesenbeck (1531–86) also played an important part.[56] The generalised approach to contract established in this period still holds good in all the major European codes: my starting point here, however, is Scottish legal history.

The Institutions of the Laws of Scotland by James Dalrymple, Viscount Stair (1619–95), first published in 1681 with a second edition in 1693, is an extraordinary work, certainly in the Scottish context; and, as I will suggest later, at least noteworthy in the European one.[57] It was quite different from anything published before on Scots law apart from Thomas Craig's *Jus Feudale*, written around 1600 and

[54] ibid 406.

[55] See chapter 2 above. Note also the following writings by J Gordley: 'Natural Law Origins of the Common Law of Contract' in J Barton (ed), *Towards a General Law of Contract* (Berlin, Duncker & Humblot, 1990); *The Philosophical Origins of Modern Contract Doctrine* (Oxford, Clarendon Press, 1991) 71–77; 'Some Perennial Problems' in idem (ed), *The Enforceability of Promises in European Contract Law* (Cambridge, Cambridge University Press, 2002) 2–10; *Foundations of Private Law: Property, Tort, Contract, Unjust Enrichment* (Oxford, Oxford University Press, 2006) chs 13, 16, 17; *The Jurists: A Critical History* (Oxford University Press, 2013) ch V. See also W Decock, *Theologians and Contract Law: The Moral Transformation of the* Ius Commune *(ca 1500–1650)* (Leiden, Martinus Nijhoff, 2013).

[56] Berman, above n 8, 156–66. See also on Wesenbeck (a Dutchman who, however, taught at Jena and Wittenberg) KP Nanz, *Enstehung des allgemeinen Vertragsbegriffs im 16. bis 18. Jahrhundert* (Cologne, J Schweitzer Verlag, 1985) 85–94. This book is helpfully reviewed for non-German speakers by WM Gordon in (1987) 8 *Journal of Legal History* 373.

[57] A luminous analysis is by DN MacCormick, 'Stair and the Natural Law Tradition: Still Relevant?' in HL MacQueen (ed), *Miscellany VI*, vol 54 (Edinburgh, Stair Society, 2009) 1–10. Hogg, above n 28, 134–42, focuses on the application of Stair's thought to obligations and contract.

first published in 1655.[58] Stair's exposition used the institutional scheme of persons, things and actions, but dealt with the first of these almost entirely in the context of persons' relations with, and obligations to, one another, ie between husband and wife, parent and child, the incapable and their guardians. His principal concern was with the *rights* of persons, ie their things, and with their constitution, transfer and extinction.[59] Before he became a lawyer, Stair taught philosophy at Glasgow University, and traditional Aristotelian thought is apparent in his legal writing. Indeed, it is a key part of what made it original from a Scots law perspective. For Stair, positive law flowed from natural equity, albeit only imperfectly. The principles of equity that were the 'efficient cause' of rights and laws were: (i) man's obedience to God; (ii) the freedom of man otherwise; which, however, being in his power, (iii) man might constrain by voluntary engagement with others. The principle of obedience produced those positive law obligations not resulting from voluntary engagement, ie what we would now call the law of delict and the law of unjustified enrichment, as well as the family law titles already referred to. Individual freedom led to personal liberty of action outside these obediential obligations, but voluntary engagement produced the law of promises and contracts, which Stair termed 'conventional obligations'.[60]

Stair followed Roman law in his general definition of an obligation:

> Obligation is a legal tie by which we may be necessitate or constrained to pay, or perform something. This tie lieth upon the debtor; and the power of making use of it in the creditor is the personal right itself, which is a power given by the law, to exact from persons that which they are due.[61]

However, he rejected the fourfold Roman division of obligations. Unlike the distinction already drawn between obediential and conventional obligations, Stair argued in Aristotelian mode that the fourfold distinction 'insinuates no reason of the cause or rise of these distinct obligations, as is requisite in a good distinct division'.[62] He subsequently gives over a whole chapter to 'Obligations Conventional, by Promise, Paction, and Contract', in which he further clearly rejected as 'unnecessary' the traditional Romanist division of contracts into 'four kinds, either perfected by things, words, writ, or sole consent'.[63] 'Every paction,' said Stair, 'produceth action.'[64] 'All pactions and contracts being now equally efficacious', the key distinction between them lay in the gratuitousness or otherwise of the transaction.[65] Stair treated 'the common requisites and properties of contracts' as 'deeds of the rational will', which therefore could not be entered by those lacking the power of reason, such as 'infants, idiots [and] furious [ie insane] persons' and those affected

[58] On Craig (*c* 1538–1608), see most recently L Dodd, 'Thomas Craig's Aetiology of Law and Society: Literary Dependence and Independence' (2016) 37 *Journal of Legal History* 121. Also note his influence in Germany, commented upon in C Fischer, 'The Reception of Magna Carta in Early Modern Germany, c.1650–1800' (2016) 37 *Journal of Legal History* 249, 254–57.

[59] James Dalrymple Viscount Stair, *Institutions of the Law of Scotland,* DM Walker ed (Edinburgh, Edinburgh University Press, 1981) I, 1, 23. This version of the text reproduces the 1693 edition.

[60] ibid I, 1, 17–23.

[61] ibid I, 1, 22.

[62] ibid I, 3, 2.

[63] ibid I, 10, 10; see also, ibid, I, 10, 7 and 11.

[64] ibid I, 10, 7.

[65] ibid I, 10, 12.

by 'fear', 'drunkenness', 'disease', or 'err[or] in the substantials of what is done'. The 'act of contracting must be of purpose to oblige', in relation to things within the parties' powers. 'Contracts of impossibilities' and 'in things unlawful' are void. He also discussed equality of exchange, abatement of price, and the principle of mutuality or reciprocity in onerous contracts.[66]

In all this, Stair is providing a Scottish contribution to the shift in thinking which had been going on across Western Europe for some time. The pre-existing obstacles in the Roman texts were not limited to the fourfold division of contracts: the famous statement against the enforceability of the bare or naked paction (the *nudum pactum*) seemed to suggest that a contract had to fit into one of the types recognised by law or otherwise fail, unless perhaps it was an innominate real contract of exchange or one of the recognised forms of unilateral promise.[67] The canon law had not applied the principle against bare pacts, however, on the basis that scripture abjured falsehood.[68] Stair himself noted that the canon law had 'taken off' the exclusion of naked pactions,[69] and his 'every paction produceth action' was in effect an abbreviated translation of the 'pacta quantumcunque nuda servanda sunt' (pacts are to be kept, however bare) found in the decretals of Pope Gregory IX promulgated in 1234.[70] But the canonists held that to bind, promissory words had to be uttered with serious intent (Stair's 'of purpose to oblige'); and in any event, the ecclesiastical courts claimed jurisdiction in these matters only if the undertaking had been supported with an oath invoking spiritual sanctions for non-performance.[71]

As Berman notes, by the mid-sixteenth century there was significant doubt amongst at least some civilians in the Protestant lands about the scope of the prohibition upon naked pactions in the secular courts.[72] Meanwhile, in Spain, Catholic scholastic theologians were fusing the philosophy of Aristotle and the thirteenth-century theology of Thomas Aquinas to produce a rational vision of natural law in which promise-keeping was a mark of the Christian life, reflecting the virtues of fidelity (keeping one's word), liberality (the sensible giving away of resources to chosen others) and commutative justice (the equivalence of exchanges so that no one was enriched at the expense of another).[73] In the seventeenth and later centuries, the great Dutch jurist Hugo de Groot (1583–1645, usually known as Grotius and whom, remarkably, Berman mentions just once, and then only in an alphabetical footnote list of jurists)[74] and other 'northern' natural lawyers (as they have been dubbed by James Gordley)[75] would be conduits by which this originally Catholic natural law thinking was transmitted to Protestant secular legal systems.

[66] For the foregoing, including all quotations, see ibid I, 10, 12–16.
[67] See above n 30.
[68] Berman, above n 1, 247.
[69] Stair, above n 59, I, 10, 4; being followed in this by 'the common custom of nations': ibid, I, 10, 7.
[70] *Decretales Gregorii P.IX*, 1.35.1 *summarium*, in E Friedberg (ed), *Corpus Iuris Canonici*, vol 2 (Leipzig, 1881) 203–204. See also Decock, above n 55, 122–30.
[71] See RH Helmholz, 'Contracts and the Canon Law' in J Barton (ed), *Towards a General Law of Contract* (Berlin, Duncker & Humblot, 1990) 49.
[72] Berman, above n 8, 157–58.
[73] For references, see above n 55.
[74] Berman, above n 8, 427 n 55.
[75] Gordley, *Philosophical Origins*, above n 55, 71.

The influence of Grotius on Stair's account of rights is apparent from both internal citation and comparison of the two men's work;[76] but it is important to note that Stair did not always agree with his predecessor. The most significant example for present purposes is that, where Grotius held that an entirely unilateral promise only became binding as to its performance upon its acceptance by the promisee, Stair took the opposite view.[77] It was a topic upon which the Spanish scholastics had also differed.[78] The view Stair preferred meant, for Scots law, not only that the unilateral promise was binding simply by virtue of having been made, but also that the undertaking of contracting parties in favour of a third party likewise created a right for that third party directly. As a result, it was not even necessary that the promisee or the third party be in existence or fully capable in order for a right to be at least inchoate from the time of its formation by the promisors.[79]

Stephen Bogle and I have argued that this disagreement with Grotius is to be explained by Stair's much stricter Calvinism.[80] It would have been unthinkable for Stair to suggest, as Grotius had done,[81] that natural law's basis in human reason meant that it would be possible even if there was no God. In Stair's world view, the distinction between the obediential obligations imposed by God and self-imposed conventional obligations was not absolute. The starting point for the recognition of conventional obligations was certainly the moral position with regard to the exercise of individual free will. Being God-given, however, this too was subject to the obediential

[76] See JJ Gow, 'The Introduction of the Theory of Justice in Scots Law' (PhD thesis, University of Aberdeen, 1952); PG Stein, 'Stair's General Concepts: The Theory of Law' in DM Walker (ed), *Stair Tercentenary Studies*, vol 33 (Edinburgh, Stair Society, 1981) 181; WM Gordon, 'Stair, Grotius, and the Sources of Stair's Institutions' in JA Ankum, JE Spruit and FBJ Wubbe (eds), *Satura Roberto Feenstra* (Fribourg, Éditions universitaires, 1985) 571 (also in WM Gordon, *Roman Law, Scots Law and Legal History: Selected Essays* (Edinburgh University Press, 2007) 255); DL Carey Miller, 'Systems of Property: Grotius and Stair' in idem and DW Meyers (eds), *Comparative and Historical Essays in Scots Law: A Tribute to Professor Sir Thomas Smith QC* (Edinburgh, Butterworths, 1992) 13; T Richter, 'Molina, Grotius, Stair and the *jus quaesitum tertio*' [2001] *Juridical Review* 219; T Richter, 'Did Stair Know Pufendorf?' (2003) 7 *Edinburgh Law Review* 367; D Reid, 'Thomas Aquinas and Viscount Stair: The Influence of Scholastic Moral Theology on Stair's Account of Restitution and Recompense' (2008) 29 *Journal of Legal History* 189; ALM Wilson, 'Stair and the *Inleydinge* of Grotius' (2010) 14 *Edinburgh Law Review* 259.

[77] Grotius, *De Jure Belli ac Pacis*, II, 11, 14–18 (see also his *Inleydinge*, III, 1, 10–12, 48); Stair, above n 59, I, 10, 4–5. *De Jure Belli ac Pacis* was first published in Paris in 1625. Current translations are R Tuck, *The Rights of War and Peace* (Oxford, Oxford University Press, 1999); SC Neff, *Hugo Grotius on the Law of War and Peace* (Cambridge, Cambridge University Press, 2012). The *Inleydinge tot de Hollantsche rechtsgeleertheit* [*Introduction to Dutch Jurisprudence*] was published in The Hague in 1631. It is translated in RW Lee, *The Jurisprudence of Holland* (Oxford, Oxford University Press, 1926).

[78] Gordley, *Philosophical Origins*, above n 55, 73–77; Decock, above n 55, 176–92.

[79] See also HL MacQueen, 'Unilateral Promises: Scots Law Compared with the PECL and DCFR' (2016) 24 *European Review of Private Law* 529, 534–35, 545; idem, 'Reforming Third Party Rights in Contract: A Scottish Viewpoint' in L Peters (ed), *Eppur si muove: The Age of Uniform Law—Festschrift for Michael Joachim Bonell, to Celebrate his 70th Birthday* (Rome, UNIDROIT, 2016) 1066, 1069–70, 1074–75, 1080–82.

[80] H MacQueen and S Bogle, 'Private Autonomy and the Protection of the Weaker Party' in S Vogenauer and S Wetherill (eds), *General Principles of Law: European and Comparative Perspectives* (Oxford, Hart Publishing, 2017) 269.

[81] Grotius, above n 77, prologue.

obligations flowing from the will of God; ultimately, conventional obligations were also obediential.[82] Like the Spanish scholastics and the other northern European natural lawyers, Stair saw promise-keeping as virtuous. But he could not give the glory for promise-keeping—for undertaking and performing promises as a virtuous act—to man alone. For the strict Calvinist, man attained virtue only through God's grace. Stair's statement that man gives up his liberty through a promise or contract, 'whereby *God* obliges us to performance, by mediation of our own will', is wholly in keeping with the orthodoxy of Calvinist theology.[83] So a promise did not need the promisee's acceptance because the obligation was owed, first and foremost, to God. Likewise, in offer and acceptance there was no requirement that the latter be communicated to the offeror; it was enough that the acceptor had declared an intention to accept the offer.[84] It was also in this sense, it is submitted, that Stair said that the promise and third party right were irrevocable even if the beneficiary did not exist.[85] The commitment that had been made was absolute in the eye of an all-seeing God and so could not be withdrawn.

VI. MERCANTILE CONTRACTS

If Stair was a revolutionary in the seventeenth century in seeking to move the Scots law of contract on from its strictly Romanist character, then it could probably be said even at the time, and certainly in the eighteenth century, that he was a failed one. His contemporaries, and most later Scottish writers up to 1750, maintained the fourfold Roman distinction of contracts at the expense of the general model. Stair himself had written five chapters on Roman nominate contracts after his general one. Most significantly, he and his successors found great difficulty in applying the system of nominate contracts to what were ever more important standard mercantile transactions. Bills of exchange and insurance were unknown to Roman law, for example; yet, as Berman and others have noted, they were crucial lubricants of international, inter-regional and inter-city trade and credit throughout Europe from the later Middle Ages on.[86] Stair placed them in the category of innominate contracts of exchange: bills of exchange ('money for money') and 'the contract of assurance, where money or things are given, for the hazard of anything that is in danger, whether it be goods or persons.'[87]

[82] Stair, above n 59, I, 1, 18. This may also explain Stair's comment (ibid, I, 10, 13) about the interaction of obligations: 'Contract may intervene where there intercedes a natural and obediential obligation … yet where obediential and conventional obligations are concurring, they are both obligatory.'
[83] ibid, I, 10, 1 (emphasis supplied). See also ibid, I, 1, 20.
[84] See on this point H MacQueen, '"It's in the Post!" Distance Contracting in Scotland 1681–1855' in F McCarthy, J Chalmers and S Bogle (eds), *Essays in Conveyancing and Property Law in Honour of Professor Robert Rennie* (Cambridge, Open Book Publishers, 2015) 47.
[85] Stair, above n 59, I, 10, 4–5.
[86] See Berman, above n 8, 164–66; see also W Swain, *The Law of Contract 1670–1870* (Cambridge University Press, 2015) chs 3 and 4; SC Styles, 'Scottish Marine Insurance before the Mid-Eighteenth Century' in ARC Simpson, SC Styles, E West and ALM Wilson (eds), *Continuity, Change and Pragmatism in the Law: Essays in Honour of Professor Angelo Forte* (Aberdeen University Press, 2016) 237; G Rossi, *Insurance in Elizabethan England: The London Codes* (Cambridge, Cambridge University Press, 2016).
[87] Stair, above n 59, I, 10, 12.

William Forbes (*c* 1668–1745), who wrote from the beginning to the middle of the eighteenth century, introduced a non-Roman mixed form, the contract 'perfect, partly by Writ, partly by Consent', within which he placed, all on its own, the bill of exchange.[88] He made insurance a real contract, presumably because the insured paid a premium for which a return would be forthcoming upon defined events not certain to happen.[89] In the mid-eighteenth century, Andrew McDouall Lord Bankton (1685–1760) took the view that a bill of exchange 'is similar to *mutuum* [ie the real contract of loan]' but 'partakes likewise of mandate and exchange, and is a compound of all three, and has something farther peculiar to itself'.[90] Insurance, on the other hand, 'is a kind of sale, for thereby the assured purchases security to his goods for a certain premium given to the assurers',[91] so Bankton treated the subject (at some length) in the same chapter as sale, ie as a consensual contract.[92] John Erskine (1695–1768), writing in the 1760s, also placed insurance as a consensual contract, though one distinct from sale; it was, he thought, an aspect of the location, or chartering, of a ship.[93] However, Erskine dealt with bills of exchange in a Forbes-like way in the chapter on obligations by word and by writing, portraying them as a form of mandate, ie consensual, but always in writing, albeit informal.[94]

These conceptual struggles in Scotland came to a sudden end with the Edinburgh Professors of Scots Law in the late eighteenth and early nineteenth centuries, Baron David Hume (1757–1838) and George Joseph Bell (1770–1843).[95] They simply bypassed the Roman structures in their expositions and, indeed, in Hume's case, the idea of any general theory or law of contract as distinct from contracts.[96] For the latter, bills and insurance were quite straightforwardly particular forms of contract alongside sale, hire and all the others. Bell, however, sought to make Scots law fit for a commercial and mercantile world. To this end, he recognised a general law of both contract and unilateral voluntary obligations—within the latter of which

[88] W Forbes, *Institutes of the Laws of Scotland* in *Edinburgh Studies in Old Scots Law* (Edinburgh, Avizandum Publishing, 2012) 207–11 (originally published 1722–1730); W Forbes, *Great Body of the Law of Scotland*, available at <www.forbes.gla.ac.uk/contents/>, folios 880–98. Forbes had earlier published two editions of *A Methodical Treatise Concerning Bills of Exchange* (1703, 1718). See also ADM Forte, '"Calculated to our Meridian"? The Ius Commune, Lex Mercatoria and Scots Commercial Law in the Seventeenth and Eighteenth Centuries' in EC Reid and DL Carey Miller (eds), *A Mixed Legal System in Transition: TB Smith and the Progress of Scots Law* (Edinburgh, Edinburgh University Press, 2005) 120.

[89] Forbes, *Institutes,* above n 88, 185–91; Forbes, *Great Body*, above n 88, folios 788–818.

[90] Andrew McDouall Lord Bankton, *Institute of the Laws of Scotland* (Edinburgh, Stair Society, 1993–95) I, 13, 1. The text was originally published between 1751 and 1753.

[91] ibid I, 19, 28.

[92] ibid I, 19, 1–37 (permutation and sale) 38–46 (policy of insurance).

[93] J Erskine, *Institute of the Law of Scotland*, 8th edn (Edinburgh, Law Society of Scotland, 1871) III, 2, 17. The text was first published in 1773.

[94] ibid III, 2, 25–38. For the struggles of early modern jurists throughout Europe to fit insurance into the Roman scheme of contracts, see G Rossi 'Civilians and Insurance: Approximation of Reality to the Law' (2015) 83 *Tijdschrift voor Rechtsgeschiedenis* 323.

[95] Hume was the nephew of the philosopher of the same name.

[96] For detailed citations see also H MacQueen, 'The Law of Obligations in Scots Law' in R Schulze and F Zoll (eds), *The Law of Obligations in Europe: A New Wave of Codifications* (Munich, Sellier, 2013) 213, 218–22; see more generally JW Cairns, 'Historical Introduction' in KGC Reid and R Zimmermann (eds), *History of Private Law in Scotland* (Oxford Oxford University Press, 2000) vol 1, 166–72.

he placed bills of exchange and also promissory notes—and divided what he called mutual contracts into sale, hire, agency, maritime contracts and, finally, insurance. But the structure of the law was governed by mercantile functionality, not Roman categories.[97]

Did all this amount to a revolution in the law in Scotland or more widely in Western Europe? James Gordley has suggested that the significance of a general law of contract was largely theoretical.[98] In Scotland, the Tory Baron Hume, who disliked too much theory, would probably have agreed with him, if we may judge from the way he framed his lectures entirely in terms of a series of named contracts.[99] But the Whiggish Bell's different approach is of interest here. He wanted a flexible law that could respond in particular to the changing practices of merchants and traders. The Roman categories had proved unable to cope with standard kinds of commercial transactions and relationships in use for centuries—and not just the novelties, like negotiable instruments and insurance. Partnership, for example, was now something very different from *societas*, and mandate was not at all like contemporary agency, brokerage or factoring.[100] A general law of contract arching over the particular forms was the means by which the law could keep moving with the times; yet it would not itself become a rigid form, by virtue of its default nature giving primacy to what the parties expressly or impliedly agreed.

In these last few paragraphs, I have been trying to justify my title's inclusion of merchants amongst the possible revolutionary forces in private law, with their trading activities ignoring, or at any rate falling outside and challenging, the scope of the traditional law. This may also be reflected in the creation of codes of commercial law alongside but separate from the European civil codes and, indeed, the Uniform Commercial Code which emerged in twentieth-century USA. But whether or not these observations have succeeded in casting any fresh light on Harold Berman's ambitious thesis about the Western legal tradition and the relationship within it between law and revolution, let me finish by observing that our ability to discuss aspects of the law under the umbrella title of Obligations is due to an insight seemingly first achieved by the otherwise obscure Roman jurist Gaius nearly 2000 years ago—a legal paradigm still not overthrown?

[97] See also H MacQueen, 'Pragmatism, Precepts and Precedents: Commercial Law and Legal History' in Simpson et al, above n 87, 10.

[98] Gordley, *Foundations of Private Law*, above n 55, 291.

[99] MacQueen, above n 97, 21.

[100] ibid 23.

4

Paradigms Lost or Paradigms Regained? Legal Revolutions and the Path of the Law

TT ARVIND*

I. INTRODUCTION: THE REVOLUTIONARY TURN IN PRIVATE LAW

FOR MUCH OF its history, private law theory was incremental and conservative, particularly when it came to the fundamental categories and principles on which its intellectual apparatus was built. Even after the emergence of tort and contract from out of the detritus of the forms of action, early treatises were so firm in their adherence to established categories and classes, and so averse to attempts to detect broader general principles in the law, that Sir Frederick Pollock would later condemn them for seeing 'nothing but shreds and patches' in the law.[1]

This is no longer true. The half-century since the publication of the first edition of *The Law of Restitution* has seen a new, revolutionary turn in private law theory, in which theorists increasingly question fundamental aspects of the way in which private law is organised. *The Law of Restitution* not only created a new taxon, but also sought to reclassify into that taxon significant portions of the law that had historically been seen as belonging to other areas. This revolutionary tendency has been taken up not only by the restitution-oriented and restitution-inspired scholarship associated with the school of Peter Birks, but also the corrective justice school and a broad range of private law scholars—seen, not least, in the fact that two of the past three Obligations conferences have borne the titles of 'Challenging Orthodoxy'[2] and 'Revolutions in Private Law'.

* I am grateful to Christine Beuermann, Joshua Getzler, Steve Hedley, Caitlin O'Neil, Andrew Robertson, Geoffrey Samuel, Jenny Steele, Ilke Turkmendag and participants at the Obligations VIII Conference for their comments on this chapter.

[1] F Pollock, 'The Province of the Law of Tort. By Percy H Winfield' (1931) 57 *LQR* 588, 589. Pollock was referring to the work of Charles Addison, a Victorian jurist who had published a treatise on contract in 1847 and one on tort in 1860. See CG Addison, *A Treatise on the Law of Contracts and Rights and Liabilities Ex Contractu* (London, W Benning, 1847); CG Addison, *Wrongs and their Remedies, Being a Treatise on the Law of Torts* (London, Stevens and Sons, 1860). Pollock's comment was directed at Addison's treatise on tort, but he described the book on contract as being even worse—see Pollock, ibid, 589.

[2] See S Pitel, J Neyers and E Chamberlain (eds), *Tort Law: Challenging Orthodoxy* (Oxford, Hart Publishing, 2013).

Far fewer people now remember another, very different, development that took place only three years after the publication of *The Law of Restitution*, and which was no less significant than the appearance of that treatise. In 1969, the Society of Public Teachers of Law, as it then was, held a joint seminar with the Law Commissions of England and Scotland on the subject of the division and classification of law.[3] The theme that emerged from the seminar was the precise opposite of the approach to legal classification taken by Goff and Jones. Rather than seeking to revive older and timeless concepts, the participants in the seminar pointed to the inadequacy of traditional ways of classifying the law even for the purpose of deciding cases:

> the value of the existing divisions and headings lies principally in the fact that they are more or less well understood; they should not be treated as possessing some kind of fundamental significance which can give to them a controlling role when it comes to the decision of individual cases. In other words, even if the law itself can be classified in accordance with the accepted terminology, care must be exercised to avoid the classification of concrete cases in such a way that their solution in terms of law appears to be dictated by their classification.[4]

What was needed was a radical move towards a more fact-based system of classification.[5] Such an approach, it was thought:

> would reveal anomalies and inequalities by bringing into juxtaposition concrete situations which are similar in their social or factual significance but are at present treated as falling under different branches of law and for that reason treated differently by the law.[6]

In purely objective terms, this seminar was as path-breaking as the development of restitution theory. It left an intellectual legacy in its influence on the work of the Law Commission and on legal scholarship more generally, not least through its introduction of fact-based categories, which continue to be influential.[7] Many of the more radical categories it introduced, like labour law and consumer law,[8] are now the subject of a broad academic consensus, unlike restitution, whose scope and fundamental principles remain the subject of considerable controversy.

It is, nevertheless, a peculiarity of the way the intellectual history of private law over the past half-century is told that this latter seminar plays no part in the story of key moments in the history of private law during the twentieth century. This chapter will argue that the reason for this peculiarity lies in a peculiar feature of legal revolutions. In the modern cultural imagination, the term 'revolution' is primarily associated with a sense of 'overthrowing'—with radical, rupturing change, where a

[3] The papers from the seminar were published in JA Jolowicz (ed), *The Division and Classification of the Law* (London, Butterworths, 1970), which also explains the reason for the seminar and the goals it hoped to achieve.

[4] JA Jolowicz and PB Fairest, 'Summary of Discussion' in Jolowicz, ibid, 86.

[5] The case for a fact-based system was put by Professor Jolowicz in a paper circulated to the membership of the SPTL prior to the seminar, which was subsequently reprinted in the final volume. JA Jolowicz, 'Fact Based Classification of Law' in Jolowicz, above n 3.

[6] Jolowicz and Fairest, above n 4, 86–87.

[7] See, eg, S Hedley 'Contract, Tort and Restitution: Or on Cutting the Legal System Down to Size' (1988) 8 *Legal Studies* 137.

[8] At the time, a 'labour lawyer' would generally have been taken to be a lawyer who supported the Labour Party (as seen, for example, in the name of the Society of Labour Lawyers).

connection to the past is broken, and older frameworks and systems are torn down to be replaced with newer, freshly devised frameworks and systems. Yet the term 'revolution' also carries an older sense not of overthrow, but of return or recovery.[9] To complete a revolution in a geometric sense is to come full circle; marking the return to, or restoration of, an imagined original position.

This older sense of 'revolution' is familiar in legal history. The English revolutionaries of the seventeenth century did not seek to destroy the existing order as much as they sought to restore the 'Ancient Constitution'—an older, more perfect and more natural order which had come to be corrupted due to human action and human innovation over the course of history.[10] In recent private law revolutions, too, it is this older sense of revolution that has dominated. Unlike scientific revolutions, such as those studied by Thomas Kuhn,[11] legal revolutions expressly seek to restore rather than rupture the law's connection with its past. The goal they espouse is that of recovering lost paradigms rather than creating new ones. The attempts to remake private law which began in the 1980s, in particular, are characterised by a strong sense of looking back and seeking to recover older forms of thinking about private law which, it is claimed, are superior to those that characterise the present day. Their radicalism is the 'radicalism of tradition'.[12]

Birksian taxonomy, for example, expressly seeks to draw on the work of jurists of the late Roman Empire—in particular, Gaius and Ulpian, whose work is said to have such an enduring and immediate relevance that engagement with them can and will improve the quality of English law.[13] Corrective justice, similarly, looks back to ideas articulated by Aristotle and Kant, which its proponents claim were once more central to English law than they now are, and which they seek to restore to that central position.[14] It has even been claimed by commentators (but not by the protagonists themselves) that the American realists were reaching back beyond the intervening period of the 'Formal Style' to the earlier, pre-Civil War, period of the 'Grand Style', in which courts were far less concerned with the dry words of rules and far more willing to adjust law in order to deal with the changing context, and better respond to social pressures and social needs.[15] Across a diverse range of schools and scholars, putative revolutions in the law are now conceptualised in terms of their relation to older and better modes of thinking about law which have now been forgotten[16]

[9] See C Calhoun, *The Roots of Radicalism: Tradition, the Public Sphere, and Early Nineteenth-Century Social Movements* (Chicago, University of Chicago Press, 2012) 76–77.

[10] JGA Pocock, *The Ancient Constitution and the Feudal Law*, reissued edn (Cambridge, Cambridge University Press, 1987).

[11] T Kuhn, *The Structure of Scientific Revolutions*, 3rd edn (Chicago, University of Chicago Press, 1996).

[12] Calhoun, above n 9, 82–120.

[13] See, eg, P Birks, 'Definition and Division: A Meditation on Institutes 3.13' in P Birks (ed), *The Classification of Obligations* (Oxford, Clarendon Press, 1997).

[14] EJ Weinrib, *Corrective Justice* (Oxford, Oxford University Press, 2012).

[15] G Gilmore, *The Ages of American Law* (New Haven, Yale University Press, 1977) 12.

[16] See, eg, A Beever, *Forgotten Justice: Forms of Justice in the History of Legal and Political Theory* (Oxford, Oxford University Press, 2013).

or from which we have fallen away,[17] and which we must seek to restore.[18] Such a restoration, so it is argued, is both possible and desirable.[19]

It is this, then, that distinguishes the 1969 seminar from the publication of *The Law of Restitution*. While *The Law of Restitution* was grounded in concepts and categories taken from the past, the 1969 seminar by express choice was not. They thus instantiate two divergent models of the contribution academic jurists can make to legal adaptation: the first a revolutionary model focusing on using the past to construct a grand theory of relevance to the present, and the second a heuristic model which seeks to devise solutions rooted in contextual details of contemporary problems and whose engagement with the past is diagnostic rather than prescriptive.

This chapter argues that the revolutionary model has failed. Restoration of lost paradigms is neither possible nor desirable. It is not possible because, whilst it is possible for older approaches and modes of thought that have been 'lost' to be reconstructed, legal revolutions cannot truly turn the wheel around to return to older positions, nor can they be put to work in the radically altered context that the present necessarily is. Even were it possible, it would not be desirable because the consequences of articulating legal doctrine in a way that emphasises its timeless continuity, even as the context in which it operates changes, are fundamentally negative. Legal revolutions which seek to recover a lost past are counter-productive because, far from leading to the establishment of a new paradigm, their tendency is to produce a phenomenon akin to incommensurability—a 'scampering discourse', as Richard Mullender has termed it,[20] with different wings of legal theory so widely separated that they can no longer even be said to be studying the same phenomenon.

The aim of this chapter is to offer a diagnosis of what it is about attempts to shape legal revolutions that leads to their having a propensity to produce deleterious effects. Section II sets the stage by demonstrating how revolutionary accounts of the law fall short of their own promises. Sections III and IV build on that argument to show, through a detailed engagement with Kuhn's work on scientific revolutions and scientific paradigms, that attempted legal revolutions differ fundamentally from scientific revolutions (section III), and that legal paradigms are characterised by features that have no counterpart in scientific paradigms (section IV). Thus, whilst they seek to return to the past, they almost invariably fail to give adequate weight to important aspects of the past and, in consequence, embed dramatically different evaluative positions from those with which they claim continuity. Legal theory has spent

[17] R Stevens, *Torts and Rights* (Oxford, Oxford University Press, 2007).

[18] See, eg, A Beever, *Rediscovering the Law of Negligence* (Oxford, Hart Publishing, 2007).

[19] It is at least arguable that some of the work, in the immense value it attaches to the past, crosses the line into committing what, in historiographic terms, is commonly termed the fallacy of nostalgia. See J Tosh, *The Pursuit of History*, 3rd edn (London, Longman, 2002) 17–18. It should, of course, be noted that interpretivist legal scholars reject the relevance of historiography for legal engagement with history: the fact that their engagement with the past is historiographically problematic is, on this account, irrelevant to their enterprise. See generally A Beever and C Rickett, 'Interpretive Legal Theory and the Academic Lawyer' (2005) 68 *MLR* 320.

[20] R Mullender, 'The Scampering Discourse of Negligence Law' (2010) 7 *The Journal Jurisprudence* 575.

too long seeking progress through revolutions. It is time to move to a more modest definition and understanding of the goals and capabilities of legal scholarship.

II. THE LIMITS OF LEGAL REVOLUTIONS

Legal revolutionaries have been criticised by their opponents for the selectivity of their engagement with the past.[21] Selective engagement with the past can lead to two types of errors. In the first instance, it can lead to a misunderstanding of how the law reached its present position, and of the choices made in that process. It can thus lead to a mistaken view of the historical inevitability of the law as it presently stands, and to inadequate attention being paid to alternatives that have in fact been present in the past of the law. Secondly, it can lead to false accounts of the law itself, by reading normative choices into it that it does not in fact make, while failing to appreciate the normative choices implicit in the types of outcomes the law currently favours.

This leaves legal revolutions prone to three different types of weaknesses. First, they tend to oversimplify the past, ignoring alternative ways of viewing the law or framing legal problems which existed in the past. Secondly, by interpreting the past in the light of the needs of the present, they also ignore the true character of the evaluative positions implicit in the past of the law, with the result that legal revolutions frequently end up embedding into legal doctrine positions which are radically different from those with which they claim continuity. Thirdly, they leave themselves prone to failures to perceive the normative shifts which characterised the transition from the past to the present, and which continue to influence the law.[22]

A. (Mis)interpreting the Past: A Revolutionary Problem

Let us begin with the first and second of these weaknesses. Both are instantiated by the restitutionary view of equity. The rejection of equity by the restitutionary revolution's protagonists is grounded in a view of equity which sees equity as a historical accident having no objectively justifiable basis as a taxon. What we call 'equity' today contains a disparate set of actions united only by their roots in a now-abolished jurisdiction. Modernising the law, they argue, requires replacing historical accidents with more logical categories.

The restitutionary view of equity claims support from the traditional division of the equitable jurisdiction into the auxiliary, concurrent and exclusive jurisdictions. As the labels suggest, this division conceptualised equity in terms of the relationship between its jurisdiction and the jurisdiction of common law courts. Yet this

[21] This is a key theme in, for example, S Waddams, *Dimensions of Private Law: Categories and Concepts in Anglo-American Legal Reasoning* (Cambridge, Cambridge University Press, 2003).

[22] A similar point has been made in relation to Kuhn's account of scientific revolutions by theorists who argue that the attention it focuses on science's past deflects attention away from the modern social role of science and the normative choices implicit in assigning it that particular role. See, eg, S Fuller, *Thomas Kuhn: A Philosophical History for Our Times* (Chicago, Chicago University Press, 2000).

division is a recent one. Although familiar from nineteenth-century writings, it first appeared only at the very close of the eighteenth century, and for the first decades of the nineteenth century it had to compete with older conceptions of equity which were wholly substantive and which continued to command support as statements of equity's jurisdiction.

The oldest of these substantive accounts is a well-known couplet printed in Rolle's Abridgment and attributed there to Thomas More:

> Three things are to be helpt in Conscience;
> Fraud, Accident, and things of Confidence.[23]

This continued to be the orthodox statement of the scope of equity jurisdiction, in various formulations, through the course of the eighteenth century. As late as 1815, an amended version was put forward by Henry Maddock:

> It will, however, be more convenient to consider the Equity Jurisdiction of the Chancellor (except what relates to the Practice, which will be treated of hereafter) under the following heads:
>
> 1. Accident and Mistake.
> 2. Account.
> 3. Fraud.
> 4. Infants.
> 5. Specific Performance of Agreements.
> 6. Trusts.
>
> According, even to this enlarged classification of the subject, it may not be very obvious how the great multiplicity of doctrines arising out of the Equity Jurisdiction, can be included; but on consulting the divisions and subdivisions of each head, it will be found, that, without any arbitrary classification, they include every branch of Equity.[24]

Others, such as Lord Redesdale, put forward accounts which were remedial, in that they sought to describe the jurisdiction of equity with reference to the remedies it granted and the situations in which they were granted, rather than the jurisdiction in which those remedies were granted.[25]

The first traceable account of equity jurisdiction which is recognisably jurisdictional is found in the editorial notes added by John Fonblanque[26] to an anonymous treatise entitled *A Treatise of Equity*, conventionally attributed to Henry Ballow.[27] It thereafter appears to have spread rapidly as a way of understanding the basis of equity jurisdiction. Fonblanque's note is brief, going no further than naming

[23] 1 Roll Abr 374.

[24] H Maddock, *A Treatise on the Principles and Practice of the High Court of Chancery* (London, W Clarke, 1815).

[25] J Mitford, *A Treatise on the Pleadings in Suits in the Court of Chancery by English Bill*, 2nd edn (Dublin, P Bryne, 1795).

[26] J Fonblanque (ed), *A Treatise of Equity* (Dublin, P Bryne, 1793).

[27] The treatise was first attributed by Fonblanque to Henry Ballow in the second edition. In a 1792 printing of the treatise (without Fonblanque's notes) in Dublin, however, it was attributed on the title page to Sir Jeffrey Gilbert. Given Gilbert's career as Chief Baron of the Irish Exchequer, the attribution merits consideration, although Macnair does not list it among Gilbert's treatises. M Macnair, 'Sir Jeffrey Gilbert and his Treatises' (1994) 15 *Journal of Legal History* 252.

and very briefly describing the auxiliary, concurrent and exclusive jurisdictions. The reasoning behind the classification is not given. The American edition of the treatise, however, goes into greater detail. Maddock's classification is acknowledged, but is expressly rejected in favour of the system proposed by Fonblanque. The rationale, as it appears in the text, is that 'such a method seems to be dictated by the character of equity as an auxiliary system engrafted on the ordinary jurisprudence'.[28] It was, in other words, expressly devised in order to help lawyers meet a very practical problem, namely, the fact that a growing range of transactions could potentially have fallen within the jurisdiction of Chancery as well as King's Bench, creating a need for some sort of system to map the relationship between the two.[29] The jurisdictional account of equity, in other words, was not put forward as a full account of what equity was about or of its place within the overall legal system. It simply reflected the need for a practical solution to a practical problem.

In treating the jurisdictional account of equity as *the* account of equity (rather than as simply one of many accounts of equity), restitutionary scholarship displays a key weakness of legal revolutions—namely, their propensity to seize upon one moment in the past, or one tendency within the past, and treat it as paradigmatic of the past, paying little attention to the fact that the past of the law also contains radically different ways of thinking about the law. This problem is not confined to equity as a taxonomic category, but also applies to theorisation about the relationship of individual equitable actions to other branches of law. As Andrew Robertson points out in his contribution to this volume, a study of how estoppel worked 300 years ago produces a very different picture from a focus on how estoppel worked 50 years ago.[30]

This also leads revolutionary theorists to a second weakness, namely, ignoring the true character of the evaluative positions embedded in the past of the law. Once again, equity provides a very good example. If we look at the substantive actions that were said to be within equity's jurisdiction even as late as the nineteenth century, equity is seen to have dealt with aspects of transactions that have normative significance, but are inadequately addressed by its restitution replacement. Haynes's *Outlines of Equity*,[31] for example, on its face discusses equity in terms of the three types of jurisdiction. Nevertheless, a closer reading reveals a clear theme uniting the actions governed by the exclusive jurisdiction. Within this heading, Haynes places four matters—trusts; administration; married women's property; and mortgages, penalties and forfeiture. It is striking that all four of these are primarily concerned with situations marked by the presence of Hohfeldian powers—that is, with situations where one person has the legal ability to alter the jural relations to which another is party.[32] This continues to find an echo in modern equity jurisprudence,

[28] A Laussat (ed), *A Treatise of Equity*, 3rd American edn (Philadelphia, John Grigg, 1831) 21–32.

[29] Fonblanque cites Redesdale's treatise as the source on which he based his jurisdictional account of equity. Redesdale's treatise itself, however, takes a remedial approach (as discussed above). It is quite significant that the only reference to auxiliary, concurrent and exclusive jurisdictions in Redesdale occurs in a discussion of demurrers in relation to the jurisdiction of Chancery. Mitford, above n 25, 103ff.

[30] A Robertson, 'Revolutions and Counterrevolutions in Equitable Estoppel', this volume, chapter 9.

[31] FO Haynes, *Outlines of Equity* (Cambridge, Macmillan, 1858).

[32] W Hohfeld, 'Some Fundamental Legal Conceptions as Applied in Legal Reasoning' (1913) 23 *Yale Law Journal* 16.

as Robertson discusses in relation to estoppel,[33] but it has no equivalent in restitutionary theory. Yet powers and immunities are juristically different from claims and privileges, and there is good reason to question an approach that does not recognise this difference.

Equity in its classical form was, in other words, distinguished not by a distinctive jurisprudence,[34] but by its concern with a distinctive set of issues. A close study of the types of matters that eighteenth- and nineteenth-century commentators treated as falling within equity suggests quite strongly that the jurisdictional conception of equity was contingent rather than inevitable, and that even after its acceptance equity had considerable internal coherence. The failure of restitutionary accounts to take adequate notice of this and their espousal of rules embedding very different evaluative positions demonstrate a fundamental weakness of revolutionary movements within law—namely, that their acceptance or rejection of aspects of the law takes inadequate account of the actual work that those aspects do within the legal system, and hence run the risk of leaving important legal needs unaddressed.

B. Normative Choices and Legal Change

The two weaknesses we have examined thus far relate to the tendency of revolutionary movements in law to overly simplify the complexity of the past and to ignore alternate possibilities present in the past. A similar point can be made in relation to the manner in which they approach legal change. This is illustrated by a second area of law, namely, public authority liability. I have discussed the complex history of this area of law in the twentieth century elsewhere, and I do not propose to repeat its details here.[35] Briefly put, however, the peculiar position of public authority liability in tort is a result of two specific motives, both traceable to Lord Diplock. The first was a desire to insulate the courts from sitting in judgment over policy decisions made by the executive, particularly in relation to the goals that a particular authority chose to prioritise and the means it adopted in their pursuit. The second was to ensure that private law did not in any way disturb the supervisory framework over executive action set up by public law. Thus, a crucial feature of the decision in *Home Office v Dorset Yacht*,[36] a case more commonly associated with the expansion of the tort of negligence rather than its retreat, was Lord Diplock's protective approach to public authorities. An action of a public authority, he suggested, should only

[33] Robertson, above n 30.

[34] M Lobban, 'Preparing for Fusion: Reforming the Nineteenth-Century Court of Chancery (Part 1)' (2004) 22 *Law and History Review* 389; M Lobban, 'Preparing for Fusion: Reforming the Nineteenth-Century Court of Chancery (Part 2)' (2004) 22 *Law and History Review* 565.

[35] TT Arvind, 'Restraining the State through Tort? The Crown Proceedings Act in Retrospect' in TT Arvind and J Steele (eds), *Tort Law and the Legislature: Common Law, Statute and the Dynamics of Legal Change* (Oxford, Hart Publishing, 2012); TT Arvind and L Stirton, 'The Curious Origins of Judicial Review' (2017) 133 *LQR* 91.

[36] *Home Office v Dorset Yacht Co Ltd* [1970] AC 1004.

ever lead to liability in tort if it was in violation of both private law and public law standards. To violate the one without violating the other should lead to no liability.

Beneath the surface of the revolution in the tort of negligence, therefore, is an approach that is extraordinarily defensive of public authorities. This approach is present in core cases, and is a part of a fundamental structure of the doctrine. To discuss public authority liability in terms of distributive and corrective justice or principle and policy, or any of the other conceptual apparatuses put forward by theorists seeking to revolutionise private law, is misleading, because it draws our attention away not only from the genealogy of the evaluative positions that we currently see embedded in legal doctrine, but from the actual evaluative position embedded in doctrine, as well as the types of outcomes which the law seeks to facilitate.

Situations of this type are not exceptional. They characterise attempts to foment revolutions in law, and reflect deep-running flaws in the structure of legal revolutions. To see this, however, we must return to scientific revolutions and study how they lead to change, before examining how legal revolutions differ.

III. SCIENTIFIC REVOLUTIONS AND LEGAL REVOLUTIONS

A. A Matter of Light

One of the more frequently cited examples of a scientific revolution is the story of the rise to dominance of the wave theory of light. The history as it is conventionally told is an arresting one. In 1818, an engineer by the name of Augustin Jean Fresnel submitted an essay to a competition that had been organised by the French Academy of Sciences. The topic of the competition was the diffraction of light, and Fresnel's paper presented an account of diffraction that dramatically, and fundamentally, challenged conventional wisdom.[37]

Diffraction was a theoretically problematic phenomenon. It was known to exist, but it was poorly accounted for. Since the publication of Newton's *Opticks*, light had been seen as particulate—a stream of tiny particles called 'corpuscles' travelling in a straight line. Why, then, did this stream seem to bend when it encountered the edges of obstructions? Newton's explanation was not consistent with the results of subsequent experiments. Theorists had come up with equations which could partially account for the bending by supposing that the corpuscles' path was influenced by forces which emanated from the objects they encountered. But it was generally acknowledged that the observed patterns of diffraction bands were hard to explain on the basis of the corpuscular theory.

[37] The story of Fresnel's paper and its role in establishing the wave theory has become part of scientific folklore, and has been told in a number of sources in a number of different versions. However, the definitive account on which the version told in this chapter is based is contained in JZ Buchwald, *The Rise of the Wave Theory of Light: Optical Theory and Experiment in the Early Nineteenth Century* (Chicago, University of Chicago Press, 1989), which is entirely based on the primary sources, including correspondence and minutes, and corrects a number of errors in the traditional accounts.

Newton was not, however, the first to formulate a theory of light. Around 25 years before *Opticks*, the Dutch scientist Christiaan Huygens had proposed that light consisted of waves. A wave theory of light could explain diffraction, but the Newtonian corpuscular theory had considerable (albeit not universal) hold in the scientific community.

Fresnel's paper proposed a solution based on the wave theory. The mathematics was ingenious, involving functions based on improper integrals which remain in use today as the 'Fresnal integrals'. But it faced an uphill task. Newton's theory was strongly defended by Pierre-Simon Laplace, the grand old man of French science. The five-member commission charged with awarding the prize included not only Laplace himself, but also Siméon Poisson and Jean-Baptiste Biot, both committed Laplaceans and supporters of the corpuscular theory of light.

In the conventional telling of the story, what transpired next was an extraordinary series of events leading to a dramatic collapse of the accepted Newtonian paradigm. In the Commission's deliberations, Poisson led the attack on Fresnel's theory. Perusing the mathematics, he noticed an implication of the equations which had escaped Fresnel. The equations, he pointed out, made a most striking prediction. They suggested that if a disc or sphere were to be placed in the path of light emanating from a small hole, there should be a bright spot in the middle of the shadow cast by the disc. This, clearly, was absurd. But another member of the Commission, François Arago, was more sympathetically disposed to the wave theory, and he suggested that the Commission put the prediction to a test. The test revealed, to general surprise, that the prediction was correct—counter-intuitively, there was indeed a black spot in the centre of the shadow. The result, as Kuhn put it, was that 'French resistance collapsed suddenly and relatively completely'. A scientific revolution had taken place, and a paradigm had shifted.[38]

B. A Legal Parallel?

There is more to the story of the wave theory of light than the received telling allows, and we will return to it in section IV of this chapter. The conventional account, however, on its face presents a striking parallel to legal revolutions in at least three ways. By the time the first edition of *The Law of Restitution* was published, it had become apparent that the traditional account of the actions that were variously called 'quasi-contract' or 'constructive contract'[39] failed to explain why they existed and functioned as they did. As with diffraction, the core insight underlying the revolutionary paradigm was not new: the theoretical concept of restitution was known before *The Law of Restitution*, just as the idea that light could be a wave was known before Fresnel presented his theory. Also like diffraction, the main shift that separated the two was an ontological one, relating to the nature of light rays in the case of Fresnel's work and to the nature of certain common law actions and remedies in

[38] Kuhn, above n 11, 155.

[39] The term was used by analogy with constructive trust, constructive notice, constructive fraud, etc. See, eg, JC Knowlton, 'Quasi Contractual Obligation of Municipal Corporations' (1911) 9 *Michigan Law Review* 671, 671.

The Law of Restitution. Likewise, what gave Fresnel's account its power was not the attractiveness of conceptualising light as waves rather than particles, nor was it merely the fact that the new theory had explanatory value. The key to its success lay in the fact that it also had predictive value. As its success in the face of Poisson's challenge demonstrated, the conceptual framework it created was capable of dealing with issues and matters that had not been anticipated and, indeed, whose existence was not suspected when the theory was devised.[40] In this, again, there is a parallel to the *Law of Restitution*, whose success sprang not as much because of the normative attractiveness of the scheme it used to explain the past cases as because of the guidance it offered on their application.

Despite these similarities, however, there are two important differences between scientific revolutions and the legal revolutions that private law theorists have attempted to foment over the past 50 years. The phenomena that are the subject of science are for the most part unchanging. Our ability to observe them and acquire accurate knowledge about them may change as we acquire better and more reliable instruments, but the phenomena themselves do not change. This is manifestly not true of law, where the social and jural relations that are its subject can and do change dramatically. Whether a society is feudal, capitalist, agrarian, industrial or post-industrial makes no difference whatsoever to the interaction between atoms and the patterns of molecular reactions or atomic decay that are the subject of the natural sciences. They do, however, fundamentally alter the patterns of social interaction and the types of social conflict with which the legal system and the laws of the realm deal. In law, as in the social sciences generally, the problem with speaking of the cumulative growth of knowledge over time is that the thing known—society—keeps changing.[41] Unlike the physical sciences, where the basic nature of atoms does not change, societies do.

The consequence is of profound significance. The statements of natural science—scientific 'laws'—apply in contexts and settings that are far removed from those in which they were originally formulated. Legal rules, doctrines and principles, in contrast, do not have universal application. Planck's constant does not depend on social understandings of electromagnetic waves. The rules for the quantification of damages in personal injury cases, and even the broad approach that is taken to the quantification of such damages, do, however, depend on the social understandings and consequences of injury that characterise a polity.

This difference is closely related to the second major divergence, namely, that in law, unlike in science, the act of describing a phenomenon alters the nature of the thing studied. In science, our articulation of a law does not change the subject of our study, merely its understanding. A new paradigm on the nature of black holes does not change the nature of black holes, much as the effect of the acceptance of Fresnel's theory did not lead to a change in the character of light rays. It only affects the scientific understanding of the phenomenon. This is not true of law, whose theories

[40] On this, see J Worrall, 'Fresnel, Poisson, and the White Spot: The Role of Successful Predictions in the Acceptance of Scientific Theories' in D Gooding, T Pinch and S Schaffer (eds), *The Uses of Experiment: Studies in the Natural Sciences* (Cambridge, Cambridge University Press, 1989).

[41] cf the argument in G Samuel, 'Is Legal Knowledge Cumulative?' (2012) 32 *Legal Studies* 448.

seek to alter the phenomena themselves. Indeed, the quest to do so is arguably the constitutive essence of legal revolutions.

Given the thrust of these two differences, the third at first sight might seem somewhat paradoxical. It relates to the way in which legal revolutions and scientific revolutions engage with the past. A scientific revolution engages with paradigms of the past only to the extent that they are part of the present. They do not seek to vindicate them, nor do they see them as having a timeless significance. Fresnel did not draw on the work of Huygens because he believed it to have a lasting authority, unlike the way in which the works of Ulpian, Kant and Aristotle have been portrayed in modern legal revolutions.[42] Unlike modern taxonomists, he did not believe that Huygens's theory was a 'software' which all theories of light had to run.[43] His paper was not an attempt to be faithful to Huygens, or even an exploration of the relevance of Huygens's thought. It was an attempt to solve a contemporary problem, in which Huygens's theory only played a role because it was part of the existing knowledge base. His use of the work of Huygens was, in other words, purely heuristic.[44]

This is typical of scientific thought and of the manner in which scientific paradigms are constructed. But it is not true of legal revolutions. There are certainly striking similarities between the heuristic guidance provided by the past in scientific progress and the role played by the past in non-revolutionary legal change, the 1969 seminar discussed in section I of this chapter being a classic case in point. But revolutionary legal change is radically different. The restitution and corrective justice revolutionaries have not sought to use Ulpian, Kant or Aristotle heuristically. Rather, they claim an authority for them that is not just enduring,[45] but also unavoidable,[46] and they accordingly seek to apply these older frameworks to the modern context in a way that is faithful to the original conception.[47] As discussed in the next section in greater detail, it is this characteristic of legal revolutions that makes them so prone to produce outcomes that are both unhelpful and deleterious to the integrity of the legal system.

IV. PARADIGMS, THEORIES AND BLACK-LETTER LAW

A. Revolutions and Paradigms

The discussion thus far has focused on legal and scientific revolutions. Revolutions, in the Kuhnian sense, reflect changes or shifts in paradigms. Kuhn's account was

[42] On the significance of the role of authority in legal scholarship and its consequences for how we understand the enterprise in which legal scholars are engaged, see G Samuel, 'Is Law Really a Social Science? A View from Comparative Law' (2008) 67 *CLJ* 288.

[43] Peter Birks famously asserted that Gaius not only provided a software for legal thought, but that this was the best software available for the purpose of analysing the law of obligations in England in the twenty-first century: P Birks, 'Introduction' in P Birks (ed), *English Private Law* (Oxford, Oxford University Press, 2000) xliv–xlvii.

[44] J Worrall, '"Revolution in Permanence": Popper on Theory-Change in Science' in A O'Hear (ed), *Karl Popper: Philosophy and Problems* (Cambridge, Cambridge University Press, 1996) 92.

[45] See, eg, P Birks, 'Roman Law in Twentieth-Century Britain' in J Beatson and R Zimmermann (eds), *Jurists Uprooted: German-Speaking Émigré Lawyers in Twentieth-Century Britain* (Oxford, Oxford University Press, 2004).

[46] See, eg, the remarks on Gaius in Birks, above n 43.

[47] See, eg, EJ Weinrib, *The Idea of Private Law* (Cambridge, Harvard University Press, 1995).

concerned with scientific paradigms. Legal reasoning and analytical frameworks are, however, conventionally described in terms of theories and doctrine, rather than paradigms. What, then, do we gain by importing the concept of paradigms from theories of revolutions in natural sciences into law?

The answer lies in certain aspects of legal disagreement which are crucial to understanding the path of the law, and on which the idea of a legal paradigm puts particular focus. When we speak in terms of theories and doctrines, we place weight on two particular aspects of the frameworks we use in law: namely, the structured set of concepts they contain and the rules that are brought to bear in associating particular sets of concepts with particular situations. If, however, we look more closely at the character of theoretical debates in private law, it becomes apparent that simply focusing on structured sets of concepts gives us an inadequate account of these debates. Speaking in terms of paradigms, rather than merely theories, in contrast makes what is at stake much clearer.

What Kuhn meant by a 'paradigm' has been much misunderstood and, particularly in the social sciences, has come to be associated largely with the high-level conceptual frameworks and world-views that we associate with theory in the social sciences and humanities. But whilst paradigms do encompass these frameworks, they are not the crucial part of a paradigm. To Kuhn, the crucial part of a paradigm was not the framework, but the exemplars—the 'paradigmatic' instances of the application of a framework to a particular problem or (in the case of law) to a particular set of facts or a particular type of situation.

Exemplars, in the form of the legal hypothetical, are endemic within law, ranging from the Roman problem of the barber who cuts the throat of a slave after having his hand jostled by a carelessly kicked ball to Peter Birks's tales of mistaken window washers. It is these exemplars, and not the mere theories and laws, that are the constitutive essence of paradigms, a point which Kuhn lamented as the 'least understood aspect' of his book.[48] Secondary discussions of Kuhn's account of how paradigms compete have tended to focus on his theory of incommensurability. But incommensurability is primarily Kuhn's explanation for why paradigm shifts are both difficult and contested. It is not the essential characteristic of a paradigm. Paradigms represent consensus not just about theories and frameworks, but also about problems and solutions which instantiate the exemplary application of those theories and frameworks, and which, additionally, are accepted as being exemplars of good science generally. Theories and frameworks are not by themselves paradigms without also containing the application of the theories to the solution of important problems and without having won broad-based acceptance for their assertion that those are exemplary in the literal sense: examples of how science can be done, of how it ought to be done and of the power of the results we get when science is done as it ought to be done.[49]

It is in this context that Kuhn, in discussing the emergence and passing of scientific paradigms, emphasises the problem-solving potentialities of paradigms. For a new paradigm to be accepted, it must promise to solve a problem that the existing

[48] Kuhn, above n 11, 187.
[49] ibid, 187–91.

paradigm cannot, and it must do so without sacrificing things that the existing paradigms can solve, whilst also demonstrating that it is good science.[50] Putative paradigms may win adherents, but they will not come to be accepted as paradigms until these criteria are satisfied through the exemplars the paradigm includes.

Kuhn thus points to the close relationship within paradigms of epistemology and method, ontology and evaluative judgments as to outcomes. This also holds true not just for the manner in which legal approaches—whether Birksian theory, corrective justice theory or legal realism—make a case for acceptance, but more fundamentally for the nature of the controversies legal revolutions cause.

Restitution, once again, provides a good example. The taxonomic approach to restitution has been criticised on the basis that the outcomes it produces are unattractive—for example, because they unacceptably widen liability[51]—but the criticisms extend much further than just this. A more fundamental criticism has been that it is no way to do good scholarship—a criticism that almost inevitably attacks the precise things that Kuhn terms exemplars, the instances showcased by the theory. David Campbell, for example, drew an unfavourable comparison between the approach of Peter Birks and the approach taken by the American Legal Realists, making the point that the approach taken by Llewellyn instantiated good scholarship in a way that the approach taken by Birks did not:

> However powerful Birks's arguments, it is perfectly laughable to think that someone sitting in his study can produce a workable revision of the whole of the law of obligations. One has only to give a moment's thought about how Llewellyn went about producing the Uniform Commercial Code to see what is needed to begin to get the job done properly.[52]

Campbell levels a similar criticism at the corrective justice school, pointing out that their very definition of the problem is misconceived:

> There is no theoretical necessity to give up the great range of social philosophical and social scientific materials on which one could and should draw in order to accept the grossly empirical limitation of abstract doctrinal scholarship, especially when, after Calabresi and Macaulay, it should be obvious that the worst problem with the common law is not the bits it might wrongly include but the great areas it leaves out if one seeks an accurate account of what the law of obligations is outwith the library.[53]

A review of the debate demonstrates that this is far from atypical. Criticisms of revolutionary theories in private law are focused at least as much on the model of legal scholarship implicit in those theories as they are on the details of the theories. Thus John Murphy's critique of *Torts and Rights* was directed as much at the particular approach to reductionism taken in that treatise as it was at the specific details of the theory it advanced.[54] Stephen Waddams's critique of a swathe of theories broadly associated with the corrective justice and taxonomic schools similarly points to the

[50] ibid, 38–39.
[51] See, eg, S Hedley, *Restitution: Its Division and Ordering* (London, Sweet & Maxwell, 2001) 27–32.
[52] D Campbell, 'Classification and the Crisis of the Common Law' (1999) 26 *Journal of Law and Society* 369, 370.
[53] Campbell, ibid, 373.
[54] J Murphy, 'Rights, Reductionism, and Tort Law' (2008) 28 *OJLS* 393.

fundamental problems raised by theories which ignore the nuances of history and context and excessively simplify the complexity of cases by forcing them into unidimensional categories such as 'contract' and 'tort'.[55]

Nor does this only run one way: critiques of relational theories of contracting have also tended to question the approach to scholarship which such a theory represents. Thus, Gava and Greene criticise Hugh Collins's theoretical approach to contract on the basis that it is *methodologically* impossible to apply:

> Collins' problem is that he asks the impossible of judges. He expects them to apply law in a way that takes into account the intimate economic and social relationships between the parties and the economic and social context of transacting more generally, and also to be sensitive to the special problems arising from contracts with the government. All this as well as, of course, having an appropriate level of expertise in law. A superhuman made up of Oliver Williamson, Max Weber, Ronald Dworkin's Hercules and Sir Humphrey Appleby might succeed at doing some of this, but even this superhuman would baulk at getting into the heads of disputing contracting parties! Judges are never going to be able to do what Collins asks of them.[56]

Even more striking are theoretical works which ignore relational contract theory altogether on the basis that they cannot be called theories of contract law.[57] This is precisely what Kuhn's theory tells us to expect of paradigms, and of disagreements centred around competing paradigms—rather than merely around theories. This suggests that, much like scientific paradigms, legal paradigms are defined by a particular approach to how we should 'do law', encompassing not just the conceptual apparatus we use to solve problems, but also the prior question of what constitutes law well done and the world-view—or 'thought style', as Mary Douglas and other neo-Durkheimian institutional theorists would put it[58]—that underlies that approach to solving problems.

B. Theoretical Revolutions and Black-Letter Law

A key feature of legal revolutions is therefore that they go to the question of the right way to do law. It is this that makes legal revolutions fundamentally unproductive, because their primary effect is to shape a growing gulf between the world of legal theory and the world of legal practice. In sharp contrast to the debate in legal theory about what constitutes 'good' or even 'acceptable' legal scholarship, legal discourse at the level of legal practice, or black-letter law, reflects the high level of consensus that Kuhn associates with paradigms. With the exception of a vanishingly small number of 'critical' textbooks,[59] a typical contract textbook is a classically Kuhnian

[55] Waddams, above n 21.

[56] J Gava and J Greene, 'Do We Need a Hybrid Law of Contract? Why Hugh Collins is Wrong and Why it Matters' (2005) 63 *CLJ* 605, 620.

[57] S Smith, *Contract Theory* (Oxford, Oxford University Press, 2004) 8.

[58] M Douglas, *How Institutions Think* (Syracuse, Syracuse University Press, 1986).

[59] Such as R Halson, *Contract Law*, 2nd edn (Harlow, Pearson, 2012); L Mulcahy, *Contract Law in Perspective*, 5th edn (London, Routledge, 2008). The US equivalents are the textbooks prepared by Macaulay and Macneil.

example of a paradigm, in that virtually every textbook reflects an extraordinarily high level of consensus and commonality in the way the subject is treated: the rules that are presented, the cases that are chosen and even the hypotheticals that are used. The same set of leading cases feature in the majority of textbooks, and the doctrines for which they are taken to stand are described in very similar ways.

Academic disagreements also do not influence the structure of legal textbooks within the law of obligations. Textbooks have remained largely unaffected by five decades of debate about taxonomy and the structure of the law, and do not depart from conventional paradigms of classification, principle and articulation of rule. Indeed, for all the debate about the law of obligations, there are virtually no student-level textbooks that treat the law of obligations as a single whole.

This point is not trivial. To Kuhn, textbooks played a crucial role in defining paradigms.[60] Paradigms, in his account, seek to capture the entirety of a phenomenon; and competition among scientific frameworks is judged with reference to their ability to account for and predict the broadest possible range of observed phenomena.[61] Textbook accounts, by showcasing the method and world-view implicit in a paradigm, as well as the problem-solving ability of the paradigm, are a key means of projecting that paradigm's ability to address a broad range of phenomena. It is precisely this that law textbooks do. Textbooks seek to draw students into legal ways of thinking (or 'thinking like a lawyer') in ways that are largely similar—for example, through a similar structure, or using similar types of hypotheticals. This demonstrates that there is something in black letter or doctrinal law strongly akin to what Kuhn termed an accepted paradigm. Kuhn's account of exemplars, in particular, closely parallels what HLA Hart called the 'core',[62] and it is the core that is the main concern of textbooks. The 'penumbra'[63] naturally has less consensus, but in the textbook treatment these are represented as the unsolved problems that can in theory be solved using the paradigm, if one draws upon the standard exemplars as instances of outstanding legal reasoning. They are presented, at best, as problems that the paradigm has not yet solved, rather than as challenges to the paradigm itself.

One reason for this consensus is that frameworks of practice are reductionist. As I have argued elsewhere, a significant portion of the work the legal system is called upon to do is dealing with the problems posed by conflicting expectations in society.[64] One of the limitations of viewing the law in terms of doctrine is that the language of doctrine—dealing in concepts such as 'reasonableness', 'unconscionable', 'merchantable' and so on—paints a picture of the law as rooted in consensus, and in the application of concepts whose meanings can be and typically are the subject of a uniform view. Yet, in reality, private law is associated with situations of conflicting

[60] Kuhn, above n 11, 136–38.

[61] See especially the discussion of responses to crises in Kuhn, above n 11, 77–91.

[62] HLA Hart, 'Positivism and the Separation of Law and Morals' (1958) 71 *Harvard Law Review* 593.

[63] ibid.

[64] TT Arvind, 'Obligations, Governance and Society: Bringing the State Back In' in A Robertson and M Tilbury (eds), *The Common Law of Obligations: Divergence and Unity* (Oxford, Hart Publishing, 2016) 267–68.

perspectives and conflicting expectations. The key 'law job'[65] discharged by private law requires it to mediate in such conflicts—between, for example, the expectations of newspapers that they have the ability to print anything they believe to be in the public interest and the expectations of their victims to privacy;[66] the expectations of secured lenders that their security merits protection versus the expectations of defrauded victims of financial scams; or the expectations of scientific researchers in relation to unimpeded access to potentially useful material versus the expectations of indigenous people in relation to their traditional knowledge.

Reductionism is an important aspect of the manner in which the law deals with conflicting expectations. This is inevitable: a social institution which sought to deal with conflicting expectations in their full complexity would find itself faced with the same underlying issues of value-incommensurability and divergent goals and understandings that produce conflicting expectations.[67] The structured sets of concepts and rules created by legal theory are accordingly reductionist devices, which serve to reduce the complexity of the situations of conflicting expectations that it is the task of the law to resolve. They may do this directly, by guiding a decision maker to take certain factors into account (for example, did a unilateral mistake as to identity relate to a face-to-face transaction or to a documentary transaction?),[68] but not to consider others (was the victim of a unilateral mistake particularly vulnerable to being influenced by a person purporting to be in a position of authority?).[69]

More significantly, they may also do this indirectly, by creating conceptual structures whose effect is to strip out aspects of the situation that might influence us were they not stripped out. Duncan Sheehan and I have suggested that the primary mechanism through which they achieve this is by the creation of ideal types—non-empirical representations of phenomena which are purely mental constructs and which do not actually exist in their pure form.[70] Many of the legal concepts used in private law, including core concepts such as 'contract', 'consent', 'reliance' and 'promise', are ideal types, in that a completely specified category which took account of all the variations that characterise these concepts as empirical phenomena would be infinitely complex.[71] Critically, however, any legal framework will at any time have within it different conceptual structures that could, potentially, be applied to any given set of facts, but whose application would simplify that set of facts in very different ways and produce very different outcomes. A central task of legal frameworks, therefore, is not only to set out sets of concepts and rules for their application, but also to provide a basis for discrimination, on which we can put a particular

[65] See K Llewellyn, 'The Normative, the Legal, and the Law-Jobs: The Problem of Juristic Method' (1940) 49 *Yale Law Journal* 1355.

[66] See, most recently, *PJS v News Group Newspapers Ltd* [2016] UKSC 26, [2016] AC 1081.

[67] Arvind, above n 64, 268.

[68] *Shogun Finance Ltd v Hudson* [2003] UKHL 62, [2004] 1 AC 919.

[69] cf the point made by Schauer in relation to the logic of formalism: F Schauer, 'Formalism: Legal, Constitutional, Judicial' in K Whittington, RD Kelemen and GA Caldeira (eds), *The Oxford Handbook of Law and Politics* (New York, Oxford University Press, 2008).

[70] D Sheehan and TT Arvind, 'Private Law Theory and Taxonomy: Reframing the Debate' (2015) 35 *Legal Studies* 480, 490–92.

[71] Sheehan and Arvind, ibid, 491.

set of facts within one particular conceptual structure within that framework rather than another.[72]

This has important implications. Because doctrinal frameworks are merely problem-solving tools which serve to reduce the complexity of fact situations, they are inherently incapable of being true or false. We can critique them on the basis that their evaluative approaches are undesirable or that the reductionist framework they embed is undesirable, but because they are simply reductionist tools, they are never true or false. This makes it possible to adopt a heuristic approach in relation to doctrinal frameworks, where the focus is not as much on what is an exemplary way of doing law grounded in a sound world-view as it is on the far simpler question of what is a useful way of doing law. Here, once again, the example of the wave theory in nineteenth-century France provides a useful parallel.

As discussed in section III, the conventional account says that the result of the tests carried out on Arago's suggestion led to the immediate collapse of the corpuscular theory of light in France. The reality was somewhat more complex. As Buchwald has shown, although the result led Poisson to accept Fresnel's mathematics and the laws of diffraction he had formulated, he continued to reject the theoretical foundation of those results. The results were valid in Poisson's view, but the theory underlying the results was not. To Poisson, because a ray of light was something that could be observed, there must necessarily exist some physical objects corresponding to rays of light. The wave theory of light could only produce this result if the 'disturbances' that constituted the waves were through some process limited to a small, clearly defined, linear geographical space. But the wave theory did not contain any basis for such a limitation. The solution proposed by the wave theory—that a ray was a mere mathematical construct, and that the real physical entity was not the ray but the wave front—was not something he accepted, because such a theory had no room for physical rays.[73] As such, he believed that it suffered from a fundamental problem, and continued to hold that view until his death.[74]

Yet, despite this fundamental 'incommensurability' between the corpuscular paradigm which Poisson held and the wave paradigm which Fresnel had put forward, Poisson had no difficulty in using the mathematical tools devised by Fresnel in his practical work. As Worrall has shown, this is because the framework within which science was conducted permitted him to use it as a heuristic—as a practical method that had demonstrated its ability to solve problems, even if aspects of it remained imperfect and potentially incorrect and even if he could not make it fit with theory.[75] The incommensurability of the underlying paradigms matter very little if the primary use of the framework in question is heuristic.

[72] On the importance of factual manipulation to the core functions of legal reasoning, see G Samuel, 'Is Legal Reasoning Like Medical Reasoning?' (2015) 32 *Legal Studies* 323.

[73] The nature of a light ray was not the only issue on which Fresnel and Poisson had fundamental conceptual differences. They also differed fundamentally in their respective conceptions of a number of other physical quantities, such as fluids. See I Grattan-Guinness, *Convolutions in French Mathematics 1800–1840: From the Calculus and Mechanics to Mathematical Analysis and Mathematical Physics* (Basel, Birkhauser Verlag, 1990) 909.

[74] Buchwald, above n 37, 188–94.

[75] Worrall, above n 40, 146–54.

The ability to engage with approaches as heuristics is fundamental to any community of practice, and it is this that underlies the surprising cohesiveness of doctrinal scholarship in the law of obligations. Consider, once again, the example of the 1969 seminar. Despite its ambition, and despite the seeming radicalism of the underlying aim of a fact-based classification of law 'according to criteria which reflect the facts of social and economic life as they now exist',[76] the final publication is striking in terms of its caution. It expressly acknowledged:

> the impracticability of abandoning altogether the traditional or conventional divisions of the law because without an accepted terminology used more or less in accordance with existing usage communication of ideas about the law itself would become impossible. The law cannot be comprehended as a whole and broad divisions on well understood lines are essential.[77]

What it sought to achieve, instead, was a situation where the law could be discussed in terms of multiple, overlapping systems of classification, none of which were perfect, but which taken cumulatively would supplement each other, and point to situations where reliance on the traditional categories produced results that were unsatisfactory.[78]

This willingness to countenance messiness, and to engage with different frameworks without worrying about the compatibility of their theoretical assumptions, is typical of a heuristic approach.[79] This reflects the primacy that its proponents assign to practice. Ideas in law, as in heuristic science, matter because they guide practice; and their correctness is judged by evaluating how successful they are when they are applied to practical life.[80] In the context of the legal system, the aim is to assist the judge or other legal actor in creating reductionist models of the social phenomena that are the subjects of the law, and in attaching evaluative significance to different aspects of these phenomena. This makes the use of a heuristic both intelligible and justifiable.

The difference with the position in legal theory is striking. The focus of doctrinal frameworks is on acceptable ways of reducing complexity, with the reasons why a particular approach is a good one taking a back seat. In revolutionary theories, in contrast, it is the reason that is the primary focus.[81] The challenges to 'good science' are accordingly given pride of place in the debate, thus making the area of maximum

[76] Jolowicz, above n 5, 7.

[77] Jolowicz and Fairest, above n 4, 86.

[78] See especially the discussions of consumer law and labour law, and the limitations of contract as a conceptual device for considering the problems these areas raised: Jolowicz and Fairest, above n 4, 87–88.

[79] cf the point recently made by Dan Priel that idealism of the sort espoused by tort theory is frequently rendered both unattainable and undesirable due to empirical constraints, and that it is the more pragmatic (or cynical) view that is a more honest position for the legal system to make: D Priel, 'Tort Law for Cynics' (2014) 77 *MLR* 703.

[80] H Putnam, 'The "Corroboration" of Theories' in PA Schilpp (ed), *The Philosophy of Karl Popper*, vol 1 (La Salle, Open Court Publishing, 1974) 239–40.

[81] cf the analogous distinction drawn by Christian Atias between 'épistémologie du droit positif' and 'épistémologie du savoir juridique': C Atias, *Épistémologie du droit* (Paris, Presses Universitaires de France, 1994) 91–92.

incommensurability the primary focus of discussions. It is hardly surprising, then, that these discussions fail to produce anything resembling an accepted paradigm.

Popper argued that the rationality of scientific revolutions lay in their ability to preserve the successes of their predecessors, unlike ideological revolutions, which often consciously sought a break with tradition.[82] The position in relation to heuristic, doctrinal change and theoretical revolutions in private law is precisely analogous. In consequence, the world of legal theory is in what Kuhn termed a pre-scientific period, characterised by the existence of significant numbers of competing schools of thought which share so little common ground that there is little likelihood of progress to an accepted paradigm. The lack of any generally accepted exemplar of what constitutes 'good' theorisation is a particular sticking point. If the world of legal doctrine is the world of a community of practice, then the world of legal theory is a world of increasingly separated epistemic communities, with ever fewer areas of overlap.

This is exacerbated by the role of exemplars. One effect of clinging on to past paradigms is to entrench the exemplars that those paradigms used. Yet if the context in which the law is applied has drastically changed, the result is that the exemplars are no longer serviceable as guides to the application of the law. One such shift, the disappearance of Hohfeldian powers from modern legal theory, and its deleterious consequences for the ability of the law to deal effectively with situations characterised by such powers, has already been noted above. But this is not the only issue. By giving a prominent place to exemplars from the past, revolution-oriented theories can also mischaracterise problems by failing to recognise that the problems the law is called upon to solve have changed, such that the models applied to solve those problems also need to change. Dan Priel provides an example of precisely such a mischaracterisation:

> Beever reads [*Fontainebleau*] as if it is concerned with the question whether one has a 'right to sunbathe'. He does that despite the fact that this right is nowhere mentioned in the case, and is not at all the right that the land owner in the case is interested in. Limited liability companies being incorporeal entities have little interest in lying 'exposed before the elements on loungers'. What the plaintiff in this case was interested in was to use nuisance law as a way of hampering a commercial competitor, and, unsurprisingly, the Court refused to play along. It is less than helpful to present it as a dispute over the existence of a 'right to sunbathe'.[83]

The result of a quest for legal revolutions, in other words, is to cause a growing divide between the worlds of legal theory and legal doctrine, and to entrench incommensurability within the world of legal theory, with little way of overcoming it. Further, to the extent the paradigms they entrench are grounded in exemplars far removed from the reality of the transactions that come before the courts, they are not only misleading, but false. Although doctrinal frameworks are neither true

[82] K Popper, 'The Rationality of Scientific Revolutions' in R Harré (ed), *Problems of Scientific Revolutions* (Oxford, Oxford University Press, 1975) 101.

[83] D Priel, 'Land Use Priorities and the Law of Nuisance' (2015) 39 *Melbourne University Law Review* 346.

nor false, theoretical paradigms are necessarily true or false. Leaving aside purely normative paradigms which make no claims about any real legal system but focus instead on constructed 'ideal' legal systems, a scholarly paradigm purports to define and describe an aspect of the approach implicit in the legal system. Claims about the outcomes the legal system uses, the goals it pursues, the evaluative judgments it embeds or some other characteristic claimed to be fundamental to or somehow immanent in the legal system are always implicit in theoretical paradigms. A paradigm which is grounded in exemplars that bear little resemblance to the reality of the law is false, because it makes claims about the operation of the legal system which are not true.[84] The combination of the propensity to entrench incommensurability in the world of legal theory and the falsity of at least some of the paradigms giving rise to that incommensurability is the reason why legal revolutions are unproductive far more frequently than productive.

V. CONCLUSION: THE FAILURE OF LEGAL REVOLUTIONS

There are no revolutions in the paradigms applied to black-letter law. There are evolutions, as the problem-solving techniques used by judges, and the frameworks of reductionism and evaluative significance on which they are based, incrementally adapt or fail to adapt in response to the changing social context in which they are applied. Legal scholarship can best make a contribution if it studies that process of adaptation—a task that necessarily requires it to attend to the social context of the law. Legal progress, seen in this light, is not progress in absolute terms, but in the relative terms of the better adaptation of law to the needs of a particular society at a particular point of time, given the broader institutional framework of the polity. This task requires an approach that is far closer to the formulation of usable heuristics than it is to the fundamental paradigm shifts that characterise revolutions. The constant quest to return to the paradigms of the past hinders the task of legal scholarship rather than helps it.

From this perspective, private law scholarship would make a stronger contribution if it were to return to the traditional business of law: a focus on local issues, on specific problems and on ways of resolving them without seeking coherence or conformity to a particular grand theory. SFC Milsom argued that many of the most influential developments in legal history were the product not of grand theorisation, but of practical persons attempting to solve practical problems.[85] This chapter has sought to suggest some ways in which scholars of the common law might return to that task. Part of the answer lies in a closer focus on legal reductionism, on the things it leaves out in specific instances of working out problems it encounters, on the consequences of it leaving those things out and on the role this leads it to play within the lives of the citizenry, as well as the other governing institutions.

[84] As I discuss briefly elsewhere, this was one of the more important insights of Scandinavian legal realism. See TT Arvind, 'Beyond "Right" and "Duty": Lundstedt's Theory of Obligations' in D Nolan and A Robertson (eds), *Rights and Private Law* (Oxford, Hart Publishing, 2011).

[85] SFC Milsom, *A Natural History of the Common Law* (New York, Columbia University Press, 2003).

The past of the law can be a tremendous resource in all of these tasks. It can contribute to a useful history of the present, which sheds light on the choices that have been made in the past, and the manner in which they have shaped the institutions of our modern society. A genealogical approach to the evolution and spread of concepts, which Jenny Steele and I have argued for,[86] is a powerful tool that can be deployed within this framework. All of these, however, require a shift in how we approach the past. They require us, in particular, to cease to view the past as the *telos* of legal revolutions or as a source of frameworks of a higher perfection which can and should be faithfully applied to present day problems. They require us, instead, to see it as a guide to how the law came to be what it is today and, hence, to the evaluative positions and normative choices that lurk beneath the surface of the doctrinal framework; and to see in it also a means of illuminating the possibilities that were implicit in the past of the law, and in particular those which have not yet wholly faded away.

[86] TT Arvind and J Steele, 'Bringing Statute (Back) onto the Radar: Implications' in Arvind and Steele, above n 35.

DOCTRINES

5

Risk Revolutions in Private Law

JENNY STEELE

I. INTRODUCTION

GENUINE REVOLUTIONS WITHIN private law appear to be thin on the ground, at least when taking the 'longer view'.[1] On some accounts, nothing deserving the title can be identified at all,[2] and the story overall seems to be one of continuity and consistency, or at least of repetition.[3] In seeking revolutionary moments in private law, this chapter turns instead to the influence in and on private law of much more general 'paradigm changes'.

This move might raise suspicions: does the choice to focus in this way tend to devalue principled or internal accounts of private law?[4] It is suggested that this focus raises pertinent questions which need not be perceived as threatening to the integrity of private law. For example, what if changes in society and styles of governance[5] give private law new and no less important roles to play compared with its past? Could private law contribute to such changes or form part of them, and, if so, is there a danger that this will take place without serious debate by legal scholars? In marked contrast to private lawyers' traditional emphasis on continuity, we might consider John Braithwaite's suggestion, in the context of shifting styles of regulation, that '[a] key to progress is to keep constructing new paradigms that sweep across the disciplines in ways that are responsive to the new realities of the world, but that fade, like Keynesianism, when those realities change'.[6] It is unlikely that private law could remain insulated from such broad changes, particularly when they affect regulatory

[1] D Ibbetson, 'Revolutions in Private Law?' this volume, chapter 2.

[2] The notion that private law has seen any revolutions was rejected by Geoffrey Samuel: G Samuel, 'Have There Been Scientific Revolutions in Law?' (Obligations VIII Conference, Cambridge, July 2016).

[3] TT Arvind, 'Paradigms Lost or Paradigms Regained? Legal Revolutions and the Path of the Law' this volume, chapter 4, arguing, however, that concepts must be understood in changing historical contexts.

[4] An argument that has, of course, been had before: see C Fried, *Contract as Promise* (Cambridge, MA, Harvard University Press, 1981) 3, pointing to the works which acted as a foil and catalyst for the development of his own argument. Fried lists works by Patrick Atiyah, Grant Gilmore, Morton Horwitz, Duncan Kennedy, Anthony Kronman and Ian Macneil, all arguing that the law of contract is open to pursuit of community goals and standards rather than 'neutrally endorsing' goals and standards of the contracting parties.

[5] See the discussion of 'Risk and Regulatory Change' in section II; see generally section IV.

[6] J Braithwaite, 'The New Regulatory State and the Transformation of Criminology' (2000) 40 *British Journal of Criminology* 222, 235.

styles. Does private lawyers' focus on internal patterns of continuity and consistency therefore risk missing significant paradigm changes in the context and function of private law?

This chapter addresses such questions by exploring the relationship between 'risk revolutions' and private law. In doing so, it examines the relationship between the development of private law and broader societal changes which, in this instance, have already been widely described as paradigm-changing. In debating the relationship between private law and broader dynamics and change, the chapter does not assume that private law is a passive recipient of external developments: significant social changes might engage and even mobilise private law, and private law may make a distinct contribution to such changes.

I will suggest that private law has been both directly and indirectly affected by broad developments in societal approaches to risk, and that it still is and will continue to be. While statutory developments form an essential element of 'private law', I will suggest that the influence of these broader developments also affects private law as it is developed in the courts. Some of this influence, historically, is clearly documented and subject to a good deal of consensus, though its nature and extent are certainly controversial. More recent changes, however, are more diffuse, and their nature, let alone their impact, is harder to discern. These changes, I suggest, tend to raise the question of the extent to which private law contributes to, and indeed helps to constitute, society's evolving responses and approaches to risk, security and responsibility.[7] A contributing role for private law seems more likely, given the observation of the increasing decentralisation of risk management and rise of meta-regulation;[8] rhetorical affirmation of a clear distinction between 'public' and 'private' despite observable blurring of the boundary between them;[9] and rebirth of uncertainty and individualised responsibility.[10] All of these have been part of latter day depictions of 'risk revolution'—and, indeed, of regulatory developments more generally.[11] If these are features of more recent risk revolutions, does private law help to shape evolving societal responses to risk and to negotiate the balance between risk, security and responsibility?

The body of this chapter comprises four sections. Section II introduces the key notions of security and responsibility developed in the chapter, and offers an overview of 'risk revolutions' for the purposes of the discussion here. Section III focuses on a first alleged paradigm shift concerning risk, which I refer to as a 'security revolution', and its potential impact on private law. Section IV explores an apparent reversal of fortunes in societal conceptions of risk from the latter part of the twentieth century onwards, and the apparent revival of both 'responsibility' and uncertainty,

[7] The role of 'security' and 'responsibility' is introduced in section II.

[8] J Black, 'The Emergence of Risk-Based Regulation and the New Public Risk Management' (2005) *Public Law* 512, 513.

[9] L Godden, F Rochford, J Peel, L Caripis and R Carter, 'Law, Governance and Risk: Deconstructing the Public–Private Divide in Climate Change Adaptation' (2013) 36 *UNSW Law Journal* 224.

[10] For example, in relation to the insurance industry, R Ericson and A Doyle, *Uncertain Business: Risk, Insurance and the Limits of Knowledge* (Toronto, University of Toronto Press, 2004).

[11] See the discussion in sections II and IV.

with attendant changes in regulation and governance: whether this is correctly seen as a new revolution or not, what is the nature of this change and of its likely effect on private law? Section V asks whether there is any evidence, particularly in tort law, of the influence of more recent 'revolution'.

II. RISK REVOLUTIONS AND PRIVATE LAW

A. Security and Responsibility

When interpreting 'risk revolutions' and their impact on private law, this paper will use two additional labels, namely 'security' and 'responsibility'. An initial risk revolution is labelled here as a 'security' revolution; later (and earlier) developments are described as more centrally engaging 'responsibility'. 'Security' in this context refers to the state of being protected from the consequences of adverse risks. This may be very general (producing a sense of or perhaps expectation of security); or it may be specific (security against particular risks may be put in place, for example through contractual terms or insurance). 'Responsibility' in this context refers principally to bearing the consequences of risks and particularly of risk decisions; it may also imply a duty to hold safe from risks (and therefore to provide security), or to act responsibly in relation to risks (for example, to minimise those risks).

These notions are to some extent in tension. However, it is important to be clear that the two are not mutually exclusive social phenomena. Rather, notions of security and responsibility are and have been mixed in different ways as notions of risk evolve: notions of responsibility are affected by the growth in security techniques, while the delivery of security is affected by changing notions of responsibility. The notions are nevertheless commonly used to typify very different responses to risk. Thus, changes in the function of risk may be interpreted as turns towards or away from security; and turns away from security are often justified or explained in terms of responsibility. Developing responses to risk may thus be typified in terms of their balance between security and responsibility; equally importantly, they may be explored in terms of the types of security and responsibility that they engage.[12] In section V, it is suggested that the cost of security is increasingly an issue of concern in private law, and that this can be observed in the courts as well as in legislation.

B. Risk Revolutions: A Brief Overview

Changing social responses to risk and uses of risk have a strong claim to be called 'revolutionary'. So far as a first and widely recognised 'risk revolution' is concerned (explored in section III), it is particularly common to use the language of a paradigm

[12] T Baker, 'Risk, Insurance, and the Social Construction of Responsibility' in T Baker and J Simon, *Embracing Risk: The Changing Culture of Insurance and Responsibility* (Chicago, University of Chicago Press, 2002).

shift. This is the shift identified with the growth of insurance, and (linked with this) the birth of social security and the welfare state, from the turn of the twentieth century onwards. Writing from a Foucauldian perspective, Francois Ewald has described the twentieth century as displaying a dominant paradigm of 'solidarity'. This, he has argued, achieved a radical transformation from a (proposed) nineteenth-century paradigm of 'responsibility'.[13] Sociologists of risk have described a 'first modernity' during the same period, where security was to be based on a 'scientific utopia', making the unsafe consequences and dangers of decisions ever more controllable.[14] If such consequences could not be avoided, they could be compensated: risks could be spread.[15] 'Late modernity', on the other hand, is associated with some features of the further risk revolutions discussed in section IV.[16] Similarly, but focusing much more narrowly on employer liability, the end of the nineteenth century has been said to have seen a shift from 'free labor' to a 'new paradigm of risk and insurance'.[17] Between them, these are broad observations. It might be noted that they also directly implicate the law of liability. Ewald's nineteenth-century paradigm of responsibility is not only exemplified but partly constituted by approaches to contractual risk allocation, and this is what is superseded in the new paradigm of solidarity; Witt's shift from free labour to risk and insurance describes the birth of workers' liability; and the 'scientific utopia' identified by Ulrich Beck is one in which foreseen and planned liabilities can transform risk exposure into risk calculation because prevention can be supplemented with compensation.

In sum, it is widely accepted that there has been at least one revolution or paradigm shift in societal responses to, or uses of, risk, emerging at the turn of the twentieth century and strengthening over the following decades. And the initial paradigm shift of so-called 'first modernity', it is argued, plainly engages private law. Indeed, it is partly defined by changes in private law and by public uses of liability.

But this chapter's title adopts the plural form of 'revolutions', and it is widely accepted that the first paradigm shift is not the end of transformation in the social significance of risk. Scholars have identified further paradigmatic challenges engaging the social role of risk. It is tempting to see some of the new paradigmatic challenges as returns to the nineteenth century and a dominant 'responsibility' mode,[18] inviting a more cyclical than binary notion of 'revolution', in which the turning

[13] F Ewald, 'The Return of Descartes's Malicious Demon: An Outline of a Philosophy of Precaution' in Baker and Simon, ibid, 273.

[14] The length of influence of this paradigm shift on private law is debated in section V. Arguably, the next paradigm shift began to make itself felt in the final quarter of the century, and particularly from the 1980s.

[15] U Beck, 'Living in the World Risk Society' (2006) 35 *Economy and Society* 329, 334: 'the security dream of first modernity was based on the scientific utopia of making the unsafe consequences and dangers of decisions ever more controllable; accidents could occur, as long as and because they were considered compensatible'. Ewald, above n 13, also speaks of a technical and scientific 'utopia' behind the paradigm of security.

[16] See, eg, D Garland and R Sparks, 'Criminology, Social Theory and the Challenge of Our Times' (2000) 40 *British Journal of Criminology* 189, 204, 198; Beck himself referred to a 'second modernity': ibid.

[17] C Witt, *The Accidental Republic* (Cambridge, MA, Harvard University Press, 2004) 206.

[18] Ewald, above n 13.

wheel returns to its initial position. For lawyers, attached to the notion of stable concepts, this may be particularly tempting.[19] But we should not assume too much from similarities in concepts and rhetoric, such as the resurfacing interest in 'individual responsibility'. Most particularly, it is unlikely that what has been learned, achieved or simply expected through the initial risk revolution could fail to influence the present shape of the law. I argue in section IV that it does not fail to do so: the influence of the security revolution continues to be a definitive frame for current questions.

What of the role of risk in our own times? Notions of 'risk' retain their vitality and continue to play a key role in theories both of evolving 'modernity' and of regulatory or governance styles. Doubtless, present changes are harder to discern than those of the past: we are faced with richer sources of information and observation, perhaps, but much less sense of the pattern of developments. More recent changes have been seen in terms of the return of uncertainty (or new appreciation of its inevitability and significance);[20] in terms of a resurgence of individual exposure to and responsibility for risk (the limits of socialisation of risk);[21] or in terms of a new willingness to 'embrace' risk and its possibilities.[22] Moreover, further new uses of risk techniques give rise, in turn, to new risk challenges. Among these might be counted the extension of financial risk management to provide social goods (mortgages, pensions and the costs of care), which would previously have been the concern of the state. The hazards of this pattern of privatisation were dramatically exposed by the crash of 2008, but the trend continues. Societal dependence on risk management by an 'expert' private financial sector could itself be regarded as revolutionary. More recently still, there has been identified a further risk revolution whose watchword is not uncertainty nor the departure from 'laws of large numbers', but the availability and exploitation of even larger numbers to predictive effect: this is the revolution signified by the algorithmic mining of 'big data'.[23] This is a development whose challenges for private law this chapter cannot begin to attempt to meet. However, it underlines not only the centrality of risk to society, but also the way that large challenges associated with risk 'revolutions' continue to occur, both for the law and for society more broadly.

C. Risk in Private Law

Risk, then, has been identified as being at the core of social paradigm shifts over the last century. What of private law? Private law discourse without reference to risk is almost unthinkable. Of course, it is by no means obvious that the term 'risk' is used in private law, either generally or in specific areas, in the same way that it is

[19] See Arvind, above n 3.

[20] Ericson and Doyle, above n 10.

[21] D Garland, 'The Rise of Risk' in R Ericson and A Doyle, *Risk and Morality* (Buffalo, University of Toronto Press, 2003) 62: neo-liberal governments 'have deregulated markets and financial institutions, emphasized free enterprise, and taken steps to shift risk and responsibility onto individuals'.

[22] Baker and Simon, above n 12.

[23] K Yeung, 'Algorithmic Regulation and Intelligent Enforcement' in M Lodge (ed), *Regulatory Scholarship in Crisis*, Discussion Paper No 84 (London, LSE, 2016).

used in risk society or regulatory theory, and plainly this complicates the inquiry in this chapter. Indeed, Pat O'Malley has argued that the law of contract is suffused not with ideas of calculable risk, but with notions of uncertainty.[24] On this basis, O'Malley suggests that private law actors—whether individual or corporate—might be seen as 'entrepreneurs of an uncertain future', not as self-regulating consumers of expert-driven risk analysis. For O'Malley, one effect of this would be that the presence of incalculable risks may not induce the paralysis of decision making that 'risk society' theory predicts—an important indicator that the logic of private actors tolerates solutions beyond the bounds of what is calculable. While the language of O'Malley's inquiry may be unfamiliar to most private lawyers, it is worth holding the thought that notions of 'risk' in private law are not equivalent to fully calculable risks; and that they are 'local' to private law, not merely transposed from public policy. At the same time, they may remain effective means of governance.

Plainly, this potential mismatch in language makes the job of identifying the role of risk in private law, and thus the possible influence of risk revolutions, much more complex. With this caveat, we can, however, note the pervasive presence of the language of risk in private law. For example, contracts are routinely analysed in terms of their allocation of risk to one party or another; remoteness of damage in tort has been analysed in terms of a so-called 'risk principle';[25] and 'voluntary assumption of risk' is both a recognised defence in the law of tort and a controversial means of assessing the extent and limits of tort duties. In occupiers' liability, it has been clarified that there is no protection for trespassers against obvious risks;[26] the field of employers' liability is suffused with duties of risk assessment both through regulation and now at common law;[27] and the 'development risks defence' is the most debated feature of the European products liability regime,[28] effecting an overt allocation of costs between consumer and producer (rather than an allocation which is the result of applying some other, more general, concept).[29] Though these notions of risk have very different origins, it might be argued that use of 'risk' terminology has more recently been on the rise in private law doctrine, but most particularly the law of tort, and this is sketched in section V. There, I will suggest that more recent uses of 'risk' in private law are associated with some distinctive ideas. The overall question is whether there is any link between these two things: the broader social developments in 'risk' and regulation roughly sketched in the current section and evolution in the internal discourse within private law using the language of risk. Do these phenomena appear to track one another in different time periods?

[24] P O'Malley, 'Uncertain Subjects: Risks, Liberalism and Contract' (2000) 29 *Economy and Society* 460.

[25] G Williams, 'The Risk Principle' (1961) 77 *LQR* 179.

[26] *Tomlinson v Congleton* [2003] UKHL 47, [2004] 1 AC 46.

[27] *Kennedy v Cordia (Services) LLP* [2016] UKSC 6, [2016] 1 WLR 597.

[28] Directive 85/374/EEC. The UK version of the development risks defence is contained in the Consumer Protection Act 1987, s 4(1)(e).

[29] The latter sort of approach can be seen as inherent in the 'neighbour principle' derived from *Donoghue v Stevenson* [1932] AC 562, in relation to the duty of care; and in the question of which risks it is reasonable to take, in relation to the standard of care. The latter is most clearly exemplified by the 'Learned Hand' approach in *US v Carroll Towing Co* 159 F 2d 169 (1947).

D. Risk and Regulatory Change

It is also important to note a deep link between regulatory change and 'risk revolutions'. This is a significant element in the influence of such revolutions over private law not least because of the changing division between and function of what would previously have been perceived as the public and private spheres. This may, in turn, signal a changed role for private law. This sub-section briefly introduces those regulatory changes and the role that scholars have identified for risk; later sections will consider the place of private law in relation to these.

While risk and security were central to the emergence of the welfare state, risk has more recently been identified as also being a key element in the rise of the 'regulatory state' or 'new regulatory state'.[30] The regulatory state is said to have been marked by a 'decentring' of the state, increased privatisation and a recommendation that governments should increasingly 'steer but not row', devolving practical implementation of policy while retaining policy control.[31] This 'has seen the state reduce its role as a direct provider but increase its role as a regulator' with the creation of a panoply of regulatory frameworks.[32] The rise of regulation in these forms has inherently led to an emphasis on risk, but, inevitably, it plays a very different role from the one it played in the emergence of a centralised welfare or security state. While there is an emphasis on the division between public and private, inherent in the very notions of privatisation and deregulation, in practice this division is blurred, since the deregulatory elements of the shift can be overstated: the emphasis is on managed self-regulation and on mechanisms of 'steering at a distance', though this may also mean perusal of internal management processes which would otherwise be perceived as private.[33] At the theoretical level, risk management is intimately linked to these developments as a pervasive 'technology of governance'[34] which facilitates self-regulation; for example, risk is an integral aspect of 'management based' regulation, by which regulators seek to assess the risk management processes of firms, rather than assessing compliance on an individual level.[35]

This section has offered a brief introduction to key aspects of the argument in this chapter. First, it has introduced the ideas of 'security' and 'responsibility' as they are used in the chapter; secondly, it has offered an overview of the 'risk revolutions', which will be explained in more detail in sections IV and V; thirdly, it has observed the extensive use of notions of 'risk' in private law, and flagged that these notions, though well established, may themselves be subject to evolution; and finally, it has

[30] Braithwaite, above n 6, 228.

[31] D Osborne and T Gaebler, *Reinventing Government* (New York, Addison-Wesley, 1992).

[32] H Rothstein, M Huber and G Gaskell, 'A Theory of Risk Colonization: The Spiralling Regulatory Logics of Societal and Institutional Risk' (2006) 35 *Economy and Society* 91, 94–95.

[33] Black, above n 8.

[34] Braithwaite, above n 6, 225, explaining the synergies between theories of the 'new regulatory state' and Foucault's interest in 'governmentality' through capacity for self-regulation.

[35] N Gunningham, 'Environmental Law, Regulation, and Governance: Shifting Architectures' (2009) 12 *Journal of Environmental Law* 179, 189; for the continued prevalence of risk-based regulation, see R Baldwin and J Black, 'Driving Priorities in Risk-Based Regulation: What's the Problem?' (2016) 43 *Journal of Law and Society* 565.

outlined the close link between risk and changing styles of regulation. The following two sections explore successive risk revolutions and their implications for private law in more detail.

III. A RECOGNISED 'SECURITY' REVOLUTION

It is widely understood that during the late nineteenth and early twentieth centuries, there were broad social changes enabled and inspired by techniques of 'risk'. As we have seen, these developments have been recognised as achieving paradigm shifts and even as giving rise to the birth of a 'first modernity'. Though it is doubtless tempting to be able to give an account of radical transformation, seismic changes plainly occurred: the birth of social security and emergence of the welfare state were among the most significant. The 'Keynesian' or welfare state has been identified as central in provision of security goods to citizens and in defining the relationship between the citizen and the state, but also in the expansion of direct state provision and regulation.

These changes, it has been argued, were facilitated by advances in technical understanding of risk and regularity, and their application to a variety of social problems.[36] To a degree, this was a 'scientific' revolution led by new expertise. Unlike more recent developments, such as the algorithmic expertise of the financial sector, this form of technical understanding could be readily comprehended and applied by government and policy makers. In essence, a collective and aggregating approach was developed which would allow risks to be shared through a range of means, including social insurance, but also, at the same time, new liabilities. 'Risk' in this context refers as much to a set of techniques as it does to exposure to uncertain adverse outcomes. In the hands of Foucauldian theorists, risk was and continues to be a technology of governing.[37]

In this guise, 'risk' (as security) may appear to be at odds with other technologies of governing, traditionally associated with private law. State provision of security goods may be associated with the growth of public rather than private law, and with increasing 'juridification' or intervention.[38] One crucial aspect of security technology which may be seen as encouraging and underlining this change is the selection of regularity and predictability across large numbers, in contrast to a focus on the individual case and its 'rights' and wrongs. This is a technique shared by both insurers and policy makers (for example, in the extension of social insurance to a range of life risks). The effective approach is to manage populations and aggregates. This might be thought a paradigmatic shift likely to weaken the impact of private law or

[36] P Bernstein, *Against the Gods: The Remarkable Story of Risk* (New York, John Wiley & Sons, 1996); TJ Lowi, 'Risks and Rights in the History of American Governments' (1990) *Daedalus* 17.

[37] Ewald, above n 13; Rose and Miller (1992) 43 *British Journal of Sociology* 173; T Lemke, '"The Birth of Bio-Politics": Michel Foucault's Lecture at the College de France on Neo-liberal Governmentality' (2001) 30 *Economy and Society* 190.

[38] H Aasen, S Gloppen, AM Magnussen and E Nilssen, *Juridification and Social Citizenship in the Welfare State* (Cheltenham, Edward Elgar, 2014); G Teubner (ed), *The Juridification of Social Spheres* (Florence, European University Institute, 1987).

to compromise its character. What, then, was the impact of the security revolution on private law? Did it simply bypass private law and replace it with more 'public' and collective solutions?

Private law has not been superseded in a wholesale way, though it has been argued that in some spheres it ought to have been, as security could be more effectively and efficiently provided in other ways.[39] To some extent, this argument depended on challenging the privateness of private law; and this was achieved by pointing to its costs and their distribution, typically through the burden of insurance. At the same time, socialised theories of private law tended to focus on the supposed absorption of contract to tort, as though tort was the more 'collective' and welfare-oriented.[40] One explanation of this move is that as the context of tort's operation became one of risk technique—security style—tort adjusted to this context by absorbing some of its thinking. The other is through the link between tort and insurance, which distributes the burden of its costs.[41]

The 'security' revolution was largely occupied with distribution, collectivisation and—in the broadest sense—'insurance'. This notably included the rise of social insurance and workers' compensation,[42] for example. The latter illustrates that there was space for new liabilities in the transformed landscape: liability was one of the techniques or responses applied, though it was plainly only one among others. Market insurance of these liabilities became the norm, so that distribution within an enterprise (the model of workmen's compensation) was met by distribution beyond it.

In the UK, the transition to workmen's compensation and social security could have marked the decline of tort; but it did not.[43] Rather, it could be said that the transition from individualised risk to collective risk or insurance was effective both within and outside the law of tort. The pre-existing bar to employers' liability under the 'fellow servant' or 'common employment' rule was itself based on an assertion about assumptions or allocations of risk, so that its removal could be perceived as part of a less individualised approach to risk. Similarly, prior to the Workmen's Compensation Acts,[44] employers' liability had been carved out to a limited extent,[45] but the statute was interpreted as subject to party risk allocation in employment contracts, at least where an employer's compensation scheme was provided. Insurance of such liabilities was also created by the market, not by policy design, and it was created immediately.[46] Both the loosening of prohibitions on employers' liability and

[39] P Cane, *Atiyah's Accidents, Compensation and the Law*, 8th edn (Cambridge, Cambridge University Press, 2013).

[40] G Gilmore, *The Death of Contract* (Columbus, Ohio University Press, 1974) 87.

[41] See the discussion in S Hedley, 'The Unacknowledged Revolution in Liability for Negligence' this volume, chapter 9.

[42] Or in the UK, workmen's compensation.

[43] For some reasons, including the commitment of the labour movement to the idea of liability based on fault, see J Steele, 'Law Reform (Contributory Negligence) Act 1945: Collisions of a Different Sort' in TT Arvind and J Steele, *Tort Law and the Legislature: Common Law, Statute, and the Dynamics of Legal Change* (Oxford, Hart Publishing, 2013).

[44] The first of which was the Workmen's Compensation Act 1897 (UK).

[45] Employers' Liability Act 1880 (UK).

[46] R Merkin and J Steele, *Insurance and the Law of Obligations* (Oxford, Oxford University Press, 2013) 285.

the creation of workmen's compensation marked a change in the perception of risk and its relation to liability. One was a change permitting liability at common law, though with limited compensation; the other was a new liability premised on risk, not fault. Was the nature of the change different, or similar? In theoretical terms, the two are very different, and in terms of the identity and fortunes of tort law as private law, these would appear to be opposite developments. But to those engaged in securing liability to workers, and to those providing insurance through the market, the two developments will have been seen as similar. From some important vantage points, therefore, tort and non-tort solutions had common effects, and also shared the common 'technology' of compensation and insurance.

In the UK, at the height of the risk revolution, there were parallel systems for distributing and allocating risk. These included: social insurance; workmen's compensation until its abolition; private first party insurance; liability insurance; contractual allocation; and tort liability. Tort liability began to expand in the same period,[47] and as it did so, it also attracted liability insurance, beginning with employers' liability. Thus, private law liability took a distributive turn in its impact, regardless of what was happening in theory. Where different forms of liability operated alongside one another, the differences in theory may have appeared less significant than the commonalities of effect. Similarly, the eventual abolition of workmen's compensation in the UK in no sense marked a reversal of the distributive turn. Instead, it was part of a broadening in social welfare provision, and industrial injuries became the subject of state, rather than industry, provision.[48]

This risk revolution is described here as a 'security revolution'. This may need justifying in a number of ways. First, are security and risk contradictory terms? The answer given here is no, on the basis that 'risk' techniques provided the means to achieving solutions based on pooling or distribution; crucially, also, they provided the means to protection from uncertainty and its effects. Secondly, why is it appropriate to define this revolution as particularly concerned with 'security'? Protection from specific life risks lay at the heart of the initial revolution, even if it later became more generalised. The application of techniques of risk to social problems appeared to enable the state to protect individuals from the uncertainties of significant life risks. On some occasions, it was openly the case that the new forms of security were alternatives to the market—that is, contract—providing security for those who could not be expected to provide it for themselves. Entitlement to income replacement was also provided to some degree, in place of mechanisms of charitable relief or other support; even so, the tort measure of full replacement of what is lost stands out as exceptional.[49] Using tort remedies to achieve security would therefore be something of an awkward fit, and this is one reason why tort was criticised as a component of the security state. Whatever the theoretical position, however, tort became part of the broader set of security provisions.

[47] The celebrated moment is the decision of the House of Lords in *Donoghue v Stevenson* [1932] AC 562. But note also the generally liberalising effects of legislative reforms, reviewed by S Hedley, 'Tort and Personal Injuries, 1850 to the Present' in Arvind and Steele, above n 43.

[48] National Insurance (Industrial Injuries) Act 1946.

[49] On the flawed provision of security through the three pillars of family, insurance and state, see C Weisbrod, *Grounding Security* (Aldershot, Ashgate, 2006).

The emphasis on security is also illustrated by road traffic liability. During this same period, road traffic also became a key concern, and the most regular form of tortious liability was developing. In the UK, through the Road Traffic Act 1930, liability insurance for road traffic accidents became compulsory. What, then, explains the introduction of compulsory liability insurance? It is suggested that it was the need to avoid insecurity (uncompensated injury) that was the most significant motivator: the trigger was, again, vulnerability to injury from a known and understood risk, which would strike with regularity, but unpredictably. This development therefore embodies both the need to secure or provide security and the use of distributive capability through both liability and insurance. If insurance was at this stage compulsory for roads but not for employers, it would reflect the fact that drivers were acknowledged to be individuals who could not necessarily provide the required compensation: the liabilities required to be secured. Now, however, we are beyond the scope of covering distinct groups who cannot be expected to cover themselves;[50] instead, we are looking to cover all those who are exposed to the risk of tortious harm arising from road vehicles. It is suggested that a different, significant judgment is thus introduced: the cost of security should be placed with motorists, not victims.

It seems unlikely that this was based on a judgment about moral ownership of the risks.[51] More likely, it is a judgment about how, practically, security from the risks of road traffic could be achieved. Road traffic liability places the risk of injury, through liability, with negligent parties, and with their insurers, and it makes that insurance compulsory; it thus seeks to provide security to all those exposed to risk, while protecting those who may be liable, at the 'tort measure' (full compensation); and it evidently uses techniques associated with risk and insurance to achieve this. Behind this is a clear public policy mandate, to the extent that insurers, by agreement with government, will also cover the liabilities of uninsured and untraced drivers.

A. Security Revolution and the Context of Private Law

We have seen that the security revolution implicated liability to some extent from the start. It led to new liabilities that superseded contractual analysis that had barred tort liability, and led to creation of rival types of liability in contrast to tort; it also led to insurance of liabilities either in practice or through legislative mandate. At the same time, tort did not shrink, but grew; in the process, over the decades, it seems to have acquired a reputation for being the 'collectivist' branch of private law. Its norms were essentially social norms; and its effect, too, was increasingly distributive. In growing, its immediate context, through social security provision, workmen's compensation and insurance, was now one of distribution and of approaches which were in some sense collective, recognising common risks and broadly insurance-like solutions. Only in a very limited sense can this be described as an 'external' revolution. Certainly, it is much broader than private law; but it operates in the immediate context of private law, and has affected the social role of private law directly.

[50] This was the notion behind the restriction of Workmen's Compensation Act compensation to restricted (though gradually expanding) categories of 'workmen'.

[51] For current notions of responsibility in relation to road traffic, see section V.

B. After Effects

How broad was the security revolution in private law, and how long did its effects last? It was as late as in the 1970s (the period when the security revolution was about to be clearly superseded) that it most clearly started to be suggested that private law was increasingly purposive, collectivised and protective, and that tort would or perhaps had begun to swallow contract.[52] Could it be argued that it was still the security revolution which continued to inspire expansion in tort liability, and perhaps the growth in status of tort at the expense of contract for several decades? Some have argued, in effect, that it was. In *Total Justice*,[53] Lawrence Friedman proposed that in the United States, but also in all Western democracies to one degree or another, an 'expectation of total justice' had evolved, which was a chip off 'a larger, more significant block', namely the welfare state itself.[54] In this process, developments that are public or private still point in the same direction. Friedman's proposal was that the reduction of uncertainty and the increase in security in some fields leads more or less inexorably to demand for the same sort of development in other fields. This proposes that the expansion of security through not only public, but also private, law is led both by demand and by the availability of techniques for reducing insecurity—primarily, in the tort field, insurance, though the very notion of duty to avoid harm should not be discounted. Allied with the techniques of uncertainty reduction is, according to Friedman, a growing 'rights consciousness'. For Friedman, there is no great surprise that private law moves in step with broader developments: a shared consciousness permeates them both, and this is in effect the consciousness of the times, as social expectation will be expressed both by claims and by the adjudication of those claims.

Of course, Friedman's analysis may be incorrect, or, at least, his claims may be exaggerated. What counts for present purposes is the existence of such a perception, and the proposal of a general shared consciousness that includes, but is much wider than, private law. More recent developments might put private law's approach to risk and uncertainty into a more distinct or specialised realm.

Friedman's proposals are consistent with a further significant feature of the law of tort during this period: its attachment to generalization—not only to broadening liability, but also to generalising principles or concepts. Is this part of the same phenomenon or not? Tort duties might naturally be seen as carving out areas of security. If tort is seen as protective, then the trend to generalise tort duties could be seen as part of a generalisation in protectiveness and security. The development of increasingly broad and general tort concepts, like the 'neighbour principle' and other uses of 'reasonable foreseeability',[55] assist with this expansion: the whole (extended) era of security revolution appears, overall, to be one of optimism in the capacity of the

[52] PS Atiyah, *The Rise and Fall of Freedom of Contract* (Oxford, Oxford University Press, 1979); Gilmore, above n 40.

[53] L Friedman, *Total Justice*, paperback edn (New York, Russell Sage, 1994).

[54] ibid 76.

[55] For example, in order to solve problems of 'remoteness' after the *Wagon Mound*: see section V below.

law and its concepts to provide not only security, but rational development through appropriate legal concepts or principles, probably mirroring optimism in the potential for improved security in general. At the same time, rising tort damages were not perceived to be an insurmountable burden for defendants, because of the prevalence of insurance. Hence the common law development in *Donoghue v Stevenson*,[56] in which it was thought logically compelling that there 'must be' a general principle to make sense of individual instances, is in harmony with the contemporaneous Road Traffic Act insistence on liability insurance. Indeed, between these two developments, the seeds were sown for considerable expansion in UK tort law.[57] None of this, of course, is entirely logical: tort could have been seen as increasingly irrelevant with the growth of the welfare state. Instead, however, it took on a security function. The cost of this security only gradually became a reason for restricting the growth of tort.

IV. BACKWARDS OR FORWARDS WITH A NEW RISK REVOLUTION

As we have seen, there has been wide consensus that a revolution in thinking placed risk techniques at the service of social welfare in the period explored above, and that this was associated with growth of the welfare state. Certainly, this altered the context in which private law operated, and I have suggested that rather than shrinking, as might have appeared logical for a branch of private law, tort instead grew during the same period. Its internal principles, though apparently independent of governmental influence, nevertheless remained in tune with the expectations of the security state.[58] The links between tort and insurance were multiple, and again encouraged the sense that tort and the security state were in harmony. More contentiously, it appears that this process of growth and the influence of security expectations continued for some considerable time. Only towards the end of this period, perhaps, were the links with social transformation fully appreciated.

More recently, there has been a more diffuse, but still broad, recognition that we have entered a new era where the social function of risk has altered in potentially revolutionary style. Further, just as the 'security revolution' was associated with change and expansion in legislation with possibly unpredictable reactions from or influences upon private law, so also changing societal approaches to risk have been closely linked with changing regulatory styles. Risk is a central concern of new forms of regulation and a core concern of regulatory theory. Again, this engages a change in the relationship between private and public domains, with potential to influence the response of private law. In relation to tort law in particular, 'risk' has become a more visible preoccupation and an increasingly significant part of the language of decision making. It will be suggested in section V that some of this is at the expense of more general concepts.

[56] Above n 29.
[57] R Lewis, 'Insurance and the Tort System' (2005) 25 *Legal Studies* 85.
[58] The expression 'security state' is used by Friedman, above n 53, Ch 4.

Putting a date on these changes is, of course, difficult. Friedman, as we have seen, thought private law worked in order to satisfy expectations of security in the 1980s; and it seems he had not altered his view in 1994.[59] In the UK, however, both private lawyers and scholars of regulation have identified significant changes at the end of the 1970s, into the 1980s. Atiyah wryly acknowledged that his work on the decline of freedom of contract had been less than prescient, given its publication a few weeks after the election of Margaret Thatcher to the office of Prime Minister, and resultant ascendancy of privatisation and contractual paradigms.[60] John Braithwaite also dates the rise of the 'New Regulatory State'[61] to the 1980s. Both in private and public law,[62] and in the UK and Australia, there is a commonality in the supposed date of revolution or paradigm shift. Given what was said above about the role of general principles in the extension of security through tort law, *Anns v Merton* was the pinnacle of attempts at stating general negligence principles in the UK,[63] giving a prima facie entitlement to security and a potential role to policy factors in restraining that entitlement. The fall of *Anns* and restriction of negligence duties in tort in *Murphy v Brentwood* by the end of the same decade is consistent both with this identification of the period of revolution and with a possible response from private law.

Unlike the security revolution, this further era of change is not necessarily premised on new discoveries about risk, at least not at the state or governmental level. But it may well reflect a belief that smarter approaches to risk can be developed through the expertise of the private sector, and particularly in finance.[64] Expertise, therefore, is devolved (and with it, it has been suggested, authority too).[65] In part, the new direction may be said to be about the perceived limits of the use of risk and of attainable security, either in practical or political terms. At the same time, there is a recognition of the limits of state action and expertise in many areas, and this has been associated with decentralisation of governance to private actors or, more subtly, the blending of private and public roles: private actors may be charged with state functions, while at the same time state entities are required to adhere to market rationality. The state itself is increasingly seen as vulnerable and in need of protection. In this process, in which 'governance' happens much more diffusely and there is a blurring of public and private entities, it is widely suggested that a 'risk management paradigm' has become 'an important framing construct', and that 'risk assessment and management have become central organising principles for many organisations and institutions'.[66] Thus, risk management can be seen as part of the decentralisation of risk decisions, rather than part of the centralisation that marked the first security revolution.

[59] This is when the paperback edition was published: see above n 53.

[60] PS Atiyah, 'Freedom of Contract and the New Right' in PS Atiyah, *Essays in Contract* (Oxford, Oxford University Press, 2001) 356.

[61] Braithwaite, above n 6.

[62] Braithwaite's influential discussion was aimed at criminologists, but drew on much broader regulatory theory to demonstrate the challenges for that discipline.

[63] *Anns v Merton* [1978] AC 728, 751–52, setting out a general two-stage 'test' for a duty of care in negligence.

[64] Examined by S Johal, M Moran and K Williams, 'Power, Politics and the City of London after the Great Financial Crisis' (2014) 49 *Government and Opposition* 400.

[65] Braithwaite, above n 6.

[66] Godden et al, above n 9, 234; Black, above n 8; Rothstein et al, above n 32.

At the same time, it is recognised that there are limits to the degree of confidence with which certain risks can be predicted: 'uncertainty', which is said to have played a diminishing role in the growing expectations of the security revolution, returns with a vengeance. It is recognised, for example, that risks are distributed partly over time, not only over cohorts; if greater risks are taken, this may be masked by the specialised nature of the expertise which sometimes devises and creates those risks, and does not always successfully control them. Equally, and importantly for the present theme, the cost of security in any general sense is recognised. Politically, this cost is attacked, and generalisation of security is questioned, on social and ethical,[67] as well as economic, grounds—though it is suspected that the last is really at the core. At the same time, protective treatment given to some classes of claimant is criticised.[68] There is a growing rhetorical focus on responsibility, particularly the responsibility of individuals to take care of their own risks or to bear the costs of their own activities or choices.

Why is it suggested that this focus is 'rhetorical'? 'Responsibility' may in part be a justification for declining support, which is, in fact, the product of the recognised costs of security. Beyond that, it is not altogether clear that renewed emphasis on responsibility is intended to lead to individual exposure to harm—though there certainly are signs of a growing willingness to allow such exposure, and a political attraction to doing this so as to influence behaviour. This is captured in the idea of the 'active welfare state', attempting to incentivise productive behaviour through highly stringent responses to failure.[69] A willingness—even intention—to create groups excluded from the provision of security is also clear.[70] But in the domain of private law in particular, it is suggested that the debate is more typically one about which source of security is most appropriate to a particular case, and to what extent, and who bears responsibility for securing the interests concerned. The core instance of this occurs where a case is brought between two insurers, in the name of insured parties, to determine which insurer bears the loss; but there are also other instances, since state support or first-party insurance continue to offer avenues for security. In commercial disputes, the tussle may concern attempts by insurers to deflect liability not to other insurers, but to uninsured parties.[71] In these instances, 'responsibility' is particularly likely to be invoked. In all these respects, the difference between the position in the nineteenth century and the position in the present era could not be more marked, despite the appearance of a common focus on responsibility: neither (non-marine) liability insurance[72] nor free health care, social security payments or

[67] Through notions such as 'compensation culture' and a returning, rhetorical attachment to 'responsibility'.

[68] Consumers, for example, may continue to be framed as vulnerable and in need of protection.

[69] See M Simpson, '"Designed to Reduce People ... to Complete Destitution": Human Dignity in the Active Welfare State' (2015) 1 *European Human Rights Law Review* 66.

[70] In the UK, this was reflected in much of the 'Leave' campaign during the Brexit referendum of 2016. See also Prime Minister Theresa May's stated preference, in her previous role as Home Secretary, to deprioritise the children of those who enter the country illegally when allocating school places: L Kuenssberg, 'Theresa May Had Plan to Deprioritise Illegal Migrant Pupils', *BBC News*, 1 December 2016, available at <www.bbc.co.uk/news/uk-politics-38165395>.

[71] Merkin and Steele, above n 46, ch 7.

[72] This point was very clearly made by Kenneth Abraham: K Abraham, *The Liability Century: Insurance and Tort Law from the Progressive Era to 9/11* (Cambridge, MA, Harvard University Press, 2008).

state occupational pensions were available before their development as constitutive parts of the 'security revolution'. For this reason, more focus on 'responsibility' and an apparent re-emphasis on the 'private' should not mislead us into thinking that we are back to the position in the nineteenth century—the context of private law is fundamentally altered, and this should inform our understanding of the concepts and principles that are applied.

Such developments do not only occur at the practical level. It is suggested that the generalised concepts that advanced the security function of the law of tort through the preceding era are also under pressure. The more recent trend is for more modulated, though equally imprecise or opaque, concepts to be deployed, permitting considerable differentiation between cases.[73] At a mundane level, these concepts are better adapted to restriction of the growth of liability than their predecessors without open-ended recourse to some apparently 'external' notion labelled 'policy'.[74] More contentiously, they may direct attention to some of the issues of risk allocation in light of rival sources of security than those general principles could. In other words, they are better adapted to assisting the choice between different sources of security than broad general principles couched in notions of fault and foreseeability: they draw attention to risk, security and the cost of security.

The continued growth of a body of private law, employing generalised 'security-type' protective concepts and serving the increasing demand for security, sometimes at the expense of the newly vulnerable state, would appear inconsistent with a mode of decentralised governance or with the ideal of the responsible risk entrepreneur. Decision in accord with very generalised principles, particularly if focused on the fault of the defendant, may also be ill-suited to recognition of rival potential security sources. Underlining the political dimension of the set of changes described, in many jurisdictions there has been movement to reform the law of tort—typically both reinforcing protection for government and re-emphasising individual responsibilities.[75] It could be argued, though, that, given the preoccupations of the regulatory state and its associated reliance on action 'at a distance', legislative reform of private law is not the expected paradigmatic response. These reforms forcibly alter those aspects of the law of tort which have become overly security-focused—or, from the reformers' perspective, insufficiently responsibility-focused—and at odds with the direction of more recent risk revolution. But intervention in tort in this way is a centralised activity resulting from collective decision and, moreover, there are signs that such intervention is insensitive to the internal preoccupations of the regulatory domain that is

[73] In the UK, this is exemplified by *Caparo v Dickman* [1990] 2 AC 605, and the subsequent developments of its 'fair, just and reasonable' and 'proximity' heads.

[74] This is not to reject the sceptical academic claim that these concepts themselves are or may be used to give effect to policy judgments. But policy arguments are at least moderated by the attempt to fit them to the applicable concepts—and it is likely that this is the intention—to narrow and shape the available reasons. Indeed, the existence of any legal concept will guide and influence the perception of applicable reasons to some extent, however malleable.

[75] On tort reform in Australia, see, eg, B McDonald, 'Legislative Intervention in the Law of Negligence: The Common Law, Statutory Interpretation and Tort Reform in Australia' (2005) 27 *Sydney Law Review* 443; K Burns, 'Distorting the Law: Politics, Media and the Litigation Crisis: an Australian Perspective' (2007) 15 *Tort Law Journal* 195.

private law. Rather than 'restoring' an earlier version of private law—as though this could be done without sensitivity to a changed context—it amounts to intervention introducing other political notions of responsibility. In the UK, this has not been typical of the development of tort law. Certainly, there has been no absence of political interest in the idea of responsibility and the possibility of 'compensation culture'. But on the whole, tort law has itself evolved to exemplify restraint.[76] Arguably, then, it has become more suited to play its role in tune with the forms of governance sketched above, with notable restraint from at least 1990. Again, arguably, it is more closely in tune with these forms of governance than it ever was with the products of the security revolution. The participants in risk management who act as the litigants in private law,[77] and the courts and lawyers themselves, may be seen as actors at a distance, steering risk more directly than central state agencies are able to do.

As we have already seen, however, these developments do not amount to a general abandonment of security. Delivery of security through a multiplicity of potential means is combined with increasing emphasis on individual, as opposed to collective, responsibility. It is suggested that this is, increasingly, responsibility for managing risks and security. This includes avoidance of some blatant risks, but it would also include management of potential sources of security where risks are worth taking, or unavoidable adjuncts of chosen activities.

The hypothesis is that consecutive risk revolutions have left a complex relationship between security/distribution and responsibility. This is likely to have both affected private law and invoked private law into arriving at the current balance. Private law is not merely a recipient of external factors, but a component of their governance, and it helps to make or shape them.

It may be asked how these developments are thought to have come about. How do changes in private law come to 'map' broader or external developments? Perhaps the answer is partly offered by what has gone before in outlining the security revolution and the transition to new forms of risk governance. Namely, these are not starkly 'external' or 'internal' changes. What happens in private law is an inherent part of what 'society' chooses to do about risk. This is partly, but only partly, because there are policy and legislative elements to what is happening. Lawyers are easily capable of being at the forefront of policy thinking—particularly in relation to law. Litigants may also seek avenues for change in relation to risk—or legal liabilities may be an important aspect of the risks they face. This is particularly, but not only, the case where litigants are either insurers or insured parties seeking to clarify their relationship to insurers. And the choice of using private law, either as litigant or legislator,

[76] This can only be stated to be 'on the whole'. The availability of tort law as a resource for litigants is heavily affected by legislative reform of costs, for example—though here, senior members of the judiciary were closely involved in reshaping the applicable regime: see, eg, R Jackson, *Review of Civil Litigation Costs: Final Report* (HMSO, 2010). More clearly, reform of employers' liability by removing civil remedies from a vast array of safety legislation is a significant outside intervention, again appearing like a reinstatement of an earlier conception of individual responsibility and deregulation: Enterprise and Regulatory Reform Act 2013 (UK), s 69.

[77] Given the notion of individuals as risk entrepreneurs, this could in principle include individuals, as well as the more obvious market and insurance participants. Lawyers, too, must manage litigation risk; in the UK, evolving models of funding make this a central part of their activities.

is itself a choice with implications for the social role of risk. Private law may either be responsive to or partly constitutive of changes in societal responses to risk. Or, of course, it may display elements of both.

For all these reasons, it is worth asking to what extent we can observe a changing emphasis within private law upon responsibility for risks, perhaps including responsibility for one's own risk in particular? Does private law appear in any sense to be increasingly 'steering' or enforcing risk management by private actors? If so, is there in any sense a move away from security and/or from the generalising concepts which encouraged private law to become increasingly protective? In the next section, we explore these questions with a focus on the law of tort.

V. TORT, SECURITY, RESPONSIBILITY AND RISK

As we have seen, tort has, at certain times in its recent history, been portrayed as security or welfare focused, and thus as more in tune with the distributive, collective approach of the security revolution than other aspects of private law. It was portrayed in this way largely in the 1970s—before the advent of a new revolution in both risk and governance. Progress towards further security might have appeared inevitable, with the main battleground being replacement of tort as a means of protecting from the consequences of harm (ie security).

This is now no longer the dominant picture of tort. Tort is perhaps unavoidably protective; however, the limits (and distribution) of its protection are being more actively defined. As we have seen, in many jurisdictions, this has taken the form of political 'tort reform' movements and reforming legislation. In the UK, the revolution has been quieter, and in some ways is more interesting. Can private law change from within either in reflection of changing social approaches and priorities or in order to influence those priorities? If private law is in some sense becoming more private, or, perhaps, more deferential about private interests and private ordering of security, and the blurring boundary between public and private is in some contexts being reworked,[78] this does not mean that tort has ceased to operate as part of broader risk 'evolution'. Rather, these developments in private law will be partly constitutive of how society responds to risk.

If tort law is indeed in some way either responsive to or constitutive of the further risk revolutions defined in the previous section, we might expect to see less universality in its principles and concepts and how they apply; more emphasis on individual responsibility to deal with, manage or avoid exposure to risk, with an awareness of alternative sources of security; more deference to contractual risk allocation; and possible mirroring of contractual styles of thinking. It is suggested that all of these things have been on the rise in the law of tort over the last 20 years or so, and that the process is, if anything, escalating, though the questions asked of or by the law of tort continue to lead to significant, if subtle, differences from contract. Indeed,

[78] This does not mean that private law has no important functions in relation to constitutional questions, for example, but in Friedman's sense it has become less welfare-oriented.

these features could be said to provide the key 'story' of the law of tort in this period. It may be objected that this is principally true only of the tort of negligence. Negligence, however, has a claim to be the key aspect of tort law where risk is concerned. Breach of duty in negligence has long been recognised as capable of being expressed in terms of reasonable risk,[79] and foreseeability of harm is an ever-present aspect of the duty of care; and I will suggest below that aspects of vicarious liability and remoteness have both been reconceptualised in terms of risk in recent years. Thus, much of the core of negligence liability can be—and often is—expressed in terms of risk. The question is whether the direction of change supports a positive answer to the question above. Three areas of development are selected here for illustration.

The first of these is the rise in voluntary assumption of responsibility and the associated concept of the scope of duty. Like 'reasonable foreseeability' in the 1970s, these notions are closely related and intended to dovetail together. While the ambition behind 'reasonable foreseeability' was to provide an overarching concept that could guide answers to both duty and remoteness questions in all cases in a clear and transparent way, the role of these newer concepts is to provide detailed reasons for differentiation between cases, and for determining the allocation of different risks between the parties.

Evidently, the shift from a broadly expressed 'duty of care' test in *Anns* to a more complex and modulated approach in *Caparo v Dickman*[80] is consistent with a felt need to control liabilities. Looking more closely at English courts' development of duty concepts, 'voluntary assumption of responsibility', or 'voluntary assumption of risk', may have a claim to be the concept that has proved most successful in the evolutionary race in recent years. Its role transcends boundaries, since it is regularly invoked in new contexts; and it appears to be taken seriously enough to transcend the need for 'fairness, justice and reasonableness' to be considered when an 'assumption' is thought to be present—it is thus, strikingly, sufficient reason on its own to recognise that a duty of care is owed.[81] Thus, on the face of it, where responsibility is assumed, it is thought to be fair, just and reasonable for liability to follow. For now, the first interesting feature of this idea is that it expresses itself directly in terms of who has responsibility for the risk and which risk is the responsibility of which party, even though the means of judging this is opaque. The second interesting feature is that very opacity, and the variety of means that may be deployed in reaching the judgment as to assumption of responsibility.

Scholars have pointed out that the notion of an 'assumption' in this context is not closely aligned with the notion of the will of the parties, despite the usual meaning of the word, and despite the addition of the word 'voluntary'.[82] Voluntary assumption of responsibility lends itself to consideration of where, given the structure of the

[79] See above n 29.
[80] [1990] 2 AC 605.
[81] *Henderson v Merrett* [1995] 2 AC 145.
[82] Use of the expression was pertinently dismantled at an early stage in its career: see K Barker, 'Unreliable Assumptions in the Modern Law of Negligence' (1993) 109 *LQR* 461; however, critical reviews appear not to have stunted its use in any way.

parties' arrangements and the nature of their activities in relation to one another, it would be reasonable for responsibility to be intended to lie—or, perhaps, where reasonable parties might be expected to think it lay. This way of putting it, however, almost certainly still uses too much contractual language. Rather, there is emphasis on the nature of the relationship between the parties and the nature of the activity undertaken by the defendant and whether it was undertaken for the claimant and with what attendant responsibilities. While this vagueness is disliked by academics, it has proved a very resilient notion: in fact, it has spread, and it seems unlikely that this could be because it is merely a veil for other, more 'real', reasons. Rather, the question can be alternatively expressed as whether the defendant took on a security duty to the claimant—and if so, which security, and security from which risks.

A linked idea underlies the relatively new approach to defining the extent of liability encapsulated in 'scope of duty' analysis.[83] Like 'voluntary assumption of responsibility', the idea has been roundly criticised by academics,[84] but it has proved more than resilient. It is not consistently used, and this inconsistency is one source of criticism; but there is no doubt that it has been added to the stock of concepts that can be used to differentiate between liability for one risk or another. Its function is to determine which risk and security duties attach to the activities of a given defendant, and in this guise, although it can be used to limit the liability owed by one party to another, it is equally designed to determine whose responsibility it is (or at least is not) to avoid a particular risk where there are multiple potential parties.

Its creation in response to a case involving losses in a rapidly falling property market is illustrative of the way that it identifies responsibility for risk management and specifies relevant risks. The notion of 'responsibility' here is not entirely vacuous; but neither is it captured by previous 'remoteness' notions. The question is not whether there was an intervening cause between the defendant's wrongdoing and the loss, nor is it the *Wagon Mound* question of whether the loss was 'reasonably foreseeable'.[85] Even leaving aside questions about the 'type of loss' which make *The Wagon Mound* test a very blunt instrument in this context, a falling market is, clearly, foreseeable, whether or not it is considered likely at any given time. Rather, what the notion identifies is the extent of the risk management role of various parties according to their functions and relationship.[86]

This underlines another feature of the restraint of tort in the era of the regulatory state, namely recognition of the potential for over-concentrated liabilities with attendant insurance costs. The same phenomenon arguably underlies the protective attitude towards public authority liabilities in tort, particularly where liability/responsibility could potentially be placed with another actor whose involvement is

[83] Originating in the House of Lords' decision in *South Australia Asset Management Corporation v York Montague Ltd* [1997] AC 191.

[84] J Stapleton, 'Negligent Valuers and Falls in the Property Market' [1997] 113 *LQR* 1.

[85] *Overseas Tankship (UK) Ltd v Morts Dock & Engineering Co Ltd (The Wagon Mound No 1)* [1961] AC 388.

[86] See also *Haugesund Kommune v Depfa ACS Bank (No 2)* [2011] EWCA Civ 33, [2012] Bus LR 230.

risk creation rather than failure to avoid risk.[87] The striking contrast between outcomes in tort claims in this context and outcomes in human rights claims[88] may be partly explained on the basis that 'damage' is not the basis of human rights claims, and that responsibility for the economic consequences of 'risk management' is not a key operator in such claims.[89]

The expanding law of vicarious liability offers a second important illustration of the centrality of risk and the emerging preoccupation with defining who bears the burden of the cost of security. The question typically is not who should have protected from harm, but much more openly who now bears the burden of the risk that harm would occur. In particular, in relation to intentional torts, the need to consider the responsibility of an employer (or other) whose purposes were not being advanced by the activities of the tortfeasor 'employee' or equivalent has led to a new question, namely whether there was a sufficiently close connection between the employment or other relationship between tortfeasor and defendant and the tort which occurred. In answering this question, the 'risk' of wrongdoing on the part of the employee or other in the course of that relationship is the key focus. But the question is not one of foreseeability of risk, for risks are by definition foreseeable, and the courts have long since stopped pinning their hopes on degrees of foreseeability.[90] Rather, the question is whose risk this is, and the idea of 'sufficiently close connection' is the means to answer that very open-ended question.

Like voluntary assumption of responsibility, the idea of 'close connection' is intended to make the question less open-ended and to offer a focus, and it is this type of concept that the courts find useful in the current risk era despite their evident imprecision. In the recent case of *Mohamud v William Morrison Supermarkets plc*,[91] there was an effort to challenge the validity of the concept and to replace it with a perhaps clearer question, namely whether a reasonable person would consider the tortfeasor to be acting as a representative of the defendant at the time of the tort. This change was rejected and, indeed, it is a far narrower question, concerned with expectations and understanding. The flexibility of the 'close connection' question is both what makes it an evaluative notion and what makes it a suitable way of narrowing the focus of a much bigger potential question, about where the responsibility for managing and avoiding risks associated with employment and other purposive activities should be said to lie. Importantly, even serious criminal wrongdoing is thus

[87] Classic cases in the UK include *Gorringe v Calderdale* [2004] UKHL 15, [2004] 1 WLR 1057; *Mitchell v City of Glasgow* [2009] UKHL 11, [2009] 1 AC 874; *Hill v Chief Constable of West Yorkshire* [1989] AC 53.

[88] In *Michael v Chief Constable of South Wales* [2015] UKSC 2, a human rights claim could proceed while a claim in negligence was struck out: here, the case concerned whether there had been a failure to respond appropriately to an emergency (999) call; in *DSD v Commissioner of Police for the Metropolis* [2015] EWCA Civ 646, [2016] QB 161, a human rights claim for failure in investigation was able to proceed in circumstances quite similar to *Hill* itself.

[89] Neither, of course, is damage the sole preoccupation of the law of tort: as explained above, the present observations are particularly aimed at the tort of negligence.

[90] See, eg, the judgments of Lord Reid in *Dorset Yacht v Home Office* [1970] AC 1004 and Oliver LJ in *Lamb v Camden LBC* [1981] QB 625.

[91] [2016] UKSC 11, [2016] AC 677.

translated into a risk, and it is plainly the management of this risk, rather than fault, that is the critical notion.

Road traffic liability provides a third important illustration of the themes explored here. Where is the balance between security and responsibility in this important context? This area of liability is a staple of tort liability, as it has been throughout the periods surveyed. And, of course, it is also a staple of the security revolution in tort. Unlike the two other illustrations offered, it is not an area where new tort concepts are being generated, and on the face of things, in relation to its concepts it is stable. However, this area of tort most neatly exemplifies the themes of risk-based governance and the layering of responsibility over structures designed to deliver security.

Does the presence of compulsory liability insurance negate the individualised responsibility of negligent drivers, while preserving the security of the injured victim? Compulsory liability insurance is itself not a responsibility-free zone. Rather, it inherently gives rise to a new responsibility, namely to insure. This responsibility is keenly enforced and promoted, not surprisingly, by insurers. In this context, the 'public' role of insurers in delivering a policy of security is plain: road traffic insurance must comply with the stringent statutory requirements, and the cases of uninsured and untraced drivers are governed by agreements between insurers and the state.[92] The public policy goal of delivering security through the insurance market in this context is plain, and can be compared with the provision of flood insurance in the era of intensified flooding events. In return, both in the case of road traffic and in the case of flooding, insurers are important contributors to policy debates. At the same time, motor insurers seek to influence behaviour directly, for example through creating information about uninsured drivers and passing relevant information to police forces. One such strategy deploys the law of tort itself. Increasingly, in recent years, the Motor Insurers' Bureau—which is responsible for compensating the victims of torts on the part of uninsured and untraced drivers—has included in its strategy the pursuit of uninsured tortfeasors.[93] As in other areas, insurers may thus be among the key promoters of 'responsibility' in the law of liability.[94] The nature of responsibility here, however, is directly derived from and oriented to the need to promote security.

VI. CONCLUSIONS: REVOLUTION UPON REVOLUTION?

The two phenomena explored—the security revolution and the apparent reversal of the wheel towards responsibility in the era of new forms of governance and regulation—have left complex relationships between security and distribution, and

[92] A new Uninsured Drivers Agreement was signed in 2015, replacing the 1999 Agreement; note also the Untraced Drivers Agreement 2003.

[93] R Merkin and J Steele, 'Policing Tort and Crime with the MIB: Remedies, Penalties and the Duty to Insure' in M Dyson (ed), *Unravelling Tort and Crime* (Cambridge, Cambridge University Press, 2014).

[94] The link between insurers and moral judgment has been demonstrated in other contexts: Baker, above n 12; R Ericson, D Barry and A Doyle, 'The Moral Hazards of Neo-liberalism: Lessons from the Private Insurance Industry' (2000) 29 *Economy and Society* 532.

between liability and responsibility, which are likely to have both affected private law and invoked private law into arriving at the current balance. As argued earlier, what has been learned and achieved through the initial risk revolution could not fail to influence the present shape of the law. 'Security' is still a working goal and ambition—it is not being given up. But the cost of security is increasingly at issue. This is as true of costs regimes and the provision of private law as a 'resource' as it is of any other aspect of the structures reviewed here.

The new era might seem to represent the triumph of truly 'private' law over a conception of the field as increasingly socialised. If this is so, the key issue might not be about changes in (internal) academic fashion, but about changes in the context of private law. However, it has been suggested that this is, in any event, not precisely to the point. What has been learned in the 'security' revolution now provides the context for the operation of private law. A more restrained—and restraining—set of concepts and principles is being promoted, sensitive to risk allocation and rival potential sources of security. These concepts may fail tests of clarity and predictability, but they do so in favour of directing decision makers to the question of where it is reasonable to place the costs of security. This is itself more in tune with the current era of risk governance than earlier tort law could hope to be in tune with the security revolution, since the practical fit between private law and security in the welfare sense was never complete at a theoretical level.

In the current era, the generalisation of principle which scholars have associated with 'autonomous' private law—which might have as its ambition a relatively timeless approach to party interactions—is heavily compromised as courts and litigants seek ways of negotiating risk and security. But it is suggested that the more complex and responsive notions, such as the assumption of responsibility and 'close connection' which have been explored herein, are themselves private law's contributions to conditions of uncertainty. Their opacity is part of the reason for their staying power, since they are highly adaptable. Nevertheless, they are not empty. Rather, they direct the courts' attention to questions about the burden of security.

Finally, and returning to the questions in this chapter's introduction, there is reason to suggest that, in the present era, private law not only reflects, but is also part of, social change; and none more so than in connection with risk, responsibility and the costs of security.

6

The Unacknowledged Revolution in Liability for Negligence

STEVE HEDLEY*

> The tort liability and insurance systems are very much like the two suns in a binary star, dependent on each other for their position in our legal system. For more than a century these two systems have influenced each other's course of development. Neither would be anything like what it is today if the other had not existed and developed along with it. Today the two systems constantly interact, and almost no effort to understand or reform one of them can take place without understanding the role played by the other.[1]

I. INTRODUCTION

IF A LEGAL discipline such as tort is to be more than a mere accumulation of regulatory details, it must have some clear internal conception of itself. And this conception—call it a theory, justification, narrative or some other expression for something that makes sense—must have at least some superficial plausibility, both descriptively (it must fit the law we have) and normatively (it must sound like a good reason for the law's being the way it is).

There are many such theories in relation to tort, almost an embarrassment of them. And it is difficult to write in the area without providing more reasons to be 'for' or 'against' particular theories. That is not, however, my primary intention. Rather, this is an exercise in meta-theory, asking why legal theorists address the questions they do, and what form their answers are likely to take. In particular, I hope to get behind the question of 'the justification of tort law', to examine whether it is the right question to be asking.

I am not the first to address this meta-theoretical question. While today many take the project of 'justifying tort' pretty much for granted, disagreeing only on how this should be done, a few have doubts. Special mention must be made of Jane

* Many thanks to my colleagues Maria Cahill, Patrick O'Callaghan, Conor O'Mahony, Catherine O'Sullivan and Bénédicte Sage-Fuller for their incisive and helpful comments. Many thanks also to those who heard this paper on 22 July 2016 at the Obligations VIII conference. I would be delighted to receive any further comment on or criticism of this chapter at s.hedley@ucc.ie.

[1] KS Abraham, *The Liability Century: Insurance and Tort Law from the Progressive Era to 9/11* (Cambridge, Harvard University Press, 2008) 1.

Stapleton, who has done so much to chart how one tort theory inevitably leads to another: adopting a particular perspective always leaves some problems unsolved, and resolving those problems often requires a fresh perspective which may threaten to supplant its predecessor, and so on ad infinitum.[2] While each theory is typically expressed as a final conclusion, it is usually only one step of the journey. Tort's voyage of self-discovery, its constant progress from one way of seeing itself to another, is the subject of this chapter.

II. ASOCIAL THEORIES

Most theories of tort tell a simple story indeed. Suppose one individual (we will call him Albus) suffers injury, insult or harm at the hands of another (let us call her Bellatrix). In many instances, tort law allows Albus to take a civil action against Bellatrix and obtain compensation. What rules are in play, and why does tort do this? Various different narratives can be found:

— The narrative of *rights and wrongs*. If Bellatrix's behaviour can be regarded as wrongful and/or as infringing Albus's rights, then Albus should have a civil action against Bellatrix. There are several of variants on this, with subtly differing conceptions of 'rights' and 'wrongs';[3] some think of tort as 'vindicating' Albus's rights,[4] others that it is an avenue of 'civil recourse',[5] or simply that it encourages peaceful dispute-resolution.[6]

— The narrative of *economics*. If the Bellatrixes of this world were free to harm the Albuses without consequences, we would all be impoverished. This narrative has a respectably long ancestry, though today it is restated in rigorous and abstract terminology. A typical modern analysis treats the problem as one of bilateral precaution (each can do something to reduce the risks) and high transaction costs (neither would have been very willing to discuss the matter beforehand). In that light, the lawyer-economist crafts rules which internalise the parties' externalities, so that as rational beings the two will both act to maximise societal wealth.[7]

— The narrative of *justice*. Albus should succeed if his claim is a just one. Again, there are several variants, reflecting different conceptions of what justice requires,[8] and to what extent the wider community should have a voice in the dispute.[9] A further layer of complexity asks whether we should consider

[2] J Stapleton, *Products Liability* (London, Butterworths, 1994).

[3] For different conceptions see M Dyson (ed), *Unravelling Tort and Crime* (Cambridge, Cambridge University Press, 2014) ch 3 (NJ McBride), ch 4 (GR Sullivan), ch 5 (R Stevens) and ch 6 (RA Duff). See also R Stevens, *Tort and Rights* (Oxford, Oxford University Press, 2007).

[4] See, eg, JNE Varuhas, 'The Concept of "Vindication" in the Law of Torts: Rights, Interests and Damages' (2014) 34 *OJLS* 253.

[5] See, eg, JCP Goldberg and BC Zipursky, 'Torts as Wrongs' (2010) 88 *Texas Law Review* 917.

[6] See, eg, A Robertson, 'On the Function of the Law of Negligence' (2013) 33 *OJLS* 31.

[7] See, eg, R Cooter and T Ulen, *Law and Economics*, 4th edn (Boston, Pearson Addison Wesley, 2004) chs 8–9.

[8] See, eg, J Gordley, *Foundations of Private Law* (Oxford, Oxford University Press, 2006) 196–97.

[9] See, eg, A Robertson, 'Policy-Based Reasoning in Duty of Care Cases' (2013) 33 *Legal Studies* 119.

how well provided-for Albus already is and whether Bellatrix can afford to compensate him (distributive justice), or whether this is irrelevant (corrective justice). Whether that distinction matters, or is even coherent, is a regular point of dispute between theorists.[10]

While these theories are usually presented as alternatives, it is not clear that they actually conflict. Tort rights wrongs and makes the community richer and implements justice—to acknowledge all three virtues does not sound like evidence of confusion.[11] And each theory does essentially the same work, which is to explain why there is a legal link between Bellatrix's behaviour and Albus's well-being. There are plenty of reasons why that link is desirable, reasons which end up being expressed as distinct theories.

These theories are as a rule asocial—that is, they make only minimal assumptions about the social world which Albus and Bellatrix actually inhabit. The rest of the community's arrangements are taken to be irrelevant, or at least they are set aside when we come to consider the parties' legal rights. In fact, these asocial models covertly make a few limited assumptions: positively, that there is a legal system which Albus may invoke, and negatively, that other social systems provide Albus with no better solution to his problem. Which actual societies are closest to this? The most obvious examples would be societies like our own but a few centuries previous: late medieval or early modern states, with well-developed legal systems and functioning legislatures, but as yet lacking other formal legal and governmental institutions we would expect today. The roots of these theories are historically very deep.[12]

Yet today these theories are not put forward as historical theories, nor (as a rule) do they account for the rather significant differences between earlier legal systems and our modern ones. For the most part, the suggestion is that these theories are timeless. The few writers who mention the historical angle treat modernity as an aberration: Aristotle's views may seem misguided to us, they argue, but Aristotle is right and we are wrong.[13] If moral philosophy or economics are taken as sources of truth, their theorists would have us believe that they are universal truths: if legal rules operate as economic incentives now, then presumably they always did—and so forth. The theorists' point seems to be an assertion of law's independence: an insistence that we can make sense of what the law does without making much reference to the rest of what goes on, or even where or when we are talking of.

These asocial theorists do not deny that Albus may today have many sources of help open to him. He may (depending on the type of harm Bellatrix has done him) call his family, his friends, his neighbours, the police, an ambulance or fire engine, his union, the safety inspector or the environmental health officer, he may claim

[10] See, eg, J Oberdiek (ed), *Philosophical Foundations of the Law of Torts* (Oxford, Oxford University Press, 2014) ch 16 (J Gardner) and ch 17 (H Sheinman).

[11] For a similar point see Gordley, above n 8, 11–12.

[12] See D Ibbetson, 'Revolutions in Private Law?' this volume, chapter 2.

[13] A Beever, *Forgotten Justice: Forms of Justice in the History of Legal and Political Theory* (Oxford, Oxford University Press, 2013) especially 13–34 and 243–77; Gordley, above n 8, ch 1. Peter Birks argued that the rot set in rather later, identifying a 'grim new rigour' by which 'money dominates the political debate as never before' commencing in the 1980s: see 'Editor's Preface' in P Birks (ed), *Wrongs and Remedies in the Twenty-First Century* (Oxford, Clarendon Press, 1996) v.

insurance or social security benefits, talk to his parliamentary representative(s), to Bellatrix's employer or to the press, or protest vocally on social media. Nor do asocial theorists really deny that, legal processes being expensive and slow, tort is little more than a longstop. Their argument is rather that tort is a distinct legal institution, and must be understood in isolation.

In short, what is notable about most theories of tort is that they are theories of tort itself, rather than of the complex social systems of which tort is part. Does this make for a good understanding or a poor one? What would we discover if we looked at tort in its modern context? An honest answer is that we very rarely look. But we must, I think, take a quick peek at least.

III. BRINGING IN THE MODERN WORLD

Of course, there are excellent reasons why legal theorists rarely look wider. Modern societies are complex. Generalisations about them are easy to make but hard to validate. Nonetheless, I suggest five broad historical propositions, true of the entire developed world, which have clear relevance for theories of tort law.

1. Over the past two centuries or more, technical understanding of the problems that societies face has improved immeasurably, and part of that understanding is an increased appreciation of human agency. Poverty, injury and disease are no longer inescapable givens, but are human problems which can be substantially mitigated if we act in a different way—more responsibly, more cleverly, more productively, more collaboratively. A vague feeling that Bellatrix does both more good and more harm than she knows has been replaced by an understanding of the risks attached to her conduct. 'Fate' no longer seems a plausible explanation of much that goes on. Chance still plays a huge role, but chance is now understood, measured and managed: indeed, many of our more important and difficult decisions are about 'risk management', as it is now called. In Ulrich Beck's famous phrase, we no longer live in scarcity societies but in risk societies.[14]
2. Growing awareness of the extent to which injury is preventable has led to increasing pressure to prevent it in fact, and while there is opposition too—on grounds of cost and convenience—overall in the past two centuries the state has taken a major role in accident prevention, with very positive results. Initially this was in relation to dangerous trades, then for transport and now on an all-pervasive basis. Long before Albus has any cause for complaint, the state's arsenal of safety compliance may have been brought to bear on Bellatrix, and the incident between the two of them perhaps headed off.
3. Over the course of the nineteenth century, it was discovered that insurance (an ancient institution) could be deployed on a very wide scale. This was of significant interest both to Albus (who could now insure against an aggressive or careless Bellatrix) and to Bellatrix (who could now insure against a

[14] U Beck, *Risk Society—Towards a New Modernity*, M Ritter trans (London, Sage Publications, 1992) especially ch 1. See more generally J Steele, 'Risk Revolutions in Private Law', this volume, chapter 5.

litigious Albus). And governments quickly appreciated that, while great benefits flowed merely from allowing people to insure themselves, sometimes even greater benefits might accrue if they were *compelled* to insure, either by forcing them to avail of the insurance market or by acting as the mandatory insurer itself. Otto von Bismarck's welfare state reforms of the 1880s were a precursor to similar innovations across Europe. The modern welfare state became a practical possibility.

4. In the same period, the law grew considerably as an instrument of social control, a process dominated by legislatures rather than courts. We no longer expect the laws and customs of the realm to remain relatively static; on the contrary, we now expect the government to change them frequently, as emerging circumstances require. Most developed nations have now transposed their traditional law into a code; even in the few that have not, statute is by far the most important source of law. And as Pat O'Malley points out, this modern growth of regulation is to a great extent a matter of money payments: it is within government's power to order individual community members to pay money, and the meaning government gives to those payments (tax, fine, rent, pension contribution, community charge, insurance premium, remuneration, price, compensation and so forth) does so much to shape the social world.[15]
5. Despite this, lawyers everywhere have a firm grasp on the basic language and grammar of the law. We are not governed by lawyers, but we accept lawyers as referees of the political game, telling us authoritatively who has won each argument over what the law should be and what the resulting law is. Indeed, private law is one of the most solid of our political institutions, one of the things that makes us who we are. In nations where the constitutional regime has a long continuous history, private law is usually assumed to be foundational; where war or revolution have interrupted continuity, private law is often the most durable institution of government still standing, and is valued for precisely that reason; and where private law has been allowed to decay, its reinvigoration is seen as a stabilising move.[16] So while the direction of modern law reform is decided politically, the conceptual framework within which reform is implemented is dominated by the lawyers.

What does all of this mean for tort?

IV. MODERN IRRELEVANCE OF ASOCIAL THEORIES?

The growth of insurance since the late nineteenth century, both through private contracts and through state insurance, knocks the stuffing out of the traditional

[15] P O'Malley, *The Currency of Justice: Fines and Damages in Consumer Societies* (Oxford, Routledge-Cavendish, 2009) 24.

[16] On private law and nationalism see G Comparato, *Nationalism and Private Law in Europe* (Oxford, Hart Publishing, 2014). See also M Raff, 'The Importance of Reforming Civil Law in Formerly Socialist Legal Systems' (2015) 1 *International Comparative Jurisprudence* 24.

justifications for tort.[17] Bellatrix increasingly safeguards her interests with liability insurance; Albus, too, increasingly finds that his interests are protected by insurance; and where Albus must sue but has a choice of defendants (either Bellatrix or her employer), he will naturally focus on whichever of them is insured. Sometimes the old tort law survives as a façade, such as where the state compels Bellatrix to take out liability insurance, which Albus is encouraged to avail of by suing her.[18]

The traditional link that tort law provides between Albus's loss and Bellatrix's behaviour has therefore been severed. When we ask for tort's justification, the old reasons no longer make much sense:

- Talk of *rights and wrongs* no longer justifies what tort does, because Bellatrix is not really treated by the law of tort as a wrongdoer. It remains true that the case concerns Albus's rights, though they have for nearly all practical purposes ceased to be rights against Bellatrix. It remains true that Bellatrix has committed a wrong: very probably, she has infringed the criminal law or road traffic law, or whatever safety regime applies to her dangerous activity. But tort no longer treats her as a wrongdoer in any serious sense. It is extremely unlikely that she will face a court. She pays no penalty, suffers no humiliation or reprimand, no demand that she apologise. She may not even be told how the civil action turned out, and if she is, it is merely a matter of courtesy. The language of wrongs remains, but it no longer describes the reality.
- Talk of *economic incentives* also looks strange, because Bellatrix does not pay any damages award, so is not much incentivised. This is an intrinsic feature of insurance regimes: the whole point of the insurance (to Bellatrix) is to liberate her from such financial pressures. Lawyer-economists often factor insurance into their analyses, but are reluctant to accept what common sense suggests and the empirical evidence confirms, that a defendant with liability insurance is not usually much influenced by the prospect of being held liable.[19] There are many legal and social factors discouraging Bellatrix from harming Albus, but tort is no longer an important one.
- Talk of *justice* between Albus and Bellatrix becomes problematic, because Bellatrix effectively drops out of any dispute. The question whether compensation should be paid is between Albus (or his insurer) and another insurer. Bellatrix's involvement in the dispute is almost entirely imaginary, and it stretches the truth to say that it is about whether justice requires her to compensate Albus—whatever the verdict, she will do no such thing.

To sum up: tort has a variety of potential functions, but by modern standards it performs none of them very well. Name any goal that tort might theoretically perform—identifying and punishing wrongful behaviour, providing compensation, deterring carelessness—and it is relatively easy to think of other institutions that

[17] GT Schwartz, 'The Ethics and Economics of Tort Liability Insurance' (1990) 75 *Cornell Law Review* 313.

[18] R Merkin and S Dziobon, 'Tort Law and Compulsory Insurance' in TT Arvind and J Steele (eds), *Tort Law and the Legislature* (Oxford, Hart Publishing, 2013) ch 15.

[19] For fuller discussion see below, text at n 24 and following.

might do it a great deal better. Tort made sense in earlier centuries, where the state did little to fulfil any of these objects, and a single institution that did *something* for all of them was clearly worth having. But as societies grew to expect better, they realised that this poor performance is intrinsic: criticism of tort's performance cannot be dismissed merely because alternative institutions are not perfect, as tort is (so to speak) not even at the races.

Clearly, a choice had to be made. Some nineteenth-century judges contemplated a ban on liability insurance, precisely because it was eating away at the system of responsibility that tort represented.[20] But it was soon obvious that if we have to choose between tort and insurance, it is insurance that should be preferred. Insurance provides quick and cheap compensation, in contrast to the law's delays. There are fewer disputes, and most are easy to resolve. It is true that insurance does little to prevent accidents, but (as reformers eventually realised) the same is true of tort: safety and compensation are distinct goals, requiring separate provision.[21]

Does tort still have a continuing behavioural impact on defendants, or potential defendants? For some of the more antiquated and rarely invoked torts, perhaps it does. The economic torts can certainly do so, which is precisely why some employers support their use as industrial discipline.[22] Nuisance and trespass to land can also influence individuals, especially if coercive equitable remedies are invoked. Defamation, too, can have a direct impact on individuals: indeed, here it is the idea of compensation that is arguably a sham, as awards typically consist merely of a sum for 'injury to feelings', ascertained by a not very rigorous system of assessment, and (strangely, if the law genuinely aspired to be compensatory) greater or smaller depending on the culpability of the defendant's conduct. And some have hopes that liability in civil rights cases could be used to deter misbehaving public officials.[23] The more medieval parts of tort, if they can be so styled, still embody medieval conceptions, though they are occasionally tweaked by legislatures to nuance their effect.

The overwhelming bulk of tort cases, though, are negligence claims, and here any hope of a coherent effect on defendants has long gone. As Gary Schwartz notes,[24] the case for tort as a general deterrent is extremely weak: numerous studies have shown that tort liability has all sorts of effects, some of which deter injuries, others of which encourage them, and many of which have no effect either way.[25] Similarly

[20] M Davies, 'The End of the Affair: Duty of Care and Liability Insurance' (1989) 9 *Legal Studies* 67, 74.

[21] For that debate in the UK see PWJ Bartrip and SB Burman, *The Wounded Soldiers of Industry: Industrial Compensation Policy 1833–1897* (Oxford, Clarendon Press, 1983) especially ch 3.

[22] See, eg, B Simpson, 'Trade Disputes Legislation and the Economic Torts' in Arvind and Steele, above n 18, ch 6.

[23] JC Schwartz, 'How Governments Pay: Lawsuits, Budgets, and Police Reform' (2016) 63 *UCLA Law Review* 1144.

[24] GT Schwartz, 'Reality in the Economic Analysis of Tort Law: Does Tort Law Really Deter?' (1994) 42 *UCLA Law Review* 377. For a broader review see C Hodges, *Law and Corporate Behaviour* (Oxford, Hart Publishing, 2015) chs 2–7, especially ch 7.

[25] In addition to Schwartz, ibid, see SD Sugarman, 'Doing Away with Tort Law' (1985) 73 *California Law Review* 555, 561–90; D Dewees, D Duff and M Trebilcock, *Exploring the Domain of Accident Law—Taking the Facts Seriously* (New York, Oxford University Press, 1996); P Cane, *Atiyah's Accidents, Compensation and the Law*, 8th edn (Cambridge, Cambridge University Press, 2013) 419–55.

compromised are more limited arguments, such as that better design of liability insurance policies (by the use of deductibles or experience-based pricing) can deter the policy holder; in fact, the effects are very variable.[26] Anecdotally, some experienced drivers report that they think of their no-claims bonus when avoiding potentially dangerous situations on the road, but there do not seem to be any empirical studies suggesting that there are fewer accidents as a consequence. New Zealand abolished tort liability for personal injuries in 1974 and replaced it with a scheme of pure accident compensation; accident rates did not skyrocket, but were in fact reduced somewhat.[27] Cane therefore seems justified in concluding that we cannot seriously treat modern tort law as a scheme to regulate unsafe behaviour.[28]

None of this is to deny that in a few limited instances tort can be shown to have a beneficial deterrent effect; there are various theories as to when and why this will be so.[29] Tort liability can therefore still form part of a rational strategy for public safety, so long as the conditions and parameters of the liability are carefully defined. That, however, is the antithesis of tort principle, the defining feature of which is that it is *not* fragmented into isolated pockets of liability but operates on a broad and systematic basis. In most contexts, where we rely on the law to promote safe conduct, it is not tort that deters, but other mechanisms: criminal penalties, licensing and qualification requirements, mandatory health-and-safety training.

Tort is therefore largely obsolete as a tool for public safety. Why not, then, simply abolish it?

V. ABOLISHING TORT?

Yet evidently enough tort does something for at least a few accident victims—money goes to real people whose injuries genuinely merit it—and a host of reasons ensure that any march away from tort is slow at best. While the public might gain hugely from the abolition of tort and its replacement with universal insurance, there is no organised body with the incentive to say so, and the huge uncertainties implicit in such a major reform discourage government action. The reform debate is dominated by professionals who earn their living from tort—after all, they are the ones who know most about it—and dissatisfaction with tort usually leads only to minor changes.

[26] See, eg, Schwartz, above n 24, 573–81; Dewees et al, ibid, 414–21; Cane, ibid, 431–53. For a more upbeat assessment see T Baker and P Siegelman, 'The Law and Economics of Liability Insurance: A Theoretical and Empirical Review' in J Arlen (ed), *Research Handbook on the Economics of Torts* (Cheltenham, Edward Elgar, 2013) 169, 178. For an argument that modern economic analysis is incapable of handling the complexities of real-world problems see SJ Bayern, 'The Limits of Formal Economics in Tort Law' (2010) 75 *Brooklyn Law Review* 707.

[27] C Brown, 'Deterrence in Tort and No-Fault: The New Zealand Experience' (1985) 73 *California Law Review* 976.

[28] P Cane, 'Tort Law as Regulation' (2002) 31 *Common Law World Review* 305.

[29] See discussion in Dewees et al, above n 25, 414–15; R Gold, 'Compensation's Role in Deterrence' (2016) 91 *Notre Dame Law Review* 1997.

While it is unlikely that the architects of modern welfare states had a very high opinion of tort law, as practical politicians it was difficult for them to argue for abolition. William Beveridge, in his famous report laying the foundations for the UK welfare reforms of the late 1940s, hinted that if decent welfare provision were made for injured industrial workers (or, for that matter, any accident victim), then the intellectual case for providing a tort remedy as well was gone:

> [I]f what is judged to be adequate compensation is provided from a Social Insurance Fund for industrial accidents, irrespective of any negligence causing them, there is no reason why this compensation should be greater because the employer has in fact been negligent. The needs of the injured person are not greater. With the inevitable uncertainties of legal proceedings, suits for heavy damages on the ground of negligence cannot escape having something of the character of a lottery. In so far as danger of such proceedings is a penalty for negligence, it is more effective to make the penalty a direct one—of criminal proceedings undertaken by the public department responsible for securing industrial safety. Employers can and normally will insure against civil liabilities; they cannot insure against criminal proceedings ...[30]

But such radicalism was politically unproductive. The issue was referred to a committee of stakeholders. The lawyers (very aware of the merits of tort) and the unions (who knew that tort would usually provide more generous benefits than any social insurance scheme) together constituted a majority of the committee.[31] So the new welfare regime, far from doing away with tort, in fact expanded its range considerably, and introduced a system of legal aid to enable litigation by those hitherto too poor to afford it.[32]

While the tort system makes no sense to a tidy-minded welfare lawyer, to those less concerned with systemic neatness it is not obviously pernicious. It channels money away from risk-creators and towards those with genuine needs, and so serves welfare goals. From that perspective, it is needlessly confrontational, oddly selective (those it helps are no more deserving than those it refuses to help) and extremely wasteful (its strange liability criteria often require complex adjudication). However, there is no simple way of appropriating the resources currently devoted to tort and devoting them to welfare proper, so there is no point in putting abolition high on the reformer's agenda. The issue has repeatedly been postponed, and it is possible that it has been postponed for ever. Tort is therefore a significant part of the welfare regime, but is effectively fenced off from the rest of that regime.

VI. TORT FROM THE GOVERNMENT'S POINT OF VIEW

Tom Baker tells a story from China. Around the beginning of the century, the Chinese government made it compulsory for car owners to take out third-party insurance

[30] W Beveridge, *Social Insurance and Allied Services* (Cmd 6404, 1942) [262] (Beveridge Report).

[31] See *Final Report of the Departmental Committee on Alternative Remedies* (Cmd 6860, 1946) (Monckton Committee Report). See further PWJ Bartrip, 'Beveridge, Workmen's Compensation and the Alternative Remedy' (1985) 14 *Journal of Social Policy* 491.

[32] See Law Reform (Personal Injuries) Act 1948 (UK); Legal Aid and Advice Act 1949 (UK).

against road accidents.[33] Baker, as a specialist in tort and insurance, was invited to lead a series of seminars. He gave the benefit of the US experience, along with its clear message: that tort's obsession with assigning blame for individual accidents devours resources that should go to the victims of those accidents. Proper resource management requires first-party insurance, which provides compensation with far greater efficiency. But the officials who heard this quickly corrected him: he was missing the point. Merely insisting on compensation for the injured would be seen as paternalistic; such a law would be unpopular and unsustainable. Rather, the aim was to remind drivers of their obligations to other road users, and to require that they took proper means to meet those obligations. By insisting on tort liability and simultaneously providing for insurance, thereby making it largely theoretical, the government would appear in the public gaze not as the overprotective friend of the injured, but as even-handedly reminding people to respect their fellow road users.[34]

This is how modern governments see tort. As a system of compensation or welfare, it is woefully inefficient. It redeems itself by delivering a constant reminder to respect the safety of others. 'Pay Your Debts!' is a more effective message than 'Help the Injured!'; to paraphrase David Howarth, appeals to collective responsibility work best when coupled with, or even disguised as, appeals to individual responsibility.[35] It is none the less so because individual responsibility is a fundamentally false description of how tort law works, proclaiming that it imposes duties to take care when in fact it merely insists on the purchase of insurance. Tort's actual workings seem tawdry and irrational, but in peoples' imagination it becomes an essential part of social discipline. The question whether tort should be abolished must focus on whether we have a satisfactory method of replacing it in *both* respects.

The modern state therefore uses tort in two quite distinct ways: to provide compensation for the injured and to remind the public of their safety obligations. As Jürgen Habermas might put it, tort is both instrumental bureaucratic action (establishing and maintaining a system of compensation rights) and symbolic communicative action (publicly encouraging considerate behaviour).[36] Both are essential: symbolic action alone cannot help the injured, but bureaucratic action alone would make no sense to the public and so would have no legitimacy. Lawyers, caught between the technical demands of the system and the rather different public perception, and sensing that an efficient welfare system would have little use for tort-based mechanisms, insist that tort is not part of the welfare system and must be kept distinct from it. Legal rhetoric therefore embraces the symbolic aspects of tort (vindication of rights, promotion of safety, justice), while doggedly implementing the bureaucratic reality (insurance, negotiation, compensation).

[33] Road Traffic Safety Law of 28 October 2003, Art 17, which also requires a social assistance fund for when insurance arrangements fall short. See generally AJ Green, 'Tort Reform with Chinese Characteristics: Towards a "Harmonious Society" in the People's Republic of China' (2008) 10 *San Diego International Law Journal* 121; W Zhang, 'Understanding the Law of Torts in China: A Political Economy Perspective' (27 October 2014), available at ssrn.com/abstract=2515449.

[34] T Baker, *The Medical Malpractice Myth* (Chicago, University of Chicago Press, 2005) 115–16.

[35] D Howarth, 'Three Forms of Responsibility: On the Relationship between Tort Law and the Welfare State' (2001) 60 *CLJ* 553.

[36] J Habermas, *The Theory of Communicative Action, Volume 1: Reason and the Rationalization of Society*, TA McCarthy trans (Cambridge, Polity Press, 1984).

To what extent can we say that this policy is deliberately deceptive? That is a question on which radically different views can reasonably be held. One the one hand, significant numbers of people are in fact misled. As an example, consider the recent social media storm when a Connecticut woman sued her nephew for injuries he accidently inflicted on her at his eighth birthday party. Widespread vilification of the plaintiff strongly suggests that the online public does not understand how the system works (she had no recourse for her considerable medical expenses without taking a civil action, any award in her favour would have been funded by an insurer and her action in no way distressed or inconvenienced her nephew).[37] In actual fact, the idea that injured people may confront their injurer and 'have their day in court' is quaint, and entirely unaffordable except in a handful of instances; belief to the contrary contradicts plain facts about the everyday operation of the legal system. So the public are, arguably, deceived in the matter. On the other hand, the actual facts are no secret to anyone who genuinely enquires into them; and there is nothing fake about official commitment to public safety and provision of compensation, though there is always debate about how to reconcile it with other governmental objectives. To what degree the government is obliged to correct public misconceptions, and to what extent they would be applauded if they did so, are matters of opinion.

The difficulty is that the gulf between the bureaucratic and the symbolic has now become very wide; the two patterns of action evolve on their own, and '[t]he instrumental rationality of the system removes decision-making from the hands of a deliberative public and passes it to bureaucrats and market forces'.[38] So the symbolic justifications given for tort grow more distant from how tort actually works, and tort faces an ongoing crisis of legitimation. The detailed story is, of course, different in each nation, as the move towards a welfare state happened from different starting points, at different times and in different circumstances[39]—but there is a degree of sameness to the national stories nonetheless. As tort increasingly turned into a welfare system, the lawyers guided the welfare state's development to protect tort law. This resulted in increased uptake of legal liability, as the nominal defendant increasingly became a mere front. Legal analysis still puts Bellatrix under the spotlight, but in reality nearly all successful claims are paid by an insurer or an employer. So tort in practice operates as part of welfare provision, though a distinctly odd part of it, and is kept distinct from the rest of the welfare system.[40]

How separate is tort from insurance law and welfare law? Legislatures are reluctant to modify traditional legal forms, but have fewer inhibitions about changing matters which do not seem very legal (such as the detail of insurance regimes) or where lawyers themselves will accept change (such as rules on procedure). Development of substantive tort law is therefore usually left up to the lawyers themselves, either by bold judicial pronouncements (as in the USA) or by legislation written

[37] See, eg, '"Aunt From Hell" and Her Nephew Speak Out after Wrist Lawsuit', *US Magazine* (15 October 2015), available at <goo.gl/XzNzv3>.

[38] P Almond, *Corporate Manslaughter and Regulatory Reform* (Basingstoke, Palgrave Macmillan, 2013) 82.

[39] For national differences see SD Sugarman, 'Compensation for Accidental Personal Injury: What Nations Might Learn From Each Other' (2011) 38 *Pepperdine Law Review* 597.

[40] For a general survey see G Wagner (ed), *Tort Law and Liability Insurance* (Vienna, Springer-Verlag, 2005).

by lawyers for lawyers and shunned by ordinary politicians (as in Ireland and the UK).[41] Even where (as occasionally happens) the legislature creates new tort-like remedies, it is left to the lawyers to say whether they are 'really' part of tort law or merely statutory anomalies.[42] The result is that courts and legislatures develop the law separately, apparently with no joint plan, indeed only occasionally acknowledging one another's existence.[43] '[T]he legislator has always confined itself to satisfying the most urgent needs rather than to providing for a coherent system of liability throughout the different areas of application.'[44] This sets the pattern for tort reform:

— Mere modifications to insurance law and practice do not attract much legal opposition.[45] So in EU nations, the awkward system of compensating road accident victims through compulsory liability insurance has slowly expanded, while leaving the substantive tort law alone. Compulsory insurance cover has been smoothly extended to cover a wider range of victims, and insurers must also compensate those injured by uninsured or untraceable drivers.[46] Meanwhile, 'the traditional peculiarities of the different tort systems have proved to be astonishingly resistant to change'.[47]
— Distinct special schemes cover meritorious claimants who fall outside ordinary tort principle. Political pressure for a remedy is satisfied without disturbing tort's conceptual structure. To a tort lawyer, responsibility for a crime rests primarily with the criminal; to a government that promised a fairer deal for the victims of crime, matters are otherwise. Hence the wide variety of victim compensation schemes across the developed world, as well as special schemes relating to particular incidents. Again, it seems odd to tort lawyers that accidental victims of voluntary vaccination schemes should expect a remedy for inevitable risks of the programme; yet to politicians who know that mass vaccination is

[41] For the genesis of a typical piece of English 'tort lawyers' law' see SH Bailey, 'Occupiers' Liability: The Enactment of "Common Law" Principles' in Arvind and Steele, above n 18, ch 9. The various Law Commissioners are, of course, all lawyers or law teachers, as the establishing legislation makes clear: see Law Commissions Act 1965 (UK), ss 1–2, Law Reform Commission Act 1975 (IE), s 3.

[42] See, eg, S Sperino 'Let's Pretend Discrimination Is a Tort' (2014) 75 *Ohio State Law Journal* 1107; A Burrows, 'Damages and Rights' in D Nolan and A Robertson (eds), *Rights and Private Law* (Oxford, Hart Publishing, 2012) 275, 290–303. See also WH van Boom, 'Torts, Courts and Legislatures—Comparative Remarks on Civil Law Codifications of Tort Law' in Arvind and Steele, above n 18, ch 2.

[43] For national reviews see, eg, W van Boom, M Lukas and C Kissling (eds), *Tort and Regulatory Law* (Vienna, Springer-Verlag, 2007). For some of the (very few) who have protested against this separation of judicial logic from legislative logic see TT Arvind and J Steele, 'Introduction: Legislation and the Shape of Tort Law' in Arvind and Steele, above n 18, ch 1; A Burrows, 'The Relationship between Common Law and Statute in the Law of Obligations' (2012) 128 *LQR* 231.

[44] S Lohsse, 'The Development of Traffic Liability in Germany' in W Ernst (ed), *The Development of Traffic Liability* (Cambridge, Cambridge University Press, 2010) 75, 110.

[45] For some of the more recent changes in one jurisdiction see J Sorabji, 'Austerity's Effect on English Civil Justice' (2015) 4 *Erasmus Law Review* 159.

[46] P Giliker, *The Europeanisation of English Tort Law* (Oxford, Hart Publishing, 2014) 74–77. On the Europeanisation of the UK's Motor Insurers' Bureau (MIB) and its gradual transformation into a regulatory agency see R Merkin and J Steele, 'Policing Tort and Crime with the MIB: Remedies, Penalties and the Duty to Insure' in Dyson, above n 3, ch 2.

[47] W Ernst, 'General Introduction' in Ernst, above n 44, 1, 7.

essential but must remain voluntary, it is rational to assuage public anxieties by compensating those fortuitously injured.[48]

- In relation to overlaps between tort and other welfare schemes, double compensation cannot fairly be permitted. No great issue of legal principle is involved, and indeed the lawyers' dogma of full compensation meshes neatly with a refusal to provide compensation twice over. As Beveridge foresaw,[49] welfare state administrators prefer not to deny tort liability where the welfare state had already met a particular need, but rather to allow the claim and claw back the excess. This is complicated to organise (it requires every tort defendant settling a case to report it to a state body and hand over the appropriate sum), but is increasingly insisted upon.[50]
- While lawyers can invoke tradition and rule-of-law considerations to protect themselves from much hostile scrutiny, fraud or waste is an undeniable ground for legislative intervention. So a government concerned with an excess of tort liability tends not to modify tort law itself, but approaches the matter through funding, procedure and the technicalities of damages rules, or may even seek to encourage the use of administrative rather than formal legal processes.[51]

None of this is to suggest that modern governments never modify tort law; however, changing legal principle is a hazardous political route, as the lawyers will emphasise the uncertainties in any such reform. UK lawyers still remember the awful example of the Pearson Commission, which was charged with considering fundamental reform to the tort system, but which, far from securing any kind of consensus on the matter, produced only minor and incremental reform proposals, even denying that their terms of reference allowed them to consider the issue of principle.[52] Politically inspired reforms to tort law tend to modify defences rather than substantive liability. Even when the Australian parliaments had to respond to a crisis where (as they saw it) tort threatened the financial stability of the entire insurance sector, they left in place central tort concepts while attempting to limit their impact through defences and other measures.[53] Revising the tort lawyer's entire mindset would be a huge undertaking; wherever possible, politicians prefer to nibble around its edges.

[48] For country reports on special compensation schemes see M Faure and T Hartlief (eds), *Financial Compensation for Victims of Catastrophes: A Comparative Legal Approach* (Vienna, Springer-Verlag, 2006).

[49] Beveridge Report, above n 30, [260].

[50] See R Lewis, 'Recovery of NHS Accident Costs: Tort as a Vehicle for Raising Public Funds' (1999) 62 *MLR* 903.

[51] See, for example, the cocktail of reforms in Ireland brought in over the last quarter of a century to restrain 'the compensation culture', including limiting access to juries, de facto restrictions on legal aid, measures against fraud, limits on occupier's liability, more intense judicial case management, standardisation of damages and mandatory administrative assessment of quantum: see E Quill, *Torts in Ireland*, 4th edn (Dublin, Gill & Macmillan, 2014) 150–60, 512–13, 538–40, 561.

[52] *Report of the Royal Commission on Civil Liability and Compensation for Personal Injury* (Cmnd 7054, 1978) (Pearson Report). For the report in its historical context see P Bartrip, 'No-Fault Compensation on the Roads in Twentieth Century Britain' (2010) 69 *CLJ* 263, 274–81.

[53] J Goudkamp, 'Statutes and Tort Defences' in Arvind and Steele, above n 18, 41–53.

There are, of course, occasional exceptions. Sometimes legislatures have insisted on strict liability, rather than fault liability as the lawyers would generally prefer: examples are the French and German provisions for strict liability for motor accidents,[54] and the EU-wide introduction of strict product liability.[55] Some legislatures have gone even further, establishing national compensation plans paid for by risk-creating groups, wholly supplanting tort law in the context of their operation: generally in the area of workers' compensation (where the UK and Ireland are rather unusual in allowing tort free rein),[56] but most famously in the New Zealand accident compensation scheme, which almost entirely replaced tort personal injury actions.

Yet these non-tortious liabilities and schemes are decidedly the exceptions rather than the rule. Enthusiasm for them has noticeably waned from the 1970s onwards, and they have a hard time escaping from the shadow of tort. While strict liability is ancient, pure strict liability is never to be found, as the liability always has exceptions of one sort or another;[57] so, far from replacing tort with a more rational system, such schemes merely trade one arbitrary criterion for another. The same is true of New Zealand-type accident compensation schemes, which from a welfare point of view seem as arbitrary as tort (why are accident victims treated so much more generously than victims of disease, who seem no less deserving?).[58] From a political standpoint, such schemes are much more vulnerable to attack, as any crisis will be blamed on the body which runs the scheme,[59] whereas responsibility for problems in the tort system is much more diffuse and disputable. These special schemes therefore face continual criticism for being no better than what they replaced and repeated pressure from lawyers to drag them back to the general legal pattern of liability only for fault.[60] Perhaps schemes of that type represent a step in the right direction, which will eventually lead to further and more productive steps—but the signs are not good.

[54] On which see R Youngs, *English, French and German Comparative Law*, 2nd edn (London, Routledge-Cavendish, 2007) 378–84; and on their history see Ernst, above n 44, ch 3 (G Viney and A Guégan-Lécuyer) and ch 4 (S Lohsse). Also, many jurisdictions have state-run no-fault schemes, which exclude tort either entirely or unless the claim exceeds a certain threshold.

[55] Stapleton, above n 2, especially ch 3.

[56] See G Wagner, 'Tort, Social Security, and No-Fault Schemes: Lessons from Real-World Experiments' (2012) 23 *Duke Journal of Comparative and International Law* 1. As Abraham notes, late nineteenth-century employment litigation can be thought of as the first 'tort crisis', and the worker's compensation legislation as 'the original tort reform': Abraham, above n 1, ch 2.

[57] On this aspect of French road traffic law see G Wagner, 'Comparative Tort Law' in M Reimann and R Zimmermann (eds), *Oxford Handbook of Comparative Law* (Oxford, Oxford University Press, 2006) 1003, 1036–38.

[58] J Stapleton, *Disease and the Compensation Debate* (Oxford, Clarendon Press, 1986) 49–51, 104–108 and 145–58.

[59] See especially differing accounts of the crisis in the 1990s, which resulted in a reduction in benefits given under the NZ scheme: 'Symposium: Looking Back at Accident Compensation: Finding Lessons for the Future' (2003) 34 *Victoria University of Wellington Law Review* 189, 189–467, especially 387–94 (R Wilson), 395–406 (D Caygill), 407–22 (J Miller) and 423–32 (L Evans and N Quigley).

[60] G McLay, 'Accident Compensation—What's the Common Law Got To Do With It?' [2008] *New Zealand Law Review* 55.

VII. MODERN THEORIES ABOUT TORT

So tort satisfies genuine welfare needs, by funnelling money away from those who create risks towards those who suffer as a result. But there are obvious objections to it, both because of the leakiness of the pipeline (a significant proportion is lost along the way in legal fees and insurance costs)[61] and because of the rather random basis on which tort's largesse is distributed. If we no longer expect a wrongdoer personally to pay damages to their victim, what is the point of insisting that a wrongdoer be identified?

In fact, in the first decades of the twentieth century, common law theorists showed a considerable degree of confusion about how tort should be seen and what it was for. Indeed, not everyone was convinced that those questions made sense: the idea that tort forms a coherent theoretical unity was quite alien to the common law (Blackstone knew of no such idea). While the project of 'tort and its justification' started to be discussed from the 1880s, most lawyers were happy, most of the time, to ignore the question.

A. Tort as Compensation or Insurance

Around the middle of the twentieth century, common law theorists began to make hay with the idea that the insured defendant was not merely a special case, but had become the norm. With nearly all of its traditional functions effectively stripped away, tort's remaining task appeared to be that of providing compensation. Bellatrix drops out of the picture, except as a taxpayer or payer of insurance premiums; tort's function is to help the injured Albus. Since it is obvious that Albus needs help, and since this arrangement makes a few token gestures in the direction of Bellatrix's guilt (in form she is held liable, and in fact the compensation is paid out of funds to which she contributed), this has at least some plausibility as a justification for the law. So, from this standpoint, tort is *compensation*: or, for those with an interest in cash flow, tort is *insurance*, paid for by the general class of people likely to cause injuries.[62] Tort is seen as part of a wider system of social security, with one foot in government and the other in the market. Bellatrix's personal legal liability plays only a very subsidiary role: occasionally, someone who neglects to insure is made to suffer as a result; the threat of legal liability becomes a spur encouraging insurance.

As a description of how tort actually operates, there is not very much wrong with this. It is true that it focuses on the tort of negligence at the expense of other torts, but then negligence is much more important today than the other torts (not least because so much had been done over the last century or more to encourage it).

[61] One estimate for the UK is that 35% of the money paid in liability insurance premiums is absorbed into managing the system rather than being paid as compensation, though the percentage varies sharply with the type of claim: Institute of Actuaries, *The Cost of Compensation Culture* (2002) 4.2, available at <goo.gl/9kz30P>.

[62] See GE White, *Tort Law in America: An Intellectual History* (New York, Oxford University Press, 1985) 147–53, 171–72.

This compensatory mindset plays down any punitive or guiding role tort might have, but this too merely reflects the reality, that the main effect of tort on behaviour is not to guide us towards an appropriate level of care but (at most) to encourage us to take out insurance.

It is from a normative or symbolic point of view that the insurance and compensation framework seems inadequate, and makes it appear that tort does either too much or too little.[63] The main proponents of tort as compensation urge that it does too little. Tort compensates those injured by negligent drivers—but what of other injured road users? This line of thought led ineluctably to the conclusion that tort should be replaced with some sort of universal accident coverage. Recognising that the political community was not yet ready for this, the theorists suggested that some intermediate solution should be devised, which would be easier to administer and less in thrall to misguided traditional ideas.[64] There were several variants on this basic idea, usually described as 'enterprise liability'.[65]

For some decades, this was a popular view in common law academic circles; indeed, some recall a pervasive sentiment that tort was living its last days, and would be gone as soon as a politically acceptable formula for universal accident insurance was found.[66] The establishment of such a scheme in New Zealand in 1974 was thought likely to be the first of many, but this was not to be, and the idea that tort was insurance and compensation began to be used to attack it as too generous.[67] What justifies this insurance coverage and its extent? Whose choice is represented in the decision to fix the availability of compensation? If Albus would not have paid for insurance voluntarily, or would only have paid for less generous cover, how can compulsion—on him, on Bellatrix—be justified? Supporters of tort began to distrust reference to insurance, precisely because it seemed to hand weapons to their opponents.[68] And so the idea of 'tort as compensation' began to lose traction, not because it was any less true as a description, but because it provided no good reason why the law should be in its current state.[69]

B. Abolition

A healthy modern school seriously disparages the intellectual pretensions of tort doctrine, spelling out the huge distance between the high ideals of responsibility it embodies and the dark, vaguely satanic settlement mills where tort's actual operation

[63] ibid 231–32.

[64] See, eg, F James Jr, 'Tort in Midstream: Its Challenge to the Judicial Process' (1958–59) 8 *Buffalo Law Review* 315.

[65] For a modern consideration of the issues see D Brodie, *Enterprise Liability and the Common Law* (Cambridge, Cambridge University Press, 2010).

[66] See, eg, PS Atiyah, 'An Autobiographical Fragment' in GP Wilson (ed), *Frontiers of Legal Scholarship* (Chichester, John Wiley & Sons, 1995) 34, 38.

[67] See, eg, GL Priest, 'The Current Insurance Crisis and Modern Tort Law' (1987) 96 *Yale Law Journal* 1521.

[68] J Stapleton, 'Tort, Insurance and Ideology' (1995) 58 *MLR* 820.

[69] For a rare modern defence see MA Geistfeld, 'Compensation as a Tort Norm' in Oberdiek, above n 10, ch 3.

is found.[70] These intellectual heirs of the 'compensation' approach insist, rightly, that widespread availability of insurance invalidates most of the arguments that have traditionally justified tort, and that better arguments are hard to discern. In short, these realists brutally insist that there is no good reason for tort to exist at all.[71] The reasons for tort's survival are predominantly political.[72]

And so they are. Lawyers gain nothing from the abolition of tort. Unions, too, can see no benefit to their members in sacrificing a substantial right to compensation with nothing in its place. Employers, by contrast, might favour abolition so long as nothing else were established as a substitute, but would rightly be apprehensive that their staff would demand a remedy of some sort, and (in the more hazardous work environments at least) cause considerable unrest until they got it—this was, after all, pretty much how tort emerged in the employment context a century and a half ago. And governments, very aware of the difficulties of managing even incremental change, would be fearful of what might result from such a sharp break with the past. None of the major stakeholders, then, are likely to be much bothered by the weakness of tort's intellectual justification, and they are all unlikely to support a major change unless something much, much better is plausibly proposed.

What, indeed, would be better? Arguments against tort have no political traction unless its opponents can unite around an alternative. Suggestions that those who desire tort-like coverage should buy it for themselves seem impractical,[73] and read more as thought experiments designed to show that tort is poor value for money, rather than as serious schemes of law reform. No doubt many would prefer that the sums currently paid in insurance premiums were applied directly to welfare aims rather than (as at present) being indirectly so applied, with much of it being lost along the way. But those who would gain from this, namely the people who would receive better and speedier compensation, are too diffuse a group to engage in any kind of political organisation;[74] and any such proposed reform would run an extremely hostile gauntlet from the more established stakeholders.

C. Symbolic Theories

Meanwhile, the last three decades have seen a revival of the old asocial theories, which are very plausible at the symbolic level, though they bear little resemblance to tort's modern bureaucratic reality. John Goldberg has described a cavalcade of

[70] See, eg, NF Engstrom, 'Sunlight and Settlement Mills' (2011) 86 *New York University Law Review* 805.

[71] See, eg, TG Ison, *Compensation Systems for Injury and Disease: The Policy Choices* (Toronto, Butterworths, 1994) especially ch 7; Sugarman, above n 25; PS Atiyah, *The Damages Lottery* (Oxford, Hart Publishing, 1997).

[72] See especially Ison, above n 71, ch 12.

[73] See, eg, PS Atiyah, 'Personal Injuries in the Twenty-First Century: Thinking the Unthinkable' in P Birks, above n 13, ch 1; D Campbell, 'Interpersonal Justice and Actual Choice as Ways of Determining Personal Injury Law and Policy' (2015) 35 *Legal Studies* 430.

[74] Though note efforts in the UK by the Association of Personal Injury Lawyers to campaign as a 'not-for-profit organisation representing injured people'—see <www.apil.org.uk>. APIL are, of course, campaigning to preserve the tort system, not to reform it out of existence.

theories, one succeeding the other in popularity as the years have gone by.[75] Initially this was all somewhat *sotto voce*. For example, Jules Coleman's reinvigoration of the theory of corrective justice considered it crucial to ask what else the community did for accident victims—and he concluded that a government which respects corrective justice might properly abolish tort so long as adequate alternative welfare provision is made.[76] With increasing confidence in this century, however, theorists have ignored such qualifications, grounding tort in ubiquitous and timeless notions such as Kantian right,[77] optimal deterrence[78] and civil recourse.[79]

As William Lucy notes, while these theories use very different language from one another and in many respects regard each other as rivals,[80] they are much more alike than they are different.[81] They are for the most part monistic: they see their very different strengths not as facets of the same big picture, but as competing indications of the 'true nature' of tort. The task of 'explaining' tort is treated as a given; they do not ask why we should expect the (unplanned and frequently chaotic) pattern of tort liability to have any unitary explanation at all. These theories largely ignore the practical workings of the system. They acknowledge that politics has a huge influence on their subject matter, but refuse to unpack that notion, seeing their role not as understanding politics but as protecting tort from it.

All of this high theory filters down to textbooks and more particularised studies, which, while they do not always accept the theories' monist assumptions (most, though not all, accept that tort is a 'mixed' or pluralistic system),[82] nonetheless find theory useful in discussing individual developments. It is here that any hope of a convincing conception of modern tort will arise, particularly as writers argue over whether the values of modern tort law are the right ones,[83] come to grips with the relation between tort and human rights[84] or try to discern what 'taking insurance into account' in tort could realistically mean.[85] As things stand, however, there is no consensus as to what tort should look like, and so no hope that tort law could be organised around consensus values.

[75] JC Goldberg, 'Twentieth-Century Tort Theory' (2003) 91 *Georgetown Law Journal* 514.

[76] See J Coleman, *Risks and Wrongs* (Oxford, Oxford University Press, 1992) especially ch 19.

[77] See, eg, A Beever, *Rediscovering the Law of Negligence* (Oxford, Hart Publishing, 2007).

[78] See, eg, S Shavell, *Foundations of Economic Analysis of Law* (Cambridge, Belknap Press, 2004) ch 2.

[79] See, eg, JM Solomon, 'Equal Accountability through Tort Law' (2009) 103 *Northwestern University Law Review* 1765.

[80] See, eg BC Zipursky, 'Civil Recourse, not Corrective Justice' (2003) 91 *Georgetown Law Journal* 695.

[81] W Lucy, 'Method and Fit: Two Problems for Contemporary Philosophies of Tort Law' (2007) 52 *McGill Law Journal* 605.

[82] See, eg, J Stapleton, 'Regulating Torts' in C Parker, C Scott, N Lacey and J Braithwaite (eds), *Regulating Law* (Oxford, Oxford University Press, 2004) ch 6.

[83] See, eg, T Keren-Paz, *Torts, Egalitarianism and Distributive Justice* (Aldershot, Ashgate Publishing, 2007).

[84] See, eg, H Collins, 'On the (In)compatibility of Human Rights Discourse and Private Law' in H-W Micklitz (ed), *Constitutionalization of European Private Law* (Oxford, Oxford University Press, 2014) ch 2; A Beever, 'What Does Tort Law Protect?' (2015) 27 *Singapore Academy of Law Journal* 626.

[85] See, eg, R Merkin and J Steele, *Insurance and the Law of Obligations* (Oxford, Oxford University Press, 2013).

This is the paradox of modern tort theory. The one thing that tort law does repeatedly and consistently—compensating injured claimants—is not regarded as a defensible function of tort law, and those who paint our mental pictures for us either reject this notion entirely (because there would be much better ways of providing compensation if that were the intention) or do their best to downplay it (because it is so much easier to justify tort if we pretend that it does other things as well). A positive picture of tort is presented by insisting that tort punishes and deters wrongdoers, or at least provides public acknowledgment that they are wrongdoers, or emphasises the need for care and restraint in our everyday dealings. But that picture is fundamentally misleading. While the modern legal system does much to promote those values, tort law has long ceased to make any serious contribution to them. The ideals of tort are alive in our imaginations, but the gap between those ideals and the reality of tort's actual workings has become a chasm.

VIII. SYMBOLIC ACTION: CURRENT DEBATES

In contrast to other areas of law bearing on personal responsibility for accidents, tort law is nearly all bark and hardly any bite. Symbolically, tort is a constant reminder that carefulness matters. As government has long since realised, actually employing tort liabilities to hold people responsible for misbehaviour is a discredited medieval policy, which has (for the most part) rightly been abandoned in favour of liability insurance. But the idea that this is still what tort law does is one that government has no incentive to dispel.

Those most receptive to this symbolism are the more doctrinal legal academics, who are extremely knowledgeable about the letter of tort law but (like most who work in offices and other safe environments)[86] rarely become acquainted with its actual operations. It is these academics, therefore, who most enthusiastically promote tort's symbolic message of personal responsibility, while ignoring its bureaucratic reality. Some even go so far as to deny that reality, claiming (for example) that we cannot describe tort as 'compensation' because this 'does not explain the boundaries of tort law: why, for example, some injured people are not given a claim by tort'.[87] But that confuses description with justification; it is rather like denying that zebras have stripes because we can think of no plausible theoretical reason why they *should* have stripes. Or again, some explain the discrepancy between tort's rhetoric and its actual operations by saying that the first is 'the law in the books' and the second is 'the law in action'.[88] But the law on insurance, on accident prevention and on procedure is in the law books; what is quietly being urged is that tort lawyers should limit their reading. This is not an issue relating to particular legal scholars or the language they use to express themselves. This is

[86] Note, however, 'Insurance Worker Wins Compensation for Falling Over Files', *Personnel Today*, 26 January 2006.
[87] Stapleton, above n 2, 215.
[88] P Cane, *Responsibility in Law and Morality* (Oxford, Hart Publishing, 2002) 225.

a legal ideology, which can only support itself by making logically doubtful assertions, such as that compensation is not really compensatory, or that only some of the law's rules are genuinely legal.

In the wider population, inevitably there is kickback, as looking out for others is an expensive and distracting task. There is always a suspicion that it would be unnecessary to take quite so much care for others, if only those others took proper care for themselves. And so tort is accused of neglecting that very 'accountability' that it claims to cherish.[89] As Paul Almond notes, official safety policy simultaneously works (because most people follow safety rules and pay for the compensation system) and does not work (because many of those people are doing what they are told rather than doing what they regard as sensible, and they resent the imposition).[90] Frustration with the entire system of injury prevention, and with periodic insurance crises, is taken out on the tort system, leading to frequent (and sometimes wildly inaccurate)[91] complaints against it. There are persistent accusations that there is a 'compensation culture'—again, the fact that tort results in compensation is stressed by tort's enemies rather than its friends—and that this has generated a 'climate of fear'.[92] Also, public tolerance of fraudulent claims may be increasing.[93] There is an increasingly ritual character to complaints against 'compensation culture', as politicians who make tiny changes to tort law nonetheless make a great fuss while doing so, to signal that they are siding with the public against the overbearing lawyers—sometimes while quietly admitting that their legislation is merely tokenistic.[94]

To those of a Machiavellian cast of mind, modern tort law is a thing of beauty: it uses the prospect of legal liability to scare people into respecting the safety of others without actually attempting to make them pay damages. The entire community benefits from the threat without the serious difficulties which would follow from actually carrying it out. Yet playing this stale trick on a sceptical public is becoming increasingly difficult: tort and minor criminal penalties are no longer scary enough, and new methods, such as high-profile health-and-safety prosecutions, so far appear ineffectual.[95] While it is perhaps naive to resent such misleading 'communicative action' when the message communicated is so evidently for the public good, there must surely be a cheaper and more effective way of persuading people that

[89] See, eg, F Furedi and J Bristow, *The Social Cost of Litigation* (London, Centre for Policy Studies, 2012).

[90] Almond, above n 38, especially ch 1.

[91] A Morris, 'The "Compensation Culture" and the Politics of Tort' in Arvind and Steele, above n 18, ch 4.

[92] *Common Sense, Common Safety* (UK Cabinet Office, 2010) 11.

[93] A Cartwright and J Roach, 'Fraudulently Claiming Following a Road Traffic Accident: A Pilot Study of UK Residents' Attitudes' (2016) 23 *Psychiatry, Psychology and Law* 446.

[94] See, for example, the debate over what became Compensation Act 2006 (UK), s 1, which was admitted by its proponents merely to restate the existing law but which was meant to 'provide reassurance to ... many ... who are concerned about possible litigation': HL Deb 28 November 2005, vol 675, col 81. Some of these tensions are explored in P Almond, 'Revolution Blues: The Reconstruction of Health and Safety Law as "Common-Sense" Regulation' (2015) 42 *Journal of Law and Society* 202. On purely symbolic legislation see D Feldman, 'Legislation Which Bears No Law' (2016) 37 *Statute Law Review* 212.

[95] This question is the main topic of Almond's *Corporate Manslaughter*, above n 38. For a possible solution—that is, wider individual participation in decision-making over safety—see ibid 190–93.

safety procedures, intelligently implemented, are good things. And while too much weight can be placed on the example of New Zealand, it is a powerful reminder that our safety culture will not necessarily disintegrate if we abandon the law of tort.[96]

IX. BUREAUCRATIC ACTION: PROSPECTS FOR THE FUTURE

Even though avoidable injury has declined significantly over the past century, in the same period tort has substantially grown—in numbers of claims, in amounts successfully claimed and in the reach of the law—and there is every reason to suppose that this will continue.[97] This is despite the quite genuine hostility from many politicians and members of the public, and even though those who benefit most from the system—successful claimants, lawyers—are unlikely to sing its praises very openly, if at all. Two major factors promote this continuing growth.

The first is that new developments—political, scientific or cultural—will always throw up new types of claimant, or novel arguments that claimants can use; inevitably some of these will be successful, and tort's upward trajectory will continue.[98] Endowment effects make it very difficult to deny compensation to established categories of claimants, whereas repeated moderate increases in insurance premiums are what everyone has come to expect. New developments encouraging greater liability may be sudden and focused (such as thalidomide, Hillsborough or 9/11) or they may be gradual and diffuse (such as the dawning recognition that 'nervous shock' can actually constitute a medical condition), but either way they boost the number of claims. This may be thought of as the 'Ralph Nader' function of tort: victims of novel types of injustice will look for some sort of recognition and rectification of their grievance, and very often they secure this more easily through the courts than by other means.[99]

The other reason for growth is that governmental efficiency drives, if successful to any degree, will make claiming quicker and cheaper, and so lead to more of it. If the cost of bringing a tort claim is reduced, claimant lawyers will be able to process more clients; if their profit from each case is reduced, they *must* do so. Tort practitioners swim in a sea of potential claims, many of which are too expensive to bring, but any of which can spring to life if market conditions make it viable; and ever more innovative methods of exploiting personal injury claims as financial assets will be used except where specifically forbidden by statute. So measures such as streamlining procedures, standardising damages and applying greater pressure to settle,

[96] See R Lilley, A Samaranayaka and H Weiss, 'International Comparison of ILO Published Occupational Fatal Injury Rates: How Does New Zealand Compare Internationally?' (University of Otago, 15 March 2013) available at <goo.gl/DsROCx>.

[97] For the UK, see R Lewis, 'Compensation Culture Reviewed: Incentives to Claim and Damages Levels' [2014] *Journal of Personal Injury Law* 209.

[98] An area of particularly rapid expansion at the moment is that of vicarious and secondary liability, on which see P Giliker, 'A Revolution in Vicarious Liability', this volume, chapter 10.

[99] On Ralph Nader see, eg, J Martin, *Nader: Crusader, Spoiler, Icon* (Cambridge, Perseus Publications, 2002). For an example of approaching tort from this political angle see M Mortazavi, 'Tort as Democracy: Lessons from the Food Wars' (2015) 57 *Arizona Law Review* 929.

while all crudely thought of as 'anti-claimant', will do nothing to reduce the scale of tort claims, and in the long term will probably have the reverse effect. Whatever may be the intention of parliamentarians, the number of tort claims therefore seems likely to continue its upward path.

Governmental hostility to 'excessive' claims will in any event become more and more of a façade, as it becomes less in their financial interests to restrict tort. To take the example of the UK: having taken the plunge in 1989, by requiring every defendant settling a tort action to account for social security payments occasioned by the tort,[100] and having extended this regime since,[101] the government's stake in tort law grows year on year. As Richard Lewis notes, this entrenches tort still further.[102] Tort's growth is certainly slow and uneven, and sudden growth spurts may result in political battles which end badly for whichever market sector is considered responsible. But the overall direction of travel is clear.

X. CONCLUSION

History has led us to a position where tort law no longer has any serious justification, but all the routes away from it are blocked by powerful interest groups. Tort is impossible to justify but equally impossible to change substantially. For theorists of tort, it is an itch which constantly irritates, but which we cannot properly scratch. We are left with only three options: to pretend that tort is rational (a pretence which leads us to deny plain facts about its practical operation); to continue to analyse emerging tort developments, in the rather forlorn hope that a defensible theory will emerge; or to admit its irrationality, note also that it satisfies *some* real needs and look for better methods of meeting those needs.

[100] Social Security Act 1989 (UK), s 22.

[101] For the current legislation see Social Security (Recovery of Benefits) Act 1997 (UK) and Health and Social Care (Community Health and Standards) Act 2003 (UK), ss 150–69.

[102] R Lewis, 'Recovery of State Benefits from Tort Damages: Legislating For or Against the Welfare State?' in Arvind and Steele, above n 18, ch 14.

7

A Revolution in Vicarious Liability: Lister, *the* Catholic Child Welfare Society Case *and Beyond*

PAULA GILIKER

'Our law no longer struggles with the concept of vicarious liability for intentional wrongdoing ... It remains, however, to consider ... where it is or is not *just* to impose vicarious liability' (Lord Steyn, *Lister v Hesley Hall Ltd*).[1]

I. INTRODUCTION

VICARIOUS LIABILITY REMAINS a controversial element of the law of torts, imposing strict liability on an innocent defendant, usually an employer, for the torts of another, typically his or her employee, committed in the 'course of their employment'. It conflicts with notions of corrective justice and with the dominance of fault-based reasoning in the common law of torts.[2] Nevertheless, it is a doctrine whose origins may be traced back to the Middle Ages.[3] It is also one which, as the quotation above indicates, has been 'on the move', as Lord Phillips famously stated in the 2012 Supreme Court decision of *Various Claimants v Catholic Child Welfare Society* (*CCWS*).[4] In this case, his Lordship identified four key ways in which the law on which he had 'cut his teeth' had changed, the most fundamental of which was the extension of vicarious liability to include not only criminal offences generally, but also the criminal act of sexual assault.[5] As late as 1998,[6] Lady Butler-Sloss had taken as read that there could not be vicarious liability for

[1] [2001] UKHL 22, [2002] 1 AC 215, [20] (emphasis added).

[2] See, eg, *Majrowski v Guy's and St Thomas's NHS Trust* [2006] UKHL 34, [2007] 1 AC 224, [8] (Lord Nicholls). See also PS Atiyah, *Vicarious Liability in the Law of Torts* (London, Butterworths 1967) 12.

[3] JG Fleming, *The Law of Torts*, 9th edn (Sydney, LBC Information Services, 1998) 433.

[4] *Various Claimants v Catholic Child Welfare Society* [2012] UKSC 56, [2013] 2 AC 1, [19] (Lord Phillips, with whom Lady Hale, Lord Kerr, Lord Wilson and Lord Carnwath agreed).

[5] The other two developments mentioned were the extension of the doctrine to unincorporated associations (of significance on the facts of *CCWS*) and the extension in *Viasystems (Tyneside) Ltd v Thermal Transfer (Northern) Ltd* [2005] EWCA Civ 1151, [2006] QB 510 to dual vicarious liability. The latter is of particular importance in permitting a formulation of the doctrine which is not tied to the requirement that the perpetrator of the tort is acting under a contract of employment.

[6] *Trotman v North Yorkshire CC* [1998] ELR 625. It should be noted that her Ladyship had experience in this area of law as the chair of the Cleveland Inquiry into allegations of child sexual abuse: *Report of*

intentional torts such as child sexual abuse. Orthodoxy dictated that in the majority of cases, intentional torts should be seen as personal acts of vengeance, malice or spite, regardless of any connection with the tortfeasor's employment.[7] The test, as set out by Sir John Salmond in his textbook *The Law of Tort*, indicated that vicarious liability would only arise if the tort could be said to be a wrongful and unauthorised mode of doing some act authorised by the master.[8] As Lady Butler-Sloss commented, 'in the field of serious sexual misconduct, [it is] difficult to visualise circumstances in which an act of the [abuser] can be an unauthorised mode of carrying out an authorised act'.[9] Yet this long-standing view was overturned by the House of Lords in *Lister v Hesley Hall Ltd*,[10] in which their Lordships discarded the tried and tested Salmond test and replaced it with an approach whose primary focus was not legal certainty, but justice and fairness. On this basis, an employer *could* be held vicariously liable for the sexual abuse of his employees when the commission of the tort was so closely connected to the employment that it would be fair and just to hold the employer vicariously liable. This is regardless of the absence of any failure to take reasonable care on the employer's part.

This chapter will examine the impact of the game-changing decision of the House of Lords in *Lister v Hesley Hall*, notably in the light of the recent UK Supreme Court decisions in *Mohamud v WM Morrison Supermarkets plc*[11] and *Cox v Ministry of Justice*.[12] It will further consider why the courts have been so willing to contemplate change in this area of law and how far it will go. *Lister* has led to modifications to both the definition of the relationship giving rise to vicarious liability and the test for 'course of employment'. We have seen the creation of what Lord Reed termed in *Cox* 'the modern theory of vicarious liability'.[13] The result has been an ever-expanding doctrine,[14] which now includes liability for vicious assaults ranging from an angry bouncer stabbing a customer in the back[15] to a racist supermarket assistant seriously

the Inquiry into Child Abuse in Cleveland 1987 (Cm 412, 1988). The report had been critical of a range of poor practices on the part of the professionals involved.

[7] See, eg, in the English courts: *Warren v Henlys Ltd* [1948] 2 All ER 935 (no vicarious liability for an act of personal vengeance by petrol pump attendant) and *Daniels v Whetstone Ltd* [1962] 2 Lloyd's Rep 1 (second assault was act of private retaliation by steward in a dance hall); in the Privy Council: *Keppel Bus Co Ltd v Ahmad* [1974] 1 WLR 1082 (no vicarious liability for violent bus conductor); and in Australia: *Deatons Pty Ltd v Flew* (1949) 79 CLR 370 (no vicarious liability for violent barmaid). See also FD Rose, 'Liability for an Employee's Assaults' (1977) 40 *MLR* 420.

[8] JW Salmond, *The Law of Tort* (London, Stevens and Haynes, 1907) 83—later found in REV Heuston and RA Buckley, *Salmond and Heuston on the Law of Tort*, 21st edn (London, Sweet & Maxwell, 1996) 443.

[9] *Trotman v North Yorkshire CC* [1998] ELR 625, 632. Indeed, initially, the doctrine of vicarious liability had not extended to intentional wrongdoing and, until *Lloyd v Grace, Smith & Co* [1912] AC 716, vicarious liability had been confined to cases where the deliberate acts could be said to have been committed for the benefit of the employer: see *Cheshire v Bailey* [1905] 1 KB 237. Nevertheless, some cases were able to satisfy the 'wrongful and unauthorised mode' test, eg, *Poland v Parr (John) & Sons* [1927] 1 KB 236 (employee striking suspected thief while seeking to safeguard his employer's property).

[10] [2001] UKHL 22, [2002] 1 AC 215.

[11] [2016] UKSC 11, [2016] AC 677.

[12] [2016] UKSC 10, [2016] AC 660.

[13] ibid [24].

[14] Lord Reed indicated in *Cox* that the evolution of vicarious liability 'has not yet come to a stop': ibid [1].

[15] *Mattis v Pollock (t/a Flamingos Nightclub)* [2003] EWCA Civ 887, [2003] 1 WLR 2158.

assaulting a customer who had made an innocent inquiry at his kiosk.[16] This chapter will examine why the *Lister* revolution occurred and the legal basis for this expansion. More fundamentally, it will question whether the revolution has gone too far. What are the implications of the Supreme Court in *Cox* and *Mohamud* applying changes initiated by *Lister* to cases not related to the sexual abuse of children, but to ordinary cases of assault and negligence? If, as these cases indicate, the changes initiated by *Lister* apply to all forms of tort law,[17] then the time has come to ask whether a doctrine moulded to respond to the horrendous sexual abuse cases which came to light in the UK in the 1990s has evolved into an uncontrolled instrument of distributive justice undermining the certainty and structure of the common law of torts.

II. TRACING THE NEED FOR CHANGE: SEXUAL ABUSE AND VICARIOUS LIABILITY

In identifying the causes of the *Lister* revolution in vicarious liability, two factors stand out: the date of the *Lister* decision (3 May 2001) and the facts of the case. *Lister* involved a number of claims alleging that the warden of the boarding annex of a school for children with emotional and behavioural difficulties had engaged in acts of sexual abuse between 1979 and 1982. Allegations that the school had been negligent in its care or in the selection and control of the warden had been dismissed at first instance, leaving only claims based on vicarious liability. Yet, under the traditional Salmond test, vicarious liability would only arise if the abuse could be said to be either (i) a wrongful act authorised by the employer or (ii) a wrongful and unauthorised mode of doing some act authorised by the employer.[18] In *Lister*, the defendants had clearly not authorised the abuse and it was inconceivable to characterise such acts as an 'unauthorised mode of looking after children'. The House of Lords was nevertheless prepared to overturn this well-established test—the traditional test for course of employment under the doctrine of vicarious liability would have to change.

The case arose at a time when the British public had been rocked by revelations of physical and sexual abuse which had occurred in North Wales children's homes between 1974 and 1990, as detailed in the 2000 Waterhouse Report.[19] A public inquiry, hearing the evidence of 259 complainants, had found evidence of the

[16] *Mohamud*, above n 11.

[17] This is certainly the indication in *Cox*, above n 12, [29]. See also Lord Clyde in *Lister*, above n 1, [48].

[18] See Salmond, above n 8. This was also a far from foolproof test. As Lord Millett rightly acknowledged in *Lister*, option (i) looks very much like primary liability, his Lordship describing it as an echo of the discredited theory of implied authority: *Lister*, above n 1, [67].

[19] R Waterhouse, *Lost in Care Report of the Tribunal of Inquiry into the Abuse of Children in Care in the Former County Council Areas of Gwynedd and Clwyd since 1974* (2000), available at <webarchive.nationalarchives.gov.uk/20130124064403/http:/www.dh.gov.uk/prod_consum_dh/groups/dh_digitalassets/documents/digitalasset/dh_134777.pdf>. The report had been triggered by an intensive investigation by North Wales Police, begun in 1991, in which around 2600 statements had been obtained from individuals and which had resulted in eight prosecutions and seven convictions of former care workers, though nevertheless speculation had continued in North Wales that the actual abuse was on a much greater scale than the convictions themselves suggested.

widespread sexual abuse of boys in children's residential establishments in Clwyd between 1974 and 1990. In total, 72 recommendations had been made. The report ended with the hope that, despite its length, it would be read fully and widely by policy makers, members of the social services profession, administrators and all others who had responsibility for the welfare of looked after children.[20] The North Wales children homes scandal was also far from an isolated case. In its 1999 report, the Home Office's Policing and Reducing Crime unit noted that 76,000 cases of child abuse were reported each year, and that the consequences of being abused in the home by a known and trusted adult were often more serious than being abused by a stranger.[21] What the Waterhouse and subsequent reports[22] have achieved is to render the existence of child abuse a fact of which no individual could be unaware. It is, further, a topic that continues to shock, as seen in the repercussions of the Jimmy Savile scandal which emerged after his death in October 2011.[23] In 2015, freedom of information requests found that reports to the police of child sexual abuse had increased by 60% over the previous four years.[24] Child abuse remains, therefore, a threat which continues to plague children, especially in an institutional environment. In 2015, an Independent Inquiry into Child Sexual Abuse was established in England and Wales to investigate whether public bodies and other non-state institutions have taken their duty to protect children from sexual abuse seriously.[25] It is examining allegations of past and ongoing failures to protect children in schools, children's homes, secure accommodation and local authority care, and the responses of institutions, including the police, health service, Crown Prosecution Service and religious bodies to allegations of child sexual abuse. Public inquiries have also been

[20] Operation Pallial, led by the National Crime Agency (NCA), continued to investigate allegations of historical allegations of child abuse in the North Wales care system until 31 August 2016: 'Operation Pallial: Update' (NCA, 20 July 2016), available at <www.nationalcrimeagency.gov.uk/news/891-operation-pallial-update>.

[21] D Grubin, 'Sex Offending against Children: Understanding the Risk' (Police Research Series Paper 99 for the Home Office Policing and Reducing Crime Unit, Research, Development and Statistics Directorate, 1999).

[22] Consider, for example, the 44 NHS reports which followed the Savile scandal (28 in June 2014 and 16 in February 2015): 'The NHS Savile Investigations' (26 February 2015), available at <www.gov.uk/government/news/the-nhs-savile-investigations>.

[23] J Halliday, 'Jimmy Savile: Timeline of his Sexual Abuse and its Uncovering', *The Guardian*, 26 June 2014. Savile's crimes included attacks on vulnerable victims in hospitals and children's hospitals across England. The BBC's own inquiry into allegations of abuse relating to his work for the BBC (undertaken by Dame Janet Smith) was published in 2016: 'The Dame Janet Smith Review' (BBC, 25 February 2016), available at <www.bbc.co.uk/bbctrust/dame_janet_smith>.

[24] A Travis, 'Reported Child Sexual Abuse Has Risen 60% in Last Four Years, Figures Show', *The Guardian*, 9 April 2015. This was based on a House of Commons library analysis using freedom of information releases by individual forces which showed that the number of offences of child sexual abuse reported to the police had soared from 5557 cases in 2011 to 8892 in 2014. At the same time, the number of arrests for child sexual abuse offences in England and Wales had fallen from 3511 in 2011 to 3208 – a drop of 9%. It is worth noting that annual police recorded crime figures still do not include an overarching category of child sexual abuse, which renders it difficult to track statistics over time.

[25] Independent Inquiry into Child Sexual Abuse (<www.iicsa.org.uk>). The inquiry is independent of government and was established under the Inquiries Act 2005. It is now led by Professor Alexis Jay, who is supported by a panel of three independent experts, a Victims and Survivors Consultative Panel, and other expert advisers. For early criticism of the inquiry under the previous chair, Dame Lowell Goddard, see D Wolchover and A Heaton-Armstrong, 'Goddard's Muddled Programme' (2016) 180 *Justice of the Peace* 202.

set up in Australia,[26] Northern Ireland,[27] Jersey[28] and Scotland,[29] all seeking to set a new and safer course for the future. Such inquiries, while costly,[30] do serve to highlight that sexual abuse is a perennial problem we can no longer sweep under the carpet.

Yet, such scandals are generally contemplated from the perspective of criminal, not tort, law. This is understandable—the heinous nature of such serious criminal offences means that the police are likely to be involved in pursuing the perpetrators in question.[31] Prosecutions have also provoked a wider discussion of the need for the police, social services and society in general to be more vigilant in identifying and bringing offenders to justice.[32] Many of the tort cases discussed in this chapter were preceded by a criminal prosecution. In *Lister*, for example, Grain (the warden of the children's home) was sentenced to seven years' imprisonment for multiple offences involving sexual abuse. In *CCWS*, the headmaster of the school, Brother James, was sentenced in 2004 to 14 years' imprisonment for 21 counts of serious sexual offences against boys.[33] In terms of compensation, therefore, it might be argued that victims are likely to look first to the criminal law, rather than tort law, either by asking the criminal court to make a compensation order[34] or by claiming under the Criminal Injuries Compensation Scheme.[35] It is important, however, to recognise

[26] See the Royal Commission into Institutional Responses to Child Sexual Abuse (est 2013) (<www.childabuseroyalcommission.gov.au>). The Royal Commission is due to report in December 2017. The Australian government has committed over $70 million until 30 June 2018 to fund community-based support services for people who participate in the Royal Commission.

[27] Inquiry into Historical Institutional Abuse in Northern Ireland (est 2014) (<www.hiainquiry.org>). This inquiry, chaired by Sir Anthony Hart, investigated the abuse of children in residential institutions (other than schools) in Northern Ireland between 1922 and 1995. Its report was published on 20 January 2017.

[28] Independent Jersey Care Inquiry (est 2014) (<www.jerseycareinquiry.org>). The Independent Jersey Care Inquiry was set up to establish what went wrong in the island's care system over many years and to find answers for people who suffered abuse as children. The inquiry was chaired by Frances Oldham QC and reported on 3 July 2017.

[29] Scottish Child Abuse Inquiry (est 2015) (<www.childabuseinquiry.scot>). This independent inquiry was established in October 2015 for a range of purposes, including: to raise public awareness of the fact of children in residential care having been abused in Scotland; to acknowledge and record the suffering of those children; to carry out investigations; and to make recommendations. The period of the inquiry is stated broadly to include the period from within the living memory of anyone who suffered such abuse up to the end of 2014. The inquiry is now chaired by the Rt Hon Lady Smith.

[30] The UK Home Secretary has reported that the England and Wales Inquiry in 2015 cost £14.9 million: HC Deb 17 October 2016, vol 615, col 581.

[31] See, eg, the Rochdale child sex grooming case: F Perraudin, 'Rochdale Grooming Case: Nine Men Jailed for up to 25 Years Each', *The Guardian*, 8 April 2016. The ringleader of a child sex exploitation ring which targeted vulnerable young girls in the Rochdale and Oldham areas of Greater Manchester was later jailed for 19 years.

[32] The Rochdale case was followed by an investigation into police conduct of the case: GMP Professional Standards Branch, Investigation into the Rochdale Child Sexual Exploitation Case—Operation SPAN (2015).

[33] He was also sentenced to seven years' imprisonment in 1990 after pleading guilty to a number of offences of sexual abuse.

[34] Compensation orders are governed by the Powers of Criminal Courts (Sentencing) Act 2000 (UK), ss 130–33.

[35] See, generally, Criminal Injuries Compensation Authority (<www.gov.uk/government/organisations/criminal-injuries-compensation-authority>). See also Ministry of Justice, *The Criminal Injuries Compensation Scheme 2012* (London, HMSO, 2012).

the limitations of both options. Despite a presumption in favour of compensation, a compensation order will not be made unless the court finds it to be 'realistic', that is, the court is satisfied that the offender either has the means available or will have the ability to pay within a reasonable time. It is also regarded as unsuitable for large and complicated cases, such as those involving sexual abuse.[36] The Criminal Injuries Compensation Scheme may seem a better option, but damages are capped (with a maximum award of £500,000) and are subject to limits. Limits exist in terms of timing,[37] but further, awards may be withheld or reduced because of the applicant's character.[38] This is likely to affect victims of abuse whose suffering may have led them to seek solace in drugs or into other criminal activities.[39] The government's 2014 guide to applying for compensation under the Criminal Injuries Compensation Scheme expressly states that:

> The Scheme is intended to be one of last resort. Where the opportunity exists for you to pursue compensation elsewhere you should do so. We will expect you to take all reasonable steps to obtain any social security benefits, insurance payments, damages or compensation to which you may be entitled as a result of your injuries.[40]

Similar problems arise in pursuing the perpetrator in the law of tort. In the case of historical sexual abuse claims, given the passage of time, the abuser may be untraceable or even dead (this was the case in a number of leading vicarious liability cases).[41] Further, even if traceable, the abuser is often not a person of means[42] and, even if

[36] See *R v Bewick* [2007] EWCA Crim 3297, [2008] 2 Cr App R (S) 31, where the Court of Appeal discouraged criminal courts from undertaking complicated investigations to establish the extent of loss.

[37] Claimants are expected to apply for compensation as soon as it is reasonably practicable for them to do so, normally not later than two years after the crime occurred. Special provisions are made for abuse cases: for example, if the incident or period of abuse took place before the applicant turned 18 but was not reported to the police at the time, claims may be made within two years from when the incident or abuse was reported to the police, but it will be subject to the provision of supporting evidence for the claim, which means that the claims officer can make a decision without further extensive enquiries and evidence that shows why the application could not have been made earlier. Nevertheless, Sugarman reports that the time limit for bringing applications continues to be a hurdle, especially in cases involving historic sexual abuse: N Sugarman, 'The Criminal Injuries Compensation Scheme 2012 and its Impact on Victims of Crime' [2016] *Journal of Personal Injury Law* 231, 233.

[38] See paras 25–27 of the 2012 Scheme, above n 35.

[39] A BBC investigation in 2015, based on a freedom of information request, found that compensation had been reduced for more than 400 sex abuse victims in Britain who later committed criminal offences: see <www.bbc.co.uk/news/uk-33707529>. Responding to this investigation, the Ministry of Justice stated that it was not prepared to change its position on this matter in view of the distress, loss and injury which had been caused to innocent third parties in addition to the cost to taxpayer money in investigating and prosecuting such offences.

[40] CICA and Ministry of Justice, *Criminal Injuries Compensation: A Guide* (26 March 2014), available at www.gov.uk/guidance/criminal-injuries-compensation-a-guide. It adds: 'We may not make a decision on your case until such times as we are satisfied that you are eligible and you could not get compensation from any other sources.' See, generally, D Miers, 'Compensating Deserving Victims of Violent Crime: The Criminal Injuries Compensation Scheme' (2014) 34 *Legal Studies* 242.

[41] See, eg, *JGE (or E) v English Province of Our Lady of Charity* [2012] EWCA Civ 938, [2013] 1 QB 722 (priest deceased); *Maga v Trustees of the Portsmouth Roman Catholic Diocesan Trust* [2010] EWCA Civ 256, [2010] 1 WLR 1441 (priest, Father Clonan, disappeared and presumed deceased); *A v Trustees of the Watchtower Bible and Tract Society* [2015] EWHC 1722 (QB) (ministerial servant who sexually abused a child in the congregation deceased).

[42] In the Irish case of *O'Keeffe v Hickey* [2009] IESC 39, for example, the victim of abuse had instituted civil assault proceedings against Hickey (the school principal who had abused her). Despite being

insured, generally speaking, liability insurance will rarely extend cover to intentional criminal acts.[43] In such cases, as McLachlin J warned in the leading Canadian case of *Bazley v Curry*,[44] seeking a claim for compensation against the abuser may prove 'a hollow remedy'.

Where, therefore, does this leave victims of abuse, seeking to rebuild their lives and obtain compensation from those who have wrongfully harmed them? For McLachlin J in *Bazley*, the answer was simple: look to the organisation that employed the offender and consider whether it should be held strictly liable for the wrong. In circumstances where it is often difficult for victims to establish that the institution was personally at fault (eg by failing to take reasonable care in its selection of employees or in monitoring their performance),[45] the only way such victims may effectively obtain compensation is through vicarious liability. Vicarious liability therefore provides a means by which abuse victims are able to gain recourse against a solvent (and insured) defendant.

III. THE *LISTER* REVOLUTION: REPLACING 'UNAUTHORISED MODE' WITH THE 'CLOSE CONNECTION' TEST

Bazley and *Lister* represent common law responses to the emerging scandal of child abuse.[46] As Lord Hope has commented: 'Child sexual abuse is an ugly phenomenon. There is a heavy responsibility on our legal system to deal as fairly and justly as it possibly can with the consequences.'[47] While Canada has faced scandals related to its residential school legacy, which led to an apology by former Prime Minister Harper in 2008[48] and the Roman Catholic Church in 1999,[49] the House of Lords could not have been unaware of the scandal involving North Wales children homes

awarded more than €300,000 in compensation, the Irish Supreme Court, in dealing with a subsequent claim for vicarious liability, noted that she had not been able to recover much, if any, of the award from the now retired teacher. See also C O'Mahony, 'State Liability for Abuse in Primary Schools: Systemic Failure and *O'Keeffe v. Hickey*' (2009) 28 *Irish Educational Studies* 315.

43 See P Case, *Compensating Child Abuse in England and Wales* (Cambridge, Cambridge University Press, 2007) 128. This may be due to public policy or a narrow construction of the wording of the policy. Consider, eg, *AXN v Worboys* [2012] EWHC 1730 (QB), [2013] Lloyd's Rep IR 207 (victims of black cab rapist could not claim against his motor vehicle insurer).

44 (1999) 174 DLR (4th) 45, [1].

45 Such claims failed in *Lister*, above n 1, and in *Bazley*, ibid (the foundation hiring a paedophile argued that it had taken reasonable care in the selection process and had immediately dismissed the employee once a complaint had been received and investigated).

46 As acknowledged recently by the High Court of Australia in *Prince Alfred College Incorporated v ADC* [2016] HCA 37, (2016) 335 ALR 1, [38] (French CJ, Kiefel, Bell, Keane and Nettle JJ). *Bazley* itself involved abuse in a residential care facility for the treatment of emotionally troubled children.

47 Lord Hope, 'Tailoring the Law on Vicarious Liability' (2013) 129 *LQR* 514, 525.

48 On 11 June 2008, the Prime Minister of Canada, Stephen Harper, made a Statement of Apology to former students of Indian Residential Schools, on behalf of the Government of Canada: 'Prime Minister Harper Offers Full Apology on Behalf of Canadians for the Indian Residential Schools System', *Indigenous and Northern Affairs Canada*, 11 June 2008, available at <www.aadnc-aandc.gc.ca/eng/1100100015644/1100100015649>.

49 See also the 2015 Report of the Truth and Reconciliation Commission, chaired by Justice Murray Sinclair, which describes how the Canadian governments and churches pursued a policy of 'cultural genocide' against the country's aboriginal people throughout the twentieth century which saw 150,000 First Nations children forcibly removed from their families and incarcerated in residential schools rife with

while deciding a case which involved sexual abuse by a warden of a boarding annex for children. In *Lister*, there was no question that Grain was an employee, but, as indicated above, the Salmond 'unauthorised mode' test seemed to block any hope of a solution based on vicarious liability. Nevertheless, following the lead of the Supreme Court of Canada in *Bazley*[50]—as noted by Peter Cane in the UK journal *The Law Quarterly Review*[51] and raised by counsel for the appellants—the House was persuaded that a test of 'close connection' could provide a means of extending the vicarious liability of employers to child sexual abuse on a basis which could be regarded as 'fair'. Vicarious liability could thus be imposed where the warden's torts were 'so closely connected with his employment that it would be fair and just to hold the employers vicariously liable'.[52]

What was less apparent from *Lister* was how this 'close connection' test would operate and to what extent the reasoning in *Bazley*—from which the 'close connection' test was taken—would now influence the underlying rationale of vicarious liability. For Lord Steyn, while the judgment in *Bazley* was 'luminous and illuminating', and would provide a starting point for the future treatment of such issues in the common law world,[53] his Lordship (in common with Lords Clyde, Hobhouse and Hutton) argued that it was unnecessary to express views on the full range of policy considerations raised in the *Bazley* decision.[54] Lord Steyn suggested that a more pragmatic approach was needed: 'Ideas divorced from reality have never held much attraction for judges steeped in the tradition that their task is to deliver principled but practical justice.'[55] In contrast, Lord Millett sought to identify the unspoken rationale of vicarious liability, focusing, in particular, on the inherent risk of sexual abuse of vulnerable people in boarding schools, prisons, old people's homes and other residential homes by those placed by their employers in authority over them.[56] Reflecting on *Lister* in the later case of *Dubai Aluminium v Salaam*,[57] Lord Nicholls commented that the various formulations of the close connection test in *Lister* and *Bazley* did no more than focus attention in the right direction when what is actually required of the court is a value judgment, having regard to all the circumstances and, importantly, having regard also to the assistance provided by previous court decisions.[58]

abuse: *Honouring the Truth, Reconciling for the Future* (Truth and Reconciliation Commission, 2015), available at <www.trc.ca/websites/trcinstitution/File/2015/Findings/Exec_Summary_2015_05_31_web_o.pdf>. For vicarious liability case law arising from this scandal, see, eg, *Blackwater v Plint* [2005] 3 SCR 3 (abuse perpetrated by a dormitory supervisor in a residential school operated by the Government of Canada and the United Church of Canada from the 1940s to the 1960s).

[50] *Bazley*, above n 44. See also *Jacobi v Griffiths* (1999) 174 DLR (4th) 71.

[51] P Cane, 'Vicarious Liability for Sexual Abuse' (2000) 116 *LQR* 21.

[52] *Lister*, above n 1, [28] (Lord Steyn).

[53] ibid, [27].

[54] ibid. See also the views of Lord Clyde at [35] and Lord Hobhouse at [60]. Lord Hutton agreed with Lord Steyn.

[55] *Lister*, above n 1, [16].

[56] ibid [83].

[57] [2002] UKHL 48, [2003] 2 AC 366, [24]–[25].

[58] ibid [26]. His Lordship did, however, favour an underlying legal policy based on the recognition that carrying on a business enterprise necessarily involves risk to others.

A further weakness of *Lister* was its inability to resolve single-handedly all the problems facing victims of sexual abuse bringing claims in the law of tort. Where, for example, it is not clear who (if anyone) employed the abuser at the time of the tort—which may be the case when dealing with agency or temporary staff—the *Lister* close connection test offers no assistance. *JGE v English Province of Our Lady of Charity*[59] raised this question in the context of abuse claims against the Roman Catholic Church. Here, the defendants argued that the church could not, as a matter of law, be held vicariously liable for the abuse committed by its priests because a priest is an office holder and not an employee working under a contract of employment.[60] If this argument was followed—and, as MacDuff J acknowledged at first instance, for many years it had appeared that vicarious liability would only attach to the employment and to no other relationship[61]—then the church had an effective barrier against vicarious liability claims. Would the courts challenge orthodoxy to prevent this happening? The answer was yes. The Court of Appeal in *JGE* opted for a test based on function, not form, influenced (like the first instance judge) by the more flexible approach to vicarious liability found in *Viasystems*.[62] A relationship 'akin to employment', that is, a relationship so close in character to one of employer/employee that it is just and fair to hold the institution vicariously liable, would suffice.[63] On that basis, Father Baldwin, while technically an office holder, was in a relationship with his bishop which was close enough and so akin to employer/employee as to make it just and fair to impose vicarious liability. The Supreme Court in *CCWS* confirmed the validity of the 'akin to employment' test, describing the judgment of Ward LJ in the Court of Appeal in *JGE* as impressive.[64]

The Supreme Court in *CCWS* also resolved the question of how to approach liability when abuse victims sought to render an unincorporated association vicariously liable. It is quite common for charitable or non-profit organisations to be unincorporated and so to lack legal personality, a prominent example being the Roman Catholic Church. The Supreme Court dealt with this simply by treating the

59 *JGE v English Province of Our Lady of Charity*, above n 41.

60 In earlier cases, such as *Maga v Archbishop of Birmingham* [2010] EWCA Civ 256, [2010] 1 WLR 1441, which also involved a claim of sexual abuse by a Roman Catholic priest, this point had not been raised. The defendant had indicated, however, that its concession that the priest could be treated as an employee of the archdiocese was for the purpose of that case only. It was therefore only a matter of time before the volume of claims against the church signified that this legal point would be raised.

61 *JGE v English Province of Our Lady of Charity* [2011] EWHC 2871 (QB), [2012] 2 WLR 709, [20].

62 Above n 5. *Viasystems* held, for the first time, that dual vicarious liability was possible for the same tortfeasor whose services had been 'loaned' from one employer to another. See also Lord Clyde in *Lister*, above n 1, [33], who made express reference to the possibility that the relationship may be other than employment.

63 *JGE v English Province of Our Lady of Charity*, above n 41, [73] (Ward LJ). Such a test is also helpful in relation to religious organisations which rely not on full-time clergy but on members of the congregation, eg, Jehovah's Witnesses, elders and ministerial servants—see *A v Trustees of the Watchtower Bible and Tract Society*, above n 41, [71].

64 Above n 4, [19]. Commentators, however, have inevitably expressed concern about how widely this relationship will be interpreted in future cases: see J O'Sullivan, 'The Sins of the Father—Vicarious Liability Extended' [2012] *CLJ* 485; P Giliker, 'Vicarious Liability beyond the Contract of Service' (2012) 28 *Journal of Professional Negligence* 291.

unincorporated association to which the abusers were affiliated as if it was a corporate body.[65] It also refused to accept that charitable or non-profit organisations should receive any different treatment regardless of their limited means.[66]

The most significant obstacle, however, was procedural. Claims for child sexual abuse are often brought many years after the event, during which memories have faded and documents lost. The reasons for this are well known. The trauma and shame of child sexual abuse, in addition to the age and powerlessness of the victims, means that many victims fail to commence proceedings (or, indeed, report the abuse), and this may be aggravated by depression, post-traumatic stress and other mental conditions which result from the abuse.[67] In 2015, a discussion paper published by the New South Wales government[68] reported that, based on its research, the average time for a victim to disclose child sexual abuse was 22 years, with men taking longer than women.[69] This does give rise, however, to problems with the strict limitation periods within which victims have to bring their claims. In *Stubbings v Webb*,[70] the House of Lords rejected as time barred a claim for damages for child abuse at a children's home on the basis that section 2 of the Limitation Act 1980 required a claim to be brought during a non-extendable period of six years from the age of majority. In 2008, the House of Lords bit the bullet (following criticism from the Law Commission)[71] and in *A v Hoare*[72] expressly acknowledged that, in the light of *Lister*, the limitation period for historical child abuse claims would have to be revised to permit extensions to the limitation period under section 33 of the Limitation Act 1980 (hence treating such claims as personal injury claims under section 11 of the Act, to which section 33 applied). As Burton QC commented in 2013, taken together, the two judgments in *Hoare* and *Lister* opened the way for multitudes of cases to be litigated, with claimants now able to seek section 33 dispensations to permit their claims for vicarious liability to proceed.[73]

[65] *CCWS*, above n 4, [33]. cf *Hickey v McGowan* [2017] IESC 6, [52]: 'It is essential to the very nature of an unincorporated association that it is not a body corporate. It cannot therefore be treated as if it was that which by very definition it is not.'

[66] See also Lord Reed in *Cox*, above n 12, [30] and McLachlin J in *Bazley*, above n 44, [47]–[56], who rejected at an early stage any exemption from vicarious liability for charitable or non-profit organisations. See, generally, M Ogilvie, 'Vicarious Liability and Charitable Immunity in Canadian Sexual Torts Law' (2004) 4 *Oxford University Commonwealth Law Journal* 167.

[67] See A Gray, 'Extending Time Limits in Sexual Abuse Cases: A Critical Comparative Evaluation' (2009) 38 *Common Law World Review* 342.

[68] *Limitation Periods in Civil Claims for Child Sexual Abuse* (NSW Department of Justice, 2015).

[69] In a May 2009 study of sexual abuse allegations by 180 victims against Anglican clergy in Australia, the average time from the alleged sexual abuse to making a complaint was 25 years for males and 18 years for females: P Parkinson, K Oates and A Jayakody, 'Breaking the Long Silence: Reports of Child Sexual Abuse in the Anglican Church of Australia' (2010) 6(2) *Ecclesiology* 183.

[70] [1993] AC 498.

[71] Law Commission, *Limitation of Actions* (2001) (Law Com No 270), which described the effect of *Stubbings v Webb* [1993] AC 498 as anomalous.

[72] [2008] UKHL 6, [2008] 1 AC 844, overturning *Stubbings v Webb*, ibid.

[73] F Burton, 'Limitation, Vicarious Liability and Historic Actions for Abuse: A Changing Legal Landscape' [2013] *Journal of Personal Injury Law* 95, 97. See, eg, *B v Nugent Care Society* [2009] EWCA Civ 827, [2010] 1 WLR 516; *Raggett v Society of Jesus Trust 1929 for Roman Catholic Purposes* [2010] EWCA Civ 1002. However, problems due to passage of time continue to exist: see, eg, *RE v GE* [2015] EWCA Civ 287; *F v TH* [2016] EWHC 1605 (QB).

IV. *LISTER* REVISITED: A MODERN THEORY OF VICARIOUS LIABILITY

The changes brought by *Lister* and subsequent case law have enabled victims of sexual abuse to rely on vicarious liability to obtain compensation. This revolution was achieved by altering the key elements of the doctrine—by extending the relationship giving rise to vicarious liability and by adopting a broader notion of 'course of employment'. Formal recognition of the impact of these developments may be found in the 2012 Supreme Court decision in *CCWS*. Giving judgment for the Court, Lord Phillips recognised the need to reformulate the test for vicarious liability more loosely into two (overlapping) stages:[74]

1. Is the relationship between D1 and D2 one capable of giving rise to vicarious liability?
2. Is there a close connection that links the relationship between D1 and D2 and the act or omission of D1?

Such a test reflects both the extension of the relationship test to those 'akin to employment' (*JGE*) and also the *Lister* close connection test, which, post-*Lister*, had been applied broadly in a number of contexts involving intentional torts.[75] It is also consistent with the finding of Ward LJ in *JGE* that vicarious liability should develop according to the policies of the law of tort, and not be tied to tests based on employment or social security law. It was therefore unsurprising that, on the facts, the De La Salle Institute, a religious foundation whose mission was to send out its lay brothers to educate children, was found to possess a relationship akin to employment with its lay brothers, and that the sexual abuse of the boys in the residential school in which the lay brothers taught was found to be closely connected to their employment. Lord Phillips acknowledged that the sexual abuse of children was now recognised as a widespread evil and that the courts had been tailoring this area of law by emphasising the importance of criteria that are particularly relevant to this form of wrong: 'In this way, the courts have succeeded in developing the law of vicarious liability so as to ensure that a remedy for the harm caused by abuse is provided by those that should fairly bear that liability.'[76]

His Lordship's judgment is also important because it acknowledges that, despite the reluctance of the House of Lords in *Lister* (with the exception of Lord Millett) to adopt a policy-based approach to vicarious liability, the degree to which vicarious liability had changed from its pre-*Lister* form required the courts to identify its underlying rationale. While Lord Phillips agreed that the broad objective was, as stated by Lord Steyn in *Lister*, to ensure, insofar as it is fair, just and reasonable, that liability for the tortious wrong is borne by a defendant with the means to compensate the victim, he added that such defendants 'can usually be expected

[74] *CCWS*, above n 4, [21]. See also Hughes LJ in the Court of Appeal: [2010] EWCA Civ 1106, [37].

[75] See, notably, *Mattis v Pollock (t/a Flamingos Nightclub)* [2003] EWCA Civ 887; *Bernard v Attorney General of Jamaica* [2004] UKPC 47, [2005] IRLR 398; *Weddall v Barchester Healthcare Ltd* [2012] EWCA Civ 25, [2012] IRLR 307.

[76] *CCWS*, above n 4, [83]. His Lordship at [85] also alluded to the Jimmy Savile scandal mentioned above.

to insure against the risk of such liability, so that this risk is more widely spread'.[77] In other words, the Supreme Court echoed Lord Millett's risk-based reasoning and conviction that vicarious liability 'is best understood as a loss distribution device'.[78] In determining whether the imposition of vicarious liability would be fair, just and reasonable, five policy reasons were identified:[79]

1. The employer is more likely to have the means to compensate the victim than the employee and can be expected to have insured against that liability (the 'deeper pockets' argument).
2. The tort will have been committed as a result of activity being taken by the employee on behalf of the employer (the delegation of task argument).[80]
3. The employee's activity is likely to be part of the business activity of the employer.
4. The employer, by employing the employee to carry on the activity, will have created the risk of the tort committed by the employee.
5. The employee will, to a greater or lesser degree, have been under the control of the employer.

The third and fourth policy reasons deal explicitly with the 'business activity' of the employer creating the risk of the tort. The relevance of such factors in the sexual abuse context was highlighted in the reasoning of McLachlin J in *Bazley* (towards which, it may be recalled, the majority in *Lister* were so non-committal). McLachlin J held that when a person or organisation puts into the community an enterprise which creates or significantly increases the risk of injury to members of the public, it is fair and just to impose liability on the employer when those risks materialise and cause injury despite the employer's reasonable efforts.[81] This approach was influenced by US law and economics reasoning, in particular the notion of enterprise liability.[82] The imposition of vicarious liability, in such circumstances, provides an adequate and just remedy for losses which result from the enterprise, with the added benefit of having a deterrent effect which will encourage organisations to take steps to prevent future incidents.[83] 'Enterprise' here extends to both charitable and non-profit-making institutions. Lord Phillips's formulation is, however, notably broader than this and includes ideas varying from delegation of task to control and

[77] ibid [34].

[78] Lord Millett in *Lister*, above n 1, [65], connecting also with the reasoning of Atiyah, above n 2, 24.

[79] *CCWS*, above n 4, [35].

[80] Lord Reed linked this argument with historical explanations of vicarious liability based on deemed authorisation or delegation: *Cox*, above n 12, [23].

[81] See further D Brodie, *Enterprise Liability and the Common Law* (Cambridge, Cambridge University Press, 2010).

[82] *Bazley*, above n 44, [31]. Notably AO Sykes, 'The Boundaries of Vicarious Liability: An Economic Analysis of the Scope of Employment Rule and Related Legal Doctrines' (1988) 101 *Harvard Law Review* 563. McLachlin J was also influenced by the policy reasoning of John Fleming: see above n 3. McIvor notes, however, that the form of risk theory used by Lord Millett in *Lister* (and by the Supreme Court subsequently) is much wider and more generalised than the economic rationale set out by McLachlin J in *Bazley*: C McIvor, 'The Use and Abuse of the Doctrine of Vicarious Liability' (2006) 35 *Common Law World Review* 268, 277.

[83] *Bazley*, ibid [32].

deeper pockets. His Lordship does, however, note a common theme in sexual abuse cases—the defendant's relationship with the abuser is such that one can say that it has used the abuser to carry on its business or further its own business in a manner which has created or significantly enhanced the risk that the victim would suffer the relevant abuse.[84] While creation of risk is not of itself enough to give rise to vicarious liability for abuse,[85] its importance is not doubted.

Such reasoning indicates, therefore, that risk-based reasoning plays a particularly significant role in child abuse cases. Indeed, if we have learnt anything from the abuse scandals of the past, it is that sexual abuse is an inherent risk in our society which arises, in particular, when vulnerable parties are placed in an institutional environment in which they are subject to the care of individual members of staff. If these risks manifest themselves in acts of abuse and victims are to be compensated—and the limitations of pursuing individual perpetrators for compensation in criminal and tort law have been highlighted above—then one is left with a stark choice between the private individual and the state. If the state is not prepared to intervene and compensate victims of institutional sexual abuse,[86] then it falls to private litigation. The path from *Lister* to *CCWS* indicates that a choice has been made—vicarious liability offers victims of child sexual abuse a means to obtain compensation and, to a certain extent, to hold accountable those institutions which failed to intervene to protect those under their care. This is a policy decision. Risk-based analysis provides the rationale to justify this line of reasoning.

While one may agree or disagree with these arguments,[87] the reasoning is clear. The question this chapter now seeks to address, however, is where this leaves non-sexual abuse cases. The reasoning discussed so far has focused on the social ill of child sexual abuse. Yet, vicarious liability is a doctrine which has been applied to scenarios varying from negligent lorry drivers having a sneaky cigarette while delivering petrol[88] to a light-fingered fumigator intentionally helping himself to the silver bars he was supposed to fumigate.[89] These cases do not raise matters of public concern or outrage. They relate to day-to-day incidents arising from human beings erring in the performance of their duties. Such matters do not lead to public inquiries or cries for justice, but are part of the workaday caseload for courts dealing with tort law claims. To what extent, therefore, does and should ordinary tort law benefit from the *Lister* revolution?

[84] *CCWS*, above n 4, [86].

[85] ibid [87].

[86] It may be noted that the public inquiries into child sexual abuse listed above are of recent origin and are focused not on compensation, but on lessons for the future, although the Australian Royal Commission has recommended that the government establishes a redress scheme for survivors/victims of child sexual abuse: see *Redress and Civil Litigation Report* (Commonwealth of Australia, 2015). Further, the progress of the UK inquiry (started in 2015) to date has been less than smooth, leading to questions as to its remit, organisation, budget and staffing in Parliament: see HC Deb 17 October 2016, vol 615, col 581.

[87] For a critique, see, eg, McIvor, above n 82; P Giliker, *Vicarious Liability in Tort: A Comparative Perspective* (Cambridge, Cambridge University Press, 2010) 237–50; J Plunkett, 'Taking Stock of Vicarious Liability' (2016) 132 *LQR* 556, 559–60.

[88] *Century Insurance Co Ltd v Northern Ireland Road Transport Board* [1942] AC 509.

[89] *Brink's Global Services Inc v Igrox Ltd* [2010] EWCA Civ 1207, [2011] IRLR 343.

V. BACK TO THE SUPREME COURT: COX, *MOHAMUD* AND THE TWO-STAGE TEST

This matter came to the fore in March 2016, when the Supreme Court, a mere four years after *CCWS*, delivered judgments in two appeals relating to vicarious liability: *Cox v Ministry of Justice*[90] and *Mohamud v WM Morrison Supermarkets plc*.[91] These cases are both notable for raising, in turn, stage one and stage two of the *CCWS* test and also for involving ordinary tort law scenarios: in *Cox*, a negligent prisoner (Inder) dropping kitchen supplies on the back of his supervisor; in *Mohamud*, a racist supermarket worker (Khan) beating up a man of Somali descent on a petrol forecourt. These are not sexual abuse cases. These are mainstream vicarious liability cases. How would the *CCWS* two-stage test fare in such (sadly) everyday scenarios?

The response of the Supreme Court, delivering two complementary judgments in which the same Justices took part, was to confirm that the extended *Lister/CCWS* test for vicarious liability would apply in all cases. On this basis, there was no reason in *Cox* why the 'akin to employment' test should not apply to prisoners working in a prison kitchen. While prisoners are clearly not prison 'employees', and, indeed, prison work is seen as part of their rehabilitation process, the Court found that Mr Inder had been integrated into the operation of the prison and had participated in the provision of low-cost meals for prisoners under the direction of prison staff. It took the view that it should make no difference to Mrs Cox's claim whether she was injured in the kitchen by the work of Mr Inder or by that of a civilian member of staff. It was also deemed irrelevant that the prison service is a public authority performing statutory functions for the public benefit.

In *Mohamud*, in applying the stage-two test, the Supreme Court was also prepared to utilise the risk-based 'close connection' test in relation to the attack on Mr Mohamud. Here, Mr Mohamud's status as a customer making an inquiry about printing services at the supermarket petrol kiosk was enough to sustain his claim that the supermarket was vicariously liable for the racist attack which consisted of Mr Khan (the kiosk assistant) following Mr Mohamud out onto the petrol forecourt, telling him in threatening words never to come back and then physically assaulting him, despite instructions from his supervisor to desist. This was, according to Lord Toulson, within the 'field of activities' entrusted by the employer to the employee. It was essential, his Lordship argued, to view the nature of the job 'broadly' and then determine whether there was a sufficient connection between the position in which he was employed and his wrongful conduct to make it right for the employer to be held liable under the principle of social justice.[92] Here, it was Mr Khan's job to attend to customers and respond to their inquiries. This was simply a foul-mouthed means of ordering Mr Mohamud to keep away from his employer's premises, albeit reinforced by violence.[93] In the words of Lord Toulson: 'There was not something personal between them.'[94]

[90] Above n 12.
[91] Above n 11.
[92] ibid [44]–[45].
[93] ibid [47].
[94] ibid.

The approach taken in these cases may be compared with parallel developments in the context of non-delegable duties. In the earlier case of *Woodland v Essex CC*,[95] Lord Sumption took the dramatic step of setting out a general non-delegable duty which would arise when the defendant has assumed a positive duty to protect vulnerable or dependent claimants from harm.[96] Whilst such liability is personal, not vicarious, its practical effect is to impose liability on employers for the torts of independent contractors to whom the 'non-delegable' duty has been entrusted, in circumstances in which, as Baroness Hale recognised, but for the outsourcing of the tasks in question, the employer would have been vicariously liable for the tort.[97] In other words, the Supreme Court saw itself as closing a gap. Employers will not be permitted to circumvent extensions to the doctrine of vicarious liability by engaging independent contractors to undertake its integral tasks.[98] On this basis, whether hiring an employee, someone akin to an employee or even an independent contractor to undertake functions integral to the custody, charge or care of the claimant, the employer may find himself liable to compensate the claimant.

In all these cases, the innocent victim is able to gain damages rather than being left to pursue an uninsured or impecunious tortfeasor. In *Woodland*, Lord Sumption noted that the non-delegable duty was a positive or affirmative duty to protect a particular class of persons, be it a patient, child or someone else who, for some other reason, is especially vulnerable or dependent on the protection of the defendant, against a particular class of risks.[99] The importance of risk-based reasoning is again emphasised by Lord Reed in *Cox*. His Lordship reappraised the five policy factors identified by Lord Phillips in *CCWS* and noted they were not equally significant. He found that the first (deeper pockets) and fifth (control)[100] factors were unlikely to be of independent significance in most cases.[101] For the Supreme Court, therefore, it was the arguments based on business activity, risk creation and delegation of task which provided interrelated justifications for extending vicarious liability. The risk

[95] [2013] UKSC 66, [2014] AC 537.

[96] ibid [23]. This category is distinct from cases involving incidents on the highway and hazards. Significantly, the court did not follow the previous practice of trying to fit the claim within an existing type of non-delegable duty.

[97] In this case, the provision of swimming lessons which were part of the school curriculum. See ibid [40]: 'It is particularly worth remembering that for the most part public authorities would have been vicariously liable to claimants who were harmed in this way until the advent of outsourcing of essential aspects of their functions.'

[98] This assumes, of course, that employers reason in this way and do not simply hire independent contractors to save costs or because they are required to put certain services out to tender.

[99] *Woodland* [2013] UKSC 66, [2014] AC 537, [23]. For commonalities between the *Woodland* non-delegable duty and the policy arguments highlighted by Lord Phillips in *CCWS*, above n 4, [35], see P Giliker, 'Vicarious Liability, Non-delegable Duties and Teachers: Can You Outsource Liability for Lessons?' (2015) 31 *Journal of Professional Negligence* 259, 266–67.

[100] Morgan is critical of the downplaying of control, arguing that the power to direct exactly how employees carry out work, even if not exercised, remains a relevant factor distinguishing employees from independent contractors: P Morgan, 'Certainty in Vicarious Liability: A Quest for a Chimaera?' [2016] *CLJ* 202. See also P Morgan, 'Recasting Vicarious Liability' [2012] *CLJ* 615.

[101] *Cox*, above n 12, [20]–[21] (Lord Reed). In contrast, in *Mohamud*, Lord Toulson approached the doctrine of vicarious liability principally in the light of the historical development of this branch of the law, finding an underlying rationale based on the principle of social justice, which, at [45], he traced back to Holt CJ in *Hern v Nichols* (1708) 1 Salk 289, 91 ER 256, 256.

of an individual committing a tort (be it negligently or intentionally) was now to be regarded as a fact of life:

> anyone who employs others to carry out activities is likely to create the risk of their behaving tortiously within the field of activities assigned to them. The essential idea is that the defendant should be liable for torts that may fairly be regarded as risks of his business activities, whether they are committed for the purpose of furthering those activities or not.[102]

This, it is submitted, is a significant step. The rationale of *CCWS* has not only been approved, but modified with an even greater focus on risk-based liability. This provides the justification for extending vicarious liability to the facts of *Cox* and *Mohamud*, but also explains the reformulation of the non-delegable duty. Here is not the place to debate the distinction between vicarious liability and non-delegable duties, which both render the employer liable for the torts of another,[103] but, taking the functionalist approach advocated by Ward LJ in *JGE*, we can identify that in both cases the approach taken by the Supreme Court is one premised on seeking to ensure that victims obtain compensation.

This takes us back to the earlier question: to what extent should ordinary tort law benefit from the *Lister* revolution when questions of abuse or the assumption of positive duties of care towards the residents in children's or old people's homes do not arise? Indeed, in *Cox*, the prisoner was not the victim, but the perpetrator of the tort! The message from the Supreme Court in *Cox* and *Mohamud* is that no distinction should be made. In terms of the 'akin to employment' test, it is submitted that this should not be viewed as a problem. The Supreme Court in *Cox* made it clear that this extension to the relationship test was a considered response to changes in the labour market. While the trigger for change was the need to ensure that office holders such as priests fell within the doctrine of vicarious liability, its underlying rationale is that the doctrine should reflect changes in the hiring practices of enterprises and the increasing complexity and sophistication of the organisation of enterprises in the modern world.[104] As I have stated elsewhere,[105] moving away from a formal definition of the employment contract utilised in labour and social security law towards a functionalist approach to the employment relationship is a positive step. *Cox* should not raise undue concerns, provided it is applied incrementally. This does not prevent, in theory, the possibility of a non-restrictive approach ignoring the underlying rationale, but it is to be hoped that the courts are sufficiently sensible to avoid this.

[102] *Cox*, above n 12, [23] (Lord Reed).

[103] For criticism of the distinction between these two doctrines see G Williams, 'Liability for Independent Contractors' [1956] *CLJ* 180; Fleming, above n 3, 433; R Stevens, 'Non-delegable Duties and Vicarious Liability' in J Neyers, E Chamberlain and S Pitel, *Emerging Issues in Tort Law* (Oxford, Hart Publishing, 2007); J Morgan, 'Liability for Independent Contractors in Contract and Tort: Duties to Ensure that Care is Taken' [2015] *CLJ* 109.

[104] See also Lord Dyson in *Mohamud*, above n 11, [55].

[105] Giliker, above n 87, 140–44. See also E McKendrick, 'Vicarious Liability and Independent Contractors—A Re-examination' (1990) 53 *MLR* 770.

It is *Mohamud*, however, that should give us pause for thought. In *Mohamud*, the Supreme Court was prepared to accept that Mr Khan's racist response to a query about a service the supermarket did not even provide was within the course of his employment. One might guess that if Mr Khan had encountered Mr Mohamud in his favourite eating establishment and Mohamud had interrupted Khan to ask him to pass the salt, Khan's reaction would have been exactly the same—to abuse the 'intruder' and require him to leave—and yet the Supreme Court was happy to interpret his actions as a violent means of ensuring Mr Mohamud left his employers' premises. It is helpful to consider at this stage the Scottish case of *Vaickuviene v J Sainsbury plc*.[106] This also involved a violent assault in a supermarket—in this case, a racist shelf-stacker, a member of the British National Party, who had fatally stabbed a fellow shelf-stacker from Lithuania. Although our knowledge of the facts is limited in that the case involved the Scottish equivalent of a striking out application, we are told that Mr McCulloch had strong views that Eastern European workers should not come to the UK to work. While the Inner House (unlike the Outer House)[107] found the murder to be outside the course of employment, it is worth considering whether it would have made any difference if Mr McCulloch's racism had led him to the declared view that Eastern European workers were lazy, illiterate and not up to the job of stacking shelves in a British supermarket. In telling Vaickuviene, therefore, to go back to his own country, could it be said that McCulloch was expressing, albeit violently and in a foul-mouthed way, his concerns that Vaickuviene was not capable of doing his job properly? While kiosk assistants are required to interact with customers, equally a shelf-stacker is expected to work with other shelf-stackers for the benefit of the supermarket and its customers. In a multi-cultural nation, there is always a risk of confrontation and linguistic and cultural misunderstandings between employees working long shifts and engaged in tiring work. Is it still too far-fetched, therefore, to regard a racist murder of a shelf-stacker as within the field of activities in which the murderer was engaged?[108] If not, then, it is submitted, we have a problem. In *Bernard*, Lord Steyn himself warned that the principle of vicarious liability should not be seen as a vague notion of justice which is infinitely extendable.[109] The course of employment test exists to ensure that the courts can justify the imposition of liability on the employer by virtue of the connection between the tortious act and the job for which the tortfeasor has been employed. In broadening the course of employment test by virtue of the doctrine of risk, can it really be said that this element of the vicarious liability test continues to operate effectively as a limit on the scope of the doctrine? Put bluntly, if vicarious liability is still on the move, where and when will it stop?

[106] [2013] CSIH 67, 2013 SLT 1032, [2013] IRLR 792.

[107] *Vaickuviene v J Sainsbury Plc* 2012 SLT 849 (Lady Clark). See J Fulbrook, 'The Outer Limits of Vicarious Liability: An Employer's Responsibility for Murder' [2012] *Journal of Personal Injury Law* 201.

[108] For similar concerns, see Morgan, above n 100, 205; G Junor, 'Vicarious Liability—Redefined?' [2016] 24 *Scots Law Times* 125.

[109] *Bernard v Attorney General of Jamaica* [2004] UKPC 47, [23].

VI. CONCLUSION

It is now time to reflect on the nature of the *Lister* revolution. As we have seen, the House of Lords in *Lister* acknowledged the need to adapt vicarious liability to respond to the emerging scandal of child sexual abuse. This led to knock-on changes to associated fields such as the rules relating to limitation, but also led to a re-examination of the very nature of the relationship that gives rise to vicarious liability. *Cox* highlights the nature of these changes at stage one of the *CCWS* test. In recognising the need to provide a more flexible approach which reflects the evolving nature of the labour market and practices such as outsourcing and increased use of agency staff, the courts are seeking to develop the law in a realistic manner which focuses on the rationale for vicarious liability in tort. This seems entirely sensible. The *Lister* revolution was, however, based on extending the concept of course of employment (stage two of the *CCWS* test). The House of Lords chose to move away from a strict, quasi-statutory formula provided by the Salmond test in favour of a looser test based on close connection. Following *Mohamud*, we are left with a formulation in which the court has to consider two questions:[110]

1. What functions or 'field of activities' have been entrusted by the employer to the employee (or, in everyday language, what was the nature of the employee's job)?
2. Is there is a sufficient connection between the position in which the employee is employed and his wrongful conduct to make it 'right' for the employer to be held liable as a matter of social justice?

It is submitted that this test, premised on the policy arguments of business activity, risk creation and delegation of task, may provide an acceptable basis for dealing with sexual abuse claims. However, in relation to mainstream claims, it runs the risk of unduly extensive liability undermining the course of employment test as a means of limiting the doctrine of vicarious liability. This was indeed the concern of the High Court of Australia in *Prince Alfred College Incorporated v ADC*.[111] The Court refused to follow the *Mohamud* test, preferring a test which determines whether the employment provides 'the occasion for the commission of the wrongful act'. It remains to be seen whether the test for 'occasion', which the Court advised should take account of particular features, including authority, power, trust, control and the ability to achieve intimacy with the victim,[112] will offer any greater clarity in practice, but it is clear that the High Court of Australia believed the *Mohamud* test to be too generous as a general 'course of employment' test for vicarious liability. In its view, what occurred after the victim had left the kiosk in *Mohamud* was not relevantly connected with the employee's employment; rather, the employment merely provided the opportunity for the tort to take place. This distinction—between close connection and mere opportunity—lay at the heart of *Lister*.[113] On this basis,

[110] *Mohamud*, above n 11, [44]–[45].
[111] Above n 46, decided on 5 October 2016.
[112] ibid [81], [83].
[113] Lord Hobhouse in *Lister*, above n 1, [62], for example, contrasted the position of the groundsman (employed to look after the grounds, but not to have anything to do with the boys) with that of

Mohamud may be seen as going beyond even the limits of the *Lister* revolution to ensure that an innocent victim obtains compensation and yet, crucially, without the justification of providing a societal response to child sexual abuse.

Baroness Hale commented in *Woodland* that the strength of the common law is its dynamism. It is, as we have seen, capable of adapting the doctrine of vicarious liability developed over centuries to respond to the modern scandal of child sex abuse. Yet, her Ladyship also acknowledged the danger of unbridled and unprincipled growth to match what the court perceives to be the merits of the particular case. I can do no more than echo her wise words—the common law 'must proceed with caution, incrementally by analogy with existing categories, and consistently with some underlying principle'.[114] If vicarious liability is to avoid imposing unduly broad forms of strict liability on employers in circumstances such as those seen in *Vaickuviene* above, then, at the very least, the lower courts must proceed with caution in their application of the *CCWS/Mohamud* test for course of employment. With the best of intentions, by extending vicarious liability, the *Lister* revolution threatens to reduce its rationale to a mere risk redistribution exercise. Nearly 20 years on, we as lawyers need to consider seriously the consequences of applying tests based on dealing with a specific social problem more broadly in the law of torts.

the warden. See also Lord Clyde at [45] and [50], Lord Hobhouse at [59] and Lord Millett at [82]. Subsequent case law has, however, made this distinction more indistinct, eg *Brink's Global Services Inc v Igrox Ltd* [2010] EWCA Civ 1207.

[114] *Woodland*, above n 95, [28]. There is some evidence that the courts immediately after *Mohamud* have heeded this warning: see *X v Kuoni Travel Ltd* [2016] EWHC 3090 (QB), [48]; *Bellman v Northampton Recruitment Ltd* [2016] EWHC 3104 (QB), [2017] ICR 543; *Fletcher v Chancery Lane Supplies Ltd* [2016] EWCA Civ 1112.

8

Revolutions in Contractual Interpretation: A Historical Perspective

JOANNA McCUNN*

I. INTRODUCTION

A SPECTRE IS haunting contractual interpretation—the spectre of history. It is well known that, in recent decades, a 'fundamental change' has overtaken the law of contractual interpretation, as 'the old intellectual baggage of "legal" interpretation' has been replaced with 'common sense' ideas about language.[1] The meaning of a contract is no longer to be determined by the meaning of its words, but by 'what the parties using those words against the relevant background would reasonably have been understood to mean'.[2] Furthermore, disparate aspects of contract law, from the implication of terms to the remoteness rule in damages, have been recast as facets of interpretation.[3] For writers outlining these changes, it has become traditional to throw them into sharp relief with a reference to what came before. Indeed, it is now almost impossible to open a book about contract law without encountering Wigmore's remark that 'the history of the law of interpretation is the history of a progress from a stiff and superstitious formalism to a flexible rationalism'.[4]

Some questions remain. Was Lord Hoffmann's judgment in *Investors Compensation Scheme* a radical move in this direction or simply one step in a more gradual trend? The basic premise, however, is rarely doubted: a stricter attitude to construction is the more 'traditional' approach of English law.[5] One reason for this is that

* The research for this chapter was funded by the Selden Society. I am grateful to Andrew Bell and Jeffrey Thomson for their comments, and to Lorenzo Maniscalco for his help with Latin translations.

[1] *Investors Compensation Scheme v West Bromwich Building Society* [1998] 1 WLR 896, 912 (Lord Hoffmann).

[2] ibid 913.

[3] See generally C Mitchell, 'Obligations in Commercial Contracts: A Matter of Law or Interpretation?' (2012) 65 *Current Legal Problems* 455.

[4] JH Wigmore, *A Treatise on the Anglo-American System of Evidence*, vol 9, 3rd edn (Boston, Little, Brown & Co, 1940) 187. See, eg, K Lewison, *The Interpretation of Contracts*, 5th edn (London, Sweet & Maxwell, 2011) 3; G McMeel, *The Construction of Contracts*, 2nd edn (Oxford, Oxford University Press, 2011) 22; J Morgan, *Contract Law Minimalism* (Cambridge, Cambridge University Press, 2013) 229; D Nicholls, 'My Kingdom for a Horse: The Meaning of Words' (2005) 121 *LQR* 577, 577; *Bank of Credit and Commerce International v Ali* [2001] UKHL 8, [2002] 1 AC 251, 265.

[5] See, eg, McMeel, above n 4, 24.

few writers venture further back than a century or so ago, when the courts were undoubtedly more wedded to the 'plain meaning' of the contract. If we have a vague idea of the further past, it is probably of a yet stricter period: a 'primitive stage of formalism when the precise word was the sovereign talisman, and every slip was fatal'.[6] It is generally admitted that no one today is an out-and-out literalist with 'two horns and a long forked tail',[7] but we are willing to believe that lawyers of the past were helpless naïfs, bedazzled by the quasi-magical power of the written word.

This chapter aims to put that idea to rest. In fact, our current liberal approach to contractual interpretation has deep roots in the history of the common law, perhaps even more so than the much-maligned 'old baggage' of strict construction. The history of the law of interpretation is not the history of a straightforward progress, but one of cyclical trends. Some eras are undoubtedly more formalist than others, but it is not clear that anyone has ever treated documents in the 'stiff and superstitious' way that is often claimed. One indication of this is that there is very little agreement as to when the bogeyman of literalism actually stalked the earth. McMeel, for example, points to the 'sclerotic 1950s',[8] while Denning LJ, in the 1950s, blamed his own forebears.[9] Perhaps he was thinking of the Victorians, who have a bad reputation in this field,[10] but Wigmore thought that they were the first to take a sensible approach.[11] Meanwhile, Lord Hoffmann has accused everyone from the Middle Ages on.[12]

This chapter will focus on the mid-sixteenth century, a foundational period for contractual interpretation in England, and the time of a revolution that dwarfed even Lord Hoffmann's. It was the setting for one of the most significant intellectual developments in common law history: the invention of legal interpretation. We will find that the sixteenth-century approach to contractual interpretation is surprisingly familiar, and that many modern debates on the subject had close counterparts in Renaissance England.

II. SOME BACKGROUND

First, though, some context is necessary, since the contract law of the sixteenth century looks very different to the law today. In fact, 'contract law' had not yet been invented. In its place were a variety of actions that could be brought on what we would now describe as kinds of contracts. These included the action of covenant,

6 *Wood v Lucy, Lady Duff-Gordon* [1917] 222 NY 88, 91 (Cardozo J).

7 R Goff, 'Commercial Contracts and the Commercial Court' [1984] *Lloyd's Maritime and Commercial Law Quarterly* 382, 388.

8 G McMeel, 'The Principles and Policies of Contractual Construction' in A Burrows and E Peel (eds), *Contract Terms* (Oxford, Oxford University Press, 2007) 29.

9 *British Movietonews v London and District Cinemas* [1951] 1 KB 190, 202.

10 T Bingham, 'A New Thing under the Sun? The Interpretation of Contract and the *ICS* Decision' (2008) 12 *Edinburgh Law Review* 374, 375.

11 Wigmore, above n 4, 189.

12 L Hoffmann, 'The Intolerable Wrestle with Words and Meanings' (1997) 114 *South African Law Journal* 656, 670.

which could only be brought on a deed, a formal instrument made under seal. There were also debt and detinue, which lay for the recovery of a definite sum of money or a specific chattel. By far the most common contractual action was debt sur obligation, brought to enforce a penalty clause in a type of deed known as a bond.[13] Although the action of assumpsit was now available to enforce some informal contracts, the number of such cases remained relatively insignificant.[14] Contracts were therefore of an overwhelmingly formal character. Deeds were commonplace, used for everything from conveyances, charterparties and building contracts to marriage agreements.[15] Edward Coke observed that the interpretation of deeds concerned 'every man (for, for the most part, every man is a lessor or a lessee)'.[16]

These contractual actions had not accrued many substantive doctrines: if the plaintiff had a deed, it would almost certainly be enforced.[17] As a result, the main legal issue was to establish the meaning of the deed.[18] And this was true for not only contractual actions, since a case that was originally brought on an action of trespass or ejectment could end up turning on a question of interpretation. The defendant might have resorted to self-help, driving the plaintiff off his land, and only after some pleading would it be revealed that the dispute centred on the meaning of a title deed.

The interpretation of deeds, then, formed a large part of the common law's bread and butter. However, before the sixteenth century, judges were not particularly interested in enunciating grand theories of interpretation. As Thorne puts it, they simply saw the reading of documents as 'an incidental, routine function of judicial administration'.[19] This is of a piece with the courts' general approach to law at the time. Baker has characterised medieval judges as referees, whose role was simply to apply certain rules in a predictable way, and who were not expected to explain the reasons for their decisions—still less to alter the settled rules of the game.[20]

However, the sixteenth century brought rapid change to the common law. Following the introduction of printing, the courts began to give greater weight to authoritative copies of written materials.[21] At the same time, new humanist scholarship was encouraging a more rational approach to the law.[22] Judges began to see it as their duty to make reasoned decisions, going beyond a rote application of the words of a

[13] AWB Simpson, *A History of the Common Law of Contract: The Rise of the Action of Assumpsit* (Oxford, Oxford University Press, 1975) 88.

[14] In Trinity term of 1572, for example, there were 503 actions of debt sur obligation and only three of assumpsit: ibid 125.

[15] J Baker, *The Oxford History of the Laws of England, Vol VI: 1483–1558* (Oxford, Oxford University Press, 2003) 819.

[16] *Walker's Case* (1587) 3 Co Rep 22a, 23a.

[17] Baker, above n 15, 814. The exceptions were pleas of duress or *non est factum*: ibid 829. There were no doctrines of mistake, fraud or undue influence in this period: Simpson, above n 13, 29.

[18] Baker, above n 15, 824.

[19] S Thorne (ed), *A Discourse upon the Exposicion & Understandinge of Statutes* (San Marino, Huntington Library, 1942) 3.

[20] Baker, above n 15, 49.

[21] See generally I Williams, '"He Creditted More the Printed Booke": Common Lawyers' Receptivity to Print, c 1550–1640' (2010) 28 *Law and History Review* 39.

[22] Baker, above n 15, 13.

text. It is unsurprising, therefore, that ideas about interpretation suddenly came to dominate the law. The courts recognised that interpretation could be a systematic process, and began to establish the rules and principles that underlay it. Techniques of interpretation were keenly debated by readers in the Inns of Court,[23] and the first English literature on the subject was produced.[24] Indeed, England was not alone in this respect: the whole of Europe was experiencing an 'interpretation boom'.[25]

It is widely recognised that elaborate theories of statutory interpretation were being developed in this period.[26] Unsurprisingly, contractual interpretation was affected too. Indeed, formal contracts were the documents that fell most frequently to be interpreted by the courts.[27] Changes to contract law, prompted by the rise of assumpsit, were also encouraging lawyers to rethink the conceptual basis of legal obligations. Ultimately, this would lead to the formulation of a general, agreement-based theory of contract law.[28] For now, however, interpretation was the only game in town. Lawyers began to formulate principles for interpreting deeds, grounded in sophisticated ideas about contractual intentions.

This chapter focuses on cases reported by Edmund Plowden and James Dyer, the two pre-eminent law reporters of their day. Dyer's reports cover his own legal career, between around 1532 and 1581,[29] while Plowden's *Commentaries* span the period from 1550 to 1580. Both sets of reports show that the courts strongly emphasised the importance of identifying and implementing the parties' intentions. This was not a wholly new feature of the law: references to contractual intentions had been rare in the fourteenth century,[30] but became increasingly common from the mid-fifteenth century on.[31] For the first time, however, the courts were developing a general theory of interpretation based on the intentions behind the contract. As a result, when faced with a choice between strictly applying the words of a deed and following the parties' intentions, the courts chose the latter in virtually every case. In fact, out

[23] See, eg, J Baker (ed), *John Spelman's Reading on Quo Warranto* (London, Selden Society, 1997) 89ff.

[24] See, eg, Thorne, above n 19, composed *c* 1565 and usually attributed to Thomas Egerton—but see J Baker, *The Reinvention of Magna Carta 1216–1616* (Cambridge, Cambridge University Press, 2017) 232–36; see also *A Treatise Concerning Statutes, or Acts of Parliament, and the Exposition Thereof* (London, Tonson, 1677), composed in the late sixteenth century and usually attributed to Christopher Hatton.

[25] I Maclean, *Interpretation and Meaning in the Renaissance: The Case of Law* (Cambridge, Cambridge University Press, 1992) 35.

[26] See, eg, G Behrens, 'Equity in the Commentaries of Edmund Plowden' [1999] *Journal of Legal History* 25.

[27] Dyer's reports, which are fairly representative of the cases he was involved in, contain only around a dozen cases on statutory interpretation, almost 30 on the interpretation of wills and over 70 on the interpretation of deeds.

[28] D Ibbetson, *A Historical Introduction to the Law of Obligations* (Oxford, Oxford University Press, 2002) 146.

[29] J Baker (ed), *Reports from the Lost Notebooks of Sir James Dyer*, vol 1 (London, Selden Society, 1994) xxiii.

[30] JM Kaye, *Medieval English Conveyances* (Cambridge, Cambridge University Press, 2009) 243.

[31] See, eg, (1440) YB Mich 19 Hen VI f 4b, pl 7; (1456) YB Mich 35 Hen VI f 16a, pl 25; *Southwall v Huddelston and Reynoldys* (1523) YB Hil 14 Hen VIII, SS vol 119, p 160, pl 1.

of almost 100 cases on the interpretation of deeds in Plowden and Dyer, there are only two in which the parties' intentions appear to have been trumped by the strict meaning of the text.[32]

III. CONTRACTUAL INTERPRETATION IN THE SIXTEENTH CENTURY

A. *Throckmerton v Tracy*[33]

Throckmerton v Tracy is a good example of a mid-century case in which the court faced a mismatch between the technical meaning of a deed and the intentions of the parties. Henry Beeley, the Abbot of Tewkesbury, had granted 100 acres of land to a tenant for life. He then leased the reversion to John Smith for 21 years, beginning on the first Michaelmas to follow the death of the life tenant. John Throckmerton succeeded to Smith's title. Fifteen years later, the monastery was dissolved and the Abbot's reversion was surrendered to Henry VIII, who granted it to Richard Tracy, a Protestant theologian and friend of Thomas Cromwell. When the life tenant died, Throckmerton entered. Tracy promptly seized his sheep, provoking a lawsuit.

When challenged, Tracy explained that there had been a drafting error in the Abbot's lease, which meant that Throckmerton had nothing in the land. The problem was that the premises of the deed granted him the 'reversion' of the land, rather than the possession. However, the reversion had been immediately destroyed on the death of the life tenant, and no longer existed for Throckmerton to take the following Michaelmas.[34] It was simply 'no longer in Being', and he had no right to claim anything else.[35]

Throckmerton argued that this was an incorrect interpretation of the word 'reversion'. He agreed that, if it were given its 'proper' legal meaning, the lease would be void. However, he claimed, the law should 'draw the Words from their proper and usual Signification to fulfil the Intention of the Parties'.[36] After all, the Abbot's intention was 'very apparent': he wanted to grant the possession of the land after the death of the life tenant, but he had fallen foul of a legal technicality by incorrectly using the word 'reversion'.[37] He concluded that 'if the Intent of the Parties appears, the Law will construe the Words in such Sense as to perform that Intent rather than in any other Sense'.[38]

Broke CJ's response has been cited as a paradigm of sixteenth-century attitudes to interpretation: indeed, it forms the basis for Wigmore's assertion that contractual

32 *Anon* (1554) Dyer 99b and *Earl of Huntingdon v Lord Clinton* (1557) Dyer 139a.

33 *Throckmerton v Tracy* (1555) Plow 145.

34 ibid 152a.

35 ibid 153. The *habendum* of the deed correctly specified the possession of the land, but, where a deed was internally inconsistent, the premises would take priority: ibid 152a.

36 ibid 153a.

37 ibid 159.

38 ibid 153a.

interpretation was labouring in an age of 'stiff and superstitious formalism'.[39] The Chief Justice objected that

> there ought to be apt Words to express the Meaning, or else the Meaning shall be void ... for if a Man should bend the Law to the Intent of the Party, rather than the Intent of the Party to the Law, this would be the Way to introduce Barbarousness and Ignorance, and to destroy all Learning and Diligence. For if a Man was assured that whatever Words he made Use of his Meaning only should be considered, he would be very careless about the Choice of his Words, and it would be the Source of infinite Confusion and Incertainty to explain what was its Meaning.[40]

Indeed, these concerns about legal certainty sound very convincing. Unfortunately, Broke's comments were not quite as authoritative as they seem. Firstly, they were made in dissent: the other three judges in the case took a very different approach. Secondly, his scruples do not seem to have troubled him for long: 'afterwards,' reported Plowden, he said that 'he was content that Judgment should be given for the Plaintiff' after all.[41] In fact, Dyer even recorded that Broke had 'prepared an argument on both sides, and if any one of his companions had been against the lease, he would have argued for it'.[42] This is not as surprising as it may at first appear: the modern doctrine of precedent was in its infancy, so there was not yet an assumption that everything said from the bench was intended as an authoritative judgment.[43] Finally, Broke's remarks were entirely unrepresentative of this period, with no other judge in Plowden or Dyer making a similar point. Much more typical were the speeches of the three remaining judges, all of whom agreed that the parties' 'Intent shall be pursued rather than the Words'.[44]

Two of these judges, Stanford and Saunders JJ, made more comprehensive attempts to set out the principles of contractual interpretation. Saunders J, for example, urged judges not to 'cavil about the Words in subversion of the plain Intent of the Parties', which was 'a kind of trickery, and an excessively clever but wicked interpretation of the law'.[45] Satirising literalism, he referred to Cicero's example of a general who made a truce for 130 days and attacked his enemy during the night. Such interpretation was 'meer Injury and Injustice'; '*summum jus*,' he warned, was '*summa injuria*'. Instead, judges should 'observe and follow the Intent of the Words', which were 'the Testimony of the Contract'.[46] However, they could also apply other principles: remembering, for example, that 'Deeds ought to have a reasonable Exposition, which shall be without Wrong to the Grantor, and with the greatest Advantage to the Grantee'.[47] Similarly, Stanford J explained that there were

> three Rules for the Understanding of Deeds. First, that they shall be taken most beneficially for the Party to whom they are made; secondly, that a Deed shall never be void, where the

[39] Wigmore, above n 4, 188.
[40] *Throckmerton v Tracy*, above n 33, 162.
[41] ibid 162a.
[42] *Throgmorton v Tracey* (1555) Dyer 124b, 126b.
[43] Baker, above n 15, 50.
[44] *Throckmerton v Tracy*, above n 33, 160.
[45] ibid 161: 'calumnia quaedam et nimis callida sed malitiosa juris interpretatio'.
[46] ibid 161a.
[47] ibid 161.

> Words may be applied to any Intent to make it good; and ... thirdly, that the Words shall be construed according to the Intent of the Parties, and not otherwise.[48]

These judgments are highly significant: they represent two of the first attempts to present the common law of interpretation as a coherent and principled system.

B. The Identification of Intentions

The most immediately striking feature of these judgments is the central place they give to the parties' intentions. This is entirely typical of interpretation cases from the period.[49] In *Colthirst v Bejushin*, for example, the defendant had been granted a life estate in certain land on condition that he live there continually. One question was whether he would have fulfilled the condition if he had lived there continually since entering the land, but did not actually enter until some time after the beginning of his term. Sjt Pollard argued that 'the Intent of a Condition ought always to be performed as well as the Words thereof'.[50] If Bejushin did not enter until ten years after the beginning of the term, he could hardly claim to have complied with the grantor's intention, even if he had technically performed the words. While the case was ultimately decided on another ground, Mountague CJ accepted Pollard's argument: 'I would readily admit that [the condition] ought to be taken according to the Intent of it, that he should be resident all the Term.'[51]

In *Chapman v Dalton*, counsel for the plaintiff cited *Colthirst* as authority for the proposition that a condition would not be performed if the words had been fulfilled but not the intention.[52] In that case, the opposite question was at issue: would a covenant be performed if the intention had been fulfilled but not the words? The defendant had agreed to make a lease to Chapman or his assigns in 21 years' time, but Chapman died before the time elapsed. The defendant argued that the covenant had become impossible to perform, because Chapman had not named any assigns in his will. The case was brought by the executor of Chapman's executrix. He claimed that the lease ought to be made to him,

> For in every Agreement made between any Parties the Intent is the chief Thing to be considered, and if ... the Agreement cannot be performed according to the Words, yet the Party shall perform it as near to the Intent of the Agreement as he can.[53]

The court agreed: although an executor was not, strictly speaking, an assign, it should be presumed that Chapman wanted him to have the lease nevertheless.

The courts, then, regarded awareness of the intention behind a legal instrument as essential to understanding its true effect. Indeed, it was more important than the

[48] ibid 160.
[49] And, indeed, of sixteenth-century law more generally: L Knafla, *Law and Politics in Jacobean England: The Tracts of Lord Chancellor Ellesmere* (Cambridge, Cambridge University Press, 1977) 44.
[50] *Colthirst v Bejushin* (1550) Plow 21, 23a.
[51] ibid 34.
[52] *Chapman v Dalton* (1565) Plow 284, 291.
[53] ibid 290.

words of the contract, which only functioned as 'testimony' of the intention.[54] But how was this intention to be identified? After all, as Christopher St German had put it, 'of the entent inwarde in the herte: mannes lawe can not Juge'.[55] And there were major impediments to ascertaining the intentions of the parties to a deed. For a start, a party to a case was prohibited from giving evidence on his own behalf in a common law court.[56] Furthermore, many deeds were not challenged in court until the original parties were long deceased.[57] Since no evidence of the parties' actual intentions was generally available, the court was required to reconstruct them after the fact.

Often, of course, the parties' intentions could simply be extrapolated from the deed itself. For example, it would be presumed that the parties had meant the words as they were 'commonly used'.[58] If a word had been used in one part of the deed, it could be assumed to have the same meaning elsewhere:[59] as Anthony Browne J and Dyer CJ observed, 'it is impossible to form a Judgment upon one Part only, without taking all the Parts into Consideration'.[60] In other cases, the courts would look at the context in which the contract had been made. In *Bold v Molineux*, for example, Bold's father-in-law had promised to pay him £30 at the Feast of St John the Baptist in 1533, unless his wife died without a son 'then living'. The question was whether 'then living' referred to the time of the Feast or of the wife's death. Bold argued for the latter, claiming that the Feast had only been named so that he 'should have the money the sooner'.[61] However, Fitzherbert and Baldwin JJ thought that the circumstances suggested a different intention. The purpose of the term had been that 'if the issue die, the payment shall immediately cease', as was 'the common practice of all men who give large sums of money with the marriage of their children'.[62]

C. Intentions and Reason

In other cases, the court did not look for the intentions of the actual parties, but resorted to general principles to establish what a reasonable party would have intended in the circumstances. This is where the other 'rules' set out in *Throckmerton* came into play. For example, Stanford J had held that 'a Deed shall never be void, where the Words may be applied to any Intent to make it good'.[63] After all, it could be assumed that the parties would have preferred their deed to take effect, 'rather than that the Intent of the Parties should be void'.[64] Thus, in *Browning*

[54] *Throckmerton v Tracy*, above n 33, 161a.
[55] C St German, *Doctor and Student*, TFT Plucknett and JL Barton eds (first published 1530, London, Selden Society, 1974) 230.
[56] Baker, above n 15, 364.
[57] J Baker, *An Introduction to English Legal History*, 4th edn (Oxford, Oxford University Press, 2007) 288.
[58] *Hill v Grange* (1556) Plow 164, 170a.
[59] *Anon* (1564) Dyer 233b.
[60] *Wrotesley v Adams* (1559) Plow 187, 196.
[61] *Bold v Molineux* (1536) Dyer 14b, 15b.
[62] ibid 17b.
[63] *Throckmerton v Tracy*, above n 33, 160.
[64] *Browning v Beston* (1555) Plow 131, 140.

v Beston, the plaintiff claimed that insufficient words had been used to reserve a rent in a lease. The defendant argued that the law would take it that there was a rent, 'as strongly as if it had been expressed in plain Terms'.[65] As Sjt Catlyn put it, 'our Law, which is the most reasonable Law upon Earth, regards the Effect and Substance of Words more than the Form of them, and takes the Substance of Words to imply the Form thereof'.[66]

Another of Stanford J's rules was that the terms of a deed 'shall be taken most beneficially for the Party to whom they are made'.[67] This is a form of the *contra proferentem* rule, which provides that a contractual term should be construed against the party 'proffering' it. Today, lawyers generally attribute its introduction into English law to Coke,[68] but in fact it has been part of the common law since at least the late fourteenth century.[69] It was certainly well established by the time of Plowden and Dyer, and one of the participants in Edward Hake's Elizabethan *Dialogue on Equity* volunteered that he had 'hearde it often sayd'.[70] However, Hake's interlocutor also pointed out that the principle was difficult to square with an intention-based approach to interpretation. How, he asked, was it possible for the courts to interpret a deed in accordance with the intention of the parties, but also more beneficially for one party than the other?[71]

It appears that the rule simply operated as a presumption, which could establish the parties' intentions if they were not otherwise clear. If the grantor had the opportunity to limit his grant in some way and failed to do so, it could be presumed that he did not intend to limit it at all. After all, it was 'the natural Principle of Mankind to act and speak according as it suits best with their own Interest and Advantage'.[72] In *Colthirst*, Sjt Saunders explained that the law 'interprets the Words and Actions of every Man most strongly against himself':[73] the courts would not deign to rescue a party if he had been so foolish as to bind himself by words he later regretted.

Finally, we come to Saunders J's admonition that 'Deeds ought to have a reasonable Exposition'.[74] He folded a rather diffident reference to *contra proferentem* into his general discussion of reasonable interpretation, claiming that 'there is a Kind of Equity in Grants, so that they shall not be taken unreasonably against the Grantor, and yet shall with Reason be extended most liberally for the Grantee'.[75] Thus, the courts would allow *contra proferentem* to be trumped by the need to construe a

[65] ibid 134.
[66] ibid 140.
[67] *Throckmerton v Tracy*, above n 33, 160.
[68] See, eg, E Peel, 'Whither Contra Proferentem?' in Burrows and Peel, above n 8, 54.
[69] *Plessington v Mowbray & Ellerton* (1382) YB Mich 6 Ric II, AF p 148, pl 17 (Sjt Rickhill): 'When a deed is made, the deed shall be taken more strongly against him who made the deed and more for him to whom the deed is made.'
[70] E Hake, *Epieikeia: A Dialogue on Equity in Three Parts* (composed *c* 1598, DEC Yale ed, New Haven, Yale University Press, 1953) 54.
[71] ibid.
[72] *Report of Plowden's argument in Basset and Morgan v Manxel, at Serjeant's Inn* (1564) Plow 6a.
[73] *Colthirst v Bejushin*, above n 50, 29. See also, in the context of pleadings, *Stradling v Morgan* (1560) Plow 199, 202a: 'It is reasonable to take it in that Sense which makes against him, for if his Complaint lies in the other Point it is his Folly that he did not shew it precisely.'
[74] *Throckmerton v Tracy*, above n 33, 161.
[75] ibid. Hake came to the same conclusion: above n 70, 55.

deed reasonably. In *Hill v Grange*, for example, the defendant was required to pay rent at the Feast of the Annunciation and at Michaelmas. He argued that the rent was not due on the first Michaelmas of his lease, because the Annunciation was named first. The first rent, therefore, ought to be paid then, 'for Reservations shall always be taken most strongly against the Reservors'.[76] The court refused to accept this argument, since the defendant's interpretation would allow him to have 'half a Year's Profit, without paying any Rent for it', which was 'no Sort of Reason'.[77] Even in *Colthirst*, the judges preferred to think in terms of finding a reasonable interpretation: none took up Saunders's discussion of *contra proferentem*, but instead approved his conclusions on the basis that 'Conditions have always a reasonable Construction' or 'Conditions have a reasonable Intendment'.[78] Again, this was linked to the parties' intentions: Hake, for example, argued that a contract should not be 'expownded contrary to reason, which no doubte it sholde be if it were construed against the intent of the parties'.[79]

Saunders and Stanford JJ were two of the first judges to try their hands at a systematic exposition of contractual interpretation. However, their presentations of the principles used by the courts were relatively crude. Stanford J, for example, presented his three rules on an equal footing. Yet, as we have seen, construing a deed in accordance with the parties' intentions was the overriding aim of the court, while the other two rules simply helped to establish the relevant intentions. Similarly, Saunders J conflated the *contra proferentem* rule, reasonableness and intention-based construction into a single approach, without explaining how they interacted with one another.

Their accounts also demonstrate how closely the parties' intentions were identified with what reasonable parties would have intended. For example, they would always want their deed to be effective, and to be treated even-handedly. Perhaps this is why judges never observed, as St German did, how difficult it was to discern the content of a man's mind. Rather, they thought that intentions were so 'apparent' that 'every Man may discover' them, simply by referring to what was reasonable in the circumstances.[80] They were not interested in the parties' beliefs and motivations, but about the 'reasonable and equal intention' that could be extracted from their agreement.[81] After all, a contract was a compromise between the two parties' interests: it could be assumed that they must have come to a 'reasonable and equal' conclusion.

D. Conceptions of Contractual Intention

The idiosyncrasies of this approach can be seen most clearly by comparing it with the construction of wills. It was well established that the testator's intentions were

[76] *Hill v Grange*, above n 58, 171.
[77] ibid 171a.
[78] *Colthirst v Bejushin*, above n 50, 30, 34.
[79] Hake, above n 70, 55.
[80] *Throckmerton v Tracy*, above n 33, 159.
[81] *Bold v Molineux*, above n 61, 15a.

of paramount importance for the interpretation of a will: as Henry Swinburne observed, 'it is the mind and not the wordes of the testator, that giveth life to the testament'.[82] Even Broke CJ admitted in *Throckmerton* that 'in Testaments the Intent only shall be observed and considered'.[83] However, when identifying the testator's intention, the courts very rarely resorted to general principles or presumptions about what it would have been reasonable for him to intend. Rather, they focused on indications of his actual intentions, such as the will itself, or the surrounding circumstances.[84] The intentions of a testator simply could not be established by reference to a general standard of reasonableness.

The intentions behind a deed, however, could. It is possible that this was a consequence of the courts' developing understanding of contractual intentions. When judges first began to consider the intentions behind a deed, they referred exclusively to 'the will of the donor'.[85] By the sixteenth century, however, their language had shifted, and what now concerned them was the 'Intent of both the Parties'.[86] This was a fundamental change: rather than expressing two parties' separate intentions, a deed was coming to be seen as the embodiment of their single, common intention.

The effects of this development can be seen in a number of mid-century cases, in which the courts struggled with the issue of whether a grant or reservation made by one party could be understood to be intended by both. For example, in *Browning v Beston*, the plaintiff argued that the 'rent' mentioned in his lease was void because it had been expressed as a grant by the lessee, rather than as a reservation by the lessor. He claimed that it would be 'utterly against Reason to take the Words of one Person as the Words of another'.[87] However, Sjt Morgan explained that this was the wrong way to think about the lease. He pointed out that debt could not be brought on the deed 'except it be adjudged a Contract in Law, and a Contract cannot be without an Assent between two or more, wherefore the Assent of both Parties is the Perfection of the Contract'.[88] Therefore, as Sjt Catlyn put it, 'in Contracts it is not material which of the Parties speaks the Words, if the other agrees to them, for the Agreement of the Minds of the Parties is the only Thing the Law respects in Contracts'.[89] Similarly, in *Reniger v Fogossa*, Sjt Pollard emphasised the minds of both the parties, defining an agreement as the 'Union, Collection, Copulation and Conjunction of two or more Minds'.[90]

Common lawyers, then, were beginning to think of a deed as the product of the parties' common intention. This emphasis on 'the agreement of the minds of the parties' was connected by lawyers to their intention-based approach to interpretation. Again in *Browning*, Sjt Catlyn explained that 'if any Persons are agreed upon a Thing ... the Law always regards the Intention of the Parties, and will apply the

[82] H Swinburne, *A Briefe Treatise of Testaments and Last Willes* (London, John Windet, 1590) 261.
[83] *Throckmerton v Tracy*, above n 33, 162a.
[84] See, eg, *Clache's Case* (1573) Dyer 330b; *Welcden v Elkington* (1578) Plow 516; *Paramour v Yardley* (1579) Plow 539.
[85] See, eg, (1344) YB 18 & 19 Edw III, RS p 362, pl 91.
[86] *Chapman v Dalton*, above n 52, 290a.
[87] *Browning v Beston*, above n 64, 136.
[88] ibid 138.
[89] ibid 140a.
[90] *Reniger v Fogossa* (1550) Plow 1, 17.

Words to that which in common Presumption may be taken to be their Intent'.[91] It was also recognised that this approach did not fit well with the *contra proferentem* rule: Sjts Stanford and Walsh argued that *contra proferentem* could not be applied to a deed made by multiple parties, 'because the law makes each Party privy to the Speech of the other'.[92] Perhaps this is why the courts often preferred to think in terms of reasonableness: it enabled them to arbitrate between the two parties without the need to distinguish between their individual intentions.[93]

Notably, this approach was very similar to the way they treated statutes. Like contracts, Acts of Parliament were made by multiple parties: 'so manie statute makers, so many myndes'.[94] Again, the intentions behind the instrument were paramount, and the courts were inclined to identify the legislator's intention with what they thought was reasonable. They used very similar presumptions: assuming, for example, that none of the Act had been intended to be void,[95] and that Parliament would never intend to pass 'a very unreasonable' statute.[96] Indeed, they were prepared to admit that these legislative intentions were sometimes all but fictional, constructed in order to legitimise the court's preferred interpretation.[97]

The courts, then, were developing a sophisticated conception of the parties' intentions, based on the meeting of their minds. Because deeds were made by the agreement of multiple parties, it was impossible to interpret them in accordance with each party's actual intentions. It was therefore necessary to construct notional reasonable parties, and the intentions that they would have had.[98] This then freed lawyers to derive contractual intentions from their own ideas of reason, something that was notably absent from the interpretation of wills. Although lawyers of this period rarely engaged in explicit philosophising about the nature of contracts, their approach to interpretation reveals that a great deal of implicit theory was lying beneath the surface.

E. Interpretation and Equity

It might be asked why the intentions of the parties were quite so important to lawyers of the sixteenth century. After all, Broke CJ had made a reasonable point: a great deal of 'Confusion and Incertainty' could be caused by the courts' creative interpretations. Since there was so little contract law theory at the time, this question can best be answered by analogy with statutory interpretation. As we have seen, the courts took strikingly similar approaches to the construction of deeds and statutes.

[91] *Browning v Beston*, above n 64, 140.
[92] ibid 134.
[93] A Lüderitz, *Auslegung von Rechtsgeschäften: vergleichende Untersuchung anglo-amerikanischen und deutschen Rechts* (Karlsruhe, CF Müller, 1966) 249.
[94] Thorne, above n 19, 151.
[95] ibid 58.
[96] *Stowel v Lord Zouch* (1564) Plow 353a, 364.
[97] See, eg, *Reniger v Fogossa*, above n 90, 13a: 'they construed the Minds of the Makers of the Statute, out of mere Necessity to avoid a Mischief'.
[98] As noted by Hoffmann, above n 12, 664.

There was also a significant cross-pollination of ideas between the two areas. For example, in *Bold v Molineux*, counsel argued that deeds were 'private laws between party and party',[99] and Fitzherbert and Baldwin JJ held that 'the intention of the makers and parties shall be expounded' in both 'deeds and statutes'.[100]

These similarities did not escape lawyers of the time. Hake, for example, observed that 'in the exposition of deedes, contractes and willes it may be affirmed withowte absurdity that *Equity* in every of them beareth rule very greatly'.[101] For Hake, equity was closely connected with the intentions of the parties. 'At all tymes and in all ages,' he declared, 'the judges of the lawe have expownded bothe deedes and contractes not precisely or strictly according to ye words, [but] by *Equity*, that is to saye, according to the intent of the parties.'[102] Similarly, statutes were 'taken and expownded according to the intent of those that were the makers of the same statute'.[103]

We can, then, better understand the courts' attachment to contractual intentions by examining their equitable construction of statutes. This was famously outlined by Plowden in his report of *Eyston v Studd*. He explained that 'it is not the Words of the Law, but the internal Sense of it that makes the Law', and warned that 'it often happens that when you know the Letter, you know not the Sense, for sometimes the Sense is more confined and contracted than the Letter, and sometimes it is more large and extensive'.[104] In order to determine whether equity should diminish or enlarge the words of a particular Act,

> it is a good Way, when you peruse a Statute, to suppose that the Law-maker is present, and that you have asked him the Question you want to know touching the Equity, then you must give yourself such an Answer as you imagine he would have done, if he had been present.[105]

This could result in an interpretation that seemed quite contrary to the words of the statute. However, this was not a problem if it was 'guided by the Intent of the Legislature ... and according to that which is consonant to Reason and good Discretion'.[106] Plowden compared the letter of the law to the shell of a nut, observing that 'you will receive no Benefit by the Law, if you rely only upon the Letter'. Rather, 'as the Fruit and Profit of the Nut lies in the Kernel, and not in the Shell, so the Fruit and Profit of the Law consists in the Sense more than in the Letter'.[107] Sjt Saunders, likewise, explained that 'Words, which are no other than the Verberation of the Air, do not constitute the Statute, but are only the Image of it'.[108]

And the same was true of the words of a contract. As Sjt Catlyn had put it, 'the Agreement of the Minds of the Parties is the only Thing the Law respects in

[99] *Bold v Molineux*, above n 61, 15a.
[100] ibid 17a.
[101] Hake, above n 70, 51.
[102] ibid.
[103] ibid 85.
[104] *Eyston v Studd* (1574) Plow 459a, 465.
[105] ibid 467.
[106] *Stradling v Morgan*, above n 73, 205a.
[107] *Eyston v Studd*, above n 104, 465.
[108] *Partridge v Strange & Croker* (1553) Plow 77, 82.

Contracts',[109] and Saunders J argued that 'the Words are no other than the Testimony of the Contract'.[110] The words of the deed were only evidence of the parties' intentions, and it was the latter that gave the contract its true force and meaning.

IV. TWO APPROACHES TO INTERPRETATION

Contractual interpretation in the mid-sixteenth century, then, was primarily concerned with implementing the intentions of the parties. These could be discovered from the document itself; from the surrounding context; or from the court's understanding of what reasonable parties would have wanted. It was understood that legal instruments gained their normative force from the intentions behind them, rather than the words that constituted them.

This is a far cry from the 'stiff and superstitious formalism' we were promised. Indeed, in many ways it is very similar to the modern approach to interpretation. A lawyer from the mid-sixteenth century, presented with Lord Hoffmann's five *ICS* principles, would find much comfortingly familiar. He would readily agree, for example, that the meaning of a document was something very different from the meaning of its words, and that even unambiguous words should be given a different meaning if it seemed clear that the parties had made a mistake with their language.[111]

The terminology of the 'factual matrix' would be new to him, but the concept would not be wholly foreign. There was a rule in his period that the words of a deed could not be varied by parol evidence,[112] but the courts would certainly consider their meaning in context. In *Hawes v Davye*, for example, Davye had agreed to pay Hawes £60 before 24 September if his ship took a prize. Davye argued that, if the ship did not take a prize, he was not bound to pay the £60 at all; Hawes, that the debt would fall due on 24 September if no prize was taken before then. The court looked to the circumstances behind the agreement to explain the term: 'it well appears that the sum of £60 was due before the bond was made, and the extremity of the payment was deferred until 24 September'.[113] In other cases, the judges considered supporting documents that helped to explain the intentions of the parties.[114]

Elsewhere, however, our lawyer would be on less certain ground. He might find himself nonplussed by Lord Hoffmann's definition of interpretation: 'the ascertainment of the meaning which the document would convey to a reasonable person having all the background knowledge which would reasonably have been available to the parties'.[115] At first glance, this looks very much like the approach of the early modern courts, but it is important not to exaggerate the similarities. While they clearly have much in common, the two approaches start from very different understandings of the nature of contracts and legal interpretation.

[109] *Browning v Beston*, above n 64, 140a.
[110] *Throckmerton v Tracy*, above n 33, 161a.
[111] *Investors Compensation Scheme*, above n 1, 913.
[112] Simpson, above n 13, 96.
[113] *Hawes v Davye* (1565) Dyer (109 SS) 119.
[114] *Vavisor's Case* (1572) Dyer 307b.
[115] *Investors Compensation Scheme*, above n 1, 912.

First, judges today ask themselves what meaning the document would convey to a reasonable reader. Sixteenth-century courts did not feel the need to introduce this cipher in order to distance themselves from their own interpretations.[116] More importantly, however, they did not ask how a reader would understand the document at all. They were much more concerned with what they thought the writer must have meant by it: with what Chen-Wishart describes as 'actor', rather than 'observer', objectivity.[117] While this may seem like a relatively minor distinction, it points to a conceptual gulf underlying the two courts' invocations of reasonableness.

In modern law, we ask ourselves how a reasonable person would understand the parties' intentions, partly for pragmatic reasons (the impossibility of knowing their actual intentions), but partly because of substantive theories about the nature of legal instruments.[118] Contracting parties are not bound to each other's unexpressed whims; this would undermine certainty and prevent parties from planning their lives on the basis of their apparent contract.[119] Observer objectivity is favoured for the fullness of the protection it gives to the reader's expectations.[120] While we recognise that this approach may thwart the parties' actual intentions, we find this justifiable given the other normative commitments of contract law.

However, these kinds of concerns were much less important for sixteenth-century judges. Attitudes had changed dramatically since the medieval period: the courts now thought that it was better to have a fair result than a predictable one. Aside from Broke CJ's abortive dissent in *Throckmerton*, and some passing references to the desirability of settling disputes,[121] legal certainty was just not something the courts worried about. When they invoked reasonableness in the context of interpretation, it was not so that the parties would have a reliable text to work from; it was because they thought that the parties would have wanted to make a reasonable contract in the first place. There was no acknowledgement that injecting reason into a contract might thwart their real intentions, or that the parties might actively prefer a more literalist approach.[122] Indeed, in the context of statutes, lawyers brushed aside concerns that it might be difficult for laymen to understand the meaning of the text: even if the court's interpretation was unpredictable, it would undoubtedly be just, and nobody could possibly take issue with that.[123] These approaches to interpretation, then, are products of convergent evolution. Two legal systems with very different commitments and values arrived at much the same result: interpretation based on the intentions of the parties, identified from what would have been reasonable in the circumstances.

[116] See *Davis Contractors Ltd Appellants* v *Fareham Urban District Council Respondents* [1956] AC 696, 728.

[117] M Chen-Wishart, 'Contractual Mistake, Intention in Formation and Vitiation: The Oxymoron of *Smith v Hughes*' in JW Neyers, R Bronaugh and SGA Pitel (eds), *Exploring Contract Law* (Oxford, Hart Publishing, 2009) 349.

[118] Hoffmann, above n 12, 664.

[119] Chen-Wishart, above n 118, 346.

[120] ibid 350.

[121] See, eg, *Colthirst v Bejushin*, above n 50, 25; *Stowel v Lord Zouch*, above n 96, 356a.

[122] As is arguably the case with commercial contracts today: see generally Morgan, above n 4, 229.

[123] Hake, above n 70, 92.

Our sixteenth-century lawyer would also be unperturbed by other aspects of modern law. For example, much angst has been caused by contract law's 'interpretive turn', in which previously free-standing legal doctrines have been rationalised as aspects of contractual interpretation. Carter and Courtney, for example, write that it is 'easy to understand the reluctance to confront the suggestion that a material chunk of the common law can be explained simply in terms of what contracts "mean"'.[124] Our lawyer would probably ask how else the law could be explained. Issues that are dealt with today by doctrines like mistake, frustration or implication were simply mopped up by interpretation.[125] The interpretive turn is, in many ways, a return to contract law before contract law proper was invented in the nineteenth century.

Critics of the law today fret that interpretation has become unprecedentedly creative, and is newly encroaching on domains that properly belong to other doctrines. Davies, for example, has accused interpretation of 'expanding beyond its proper scope' into areas 'traditionally encompassed' by the doctrines of implication and rectification.[126] There is widespread fear that we are journeying into the unknown: Wee argues that judges have 'never' before had such a 'broad, unstructured and unfettered discretion' to construe contracts.[127] He predicts that 'insurmountable theoretical and pragmatic problems' will be the result,[128] as the meaning of contracts becomes 'dangerously unpredictable'[129] and established rules are undermined.[130] But interpretation has certainly gone as far and even further before. The reading of 'reversion' to mean 'possession' in *Throckmerton* was just as radical as a modern interpretation of 'landlord' to mean 'tenant',[131] and rendered rectification just as unnecessary.[132] And this excursion into the past is not merely of antiquarian interest. Rather, it allows us to peer into the future. These critiques of the modern law could be equally applied to interpretation in the sixteenth century. How, then, did this earlier experiment with liberal interpretation play out?

[124] JW Carter and W Courtney, 'Belize Telecom: A Reply to Professor McLauchlan' [2015] *Lloyd's Maritime and Commercial Law Quarterly* 245, 249.

[125] On implication, see, eg, *Reniger v Fogossa*, above n 90, 15; *Kidwelly v Brand* (1551) Plow 69, 70; *Ayer v Orme* (1563) Dyer 221b, 222b. On mistake and frustration, see generally D Ibbetson, 'Fault and Absolute Liability in Pre-Modern Contract Law' [1997] *Journal of Legal History* 1.

[126] PS Davies, 'Recent Developments in the Law of Implied Terms' [2010] *Lloyd's Maritime and Commercial Law Quarterly* 140, 145; PS Davies, 'Rectification versus Interpretation: The Nature and Scope of the Equitable Jurisdiction' (2016) 75 *CLJ* 62, 66.

[127] PCK Wee, 'Contractual Interpretation and Remoteness' [2010] *Lloyd's Maritime and Commercial Law Quarterly* 150, 176.

[128] ibid 175.

[129] ibid 166.

[130] ibid 176.

[131] *Littman v Aspen Oil (Broking)* [2005] EWCA Civ 1579, [2006] 2 P&CR 2.

[132] It was possible to have a deed rectified in Chancery during the sixteenth century: see, eg, 117 SS 260, [220] and [221]. However, rectification cases were very rare. In *Goodfellow v Morris and Others* (1618), precedents had to be shown to prove the existence of the jurisdiction: J Ritchie, *Reports of Cases Decided by Francis Bacon in the High Court of Chancery, 1617–1621* (London, Sweet & Maxwell, 1932) 133. I am grateful to Astron Douglas for this point.

V. THE SEVENTEENTH CENTURY AND BEYOND

First, it is clear that similar concerns were creeping in throughout the sixteenth century. Although they had not yet filtered through to the courts, complaints were beginning to appear in the literature of the time. Thomas Wilson castigated lawyers in his book on rhetoric, griping that

> rather than fail, they will make doubts oftentimes where no doubt should be at all. 'Is his lease long enough,' quod one? 'Yea sir, it is very long,' said a poor husbandman. 'Then,' quod he, 'let me alone with it; I will find a hole in it, I warrant thee.'[133]

Thomas Elyot lamented that it was impossible to 'devise so sufficient an instrument, to bynde a man to his promyse or covenaunt, but that there shall be some thinge therein espied to brynge it in argument'.[134] Even Hake raised the argument that it might be 'daungerous' to allow judges too much discretion in interpreting, although he was quick to dismiss it.[135]

By the beginning of the seventeenth century, however, judges were beginning to express similar anxieties. These were part of a wider phase of uncertainty about the law: the intellectual blossoming of Renaissance scholarship and the recent proliferation of printed texts had left the legal profession floundering in a mass of new materials.[136] Furthermore, litigation rates were rocketing to unprecedented levels, leading to accusations that the law was fomenting dispute and undermining social order.[137] Lawyers were starting to point the finger at interpretation as a force behind both of these developments.

Edward Coke, for example, argued that the courts were spending too much time trying to save badly drafted contracts. Uncertainty in the law, he explained, was not caused by 'any of the rules of the common law', but by 'conveyances and instruments made by men unlearned',[138] which forced judges to 'so often and so much perplex their heads, to make attonement and peace by construction of law between insensible and disagreeing words, sentences, and provisoes'.[139] New and increasingly complex forms of drafting led to the 'miserable slavery' of legal uncertainty, since nobody could determine their meaning.[140] Coke also criticised the parties in interpretation cases, whom he saw as 'eagle-eyed' predators, exploiting the law to raise questions about perfectly straightforward documents.[141] Their 'strained' and

[133] T Wilson, *The Art of Rhetoric (1560)*, PE Medine ed (University Park, Pennsylvania State University Press, 1994) 130.

[134] T Elyot, *The Boke Named the Governour* (London, Thomas Berthelet, 1531) 195v.

[135] Hake, above n 70, 25.

[136] DC Smith, *Sir Edward Coke and the Reformation of the Laws: Religion, Politics and Jurisprudence, 1578–1616* (Cambridge, Cambridge University Press, 2014) 19, 144.

[137] CW Brooks, *Pettyfoggers and Vipers of the Commonwealth: The 'Lower Branch' of the Legal Profession in Early Modern England* (Cambridge, Cambridge University Press, 1986) 133. The number of cases brought at common law had increased from around 5000 in 1560 to over 23,000 in 1606: ibid 51.

[138] 2 Co Rep ix.

[139] ibid x.

[140] *Sir Anthony Mildmay's Case* (1605) 6 Co Rep 40a, 42a: 'misera est servitus, ubi jus est vagum'.

[141] 10 Co Rep xiv.

opportunistic constructions undermined conveyances, to 'the disherison of the subject, and against the true reason and ancient rule of the law'.[142]

In response to these concerns, the courts' approach to interpretation was evolving. The words the parties had chosen to use were associated ever more closely with their intentions: judges were increasingly likely to ask what 'the intent and the words import',[143] and slid between references to the meaning of the parties and the meaning of the document.[144] They also began to present interpretation as a logical system of principles and maxims, rather than an amorphous discretion. The arguments in *Shelley's Case*, for example, focused primarily on establishing the intentions of Edward Shelley, but the court's decision was reported as a formal rule of law.[145] Judges resorted to authority to bolster principles, like the *contra proferentem* rule, that had previously been taken for granted,[146] or to support their interpretation of a particular word. In *Edward Altham's Case*, for example, a dozen cases were cited to help define the word 'right',[147] whereas, 35 years earlier, Plowden had simply plucked his definition from 'Reason … the Key which pierces and opens the Sense of obscure Words'.[148] While intentions remained central to interpretation, the courts attempted to play this down, instead emphasising the words of the document, the primacy of legal rules and the reliability of precedent.

Judges were also keen to stress that the parties' intentions could not ride roughshod over existing legal rules. Typically, they now pronounced that 'the law will not make an exposition against the express words and intent of the parties, when it may stand with the rule of law': a striking change of emphasis.[149] In *The Lord Cromwel's Case*, for example, it was held that an understanding of a contract based on reason must bow to established rules. 'There should be no departure from common usage,' the court maintained, 'and those things which have had a certain interpretation should be changed least.'[150] Coke approvingly quoted the philosopher Theophrastus: 'he who seeks reason in everything, subverts reason'.[151] Providing certainty for the parties was a growing preoccupation of the courts, and was again beginning to displace their dedication to finding a reasonable result.

However, the courts were by no means plunging headlong into literalism. Instead, they were trying to steer a middle course. Thus, while Coke rejected a law of interpretation that focused too much on reason, he also argued that a 'nice and captious pretence of certainty, confounds true and legal certainty, and it is a bad exposition

[142] *Roger Earl of Rutland's Case* (1608) 8 Co Rep 55a, 56b.

[143] *Englefields Case* (1590) Moore 303, 336: 'l'entent & les p[ar]ols emporto[n]t'.

[144] *Mildmay's Case* (1584) 1 Co Rep 175a, 177a.

[145] *Shelley's Case* (1581) 1 Co Rep 93b. See DA Smith, 'Was There a Rule in Shelley's Case?' (2009) 30 *Journal of Legal History* 53, 69; AWB Simpson, *Leading Cases in the Common Law* (Oxford, Oxford University Press, 1995) 34.

[146] *Humfrey Lofield's Case* (1612) 10 Co Rep 106a, 106b.

[147] *Edward Altham's Case* (1610) 8 Co Rep 150b, 151b.

[148] *Nichols v Nichols* (1575) Plow 477, 488.

[149] *Butt's Case* (1600) 7 Co Rep 23a, 24a. The rules in question were usually rules of property law, such as the rule against perpetuities.

[150] *The Lord Cromwel's Case* (1601) 2 Co Rep 69b, 74a: 'non est recedendum a communi observantia, & minimè mutanda sunt quae certam interpretationem habuerunt'. See also Justinian's *Digest*, D.1.3.23.

[151] ibid 75a: 'qui rationem in omnibus quaerunt, rationem subvertunt'.

that corrupts and confounds the text'.[152] He was well aware that 'a literal and strict construction' could thwart the parties' intentions,[153] and argued that documents 'should be liberally and beneficially expounded' to quash opportunistic quibbling.[154] The courts strove to find a balance between unrealistic strict construction and a broad-brush approach that failed to provide certainty.

Attitudes to contractual interpretation, then, were gradually shifting: unsettled by the uncertainties of liberal construction, the courts tacked towards a more predictable approach. While mid-century lawyers like Plowden and Hake had been supremely confident in the powers of interpretation, the next generation were more diffident. Their views of legal interpretation became more nuanced, and perhaps more realistic.

VI. CONCLUSION

Revolutions in contractual interpretation are not a phenomenon new to English law. Arguably the greatest innovation came in the mid-sixteenth century, when the courts first began to engage in interpretation as a self-conscious and systematic activity. It does a disservice to the common law to ignore this fascinating period, or indeed to assume that all lawyers before the mid-twentieth century suspended their intellectual faculties when presented with a contract to construe. In fact, examining earlier approaches to this perennial issue can help to provide a new perspective on the law of our own time.

On this view, it seems clear that recent changes to contractual interpretation follow a pattern that is well established in the history of the common law. The development of contractual interpretation has not been a straightforward progress; rather, it has oscillated between more or less liberal and literal approaches for centuries. Some of these shifts have been prompted by social and cultural changes: new technology, perhaps, or a more sophisticated understanding of language. They may also form part of a wider legal trend, as lawyers react to the perceived shortcomings of the past. Indeed, lawyers' perceptions that their law is causing problems seem to have been much more influential than any complaints by laymen.

As a result, we should not be surprised if contractual interpretation continues to evolve: *ICS* was not the end of history. Indeed, adverse commentary on Lord Hoffmann's approach is already having its effect, as the courts stress the importance of the parties' words[155] and established legal rules[156] in the context of construction. Lawyers will, undoubtedly, continue to argue over the best approach to interpretation. However, it is no defence of any theory to hearken wistfully back to the 'traditional approach' of English law. There is no such thing. The evolution of the common law of interpretation has been much more complex, and more interesting, than that.

[152] *Roger Earl of Rutland's Case*, above n 143, 56b: 'et maledicta expositio est quae corrumpit et confundit textum'.

[153] ibid.

[154] *Twyne's Case* (1601) 3 Co Rep 80b, 82a.

[155] *Rainy Sky SA v Kookmin Bank* [2011] UKSC 50, [2011] 1 WLR 2900, 2908.

[156] *Marks and Spencer plc v BNP Paribas Services Trust Co (Jersey) Ltd* [2015] UKSC 72, [2016] AC 742, 757.

9

Revolutions and Counterrevolutions in Equitable Estoppel

ANDREW ROBERTSON

I. INTRODUCTION

THE 'REVOLUTIONS' OF equitable estoppel, like those of other legal and equitable doctrines, have primarily taken the form of circular movements rather than upheavals.[1] Some of the most far-reaching decisions, such as *Jorden v Money*[2] and *Waltons Stores (Interstate) Ltd v Maher*,[3] might be characterised as revolutionary in the sense that they overthrew an existing order and ushered in a new regime. But even those decisions were grounded in the past, justified by reference to precedent and purported to do no more than interpret the existing law. What is clearly discernible in this field of obligation, however, is a tendency for the law to cycle through expansionary and contractionary movements. Equitable estoppel, particularly in its application to assumptions about future conduct, seems to wax and wane more than other doctrines. For that reason, the doctrine appears to occupy a relatively uneasy and insecure place on the edge of the law of obligations.

The common thread that unites equitable estoppel is the following principle. Where (i) one person (the inducing party) plays a role in the adoption by another person (the relying party) of an assumption of fact, existing legal rights, or future conduct; (ii) in the circumstances, the inducing party ought reasonably to expect that the relying party might act in reliance on the assumption in such a way that he or she will suffer detriment if the inducing party behaves inconsistently with that assumption; and (iii) the relying party does act on the assumption in such a way, then it is unconscionable for the inducing party to act inconsistently with the assumption, at least without taking steps to ensure that the relying party suffers no detriment as a result of the action he or she took in reliance on the assumption.

The underlying justification for the principle is that a person who induces an assumption of fact, legal rights or future conduct, in circumstances where he or she should reasonably expect reliance by another, creates a risk of a distinctive kind of

[1] 'Revolution' (*Oxford English Dictionary Online*, Oxford University Press, March 2016), <www.oed.com>.
[2] (1854) 5 HLC 185, 10 ER 868.
[3] (1988) 164 CLR 387.

harm. The relying party stands to suffer harm if he or she acts or refrains from acting in reliance on the assumption, and the inducing party then engages in inconsistent behaviour. Once the relying party acts on the assumption, the risk of this kind of harm is entirely within the control of the inducing party. Having created a risk of reasonably foreseeable harm that is within his or her control, good conscience requires the inducing party either to prevent that harm by behaving consistently or to answer for the harm if he or she behaves inconsistently with the assumption.

The most controversial aspect of that principle is its capacity to generate liability from reliance on an assumption about the inducing party's future conduct. It is this application of equitable estoppel that has seen the most expansion and contraction, and it is this application of the doctrine that constitutes the focus of this chapter. Future conduct is not only the most controversial application of reliance-based liability, but is also potentially the most expansive. While people commonly rely on assumptions of fact induced by others, any harm resulting from such reliance is usually caused by the fact being untrue rather than by the inducing party behaving inconsistently with it. Reliance on assumptions as to existing legal rights is more common, particularly in the property context, and there is some scope for an inducing party to cause harm by asserting inconsistent rights. But there is vastly greater scope for harm to result from reliance on an assumption as to the inducing party's future conduct. The reason for this is that, while all estoppels by conduct arise as a result of one person trusting another, the degree of trust is higher when the assumption relates to the way in which another person will behave in the future. Where an inducing party leads a relying party to believe that the inducing party will, at some point in the future, act in a way that is beneficial to the relying party, the reliability of that assumption is almost entirely in the hands of the inducing party.

The fact that the relying party's fate lies in the hands of the inducing party provides a justification for imposing liability on the inducing party, but also provides a reason for denying liability. This application of equitable estoppel may be controversial because, unlike the situation with assumptions as to facts and existing rights, the relying party knows at the time of relying on an assumption as to future conduct that his or her fate is dependent on the inducing party behaving consistently with the assumption. The relying party knows that his or her fate is dependent on the inducing party conferring the benefit that the relying party has been led to assume will be forthcoming (eg property rights, contractual rights, money or commercial benefits) or refraining from imposing the disbenefit that the relying party has been led to assume will not be imposed (eg eviction from land, enforcing a contract or taking action to recover a debt). Action in reliance on an assumption about future conduct therefore involves a higher degree of trust than action on assumptions about facts and rights. The cases show, however, that it is not uncommon for people to adopt and act upon assumptions that others will behave in certain beneficial ways in the future. Whether responsibility for any resulting harm should, as a general matter of interpersonal responsibility, be attributed to the relying party's misplaced trust or the inducing party's inconsistent behaviour is a finely balanced question on which opinions clearly differ.

In English law, an assumption relating to the future conduct of the inducing party can give rise to a promissory estoppel (if it is an assumption that the inducing party will not exercise rights which the inducing party has against the relying party)[4] or a proprietary estoppel (if it is an assumption that the inducing party will create or transfer a property interest to the relying party at some point in the future).[5] In Australia, equitable estoppels have also been held to arise from assumptions that the inducing party will at some future point confer non-proprietary rights on the relying party. The best-known example of this is *Waltons Stores (Interstate) Ltd v Maher*, where a prospective tenant led the prospective landlord to believe that the prospective landlord would be given contractual rights by way of a lease.[6] But equitable estoppels have also been held to arise from assumptions that the inducing party will in the future confer other non-proprietary benefits on the relying party, including the payment of money, the provision of financial support and other commercial benefits.[7] In the USA, it is well accepted that a promissory estoppel might arise from a promise relating to future conduct that does not involve the conferral of property or other legal rights.[8] Promissory estoppel can arise from a promise to confer any benefit. It is noteworthy that the first illustration to section 90 of the Second Restatement of Contracts involves reliance (the expenditure of time and effort) on a promise that the inducing party will pay money to the relying party at a certain point in the future.[9]

II. EARLY EXPANSIONISM: MAKING REPRESENTATIONS GOOD

The idea that liability can arise from reliance on an assumption as to the future behaviour of the inducing party has a respectably long history in English law. It is reflected in the equitable doctrine, widely applied from the seventeenth to the

[4] *MWB Business Exchange Centres Ltd v Rock Advertising Ltd* [2016] EWCA Civ 553, [2016] 3 WLR 1519, [61] (Kitchin LJ, with whom McCombe LJ agreed). The best examples of the application of the principle are Australian cases such as *Je Maintiendrai Pty Ltd v Quaglia* (1980) 26 SASR 101 (landlord agreed to accept reduced rent) and *Anaconda Nickel Ltd v Edensor Nominees Pty Ltd* [2004] VSCA 167, (2004) 50 ACSR 679 (buyer of shares promised not to rely on due diligence clause which operated as a contingent condition).

[5] *Thorner v Major* [2009] UKHL 18, [2009] 1 WLR 776.

[6] Above n 3.

[7] eg *W v G* (1996) 20 Fam LR 49 and *Gray v National Crime Authority* [2003] NSWSC 111 (financial support); *ACN 074 971 109 Pty Ltd (as Trustee for the Argot Unit Trust) v The National Mutual Life Association of Australasia Ltd* [2008] VSCA 247, (2008) 21 VR 351 (other commercial benefits).

[8] *Restatement of Contracts (2d)* (American Law Institute, 1981) s 90:

> (1) A promise which the promisor should reasonably expect to induce action or forbearance on the part of the promisee or a third person and which does induce such action or forbearance is binding if injustice can be avoided only by enforcement of the promise. The remedy granted for breach may be limited as justice requires.

[9] The promisor, knowing the promisee is going to college, promises to pay him a sum of money on completion of his course. In reliance on that promise, the promisee borrows and spends money on college expenses. On the facts as stated, it is not clear that the promisee has altered his position to his detriment in reliance on the promise, though that could be made clear with only a minor addition to the illustration.

nineteenth century, by which relied-upon representations were required to be made good.[10] That doctrine operated in relation to assumptions of fact, assumptions as to existing rights, assumptions as to future rights and assumptions as to the future conduct of the inducing party. Indeed, it is a feature of this line of cases that distinctions were not drawn between assumptions of fact, existing rights and future conduct. Reliance on assumptions of fact or existing rights did not simply prevent the inducing party from asserting inconsistent facts or rights, but in some cases bound the inducing party to behave in a particular way in the future. In the seventeenth century case of *Hunsden v Cheyney*, for example, the defendant was present at the marriage treaty of her son when he declared that a particular term was to come to him on the defendant's death.[11] Though the defendant was ignorant of the fact that she had more than an estate for life, she was compelled by the Lords Commissioners, on a bill brought by her grandson, to make good the representation by settling the reversion of the term on the issue of the marriage after her death. In the nineteenth century case of *Piggott v Stratton*, the defendant represented to the plaintiff's predecessor in title that the defendant's lease did not allow him to build houses closer than 30 feet apart.[12] That representation was true when it was made, but the defendant's lease was later surrendered and a new lease was granted which did not impose such a restriction on the defendant. The plaintiff was held to be entitled to an injunction on the basis that the defendant had led the plaintiff's predecessor in title to believe that 'during the currency of the lease he, Harbour [the plaintiff's predecessor in title], would be safe from the apprehended obstruction'.[13]

Most of the cases in which representations were required to be made good involved marriage settlements and other property arrangements in contemplation of marriage, where the marriages took place on the assumption that the settlements would be made. The best-known example is *Hammersley v De Biel*.[14] In that case, Mr Thomson led his prospective son-in-law (Baron De Biel) to believe that Mr Thomson would in his will settle the sum of £10,000 on his daughter and her future children. In reliance on that assumption, Baron de Biel settled a jointure

[10] See, eg, LA Sheridan, 'Equitable Estoppel Today' (1952) 15 *MLR* 325; D Jackson, 'Estoppel as a Sword (Part 1)' (1965) 81 *LQR* 84; IW Duncanson, 'Equity and Obligations' (1976) 39 MLR 268; PS Atiyah, *The Rise and Fall of Freedom of Contract* (Oxford, Oxford University Press, 1979) ch 15; F Dawson, 'Making Representations Good' (1982) 1 *Canterbury Law Review* 329; M Lunney, '*Jorden v Money*—A Time for Reappraisal' (1994) 68 *Australian Law Journal* 559; J Ngugi, 'Promissory Estoppel: The Life History of an Ideal Legal Transplant' (2007) 41 *University of Richmond Law Review* 425.

[11] (1690) 2 Vern 150, 23 ER 703.

[12] (1859) 1 De G F & J 33, 45 ER 271.

[13] ibid 50, 277. *Jorden v Money*, above n 2, was distinguished (at (1859) 1 De G F & J 33, 51–52, 45 ER 271, 278) on the basis that it stood only for the principle that 'a mere expression of intention, although acted upon, is no ground for equitable interference', whereas here the defendant 'absolutely asserted that there was no power to do the act, and that the act could not be done during the currency of the lease. There was no room left for change of intention. It would be childish to suppose that he meant to be understood to say that, although he then had no power to do the act, he might afterwards acquire the power by surrendering the lease. He clearly gave Harbour to understand that he would have no power to disturb the sea view during the currency of the lease, and that during the currency of the lease the sea view could not be disturbed.'

[14] (1845) 12 Cl & F 45, 8 ER 1312.

on Miss Thomson and married her. When Mr Thomson died without making any such provision, his estate was held liable to pay the sum. A decree to that effect was made by the Master of the Rolls, and was upheld on appeal by the Lord Chancellor and subsequently by the House of Lords. In a well-known passage quoted by Lord Campbell, Lord Cottenham LC said in his judgment on the intermediate appeal:

> A representation made by one party for the purpose of inducing the conduct of the other party, and acted upon by him, will in general be sufficient to entitle him to the assistance of this Court for the purpose of realizing such representation. Of this, *Hodgson v Hutchenson* (5 Vin Abr 522), *Cookes v Mascall* (2 Vern 200), and *Wankford v Fotherley* (2 Vern 322), which last case was affirmed by the House of Lords, afford strong instances.

In the seventeenth-century case of *Wankford v Fotherley*, the prospective father-in-law said he would give his daughter a marriage portion of £3000, but countermanded his proposal when the couple were ready to go to church.[15] The Lord Keeper decreed that it should be paid and that decision was upheld by the House of Lords. An interesting aspect of the case is that the detrimental reliance did not consist of marrying, because the father-in-law's proposal was countermanded before the marriage took place. The Lord Keeper disregarded the countermand, however, because by then 'the young people's affections were engaged'.[16] The case therefore provides an early example of detrimental reliance of a genus that is not uncommon in the modern proprietary estoppel cases, taking the form of 'life-changing decisions with irreversible consequences of a profoundly personal nature'.[17]

The making good representations cases were not, however, confined to marriage settlements. *Hobbs v Norton* provides an early example of the application of the doctrine to a situation involving an assumption as to the future conduct of the inducing party that did not involve a marriage settlement, and action in reliance other than marriage.[18] In that case, a testator purported to create, in favour of his younger son, an annuity charged on land that passed under the testator's will to his older son. Some 20 years after the father had died, the younger son sought to sell the annuity. The prospective purchaser asked the defendant—the older son who had inherited the land—whether his younger brother had good title and his father had been seized in fee at the time the settlement was made. The defendant indicated that there was some doubt about the validity of the annuity, but encouraged the plaintiff to proceed with the purchase on the basis that he had paid the annuity for 20 years and would continue to do so. The following facts were reported:

> Sir George Norton told him, he believed his brother had a good title to it, and that he had paid him this annuity these twenty years, but withal told him, that he heard there was a settlement made of his father's lands before the will; and that the said settlement was in Sir Timothy Baldwin's hands, and that he had never seen it, and therefore could not tell him what the contents of it were, but *encouraged him to proceed in his purchase; telling him, he had not only paid his brother his annuity to that time, but had paid to his sisters £3000*

[15] (1694) 2 Freem 201, 22 ER 1159.
[16] ibid 201, 1160.
[17] *Donis v Donis* [2007] VSCA 89, (2007) 19 VR 577, [34] (Nettle JA).
[18] (1682) 1 Vern 136, 23 ER 370.

under the same will. Afterwards Sir George Norton gets this settlement into his hands, and would avoid this annuity, the lands being thereby entailed.[19]

The report records that the Lord Keeper 'decreed the payment of the annuity, purely on the encouragement Sir George gave Hobbs to proceed in his purchase'.[20] Although the defendant made a representation of fact, that representation was accompanied by an expression of doubt as to whether it was true, and by encouragement to proceed with the purchase on the basis that the defendant had been making payments under the will for the last 20 years and would continue to do so. What is significant about the case is that it involves an obligation arising from reliance on an assumption that the inducing party would make certain payments in the future, regardless of the validity of the instrument under which the payments were to be made. The inducing party made no promise in the sense of any commitment to make the payments, but clearly induced the assumption that the payments would be made, and did so with the apparent intention of inducing reliance.

III. THE NINETEENTH-CENTURY CONTRACTION

The equitable jurisdiction to order the making good of representations that had been relied upon was effectively brought to an end by two decisions of the House of Lords handed down five months apart in 1854: *Maunsell v Hedges*[21] and *Jorden v Money*.[22] The appellants in *Maunsell v Hedges* married on the faith of an assurance given to the groom by his uncle that 'my county of Tipperary estate will come to you at my death, unless some unforeseen occurrence should take place'.[23] *Hammersley v De Biel* was rightly distinguished: the uncle's assurance was no more than a qualified statement of intention which could not reasonably be relied upon by the appellants, nor reasonably be expected by the uncle to be relied upon. Lord Cranworth LC, however, undermined the entire making good representations line of cases by insisting that the basis of obligation in *Hammersley v De Biel* was, and could only be, contract:

> Where a man engages to do a particular thing, he must do it; that is a contract; but where there are no direct words of contract, the question must be, what has he done? He has made a contract, or he has not; in the former case he must fulfil his contract; in the latter there is nothing that he is bound to fulfil.[24]

[19] ibid 136, 370 (emphasis added).
[20] ibid 137, 370.
[21] (1854) 4 HLC 1039, 10 ER 769.
[22] Above n 2.
[23] The relevant passage of the letter was: 'My sentiments respecting you continue unalterable; however I shall never settle part of my property out of my power while I exist; my will has been made for some time, and I am confident that I shall never alter it to your disadvantage. I have mentioned before, and I again repeat, that my county of Tipperary estate will come to you at my death, unless some unforeseen occurrence should take place. I have never settled anything on any of my nephews, and I should give cause for jealousy if I was to deviate in this instance from a resolution I have long made.'
[24] Above n 21, 775. See further Lunney, above n 10, 569–70.

Lord St Leonards also characterised the obligation as contractual, but recognised that it was founded on induced reliance:

> I do not dispute the general principle, that what is called a representation, which is made as an inducement for another to act upon it, and is followed by his acting upon it, will, especially in such a case as marriage, be deemed to be a contract.[25]

In *Jorden v Money*, a majority of the House of Lords denied that any liability could arise from reliance on an assumption relating to the future conduct of the inducing party. The defendant was a close family friend of the plaintiff and was said to have 'treated him as a mother would treat her child'.[26] The defendant inherited from her brother a debt, secured by a bond and a warrant of attorney, which the plaintiff had incurred some years before as a result of a speculative investment venture he had entered into as a young man. Because the plaintiff's father had been very generous to the defendant, because of the defendant's great affection for the plaintiff and because of her sympathy for the plaintiff in relation to the circumstances in which the debt was contracted, the defendant promised on numerous occasions that she would not enforce the debt. The defendant repeated the promise in the knowledge that the plaintiff intended to marry on the faith of it, which he duly did. The defendant herself married late in life, and she and her husband then sought to enforce the debt. The plaintiff sought relief in Chancery, which was granted by the Master of the Rolls, affirmed by an evenly divided Court of Appeal in Chancery and overturned by a divided House of Lords.[27]

In the House of Lords, Lord Cranworth observed that the plaintiff's case was 'put entirely on the ground of representation' and not contract, and that it could not have been put in contract because it was not in writing and signed.[28] Lord Cranworth held that the principle of estoppel by representation had no application because that doctrine does not apply to a case where the representation is not a representation of fact, but a statement of something which the party intends or does not intend to do.[29] Lord Brougham concerned himself only with authorities on representations of fact, concluding that the principle applied in those cases could have no application in this case, where the inducing party asked only to be trusted not to enforce the bond:[30]

> In my opinion, there was a misrepresentation by Louisa Marnell of an intention as to her will, and a promise was made by her; but of misrepresentation of fact there was none. She simply stated what was her intention; she did not misrepresent her intention; and I have no

[25] ibid 1059–60, 777.

[26] Above n 2, 889.

[27] Lunney, above n 10, 560 has noted that, since Lord Cranworth was one of the two judges who heard the case in the Court of Appeal in Chancery, this meant that three of the judges who heard the case thought the plaintiff should succeed (Sir John Romilly MR at first instance, Knight-Bruce LJ in the Court of Appeal in Chancery and Lord St Leonards in the House of Lords), whereas only two (Lord Cranworth LC and Lord Brougham) held the view that prevailed.

[28] ibid 215, 882.

[29] ibid 214–15, 882. Lord Cranworth LC was also concerned (ibid 221–22, 884) that the defendant's promise was intended to be binding in honour only, as evidenced by the fact that the defendant retained the bond and refused to give it up or destroy it.

[30] ibid 228–29, 887.

> manner of doubt that, at the time she made that statement, she had the intention which it is stated she professed, of never putting William Bailey Money in trouble, by proceeding upon the bond.[31]

In his dissenting speech, Lord St Leonards accepted the existence of a principle of equity to the effect that a person who has said that he or she will not enforce a security cannot

> enforce that right after an act has been done upon the faith of that declaration; an act which cannot be undone as to the party whom he has induced so to act. The whole current of authorities is the other way.[32]

Lord St Leonards took the evidence to establish that, in return for the defendant's undertaking not to pursue the debt, the plaintiff's father had undertaken not to pursue certain rights against the defendant in relation to a property at Midnapore. The father's undertaking was not essential to the plaintiff's case, however, because the plaintiff's reliance on the promise was sufficient to render it enforceable:

> we may assume that there was an undertaking by the one party not to pursue the right as against Midnapore, which was met by an undertaking by the other not to pursue the right upon the bond. That is a very important circumstance, but it is not a necessary circumstance, for the marriage of William was itself a sufficient consideration. If, without having a shilling of interest in Midnapore, if Midnapore had never existed, she had said, previous to the marriage, intending the parties to believe her, and to act upon that belief, 'I will never enforce this bond,' I apprehend the law to be that she never could enforce it afterwards.[33]

Lord St Leonards's reference to a 'sufficient consideration' must be understood in light of his earlier explanation that in his view the facts 'raise an equity which is not to be resisted, according to the rules of equity, as I understand them'.[34] He observed in relation to the agreement between the plaintiff's father and the defendant that:

> It is now argued that that, if anything, was a contract; but I will not so treat it, and I am not arguing that your Lordships are driven to treat it as a contract in the proper sense of the word. It is, however, a representation by one party of an intention to do an act which he refrains from doing in consideration of another party giving up a right to something else, and refraining from doing another act; and I will show your Lordships that that is perfectly good in law, and can be enforced without any legal contract at all.[35]

The majority of the House of Lords thus denied the existence of the equitable jurisdiction to make good an assumption as to the future conduct of the inducing party which has been relied upon. Their Lordships did so in spite of a wealth of authority to the contrary stretching back over the preceding two centuries. Neither Lord Cranworth nor Lord Brougham cited any of the cases in which the making good representations doctrine had been applied to assumptions as to future conduct, while only *Cookes v Mascall*[36] was cited by Lord St Leonards.[37] Taken in

[31] ibid 226–27, 886.
[32] ibid 249, 895.
[33] ibid 243, 893. The applicable principle is discussed further at 249–56, 895–98.
[34] ibid 239, 891.
[35] ibid 239–40, 891.
[36] (1690) 2 Vern 200, 23 ER 730.
[37] On the authorities that were cited and discussed, see Lunney, above n 10, 564–69.

isolation, the majority speeches in *Jorden v Money* may be understood simply to have been made *per incuriam*. Lord Cranworth's claim that 'there is nothing within the meaning of the authorities or of principles to make this a representation by which Mr and Mrs Jorden are to be bound' was plainly incorrect.[38] On the other hand, Lord Cranworth had rationalised and explained away *Hammersley v De Biel* only five months earlier in *Maunsell v Hedges*, and key authorities such as *Wankford v Fotherley* and *Cookes v Mascall* were cited in *Hammersley v De Biel*. The move to shut down reliance-based liability arising from induced assumptions about future conduct must therefore have been deliberate. Professor Atiyah has argued that the driving force behind *Jorden v Money* was a concern that the recognition of such non-contractual reliance-based liability would undermine the Statute of Frauds and effectively confine it to executory contracts.[39] A deeper explanation, supported by the work of Atiyah and others, is that the decision reflected the political and economic ethos of the Victorian age, which favoured individualism and self-reliance, and was therefore hostile to the notion of liability arising from reliance on non-bargain promises.[40] Those who relied on informal assurances made by others 'might have been deemed morally unworthy of recompense due to their foolishness'.[41]

IV. RE-EXPANSION: PROPRIETARY AND PROMISSORY ESTOPPEL

A. Proprietary Estoppel

Since both the decision and the reasoning in *Jorden v Money* were inconsistent with long-standing authority, and given the failure of the judges in the majority to deal with the relevant authorities, it is not surprising that the decision was itself undermined by the continued imposition of liability arising from reliance on assumptions as to future conduct.[42] *Dillwyn v Llewelyn* was an important case in the immediate aftermath of *Jorden v Money* in which reliance on an assumption relating to future conduct was found to create a binding obligation.[43] In that case, the plaintiff's father offered him a farm so that he might build a house on it and live near his father. On the plaintiff's acceptance of the offer, his father signed a memorandum 'presenting' the farm to him. The son's subsequent expenditure in reliance on the statement 'supplied a valuable consideration originally wanting, the memorandum signed by the father and son must be thenceforth regarded *as an agreement* for the soil extending to the fee-simple of the land'.[44] Accordingly, '*the intention* to give the fee

[38] Above n 2, 885.

[39] PS Atiyah, *Essays on Contract* (Oxford, Clarendon, 1986) 233–38.

[40] The extensive literature on this topic, which includes PS Atiyah, *The Rise and Fall of Freedom of Contract* (Oxford, Clarendon, 1979), is surveyed in A Robertson, 'Situating Equitable Estoppel within the Law of Obligations' (1997) 19 *Sydney Law Review* 32, 33–37.

[41] MB Metzger and MJ Philips, 'The Emergence of Promissory Estoppel as an Independent Theory of Recovery' (1983) 35 *Rutgers Law Review* 472, 502.

[42] See Lunney, above n 10, 570–73.

[43] (1862) 4 De G F & J 517, 45 ER 1285.

[44] ibid 522, 1287 (emphasis added).

simple must be performed'.[45] Just like Lord St Leonards in *Jorden v Money*,[46] Lord Westbury LC was discussing the principles on which a court of equity proceeds, and his reference to valuable consideration must have meant no more than an act which creates a binding obligation.[47]

A more explicit challenge to *Jorden v Money* was the decision of Sir John Stuart VC in *Loffus v Maw*.[48] The plaintiff cared for her infirm uncle and performed housekeeping services for him in reliance on the uncle's representation that he would leave her the rents and profits of certain houses upon his death. Sir John Stuart VC decreed that trusts which had been declared and revoked by codicil should be performed. The Vice Chancellor held that neither the Statute of Frauds nor the decision in *Jorden v Money* stood in the way of the plaintiff's claim, which was founded on the principle applied in *Hammersley v De Biel*:

> As to the reliance which the Defendant's counsel placed on the decision of the House of Lords in the case of *Jorden v Money*, although the decision in that case is no doubt binding, it cannot be considered as a reversal of the decision of the House of Lords in *Hammersley v De Biel*; and the proposition attributed to Lord Cranworth in the printed report, that a statement or representation of what a person intends or does not intend is not sufficient, seems irreconcilable with the decision of the House of Lords in *Hammersley v De Biel*, and with the law as laid down by all Judges of the highest authority. It is remarkable that the case of *Hammersley v De Biel* was not referred to by any of the counsel or Law Lords in the case of *Jorden v Money*.[49]

Although the principle applied in *Loffus v Maw* went into abeyance for some decades, the case would undoubtedly be decided the same way today. Claims following that fact pattern are now commonplace, with English and Australian courts routinely granting remedies to claimants in similar situations by way of compensation or specific relief under the banner of proprietary estoppel.[50] In *Jennings v Rice*, for example, the claimant worked unremunerated for several years providing personal care for an elderly woman in failing health, on the faith of assurances that he would receive her house and furniture on her death. He was held to be entitled to an award of compensation on the basis of proprietary estoppel. The major issue in such cases is not the availability of equitable relief in these circumstances, but the nature and extent of such relief.[51] The correctness of the principle applied in these cases was confirmed by the House of Lords in *Thorner v Major*, which will be discussed below.[52]

[45] ibid 523, 1287 (emphasis added).

[46] See above, text accompanying above nn 33–35.

[47] In a similar vein, in *Jorden v Money*, Lord Cranworth explained the distinction between reliance on a statement of fact and reliance on a statement as to what a party 'intends or does not intend to do' on the basis that '[i]n the former case it is a contract, in the latter it is not': above n 2, 882.

[48] (1862) 3 Giff 592, 66 ER 544.

[49] ibid 604, 549.

[50] See the cases cited by B McFarlane, *The Law of Proprietary Estoppel* (Oxford, OUP, 2014) 1.16.

[51] See A Robertson, 'The Reliance Basis of Proprietary Estoppel Remedies' (2008) 72 *The Conveyancer and Property Lawyer* 295.

[52] Above n 5.

B. Promissory Estoppel

Jorden v Money was also undermined in its immediate aftermath by the development of promissory estoppel. In *Hughes v Metropolitan Railway Co*, the House of Lords held that a person who has led another to believe that legal rights will not be enforced, or will be kept in suspense or held in abeyance, will not be allowed to enforce those rights 'where it would be inequitable having regard to the dealings which have thus taken place between the parties'.[53] That principle remains good law in England, with the clarification that what renders it inequitable for the inducing party to enforce his or her rights is that the relying party has altered his or her position in reliance on the representation.[54] The principle cannot, in English law, be relied upon as an independent source of rights arising from reliance on an assumption that the inducing party will confer a benefit on the relying party.[55] In *MWB Business Exchange Centres v Rock Advertising*, Kitchen LJ stated the principle as follows:

> Drawing the threads to together, it seems to me that all of these cases are best understood as illustrations of the broad principle that if one party to a contract makes a promise to the other that his legal rights under the contract will not be enforced or will be suspended and the other party in some way relies on that promise, whether by altering his position or in any other way, then the party who might otherwise have enforced those rights will not be permitted to do so where it would be inequitable having regard to all of the circumstances.[56]

In Australian law, a further expansionary turn was taken in *Waltons Stores (Interstate) v Maher*,[57] where the principle of promissory or equitable estoppel was held to operate where one party leads or encourages another to believe that a contract will be made on terms which have been agreed, at least in circumstances where the inducing party's knowledge of the action being taken on the faith of the assumption by the relying party and the circumstances as a whole render it unconscionable to act inconsistently with the assumption. What was not clear from the judgments in *Waltons Stores v Maher* was whether this expanded principle could operate only where the inducing party leads the relying party to believe that the inducing party would confer enforceable legal rights on the relying party, or whether it could operate where the inducing party leads the relying party to believe that any benefit would be conferred. On the narrower view, the principle does not operate as an independent source of rights, but only operates as a basis for enforcing the legal rights which the relying party had been led to believe that he or she would be granted. On the broader view, the principle operates as an independent source of rights, providing the relying party with a cause of action to enforce the provision of the benefits or recover compensation for harm suffered as a result of action taken in reliance on the expectation of receiving them.

[53] ibid 448 (Lord Cairns LC).
[54] *BP Exploration (Libya) v Hunt (No 2)* [1979] 1 WLR 783, 782 (Goff J).
[55] *Combe v Combe* [1951] 2 KB 215 (CA).
[56] Above n 4, [61].
[57] Above n 3.

In some Australian cases, that broader interpretation of the principle has been adopted, and promissory or equitable estoppel has been allowed to operate as an independent source of rights. The broader principle has been applied in relation to assumptions that the inducing party would pay money to the relying party,[58] would provide financial support to the relying party[59] and would provide other commercial benefits to the relying party.[60] If this broader view is correct, then there is no real distinction between the operation of promissory and proprietary estoppel in Australian law. Rather, there is a unified and substantive doctrine of equitable estoppel, the scope of application of which is not limited to any particular types of fact situations.

V. CONTEMPORARY CONTRACTIONARY TURNS

In recent years, there have been attempts to limit the application of both proprietary estoppel and promissory estoppel to assumptions about future conduct. In *Cobbe v Yeoman's Row Management Ltd*, Lord Scott (with whom Lord Hoffmann, Lord Brown and Lord Mance agreed) sought to reinterpret and radically circumscribe the ambit of proprietary estoppel. Lord Scott held that an 'estoppel' could only operate as a bar to the assertion of a fact, or a mixture of fact and law, that stands in the way of a right claimed by the relying party.[61] An estoppel, Lord Scott suggested, is a proprietary estoppel if the right in question is a proprietary right. On this view, proprietary estoppel is not a substantive doctrine and could not operate as an independent cause of action where the inducing party has led the relying party to believe that the inducing party would in the future confer rights in relation to property on the relying party. If correct, this would have severely circumscribed the doctrine, and would have rendered incorrect decades of prominent decisions of the Court of Appeal.[62] In the same case, Lord Walker held that proprietary estoppel could not arise from an assumption that the inducing party would act in a particular way in the future, but only from an assumption that the inducing party would be bound to act in a particular way in the future.[63]

Neither of those restrictions was accepted by the House of Lords in *Thorner v Major*. In that case, the claimant worked for nearly 30 years without wages on his father's cousin's farm, on the faith of an assumption, induced by the cousin, that the claimant would inherit the farm on the cousin's death. When the cousin died intestate, the claimant was held to be entitled to the farm. The capacity of equitable

[58] *Lee Gleeson Pty Ltd v Sterling Estates Pty Ltd* (1991) 23 NSWLR 571; *Chanrich Properties Pty Ltd v Baulkham Hills Shire Council* [2001] NSWSC 229.
[59] *W v G*, above n 7; *Gray v National Crime Authority*, above n 7.
[60] *ACN 074 971 109 Pty Ltd (as Trustee for the Argot Unit Trust) v The National Mutual Life Association of Australasia Ltd*, above n 7; *Yarrabee Chicken Company Pty Ltd v Steggles Ltd* [2010] FCA 394 (a point not challenged on appeal: *Steggles Ltd v Yarrabee Chicken Company Pty* Ltd [2012] FCAFC 91).
[61] [2008] UKHL 55, [2008] 1 WLR 1752 [14].
[62] B McFarlane and A Robertson, 'The Death of Proprietary Estoppel' [2008] *Lloyd's Maritime and Commercial Law Quarterly* 449, 453–56.
[63] Above n 61, [63]–[71].

estoppel to operate where assumptions as to future conduct are relied upon was thus established beyond question. Proprietary estoppel provided an independent source of rights and a cause of action in those circumstances, and was not defeated by the fact that the relying party did not believe that the inducing party was legally bound to make the testamentary disposition in question. The High Court of Australia has also upheld proprietary estoppel claims arising from assumptions that the inducing party would, in the future, transfer a property interest to the relying party.[64]

In Australia, the contractionary turn has involved promissory, rather than proprietary, estoppel. In a series of cases, the New South Wales Court of Appeal has sought to bring the Australian law of promissory estoppel back into line with English law.[65] The New South Wales Court of Appeal has maintained that promissory and proprietary estoppel remain entirely separate principles, and that promissory estoppel is negative in substance and can only operate to prevent a person from enforcing a legal or equitable right. On this view, proprietary estoppel provides a cause of action, but promissory estoppel does not: the latter can only arise from a promise not to enforce a right. This understanding of promissory estoppel was first outlined by Ken Handley in his 2006 book *Estoppel by Conduct and Election*, and was then applied by him as an acting judge of the New South Wales Court of Appeal in *Saleh v Ramanous*.[66]

In *Saleh v Ramanous*, a buyer of land contracted with the seller on the faith of the seller's statement that the buyer would be released from the contract if he was unable to conclude a development joint venture agreement with the seller's brother, who was the owner of adjoining land. The buyer was unable to negotiate such an agreement and purported to terminate the contract. The primary judge held that the contract was unenforceable, and ordered repayment of the deposit by way of relief to give effect to a promissory estoppel. An appeal by the seller was dismissed, although the Court of Appeal justified the order for repayment of the deposit on a different basis. Handley AJA, with whom Giles JA and Sackville AJA agreed, held that promissory estoppel prevented the seller from enforcing the contract, but could only operate negatively and could not therefore ground an order for repayment of the deposit. Nevertheless, the court was able to order repayment of the deposit pursuant to an independent statutory power.[67] The restrictive nature of the principle applied by Handley AJA in that case was relevant to the decision, but was not essential to it because the appeal was dismissed. There is therefore scope for debate as to whether the restrictive principle formed part of the ratio. The principle has nevertheless been reiterated in subsequent decisions and now appears to be accepted as part

[64] *Giumelli v Giumelli* [1999] HCA 10, (1999) 196 CLR 101; *Sidhu v Van Dkye* [2014] HCA 19, (2014) 251 CLR 505.

[65] See A Robertson, 'Three Models of Promissory Estoppel' (2013) 7 *Journal of Equity* 226.

[66] [2010] NSWCA 274, (2010) 79 NSWLR 453 (Giles JA and Sackville AJA agreed with Handley AJA).

[67] Conveyancing Act 1919 (NSW), s 55(2A): 'In every case where the court refuses to grant specific performance of a contract, or in any proceedings for the return of a deposit, the court may, if it thinks fit, order the repayment of any deposit with or without interest thereon.'

of the law of New South Wales.[68] In the most recent discussion of the principle in the New South Wales Court of Appeal, Bathurst JA observed that:

> These decisions are to the effect that a promissory estoppel only operates as a restraint on the enforcement of rights and, unlike a proprietary estoppel, must be negative in substance; that is, it will only apply to assumptions or expectations that existing or future rights will be suspended or extinguished rather than created.[69]

The idea that promissory estoppel can only operate defensively as a restraint on rights in Australian law would seem to be plainly inconsistent with *Waltons Stores v Maher*, where a majority of the High Court of Australia held that a promissory or equitable estoppel arose from the Mahers' reliance on an assumption induced by Waltons that Waltons would sign and exchange a lease on terms that had been negotiated. The contractionary movement led by Handley AJA depends on a reinterpretation of *Waltons Stores v Maher* as a decision based on proprietary estoppel, with the unusual feature of the case being that the estoppel was asserted by the land owner against a person who had promised to take an interest in the land by way of lease.[70] This explanation is, however, very difficult to reconcile with the judgments of Brennan J, Mason CJ and Wilson J in that case.[71] If the restraint on rights view of promissory estoppel is correct, then the cases applying the broader principle mentioned above, which include decisions of the Supreme Court of New South Wales, the Federal Court of Australia and the Victorian Court of Appeal, were wrongly decided.[72]

The net result of all of those expansionary and contractionary movements to date is as follows. In both England and Australia, an assumption relating to the future conduct of the inducing party can found an equitable estoppel, and can operate as an independent source of rights and provide a cause of action if the assumption is that the relying party will be granted an interest in property. In England, an assumption as to future conduct can establish a promissory estoppel only if the assumption is that the inducing party will not enforce, or will suspend, existing legal rights or powers. In Australia, the law is uncertain. On one view, the Australian law of promissory estoppel does not differ from English law. On a broader view, promissory estoppel can operate in Australia where the relying party has been led to believe that he or she will in the future be granted legal rights, such as rights under a contract, and the doctrine allows the relying party to enforce those rights as though they had been granted.[73] On a still broader view, the Australian law of promissory estoppel is vastly more expansive, and is capable of operating as an independent source of

[68] *DHJPM Pty Ltd v Blackthorn Resources Ltd* [2011] NSWCA 348, (2011) 83 NSWLR 728, [93]–[94]; *Hammond v JP Morgan Trust Australia Ltd* [2012] NSWCA 295, [26], discussed in Robertson.

[69] *Ashton v Pratt* [2015] NSWCA 12, (2015) 88 NSWLR 281, [102]. Bathurst JA acknowledged (ibid [138]) that 'there is significant dicta contrary to this limitation' but did not find it necessary to resolve the controversy because the relying party in that case had failed to establish detriment.

[70] KR Handley, *Estoppel by Conduct and Election* (London, Sweet & Maxwell, 2006) [11-032]. See also *DHJPM Pty Ltd v Blackthorn Resources Ltd* [2011] NSWCA 348, (2011) 83 NSWLR 728, [122].

[71] See A Robertson, 'Three Models of Promissory Estoppel' (2013) 7 *Journal of Equity* 226, 231–33.

[72] See above nn 58–60.

[73] ibid 238–43 (discussing the 'legal relationship model' of promissory estoppel).

rights or cause of action wherever one party induces another to assume that the inducing party will confer a benefit on the relying party.[74]

VI. CONCLUSION

Reflecting on the pace of development of the strand of proprietary estoppel involving promises to confer interests in land, Ben McFarlane has noted that this kind of liability was 'not known to lawyers practicing fifty years ago'.[75] Tellingly, however, such liability would appear to have been well known to Chancery lawyers practising 300 years ago. The expansionary turns discussed in this chapter, and the application of the underlying principle in different eras and across vastly different fact situations, point to a persistent and widely held notion that justice demands liability where one person leads another to act to his or her detriment on the faith of an assumption relating to the inducing party's future conduct. The contractionary counterturns discussed in this chapter point to a persistent scepticism about this species of liability. As noted in the introduction to this chapter, it is understandable that there are conflicting views about this kind of liability because it involves a higher degree of trust than assumptions about facts and existing rights. For some, that higher degree of trust weighs on the inducing party's conscience and justifies liability. For others, the inherent unreliability of informal assurances supports the view that the relying party should be responsible for the consequences of his or her own risky behaviour. The notion of interpersonal responsibility that underlies a principle of estoppel relating to assumptions as to future conduct appears to lie at the outer limits of common understandings as to what people are entitled to expect from one another to the extent required to justify a legal obligation. Whether it lies just within or just outside those limits has been, and seems destined to remain, a matter on which views differ.

[74] ibid 243–45 (discussing the 'independent source of rights model' of promissory estoppel).
[75] McFarlane, above n 50, 1.17.

10

Reflections on the Restitution Revolution

IN 1966, ROBERT Goff and Gareth Jones published the first edition of *The Law of Restitution*. This book has had a profound impact on the development of the law of restitution and of unjust enrichment throughout the common law world. The Eighth Obligations Conference, which took place in Cambridge in July 2016, provided an ideal opportunity to celebrate the golden jubilee of *The Law of Restitution*. Four academics and a senior judge were invited to reflect on the impact of this book on the law from their particular jurisdictional perspectives and contemplate how the law might develop in the future. Gareth Jones accepted an invitation to attend this symposium. Sadly, he died earlier in 2016. Robert Goff died a few months later. The papers which follow are based on those which were delivered at the conference. They are published here in honour of Robert Goff and Gareth Jones, and signify the exceptional impact both of these great lawyers had on the evolution of the law of obligations.

1. England and Wales

AMY GOYMOUR

I. INTRODUCTION

The year 2016 will be remembered with great sadness within the legal community as the year which saw the deaths of Robert Goff and Gareth Jones, exactly 50 years after the publication of their first edition of *Goff and Jones: The Law of Restitution* in 1966.[1] Metaphors abound, from the highest levels, as to the significance of their mighty book: for Lord Millett, Goff and Jones were the 'progenitors' of the subject;[2] for Lord Rodger, they were 'the Romulus and Remus of the English Law of Restitution' who 'out of a few weak and scattered settlements founded a powerful city

[1] R Goff and G Jones, *The Law of Restitution* (London, Sweet & Maxwell, 1966).

[2] P Millett, 'Restitution and Constructive Trusts' in W Cornish, R Nolan, J O'Sullivan and G Virgo (eds), *Restitution: Past Present and Future—Essays in Honour of Gareth Jones* (Oxford, Hart Publishing, 1998) ch 13.

whose territory now extends far and wide'.[3] Significantly, 2016 marked the twenty-fifth anniversary of that 'city' gaining official recognition by the House of Lords, in *Lipkin Gorman v Karpnale*, in 1991.[4]

The speed and richness with which restitution law has developed in England and Wales, both academically as well as judicially, over the past 50 years is arguably unparalleled in any other branch of private law, and perhaps the law more generally. *Goff and Jones* itself has developed: it is into its ninth edition, under the authorship of a new team—Charles Mitchell, Paul Mitchell and Stephen Watterson—and sporting a new title, *The Law of Unjust Enrichment.*[5]

Now is a fitting time to pause and reflect on the developments which the subject has undergone since 1966. This short contribution seeks to do that, via three main themes. First, to continue Lord Rodger's metaphor, it examines (in section III) the development of the modern-day 'city' (whether we call that city 'restitution' or 'unjust enrichment'): the size and shape of its territory; its governance; its in(ter) dependence; and how it has coped with evolutionary or revolutionary changes. Secondly, it reflects (in section IV) on the legacy of the first edition of *Goff and Jones*, by evaluating the precise role the book has played in the subject's foundation and subsequent development. And thirdly, it considers (in section V) some future challenges facing the subject.

To provide a backdrop for the discussion of these three themes, we must first go back to 1966, to the first edition of *Goff and Jones*.

II. THE FIRST EDITION OF *GOFF AND JONES*

A. The Pre-existing Legal Landscape

In 1966, the landscape within which Goff and Jones founded their 'city' was bleak: it consisted of isolated clusters of cases concerning particular 'actions', with little to unite them, except for unhelpful and artificial notions of implied (or quasi) contracts.[6] Thus, what became Goff and Jones's metaphorical 'city' of Restitution began as a disorganised collection of hamlets, lacking any obvious sense of common identity.[7]

[3] A Rodger, 'Recovering Payments under Void Contracts in Scots Law' in W Swadling and G Jones (eds), *The Search for Principle: Essays in Honour of Lord Goff* (Oxford, Oxford University Press, 2000) ch 1.

[4] *Lipkin Gorman v Karpnale* [1991] 2 AC 548.

[5] C Mitchell, P Mitchell and S Watterson, *Goff and Jones: The Law of Unjust Enrichment*, 9th edn (London, Sweet & Maxwell, 2016).

[6] Note various chapters in English textbooks, eg P Winfield, *The Province of the Law of Tort* (Cambridge, Cambridge University Press, 1931), which contained a chapter on quasi-contracts.

[7] Goff himself described the territory as 'undeveloped', and with 'undefined' 'boundaries': R Goff, 'Reform of the Law of Restitution' (1961) 24 *MLR* 8.

The equivalent territory in the USA looked very different in 1966. Restitution had begun to emerge as a coherent subject in 1887, via the work of James Barr Ames (and his peers, including William Keener) at Harvard Law School, who identified that previously disparate bodies of case law belonged together, and were explained by a principle of reversing unjust enrichment.[8] Fifty years later, in 1937, the American Law Institute (under the supervision of Austin Scott and Warren Seavey) mapped out 'for general use' the territory which Ames had discovered,[9] in its *Restatement on the Law of Restitution: Quasi Contracts and Constructive Trusts.*[10]

Back on English soil, in the late 1950s, Goff (by then at the Bar, and formerly a Fellow at Lincoln College, Oxford) and Jones (a Fellow at Trinity College, Cambridge, who had studied restitution under Seavey at Harvard) were introduced to each other, and began to attempt what had already happened in the USA: the discovery, mapping and building of a law of restitution, around a common principle. Key to that project was their belief that lurking beneath the messy territory was an untapped 'fountain'[11] which had the potential to unite and invigorate the existing, disparate settlements. This was the principle of 'unjust enrichment', whose source could be traced (at least) back to statements of Lord Mansfield in *Moses v Macferlan*, to the effect that those who receive money by mistake (or for other defined reasons) are 'obliged by the ties of natural justice and equity to refund the money'.[12]

B. Ambitions of the First Edition

The first edition of *Goff and Jones* was the fruit of over six years of hard—and seemingly fun[13]—labour. Remarkably, each chapter was initially written independently by both authors, and then 'blended', after much discussion, to form a genuinely joint product.[14] The book conveys a broad and confident ambition—'to state, in a coherent and rational form, the principles of the English Law of Restitution'.[15] The authors gave little insight into the book's intended audience, nor any detail as to its intended impact; these were masterful omissions, for they would enable the book to command wide appeal and interest. Despite the book's deliberately broad ambitions, four specific objectives are evident from the text.

First, in terms of subject matter, the authors 'cast [their] net very wide',[16] to include all claims, whatever their source, that might be explained by the unjust enrichment

[8] A Kull, 'James Barr Ames and the Early Modern History of Unjust Enrichment' (2005) 25 *OJLS* 197, 302–303.

[9] ibid 317.

[10] WA Seavey and AW Scott, *Restatement of the Law of Restitution: Quasi Contracts and Constructive Trusts* (St Paul, American Law Institute Publishers, 1937). See also WA Seavey and AW Scott, 'Restitution' (1938) 54 *LQR* 29.

[11] F Rose, 'Preface' [1997] *Restitution Law Review* 1.

[12] *Moses v Macferlan* (1760) 2 Burr 1005, 1021, 97 ER 676, 681.

[13] See R Goff, 'Preface' to Cornish et al, above n 2, vii–viii.

[14] G Jones, 'The Law of Restitution: The Past and the Future' in A Burrows (ed), *Essays on the Law of Restitution* (Oxford, Oxford University Press, 1991) ch 1.

[15] Goff and Jones, above n 1, v.

[16] ibid.

principle. They explained that 'only through the study of Restitution at its widest can the principles underlying the subject be fully understood'.[17] Crucially, and in striking contrast to the US *Restatement*, their work cut across 'the boundaries that traditionally separate law from equity'.[18]

Secondly, in terms of legal technique, the authors stated that they had approached the subject 'empirically',[19] rather than from a theoretical, political or moral perspective. The English cases were their starting point, and from those they sought to extract principles and find coherence. Inevitably, however, this enterprise cannot have been purely 'empirical', for the authors recognised that certain cases were 'open to criticism'.[20] The extraction of principles and systems from the sources must have required the authors to make certain value judgments, especially where the sources seemed inconsistent, as to what the relevant principles and systems ought to be.

Thirdly, the authors were keen to pre-empt and dismiss any criticism that the unifying 'principle' of unjust enrichment might invite 'sloppiness of thought', when applied in practice to novel situations.[21] To avoid such 'sloppiness', they distinguished between 'principles', which serve as abstract principles of justice, and 'concepts'—precise rules derived from the principles, which guide results in particular cases.[22] The authors then articulated the now-familiar 'conceptual' ingredients of cases where unjust enrichments are typically reversed: a defendant's enrichment; which comes at the expense of the claimant; where it would be unjust for the defendant to retain the benefit. The presence of these ingredients would normally justify a restitutionary claim, subject to certain 'limiting principles'—classified today as bars, denials or defences—for example, where the claimant acts officiously.[23] Whilst, in 1966, English law did not recognise a generalised right to restitution in every unjust enrichment case, Goff and Jones asserted that 'the law of restitution should not lightly be presumed to be past the age of child-bearing',[24] and might in the future recognise a free-standing claim, structured around the conceptual framework they had identified.

Finally, Goff and Jones advocated some areas where substantive legal change or development was required. Particularly prescient were the book's recommendations for the recovery of payments made under a mistake of law, and for the recognition of a change of position defence.

C. Contemporary Critical Reception

The book received immediate critical acclaim. Within weeks, it was deemed 'admirable' by the High Court in *Chesworth v Farrar*.[25] And academic reviewers—including

[17] ibid.
[18] ibid. See also A Denning, ['Review of *Goff and Jones*'] (1967) 83 *LQR* 277.
[19] ibid.
[20] ibid.
[21] *Holt v Markham* [1923] 1 KB 504, 513 (Scrutton LJ).
[22] Goff and Jones, above n 1, 12; Seavey and Scott, above n 10, 36–37.
[23] Goff and Jones, above n 1, 13–14, 16–17.
[24] ibid 13–14.
[25] [1967] 1 QB 407, 417 (Edmund Davies J).

Lord Denning,[26] Donald Harris[27] and William Cornish[28]—heaped much-deserved praise on Goff and Jones for the magnitude of their achievement, in not only 'assembling and marshalling so much material'[29] and 'piecing together the jigsaw', but also in having exposed a 'new subject'[30] or 'new [legal] category in the law'.[31] Indeed, so novel was the subject matter that, according to Cornish, it caused 'some perplexity' among some of those tasked with classifying academic books. It seems astonishing, with hindsight, that 'the library of one ancient university ... classified [*Goff and Jones*] as Criminal law' and the 'library of one Inn of Court refused to take it at all'.

Notwithstanding the overwhelmingly positive reaction, two notes of caution were sounded by the reviewers. First, Harris was concerned about the book's breadth and suggested that some topics would be better left to more specialist texts. Why, for example, should *Goff and Jones* give an account of 'rescission' when books on contract law already, and appropriately, covered the material?[32] Secondly, Cornish, whilst sharing Goff and Jones's enthusiasm for the development of a free-standing unjust enrichment claim, nonetheless recognised that practical hurdles stood in the way of that goal. In particular, he noted that reform would 'depend a great deal on the acceptance and promulgation of [Goff and Jones's] ideas by teachers', but that finding a place for restitution in legal curricula was intrinsically problematic. He explained that restitution governs the consequences of transactions going *wrong*, whereas students necessarily need to learn the legally *right* way of transacting—'governed by some other branch of the law' (for example contract law)—before being equipped for studying the consequences of things going wrong. Thus, he concluded that restitution 'as a whole is not easy to expound to a new student' and would be better suited to 'postgraduate work'.

How discerning Harris and Cornish proved to be with these cautionary notes. As we shall see, disagreement about the breadth of the subject and its place on legal curricula have plagued the subject since its inception, and continue to do so.

III. THE DEVELOPMENT OF THE SUBJECT SINCE 1966

It is impossible in such a short contribution to capture, or indeed do justice to, the depth and breadth of the developments within the 'city' of restitution or unjust enrichment since 1966. Nonetheless, this section gives some edited highlights, by focusing on (i) the manner in which the subject has evolved, and (ii) how it has responded to attempts at revolution and regime change. As we shall see, much has been written by restitution law's critics to cause the city's foundations to be rattled; the city has not (yet) been toppled, but these 'insurgencies' have played, and continue to play, a very important role in the rich development of the subject.

[26] Denning, above n 18.
[27] D Harris, ['Review of *Goff and Jones*'] [1967] 25 *CLJ* 114.
[28] W Cornish, ['Review of *Goff and Jones*'] [1966] 29 *MLR* 579.
[29] Harris, above n 27, 114.
[30] Cornish, above n 28, 580.
[31] Denning, above n 18, 277.
[32] Harris, above n 27, 114. See also, implicitly, Cornish, above n 28, 580.

A. Evolution

(i) Tracking Evolution via Statistics

What metrics might be used to track the evolution of a legal subject? History might suggest that the vitality and evolution of a given legal territory depends on the quality and extent of at least three intertwining factors: (i) law-making—both judicial and legislative; (ii) academic writing—of both supporters and critics; and (iii) teaching. The last 50 years have witnessed striking growth in all three fields, although it would appear that, in terms of quantity, the most restitution-related growth has occurred in the areas of law making and academic writing; the teaching of the subject has grown less quickly.

A rough-and-ready view of the extent of law making and academic writing can be gleaned from the data captured by *Restitution Law Review*, which began in 1993. In each annual edition, the journal's 'Regional Digest' has collated cases, articles and books on the subject for each jurisdiction. The collection is necessarily impressionistic, much depending, of course, on value judgments made by the Regional Digester[33] for any particular year. Nonetheless, the numbers, shown in Figure 1,[34] reveal a consistently large amount of judicial and scholarly activity in England and Wales, including a significant number of cases from the House of Lords/Supreme Court. It is particularly noteworthy that the number of annual academic outputs—books and articles—has remained relatively constant, which runs counter to a suggestion made by John Langbein in 1998 that scholarly 'excitement' in restitution was owing to its 'newness' as a subject, implying that such interest might wane as the subject comes of age.[35]

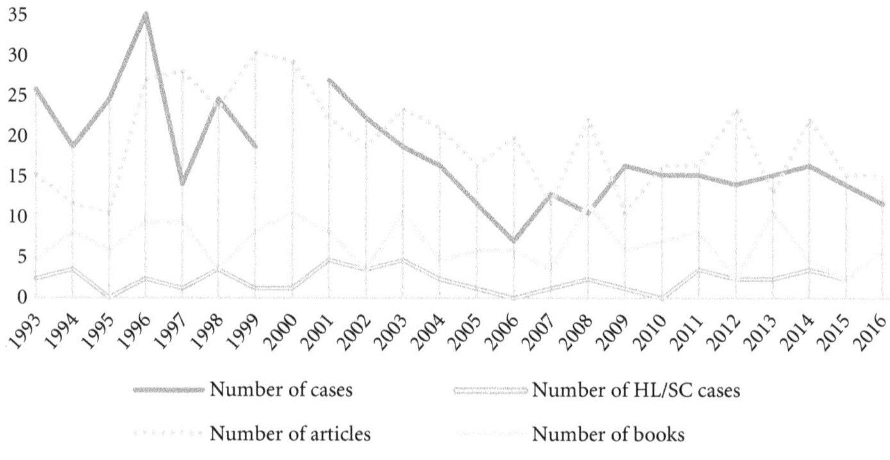

Figure 1: Restitution Law Review Regional Digest Statistics, 1993–2016

[33] These were, for England and Wales, William Swadling (1993–99); Charles Mitchell (2000); and Gerard McMeel (2001–16).

[34] Note that some 80 cases were included in the Regional Digest for England and Wales in the 2000 volume of *Restitution Law Review*, which coincided with Charles Mitchell's one-year tenure of the Regional Digester role. Without wishing to diminish the significance of this impressive statistic, it has been omitted from Figure 1 out of a concern not to distort the scale of the graph's *y*-axis.

[35] J Langbein, 'The Later History of Restitution' in Cornish et al, above n 2, ch 4.

As Cornish had predicted, the growth of the teaching of restitution/unjust enrichment has been more limited: although many law schools offer restitution-based courses, most of these are advanced offerings, pitched at postgraduate students. Undergraduate law students continue to leave university with little or no understanding of the subject matter. Time will tell whether, and to what extent, this might affect the future general evolution of the subject.[36]

(ii) Tracking Evolution via Substantive Developments

These quantity-based statistics give only a superficial snapshot of the subject's evolution; they take little or no account of its substantive and qualitative growth. Substantive developments within the law of restitution since 1966 have been far reaching; four themes are highlighted here.

First, the subject has morphed from being an academic analytical tool into a fully-fledged legal doctrine. This significant development was a slow one. It took 11 years for Parliament to acknowledge the concept of unjust enrichment, via an oblique reference in the Torts (Interference with Goods) Act 1977.[37] The recognition of unjust enrichment as a distinct claim took much longer. Even in 1987, Robert Sutton, reviewing the second edition of *Goff and Jones*, said that 'after twenty years under [Goff and Jones's] care, the subject still wanders indiscriminately through the halls of property law, tort and contract, without any clear lines of demarcation'.[38] It was not until 1991 that unjust enrichment was finally recognised as a distinct concept, by the House of Lords in *Lipkin Gorman v Karpnale*.[39]

A second major development concerns the name and shape of the subject. Spearheaded by Peter Birks in 1998,[40] most scholars now concur that 'restitution' and 'unjust enrichment' are analytically distinct, and do not 'quadrate':[41] Restitution is a remedy; unjust enrichment is a cause of action that might yield a restitutionary remedy. Most, though not all, treatises on the subject now have as their focus the cause of action, rather than the remedy. Even *Goff and Jones*, under the care of its new team of authors, has been rebranded *The Law of Unjust Enrichment*.[42] So, perhaps unjust enrichment is the heart of the city built by Goff and Jones, and Restitution the name for the urban sprawl that surrounds it.

Thirdly, our understanding of the cause of action has, since it was recognised in 1991, been refined via further significant judicial developments. These include: recognising the fourfold shape of the unjust enrichment inquiry (as advocated by the

[36] See Langbein, ibid, for a discussion of the link between teaching and the vitality of subjects.

[37] Section 7(4). Note that Patrick Atiyah, in his review of the second edition of *Goff and Jones*, asserted that the 1977 Act had 'canonised' the concept of unjust enrichment: P Atiyah (1979) 42 *MLR* 727, 728.

[38] R Sutton, ['Review of *Goff and Jones*, 2nd edn'] [1987] 46 *CLJ* 509.

[39] *Lipkin Gorman*, above n 4. See Burrows's early acknowledgement of the importance of *Lipkin Gorman* in the preface to Burrows, above n 14, ch 1, ix. See more recently *HMRC v The Investment Trust Companies* [2017] UKSC 29, [39] (Lord Reed).

[40] P Birks, 'Misnomer' in Cornish et al, above n 2, ch 1.

[41] See also *Sempra Metals Ltd v IRC* [2007] UKHL 34, [2008] 1 AC 561. Note, too, R Jackson's early consternation as to the taxonomical alignment of contract, tort and restitution in 'The Restatement of Restitution' (1938) 10 *Mississippi Law Journal* 95, 95–96.

[42] Mitchell et al, above n 5, esp v.

first edition of *Goff and Jones*);[43] extending the reach of a mistake-based restitution claim beyond liability mistakes, to encompass other mistakes;[44] permitting recovery for mistakes of law;[45] recognising the change of position defence;[46] permitting recovery against public bodies in respect of ultra vires receipts;[47] and refining the nature of the 'enrichment' inquiry.[48] The extraordinary speed with which these case-based developments have occurred might be explained by the chance coincidence of four particular catalysts: (i) pressure exerted by the surge in academic interest and associated scholarship;[49] (ii) the existence of waves of high-value litigation on particular restitutionary matters (arising in particular legal-economic climates), for example void 'swaps' contracts and unlawfully levied taxes; (iii) pressure from EU law to provide restitutionary remedies in certain settings; and (iv) indirect pressure from domestic legal obstacles (such as limitation periods) causing the law to develop in certain directions. We might question in which direction the law will develop—and at what pace—once certain catalysts expire and new ones take their place. In particular, catalyst (iii) will expire upon Britain's exit from the EU, but it is likely that the same event will cause fresh waves of high-value litigation, raising new problems for restitution law to tackle.[50]

Finally, hand in hand with this judicial evolution has been an explosion of academic scholarship on restitution/unjust enrichment which, in terms of its depth, breadth and quality, is probably unrivalled in private law. As discussed below, this scholarship has broadly tracked a path from 'discovery' of restitutionary cases and principles to 'mapping' and 'quasi-codification',[51] and, more recently, to engaging in more normative/theoretical inquiries. Throughout, there has also been a healthy interaction with other disciplines—not only within private law, but also with, inter alia, public law, EU law and criminal law.

B. Attempts at Revolution

Equally important in understanding the historical development of restitution/unjust enrichment are the 'attacks' that have been attempted on its existence, size and

[43] See, inter alia, *Banque Financière de la Cité SA v Parc (Battersea) Ltd* [1999] 1 AC 221. Note, however, the contrasting comments by Lord Clarke in *Menelaou v Bank of Cyprus Plc* [2015] UKSC 66, [2016] AC 176, [19]. See also *Investment Trust Companies* [2017] UKSC 29, [41]–[42] (Lord Reed); *Lowick Rose LLP v Swynson Ltd* [2017] UKSC 32, [56] (Lord Mance) and [110] (Lord Neuberger).

[44] *Barclays Bank Ltd v WJ Simms & Cooke* [1980] QB 677.

[45] *Kleinwort Benson v Lincoln City Council* [1999] 2 AC 349.

[46] *Lipkin Gorman*, above n 4.

[47] *Woolwich Equitable Building Society v IRC* [1993] AC 70.

[48] *Sempra Metals Ltd v IRC* [2007] UKHL 34, [2008] 1 AC 561; *Benedetti v Sawiris* [2013] UKSC 50, [2014] AC 938.

[49] See F Rose, 'Editorial' [1995] *Restitution Law Review* 1; F Rose, 'Editorial' [1996] *Restitution Law Review* 1.

[50] Contextual waves of litigation, throwing up new challenges for restitution law, might also flow from other economic/political events, for example the 2008 global financial crisis and ensuing recession, and the election of President Trump.

[51] See A Burrows, *A Restatement of the English Law of Unjust Enrichment* (Oxford, Oxford University Press, 2013); see also A Burrows, 'Unjust Enrichment' (lecture delivered at the Honourable Society of the Inner Temple, 17 February 2014).

internal governance. They take four different forms, which are summarised here.[52] None has toppled the city, but each attack has made a lasting and significant mark on its character.

First, the very existence of the subject has been challenged, as has the size of its territory. Chief among the attackers is Steve Hedley,[53] who most recently expressed doubt as to whether the subject has a 'heart', and suggested that 'unjust enrichment orthodoxy' may actually be a 'cover for something very different'.[54] Previously, he had asserted that:

> The various cases usually thought to constitute 'restitution' are in fact linked by little except their ejection from the traditional mega-theories of private law. To leave them as pariah doctrines is unacceptable; the question is where they should go ... I suggest they should be fairly divided into four groups: some to be returned to contract law, some to wrongs, some to property, and the remainder to the law of adjustment of liabilities.[55]

Thus, for Hedley, Goff and Jones were wrong in 1966 to transform the hamlets they had discovered into a city of restitution/unjust enrichment; they should instead have merged the settlements into other, pre-existing, townships. Whilst the attacks by Hedley and others have not, of course, brought down the subject—unjust enrichment seems to be thriving—they may be contributing to a welcome shrinkage of its core territory. Take, for example, the rules governing the availability of contractual rescission, which the first edition of *Goff and Jones* accounted in detail;[56] today's texts (including the current *Goff and Jones* edition) include rescission as a restitutionary remedy but defer, appropriately, to other texts—for example, contract law books—for the specific rules governing its availability.[57]

The second attack on unjust enrichment orthodoxy came from within: Peter Birks argued that the 'unjust' element of the unjust enrichment formula should no longer be judged by reference to a series of 'unjust factors' (for which he had previously been a strong proponent); instead, recovery should depend on there being an 'absence of basis' for the defendant's enrichment.[58] The House of Lords has rejected the regime change that Birks sought,[59] and the Supreme Court in *Swynson* recently affirmed the importance of 'unjust factors' as reflective of 'legal norm[s]'. Nonetheless, the attempted coup has resulted in welcome academic attention being given to the relevance of a 'presence of basis' or 'justifying ground' in limiting restitutionary actions.[60]

[52] In this short chapter, it is impossible to do justice to the complexity of these attacks.

[53] S Hedley, *Restitution: Its Division and Ordering* (Oxford, Oxford University Press, 2001); S Hedley, *A Critical Introduction to Restitution* (London, Butterworths, 2001). See also Sutton, above n 38; Atiyah, above n 37; and SJ Stoljar, *The Law of Quasi-Contract*, 2nd edn (London, Sweet & Maxwell, 1989).

[54] S Hedley 'What is "Unjust Enrichment" for?' [2016] 16 *Oxford University Common Law Journal* 333, which is a review of C Webb, *Reason and Restitution: A Theory of Unjust Enrichment* (Oxford, Oxford University Press, 2016).

[55] Hedley, *Restitution: Its Division and Ordering*, above n 53, 232.

[56] Goff and Jones, above n 1, 101–35.

[57] Mitchell et al, above n 5, 1001.

[58] P Birks, *Unjust Enrichment*, 2nd edn (Oxford, Oxford University Press, 2005) chs 5–6.

[59] *Sempra Metals Ltd v IRC* [2007] UKHL 34, [2008] 1 AC 561; *Deutsche Morgan Grenfell Group Plc v IRC* [2007] UKHL 49, [2007] 1 AC 558.

[60] See, eg, G Virgo, *The Principles of the Law of Restitution*, 3rd edn (Oxford, Oxford University Press, 2015) ch 7; Mitchell et al, above n 5, chs 2–3.

Thirdly, domestic restitution law has been challenged as a result of Britain's membership of the EU. The potential importance of EU law to the subject's development was foreseen by the editor of *Restitution Law Review* which, since 1996, has included an EU Law section in its annual Regional Digest. The EU's '*San Giorgio* principle' requires a member state to ensure that restitution is made where a person pays charges levied by a member state contrary to EU rules,[61] notwithstanding that the defendant's position might have changed, and even where domestic law would not itself provide for a restitutionary claim. This EU principle, being more generous to claimants than English restitution/unjust enrichment law might be, had the potential to revolutionise the domestic system, resulting in the unjust enrichment formula being rewritten. But that dramatic revolution has not occurred. Instead, EU law's claimant-friendly formula has applied (to the exclusion of incompatible domestic rules) only in those cases with a direct EU dimension. Crucially, the domestic formula has remained intact for non-EU-related cases. As discussed above, the real significance of Britain's EU membership has been its role in catalysing the evolution (not revolution) of domestic restitution law, by providing a wealth of difficult factual scenarios for which domestic law has needed to provide legal solutions. For example, EU law was the reason for the invalidity of the tax receipts in *Woolwich v IRC*;[62] that case, of course, prompted domestic law to develop a new unjust factor, justifying recovery in respect of ultra vires state receipts. Thus, as Rebecca Williams has aptly written, EU-related cases have 'been fertile ground for development of the domestic law, without which the latter may not have reached its current stage of development'.[63] It is likely that Britain's forthcoming exit from the EU will bring about a fresh set of challenges for the law of restitution/unjust enrichment.

Finally, English law might have been susceptible to revolutionary changes following developments to the law of restitution in other jurisdictions. However, English law has (to date, at least) resisted the pressure to align itself with other jurisdictions' developments. In particular, it has not followed the Canadian preference for assessing 'unjustness' by reference to an 'absence of juristic reason' for the relevant enrichment;[64] or the Canadian preference to deal with restitutionary claims against public bodies via a separate public law system;[65] and it has resisted the Australian preference for 'unconscionability' over 'unjust enrichment' as the relevant organising concept.[66]

We might conclude that none of these four attacks have resulted in revolution. But each has contributed to valuable evolutionary developments. Judges and

[61] See Case R-199/82 *Amministrazione delle Finanze dello Stato v SpA San Giorgio* [1983] ECR 3595. See also *Woolwich Equitable BS v IRC* [1993] AC 70, 177 (Lord Goff).

[62] ibid.

[63] R Williams, *Unjust Enrichment and Public Law* (Oxford, Hart Publishing, 2010) 272.

[64] *Garland v Consumers' Gas Co* [2004] 1 SCR 629.

[65] *Kingstreet Investment Ltd v New Brunswick* [2007] 1 SCR 3.

[66] See, eg, *Roxborough v Rothmans of Pall Mall Australia Ltd* [2001] HCA 68, (2001) 208 CLR 516; *Australian Financial Services and Leasing Lty Ltd v Hills Industries Ltd* [2014] HCA 14, (2014) 253 CLR 560.

scholars have been compelled to challenge orthodox thinking, and therefore address the subject's vulnerabilities and weaknesses sooner than would otherwise have been the case.

IV. THE PLACE OF *GOFF AND JONES* IN THE SUBJECT'S INTELLECTUAL EVOLUTION

What has been the contribution of *Goff and Jones* in the subject's evolution since 1966? This question commands answers at two levels: one general; the other more specific.

A. 'But for' the Publication of *Goff and Jones* in 1966 ...

First, it is no exaggeration to make the bold claim that *Goff and Jones* in 1966 has been a 'but for' cause of the development of the subject in England and Wales.[67] The House of Lords, albeit in a judgment of Lord Goff, referred to *Goff and Jones* in *Lipkin Gorman* when recognising the concept of unjust enrichment for the first time, and it has been the inspiration behind other judicial developments. Moreover, the book, by 'collecting together for easy consultation ... and rationalis[ing] ... the grounds of liability',[68] has been the fountain, the vital source—directly or indirectly—for all subsequent academic work. On turning 80, Gareth Jones noted, in a lecture published in Trinity College's 2011 Annual Record, that he had taken joy in 'inspir[ing] many younger Dons' and 'notably ... Peter Birks'. That was an understatement: Peter Birks, himself a 'but for' inspiration for so many after him, asserted, in his 1985 *An Introduction to the Law of Restitution*, that '*Goff and Jones* has an absolute monopoly' over the 'English law of restitution',[69] and that the relationship between his own work and *Goff and Jones* could 'be shortly stated ... without *Goff and Jones* this [Birks's book] would never have been so much as attempted'.[70] Indeed, it is inconceivable that anyone who has engaged with the English Law of unjust enrichment over the past 50 years, whether as a supporter or critic, has emerged without owing a debt to Goff and Jones.

[67] M McInnes, 'Review—Goff and Jones: The Law of Unjust Enrichment, 8th ed' [2014] 55 *Canadian Business Law Journal* 323, 323.

[68] ibid.

[69] P Birks, *An Introduction to the Law of Restitution* (Oxford, Oxford University Press, 1985) 2–3. See also Birks, *Unjust Enrichment*, above n 58, xi–xii.

[70] To similar effect, Langbein described *Goff and Jones* as having 'launched the modern era [of restitution] in England': Langbein, above n 35, 61. Jack Beatson has concurred with Birks's statement that the book's publication was 'the most important English event in a wider movement by which Anglo-American common law set about rectifying the error of having overlooked the subject': J Beatson, 'Should There Be Legislative Development of the Law of Restitution?' in Burrows, above n 14, ch 11, 279, quoting Birks, *Introduction*, above n 69, 5. See also J Edelman, ['Review of *Goff and Jones*, 8th edn'] (2012) 128 *LQR* 619.

B. Viewing the Precise Contribution of *Goff and Jones*, with the Benefit of Hindsight

Secondly, on the (sound) assumption that *Goff and Jones* has been a 'but for' cause of the subject's growth, we might probe more deeply—and with the benefit of hindsight—to ask what has been the book's precise contribution to the evolutionary process. This inquiry requires a preliminary understanding of the stages in the subject's modern intellectual development.

(i) Stages in the Subject's Intellectual Evolution

It is impossible to do justice to the complexities of, and controversies surrounding, the subject's modern evolution in this short contribution. Nonetheless, few would disagree that the subject has tracked the following eight broadly chronological (but sometimes overlapping) evolutionary stages: (i) the subject began, in the typical common law tradition, as a nascent body of scattered case law; (ii) next came an awareness of an underlying unifying principle (spearheaded by James Barr Ames in America),[71] leading to a preliminary gathering together of relevant cases to form the 'city'; (iii) this was followed by a more thorough, and more 'empirical', exercise (undertaken by the American Law Institute in America, and by Goff and Jones in England and Wales) in unearthing and exposing the relevant case law; (iv) from these authorities, principles were more finely 'distilled' and theories found to explain the rules;[72] and, following this, and in combination, (v) the newly founded subject began to be mapped: boundaries were pegged out around its territory; material was organised within the subject's boundaries, to ensure like cases were treated alike; and previously decided cases were then appraised by reference to the charted map. As a result of multiple 'cartographers' undertaking this work—chief among them Robert Goff and Gareth Jones, Peter Birks,[73] Andrew Burrows, and Graham Virgo[74]—numerous, and inconsistent, maps emerged. The mapping process was then followed (and, to an extent, accompanied) by (vi) critical and theoretical appraisal of the extent of the subject's territory (and indeed the subject's existence), and the style and content of the maps by, for example, Steve Hedley and Charlie Webb;[75] (vii) the addition of detail to the maps, especially via judicial refinements to particular rules; and (viii) an attempt at loosely codifying the rules to 'enhance our understanding' and to 'make [the subject] more accessible', in the form of Andrew Burrows's *Restatement of the Law of Restitution* from 2013.[76]

[71] See text to n 8.
[72] Virgo, above n 60, preface.
[73] See R Rose, 'The Evolution of the Species' in A Burrows and A Rodger, *Mapping the Law: Essays in Memory of Peter Birks* (Oxford, Oxford University Press, 2006) ch 1.
[74] Note that Virgo defines the ambition of the third edition of his book as 'seek[ing] to provide a map for those who are trying to climb to the top of' what he calls the '[restitution] mountain': Virgo, above n 60, v.
[75] See n 54.
[76] Burrows, *Restatement*, above n 51, x.

(ii) The Place of Goff and Jones *in the Evolutionary Process*

Fifty years on, it is clear that *Goff and Jones* was not only fundamental to, but actually constituted, the third stage of the subject's growth in England and Wales. The authors undertook the laborious and largely 'empirical' task of unearthing and 'drawing together' the relevant 'mass of cases from apparently disparate areas', rather like Emperor Justinian had done in the early sixth century AD, in respect of classical Roman law developed four centuries earlier, which had by that point become buried. As Lionel Smith has written, *Goff and Jones* was the 'Domesday book of restitution: foundational, authoritative and exactingly comprehensive'. Without Goff and Jones's encyclopaedic work, none of the subsequent stages of development ((iv)–(viii)) would have been reached, and certainly not in the brief fifty-year time frame: almost all subsequent academic work has used as its base—directly or indirectly—the cases unearthed in *Goff and Jones*.

But Goff and Jones's work was not, and could not have been, purely empirical. By grouping cases around common principles, Goff and Jones necessarily also began the process, which was continued by others, of distilling rules from the cases (stage (iv)) and sketching out a map (stage (v)). It is, however, crucial to understand the limits of Goff and Jones's ambition: their work predominantly involved the unearthing of sources, not the formulation of fixed rules—nor, it seems, an exhaustive statement of the subject's territorial boundaries. Yet their book became the principal source—a much-revered collection of materials—for those who took up the task of developing the subject after 1966: rules and theories were formulated by others almost exclusively by reference to the cases unearthed by *Goff and Jones*, and the subject's boundaries were shaped, at least initially, by the book's own territorial limits. Whilst Goff and Jones, back in 1966, had intended to kick-start the subject's evolution, it seems unlikely that they expected their book to have such a firm grip on the precise future shape and contours of the subject.

(iii) Evaluating this Mode of Intellectual Evolution

With hindsight, it is possible to discern problems associated with the manner of the subject's intellectual evolution. Much of the subject's post-1966 development (stages (iv)–(viii)) has treated *Goff and Jones* as an almost sacrosanct collection of legal materials. Many scholars, spearheaded by Peter Birks, placed *Goff and Jones* on a pedestal, and then searched for principles and theories which might rationalise its content. It is not obvious that Goff and Jones ever intended for their book to occupy this lofty position, and in so doing circumscribe the subject's future development.

This mode of evolutionary development might prove problematic for the subject, for two reasons. First, it assumes that there is an internal logic in the historic cases—which there may not be, given the sporadic nature of their own evolution; secondly, it constrains the intellectual inquiry and the search for principle—somewhat artificially—to the selection of cases made by Goff and Jones for inclusion in their 1966 book, when 'founding' the subject. Thus, any rules and principles which emerge are vulnerable to the criticism that they are themselves premised on a manufactured body of law, albeit manufactured by the very finest of makers. But very few judges have, to date, preyed on this vulnerability;[77] to the contrary, the Supreme Court has continued to reaffirm the subject's structural framework, and that it is right to put faith into the decided cases, old and new.[78]

V. THE FUTURE (R)EVOLUTION OF THE SUBJECT

As we celebrate, and learn from, the subject's past 50 years, we must look to the future. Some potential challenges might be anticipated—some at the micro-level (which might cause evolutionary development) and others at a more macro-level (bringing the possibility of more revolutionary change).

A. Some Micro-level Concerns

Concerns at the micro-level assume that the subject will broadly retain its current shape, so instead focus on the detail of its rules. They cluster around two themes.

First, there are many continuing uncertainties within the subject that will require future resolution. Some pressing examples include: the applicability of the change of position defence (especially in relation to claims against public bodies, and as to its availability in respect of claims for a proprietary remedy); the relevant test for recovering mistaken gifts or other unilateral dispositions; the precise reach of unjust enrichment claims against indirect recipients;[79] the relevance and meaning of the claimant's being a risk-taker; and the proper role for unconscionability—and therefore the associated judicial discretion that might follow—in respect of restitutionary claims. Furthermore, it is likely that Britain's now-inevitable exit from the EU may create new (as-yet-unpredictable) patterns of restitution-based litigation, which may in turn raise new legal problems.

Secondly, it is crucial, for the coherent evolution of the subject, that the developing case law and associated scholarship are widely accessible. The wide promulgation of the subject was one of Goff and Jones's core ambitions in 1966, when, of course, the printed book was the appropriate publicity vehicle. Fifty years on, if we are to

[77] Perhaps the most obvious voice of discontent has been that of Lord Clarke, who hinted at some dissatisfaction at being constrained by the law's ever-more-rigid and more finely grained restitutionary rules, and expressed a preference for engaging in a more open-textured inquiry into the justice of the case: *Menelaou v Bank of Cyprus Plc* [2015] UKSC 66, [2016] AC 176, [19].

[78] See especially *Investment Trust Companies* [2017] UKSC 29, [40] (Lord Reed) (see text to n 81 below).

[79] In *Investment Trust Companies* [2017] UKSC 29, Lord Reed set out a test for the extent to which unjust enrichment claims might reach indirect recipients, but nonetheless acknowledged that the rules would require further clarification in future cases: 'it would be unwise' in that judgment 'to arrive at a definitive statement of the circumstances in which the enrichment of a defendant can be said to be at the expense of the claimant': [38].

realise Goff and Jones's vision of continued accessibility, it is essential that dedicated courses on restitution/unjust enrichment are given space on more universities' core curricula and, crucially, that relevant resources are available electronically. It is heartening that the subject's dedicated journal—the *Restitution Law Review*—has now acquired a much-needed online presence.[80]

B. Some Macro-level Concerns

The subject also faces some fundamental 'macro-level' challenges, which threaten not merely evolutionary, but potentially revolutionary, change. Three overlapping concerns are highlighted here.

First, the 'city' of restitution/unjust enrichment has been mapped by multiple cartographers, yielding: (i) vastly different maps of the same geographical area; (ii) disagreement as to which geographical area should be mapped; and (iii) further disagreement as to whether the city/subject exists at all. There is a real risk that, unless reconciled, these diametrically opposed visions of the 'city' of restitution/unjust enrichment—concerning its shape, content and very existence—might serve to undermine the subject's stability, and therefore its future place on any legal map.

Secondly, as discussed in section IV, the current legal framework has been built upon cases and principles exposed by Goff and Jones in 1966. Hedley, among others, has questioned whether 'unjust enrichment', as a core organising principle, and its associated case law can be normatively justified (in the way that tort and contract can be) and, further, whether scholars and judges have been right to put their faith in the decisions reached in previous cases. Concluding that unjust enrichment has an 'empty heart', he has written that

> [e]nrichments are not intrinsically objectionable—in fact the reverse is true—and no writer has identified any coherent theory to identify which of these are truly *unjust*, the leading twentieth [century] scholarship having dismissed any attempt to do so in favour of 'bring[ing the concept] down to earth'—in other words, describing what the courts actually do rather than asking what they should do. There is no reason to suppose that there is any good theory to be had.[81]

If Hedley's views gain traction, they threaten to bring down the subject as we know it. The most recent pronouncement from the Supreme Court in *Investment Trust Companies*, however, suggests that this kind of revolution is unlikely. Lord Reed, speaking for the Court, stated that

> the adoption of the concept of unjust enrichment in the modern law, as a unifying principle underlying a number of different types of claim, does not provide the courts with a tabula rasa, entitling them to disregard or distinguish all authorities pre-dating

[80] Note that in 1994 Birks and Rose (the then editors of *Restitution Law Review*) foresaw the importance of electronic access to their journal; the journal was available on disk: [1994] *Restitution Law Review* 1.

[81] Hedley, above n 54, 343 (footnotes omitted).

> *Lipkin Gorman* ... Although judicial reasoning based on modern theories of unjust enrichment is in some respects relatively novel, there are centuries' worth of relevant authorities, whose value should not be underestimated. The wisdom of our predecessors is a valuable resource, and the doctrine of precedent continues to apply. The courts should not be reinventing the wheel.[82]

Thirdly, restitution/unjust enrichment has, to date, grown up in relative isolation from other academic disciplines. An obvious next step, as the subject matures, is for greater cross-disciplinary engagement of restitution/unjust enrichment scholarship with (i) other legal disciplines (for example, public law, real property law and corporate law) and (ii) non-legal disciplines (for example behavioural economics, to ascertain the likely practical impact of certain rules, or neuroscience, to better understand the concept of a mistaken belief). It is surely right, for the intellectually sound development of the subject, to take account of evidence-based insights from other disciplines. However, the incorporation of cross-disciplinary insights must be managed carefully, to avoid subverting the legal doctrinal clarity achieved within the law of restitution over the past 50 years. As Langbein has observed, when too much weight is afforded to the principles of another discipline, for example economic theory, there is a risk of the pre-existing legal structure being taken over by, and reoriented around, the other discipline's own taxonomical structure. The fourfold unjust enrichment inquiry might, for example, collapse into a broader inquiry into the economic impact of particular outcomes.[83] That would be *revolutionary*. But cross-disciplinary engagement need not result in revolution. Managed carefully, insights from other disciplines might fruitfully inform aspects of the current legal rules in a way that is less subversive, more *evolutionary* and more 'respect[ful]' to current 'legal doctrine'.[84] Drawing on external insights in this controlled manner need not result in a complete overhaul of the entire pre-existing legal structure.

C. *Goff and Jones* at 100?

Given these future challenges, it is impossible to predict the shape that the 'city' of restitution/unjust enrichment might take when *Goff and Jones* reaches its hundredth anniversary, and whether indeed that 'city' will still exist. Whatever happens over the next 50 years, it is to be hoped that the subject continues to be as much a source of intellectual fodder and fun for future generations of law students, scholars and judges as it has been for past and present restitution lawyers.

[82] *Investment Trust Companies* [2017] UKSC 29, [40]. See also *Swynson*, above n 43, [22] (Lord Sumption).

[83] Langbein, above n 35.

[84] ibid.

2. Australia

ELISE BANT

I. A POTTED HISTORY OF UNJUST ENRICHMENT IN AUSTRALIA PRE-*AFSL* V *HILLS INDUSTRIES*

The trials and tribulations of unjust enrichment law and theory in Australia are well documented. Scholars have charted the early enthusiasm of the High Court of Australia for the clarity unjust enrichment analysis brought to the muddied waters of implied contract and quasi-contractual reasoning.[85] *Pavey & Matthews Pty Ltd v Paul*,[86] *Australia and New Zealand Banking Group Ltd v Westpac Banking Corporation*,[87] *David Securities Pty Ltd v Commonwealth Bank of Australia*[88] and *Baltic Shipping Company v Dillon*[89] seemed to lead the way in developing a sophisticated and coherent understanding of the nature and place of the law of unjust enrichment. Unjust enrichment scholarship was embraced as an integral part of that work. But this welcoming atmosphere quickly cooled in a series of decisions in which the High Court repeatedly cautioned against the unthinking acceptance of unjust enrichment analysis,[90] which threatened to introduce an ahistorical incoherence to the law. Unjust enrichment theory became synonymous with 'top-down' reasoning, at the expense of and alien to more traditional common law and equitable modes of analysis. On this view, unjust enrichment reasoning offered a one-size-fits-all analytical framework that was simply inappropriate to necessarily diverse and complex common law and equitable claims.

In that context, Australian unjust enrichment scholars understandably welcomed the 2012 High Court of Australia decision in *Equuscorp Pty Ltd v Haxton*.[91] The joint reasons of French CJ, Crennan and Kiefel JJ appeared clearly to vindicate the value of unjust enrichment analysis in Australia. They affirmed that it was not an illegitimate, unhelpful form of top-down reasoning and that it did not purport to found or reflect any 'all-embracing theory of restitutionary rights and remedies'.[92]

[85] See, eg, A Burrows, 'The Australian Law of Restitution: Has the High Court Lost its Way?' in E Bant and M Harding (eds), *Exploring Private Law* (Cambridge University Press, Cambridge, 2010) 67; K Mason, 'Strong Coherence, Strong Fusion, Continuing Categorical Confusion: The High Court's Latest Contributions to the Law of Restitution' (2015) 39 *Australian Bar Review* 284.

[86] (1987) 162 CLR 221.

[87] (1988) 164 CLR 662.

[88] (1992) 175 CLR 353.

[89] (1993) 176 CLR 344.

[90] *Roxborough v Rothmans of Pall Mall Ltd* [2001] HCA 68, (2001) 208 CLR 516; *Farah Constructions Pty Ltd v Say-Dee Pty Ltd* [2007] HCA 22, (2007) 230 CLR 89; *Lumbers v W Cook Builders Pty Ltd (in liq)* [2008] HCA 27, (2008) 232 CLR 635; *Bofinger v Kingsway Group Ltd* [2009] HCA 44, (2009) 239 CLR 269.

[91] [2012] HCA 7, (2012) 246 CLR 498; E Bant, 'Illegality and the Revival of Unjust Enrichment in Australia' (2012) *LQR* 341.

[92] ibid [30].

Rather, unjust enrichment served a useful, taxonomical function in identifying and understanding categories of cases in which the law allows restitution. In this regard, their Honours adopted and endorsed the fourfold inquiry now well established in English courts, which directs attention to the presence of (i) an enrichment, (ii) that has come at the expense of the plaintiff, (iii) a vitiating or 'unjust factor' and (iv) potential defences.

II. *AFSL v HILLS INDUSTRIES*

Seen against this turbulent background, the High Court's most recent, extended consideration of the law of unjust enrichment in *Australian Financial Services and Leasing Pty Limited v Hills Industries Limited*[93] necessarily invites renewed reflection on its future development in Australia. Stated in brief, AFSL was induced by the fraud of a third party to make mistaken payments to the defendants, Hills and Bosch. The issue before the High Court was whether the defendants were protected from the obligation to make restitution of the value of the mistaken payments by virtue of various changes of position they had made in reliance on their receipts. The members of the High Court engaged in careful analyses of the nature of the change of position defence, which have significantly advanced our understanding of its purpose and effect. The defence is, broadly speaking, designed to protect good faith defendants from being placed unjustly by an order for restitution in a worse position than they occupied prior to their receipt.[94] When addressing this purpose, the High Court explained that courts should not take an overly restrictive approach to the question of the detriment to be avoided: the defence is not solely concerned with a mathematical inquiry into disenrichment, for example, but encompasses a vast array of diverse changes that can prevent return of the parties to their former positions.[95] This aspect of the judgment has been broadly welcomed in Australia as providing a nuanced approach to the defence that draws on the rich body of learning concerning analogous concepts in estoppel and charts a sure course for its future development.

However, from a broader perspective, the language of the decision has puzzled scholars and practitioners alike. Redolent with references to the equitable foundations of unjust enrichment, all judgments speak of the importance of concepts of unconscionability and inequitability in determining restitutionary liability.[96] It is not clear how these references should be understood or what their significance is for the future development of the law of unjust enrichment in Australia.[97] Some

[93] [2014] HCA 14, (2014) 253 CLR 560.

[94] ibid [23] (French CJ), [84]–[85] (Crennan, Kiefel, Bell and Keane JJ), [157] (Gageler J).

[95] ibid [22]–[25] (French CJ), [78]–[84] (Crennan, Kiefel, Bell and Keane JJ), [147]–[148] (Gageler J).

[96] ibid [1] (French CJ), [65]–[77] (Hayne, Crennan, Kiefel, Bell and Keane JJ), [155] (Gageler J).

[97] See, eg, K Mason, J Carter and G Tolhurst, *Mason & Carter's Restitution Law in Australia*, 3rd edn (Chatswood, LexisNexis Butterworths, 2016) [123]; J Edelman and E Bant, *Unjust Enrichment*, 2nd edn (Oxford, Hart Publishing, 2016) 25–28.

commentators have also been concerned that the joint judgment of Crennan, Kiefel, Bell and Keane JJ in *AFSL* marks a fresh rejection of unjust enrichment analysis.[98] In the course of eschewing the 'disenrichment' approach to change of position, their Honours stated that 'the concept of unjust enrichment is not the basis of restitutionary relief in Australian law'.[99]

This particular passage certainly proved influential in the subsequent Victorian Supreme Court of Appeal case of *Southage Pty Ltd v Vescovi*.[100] As in *AFSL v Hills Industries*, that case concerned the application of the change of position defence in the context of a claim for restitution of a mistaken payment induced by a third party's fraud. In the course of upholding the result reached at first instance, the Court criticised the trial judge for adopting an analysis based on the fourfold inquiry.[101] Citing the passage, their Honours concluded that 'authority binding on this Court is against liability to restitution being established by … [the] questions identified by the judge'.[102] Rather, their Honours adopted the 'two stage analysis'[103] developed in *David Securities Pty Ltd v Commonwealth Bank of Australia*.[104]

What, however, was that two-stage analysis? In *AFSL v Hills Industries*, Gageler J described it in the following way:[105]

> [T]he concept of unjust enrichment inform[s] both: [1] the circumstances in which, if proved by a plaintiff, enrichment of the defendant at the expense of the plaintiff will be prima facie unjust and in which the law will therefore recognise a prima facie obligation to make restitution of a payment; and [2] the circumstances which, if proved by the defendant, will "show[] that his or her receipt (or retention) of the payment is not unjust" and in which the law will therefore recognise a defence.

On this analysis, the Victorian Supreme Court of Appeal's apparent wholesale rejection of the role of unjust enrichment reasoning merely serves to underscore its inevitable potency.[106] It is certainly the case that unjust enrichment reasoning underpins a raft of cases[107] handed down since *AFSL v Hills Industries*. These include a subsequent and unanimous High Court decision on the equitable doctrine

[98] K Mason, 'Strong Coherence, Strong Fusion, Continuing Categorical Confusion: The High Court's Latest Contributions to the Law of Restitution' (2015) 39 *Australian Bar Review* 284: 'On one reading, the jurisprudence of the past three decades has been ditched without a backward glance …' cf the cautiously more optimistic discussion in K Mason, J Carter and G Tolhurst, *Mason & Carter's Restitution Law in Australia*, 3rd edn (Chatswood, LexisNexis Butterworths, 2016) [123].

[99] ibid [78].

[100] [2015] VSCA 117.

[101] ibid [49].

[102] ibid [49].

[103] ibid [51].

[104] [1992] HCA 48, (1992) 175 CLR 353, 379 (Mason CJ, Deane, Toohey, Gaudron and McHugh JJ).

[105] [2014] HCA 14, (2014) 253 CLR 560, [136].

[106] See further Edelman and Bant, above n 97, 26.

[107] eg *Electric Life Pty Ltd v Unison Finance Group Pty Ltd* [2015] NSWCA 394; *Belgravia Nominees Pty Ltd v Lowe Pty Ltd* [No 3] [2015] WASC 442; *Comgroup Supplies Pty Ltd v Products for Industry Pty Ltd* [2016] QCA 88; *Fistar v Riverwood Legion and Community Club Ltd* [2016] NSWCA 81, [53] (Leeming JA, Bathurst CJ agreeing), [90]–[93] (Sackville AJA); *Great Investments Ltd v Warner* [2016] FCAFC 85, [68]–[69] (the Court).

of contribution, which explained the claim in terms of unjust enrichment and the fourfold analysis.[108]

III. THE FUTURE OF UNJUST ENRICHMENT AND RESTITUTION LAW IN AUSTRALIA

The conclusion that *AFSL v Hills Industries* supports the continued evolution of unjust enrichment reasoning in Australia prompts a further question: in what direction? The High Court's repeated consideration of that body of law in recent years suggests a number of possibilities.

A. Evolution and Refinement of the Fourfold Inquiry

The High Court has repeatedly stated that unjust enrichment is not 'a principle of direct application'.[109] Unjust enrichment is not a concept to be applied in the round, at a high level of generality, to the specific facts of pleaded cases. Rather, it is a taxonomical construct that helps us understand the common features of a certain category of claims. The fourfold inquiry provides guideposts to relevant considerations that commonly characterise, and help to analyse and explain, these more specific claims. But its elements are not legislative requirements, and close regard must always be had to the particular requirements of the claims as they appear from the cases. Thus, the High Court has cautioned that blunt application of the usual fourfold inquiry may be overly restrictive of, or obscure, the relevant considerations for restitutionary liability.[110] This concern may inform the High Court's recent emphasis on the equitable foundations of unjust enrichment. This approach aims to counter a common law-like loyalty to bright line rules in favour of a more open-textured approach that leaves room for relevant considerations not evident on the face of the fourfold (or two-stage) inquiry.

There are a number of areas that illustrate the danger of an overly rigid adherence to the fourfold inquiry. It is increasingly evident that a plaintiff who has made a mistaken payment to a defendant (and thus seemingly satisfies the first three elements of the inquiry) may nonetheless not be entitled to restitution—even in the absence of a recognised defence. An example was given by Lord Walker in *Pitt v Holt*,[111]

[108] *Lavin v Toppi* [2015] HCA 4, (2015) 254 CLR 459, [41] (the Court).

[109] *Farah Constructions Pty Ltd v Say-Dee Pty Ltd* [2007] HCA 22, (2007) 81 ALJR 1107, [151] (the Court); *Lumbers v W Cook Builders Pty Ltd (In liq)* [2008] HCA 27, (2008) 232 CLR 635, 665 [85] (Gummow, Hayne, Crennan and Kiefel JJ); *Bofinger v Kingsway Group Ltd* [2009] HCA 44, (2009) 239 CLR 269, [85] (the Court); *Friend v Brooker* [2009] HCA 21, (2009) 239 CLR 129, 141 [7].

[110] eg *Roxborough v Rothmans of Pall Mall Ltd* [2001] HCA 68, (2001) 208 CLR 516; *Farah Constructions Pty Ltd v Say-Dee Pty Ltd* [2007] HCA 22, (2007) 230 CLR 89; *Lumbers v W Cook Builders Pty Ltd (in liq)* [2008] HCA 27, (2008) 232 CLR 635.

[111] *Pitt v Holt* [2013] UKSC 26, [2013] 2 AC 108, [114] (Lord Walker, delivering the judgment of the Court).

namely where a plaintiff has assumed the risk of error in making a payment to the defendant. The relevance of risk-taking in cases of mistake has been well recognised by Australian courts,[112] and properly so. However, too rigid or automatic an application of the fourfold inquiry may fail to appreciate the nuanced, lower-level inquiry necessary to determine restitutionary liability, including the relevance of any assumption of risk by the plaintiff in the context of mistake.

Another example relates to the increasing appreciation of the demands of what Keith Mason has called 'conceptual coherence' in the unjust enrichment inquiry.[113] The High Court has emphasised that a claim for restitution of unjust enrichment cannot contradict or confound another overriding requirement, principle or policy of the law. An example of where this occurred, and had to be corrected by the High Court, is *Lumbers v W Cook Builders Pty Ltd (In liq)*.[114] In that case, the presence of a valid contract justifying the receipt and retention of the plaintiff's services by the defendant demanded that any claim for restitution must inevitably fail. Coherence thus dictates that it is not enough to show that there is some vitiating or 'unjust factor' that led to the transaction that enriched the defendant: the plaintiff must also negate any juristic reason the defendant may have to retain the benefit (such as pursuant to a contract, statute or debt owed by the plaintiff to the defendant). This requirement of coherence applies more generally in the law of unjust enrichment, in a way which is not explicit on the face of the fourfold inquiry and is only now starting to be articulated by commentators.[115]

B. Unjust Enrichment and Restitution

The principle of coherence also demands that we examine closely another potential overreach that might occur from overly rigid application of the unjust enrichment analysis. The statement in the joint judgment in *AFSL* that 'the concept of unjust enrichment is not the basis of restitutionary relief in Australian law' is consistent with increasing recognition that restitution is 'multi-causal': that is, it responds to categories of legally significant events other than unjust enrichment. The implications of this point have perhaps been under-appreciated to date. The chief, generally recognised examples of independent reasons for restitution are legal or equitable wrongdoing. However, it is strongly arguable that claims for restitution on grounds of policy are also normatively and doctrinally distinct.

[112] eg *Qld Alumina Ltd v Alinta DQP Pty Ltd* [2007] QCA 387, [70]–[72] (Holmes JA); *Re Magarey Farlam Lawyers Trust Accounts (No 3)* [2007] SASC 9, (2007) 96 SASR 337, [172] (Debelle J); *Lahoud v Lahoud* [2010] NSWSC 1297, [180] (Ward J); *Salib v Gakas* [2010] NSWSC 505, [333] (Ward J).

[113] K Mason, 'Strong Coherence, Strong Fusion, Continuing Categorical Confusion: The High Court's Latest Contributions to the Law of Restitution' (2015) 39 *Australian Bar Review* 284.

[114] [2008] HCA 27, (2008) 232 CLR 635.

[115] Notably led by C Mitchell, P Mitchell and S Watterson, *Goff and Jones' The Law of Unjust Enrichment*, 8th edn (London, Sweet & Maxwell, 2011). See now also A Burrows, *A Restatement of the English Law of Unjust Enrichment* (Oxford, Oxford University Press, 2012) s 3(6); Edelman and Bant, above n 97, chs 6 and 7. Courts arguably have been alive to the issue for far longer: see, eg, *David Securities Pty Ltd v Commonwealth Bank of Australia* (1992) 175 CLR 353, [6] (Brennan J).

Policy-based reasons for restitution apply even though the plaintiff's consent to the transaction may have been perfect. They constitute reasons external to the justice of the transaction between the parties which require restitution of the enrichment from the plaintiff. Examples of this category of claim include claims based on the *Woolwich* principle,[116] claims involving members of a protected class,[117] withdrawal from an illegal transaction,[118] incapacity[119] and reversal of judgment restitution.[120] In all cases, there are aspects of the policy-based claims that simply do not align with the usual unjust enrichment inquiry. For example, questions of intention and causation are usually irrelevant or marginalised in the policy cases, and application of the change of position defence will undermine or stultify the policy demanding restitution. To lump these claims together with others solely concerned with impaired or imperfect consent is to invite confusion and incoherence in the law.

The evolution of the policy-based *Woolwich* claim illustrates the dangers of confusing the two categories. Courts' and commentators' assumptions that this category of claim forms part of the law of unjust enrichment for a long time led to the further natural, but incorrect, conclusion that the change of position defence must apply.[121] However, any application of the change of position defence to *Woolwich*-based claims necessarily undermines the informing policy of no taxation without legislation. Fortunately, this error is now being corrected, specifically by reference to the demands of coherence.[122] The same principled approach to the application of the defence is now also being taken to mistake-based or pressure-based claims brought for restitution of tax.[123]

It is an interesting feature of the post-*AFSL v Hills Industries* jurisprudence that Australian courts seem to favour categorising the claim by reference to the specific reason for restitution (mistake, duress, want of authority and the like) or, less happily, the language of the old forms of action over the more generalised language of unjust enrichment. This preference runs the risk of losing sight of the commonalities between related forms of claim.[124] However, it does have the merit of avoiding unfounded assumptions of a generalised correlation between availability of a remedy of restitution and the many and varied reasons for restitution.

[116] Named after *Woolwich Equitable Building Society v Inland Revenue Commissioners* [1993] AC 70.

[117] eg *Amadio Pty Ltd v Henderson* (1998) 81 FCR 149, 197 (the Court); *South Australian Cold Stores Ltd v Electricity Trust of South Australia* (1965) 115 CLR 247, 257 (Kitto J).

[118] eg *Nelson v Nelson* (1995) 184 CLR 538, 562.

[119] eg *Auckland Harbour Board v The King* [1924] AC 318, 327 (Viscount Haldane, delivering the opinion of the Board); *Gibbons v Wright* (1954) 91 CLR 423.

[120] eg *Woolworths Ltd v Strong (No 2)* [2011] NSWCA 72, (2011) 80 NSWLR 445.

[121] eg *Commissioner of State Revenue (Vic) v Royal Insurance Australia Ltd* (1994) 182 CLR 51, 64 (Mason CJ); *Test Claimants in the FII Group Litigation v Revenue and Customs Commissioners* [2008] EWHC 2893, [2009] STC 254.

[122] *Prudential Assurance Co Ltd v Revenue and Customs Commissioners* [2013] EWHC 3249, [2014] 2 CMLR 10 [188] (Henderson J); *Test Claimants in the FII Group Litigation v HM Revenue & Customs* [2014] EWHC 4302, [2015] STC 1471, [310]–[315] (Henderson J).

[123] ibid.

[124] See, eg, *SunWater Limited v Drake Coal Pty Ltd* [2016] QCA 255, [19] (Philippides JA), [36] (Philip McMurdo JA).

C. Equity and Unjust Enrichment

One of the most important areas of potential development in the Australian law of unjust enrichment lies in its ongoing relation with equitable principles. The High Court in *AFSL v Hills Industries* repeatedly emphasised the equitable foundations of unjust enrichment and that the law of unjust enrichment concerns 'unconscionable' or 'inequitable' retention of benefit. We have seen that this likely reflects resistance to an overly rigid characterisation and application of unjust enrichment principles. However, there are additional possibilities that merit brief discussion.

One possibility must be immediately and emphatically rejected. It is clear that the High Court's linguistic shift did not signal recognition of a model of liability in which unjust enrichment is founded on legal or equitable wrongdoing. Both the defendants and plaintiff in *AFSL v Hills Industries* were the innocent victims of a third party's fraud. Indeed, although it had been argued variously in the courts below that either the plaintiff or the defendant could have avoided the whole problem by being more careful, it was accepted that neither party was particularly careless and there was no value to be had in throwing allegations of blame either way.[125] Moreover, in *David Securities*,[126] the joint judgment expressly rejected the defendant's contention that, over and above having received a mistaken payment, some element of unconscionability must be proven for prima facie liability in unjust enrichment. *David Securities* has never been challenged or doubted on this point. This was re-emphasised by Gageler J in *AFSL v Hills Industries*.[127] As the joint judgment separately emphasised, restitution for a mistaken payment is entirely independent of tort, and considerations of fault form no part of the conditions for prima facie liability.[128]

Another possibility is that the language of 'unconscionable retention of benefit'[129] alludes to the requirement (discussed earlier) that a plaintiff must negate any juristic reason the defendant has to retain the benefit.[130] However, if so, it may be better to reframe the requirement in those terms, to avoid confusion over any role for fault in the inquiry.

Justice Edelman has suggested that the High Court's language of inequitability and unconscionability refers to the overarching norms motivating restitutionary liability in this field, rather than to the discrete conditions or requirements of liability.[131] On this approach, the concepts reflect high-level normative standards of corrected conscience, in which a defendant who has been unjustly enriched at the expense of another must make restitution to that other. 'Unconscionability' is a statement of

[125] ibid [55]–[57], [64], [69] (Hayne, Crennan, Kiefel, Bell and Keane JJ).
[126] (1992) 175 CLR 353, 378.
[127] [2014] HCA 14, (2014) 253 CLR 560, [134]–[135].
[128] ibid [83] (Hayne, Crennan, Kiefel, Bell and Keane JJ).
[129] *Perpetual Trustees Australia Ltd v Heperu Pty Ltd* [2009] NSWCA 84, (2009) 76 NSWLR 195; *Heperu Pty Ltd v Belle* [2009] NSWCA 252, (2009) 76 NSWLR 230.
[130] Edelman and Bant, above n 97, 28, chs 6 and 7.
[131] *Lampson (Australia) Pty Ltd v Fortescue Metals Group Ltd (No 3)* [2014] WASC 162, [45]–[55].

conclusion, rather than reflective of the process of reasoning that leads to it.[132] In the words of the joint judgment in *AFSL v Hills Industries*:[133]

> The issues of conscience which fall to be resolved assume a conscience 'properly formed and instructed' by established equitable principles and doctrines. As was said in *Kakavas v Crown Melbourne Ltd*, '[t]he conscience spoken of here is a construct of values and standards against which the conduct of "suitors"—not only defendants—is to be judged'.

This high-level conception is, as the High Court has also repeatedly recognised, not itself a principle of direct application. As Gageler J noted in *AFSL v Hills Industries*: 'No less than its traditional synonyms, "unconscionable" and "unconscientious", "unjust" has the potential to "mask rather than illuminate the underlying principles at stake".'[134] Rather, as French CJ stated: 'Guiding criteria are indispensable to judicial decision-making in the application of broad normative standards to particular classes of case.'[135] In this context, the guidance offered by the fourfold inquiry is a critical starting point to a more nuanced inquiry, at an even lower level of generality, into the conditions for liability. This is not a matter of unarticulated judicial discretion but the search for recognised principles, by exegesis of the cases, drawing from common law, equitable and potentially even statutory sources.

This raises the final, and perhaps most intriguing, possibility for the future development of the Australian law of unjust enrichment. The High Court's emphasis on the equitable foundations of unjust enrichment does not deny, contrary to history, the common law origins of, for example, the action for money had and received.[136] But that emphasis, alongside the weight placed on the principle of coherence, strongly suggests that equitable and common law concepts and doctrines will increasingly be integrated within the Australian law of unjust enrichment. Recent judicial recognition of an alternative, strict liability claim for restitution that works alongside the fault-based equitable wrong of knowing receipt may be an early example of this development.[137]

If correct, we should expect to see, for example, formal recognition of undue influence as a reason for restitution alongside mistake and duress, with which it shares so much in common.[138] These strict liability forms of claim could then stand alongside wrong-based claims of deceit, intimidation and abuse of influence, the remedies for which would include but not be limited to restitutionary relief.[139] Equitable doctrines such as unconscionable dealing[140] may likewise evolve strict wrongs-based

[132] *Garcia v National Australia Bank* [1998] HCA 48, (1998) 194 CLR 395, [34] (Gaudron, McHugh, Gummow and Hayne JJ).

[133] [2014] HCA 14, (2014) 253 CLR 560, [76] (citations omitted).

[134] ibid [140].

[135] ibid [25].

[136] ibid [65]–[69] (Hayne, Crennan, Kiefel, Bell and Keane JJ).

[137] *Fistar v Riverwood Legion and Community Club Ltd* [2016] NSWCA 81; *Great Investments Ltd v Warner* [2016] FCAFC 85, [68] (the Court).

[138] *David Securities Pty Ltd v Commonwealth Bank of Australia* (1992) 175 CLR 353, 374 [36] (Mason CJ, Deane, Toohey, Gaudron and McHugh JJ); *Benedetti v Sawiris* [2013] UKSC 50, [2014] AC 938, [175] (Lord Neuberger); *Hart v Burbidge* [2014] EWCA Civ 992, [43] (Vos LJ, Black and Richards LJJ concurring).

[139] cf *Great Investments Ltd v Warner* [2016] FCAFC 85, [53] (the Court).

[140] *Blomley v Ryan* (1956) 99 CLR 362; *Commercial Bank of Australia v Amadio* (1983) 151 CLR 447; *Kakavas v Crown Melbourne Ltd* [2013] HCA 25, (2013) 250 CLR 392.

forms, the one focusing on impaired judgment arising from circumstances of special disadvantage, the other on exploitation of special disadvantage. Such claims would have different elements and give rise to distinct remedial relief. We may expect that courts will seek to integrate the law of rescission into the law of unjust enrichment and restitution, drawing on its many insights for the defence of change of position, the concept of enrichment and, of course, its role in negating juristic reasons to retain benefits.[141] Finally, in Australia, this work in developing a coherent private law will also need to take into account statutory principles[142] that notably draw equally from common law and equitable sources and play an increasingly dominant role in circumstances of unjust enrichment.

The task of developing an integrated and coherent law of unjust enrichment is not an easy one: as the use of estoppel as a guiding analogical source of principle in *AFSL v Hills Industries* itself illustrates,[143] the promises of coherence may also present traps for the unwary. Overall, however, the prospect is an exciting one that ultimately bodes well for the future for the law of unjust enrichment, and unjust enrichment scholarship, in Australia.

IV. CONCLUSION

In concluding this brief reflection, the future of unjust enrichment in Australia remains bright following *AFSL v Hills Industries*. Unjust enrichment reasoning has not been abandoned, but, rather, has been put onto a potentially more integrated and nuanced footing. Only time will tell whether any of the speculation as to its future evolution in this piece is well founded. Much will depend on the evolving constitution of the High Court bench, as it has always done.[144] However, what is clear is that Australian law and jurisprudence will continue to provide important insights for companion jurisdictions seeking to map and clarify their own laws of unjust enrichment and restitution.

[141] E Bant, 'Rescission, Restitution and Compensation' in J Varuhas and S Degeling (eds), *Equitable Compensation and Disgorgement* (Oxford, Hart Publishing, 2017) ch 13.

[142] Such as the overarching norms against misleading and unconconscionable conduct found throughout the consumer, company and securities acts.

[143] See, eg, Gageler J's *obiter* suggestion that change of position, like estoppel, operates as a complete defence subject to a disproportionality requirement, which would invert the usual, proportionate operation of the change of position defence: [2014] HCA 14, (2014) 253 CLR 560, [158]. This suggestion seems not to have been taken up by courts subsequently applying his Honour's analysis: see *Comgroup Supplies Pty Ltd v Products for Industry Pty Ltd* [2016] QCA 88.

[144] Compare, eg, Deane J in *Pavey & Matthews Pty Ltd v Paul* (1987) 162 CLR 221 and Gummow J in *Roxborough v Rothmans of Pall Mall Ltd* [2001] HCA 68, (2001) 208 CLR 516. In England, the influence of Lord Goff through decisions such as *Barclays Bank Ltd v WJ Simms Son & Cooke (Southern) Ltd* [1980] QB 677 and *Lipkin Gorman v Karpnale Ltd* [1991] 2 AC 548 arguably parallels that of Deane J, but without a counteracting equivalent to Gummow J.

3. Canada

MITCHELL McINNES

I. INTRODUCTION

Within the broader topic of *Revolutions in Private Law*, this paper was assigned the task of providing an overview of the modern Canadian law of unjust enrichment. At first glance, that might seem a fairly simple task. During the second part of the twentieth century, Canadian law split from orthodoxy on a number of important points: its peculiar perception of equity, its relaxed view of remedial constructive trusts, its fixation on family cases, and so on. It seems a stretch, however, to characterise any of those developments as truly revolutionary, in the sense of fundamentally transforming the concept's core. Revolution, by its nature, is rare.

That label nevertheless fits the decision taken in *Garland v Consumers' Gas Co*,[145] to adopt a model of juristic reasons for deciding the availability of restitution. Since 2004, Canadian law has framed the issue of injustice in terms of reasons for retention rather than reasons for reversal. A more profound shift is difficult to imagine, and to their credit, Canadian courts have managed the task admirably well. The future, however, is not yet secure. Unhappy with change, one influential scholar has argued for a curious compromise that would subject some cases to the new regime, but others to the old. Nothing could be worse.

II. HISTORY

Restitution had always been available in Canada, under various labels and in specific instances, but the law traditionally lacked any guiding principle or coherent scheme. That changed in 1954, with *Deglman v Guaranty Trust Co*.[146] More than a decade before *Goff & Jones*[147] appeared, the Supreme Court of Canada became the first Commonwealth court to connect restitution to an independent principle of unjust enrichment. Truth be told, however, the impact was far from revolutionary. Claims continued to be resolved much the same as before and the subject excited little interest.

An opportunity for more meaningful change arose, a quarter of a century later, at the intersection of private law and public policy. Upon the dissolution of a cohabitational relationship, a woman was apt to be treated shabbily by both her former partner and the law. By tradition, she laboured in the home while he earned income and acquired assets. The courts, operating within the same paradigm, seldom saw grounds for intervention where such traditional arrangements ended in separation

[145] [2004] 1 SCR 629.
[146] [1954] SCR 725.
[147] R Goff and G Jones, *The Law of Restitution* (London, Sweet & Maxwell, 1966).

and assets were accordingly divided. Few couples predetermined the economic consequences of their relationship by contract, and the conventional constructive trusts did not extend to such circumstances. A resulting trust would exist if the woman financially contributed to the purchase of enduring assets, but few women worked outside the home and those who did often directed their incomes to household expenses. Something had to be done.

During the 1970s, provincial legislatures began exploring mandated sharing, at least between former spouses.[148] The Supreme Court of Canada similarly searched for a way forward. A solution was found in the 'equitable' doctrines of unjust enrichment and constructive trust, both of which were usefully venerable and obscure. Age lent the effort an air of respectability; lack of familiarity within the profession afforded the courts considerable flexibility.

That strategy[149] was implemented in 1980 in *Pettkus v Becker*.[150] The decision was important in several respects. Most obviously, it explained why relief was available when couples parted. The defendant was held to have freely accepted the plaintiff's services despite knowing that she expected, in exchange, to share the accumulated assets. A constructive trust then achieved an equitable division of assets.[151] As evidenced by the fact that it remains a staple of family law practice, *Pettkus v Becker* undoubtedly was good social policy.

The extent to which *Pettkus v Becker* was good law is more contentious. Dickson J's judgment became the template for restitutionary claims regardless of context. And though there is much to admire, several aspects of the decision are problematic. The perverse belief that unjust enrichment, as a whole, is equitable in origin and nature[152] continues to jeopardise legitimate claims[153] and encourages judges to broadly assess 'the equities of the case'.[154] The desire to fulfil expectations, while appropriate in the context of failed intimate relationships, is difficult to accommodate within a principle designed to reverse unwarranted transfers. Canadian courts nevertheless insist that in every case of unjust enrichment, 'the fundamental concern is the legitimate expectation of the parties'.[155] Likewise, while proprietary relief may be readily justified as between former spouses or partners, it otherwise has proven

[148] The common law action is available even if the legislation applies: *Rawluk v Rawluk* [1990] 1 SCR 70.

[149] The development began with Laskin J's dissent in *Murdoch v Murdoch* [1975] 1 SCR 423 and continued with Dickson J's concurrence in *Rathwell v Rathwell* [1978] 2 SCR 436.

[150] [1980] 2 SCR 834.

[151] The trust ultimately failed to achieve its goal. Lothar Pettkus, rotten to the end, used various ploys to frustrate Rosa Becker's efforts to satisfy judgment. Exhausted by the dispute and disillusioned by the legal system, she committed suicide without having obtained relief.

[152] *Pettkus v Becker* [1980] 2 SCR 834, 848; *Garland v Consumers' Gas Co* [2004] 1 SCR 629, [44]; *Air Canada v British Columbia* [1989] 1 SCR 1133, 1213; cf *Communities Economic Development Fund v Canadian Pickles Corp* [1991] 3 SCR 388, 415.

[153] *R v S* (1988) 17 RFL (3d) 170 (unjust enrichment cannot be applied by courts that lack equitable jurisdiction); *Toronto-Dominion Bank v Bank of Montreal* (1995) 22 OR (3d) 362, 373 (restitution unavailable if claimant lacks clean hands).

[154] *Upham (cob MU Rhino Renovations) v Dora Construction Ltd* 2016 NSSC 90, [78].

[155] *Peter v Beblow* [1993] 1 SCR 980, 990. See also *Garland v Consumers' Gas Co* [2004] 1 SCR 629, [46].

problematic. Canadians seem broadly agreed that a purely personal response may be inadequate if a cohabitee acted in the expectation of sharing title. The lack of analytical rigour, however, creates substantial problems outside of family matters. While proprietary disgorgement of wrongful gains is governed by a comprehensive scheme,[156] the availability of a truly restitutionary constructive trust turns on the individual judge's treatment of a long list of inconclusive criteria.[157]

III. A FALSE START

Pettkus v Becker's most enduring legacy, of course, is the formulation of the autonomous cause of action. Since 1980, Canadian lawyers have framed restitutionary claims simply in terms of the three-part principle. Notwithstanding occasional lapses into the language of ancient writs,[158] courts routinely reckon liability directly in terms of enrichments, corresponding deprivations and reasons to reverse.[159]

Unrecognised at the time, however, the three-part action sowed seeds of confusion. Rather than simply refer to 'a reason to reverse', Dickson J held that an unjust enrichment required 'an absence of any juristic reason'.[160] The language is civilian. Whereas the common law had always required the plaintiff to prove an *unjust factor* (ie a positive reason for restitution, such as a mistake), civil law traditionally allowed recovery unless the defendant pointed to some *juristic reason* for the transfer (ie a reason for retention, such as a contract). The two systems essentially operate in opposite directions. One says 'No restitution unless …'; the other says, 'Restitution unless …'.

Dickson J clearly had no intention of revolutionising liability. He made no mention of the matter, and, regardless of terminology, he tied recovery to the unjust factor of free acceptance. The explanation for his use of the civilian phrase may never be known, but it most likely was an accident of bijuridicalism. Three years before *Pettkus v Becker*, Dickson J concurred in a colleague's formulation of the action for unjustified enrichment that exists in Quebec.[161] On that occasion, Beetz J naturally said that the civilian claim involves 'the absence of justification' for the defendant's enrichment. That phrase, it seems, simply stuck in Dickson J's mind.

For the next quarter century, virtually every case reflected Dickson J's lead. Decisions were civilian in form, but common law in substance.[162] Running parallel

[156] *Soulos v Korkontzilas* [1997] 2 SCR 217, [45].

[157] M McInnes, *The Canadian Law of Unjust Enrichment and Restitution* (Markham, LexisNexis, 2014) 32.

[158] *BMP Global Distribution Inc v Bank of Nova Scotia* [2009] 1 SCR 504; *Barafield Realty Ltd v Just Energy (BC) Limited Partnership* 2015 BCCA 421.

[159] *Peel (Regional Municipality) v Canada* [1992] 3 SCR 762, 786; cf *Ileman v Rogers Communications Inc* 2014 BCSC 1002, [117], affd 2015 BCCA 260, [68]–[70] (ancient writs subsumed within unjust enrichment).

[160] [1980] 2 SCR 834, 848.

[161] *Cie Immobilière Viger Ltée v Lauréat Giguère Inc* [1977] 2 SCR 67, 77.

[162] *Nepean (Township) Hydro Electric Commission v Ontario Hydro* [1982] 1 SCR 347 (mistake); *Re Eurig* [1998] 2 SCR 565 (compulsion); *Palachik v Kiss* [1983] 3851 SCR 623 (failure of consideration). *Sorochan v Sorochan* [1986] 2 SCR 38 (free acceptance).

to that line of authority, however, a sliver of precedence took the terminology at face value and imposed liability for enrichments that lacked juristic reason.[163] Canadian law became confused. While courts usually said one thing but did another, litigants could never be sure how their disputes would be resolved. The situation was intolerable.

IV. A NEW DIRECTION

Canadian law had a choice. The simpler solution merely required a semantic shift back to the common law language of unjust factors. Judges could otherwise continue with what they had been doing. The alternative was distinctly unattractive. Holding firm to the civilian phrase, courts could make the enormous leap into civilian analysis. Academic opinion ran against that option, primarily for fear of the associated costs.[164] A civilian test of liability would require more than a change in perspective. A comprehensive scheme of juristic reasons would have to be devised and the new regime would have to be reintegrated into the private law matrix.

The more difficult path was chosen. Iacobucci J presented *Garland v Consumers Gas Co*[165] as a modest exercise in 'redefinition and reformulation', but it actually pointed Canadian law in a radically different direction. Restitution no longer is triggered by the common law's unjust factors. It now responds to a unique variation on the classic civilian model. The plaintiff must disprove the 'established categories' of juristic reason: contract, donative intent, disposition of law and other valid common law, equitable or statutory obligations. If that burden is satisfied, the defendant may still avoid liability by demonstrating some other reason—based on public policy or the parties' reasonable expectations—for denying recovery. Defences may then be invoked at a separate stage of analysis.

V. POSITIVE DEVELOPMENTS

Garland created difficulties. Some were to be expected. It will take many years to settle the content of the four 'established categories' of juristic reason. The curious division of labour[166] between the parties has also proved to be awkward.[167] It would

[163] *Peter v Beblow* [1993] 1 SCR 980 (McLachlin J); *Reference Re: Goods and Services Tax* [1992] 2 SCR 445, 477; *Nova Scotia (Attorney General) v Walsh* [2002] 4 SCR 325, [165].

[164] L Smith, 'The Mystery of "Juristic Reason"' (2000) 12 *Supreme Court Law Review* (2d) 211; M McInnes, 'The Canadian Principle of Unjust Enrichment: Comparative Insights into the Law of Restitution' (1999) 37 *Alberta Law Review* 1.

[165] [2004] 1 SCR 629, [44].

[166] There is some confusion regarding *Garland*'s second branch. Iacobucci J invited the defendant to 'rebut' the prima facie right to restitution that arises once the plaintiff has negated the 'established categories' of juristic reason. Some courts, however, have turned the analysis around by allowing claimants to invoke policy or expectations in order to rebut proven juristic reasons: *KBA Canada Inc v 3S Printers Inc* 2012 BCSC 1078, revd 2014 BCCA 117; *Frame v Rai* 2012 BCSC 1876.

[167] *Solarblue LLC v Aus* 2014 ONSC 3482 (conflating *Garland*'s second branch with the change of position defence); *College of the North Atlantic v Newfoundland and Labrador Assn of Public and Private Employees* (2009) 184 LAC (4th) 25 (change of position treated as a juristic reason).

be far simpler to require the plaintiff to demonstrate that the impugned transfer was either undertaken for a purpose that failed[168] or not intended at all.[169]

Other pitfalls became apparent only after *Garland* was decided. It is now clear that certain concepts, largely superfluous under the traditional common law model but indispensable to a regime of juristic reasons, are woefully underdeveloped in Canadian law.[170] *Garland* has also revealed the extent to which legal minds resist new modes of thought. Long accustomed to being satisfied upon proof of a single unjust factor, judges sometimes allow recovery as soon as a claimant disproves a single potential juristic reason.[171] Properly applied, of course, the civilian model requires the absence of all juristic reasons.

The preceding problems are easily forgiven as the costs of change. On the whole, Canadian judges have adjusted remarkably well to the civilian-inspired test of reversibility. The burden perhaps was lightened by familiarity with the terminology, the secondary line of authority that developed between 1980 and 2004, and occasional contact with civil law in Quebec. The shift nevertheless has been managed as well as anyone could have reasonably hoped.

Indeed, evidently reinvigorated, Canadian courts have moved forward on a number of issues. The error remains oddly enduring, but there is growing recognition that most instances of restitutionary liability are not equitable after all.[172] Similarly, while the ambiguous use of 'unjust enrichment' and 'restitution' continues to befuddle,[173] judges increasingly distinguish between reversing unwarranted transfers and stripping wrongful gains.[174] The rules of tracing have been modernised with recognition that the 'evidentiary process' may operate despite a commingling of funds.[175] And perhaps most remarkably, courts have begun to acknowledge that true restitution—the restoration of a *status quo ante*—is ill-suited to cohabitational property disputes. Whereas unjust enrichment redresses past transfers, intimate relationships look forward. The parties join together to share life's benefits and

[168] The 'established categories' suggest examples. A claimant might prove that services were rendered under a contract that was void for uncertainty; that a gift was given in the erroneous belief of a special occasion; that money was paid pursuant to a subsequently overturned judgment; or that a benefit was conferred under a misinterpretation of a statutory obligation.

[169] That would be true if the plaintiff either utterly lacked intention (as in cases of theft and finding) or intended to create a benefit but did not intend for the defendant to receive it (as when property is improved under a mistake as to ownership).

[170] That is true of natural obligations, incidental benefits and officiousness: see M McInnes, above n 157, chs 27, 41, 42.

[171] *Pacific National Investments v Victoria (No 2)* [2004] 3 SCR 575; *1318847 Ontario Ltd v Laval Tool & Mould Ltd* 2015 ONSC 2664; *Low v Pfizer Canada Inc* 2014 BCSC 1469; *Hike Metal Products Ltd v Rose City Cruises (cob Royal Windsor Cruises)* (Ont SCJ, 17 January 2012). The same error arguably occurred in *Garland* itself. Satisfied that the defendant's enrichment was not justified by a statutory provision, Iacobucci J imposed liability without observing that the transfers occurred under persisting contracts.

[172] *Klein v Wolbeck* 2016 ABQB 28, [260]; *Safety First Consulting Professional Corp v Scipione* (Ont SCJ, 16 June 2015) [23].

[173] *Lac Minerals Ltd v International Corona Resources Ltd* [1989] 2 SCR 574; *Pro-Sys Consultants Ltd v Microsoft Corp* [2013] 3 SCR 477.

[174] *Indutech Canada Ltd v Gibbs Pipe Distributors Ltd* 2011 ABQB 38, [507], affd 2013 ABCA 111; *Nunavut Tunngavik Inc v Canada (Attorney General)* 2012 NUCJ 11, [308], revd on other grounds 2014 NUCA 2; *Chatfield v Bell Mobility Inc* 2014 SKQB 82, [38].

[175] *BMP Global Distribution Inc v Bank of Nova Scotia* [2009] 1 SCR 504, [78]–[79].

burdens. When the love dies, the appropriate response is to fulfil that shared expectation. To that end, *Kerr v Baranow*[176] formulated the concept of 'joint family ventures' to identify those relationships that warrant such relief. The analysis still hangs awkwardly within the unjust enrichment framework, but there is hope that the new concept eventually will serve as a unique cause of action for a unique social problem.[177]

VI. A VERY BAD IDEA

In the past decade, Canadian judges have done remarkably well in a notoriously difficult area. In that sense, the future looks bright—the *Garland* revolution has set unjust enrichment on a promising path. Danger nevertheless remains. Some commentators, resistant to change or unwilling to adapt, threaten to render the project incoherent.

In 2004, *Garland* made a clean break with the past. After 25 years of civilian form and common law substance, the Supreme Court of Canada decided that the availability of restitution depended upon the absence of juristic reasons. Iacobucci J was unequivocal. He said nothing to suggest that the new test was applicable in some cases, but not in others. His colleagues followed suit. During the next decade, the court heard at least one unjust enrichment appeal per year. And with one peculiar exception,[178] it applied *Garland* across the board. Whether it dealt with family matters,[179] transfers between commercial parties,[180] disputes in the highly nuanced context of Aboriginal–Crown relations[181] or more esoteric circumstances[182]—and whether a case arose in familiar territory or broke new ground—the court demanded proof that there was no legal explanation for the impugned enrichment.

The point was made clear in *Kerr v Baranow*,[183] the latest in the court's long line of cohabitational property decisions. On every occasion between 1980 and 2004,[184] liability was determined by the unjust factor of free acceptance. The plaintiff had to prove that the defendant received her services despite knowing that she expected some benefit in return. Nevertheless, while acknowledging that free acceptance had

[176] [2011] 1 SCR 269.

[177] cf *Guay v Pruneau* (Ont SCJ, 5 August 2015) [114] (recognising 'three streams' of unjust enrichment: the 'autonomous form ... wrongdoing [and] joint family venture').

[178] *BMP Global Distribution Inc v Bank of Nova Scotia* [2009] 1 SCR 504.

[179] *Kerr v Baranow* [2011] 1 SCR 269.

[180] *Pacific National Investments v Victoria (No 2)* [2004] 3 SCR 575; *Jedfro Investments (USA) Ltd v Jacyk* [2007] 3 SCR 679; cf *Kingstreet Investments Ltd v New Brunswick* [2007] 1 SCR 3.

[181] *Gladstone v Canada (Attorney General)* [2005] 1 SCR 325; *Ermineskin Indian Band and Nation v Canada (Attorney General)* [2009] 1 SCR 222.

[182] *Alberta v Elder Advocates of Alberta Society* [2011] 2 SCR 261; *Professional Institute of the Public Service of Canada v Canada (Attorney General)* [2012] 3 SCR 660; *Pro-Sys Consultants Ltd v Microsoft Corporation* [2013] 3 SCR 477.

[183] [2011] 1 SCR 269.

[184] *Pettkus v Becker* [1980] 2 SCR 834; *Sorochan v Sorochan* [1986] 2 SCR 38; *Rawluk v Rawluk* [1990] 1 SCR 70; *Peter v Beblow* [1993] 1 SCR 980; *Nova Scotia (Attorney General) v Walsh* [2002] 4 SCR 325. See also *Murdoch v Murdoch* [1975] SCR 423 (Laskin J); *Rathwell v Rathwell* [1978] 2 SCR 436 (Dickson J).

previously governed 'domestic unjust enrichment claims', Cromwell J explained that that analysis 'has ... been overtaken by ... *Garland* [which has] mandated a two-step approach to the juristic reason analysis'.[185] The non-titled spouse's claim consequently succeeded simply because her services were not rendered pursuant to a contract, with a donative intent or in satisfaction of some obligation.

BMP Global Distribution Inc v Bank of Nova Scotia[186] is the only post-*Garland* claim to which the Supreme Court of Canada did not apply the juristic reason test. A rogue's forged cheque caused the plaintiff bank to pay about $900,000 to the defendants. Although the defendants carelessly facilitated the fraud, and although their windfall was subtracted from the plaintiff, they wished to keep the money. Liability quite properly was imposed and there are aspects of the decision (particularly pertaining to tracing) that are most welcome. On the reason for restitution, however, the judgment is deeply perplexing. There is no mention of 'juristic reasons' or *Garland*, or even 'unjust enrichment'. The claim is analysed instead in terms of the 'doctrine of mistake of fact'. The only plausible explanation is that the judge, a civilian who had not previously written on the action for unjust enrichment, took her lead from the parties. And, for whatever reason, counsel drafted their pleadings without regard to developments after 1953.

BMP nevertheless is tendered by Professor McCamus as proof of a startling proposition.[187] 'Routine' restitutionary claims, he says, continue to be governed by the common law's unjust factors. That is why *BMP* was analysed in terms of the 'doctrine of mistake of fact'. *Garland*, he insists, is confined to 'novel' cases. Juristic reasons are relevant only at the margins, where precedent has been exhausted and there is no alternative to creating new law.

McCamus's thesis is the subject of ongoing debate.[188] Detailed discussion is beyond this essay. A few comments are nevertheless warranted in light of two factors. The first is Professor McCamus's status as the doyen of Canadian unjust enrichment. His text,[189] published in 1990 and updated in 2004, until quite recently stood unchallenged. The second factor is the profound damage that adoption of his position would entail.

It undoubtedly is possible for a legal system to embrace two models of injustice if, for instance, it is thought that property transfers are better governed by unjust factors, whereas services respond well to juristic reasons.[190] Different circumstances

[185] [2011] 1 SCR 269, [118], [121].

[186] [2009] 1 SCR 504.

[187] JD McCamus, 'Mistake, Forged Cheques and Unjust Enrichment' (2009) 48 *Canadian Business Law Journal* 76.

[188] M McInnes 'Revising the Reason for Restitution: *Garland* Ten Years After' (2015) 57 *Canadian Business Law Journal* 1; M McInnes '*Garland*'s Unitary Test of Unjust Enrichment: A Response to Professor McCamus' (2011) 38 *Advocates' Quarterly* 165; M McInnes 'The Reason to Reverse: Unjust Factors and Juristic Reasons' (2012) 92 *Boston University Law Review* 1049.

[189] PD Maddaugh and JD McCamus, *The Law of Restitution* (Aurora, Canada Law Book Inc, 1990).

[190] Quebec is such a system. The claim for *réception de l'indu* reverses transfers of property (including payments of money) if the plaintiff can establish a mistake or compulsion; the *actio de in rem verso* allows recovery for beneficial services rendered without juristic reason: *Willmor Discount Corp v Vaudreuil (City)* [1994] 2 SCR 210; *Cie Immobilière Viger Ltée v Lauréat Giguère Inc* [1977] 2 SCR 67; *Civil Code of Quebec*, SQ 1991, c 64, art 1493.

raise different concerns that may be addressed by different concepts.[191] In contrast, even if it was possible to sensibly distinguish between 'routine' and 'novel' cases,[192] there can be no principled justification for deciding the former in accordance with common law tradition and the latter along civilian lines. Being 'novel' as of 22 April 2004 is an analytically neutral fact.

Fortunately, McCamus's proposal has literally no precedential support. The vast majority of decisions have applied *Garland* without discussion. On the few occasions when the issue has arisen, courts have emphatically denied that the traditional common law analysis survives. The Alberta Court of Appeal did not entertain any doubt when it explained that *Garland* 'fundamentally re-conceived the basis for restitutionary liability. The plaintiff no longer needs to establish a positive reason, such as failure of consideration, for reversing a transfer.'[193]

The practical implications of McCamus's thesis are difficult to comprehend. If a claim is deemed to be novel on its first appearance in court, does it thereafter become routine? If so, then two instances of the same type of claim, perhaps arising from a single set of events, would be subject to juristic reasons the first time and unjust factors the second time. The situation becomes even stranger once it is realised that while the two models of injustice usually arrive at the same conclusion, they occasionally point in opposite directions.[194] A court would find for one side on Monday and the other side on Friday. Lawyers would be hard-pressed to explain such inconsistencies to their clients.

[191] That is Professor Lionel Smith's position: 'Defences and the Disunity of Unjust Enrichment' in A Dyson, J Goudkamp and F Wilmot-Smith (eds), *Defences in Unjust Enrichment* (Portland, Hart Publishing, 2016) 27, 48. He doubts that Canada has adopted a unified action in unjust enrichment, but he provides no support for the belief that *Garland* is confined to 'novel' cases: LD Smith 'The State of Unjust Enrichment in Common Law Canada' (2015) 57 *Canadian Business Law Journal* 39.

[192] The common law works by analogy. However unorthodox, a claim never requires a court to start from scratch. At the same time, no two cases are identical, even if they arise from the same factual events: *Overseas Tankship (UK) Ltd v Morts Dock & Engineering Co Ltd (Wagon Mound No 1)* [1961] AC 388; *Overseas Tankship (UK) Ltd v The Miller Steamship Co (Wagon Mound No 2)* [1967] AC 617. The impossibility of sensibly distinguishing between routine and novel cases is evidenced by the decisions delivered since *Garland*. To accept McCamus, one must believe that, other than *BMP*, every case in the Supreme Court of Canada has been novel—even those that cover familiar ground. Moreover, because almost all have been resolved by reference to juristic reasons, one must also conclude that, with rare exceptions, claims in lower courts have been universally novel. Of course, if every claim is novel, then McCamus's thesis is self-defeating.

[193] *VanCamp v Laurentian Bank of Canada* 2015 ABCA 83, [41]. See also *Bond Development Corp v Esquimalt (Township)* 2006 BCCA 248, [47] (traditional tests of liability 'have given way to the *Garland* juristic reason analysis'); *TD Canada Trust v Mosiondz* 2005 SKQB 540, [20] (precedents dealing with unjust factors 'are useful in outlining the history and development of the law [but] the analysis to be applied has been settled in … *Garland*'); *Annapolis (County) v King's County Transit* 2012 NSSC 401, [56]; *MacMichael v MacMichael Estate* 2009 BCSC 290, [27].

[194] *KBA Canada Inc v 3S Printers Inc*, above n 144, turned on essentially the same issue that previously had been resolved in *Central Guaranty Trust Co v Dixdale Mortgage Investment Corp* (1994) 121 DLR (4th) 53. The British Columbia Court of Appeal nevertheless rejected the earlier decision on the ground that it was 'decided twenty years ago [and] has been overtaken by … the Supreme Court of Canada's analysis of "juristic reason"': 2014 BCCA 117, [33]–[43]. See also *Sempra Metals Ltd v IRC* [2007] UKHL 34, [2008] 1 AC 561.

Alternatively, McCamus might say that once a claim is labelled 'novel', it must forever be treated that way. If so, then Canadian unjust enrichment would be permanently split. Based entirely on the arbitrary element of timing, half the subject would maintain the common law tradition while the other would pursue *Garland*. In all but the clearest cases, counsel would have to plead both ways, unsure how the judge ultimately would classify the matter. The parties would win and lose depending not on the substantive merits of their arguments, but rather on the court's conception of novelty. Inevitably, given the subjectivity of that exercise, like cases would not be decided alike.

VII. CONCLUSION

The Canadian law of unjust enrichment has embarked on a remarkable experiment. So far, so good. The success of the project, however, ultimately will depend upon the courts' commitment to principle.

4. South Africa

HELEN SCOTT*

I. THE IDEA OF UNJUSTIFIED ENRICHMENT

There are several candidates for the invention of the law of restitution or unjust enrichment, but Robert Goff and Gareth Jones's *Law of Restitution*, first published in 1966,[195] must surely be among the front-runners. Even if one dates the invention of the subject instead to the first American Restatement of 1937,[196] or to the work of James Barr Ames and his pupils leading up to its publication, there can be no doubt that the idea of unjust enrichment is a twentieth-century one. The idea of unjustified enrichment, on the other hand, is much older. Although the Roman jurists recognised no such unitary category, Roman law included a range of remedies which South African lawyers would now classify as causes of action arising in unjustified enrichment: in particular, the *condictiones* which form the subject matter of Books 12.4, 5, 6 and 7 of Justinian's Digest.[197] Unjustified enrichment as a conceptual unity within the civilian law of obligations was first identified early in the seventeenth century by Hugo Grotius. In his *Introduction to the Jurisprudence of Holland*, the first

* Many thanks to Robin Evans-Jones for his helpful comments on a late draft of this paper.

[195] R Goff and G Jones, *The Law of Restitution* (London, Sweet & Maxwell, 1966).

[196] WA Seavey and AW Scott, *Restatement of the Law of Restitution: Quasi Contracts and Constructive Trusts* (St Paul, American Law Institute Publishers, 1937).

[197] The status of the *condictio furtiva* recognised in Book 13.1 is more uncertain.

edition of which appeared in 1631,[198] Grotius included a title called 'Of Obligations Arising from Enrichment'.[199] Although its content is limited—Grotius deals only with a subset of the Roman *condictiones*—its first sentence seems to constitute a workable framework for a modern law of unjustified enrichment: 'Obligation from enrichment arises when someone without legal title derives or may derive advantage from another person's property.'[200]

However, the subsequent development of the subject in the civilian tradition has been much more hesitant and erratic than this ringing definitional statement suggests. In truth, it left several important questions unanswered. First, what was the subject's content? Again, 'Of Obligations Arising from Enrichment' is rather skimpy.[201] The subject remained to be populated—with enrichment actions culled from elsewhere in the civilian canon, such as that modelled on the action of the *negotiorum gestor* against the *dominus* for expenses incurred, and the action of the unauthorised improver of property against its owner—over the course of the following centuries. On the other hand, the status of Grotius's general principle was unclear: could liability be recognised in previously unregulated cases on the basis of the principle alone? In other words, did it amount to a species of 'general enrichment action'? And if so, what was its relationship to the established enrichment remedies?

The genesis of the modern subject in South Africa can be traced to the publication of Wouter de Vos's *Enrichment Liability in South African Law* (*Verrykingsaanspreeklikheid in die Suid-Afrikaanse Reg*) in 1958,[202] just eight years before the first edition of Goff and Jones. In chapter V, 'The Rules of the General Enrichment Action in Modern South African Law', De Vos identified three such rules or elements: the defendant must be enriched; enrichment must be at the expense of the plaintiff; and the enrichment must be unjustified.[203] He argued that a general enrichment action founded directly on these principles already existed in South African law, although this action was subsidiary in the sense that it would arise only where the case could not be allocated to one of the classical enrichment actions, and where

[198] The Dutch title is *Inleydinge tot de Hollandsche Rechtsgeleertheid*. Translations into English given here are taken from RW Lee, *The Jurisprudence of Holland by Hugo Grotius*, vol 1 (Oxford, Clarendon Press, 1926), although I have modified them where necessary.

[199] Grotius, *Inleydinge*, III.30. In the original Dutch, 'Van verbintenisse uit baet-trecking'. As Robert Feenstra points out, this is perhaps better translated as, 'Of obligation from deriving profit': see R Feenstra, 'Grotius' Doctrine of Unjust Enrichment as a Source of Obligation' in EJH Schrage (ed), *Unjust Enrichment: The Comparative Legal History of the Law of Restitution*, 2nd edn (Berlin, Duncker & Humblot, 1999) 197, 204.

[200] The phrase 'without legal title' is given further content in the next fragment: 'that is, without antecedent gift or other contract': Grotius, *Inleydinge*, III.30.1–2.

[201] Regarding Grotius's treatment of enrichment in the introductory chapter to Book III of the *Inleydinge*, and in particular the example(s) that he gives there, see section III below.

[202] W de Vos, *Verrykingsaanspreeklikheid in die Suid-Afrikaanse Reg* (Cape Town, Juta, 1958). All three editions of this work appeared in Afrikaans. The translations into English given here are mine.

[203] The claim thus arising would lie in respect of either the defendant's enrichment or the plaintiff's impoverishment, whichever was the lesser: see ibid 180. In effect, then, De Vos recognised a fourth rule or element, that the plaintiff must be impoverished. For modern statements of these principles see, eg, D Visser, *Unjustified Enrichment* (Cape Town, Juta, 2008) ch 3; JE du Plessis, *The South African Law of Unjustified Enrichment* (Cape Town, Juta, 2012) ch 2; HJ Scott, 'Unjustified Enrichment' in *Wille's Principles of South African Law*, 10th edn, G Bradfield ed (Juta, Cape Town, 2017) ch 39 (forthcoming).

there was no legal rule in existence which precluded it.[204] There is thus a remarkable similarity between De Vos's general enrichment action and the principle of unjust enrichment recognised in the first edition of *Goff and Jones*, the first chapter of which sets out three subordinate principles: that the defendant has been enriched by the receipt of a benefit; that he has been so enriched at the plaintiff's expense; and that it would be unjust to allow him to retain the benefit. It must be admitted, however, that De Vos's influences were exclusively Continental—most prominently, the German Civil Code[205]—and, indeed, *Verrykingaanspreeklikheid* exhibits a remarkable hostility towards English law on account of its perceived casuistry.[206]

In the same year in which *Goff and Jones* first appeared, De Vos's generalising project suffered a serious setback in the form of the decision of the South African Appellate Division in *Nortjé v Pool NO*.[207] In denying the plaintiffs' claim—in respect of expenditure incurred in prospecting for kaolin on the defendant's farm, the discovery of which substantially increased the land's value—a majority of the court rejected out of hand the possibility of a general enrichment action in South African law: only incremental development of existing common law actions would be permitted. It is clear that this view was stimulated largely by fear of the open-ended liability that might arise out of De Vos's broadly formulated principles. But in the event, the effect of this decision was to halt even the analogous development of existing claims.[208] More recently, however, the position has changed again, with the handing down of the decision in *McCarthy Retail (Pty) Ltd v Shortdistance Carriers CC*[209] in 2001. Influenced by a series of academic articles,[210] Schutz JA gave judicial recognition (in the form of an *obiter dictum*) to the existence of a general principle of enrichment liability or subsidiary[211] general enrichment action which could be used either to extend liability to new, previously unrecognised cases or to rationalise existing common law claims.[212] The principles identified by De Vos were explicitly approved.[213] Although technically it decided nothing, the *McCarthy*

[204] De Vos, above n 202, ch 7.

[205] cf the detailed account of the provision of the BGB dealing with unjustified enrichment at pp 77–88 of the first edition. On the general clause contained in §812, see further section II(2) below.

[206] See pp 98–100 of the first edition: 'Although it must be admitted that in its present state English law will probably be able to reach an equitable solution in most cases of unjustified enrichment, reference to English law in this connection can in my opinion only pose a danger to our law'. Although the equivalent section in the third edition (pp 149–51) contains some acknowledgement of the impact of Goff and Jones (with references to the second edition of 1978), the warning against the influence of English law remained: see p 151.

[207] *Nortjé v Pool NO* 1966 (3) SA 96 (A).

[208] '[T]he law of unjustified enrichment remained essentially the same for almost three decades': Visser, above n 203, 50.

[209] 2001 (3) SA 482 (SCA).

[210] See in particular JE Scholtens, 'The General Enrichment Action That Was' (1966) 83 *South African Law Journal* 391 and Feenstra, above n 199, both of which are cited in the *McCarthy* case at [9].

[211] That Schutz JA envisaged a subsidiary or 'weak' general enrichment action only appears clearly from [8] to [10] of the judgment. In fact, De Vos had argued in the first edition of his book, and continued to argue in the third and final edition in 1987, for the creation by statute of a 'strong' general enrichment action which would replace the common law actions entirely: see ch 6 in the first edition and ch 8 of the third edition.

[212] See, in particular, 2001 (3) SA 482 (SCA), [8].

[213] ibid [8].

case has given rise to a sea change in the fortunes of the subject, producing not only a dramatic upswing in academic interest,[214] but also a marked increase in the frequency of litigation.[215] The parallels with the decision of the House of Lords in *Lipkin Gorman v Karpnale*[216] in 1991 and with the decision of the Scottish Court of Session in *Shilliday v Smith*[217] in 1998 are clear. However, this does not mean that the interior landscape of the modern subject is either orderly or uncontroversial. In a sense, the decision in *McCarthy* marked only the beginning of a new and difficult phase in its evolution, the project of converting the scattered fragments of the uncodified civil law into a body of rules characterised by transparent rationality.

II. THE RATIONALISATION OF UNJUSTIFIED ENRICHMENT

One of the principal challenges facing enrichment lawyers in South Africa today is the continued dominance of the historical forms of action inherited ultimately from Roman law. This is, of course, closely analogous to the difficulties faced by English lawyers in seeking to extricate themselves from the forms of action of the ancient common law. Yet the progress made by common lawyers in this respect is evident even in the first edition of *Goff and Jones*. The common *indebitatus* counts for money had and received and for money paid, as well as *quantum meruit* and *quantum valebat*, are summarily dispatched in the first few pages of chapter 1—'Historical accident is an unsatisfactory basis for classification ...'[218]—and the subsequent chapters organised at least in part according to what would come to be referred to as unjust factors: mistake, compulsion and necessity. By contrast, De Vos's work was arranged according to historical period in all three of its editions: Roman law, Roman-Dutch law and South African law. Within those chapters, De Vos's treatment followed the original Roman categories: *condictio causa data causa non secuta*, *condictio ob turpem vel iniustam causam*, *condictio indebiti*, *condictio sine causa*, *condictio furtiva*, *actiones negotiorum gestorum*, *actio de in rem verso* etc.

This is not to diminish the conceptual sophistication of De Vos's treatment. The contents of the chapters show that he was alive to the ways in which the general principles of 'enrichment', 'at the expense of' and 'unjustified' were expressed through the ancient categories. Nevertheless, it is striking that the table of contents of the third edition of *Verrykingsaanspreeklikheid*, published in 1987, would have been immediately and readily intelligible to the third-century Roman jurist Ulpian. Conversely, the plaintiff's substantive cause of action remained almost entirely opaque to

[214] See, eg, JC Sonnekus, *Ongegronde Verryking in die Suid-Afrkaanse Reg* (Durban, LexisNexis, 2008); Visser, above n 203; du Plessis, above n 203; H Scott, *Unjust Enrichment in South African Law: Rethinking Enrichment by Transfer* (Oxford, Hart Publishing, 2013).

[215] See, eg, the chapters on 'Unjustified Enrichment' in the *Annual Survey of South African Law* over the course of the past 15 years for a sense of the increase in the number of decided cases, and in particular the increase in the number of decisions on unjustified enrichment by appellate courts.

[216] [1991] 2 AC 548.

[217] 1998 SC 725. See also *Dollar Land (Cumbernauld) Ltd v CIN Properties Ltd* 1998 SC (HL) 90.

[218] Goff and Jones, above n 195, 3–5.

the contemporary reader. The effects of such historical formalism are discernible in modern South African law. Its most noticeable consequence is the fact the *condictio* remains limited, as in Roman law, to claims in respect of the deliberate transfer of money and property (or rather its value).[219] Claims can be raised in respect of the deliberate conferral of services, but only if they can be brought within the scope of one of the other enrichment actions. As a result, the analysis of services claims is often distorted. For example, the action in *Nortjé v Pool* was pleaded as a claim (in respect of the plaintiffs' expenditure) arising from the improvement of the defendant's land. It failed because the plaintiffs could show no tangible, physical improvement: the kaolin had been there all along, the plaintiffs having merely detected it. It would have been far more natural to construe the claim as one arising from the deliberate conferral of a benefit (the plaintiffs' prospecting activities) in the context of a void contract:[220] as an instance of the *condictio indebiti* (in respect of a service not owed conferred by mistake) or (preferably) a *condictio causa data causa non secuta* (in respect of a service conferred in anticipation of a future event, ie the acquisition of the exclusive right to exploit kaolin if, indeed, any were discovered). Yet that analysis—and thus the possibility of any claim at all in respect of the value of the services—was precluded by the historically determined restriction on the scope of the *condictiones*.[221]

In short, South African law has thus far failed definitively to detach causes of action from forms of action. This is to be contrasted not only with the position in the common law, but also with the closely analogous Scots law of unjustified enrichment. Here, the combining of Stair's response-based classification of restitution, recompense and reparation with the original Roman scheme of obligations produced profound confusion: in particular, 'the *response* of "recompense" in a range of obediential obligations came to be understood as a group of *causes of action*'.[222] Yet, in *Shilliday v Smith*[223] in 1998, the 'three Rs' were definitively reduced to the role of responses, leaving causes of action to develop independently.[224] Crucially, Lord Rodger identified the *condictio* in its various manifestations as representative of a

[219] See in particular du Plessis, above n 203, 63–64.

[220] R Evans-Jones, 'Searching for "Imposed" Enrichment in Improvements' (2008) 16 *Restitution Law Review* 1. The plaintiffs had been granted the exclusive right to prospect for kaolin on the defendant's farm and, if they should find it, then also the exclusive right to exploit it, but the parties had failed to notarise their agreement as required by legislation. When this defect was discovered, subsequent to the defendant's death, the executor of his estate refused to assent to attestation.

[221] But cf the discussion of compensation for work done in the context of an invalid contract in the minority judgment of Rumpff JA, 119ff.

[222] R Evans-Jones, 'Thinking about Principles and Actions: Unjustified Enrichment in Scots and South African Law' in A Simpson, D Bain, R Paisley and N Tait (eds), *Northern Lights: Essays in Memory of Professor David Carey Miller* (Aberdeen, Aberdeen University Press, 2017) (forthcoming).

[223] *Shilliday v Smith* 1998 SC 725.

[224] The work of Peter Birks was deeply influential in helping to sweep away the '"classificatory muddles" into which Scots law had sunk': Evans-Jones, above n 222, 4. See PBH Birks, 'Six Questions in Search of a Subject—Unjust Enrichment in a Crisis of Identity' [1985] *Juridical Review* 227; 'Restitution: A View of Scots Law' (1985) 38 *Current Legal Problems* 57.

group of causes of action only.[225] Unlike its South African counterpart, then, the Scottish *condictio* lies in respect of services as well as goods and money.[226]

The path out of the enrichment forest[227] for South Africa appears to lie in paying greater attention to the internal taxonomy of the subject. In fact, in the case of both South African and Scotland, the influence of German law as a source of ordering principle and stimulus for reform has been considerable. Since the decisions in the *McCarthy* and *Shilliday* cases, writers on enrichment such as Jacques du Plessis, Danie Visser, Robin Evans-Jones, Martin Hogg, Hector MacQueen and Niall Whitty have drawn on the Wilburg/Von Caemmerer taxonomy of the general enrichment claim set out in §812, paragraph 1, sentence 1[228] of the German Civil Code in organising the Scots[229] and South African[230] laws of unjustified enrichment according to the manner in which the enrichment occurred: by transfer or deliberate conferral of the benefit by the plaintiff on the defendant (roughly equivalent to the German *Leistungskondiktion*); by imposition of the benefit by the plaintiff upon the defendant, a category which in South Africa in generally understood to comprise both enrichment through unauthorised improvements to land or goods (roughly equivalent to the German *Verwendungskondiktion*) and the payment of another's debt (roughly equivalent to the German *Rückgriffskondiktion*);[231] and by invasion of or interference with the plaintiff's rights by the defendant (roughly equivalent to the German *Eingriffskondiktion*).

This classification is not simply a useful organising principle, but is grounded in meaningful substantive distinctions between different classes of claims: it acts as an intermediate generalisation between the general principles of enrichment liability identified above and individual causes of action. As such, it has exercised a profound influence over South African law, encouraging the standardisation and rationalisation of the ancient actional categories. Recognising that the *condictio* cases form part of a wider class organised around deliberate conferral encourages the abrogation of the traditional restriction of such claims to the transfer of goods

[225] Evans-Jones, above n 222, 5. Since the decision in the *Shilliday* case, Scots law has experienced an upswing in academic writing comparable to that in South Africa: see, eg, R Evans-Jones, *Unjustified Enrichment*, vols I and II (Edinburgh, W Green, 2003 and 2013).

[226] See Evans-Jones, *Unjustified Enrichment*, above n 225, vol I, especially ch 7.

[227] cf R Zimmermann, 'A Road Through the Enrichment-Forest? Experiences with a General Enrichment Action' [1985] *Comparative and International Law Journal of Southern Africa* 1.

[228] For an overview of German law in English see G Dannemann, *The German Law of Unjustified Enrichment and Restitution* (Oxford, Oxford University Press, 2009).

[229] N Whitty, 'The Scottish Enrichment Revolution' (2001) 6 *Scottish Law and Practice Quarterly* 167, 175; N Whitty, 'Rationality, Nationality and Taxonomy' in D Johnston and R Zimmermann (eds), *Unjustified Enrichment: Key Issues in Comparative Perspective* (Cambridge, Cambridge University Press, 2002) 658, 686–87; M Hogg, 'Unjustified Enrichment in Scots Law' (2006) 14 *Restitution Law Review* 1; H MacQueen, *Unjustified Enrichment*, 3rd edn (Edinburgh, W Green, 2013) 17; Evans-Jones, above n 225, vols I and II.

[230] Visser, above n 203, especially 78–85; du Plessis, above n 203.

[231] See, eg, Visser, above n 203, ch 10; du Plessis, above n 203; see also H McQueen, *Unjustified Enrichment*, 3rd edn (Edinburgh, W Green, 2013) 16–18. Evans-Jones, above n 225, vol II separates out the payment of another's debt (in ch 6) from the imposition of unauthorised benefits (in ch 5), following the Wilburg/Von Caemmerer scheme.

and money.[232] Another example is the reforms proposed by Jacques du Plessis to the extended action of the *negotiorum gestor*, one of two subclasses (along with claims arising from unauthorised improvements) within the category of imposed enrichment, reforms which draw heavily on the *Rückgriffskondiktion*, the claim arising from the discharge of another's debt.[233]

III. FAREWELL TO UNJUSTIFIED ENRICHMENT?

Yet the influence of the Wilburg/Von Caemmerer taxonomy on Scottish and South African law may not be entirely benign. Dividing up the subject in this way threatens to fragment it: perhaps, after all, taxonomy contains the seeds of the destruction of the unitary law of unjustified enrichment? In fact, as Nils Jansen has recently reminded us, the general principle of unjustified enrichment conceals a profound historical schism within the subject.[234] Whereas modern civilians emphasise 'unjustified' as the central unifying concept,[235] the natural lawyers whose work strongly informed that of Grotius focused on 'enrichment'.[236] Indeed, Grotius's own treatment is somewhat schizophrenic in the way that it veers between these two organising principles, not only as between the *Introduction* (which deals with the positive civil law of Holland) and *On the Law of War and Peace* (which deals with universal natural law), but also within the former work.[237] Whereas the first idea is strongly associated with the *condictiones*[238]—deliberate conferral—the natural-law doctrine of restitution focuses on enrichment 'from the property of the plaintiff'[239]—cases of imposed enrichment (as where a possessor improves another's property) or infringement of rights (as where one man is fed with another's food).[240] Having set out the second idea at the beginning of his treatment of the law of obligations in Book III of the *Introduction*,[241] at the beginning of the chapter dealing specifically with obligations arising from enrichment, Grotius appears to attempt to fuse it with the 'unjustified' principle: 'Obligations from enrichment [*verbintenisse door baet-trecking*] arise when someone without legal title [*zonder voorige recht-gunninge*] is enriched [*baet treckt*] or may be enriched from another person's property'.[242] But this attempted

[232] As argued by Visser, above n 203, 265–68; du Plessis, above n 203, 64–65.
[233] See generally du Plessis, above n 203, chs 8 and 10.
[234] See N Jansen, 'Farewell to Unjustified Enrichment?' (2016) 20 *Edinburgh Law Review* 123.
[235] In the original Latin of *Digest* 12.7, 'sine causa'; in Grotius's Dutch, 'zonder voorige recht-gunninge' or 'zonder rechtelicke oorzake'.
[236] Jansen, above n 234, s B(2).
[237] For a detailed analysis of Grotius's treatment see ibid, s B(2).
[238] Grotius, *Inleydinge*, III.30.
[239] cf Grotius, *De Iure Belli et Pacis* II.10.II.1: 'Regarding property which no longer exists, the human race has decided as follows: if you have been enriched from my property, while I did not have possession of it, you will be liable to the extent that you have been enriched; because to the extent that you have been enriched by my property, you have more, while I have less.' This is my translation of the modern 1939 edition by BJA de Kanter-van Hettinga Tromp, published by EJ Brill, Leiden.
[240] Grotius, *Inleydinge*, III.1.15, as amended in manuscript by Grotius himself: see Feenstra, above n 199, 202ff.
[241] At III.1.15.
[242] At III.30.1. This is an amended version of Lee's original translation. See also the reference to 'repetition of anything which in any other way, without gift, payment, or promise, has come to a man from another man's property apart from any lawful cause' in III.30.18.

fusion is not pursued further: Grotius simply sets out the law relating to several of the *condictiones* without further adverting to their theoretical foundation. Thus, it does not seem that Grotius's 'unjustified' principle originally encompassed anything other than the *condictiones*; he made no attempt to explain enrichment 'in another way' with reference to this principle. Conversely, it does not seem that the *condictiones* were really treated by Grotius as cases of 'enrichment' in the sense identified by the natural lawyers;[243] certainly, enrichment by transfer arises 'from another's property' in a far less direct sense than that intended by them. In truth, neither of these general principles could satisfactorily account for the cases which constituted the focus of the other.

Thus, it appears that the unity created by the general clause in §812 BGB, pioneered by Friedrich von Savigny in the nineteenth century[244] and clearly De Vos's primary influence,[245] is anomalous when viewed against the backdrop of the deeper civilian tradition. But with the increasing prominence of the Wilburg/von Caemmerer typology, not only in Germany but in uncodified civilian jurisdictions such as Scotland and South Africa, the ancient fault-lines are re-emerging. The general principles with which we began appear, on closer examination, to be deeply fractured. Whereas the rules on improvements look to enrichment surviving in the hands of the defendant at the time that action is instituted,[246] the rules on enrichment by transfer are in effect restitutionary: the defendant is liable in the first instance to restore what he received (or its value).[247] This fundamental distinction is underlined by the fact that a defence of loss of enrichment to *condictio* claims was recognised by the South African Appellate Division only in 1977.[248] Similarly, the concept of 'unjustified' has profoundly different significance depending on its context: whereas the absence of a legal ground may be sufficient in itself to trigger the restitution of transfers,[249] and is certainly an important part of the reason for restitution in such cases,[250] it figures far less prominently in cases of imposed enrichment or enrichment by invasion of rights. I have argued elsewhere that 'unjustified' constitutes a necessary condition for

[243] In *De Iure Belli et Pacis*, Grotius mentions the *condictiones* briefly in the context of his general treatment of obligations at II.1.II.1, but not at all in his discussion of 'the obligation which arises from ownership' in II.10.

[244] For details see Jansen, above n 234, s C.

[245] See section I above.

[246] Subject, at least in South African law, to the loss-cap imported from the *condictiones*. The rules on enrichment by invasion of rights are different, in that the risk of loss of enrichment often falls on the defendant.

[247] See, eg, du Plessis, above n 203, ch 13, especially 379–80 and 381–82.

[248] *African Diamond Exporters (Pty) Ltd v Barclays Bank International Ltd* 1978 (3) SA 699 (A); *Senwes Ltd v Jan van Heerden & Sons* CC [2007] 3 All SA 24 (SCA).

[249] See, eg, JC van der Walt, 'Die Condictio Indebiti as Verrykingsaksie' (1966) 29 *Tydskrif v Hedendaagse Romeins-Hollandse Reg* 220; see more recently the work of Danie Visser and Jacques du Plessis: Visser, above n 203, 171–93; du Plessis, above n 203, 52–58.

[250] I have argued that these claims are triggered not solely by transfer in the absence of a legal ground, but also require the presence of a specific reason for restitution, such as mistake or compulsion: see H Scott, 'Rationalising the South African Law of Enrichment' (2014) 18 *Edinburgh Law Review* 433; see also Scott, above n 214.

the plaintiff's claim in cases of enrichment 'in another way', and that the 'unjustified' principle therefore links all the cases comprised within the modern subject.[251] But although the presence of a legal ground would surely preclude the existence of a claim in such cases,[252] it is unclear whether it is really any stronger than a defence. It is for reasons such as these that Jansen argues that the time has come to break apart the components of the Wilburg/von Caemmerer taxonomy: to bid farewell to a unified law of unjustified enrichment. Indeed, he argues that 'unjustified enrichment' should be extinguished entirely, with transfer cases and in particular three-party cases assigned to contract, and cases of rights invasion to a wider category of non-contractual obligations, along with delict.[253]

In my view, the latter claim cannot be applied to South African law. Focusing exclusively on the transfer cases for the moment, whilst Jansen is surely right to insist on greater consistency in the treatment of the restitution of bilateral performances,[254] which might conceivably require the assimilation of enrichment claims in the context of failed contracts to the law of contract, that leaves a large body of well-defined claims in respect of unilateral transfers which cannot be construed as contractual: a plaintiff who has misconstrued his obligations under a valid contract and paid when he was not bound to do so, or paid the wrong person or transferred the wrong thing, cannot be forced back to a contractual claim without resort to the crudest of fictions. Nor could South African law solve these cases merely by reference to 'general rules and principles of the law of obligations'.[255] Autonomous unjustified enrichment lives on, though it does seem that the unity assumed by De Vos's general principles is a looser one than is often acknowledged. Grouping causes of action according to the Wilburg/Von Caemmerer taxonomy permits us to notice important conceptual and functional differences between claims and thus handle them differently where appropriate.[256] It may also help to restrain courts and academics in South Africa and Scotland from taking too seriously the promise of a general enrichment action, and so rein in a general principle which retains its potential for uncontrolled and, indeed, destructive proliferation.

[251] ibid, Scott (2014), 449: 'in South African law, as in German law, the "big idea" which holds the entire law of enrichment together is the absence of a legal ground for the enrichment. But ... although it may be a big idea, it is also rather a thin one'.

[252] cf *St Helena Primary School v The MEC, Department of Education, Free State Province* 2007 (4) SA 16.

[253] See Jansen, above n 234, E and F, especially at p 144: 'Claims under this category [enrichments by transfers] can no longer be understood as "independent claims in corrective justice" beside obligations arising from contracts and from delicts. Rather, they have become *remedies* in contract law. From the point of view of German private law, their proper systematic place is hence within general contract law.'

[254] See ibid D(5).

[255] ibid 146.

[256] Evans-Jones, above n 222, 7–8.

5. A Judicial Perspective

SIR TERENCE ETHERTON MR

In 1972, I started to study for the restitution paper for the Cambridge LLB. I had the great privilege of having Gareth Jones as the lecturer. He was a charismatic figure. The combination of his personality, outstanding knowledge and intellect and the nature of the subject matter made the course thoroughly absorbing, with no time for day dreaming in the back row. I have always been very grateful for the intellectual rigour of that course. That rigour has been imparted to successive generations of students, lawyers and judges by Goff and Jones's leading work on restitution for unjust enrichment. It is a work that has an essential place on the bookshelf of anyone interested in the subject, including judges, like myself, whose job is to resolve a wide range of civil law disputes.

Restitution of payments made under mistake is the archetype of restitution for unjust enrichment. Of all the areas of restitution, it has seen, in the period since the publication of Goff and Jones, perhaps the greatest rationalisation and liberalisation from the unjustified complications and constraints of past jurisprudence. It therefore seems fitting to look at one aspect of mistake which seems to me to raise interesting issues, both particular and general, about the interrelationship between the common law cause of action and equitable relief.

In *Pitt v Holt*, the Supreme Court ordered that the 'Special Needs Trust', which had been set up by Mrs Pitt (as Mr Pitt's Mental Health Act receiver) for the benefit of Mr Pitt, who had been badly injured in a road accident, should be set aside because of Mrs Pitt's grave mistake in believing that the trust would have no adverse tax consequences.[257]

In his judgment, with which all the other members of the Supreme Court agreed, Lord Walker set out the following criteria for the exercise of the equitable jurisdiction to grant rescission for a causative spontaneous mistake in the case of a unilateral (that is to say, voluntary or non-contractual) transaction:

(1) the mistake must take the form of an incorrect conscious belief or an incorrect tacit assumption (as distinct from mere ignorance or disappointed expectations);
(2) the mistake must be of sufficient gravity as to make it unconscionable and unjust to leave the transaction uncorrected;
(3) that test will not normally be satisfied unless the mistake was either as to the legal character or nature of the transaction or as to some matter of fact or law which is basic to the transaction; and
(4) unconscionability and injustice in this context are to be evaluated objectively by looking in the round at the degree of centrality of the mistake to the transaction in question and the seriousness of its consequences.

[257] [2013] UKSC 26 [2013] 2 AC 108.

There is a general acceptance that a 'but for' causation test applies to a common law personal claim for restitution for unjust enrichment due to a mistaken payment.[258] Lord Walker's criteria (2) to (4) lay down a much more stringent test for equitable relief. At first sight, it would appear anomalous that rescission in equity should be more difficult to obtain than a common law remedy. I have, however, suggested elsewhere that this difference is justified on the policy ground that a personal remedy does not have the same potentially disruptive consequences for third parties as rescission.[259] In policy terms, therefore, the distinction is not so much between common law and equity as between personal and proprietary relief.

This then brings us to the question whether there is or should be any difference between common law proprietary restitution, assuming for present purposes that such relief exists in law,[260] and equitable rescission. The main decision here is *Chase Manhattan Bank NA v Israel-British Bank (London) Ltd.*[261] Lord Browne-Wilkinson in *Westdeutsche Landesbank Girozentrale v Islington LBC*[262] explained and justified Goulding J's decision in the *Chase Manhattan Bank* case on the footing that—although the mere receipt of the money in ignorance of the mistake did not give rise to a trust—the retention of the money after the recipient bank learned of the mistake may well have given rise to a constructive trust (that is to say, equitable proprietary restitution). Both judgments are controversial. Lord Browne-Wilkinson's analysis would, however, fit both the policy point I have mentioned about the need for a more stringent test for proprietary relief than for a personal claim and Lord Walker's criteria for rescission of a voluntary transaction for causative mistake.

This policy distinction between proprietary and personal relief would seem to be a more coherent rationale than one based on notions of the need to respect the autonomy of a donee,[263] that gifts transactions are a distinct class which require special treatment[264] or that gifts into settlements are to be treated as a special class.[265]

This leaves us with two further criticisms of Lord Walker's test. The first is that it is wrong to exclude cases of 'mere causative ignorance' from the category of relevant

[258] A Burrows, *The Law of Restitution*, 3rd edn (Oxford, Oxford University Press, 2011) 209; G Virgo, *The Principles of the Law of Restitution*, 3rd edn (Oxford, Oxford University Press, 2015) 170ff; R Goff and G Jones, *The Law of Unjust Enrichment*, 8th edn (London, Sweet & Maxwell, 2016) [9-50].

[259] T Etherton, 'The Role of Equity in Mistaken Transactions' (2013) 27 *Trust Law International* 159; see also Goff and Jones, ibid, [9-111].

[260] An important debate on which I do not wish to express a view in this essay.

[261] [1981] Ch 105.

[262] [1996] AC 669.

[263] Tang Hang Wu, who emphasises the need to respect the autonomy of the donee and his or her life choices and the importance of the transformative social effect of a gift, which promotes trust so as to form the source of future action, argues for a hybrid failure of basis test and a serious mistake test: HW Tang, 'Restitution for Mistaken Gifts' (2004) 20 *Journal of Contract Law* 1.

[264] Goff and Jones, above n 258, [9-110]; Virgo, above n 258, 182–83; S Watterson, 'Reversing Mistaken Voluntary Dispositions' (2013) 72 *CLJ* 501, 503–504; this was the joint approach of counsel in *Pagel v Farman* [2013] EWHC 2210, [39].

[265] Goff and Jones, above n 258, [9-112]; Virgo, above n 258, 182, 200 (distinguishing between gifts with and without a deed).

mistakes.[266] The authors of *Goff and Jones*, who favour mere causative ignorance as a ground for restitution, argue that the boundary line would otherwise be difficult to draw in practice and is susceptible to judicial manipulation, according to whether it is felt that relief should be afforded—with the courts finding or declining to find incorrect conscious belief or tacit assumptions according to the court's perception of the merits of the claim.[267] I have little enthusiasm for this criticism. The authors themselves recognise that true cases of causative ignorance are likely to be exceptional,[268] and that, in terms of principle, the question whether mere causative ignorance can ground a claim to restitution is finely balanced.[269]

Ultimately, the ground for relief either at common law or in equity is for a 'mistake', so it is necessary to provide some legal definition of what constitutes that frame of mind. 'Mere causative ignorance' is itself a rather elusive concept in this context. I doubt whether, as a concept distinct from incorrect conscious belief or incorrect tacit assumption, it would generally be recognised as falling within the meaning of 'mistake' in ordinary speech. In truth, the real basis of the criticism seems to be a view that relief should not be restricted to cases of causative mistake but—subject to defences of change of position and so forth—should extend to any transaction where the voluntary disposition would not have been made had the transferor then known what he or she subsequently became aware of. That seems to me to be a new and different cause of action.[270]

It might be said that, the Court of Appeal and the Supreme Court having found, contrary to the trial judge, that as a matter of fact Mrs Pitt was motivated by an incorrect conscious belief or an active mistake, the judgment of Lord Walker on the actionability of mere causative ignorance was strictly *obiter*. Even if that were correct, I am far from certain that the arguments so far advanced by critics would carry the day for a change of view at the highest appellate level.

The question of 'judicial manipulation' is also, and more fundamentally, raised by the final issue I wish to address, namely the importation of a test of unconscionability as part of the criteria. The criterion of unconscionability in this area has been powerfully criticised as introducing too much vagueness and judicial discretion.[271] It has been said that Lord Walker's use of the word 'unconscionableness' interchangeably with that of 'justice' and 'unfairness' means that 'the test of gravity appears to turn simply upon an assessment of fairness determined through the exercise of judicial discretion ... and judicial whim'.[272] This is a strong statement, but it is, in

[266] This is described in Goff and Jones, above n 258, [9-37] as the situation 'where the claimant made neither an active nor a tacit mistake and simply acted in a state of mere causative ignorance. He would not have acted as he did had he known of some fact of which he was ignorant; but when he acted, he held no belief or assumption about that fact conscious or tacit.'

[267] Goff and Jones, above n 258, [9-41]; Virgo, above n 258, ch 8 argues for ignorance as a ground of restitution.

[268] Goff and Jones, above n 258, [9-38].

[269] ibid [9-40].

[270] cf the analysis of ignorance as a distinct ground for restitution, so far unrecognised by the courts, in Virgo, above n 258, ch 8.

[271] P Davies and G Virgo, 'Relieving Trustees' Mistakes' (2013) *Restitution Law Review* 74.

[272] ibid; Virgo, above n 258, 201–202.

truth, reflective of a fundamental issue about the appropriateness of unconscionability as a criterion for judicial decision making in civil claims. The common law cause of action for restitution for unjust enrichment, unlike much equitable relief, is not dependent on judicial discretion. Many scholars in the field of restitution for unjust enrichment see a test of unconscionability, which is at the heart of so many equitable rights and obligations, as synonymous with judicial discretion in legal proceedings, and discretion as objectionable for giving rise to uncertainty in the application of the law to particular facts and to commerce generally.

This is a broad and important subject, which cannot be adequately addressed in this short essay. I wish, however, to make the following brief points.

First, one of the important facets of the rule of law is that the law should be, so far as possible, coherent and predictable.[273] Peter Birks once said that 'conscience of the intuitive kind is … antithetical to the rule of law'.[274] If 'conscience of the intuitive kind' is equated with an unfettered judicial discretion, I can see the force of that point. I would respectfully suggest, however, that there is no such thing as an unfettered judicial discretion, and it is simply inconceivable that the application of a principle of 'unconscionability', woven into our law over centuries, would be regarded by any judge of the UK, the European Court of Human Rights or the Court of Justice of the European Union as a carte blanche for unconstrained and unprincipled judicial decision-making inconsistent with the rule of law.

Secondly, in historical terms, conscience lies at the heart of equity and the Court of Chancery as the court of equity.[275] Equity was intended to mitigate the rigour of the strict common law, to be responsive to the particular circumstances of individual cases and to provide remedies in appropriate circumstances where the defendant had behaved unconscionably but no relief was available at common law. This is not, however, an unfettered discretion. By the time of Lord Nottingham as Lord Chancellor in the second half of the seventeenth century, equity and principles of conscience, far from introducing a general judicial discretion, had become severely constrained by rules. As Lord Eldon famously said some 130 years later:[276]

> The doctrines of this Court ought to be as well settled and made as uniform almost as those of the common law, laying down fixed principles, but taking care that they are to be applied according to the circumstances of each case. I cannot agree that the doctrines of this Court are to be changed with every succeeding judge. Nothing would inflict on me greater pain, in quitting this place, than the recollection that I had done anything to justify the reproach that the equity of the Court varies like the Chancellor's foot.

[273] See Lon Fuller's eight desiderata: L Fuller, *The Morality of Law* (New Haven, Yale University Press, 1969) 41ff.

[274] P Birks, 'Equity, Conscience and Unjust Enrichment' (1999) 23 *Melbourne University Law Review* 1, 22, quoted in D Klink, 'The Unexamined "Conscience" of Contemporary Canadian Equity' (2000–2001) 46 *McGill Law Journal* 571.

[275] Aristotle called the virtue of an even-handed willingness to refrain from insisting upon the full measure of one's legal rights 'epieikeia'—in latin 'aequitas' and in English 'equity': PA Keane, 'The 2009 WA Lee Lecture in Equity: The Conscience of Equity' (2010) 10(1) *Queensland University of Technology Law and Justice Journal* 106.

[276] *Gee v Pritchard* (1818) 2 Swanston 402, 414.

The criticism of a test of unconscionability does indeed have the appearance even in the twenty-first century of a criticism that the application of the concept of unconscionability varies like the foot of the judge who happens to try the case in question. Such a criticism is an exaggerated and extravagant one which, even if justified to some extent, is nevertheless equally applicable to other central concepts of our adjudicative processes, such as the common law's reasonable person or notion of reasonableness, the public law concept of proportionality and the touchstone of 'common sense' beloved by judges. Indeed, it may be said that the principles which lie at the heart of a liberal Western democracy, such as ours, are those very principles of reasonableness, proportionality and conscience. If 'unconscionability' in this context is to be labelled as discretionary, it is what Peter Birks described as 'weakly discretionary'.[277]

Thirdly, criticism of the concept of unconscionability in the *Pitt v Holt* context is inconsistent with acceptance of the same concept in the defence of change of position, that is to say, in the need to show that the circumstances of the change of position are such that it would be inequitable to require the defendant to make restitution to the claimant. Tellingly, in that context, too, the notion of what is inequitable does not confer a carte blanche discretion.[278]

Fourthly, for equity as much as the common law, the development of the law through precedent is the genius of our legal system, for it enables the law to develop from generation to generation, adapting to new societal conditions. Precedents provide guidance for what may be considered to be reasonable, proportionate and unconscionable in particular factual situations while acting as a litmus test for changes in attitudes within our society.[279]

Fifthly, while it is a truism that uncertainty is particularly inimical to business, the suggestion that there should be no scope for the concept of unconscionability or for equitable relief involving judicial discretion in business law is overblown. Many equitable principles involving discretion are vital to trade: injunctions, including against disposal of assets, processes for seizure and search of the defendant's property, and tracing in equity, to name but a few.

For all those reasons, I do not baulk at the inclusion of unconscionability in Lord Walker's formulation of the principles for rescission of a voluntary transaction for causative spontaneous mistake. It is consistent with precedent and other applications of equity where unconscionability is an ingredient, such as the defendant's obligation to account as a constructive trustee for money received with notice of breach of fiduciary duty, and, indeed, Lord Browne-Wilkinson's explanation of the decision in the *Chase Manhattan Bank* case.[280]

[277] P Birks, 'Rights, Wrongs and Remedies' (2000) 20 *OJLS* 1, 23.

[278] Goff and Jones, above n 258, [27-02].

[279] In *Re Hallett's Estate* (1880) 13 Ch D 686, 710 Jessel MR refers to 'the modern rules of Equity' as refined by precedent.

[280] For an analysis of objective and subjective interpretations of unconscionability, see G Virgo, 'Whose Conscience? Unconscionability in the Common Law of Obligations' in A Robertson and M Tillbury (eds), *Divergences in Private Law* (Portland, Hart Publishing, 2016).

On the other hand, underlying that criticism is an important wider policy issue about the desirability of applying common law restitution principles to areas otherwise covered by equity and concepts of conscience.

The study and exposition of the principles of restitution for unjust enrichment as a distinct subject since the middle of the last century has been of immense importance in the development of our civil law for it has enabled a scholarly spotlight to be focused on weaknesses and inconsistencies within and across what had previously been considered separate areas and disciplines. It has introduced a highly desirable rigour into legal analysis. The result is that in some areas we have arrived at a stage when the coherent development of the common law cause of action for restitution for unjust enrichment calls into question both the need and the appropriateness of doctrines and rules governed by equitable concepts. In other words, the principles of equity which historically were justifiably applied to soften the strict consequences of the common law, where that would cause unfairness and injustice, are now themselves being called into question by a coherent development of the common law.

This is illustrated graphically in the area of which *Pitt v Holt* forms part, namely mistaken payments. It has been said that if a defendant was enriched at the claimant's expense as a result of an operative mistake, then—subject to the usual defences to an unjust enrichment claim, such as change of position—a restitutionary remedy should be available to recover the value of the enrichment, regardless of the nature of the benefit received.[281] The equitable rule expounded in *Pitt v Holt* permits relief in much more limited circumstances.

If the common law rule was as stated above, the equitable rule might in effect be deployed as a defence to the common law cause of action on the basis of the unconscionability of the claimant relying on a strictly legal right to recover the payment or its equivalent value. If that was the outcome, it would be the result of a policy that deemed the defences to the common law cause of action to be inadequate to protect the legitimate interests of the recipient or, in the event of insolvency, his or her creditors. If and insofar as proprietary restitution is proper relief for unjust enrichment, one policy justification for such an equitable defence might be, as I have suggested in relation to the *Pitt v Holt* formulation, that proprietary relief should be more constrained that personal relief. If, on the other hand, there is no legitimate ground for providing any further defences than the standard ones in claims to restitution for unjust enrichment, the equitable doctrine would have become redundant and would no longer be of any relevance.

The same issue arises in relation to 'knowing receipt' liability. In *BCCI (Overseas) Ltd v Akindele*,[282] the Court of Appeal held that the defendant recipient is liable if his or her state of knowledge makes it unconscionable for the benefit of the receipt to be retained. Here, again, it has been suggested that the position should be governed by the ordinary principles of restitution for unjust enrichment.[283] There is, from one point of view, a particularly powerful ground for such an argument, since such a

[281] Burrows, above n 258, 214–17; Goff and Jones, above n 258, [9-02]; Virgo, above n 258, 183.
[282] [2001] Ch 437.
[283] Burrows, above n 258, 416; Goff and Jones, above n 258, [8-50], [8-63]ff.

person is not a true trustee but only liable to account as if he or she were—although that does not preclude proprietary relief.[284] If that argument were correct, again the equitable doctrine would be redundant. This again raises the policy issue of whether a more stringent test is appropriate for proprietary relief and whether absence of unconscionability on the part of the defendant is, for policy reasons, a necessary addition to the limited defences to a common law restitution claim.

So, in conclusion, we can see the civil law in a continuing cycle of development: strict common law rules; qualified by the application of equity; the subsequent tightening of equitable rules, but with elements of unconscionability at their heart and some judicial discretion remaining; then further refinement of the common law and the calling into question of equitable rules as producing incoherence in the new legal order. *Pitt v Holt* is unlikely to be the last word.

[284] *Williams v Central Bank of Nigeria* [2014] UKSC 10, [2014] AC 1189.

11

Revolutions in Personal Property: Redrawing the Common Law's Conceptual Map

SARAH WORTHINGTON

I. INTRODUCTION

LAWYERS TYPICALLY DESCRIBE the common law—and its property law in particular—as more flexible, more commercial, more responsive, and therefore more useful and more attuned to modern times, than the equivalent laws in civilian jurisdictions.[1] If true, then the common law must have pursued a different development route from its civilian counterparts: if not a revolutionary route, then at least a different evolutionary route. What impelled this different course? Explanations invariably showcase the trust and its exalted status as an ancient invention of English Chancery Courts, but one with great modern utility.[2] I suggest this does not quite nail the genius of English property law. Instead, it is a far less obvious feature that seems to merit such accolades. It is the genuinely innovative English approach to sharing assets, an approach now adopted by all common law jurisdictions.

Early English law took the startling step of ignoring the *numerus clausus* principle, refusing to limit either the number of things that might count as property or the types of interests that might count as property interests. This move rendered the civilian-style concept of property almost meaningless, and thus raised very starkly the question, 'What is English property law about?' For common lawyers, the answer to this question might turn out to be surprisingly simple but quite unexpected. The insight advanced here is that the common law's approach to property has everything to do with the sharing of assets and very little to do with classifying either the assets themselves or the particular interests in those assets as property. This novel suggestion might pinpoint the simple, but crucial and revolutionary, contribution of the common law to modern conceptions of property. If true, then this is the real revolutionary genius of English property law.

[1] JH Dalhuisen, 'European Private Law: Moving from a Closed to an Open System of Proprietary Rights' (2001) 5 *Edinburgh Law Review* 273.

[2] 'The trust is the greatest contribution made by English lawyers to international legal thought': P Matthews, 'The Place of the Trust in English Law and in English Life' (2013) 19 *Trusts & Trustees* 242, 242.

Hindsight is a wonderful thing, but if we examine the legal landscape from our modern vantage point, we can now see that the property category, in the sense of defining things that might count as 'property' as distinct from 'obligation', is too unstable to be meaningful. Rather, what does define property is the possibility that an owner can share with others. This is done when owners grant derivative or secondary interests in their property to others without giving up their own ownership: this is the essence of sharing. As with every form of sharing, the owner's rights will inevitably be constrained by the arrangement to share, and the sharing party will have rights in the underlying asset that did not exist before. These sharing arrangements display several notable features.

First, these shared interests in property—these derivative interests—currently take only a limited number of forms, but these are 'family' forms that are almost infinitely variable in their precise characteristics. As presently conceived, these include not only shared ownership, but also the far more imaginative sharing achieved by dividing ownership and possession; or ownership and interests under a trust; or ownership and an equity of redemption; or ownership and interests by way of charge. Note that each of these derivative interests is equally amenable to further sharing by way of sub-interest (sub-bailment, sub-lease, sub-trust, a charge over a trust interest, and so on). Note, too, that although we typically assert that these derivative or secondary interests come in limited varieties—ie that they obey a *numerus clausus* as to types of interests—this is clearly not an immutable rule. It was precisely the English judiciary's disregard for limited categories that gave us the trust, the equity of redemption, the equitable charge and, later, the floating charge. Thus, in principle (even if unlikely in practice), it is conceivable that other shared interests might emerge as parties structure their sharing arrangements in still more imaginative ways to achieve their commercial or social ends, and the courts are persuaded to accept that new proprietary interests in the underlying assets have thus been invented.[3]

Finally, note that these shared interests have a unique ability to deliver bilateral insolvency protection. The owner, O, agrees to share with S. If this were simply a personal arrangement, S would not be protected on O's insolvency. But if the arrangement gives S a derivative or secondary interest in O's assets, then S is protected: S's property interest is an independent interest in the underlying asset, and is not dragged into the funding of O's insolvency.[4] Indeed, as discussed later, some of the most difficult remedial issues relating to property seem more readily explained as mechanisms for protecting the underlying sharing relationship rather than mechanisms for protecting the interest holder 'against all the world'.[5]

[3] Practicalities rather than law may be against this. The modern trust is now so flexible and so amenable to manipulation of the sharing arrangement that it seems impossible to conceive of objectives that could not be achieved by way of a carefully structured trust arrangement.

[4] However, note that the extent of the protection depends entirely on the type of shared interest at issue, which, in turn, depends on the particular terms agreed between the parties. For example, S is differently protected if S's interest is possession, a trust interest or an interest by way of charge. Note, too, that it is often immaterial whether the underlying asset is itself classified as property: for example, a trust of a business undertaking or a floating charge over it delivers trust or security interests in all the underlying assets, whether those are deemed 'property' or 'obligation' under orthodox classifications.

[5] See below, section V.

Putting this another way, the simple civilian opposition between 'property' and 'obligation' is not informative for common lawyers. A common lawyer's insight is only derived from fully understanding property law's secondary or derivative interests. It is only here that the property/obligation distinction is crucial. But consider what particular distinction is then crucially in play. It is nothing to do with whether the underlying asset is property or obligation. Regardless of that, the crucial distinction is between an agreement 'to share' (and then the specific creation by O of some derivative or secondary property interest in S) and, by contrast, a mere agreement by O 'to do' or to act in some way in relation to S.

Expanding on this, two key insights and several crucial consequences are presented in this chapter. The first insight is that an asset is not 'property' if it cannot be shared, and shared in the ways just described. This characteristic holds true for all the assets commonly regarded as property—land, shares, copyright, debts, and so on: all can be shared in some or all of the ways just noted here (possession being an inherently restricted option). As it turns out, most, if not all, assets are 'property' under this definition—they are usable wealth. Secondly, the various secondary or derivative sharing interests have far more uniting them than dividing them. Secondary interests by way of possession, trust, mortgage and charge are in truth simply functionally different ways of dividing assets between two or more people. That common objective of sharing assets is far more important in analysing the associated property rights and their incidents than any notion of some distinctive historical common law or equitable origin, or any resort to the legendary status of the trust.

The analysis in this chapter proceeds in steps. Successive sections consider in turn what English law has done with the *numerus clausus* principle generally, how it ignored what 'things' count as property and what 'interests' count as proprietary interests, and, finally, what consequences follow for English (and thus common law) property law. The first sections are essential precursors, but the innovative genius of English law emerges most clearly in the fourth and fifth sections.

II. WHAT HAS ENGLISH LAW DONE WITH THE *NUMERUS CLAUSUS* PRINCIPLE?

The *numerus clausus* principle is seen as foundational in civilian legal systems, although commitment to it is not uniform.[6] The term itself is Latin for 'closed number', but a closed number of what? It could mean there is a limit to the types of *things* that are classified as property, or a limit to the types of *interests* that are classified as property. In all the writing on *numerus clausus*, this fundamental question is typically not confronted. In most civilian jurisdictions, however, both aspects seem to be embraced; there is commonly some notion that only certain things count as property, and that only certain limited interests count as property. Outside those things and those interests, whatever is done—even if it concerns property—is done by way of contract or obligation, not by way of property.

[6] Dalhuisen, above n 1, 281–89.

To illustrate, if the *numerus clausus* principle tells us that only certain things count as property, then we might have a rule that land and tangible goods count as property but nothing else does. It would not matter what else might be invented—computer codes, shares, copyright interests—none of these would count as property because the list is closed to anything beyond land and tangible goods.[7] Of course, the list might include computer codes, shares, copyright, body parts, genetic code, carbon trading units, bitcoins and so on. So the agreed list might equally be a very long list. All would seem to depend on the purpose of having such a list. The principal object of categorisation is to have useful categories, and thus typically a limited number of them—but useful for what?

Alternatively, if the principle tells us that only certain types of interest count as property but nothing else does, then we might have a rule that ownership, possession and security interests count as property but nothing else does. It would then follow that licences, options and so forth were not property.

In either case, the consequence is that the privileges accorded to property are reserved for things or interests that fall within the defined categories of property. Quite why this should be so, and whether a limited list is a good idea, is fiercely contested, but that need not detain us, since the common law has ignored both limitations, and profitably so.[8] Each aspect is considered below.

III. WHICH 'THINGS' COUNT AS PROPERTY?

Lawyers are brought up on the notion of a significant conceptual divide between property and obligation. Recognising this divide, the law allocates distinctive rights and protections to each distinctive category. The idea was recognised in Roman law, with its classification of law into categories dealing with persons, things and actions.[9] The same distinction now appears universal. Roy Goode put it well, noting that all legal systems sharply distinguish 'property rights from mere personal rights to the delivery or transfer of an asset. I *own* property; I am *owed* performance of a transfer obligation.'[10]

In identifying the attributes that mark an asset out as 'property', not simply 'obligation' or 'wealth', the work of Tony Honoré[11] and Kevin Gray[12] has proved

[7] For a classic analysis of what counts as property and what does not, see the Australian High Court case of *Victoria Park Racing and Recreational Ground Co Ltd v Taylor* (1937) 58 CLR 479. See also P Kohler and N Palmer, 'Information as Property' in N Palmer and E McKendrick (eds), *Interests in Goods*, 2nd edn (London, Lloyd's of London Press, 1998) ch 1.

[8] For the relevant references and a short discussion, see S Worthington, 'The Disappearing Divide between Property and Obligation: The Impact of Aligning Legal Analysis and Commercial Expectation' in S Degeling and J Edelman (eds), *Equity in Commercial Law* (Sydney, Law Book Co, 2005), 101–103.

[9] M Radin, 'Fundamental Concepts of the Roman Law' (1925) 13 *California Law Review* 208; A Wajenberg and D Gorecki, 'Classification of Roman Law: Problems and a Suggested Classification Scheme' (1981) 74 *Law Library Journal* 632.

[10] RM Goode, 'Ownership and Obligation in Commercial Transactions' (1987) 103 *LQR* 433, 433 (emphasis in the original).

[11] AM Honoré, 'Ownership' in AG Guest (ed), *Oxford Essays in Jurisprudence* (Oxford, Oxford University Press, 1961). See especially 107, where a list of the attributes of property is provided.

[12] K Gray, 'Property in Thin Air' (1991) 50 *CLJ* 252.

especially influential. Following their lead, common lawyers would typically insist that all property has the following distinctive characteristics:

1. *Assignability*: owners of property can determine who will have the benefit of their property in the future. I can determine who will be the next owner of my car, but I cannot determine who will be the next incumbent of my job. Property comes with assignability; obligation does not.
2. *Excludability*: owners of property can determine who will *not* have the benefit of their property in the future. This is the flipside of the previous attribute, but serves to emphasise that property rights are good against the world without the need to negotiate individual agreements with all the world. My car is protected from thieves, vandals and joyriders merely because it is property, without my negotiating any of these exclusions with the relevant parties.
3. *Insolvency protection*: owners of property can remove their property from the pool of assets held by an insolvent debtor; they do not share *pari passu* in the insolvency losses as do those whose claims lie only in obligation. This is well illustrated by the potentially different outcomes for vendors who sell goods subject to retention of title agreements and those who simply sell on personal credit.
4. *Entitlement to the fruits derived from the property*: owners of assets also own the fruits these assets generate. If I own sheep, their lambs are automatically mine; if I own apple trees, the apples are mine; the same is true of shares and their dividends, or debts and their proceeds. I can make agreements about alternative ownership of the fruits, but absent those agreements the fruits are mine.[13]

Of these four characteristics, the key attributes of property are often said to be the first two, assignability and excludability.[14] These enable property owners to control allocation and access; they reinforce the idea that property is usable wealth.

That idea of usable wealth is important, yet it is precisely at this point that the carefully constructed and widely agreed classification system seems to break down rather alarmingly. Neither of these key attributes needs to be absolute for an asset to be classified as property. Moreover, neither applies exclusively to 'property' or to 'obligation'. There is thus little, if anything, marking a clear divide between property and obligation, notwithstanding our insistence that the divide is crucial and determines a significant disjunction between rights and protections afforded to an asset's owner.[15]

[13] In what may be a confusion between the first and the last of these four characteristics, it is often said that an owner of property also automatically owns the exchange products generated from any dealing with the property. This is clearly true if the owner makes the exchange: if I sell my car, then the proceeds of the sale belong to me. But is the same true if the exchange is made by a third party? For example, if a third party somehow obtains the owner's property and sells it, investing the proceeds remarkably successfully, does the benefit of the successful investment belong to the original owner? We routinely hold the answer to be 'yes' if the person selling the asset is a fiduciary or a fraudster. Otherwise, however, the answer is far more difficult: see the discussion in Worthington, above n 8, ch 5 (reprinted in [2007] 42[3] *Texas International Law Journal* 917); S Worthington, 'Justifying Claims to Secondary Profits', EJH Schrage (ed), *Unjust Enrichment and the Law of Contract* (Kluwer, 2001) 451.

[14] Gray, above n 12.

[15] This assertion, and the evidence for it, is discussed in detail in Worthington, above n 8, ch 5.

Consider assignability. It is impossible to suggest that 'property' is assignable but 'obligations' are not. The modern rule is that both are assignable, although assignment may be subject to practical or procedural limitations imposed for reasons of public policy.[16] These imposed limitations do not distinguish property from obligation. Indeed, even though property is typically thought to be assignable by its very nature, greater restrictions often apply to the assignment of property than to the assignment of obligations. Consider the restrictions on assignment of certain categories of land or certain categories of goods—such as national art treasures, or petrol in periods of national shortage. Put another way, public policy determines whether a particular bundle of rights is assignable, and it does this without regard to some fixed property/obligation divide. When public policy determines whether it is appropriate to sell human beings into slavery, cell lines to research laboratories or rights to litigate to the highest bidder, it does not first decide whether these rights are property; it moves immediately to the core controversies. In short, the attribute of assignability does not serve to characterise a given right as 'property' rather than 'obligation'.

Turning instead to excludability, or protection from interference, we routinely assert that 'property' is better protected than 'obligation'. This remedial insight was famously articulated by Calabresi and Melamed 45 years ago.[17] They suggested that property rights are distinguishable because they are protected through 'property rules', not merely through 'liability rules'. Put in more familiar language, injunctions and specific performance are the norm in protecting property rights, rather than mere payment of compensation.[18] Once again, however, we might notice that this preferential remedial approach no longer seems to track any meaningful property/obligation divide.

Take some obvious examples. Rights that we might classify as purely personal—that is, as obligation rather than property—are often protected by 'property rules'. For example, tort claims may be remedied by compensation or by positive or negative injunctions,[19] and the choice does not turn on whether the rights infringed are 'proprietary'.[20] Contract rights, too, are enforced using the full panoply of 'property' and 'liability' rules. This remains true even when the rights infringed appear to be especially personal rather than proprietary, such as those requiring personal services to be performed by the defendant for the claimant.[21] Generalising, it seems

[16] See, eg, RM Goode, 'Inalienable Rights?' (1979) 42 *MLR* 553.

[17] G Calabresi and AD Melamed, 'Property Rules, Liability Rules, and Inalienability: One View of the Cathedral' (1972) 85 *Harvard Law Review* 1089.

[18] See the extended discussion of this issue in R Chambers, 'The Importance of Specific Performance' in Degeling and Edelman, above n 8, ch 17, especially his consideration of *Smelhago v Paramedevan* (1996) 136 DLR (4th) 1 and *Tanwar Enterprises Pty Ltd v Cauchi* [2003] HCA 57, (2003) 217 CLR 315.

[19] Even when the damage is still only threatened, the claimant may be obliged to take compensation for the likely harm that will be caused, rather than be afforded an injunction: Lord Cairns' Act (Chancery Amendment Act 1858, 21 & 22 Vict c 27 (UK)), now re-enacted in the Senior Courts Act 1981 (UK), s 50.

[20] 'Proprietary' in the sense that the tort interferes with claimants' property rights, not their personal rights. Assessed on other criteria, all tort 'rights' are sometimes considered 'proprietary', since they can be enforced against all the world.

[21] See the discussion in *Co-operative Insurance Society Ltd v Argyll Stores (Holdings) Ltd* [1998] AC 1 and contrast *Lumley v Wagner* (1852) 1 De GM & G 604, 42 ER 687, where the courts were prepared to order an injunction, although not specific performance.

that obligations are sufficiently commonly protected by 'property rules', and vice versa, for this form of enhanced legal protection to be of little use in distinguishing property from obligation.[22]

The inability of these remedial attributes to provide a distinguishing test appears all the more stark when the issues are examined from the property perspective. Then we may notice that our legal system does not necessarily protect some of the most uncontroversial property forms by means of property rules, but prefers, instead, to limit protection to liability rules. This is the approach taken by the common law in protecting goods. These assets are clearly property, but they are not—or not generally—protected by property rules: an owner whose goods have been converted by another is generally entitled only to compensation rather than to specific recovery unless the court can be persuaded to exercise its statutory discretion to order the latter.[23]

Generalising again, the more accurate analysis seems to be that the special protective regimes which deliver performance rather than damages (Calabresi and Melamed's 'property rules') are not afforded exclusively to property rights. Rather, they are afforded to *all* scarce rights, whether property or obligation. Once again, this aspect of the law's remedial regime does not enable us to distinguish between property and obligation.

Pursuing another aspect of excludability, it is often said that property rights are 'good against the world'. But even here, the degree of protection varies with the type of asset being protected, rather than with whether it is 'property' or 'obligation'. Contrast the protection of land with the protection of ordinary goods. Indeed, the law increasingly protects all assets from external interference, regardless of whether they are categorised as property or obligation. For example, both intellectual property rights and pure contract rights may be subject to injunctive and compensatory rules protecting parties from third-party interference with the underlying rights. There is perhaps a greater range of techniques in the court's armoury in relation to tangible assets, whether land or goods, but that surely only reflects the greater range of infringements that are possible. Otherwise, the line between property and obligation is blurred in the extreme.

And if, in desperation, we turn to insolvency protection as being the essential marker distinguishing property and obligation, we see that the test then becomes irretrievably circular. 'Wealth' is protected if the creditor has a proprietary interest, but not otherwise, and yet the marker distinguishing one category from the other is, as just revealed, fuzzy in the extreme. In fact, insolvency protection seems to be tracking something else entirely. Note that the 'wealth' itself need not be 'property'. The creditor can have a protected proprietary interest (by way of trust or security interest) in a contract right, but will not have a proprietary interest in tangible assets sold and delivered to the insolvent debtor but not yet paid for. The creditor has insolvency protection in the former case, but not in the latter. A better explanation of the focus of insolvency protection is needed, and is given later in this chapter.

[22] See the similar conclusion in L Smith, 'Understanding Specific Performance' in N Cohen and E McKendrick (eds), *Comparative Remedies for Breach of Contract* (Oxford, Hart Publishing, 2005) 221 and 233.

[23] Torts (Interference with Goods) Act 1977 (UK), s 3.

This is all by way of showing that there are no characteristics that successfully distinguish 'property' from 'obligation'. It would thus seem impossible to hold to a hard *numerus clausus* line on the types of assets that might count as property, since the class is not watertight. Indeed, even cursory reflection confirms that both English legislatures and English judges have shown little regard for such a dividing line.[24]

Legislative additions to the property category are increasingly common. This is familiar in the context of copyright, patents, trademarks, carbon trading units and so on. But the same imagination that is now directed towards statutory expansion led to equally dramatic developments in the early common law, all brought about by judicial fiat.[25] The early common law only accorded proprietary status to real property and tangible personal property, not to intangible property: intangible property was not assignable, it was not usable wealth and it embraced only personal rights against specific parties. But now the picture is quite different. The judges have effectively turned obligation into property.[26]

Consider debts. A debt is simply a contract, and perhaps the purest example of 'obligation' not 'property'. A debt which is assignable, however, against which security can be granted, which security then delivers insolvency protection, begins to look a lot like property, even if the financial value of the property is essentially determined by the solvency of the debtor. Although the common law judges initially regarded debts as unassignable, equity judges—in one of their more flexible and imaginative periods—saw the commercial sense and broad benefit in permitting all of these various uses of debts, and did permit them. It is only the benefits of a debt obligation that can be assigned: the creditor can assign the debt; the debtor cannot assign the obligation to pay. But it is the benefits, not the burdens, that the parties are typically keen to assign, so as to capitalise on their value. Indeed, precisely analogous rules apply to transfers of tangible property, where it is exceedingly difficult, although not impossible, to ensure that positive burdens run with the property.[27]

By this simple step, 'obligation' in the form of a debt was converted into something that could be used as 'property'.

It should be noted at this point that the equity judges were not doing quite the same thing as the legislators. The legislators were making provision for absolute assignments.[28] The equity judges, by contrast, were making provision for sharing: the debt was indeed treated by them as property, but as property still owned by the

[24] See S Worthington, *Equity*, 2nd edn (Oxford, Oxford University Press, 2006) ch 3; Worthington, above n 8.

[25] Now see the same careful attention directed to the ownership of body parts: *Yearworth v North Bristol NHS Trust* [2009] EWCA Civ 37; *R v Kelly* [1999] QB 621; *Moore v Regents of University of California* 249 Cal Rptr 494 (1988).

[26] Further detail appears in Worthington, above n 24, ch 3. There, however, the argument is simply that equity dramatically expanded the notion of property. Nothing is made of the further point that there is no longer an effective distinction between property and obligation.

[27] B Rudden, 'Economic Theory v Property Law: The *Numerus Clausus* Problem' in J Eekelaar and J Bell (eds), *Oxford Essays in Jurisprudence*, 3rd series (Oxford, Oxford University Press, 1987) 239.

[28] Law of Property Act 1925 (UK), s 136. Note that the statute only permits the assignment of the whole debt; a part only of the debt cannot be assigned. Moreover, the debtor must be notified, and set-off between the initial contracting parties then ceases, so the statutory mechanism is effectively a novation of the debt contract from a particular point in time.

creditor and merely shared with the assignee, who became entitled to the economic benefit of the debt (or, in orthodox language, the equitable or beneficial interest). True, the equity judges 'converted obligation to property'—they ignored the then current common law view that contract was not property—but they did this by conceding that contract might be treated as property and then by allowing its sharing, not by any other step. A moment's consideration suggests that this idea of 'sharing', of giving the assignee the economic benefit of the asset but assessing that interest as the net economic benefit in the light of the rights and obligations between the original debtor and creditor, is both a more realistic and, perhaps, a more helpful take on what is intended by those effecting an assignment of the benefit of a debt and the consequential creation of a triangulated relationship between the relevant parties.

Taken together, these various moves suggest that a line between 'property' and 'obligation' is well nigh impossible to draw. Indeed, we might now have reached the point where all assets, whether tangible or intangible, whether 'property' or 'obligation' on an orthodox or civilian view, are effectively treated as if they were 'property', at least in the sense of the key characteristics identified earlier. In short, the common law does not recognise a *numerus clausus* as to the things that might count as property: all assets are potentially amenable to the rights and obligations that might be classified as 'property rules'.

IV. WHICH 'TYPES OF INTERESTS' COUNT AS PROPERTY?

The alternative claim of the *numerus clausus* principle is that it constrains the types of interest that count as property. As noted earlier, it might prescribe that ownership, possession and security interests count as property but nothing else does. That would mean that licences and options, for example, are not property. The consequence would be that the privileged protection given to property is reserved exclusively for the interests falling within particular defined categories.

Here, too, English law ignored such limitations. Instead, over time, it slowly recognised new types of property interests, most notably trusts, the equity of redemption in mortgages and, finally, equitable charges, including floating charges.[29] This evolution undoubtedly required remarkably innovative leaps. This is evidenced by the fact that the modern trust is still not fully mimicked in civilian statutory provisions, no matter how sophisticated their attempts.

Remarkable though the English trust is, however, note that at root it is merely a property-sharing arrangement. As such, it is perhaps not quite so remarkable, or so remarkably different from other derivative or shared interests in property, as is commonly insisted. Admittedly this is not how trusts are typically described, but the family resemblance of sharing may provide an important if novel insight, and one that may be crucial to a clearer understanding of the proper function of property in modern English law.

To see this more dramatically, note that dividing interests in property and allowing several parties to share an asset is both commercially and socially attractive.

[29] 'Floating charges' are described below, in the text at n 64.

The early common law recognised that different divisions were possible. Tangible things (land and goods) could be co-owned. Division of rights between co-owners could give them interests that were qualitatively the same, even if quantitatively different. Co-ownership of a horse, for example, might divide ownership rights amongst a number of people in agreed proportions. More sophisticated strategies could allow different parties to have different types of interests in the same asset, not merely different shares of the same interest. With tangible personal property, the common law allowed the parties to split ownership and possession between different parties. With land, the common law went still further, and allowed different parties to have concurrent or sequential legal interests along a timeline via the doctrine of estates. In this way, the practical and commercial benefits of divided property ownership were recognised and accommodated as 'common law property rights'.

Although these options for divided ownership appear limited, especially for personal property, their innovative potential should not be underestimated. Take the simple division of ownership and possession. Because the terms on which this division might be organised are so inherently flexible by agreement between the parties, the result is that tangible assets can be subjected to different types of leases with all manner of associated covenants, to hire-purchase agreements, pledges, contractual liens, retention of title sales, bailments and so forth. Note that some of these provide insolvency protection and some do not: all depends on the precise terms agreed between the parties.[30] And all these various options are made possible through the inventive use of a single type of derivative or shared property interest, being possession.

Even more substantial innovations came later, introduced by Chancery judges. These judges dramatically expanded upon the still relatively meagre common law possibilities for shared or divided interests. They did this to greatest effect through the creation of trusts and charges. These two structures, especially the first, are often said to be equity's greatest legacy to the law. Maitland described the trust as 'perhaps … the most distinctive achievement of English lawyers',[31] created and developed over almost 1000 years by Chancery judges operating until the late nineteenth century in separate courts, delivering different substantive rules and utilising different practices from the common law courts. The trust's antiquity makes its modern role all the more remarkable. Its mechanical analogue is the ancient invention of the wheel and its prodigious modern usage.

[30] Consider the very different effects on the owner and the person entitled to possession on the insolvency of either of them under a typical lease, or a pledge, or a hire-purchase or retention of title agreement. Note that, other than with a pledge, it is the possessory interest which is typically terminated under the express terms of the sharing arrangement on the possessor's insolvency, not the owner's interest on the owner's insolvency. Absent the creation of effective legal security, the latter would offend the anti-deprivation principle: *Belmont Park Investments Pty Ltd v BNY Corporate Trustee Services Ltd* [2011] UKSC 38, [2012] 1 AC 383. This is for reasons explained in S Worthington, 'Good Faith, Flawed Assets and the Emasculation of the UK Anti-Deprivation Rule' (2012) 75 *MLR* 112; S Worthington, 'The Scope and Application of the Anti-deprivation Rule' in D Faber and N Vermunt (eds), *Bank Failure: Lessons from Lehman Brothers* (Oxford, Oxford University Press, 2017).

[31] FW Maitland, *Equity: A Course of Lectures*, John Brunyate ed, 2nd edn (Cambridge, Cambridge University Press, 1936) 23.

The trust's enormous commercial significance goes without saying. But note that these arrangements began as mere personal obligations for the management of the owner's property so as to deliver certain of its economic benefits to others. These arrangements slowly evolved until eventually they were recognised unequivocally as delivering new, shared, property interests in the underlying assets to those intended as the economic beneficiaries.[32] As with the common law shared interest by way of possession, here, too, the terms 'trust' and 'charge' disguise the enormous individual flexibility permitted within these two broad family categories.

In trying to expose the essence of trusts, commentators have noted that English trusts may never have evolved if English contract law had been more sophisticated, especially in allowing for the enforcement of contracts for the benefit of third parties,[33] and doing so specifically. This suggestion is reinforced by comparisons with civil law jurisdictions. These jurisdictions generally permit enforcement of contracts for the benefit of third parties,[34] and enforcement *in specie* rather than merely by damages remedies, and these jurisdictions have survived for long periods without the need for the trust. In the USA, too, contracts for the benefit of third parties are enforced.[35]

But trusts are far more than a camouflage for much needed developments in the law of contract.[36] The real ingenuity of the trust lies in its insolvency effect. This is one of the trust's most valuable commercial functions, now commonly described as delivered through 'asset partitioning'.[37] Thus it is typically said that trust vehicles isolate a fund of assets, separating them from the general patrimony of the trustee and ensuring that they are held preferentially for the trust beneficiaries, thereby avoiding all the complications that would otherwise result in the event of the trustee's insolvency.[38] To English eyes, this remains a remarkable achievement. Outside the exceptions provided by the trust and equitable security, the English rule is that

[32] Again, see Worthington, above n 24, ch 3. 'Asset' is used very loosely as shorthand for bundles of rights, whether proprietary or personal under orthodox classifications.

[33] Maitland, above n 31, 28; AL Corbin, 'Contracts for the Benefit of Third Persons' (1930) 46 *LQR* 12, 16–17; AJ Waters, 'The Property in the Promise: A Study of the Third Party Beneficiary Rule' (1985) 98 *Harvard Law Review* 1109. Some even suggest that the difference between trust and contracts for the benefit of third parties is largely lawyers' conceptualism: J Langbein, 'The Secret Life of the Trust: The Trust as an Instrument of Commerce' (1997) 107 *Yale Law Journal* 165, 185; FH Lawson, *A Common Lawyer Looks at the Civil Law* (Ann Arbor, University of Michigan School of Law, 1953) 200. See also JH Langbein, 'The Contractarian Basis of the Law of Trusts' (1995) 105 *Yale Law Journal* 625.

[34] H Kötz, 'Rights of Third Parties, Third Party Beneficiaries and Assignment' (1992) 7 *International Encyclopedia of Comparative Law* 7–11.

[35] AJ Waters, 'The Property in the Promise: A Study of the Third Party Beneficiary Rule' (1985) 98 *Harvard Law Review* 1109, 1111–12; JH Langbein, 'The Contractarian Basis of the Law of Trusts' (1995) 105 *Yale Law Journal* 625, 646; CHS Fifoot, *History and Sources of the Common Law* (London, Stevens, 1949) 257–59.

[36] For the detail, see S Worthington, 'Property as Proxy for Policy in Common Law Adjudication' (2006) 25(2) *University of Queensland Law Journal* 329.

[37] H Hansmann and R Kraakman, 'The Essential Role of Organizational Law' (2000) 110 *Yale Law Journal* 387; H Hansmann and U Mattei, 'The Functions of Trust Law: A Comparative Legal and Economic Analysis' (1998) 73 *New York University Law Review* 434; GL Gretton, 'Trusts without Equity' (2000) 49 *International and Comparative Law Quarterly* 599.

[38] Some other seemingly 'proprietary' features are not necessarily unique to trusts: GL Gretton, ibid, 603. Also see R Nolan, 'Equitable Property' (2006) 126 *LQR* 232.

each individual holds one undivided patrimony. Whether a human or a corporation, an individual's entire patrimony is exposed to the claims of the individual's creditors. By contrast, many civil law jurisdictions are familiar with divided patrimony in different contexts, so the trust's achievement may seem less remarkable. Indeed, this civil law recognition of divided patrimony is essential to its ability to mimic by statute the effects of the English trust.

The trust is one of the earliest English vehicles to achieve this goal of divided patrimony, or asset partitioning, and to recognise the commercial advantages it could deliver.[39] Companies evolved later, and modern security law later still. Despite that chronology, the form of asset partitioning delivered by the trust is still beyond anything that companies and contractual security arrangements can possibly achieve, even ignoring transaction costs.[40]

The term 'asset partitioning' may seem to add a layer of complication to a relatively simple idea, but the particular simple idea at issue needs emphasising. There is a risk that the 'partitioning' terminology is distracting, too suggestive of the civilian model which has one individual holding two segregated pots of assets—one 'belonging' to the legal owner and one 'belonging' to the beneficiaries. The analogy is encouraged by calling the trustee 'the legal owner' and the beneficiary 'the equitable owner', thus naming both as 'owners'.

However, the reality is that the English trust simply reflects a new form of permitted sharing of assets. The trustee remains the legal owner, although with greatly cored out rights, while the beneficiary has the economic benefit, either in its entirety or in some defined and limited part. Like any absolute owner, the trustee can pursue claims to recover the trust property or claim damages for harm done to it. Unlike a sole owner, however, the real benefit or the real economic loss will not fall solely on the trustee. Furthermore, the trustee cannot with impunity destroy the property or give it away, and the trust property cannot serve as a substitute for the obligations of the trustee either by execution or by consensual security.[41]

The position of the beneficiary is equally not as 'owner'. The beneficiary shares in some way with the trustee in the totality of the property in the asset, and is accordingly entitled to some defined economic benefit from the asset; but the beneficiary does not have title to the trust property and cannot deal with it at will, nor deal with third parties in relation to it.[42] Put like this, the structure of the trust arrangement is not inherently very different from the structure of an arrangement involving an

[39] The implications of an elective divided patrimony are enormous: B Wedderburn, 'Trust, Corporation and the Worker' (1985) 23 *Osgoode Hall Law Journal* 203, 203.

[40] JH Langbein, 'The Contractarian Basis of the Law of Trusts' (1995) 105 *Yale Law Journal* 625, 667; H Hansmann and R Kraakman, 'The Essential Role of Organizational Law' (2000) 110 *Yale Law Journal* 387.

[41] B Rudden, 'Things as Things and Things as Wealth' (1994) 14 *OJLS* 81, 82.

[42] Other than in proving priority claims to the economic/beneficial interest (as in claims asserting a recipient is not a bona fide purchaser for value) or personal claims against such parties for knowing abuse of the beneficiaries' economic interests. As to the latter, and to the parallels with beneficiaries' claims against defaulting trustees, see S Worthington, 'Exposing Third Party Liability in Equity: Lessons from the Limitation Rules' in PS Davies and JE Penner (eds), *Equity, Trusts and Commerce* (Oxford, Hart Publishing, 2017).

owner sharing possession with another, despite the very significant differences in the nature of the interests held by those sharing the asset.

Furthermore, note that the asset partitioning insolvency effect of trusts is achieved solely because of this sharing relationship, not because of anything else. As a general rule, if X becomes insolvent, then all the assets belonging to X fall into the insolvency pot, but assets belonging to others do not. The 'assets belonging to X' include X's shared interests in assets, as well as assets owned absolutely. Equally, 'assets belonging to others' similarly include both absolute and shared interests. It is then a simple matter of looking to the particular terms of the sharing agreement to determine whether, and to what extent, the particular shared interest survives the insolvency. Note that it is the particular terms that are vital, not simply the family type of the interest at issue. Consider the special fragility of X's ownership of assets if those assets have been pledged or charged,[43] or of X's trust interests if they are held under a protective trust,[44] or, similarly, the fragility of X's possessory interests under a lease or hiring arrangement.[45] Moreover, note that the nature of the underlying asset is very much a secondary issue. In all of this, it does not matter that X may also be a trustee. The only change is that X's interests in those assets held by X on trust will be shared interests, not absolute interests, so X's insolvency pot will include X's share but not the trust beneficiaries' share in the underlying asset.

To arrive at this point required a remarkable leap in conceptualising the possible forms of sharing of assets. The courts went well beyond an owner's sharing of possession of tangibles to an owner's sharing of the economic benefits in almost any form of wealth.[46] This recognition evolved slowly. Initially the courts acted only *in personam* in dealing with these arrangements, but eventually they acted in relation to the underlying assets: in short, they moved from enforcing obligations of the parties in relation to the property to the sharing of the property itself.

Under this form of sharing recognised early on by the Chancery courts, assets can be shared in different ways at will, with different types of benefits parcelled out to different parties.[47] For example, by using a trust, the rights associated with company shares can be divided to give certain parties the voting rights, others the dividend rights and still others the rights to bonus issues. Even this does not exhaust the divisions that are possible by way of trust. Recall the many formal and informal arrangements that are now considered to deliver trust structures of divided ownership or shared interests in some underlying asset, whether consensually or by operation of law. These go well beyond standard commercial and family trusts,

[43] Note that the sharing here involves giving the security holder either a possessory interest or an interest by way of equitable charge. The insolvency consequences do not depend especially on this, but on the particular terms of the sharing agreement itself (and any relevant legislation, of course).

[44] Where rights to income from the trust assets will cease on X's insolvency: Trustee Act 1925 (UK), s 33.

[45] Which may or may not include terms making it determinable on X's insolvency.

[46] Although the common law form of *profits à prendre* in land law has some similarities.

[47] Hansmann and Mattei, above n 37; S Worthington, 'The Commercial Utility of the Trust Vehicle' in DJ Hayton (ed), *Extending the Boundaries of Trusts and Similar Ring-Fenced Funds* (The Hague, Kluwer, 2002) 135.

and include Quistclose trusts,[48] building retention trusts[49] and constructive trusts arising in response to contracts of sale[50] and, occasionally, in response to family agreements.[51]

The evolution of equitable charges tracked a parallel course. These, too, now provide enormous flexibility, enabling contracting parties to structure security arrangements to accommodate security over future property (after-acquired assets),[52] floating charges,[53] automatic crystallisation clauses[54] and even charges over the debtor's account with its lending bank ('charge backs').[55] The powerful protection thus able to be delivered to well-advised creditors by these flexible security arrangements soon led to Parliament providing statutory protection for particular classes of unsecured creditors, especially against floating charge holders.[56] This, in turn, led to fresh rounds of litigation concerning the accurate characterisation of particular derivative security arrangements: did they indeed create these vulnerable floating charges, or instead some other preferable form of proprietary protection by way of fixed charge,[57] contractual lien,[58] trust or even outright legal ownership?[59] For present purposes, these debates are not important in themselves. What is important is that they reinforce the idea that certain types of agreed 'obligations' between parties have, in English law, come to count as 'property' of one sort or another when those obligations concern the sharing of benefits and burdens in an asset, with each party agreeing to have and hold different interests in the same asset.[60]

This is all typically presented as a remarkable legal development by equity judges. At one level it is. But at another level these equitable interests merely reflect different types of sharing by way of newly recognised and novel forms of derivative proprietary interest in the underlying asset. Where the derivative interest is possession, we barely pause to think of 'sharing'. Yet note that all forms of property sharing,

[48] W Swadling (ed), *The Quistclose Trust: Critical Essays* (Oxford, Hart Publishing, 2004).

[49] See *Mac-Jordan Construction Ltd v Brookmount Erostin Ltd (in rec)* [1992] BCLC 350.

[50] Other than sales of goods, where the Sale of Goods Act 1979 (UK) and its Commonwealth equivalents provide an even more aggressive default rule, so that legal property is rebuttably presumed to pass to the buyer at the time of the contract of sale, notwithstanding that delivery and payment of the price occur at some later stage.

[51] The relevant cases are listed in S Worthington, *Proprietary Interests in Commercial Transactions* (Oxford, Oxford University Press, 1996) chs 3 and 8; S Worthington, *Personal Property Law: Text and Materials* (Oxford, Hart Publishing, 2000) [3.9] and [4.10]–[4.14]. For brief comment on the interests arising by operation of law, see below, text at n 68.

[52] *Holroyd v Marshall* (1862) 10 HLC 191, 11 ER 999.

[53] *Re Yorkshire Woolcombers Association Ltd* [1903] 2 Ch 284.

[54] *Re Brightlife Ltd* [1987] Ch 200.

[55] *Re Bank of Credit and Commerce International SA (No 8)* [1998] AC 214.

[56] Insolvency Act 1986 (UK), ss 40 and 175(2)(b), and, more recently, s 176A.

[57] See *National Westminster Bank plc v Spectrum Plus Ltd* [2005] UKHL 41, [2005] 2 AC 680, approving the analysis in S Worthington, 'An "Unsatisfactory Area of the Law"—Fixed and Floating Charges Yet Again' (2004) 1 *International Corporate Rescue* 175.

[58] In the context of construction contracts: *Re Cosslett (Contractors) Ltd* [1998] Ch 495 (analysis not affected by the subsequent appeal to the House of Lords in *Smith (Administrator of Cosslett (Contractors) Ltd) v Bridgend County Borough Council* [2002] 1 AC 336).

[59] In the context of retention of title agreements: *Borden (UK) Ltd v Scottish Timber Products Ltd* [1981] Ch 25.

[60] It is then a matter of proper construction of the agreement and arrangements between the parties to determine the precise and particular nature of the sharing arrangement between them.

whatever the type of shared or derivative interest, follow the same model: the owner retains legal ownership, but that ownership is constrained by derivative rights given to another. True, the trust beneficiary's rights are not the same types of rights as those arising under common law leases or equitable security arrangements, but the analogous sharing of the totality of the 'bundle of property rights' is clear.

The observant might comment that a trust is different because the trustee is subject to a variety of rather onerous obligations. But every owner who grants derivative rights to a third party is subject to some distinctive package of personal obligations. A derivative property right cannot be created without this. For example, an owner who grants her lender a security interest by way of pledge or by way of charge inevitably restricts her own ability to exercise ownership rights over the secured property; so too does an owner who agrees to hire out an asset or to transfer possession under a retention of title agreement. In each case, the obligations to which the owner and the counterparty are subjected arise from the particular agreement between the parties, supplemented by common law default rules. These increasingly sophisticated default rules are derived from the steady and sustained intervention of common law and equity judges reviewing these cases and determining what is needed to make the shared proprietary interests work effectively in different contexts.[61]

In this crucial sense, a trust interest is not essentially different from every other type of derivative interest. If there is any magic, it is that the English courts were imaginative enough to recognise the potential value of this particular form of derivative interest. Trusts are now ubiquitous, used in dealing with every form of property and in all manner of contexts, whether in self-declared or consensual contexts, in private or commercial arrangements, or in court-mandated contexts where trusts arise by operation of law.[62] Yet the insight that they merely provide yet another mode of sharing assets might help to close the seemingly endless debates over the special or even unique nature of the beneficiaries' rights.[63]

Equitable charges can be seen in precisely the same light. They too have their ready common law parallels. Just as security by way of pledge at common law involves the sharing of ownership and possession between the borrower and the lender, so too with charges, although the sharing is rather more sophisticated.

Determining precisely how far the parties can go in tailoring these sharing arrangements to suit their own needs can be testing. Their arrangements cannot go so far as to give one side all the rights in the underlying assets, leaving the other with nothing that amounts to a proprietary interest. This issue came to a head a century ago in the context of charges. A 'floating charge' is a charge over circulating assets: it permits

[61] In the shared property context, consider the tomes written on leases, hire purchase, bailments, security interests, etc, as well as on trusts. And if the history is seen as relevant, note Ibbetson, 'Revolutions in Private Law?', chapter 2 of this volume, especially his Introduction.

[62] Although this is not as novel as sometimes assumed. Derivative interests arising by operation of law are not confined to trusts (constructive and resulting trusts) and charges (equitable liens). Consider common law liens. More controversially, perhaps, an equitable lease does not connote a trust, nor some novel and peculiar form of 'equitable possession', but merely a lease arising by operation of law where the formalities for a legal lease are not met, but where enough has been done to warrant enforced sharing of the leased property under and terms proposed.

[63] See below, section V, text at n 81.

the debtor to continue to deal with the 'secured' assets, removing them from the ambit of the charge at the debtor's discretion and for the debtor's personal benefit when acting in the ordinary course of business. The borrower's wide-ranging rights over the secured assets persist until determined according to the parties' contract or the common law's default rules.[64] When the possibility of this sort of security interest was litigated in the English courts over 100 years ago, the courts held that the parties could indeed agree to such a security interest. The arrangement did create a charge: it followed the core model of a charge; it gave the lender a shared interest in a defined pool of secured assets, albeit a much less stable pool of assets than earlier security arrangements had necessarily specified.[65] By contrast, when the issue was litigated in the USA at around the same time, those courts held that the arrangement allowed the debtor to retain such extensive ownership rights over the underlying assets that the lender could not be seen as having any residual proprietary interest: to hold otherwise would be a fraud on the creditors. History favours the English judges, since the Uniform Commercial Code now provides for something that is the functional equivalent of the English floating charge. But note the real issue before the judges in these cases. At root, it was whether the parties' arrangements could be treated as one 'to share' the underlying asset, giving the derivative interest holder some part of the property in the underlying asset, or only one 'to do' particular things with the underlying asset in certain future eventualities. The same issue can infect any proposed sharing arrangement.[66]

To summarise, this discussion suggests that English courts have ignored the *numerus clausus* as to types of interests in property. This is a dramatic step, not undertaken lightly. Recall Lord Wilberforce in *National Provincial Bank Ltd v Ainsworth*:[67]

> Before a right or an interest can be admitted into the category of property, or of a right affecting property, it must be definable, identifiable by third parties, capable in its nature of assumption by third parties, and have some degree of permanence or stability.

However, over time, and to great commercial and social effect, the courts treated certain arrangements to share assets as themselves creating new forms of derivative property interests. Put bluntly, the old Chancery courts were occasionally persuaded to convert obligations into property where those obligations related to the intentional sharing of underlying assets.

[64] That is, once the debtor ceases to carry on business in the ordinary course, typically by selling all its assets and undertaking, or by going into liquidation.

[65] As noted above, the legislature then intervened to subject these floating charges to increasingly severe claw-back provisions in favour of unsecured creditors and to the detriment of the secured lender relying on this form of security.

[66] Sometimes the problem is not whether both sides have proprietary interests in the underlying asset, but what types of interests they have. That problem is seen in dramatic form in retention of title agreements in sale transactions: sharing of ownership and possession (via retention of title) can easily tip over into a security arrangement if the buyer is given so many rights that it is the buyer, not the seller, who must be seen as having ownership. The contract terms may then go still further to suggest that the buyer, having acquired title from the seller, now perhaps holds the asset subject to a charge in favour of the seller, but this is typically a charge which is ineffective since it is not registered (for the simple reason that the parties did not intend to create it). See, eg, *Re Bond Worth Ltd* [1980] Ch 228.

[67] [1965] UKHL 1, [1965] AC 1175, 1247–48.

Finally, a comment is needed on proprietary interests arising by operation of law. If the law is as described here when the sharing is arranged consensually, then it might be thought apt for the law to intervene in a strictly analogous fashion whenever the parties have not expressly provided for such sharing, but where their relationship and conduct is such that it would be appropriate to treat them as if they had. This broad idea seems to underpin the law in this area, and to provide a potentially useful guiding principle, although space prevents proper exposure of the idea in this chapter.[68]

V. CONSEQUENCES

The preceding sections suggest that very early in its development the common law effectively ditched the *numerus clausus* principle. It did not respect limits to the things that count as property, nor to the types of interests that count as property.[69] Indeed, going further, the idea advanced here is that English property law is not at all concerned with which assets count as property and which do not,[70] nor which types of interests are proprietary and which are not;[71] instead, it is exclusively concerned with the sharing of assets, and how that might be done.

To that end, note that the only time property interests really matter is when sharing is an issue. Then we need to know what rights each party has in the underlying asset. For example, on insolvency we need to know whether assets in the possession of the insolvent debtor are owned by the insolvent or owned by an unpaid creditor, perhaps under a hire agreement or a retention of title agreement. Equally, we need to know whether assets owned by the insolvent debtor are subject to security interests held by an unpaid creditor by way of equitable charge. Similarly, in trust contexts, we need to know which assets owned by the trustee are held for the economic benefit of the beneficiaries and which are not. This remains the relevant question regardless of whether the 'trustee's assets' are those held properly or improperly,[72] or whether the sharing arrangement arises consensually or by operation of law.[73] The list could go on.

[68] These arrangements are dealt with in detail in all standard equity and property texts, although not explained like this. See Worthington, above n 24; Worthington, *Proprietary Interests in Commercial Transactions*, above n 51. The mechanisms, of course, include resulting trusts, constructive trusts and equitable liens, but also equitable leases, proprietary estoppel remedies, common law liens, etc.

[69] The result has not been detrimental to English property law because the perceived advantages of the *numerus clausus* principle are overrated: the arguments and their authorities are summarised in Worthington, above n 8.

[70] Hence the difficulty in drawing the line between property and obligation: see ibid, and the references cited therein.

[71] Hence the variety of contexts giving rise to proprietary interests arising by operation of law: see the relevant chapters in Worthington, above n 24; Worthington, *Proprietary Interests in Commercial Transactions*, above n 51.

[72] As in *Foskett v McKeown* [2001] 1 AC 102; *FHR European Ventures LLP v Cedar Capital Partners LLC* [2014] UKSC 45, [2015] AC 250.

[73] For all of these, see the summary in the appropriate chapters in Worthington, above n 24; Worthington, *Proprietary Interests in Commercial Transactions*, above n 51.

Even when the question does not seem to be one of sharing, but simply one of identifying the single owner by following assets or by determining issues of priority, this is often not quite so. Note that when assets are stolen or dealt with without authority, the legal problem typically presents itself because the thief has possession, even if the owner has not lost legal title, or, alternatively, the stranger has legal title even though the original owner still has the economic or beneficial interest. Of course, pursuing the analysis to its proper legal ends may entail finding that the victim of the theft or of some other misdealing no longer has *any* proprietary interest: there is no sharing, no split of ownership and some derivative interest, whether by way of possession or trust interest. But getting to this point requires an analysis of each step in the transfer chain to decide whether the underlying asset is shared or not (eg whether legal title is in one person's hands, but possession or a trust interest is in another's). That analysis typically depends on a combination of the agreed dealing between the relevant parties in the chain[74] and the common law's default rules concerning property.[75]

Note, too, that this sharing analysis may prove useful in assessing remedies. Reliable analysis depends on identifying precisely the particular breach of duty at issue and its protective objective. That may be easier if the context is clearer. If all parties to sharing arrangements are recognised as owing a range of different duties to each other, then the relevant remedies would be seen more clearly to depend straightforwardly on the particular breach of duty at issue and its particular context.[76] Similarly, when third parties interfere, the remedies again depend on identifying the particular breach and the context in which it occurs.[77] These remedies may be personal or proprietary; they may be quantified by compensatory measures or disgorgement measures; and any such compensation may be assessed by focus on the loss to the person with a shared interest or on the loss suffered to the underlying shared asset.[78] Crucially, though, the answers to all these questions will be recognised as depending on the precise nature of the sharing arrangement and the rights and obligations thereby created, both as between the parties sharing and as against outsiders.[79]

[74] For example, whether it is a sale or a gift, a completed transfer or an executory arrangement.

[75] Including its priority rules when inconsistent shared interests are claimed, eg the bona fide purchaser for value defence, the currency rules for money. The further protections provided to holders of proprietary interests by the tracing rules and the resulting interests in substitute assets are in a different class.

[76] Contrast the remedies available against lessors, bailees, chargors and trustees. Similarly, the owners may have claims to remedies against their lessees, chargees and beneficiaries.

[77] Contrast the remedies available against accessories to a breach of trust, vandals of leased property or purchasers of secured assets, etc.

[78] With that distinction being absolutely critical to any proper analysis. With breaches of trust (as with many other sharing arrangements), the duties relate to managing the shared asset, and compensation claims are assessed on the basis of losses to that underlying asset, not losses to the affected beneficiaries: see *AIB Group (UK) Plc v Mark Redler & Co Solicitors* [2014] UKSC 58, [2015] AC 1503. For a discussion of this poorly understood case, see S Worthington, 'Four Questions on Fiduciaries' (2016) 2 *Canadian Journal of Comparative and Contemporary Law* 723, 754–64.

[79] This approach could be applied in contexts as diverse as *AIB v Redler*, ibid; *Akers v Samba Financial Group* [2017] UKSC 6; *FHR European Ventures LLP v Cedar Capital Partners LLC* above n 72; *Pitt v Holt; Futter v Futter* [2013] UKSC 26, [2013] 2 AC 108.

The suggestion that property law is primarily about the sharing relationship and not the underlying asset has several significant consequences. A number of these are implicit in what has been said already, but a few merit special attention.

First, all shared property interests, whatever their type, necessarily involve each party having a proprietary interest in the underlying asset, and each party also having personal rights and obligations arising from the sharing relationship. These property and obligational aspects are defined by the particular arrangement creating the interest, and each may be supplemented by the common law's own mandatory or default rules.[80] This is as true of leases, bailments, pledges and charges as it is of trusts. This is the essence of all derivative interests: sharing of every sort requires the detailed definition of both property and obligation. This insight, and its generality in applying to all derivative interests, including both common law possession and equitable interests by way of trust and charge, might inspire closure of the seemingly endless debates concerning the special nature of a beneficiary's interest under a trust.[81] The trust interest is innovative, certainly, but it is not uniquely 'special' or inescapably 'equitable'.

Secondly, it is this closed bilateral sharing arrangement that is protected by 'property law'; it is not the owner or even the owner's assets that are protected 'against the world'. Certainly, a lot of law is about assets (with a fuzzy divide between property and obligation) and their protection against the world,[82] but property law is about the sharing of those assets, and the consequences of those sharing relationships for the individuals concerned and for their interests in the underlying property. This is true whether the claims are between owner and derivative interest holder, between owner and outsider or between derivative interest holder and outsider. In each case, it is crucial to consider the particular claim at issue, and the relevant remedies and their proper quantification for that claim.

This particular focus explains a lot of law that is already familiar: consider a beneficiary's compensation claims[83] or insolvency claims[84] arising from dispositions by defaulting trustees. But it might also better explain why the beneficiary's claim against a third-party accessory is strikingly similar to the beneficiary's claim against the trustee/fiduciary.[85] Moreover, it might be possible to see some especially difficult

[80] As an example, consider the various mandatory and default rules imposed on bailees and bailors, pledgees and pledgors, beneficiaries and trustees, each of whom is routinely considered to have some sort of proprietary interest in the underlying asset. The combination of 'property + obligation' has been most recently noted by Jaffey, but even he has pursued that line in a context which places trusts in a special category requiring a unique explanation: P Jaffey, 'Explaining the Trust' (2015) 131 *LQR* 377. That uniqueness is doubted here.

[81] Many commentators could be cited. There are some excellent articles. See especially Maitland, above n 31; DWM Waters, 'The Nature of the Trust Beneficiary's Interest' (1967) 45 *Canadian Bar Review* 219; Nolan, above n 38; B McFarlane and R Stevens, 'The Nature of Equitable Property' (2010) 4 *Journal of Equity* 1; E Hargreaves, 'The Nature of Beneficiaries' Rights under Trusts' (2011) 4 *Trust Law International* 163; W Swadling, 'The Fiction of the Constructive Trust' (2011) 64 *Current Legal Problems* 399; Jaffey, above n 80.

[82] See the discussion in section III above.

[83] See the earlier comment on *AIB v Redler*, above n 78.

[84] *Akers v Samba Financial Group*, above n 79.

[85] To the contrary, see *Williams v Central Bank of Nigeria* [2014] UKSC 10, [2014] AC 1189; but consider the discussion in Worthington, above n 42.

cases in a new light. For example, since a person in possession can sue in tort for economic loss, it might not be such a leap to consider that so too might a beneficiary holding the economic interest under a trust: both have shared interests in the underlying asset, and perhaps both should be treated alike in pursuing tort defendants who damage that property.[86]

Thirdly, note that all these sharing arrangements are upheld at law and treated as 'enforceable' regardless of the perfectly ordinary nature of the underlying assets.[87] Put another way, a trust arises because the settlor intended to share an asset in this particular way, not because some underlying undertaking must be found, with its personal obligations then deemed specifically enforceable because the underlying asset is special and damages are inadequate. Nothing in the context of trusts suggests such limitations. It is the same with security interests.[88] Nor do we typically stumble at this step. But we can be seduced into thinking that such specific enforcement is crucial in other contexts where consensual sharing is at issue.[89] A clearer understanding of the sharing objective might aid analysis. Thus, subject to any statutory rules on formalities, it follows that all intended equitable assignments are effective, even if gratuitous, provided the property exists: an owner's intended equitable assignment *is* an intended trust; there is no other way to conceive of such an intended arrangement.[90] In this context, there is no concern for whether the asset is special and no concern for whether there is consideration supporting the arrangement. The transaction 'to share' is complete in itself.[91] But the issues are quite different with intended assignments of future property or intended but failed outright transfers of title: in both those contexts, specific enforcement of the agreement and 'equity treats as done …' is of the essence in protecting the parties where their intentions remain executory.

Fourthly, as noted earlier, this analysis might clarify the issues in finding shared property interests arising by operation of law. The focus might then usefully settle on determining when the law should impose a particular sharing relationship, rather than simply compelling the defendant to do something for another person.

[86] See the controversial decision in *Shell UK Ltd v Total UK Ltd* [2010] EWCA Civ 180. I suggest that the decision is controversial because of its reasoning, not its conclusion, although see J Edelman, 'Two Fundamental Questions for the Law of Trusts' (2013) 129 *LQR* 66. An extended view of the law on economic loss would not enable the beneficiary to escape the hurdles of proving a duty is owed, and that remoteness and foreseeability issues are met. It seems they would have been on the facts in *Shell*, but may not be in other instances.

[87] It is tempting to think this is not true with ownership and possession of ordinary chattels, but the insolvency response is to the contrary: *Bristol Airport Plc v Powdrill* [1990] Ch 774. Note, however, that if the lessee becomes insolvent, the express terms of the sharing agreement typically terminate the arrangement. The issue is controversial. See W Swadling, 'The Proprietary Effect of a Hire of Goods' in N Palmer and E McKendrick (eds), *Interest in Goods*, 2nd edn (London, LLP, 1998) ch 20; G Watt, 'The Proprietary Effect of a Chattel Lease' [2003] *Conveyancer and Property Lawyer* 61; S Worthington, 'Review Article: Interests in Goods' (2000) 34 *Canadian Business Law Journal* 269 (Review of Palmer and McKendrick (eds), n 86).

[88] Although there, of course, it is easy to say that damages are inadequate.

[89] Some of the discussions of chattel leases are in this vein: eg, S Douglas, *Liability for Wrongful Interferences with Chattels* (Oxford, Hart Publishing, 2011) 35. He cites others who agree.

[90] See the unanswerable analysis to that effect in J Edelman and S Elliott, 'Two Conceptions of Equitable Assignment' (2015) 131 *LQR* 228.

[91] Subject to any necessary formalities, of course.

Fifthly, this contrast between 'sharing' and 'doing' in assessing the obligations imposed on the owner—and on the counterparty—is crucial in assessing remedies. In particular, the focus of remedies in 'doing' cases is typically on the harm caused to the counterparty; in 'sharing' cases, it is typically on the harm to the underlying asset. In assessing losses, therefore, the relevant measure is respectively the loss to the counterparty or the loss to the counterparty's property when compared with the status each might have had if the relevant duties had been carried out properly. That means the focus of the particular duty at issue is crucial: is it protection of the counterparty or protection of the property?[92]

VI. CONCLUSION

In summary, it is suggested here that the core of English property law is not concerned with 'assets', and which assets are classed as property and which are not. Nor is it concerned with which 'interests' are proprietary and which are not. Instead, it is about the sharing of assets, and which shared or derivative interests are possible. We could say that any asset that can be shared is 'property', so long as we then recognise that the key 'property' questions are exclusively concerned with the various possible sharing arrangements and shared interests in that asset. One of the clearest examples of this is with debt. In a classificatory system that divides property and obligation, a contract creating a debt is the clearest example of 'obligation'. Yet this asset can be 'shared': it can be held on trust or used as security, and those arrangements can be put in place by agreement or by operation of law. So is a debt really 'property', rather than obligation, despite the initial assertion to the contrary? Or is the real insight simply that all property questions are concerned with 'sharing', and this asset can be shared? I suggest the latter is the important issue.

So perhaps the most incisive and revolutionary contribution of English property law lies in this novel suggestion: that it is English law's greater flexibility and innovation in recognising sharing arrangements, and its concession that perhaps all wealth can be shared in some way, that is the true English 'genius'. It is this that has enabled English 'property law'—the English law of sharing assets—to be more flexible, more commercial, more responsive, and therefore more useful and more attuned to modern times than the equivalent laws in civilian jurisdictions. And so I end with what I think might be an answer to my opening question. English property law has redrawn the civilian's conceptual map, recognising that 'property' is about sharing, and permitting innovative, perhaps revolutionary, forms of sharing of all manner of assets.

[92] See the comments earlier on *AIB v Redler*, above n 78, a case concerning the protection of the property held on trust. Contrast that with protection of the solicitor's client in *Bristol and West Building Society v Mothew* [1998] Ch 1 (CA).

GENERAL ISSUES

12

Modern Equity: Revolution or Renewal from Within?

PAULINE RIDGE*

I. INTRODUCTION

A REVOLUTION IN thinking about equity began during the latter part of the twentieth century and was spearheaded by Professor Peter Birks.[1] That revolution sought to collapse a perceived divide between the principles and methods of the common law and those of equity. Its influence can clearly be seen in English private law and, to a lesser extent, in Australian law. This chapter asks how successful the revolution has been: has the common law/equity divide collapsed or does there remain something distinctive about modern equitable principle and method?

This question may be construed in various ways and different answers may be given depending on one's jurisdiction, legal education and ideology.[2] My approach is as follows. I first describe three strands of the revolutionary narrative for modern equity (section II).[3] I then describe the corresponding strands of a counter narrative that is apparent in contemporary case law (section III). This counter narrative is suggestive of an internal and ongoing renewal in equity quite different to that envisaged by the revolutionary narrative. According to the counter narrative, equitable principle and method retain distinctive genetic features, but these are not antithetical to those of the common law and may in fact be shared. I discuss the three strands of these two narratives in sections IV–VI in relation to the law of particular interest to me, namely, third-party ancillary liabilities that protect equitable rights and interests. I also refer in passing to the law concerning undue influence, the change of position defence, mistaken gifts and private law claims tainted by illegality.

My choice of illustrative subject matter is certainly selective and perhaps my representation of the two narratives will be considered exaggerated; however, this does

* I thank Joachim Dietrich and Jane Stapleton for their feedback on an earlier version of this chapter.

[1] There were other revolutionary influences upon private law during this time, of course, such as the economic analysis of law and corrective justice movements.

[2] For an analysis grounded in legal philosophy, see M Harding, 'Equity and the Rule of Law' (2016) 132 *LQR* 278.

[3] There is a fourth strand to each narrative, concerning remedies, but its discussion is beyond the scope of this chapter. In particular, the two narratives differ as to the legitimacy of remedial discretion.

allow for discussion of larger questions concerning judge-made law. In reality, there are as many 'narratives' of modern equity as there are narrators. For that reason, I will avoid linking either of the two narratives discussed here to particular individuals, other than to acknowledge the enormous contribution of Peter Birks.[4]

II. A REVOLUTIONARY NARRATIVE OF MODERN EQUITY

Peter Birks and others following him challenged orthodox understandings of equity's doctrines and methods. This appears to have been the by-product of a desire to better understand the operation and arrangement of the general law as a whole, especially the relevance of unjust enrichment reasoning to equitable doctrines.[5] The objective was to formulate a doctrinal taxonomy ordered according to principle, rather than historical jurisdiction. In the course of the taxonomy project, perceived inconsistencies were identified in the formulation and elements of equitable doctrines compared with common law doctrines operating in the same contexts.[6] The highlighting of such inconsistencies led to a broader inquiry into the legitimacy of equity's method where it differed from that of the common law.[7]

The revolutionary narrative was driven by the academy, not the courts, although it has had judicial supporters. Due to its internally focused inquiry (eschewing policy concerns,[8] for instance), as well as its ahistorical doctrinal labelling and abstract conceptual reasoning, it is challenging for sympathetic judges to incorporate into law.[9]

There are at least three strands in the revolutionary narrative that pertain to the organisation, principles and methods of modern equity:

1. The first strand concerns the integration of common law and equity: the historical jurisdictional divide between common law courts and the Court of Chancery caused doctrinal anomalies of principle which should be corrected (generally by removing the anomalous features of equitable doctrines). Furthermore, where there is already commonality of principle across the common law and equity, this should not be obscured by jurisdictional labelling: the relevant law can be organised more coherently. For instance, the principle of unjust enrichment is proposed as a more coherent organising principle for some equitable doctrines,

[4] For a portrayal of two 'combative giants' of the revolution, see K Mason, 'Strong Coherence, Strong Fusion, Continuing Categorical Confusion: The High Court's Latest Contributions to the Law of Restitution' (2015) 39 *Australian Bar Review* 284, 290–91.

[5] A seminal article is P Birks, 'Equity in the Modern Law: An Exercise in Taxonomy' (1996) 26 *Western Australian Law Review* 1. See also A Beever and C Rickett, 'Interpretive Legal Theory and the Academic Lawyer' (2005) 68 *MLR* 320, where Birks's approach is described as an 'interpretive legal theory' rather than a historical, prescriptive or descriptive account of the law. See also J Dietrich, 'What is "Lawyering"? The Challenge of Taxonomy' (2006) 65 *CLJ* 549.

[6] See, eg, A Burrows, 'We Do This At Common Law But That In Equity' (2002) 22 *OJLS* 1.

[7] See, eg, Birks, above n 5.

[8] See, eg, Beever and Rickett, above n 5, 328, 335.

[9] See comments to this effect by A Phang Boon Leong JA in *Wee Chiaw Sek Anna v Ng Li-Ann Genevieve* [2013] 3 SLR 801, [144].

the constituent elements of this principle (in Birksian terms) being: (i) an enrichment of the defendant; (ii) at the claimant's expense; and (iii) a recognised unjust factor.[10]

2. The second strand concerns the use of conscience-based reasoning in equity: reliance upon the concept of 'conscience' in legal reasoning is said to be obfuscatory and unnecessary.[11]
3. The third strand concerns judicial method: according to the revolutionary narrative, holistic determination of liability by reference to basal principle and criteria of indeterminate weight is unprincipled and antithetical to the rule of law.[12]

The language of this revolutionary narrative is one of simplicity, order, fixed categories, predictability of outcome, certainty and clarity.

III. A COUNTER NARRATIVE OF MODERN EQUITY

There is a counter narrative to the revolutionary narrative that has made its presence felt, particularly in Australia.[13] It also emerged in the latter part of the twentieth century, but was more accepting of existing equity jurisprudence. It originated in the courts,[14] rather than in the academy.[15] Accordingly, I would characterise it as a renewal from within, rather than as a revolution. It is not the only possible counter narrative in Australia to that of the Birksian-inspired revolution,[16] but I find it more persuasive than alternative counter narratives on the whole and it offers a useful counterpoint. Strands in this narrative that correspond with those of the revolutionary narrative concerning integration, conscience-based reasoning and judicial method are:

1. Principled integration of common law and equitable doctrine is desirable[17] and consistent with historical practice.[18] However, further integration is likely to be

[10] See, eg, P Birks, *Unjust Enrichment*, 2nd edn (Oxford, Oxford University Press, 2005) 39.

[11] See, eg, Birks, above n 5.

[12] ibid.

[13] cf the counter narrative suggested by Dietrich, above n 5, 575–78.

[14] The judgment of Gummow J in *Roxborough v Rothmans of Pall Mall Australia Ltd* [2001] HCA 68, (2001) 208 CLR 516 has been particularly influential, as has the equity jurisprudence of the Mason High Court. On the latter point, see P Finn, 'Common Law Divergences' (2013) 37 *Melbourne University Law Review* 509.

[15] Nonetheless, the productive interaction of judges and academics can be seen in Paul Finn's celebrated series of edited essays: P Finn (ed), *Essays in Equity* (Sydney, Lawbook Co, 1985); P Finn (ed), *Equity and Commercial Relationships* (Sydney, Lawbook Co, 1987).

[16] There is an alternative, perhaps overlapping, counter narrative that is more conservative in nature and adheres strictly to the historical formulation of doctrine. It is epitomised by the joint judgment of the High Court concerning equitable accessory liability and recipient liability: *Farah Constructions Pty Limited v Say-Dee Pty Limited* [2007] HCA 22, (2007) 230 CLR 89. See also M Kirby, 'Overcoming Equity's Australian Isolationism' (2009) 3 *Journal of Equity* 1.

[17] See, eg, *Baltic Shipping Co v Dillon* (1993) 176 CLR 344, 376 (Deane and Dawson JJ); *Roxborough*, above n 14, 554 (Gummow J). See also P Finn, 'Equitable Doctrine and Discretion in Remedies' in W Cornish, R Nolan, J O'Sullivan and G Virgo (eds), *Restitution: Past, Present and Future* (Oxford, Hart Publishing, 1995) 251, 252.

[18] *Roxborough*, above n 14, 553–54.

uncommon. This is not because of the jurisdictional divide per se, but because of the generally different purposes, values and subject matter of the two bodies of law.[19] Where there is integration, the Birksian unjust enrichment framework is not favoured; however, unjust enrichment as an analytical, explanatory concept is accepted.[20]

2. The concept of conscience has two overlapping roles, one of which is as a shorthand expression of the judicial norms underpinning doctrine (a rationale). Conscience in its second role is a tool of judicial reasoning and refers either to a discrete doctrinal element of or an overall doctrinal threshold for liability. These roles are not necessarily confined to equity.
3. A legitimate trait of many, but by no means all, equitable doctrines is the use of 'basal principle'[21] and 'guiding',[22] rather than fixed criteria: a holistic judgment that balances relevant factors must be made. This methodology is not confined to equity, but is a trait of legal reasoning more generally.

The language of this counter narrative is one of nuance, complexity, metaphor, gradations and spectrums in which the haphazard evolution of the law is acknowledged.[23]

In the remainder of this chapter I consider some manifestations of the three strands of both the revolutionary and counter narratives in Australian and English law.

IV. THE INTEGRATION OF COMMON LAW AND EQUITY

A. The Revolutionary Narrative: Undue Influence

The revolutionary narrative of modern equity sparked many debates regarding the proper characterisation of equitable doctrines and how they might be better

[19] Integration does not necessarily require that there be uniformity in doctrinal requirements. Contrast P Davies, *Accessory Liability* (Oxford, Hart Publishing, 2015) with J Dietrich and P Ridge, *Accessories in Private Law* (Cambridge, Cambridge University Press, 2015). Both books accept that accessory liabilities across private law have a common analytical framework. Davies argues that therefore a uniform claim for 'knowing assistance or inducement should apply' across equity, tort and contract law. Dietrich and I disagree that there should be a uniform test. The content of the three elements of the analytical framework (the nature of the primary wrong; the accessory's involvement, through conduct, in that wrong; and the accessory's mental state) will vary according to the purposes, values and historical development of the primary wrong. Integration of the common law and equity operates at the conceptual level of the analytical framework, but this does not dictate uniformity in doctrinal requirements.

[20] *Equuscorp Pty Ltd v Haxton* [2012] HCA 5, (2012) 246 CLR 498, [30] (French CJ, Crennan and Kiefel JJ): the concept 'has a taxonomical function referring to categories of cases in which the law allows recovery by one person of a benefit retained by another'. In this sense, it is used to explain equitable contribution: *Burke v LFOT Pty Ltd* [2002] HCA 17, (2002) 209 CLR 282, [38] (Gaudron ACJ and Hayne J); *Lavin v Toppi* [2015] HCA 4, (2015) 254 CLR 459, [41] (French CJ, Kiefel, Bell, Gageler and Keane JJ). See generally E Bant, 'Australia', in chapter 10 of this volume.

[21] Finn, above n 14, 518.

[22] *Australian Financial Services and Leasing Pty Ltd v Hills Industries Limited* [2014] HCA 14, (2014) 253 CLR 560, [23] (French CJ) (*AFSL*).

[23] See, eg, *Fistar v Riverwood Legion and Community Club Ltd* [2016] NSWCA 81, (2016) 91 NSWLR 732, [53]. Leeming JA referred to 'the essential disorderliness of the Australian legal system, in which overlapping causes of action are a familiar feature'. His Honour questioned whether the resulting complexity 'is desirable or otherwise': [51].

integrated with their supposed common law counterparts.[24] A well-known example which will only be briefly noted here concerns the doctrine/s of equitable undue influence (actual and presumed). In an influential paper, Professors Birks and Chin conceptualised undue influence as a strict liability unjust enrichment claim.[25] They argued that the language of equitable wrongdoing which pervaded the cases was anomalous and redundant: the true basis for rescission of a gift or contract tainted by undue influence was not presumed or actual wrongdoing by the influencing party, but rather the vitiated autonomy of the influenced party. 'Undue influence' cases that, in fact, were decided on illegitimate pressure grounds 'should be treated as duress', (although duress was also explained on the basis of vitiated autonomy).[26] The resulting pared-down undue influence doctrine was said to be wholly 'claimant-sided' (that is, focused solely upon the influenced party's state of mind, rather than the influential party's conduct), and of the same genre as common law restitution claims for duress and mistake.

Birks and Chin's thesis was valuable in exposing ambiguity in judicial understandings of the rationale and function of undue influence. However, their refiguring of equitable undue influence as an unjust enrichment claim alongside common law vitiated autonomy claims has not, as yet, been universally accepted by the courts. Although the revolutionary narrative of undue influence is quite popular in Australia,[27] there are two competing models of undue influence also applied by the courts: a fiduciary model (whereby the influential party comes under a fiduciary-like duty that is prophylactic and policy-based in nature)[28] and a 'wrongful exertion of influence' model[29] (the dominant English approach).[30] The commentators are similarly divided.[31] Even scholars who accept the emphasis placed upon the

[24] See, eg, the debate concerning equitable subrogation, which has become an unjust enrichment claim in England: *Banque Financière de la Cité v Parc (Battersea) Ltd* [1999] 1 AC 221; *Bank of Cyprus UK Limited v Menelaou* [2015] UKSC 66, [2016] AC 176. The High Court has emphatically rejected the revolutionary narrative for subrogation: *Bofinger v Kingsway Group Limited* [2009] HCA 44, (2009) 239 CLR 269.

[25] P Birks and Chin Nyuk Yin, 'On the Nature of Undue Influence' in J Beatson and D Friedmann (eds), *Good Faith and Fault in Contract Law* (Oxford, Clarendon Press, 1995) 57. It is beyond the scope of this chapter to do justice to recent detailed accounts of undue influence and I have not attempted to do so. See, eg, J Edelman and E Bant, *Unjust Enrichment*, 2nd edn (Oxford, Hart Publishing, 2016) ch 10.

[26] ibid 63.

[27] *Hart v Burbidge* [2014] EWCA Civ 992, [43] is a possible example of English endorsement. The English Court of Appeal accepted, without any analysis of the case law, that the 'juridical basis' for undue influence was unjust enrichment: citing C Mitchell, P Mitchell and S Watterson (eds), *Goff & Jones on the Law of Unjust Enrichment*, 8th edn (London, Sweet & Maxwell 2011). With respect, the case is weak authority, given the lack of reasoned analysis of the point and the apparent unawareness (at [44]) of case law addressing the Court's *obiter* question whether a third-party volunteer to a relationship of influence could rely on lack of knowledge of the relationship as a defence. See, eg, *Bridgeman v Green* (1757) Wilm 56, 97 ER 22; *Huguenin v Baseley* (1807) 14 Ves 273, 33 ER 526.

[28] See, eg, *Johnson v Buttress* (1936) 56 CLR 113, 134–36 (Dixon J); R Honey, 'Divergence in the Australian and English Law of Undue Influence: Vacillation or Variance?' in A Robertson and M Tilbury (eds), *Divergences in Private Law* (Oxford, Hart Publishing, 2016) 271, 273–74.

[29] Honey, ibid, argues that this is the model laid down in *Royal Bank of Scotland Pty Ltd v Etridge (No 2)* [2001] UKHL 44, [2002] 2 AC 773.

[30] Honey, ibid, 271.

[31] Contributions to the debate include R Bigwood, 'Undue Influence: "Impaired Consent" or "Wicked Exploitation"?' (1996) 16 *OJLS* 503; M Chen-Wishart, 'Undue Influence: Vindicating Relationships of Influence' (2006) 59 *Current Legal Problems* 231.

influenced party's autonomy argue for a much more complex and nuanced approach to autonomy concerns.[32]

In my view, one reason why the revolutionary narrative has not yet prevailed over competing explanations of equitable undue influence is because it does not give sufficient weight to the prophylactic function of the doctrine.[33] It is the danger of wrongdoing (in the equitable sense of that term), rather than actual wrongdoing, that is addressed. As with fiduciary law's onerous conflict and profit obligations, which are removed entirely once fully informed consent is given, the doctrine of undue influence presumes the worst until convinced otherwise. A further weakness with the revolutionary narrative of undue influence is that it does not acknowledge the doctrine's holistic concern with both the influenced party's autonomy and the influencing party's conduct.[34] Clearly, vitiated autonomy is a crucial factor in why relief is given, but it is not the only factor at play. The case law displays a spectrum of scenarios in which either autonomy or wrongdoing concerns may be dominant. The revolutionary narrative addresses this by differentiating a strict liability, vitiated autonomy claim (with a restitutionary remedy) and a wrong-based claim (with a range of remedies), but this solution lacks the subtlety and flexibility of the original doctrine.

In one respect—actual undue influence—Birks and Chin's integration proposals are more persuasive. It is clear that such scenarios were dealt with in the same way at common law (duress) and in equity (actual undue influence).[35] There seems little point in maintaining the jurisdictional distinction other than, perhaps, for remedial purposes. As Birks and Chin argue:

> It is unfortunate if this must still be expressed as transferring them from equity to common law. It is time that in this field we overcame the old jurisdictional duality. It would be better to say simply that pressure should be litigated as pressure ...[36]

Nonetheless, such an integration does not necessarily entail accepting actual undue influence/duress as a claimant-sided, unjust enrichment claim. Interestingly, the High Court of Australia, in *obiter*, has suggested that common law duress could fall within 'unconscionable conduct within the meaning of the unwritten law' for the purposes of section 51AA of the Trade Practices Act 1974 (Cth).[37] This is consistent with the revolutionary narrative's desire to remove unhelpful jurisdictional differences, albeit that the suggested shift is from a common law to an equitable characterisation of the claim.

[32] See, eg, Chen-Wishart, ibid.

[33] Although Birks and Chin acknowledge that undue influence has a 'remoter justification as a prophylactic instrument against wicked exploitation', the latter phrase does not accurately capture the essence of equitable wrongdoing in this context: Birks and Chin, above n 25, 63.

[34] See, eg, *Johnson v Buttress*, above n 28, 134–35 (Dixon J).

[35] cf *Williams v Bayley* (1866) LR 1 HL 200 (undue influence; threat to prosecute son); *Kaufman v Gerson* [1904] 1 KB 591 (duress; threat to prosecute husband).

[36] Birks and Chin, above n 25, 63.

[37] *Australian Competition and Consumer Commission v CG Berbatis Holdings Pty Ltd* [2003] HCA 18, (2003) 214 CLR 51, [45].

B. The Counter Narrative: The Claim for Money Had and Received

A counter narrative of the integration of common law and equity that favours equitable concepts, terminology and method has emerged in Australia in relation to the common law claim for money had and received. The High Court favours an equity-infused understanding of the common law claim, and in so doing is developing a conscience-based jurisprudence of 'unjust enrichment' that is at odds with the Birksian unjust enrichment framework.[38] Two long-standing equitable features of the claim for money had and received have been emphasised. The first is that the action is available, in at least some circumstances, to recover monies to which a claimant is entitled in equity.[39] The second is that the action has been formulated in equitable terms since the eighteenth century and should continue to be so.[40] The use of equitable norms to explain and shape the claim for money had and received was given imprimatur by the judgment of Gummow J in *Roxborough v Rothmans of Pall Mall Australia Limited* and has been supported by other members of the High Court both before and after that case.[41] Thus, 'notions derived from equity have been worked into and in that sense have become part of the fabric of the common law'.[42]

A recent example of this approach to the integration of the common law and equity—merely noted here—concerns the change of position defence to the common law claim to recover a mistaken payment. The High Court in *Australian Financial Services and Leasing Pty Ltd v Hills Industries Limited* disavowed a (Birksian) 'disenrichment' formulation of the defence in favour of a broader, estoppel-based, formulation aimed at preventing irreversible detriment and that is 'conducted by reference to equitable principles'.[43] This is welcome:[44] the Australian version of the change of position defence allays concern that strict liability operates too harshly upon innocent defendants and makes an unjust enrichment explanation of the mistaken payment claim more palatable. Furthermore, the estoppel jurisprudence upon which the Court relied provides a wealth of material to draw upon in further shaping of the defence.

[38] See, eg, *AFSL*, above n 22, [20] (French CJ), [65], [68], [70]–[71] (Hayne, Crennan, Kiefel, Bell and Keane JJ), [138] (Gageler J).

[39] See generally *Roxborough*, above n 14, 541 [66]–[67] (Gleeson, Gaudron and Hayne JJ). For one example, see *Fischer v Nemeske Pty Ltd* [2016] HCA 11, (2016) 330 ALR 1, [16]–[17] (French CJ and Bell J), [81] (Kiefel J), [105] (Gageler J), [187] (Gordon J). See also *Fistar*, above n 23, [31].

[40] *Moses v Macferlan* (1760) 2 Burr 1005, 97 ER 676. See also Lord Wright in *Fibrosa Spolka Akcyjna v Fairbairn Lawson Combe Barbour Ltd* [1943] AC 32, 61. cf P Birks, above n 10, 290.

[41] *Roxborough*, above n 14. See further K Mason, 'R3RUE, the Taxonomy of the Constructive Trust and the Fusion of Law and Equity' in E Bant and M Bryan (eds), *Principles of Proprietary Remedies* (Sydney, Lawbook Co, 2013) 97.

[42] *Roxborough*, above n 14, 554 [100] (Gummow J), quoted in *AFSL*, above n 22, [12] (French CJ).

[43] *AFSL*, above n 22, [78] (Hayne, Crennan, Kiefel, Bell and Keane JJ); see also [24] (French CJ), [77]–[78], [84] (Hayne, Crennan, Kiefel, Bell and Keane JJ), [157]–[158] (Gageler J). See further Bant, above n 20.

[44] But see Mason, above n 4.

C. Ancillary Liabilities for Receipt of Trust Property

Both narratives of modern equity are clearly evident in recent Australian developments concerning ancillary liabilities for receipt of misappropriated property. I shall now explore this area in more depth.

(i) Background: The Knowing Receipt and Persisting Property Claims

By way of background, it is first necessary to note the two most commonly litigated equitable ancillary claims against a defendant,[45] D, who is the recipient for personal benefit of misappropriated trust property or its traceable proceeds. These claims apply not only to property that is the subject of an express trust, but also to constructive trust property, which includes stolen property.[46] Hence, they are of great practical importance in unwinding the proprietary consequences of fraud. Until late last century, the two claims—'unconscionable'[47] (or, in Australia, 'knowing')[48] receipt and 'the persisting property claim'[49]—dominated the consciousness of lawyers in this area of practice. The former liability is personal and fault-based. Fault is determined according to the recipient's mental state at the time of receipt.[50] D is liable whether or not D retains the trust property or its traceable proceeds. Relief may be personal or proprietary (if D in fact retains the property). The persisting property claim is available if D retains trust property or its traceable proceeds and is not a bona fide purchaser of the legal interest without notice. It comprises 'proprietary, in rem, proceedings to make specific restitution to the "true owner" of such trust property (or its traceable proceeds) as remains in [D's] hands'.[51] In other words, the claim is fundamentally proprietary in nature.

Both the revolutionary narrative and the counter narrative with respect to the integration of the common law and equity have radically changed the late twentieth-century understanding of this area. Overlooked pockets of law have been revived and reshaped by the courts. In doing so, both common law and equitable concepts have been utilised, as will now be explained. The focus is upon Australian law.

[45] By 'ancillary' I mean those liabilities predicated upon the equitable wrongdoing of another and by which the law seeks to protect the beneficiary of a relationship governed by equity from third-party interference or exploitation. See further Dietrich and Ridge, above n 19, ch 7.

[46] See further *Fistar*, above n 23, [36]–[39].

[47] *Bank of Credit and Commerce International (Overseas) Ltd v Akindele* [2001] Ch 437, 455.

[48] *Farah*, above n 16. I will use the traditional label of 'knowing receipt' in the following discussion.

[49] The persisting property claim is described in various ways, including as 'the tracing doctrine': *Federal Republic of Brazil v Durant International Corpn* [2015] UKPC 35, [2016] AC 297; and the doctrine of 'purchaser without notice': *Re Montagu's Settlement Trusts* [1987] Ch 264, 272–73. 'Persisting property' captures the essence of the claim, which is that the claimant's proprietary rights persist in property now held by D. See also C Mitchell and S Watterson, 'Remedies for Knowing Receipt' in C Mitchell (ed), *Constructive and Resulting Trusts* (Oxford, Hart Publishing, 2010) 115, referring to 'persisting property'.

[50] In Australia, the question is whether D had sufficient knowledge of the breach of trust or fiduciary duty: *Farah*, above n 16. In England, it is whether D's knowledge made it 'unconscionable for [D] to retain the benefit of the receipt': *Akindele*, above n 47, 455.

[51] *Grimaldi v Chameleon Mining NL (No 2)* [2012] FCAFC 6, (2012) 200 FCR 296, [251].

(ii) The Revolutionary Narrative and Knowing Receipt

Initially, the revolutionary narrative was that knowing receipt should be reformulated as a strict liability, unjust enrichment claim (by discarding the fault element, adding defences of change of position and bona fide purchaser, and mandating a restitutionary remedy).[52] The fault element was said to be anomalous when the claim was compared with analogous common law recipient liabilities and with other pockets of equity.[53] This integration argument was later modified so as to retain the existing fault-based claim, but to add, as an alternative, a strict liability unjust enrichment claim that would operate alongside the fault-based claim.[54] The English courts and, so far, the Australian courts have rejected the revolutionary narrative regarding knowing receipt.[55] It continues to be a fault-based claim with a range of possible remedies. This appears to tell against the integration of the common law and equity in relation to the recipient of misappropriated trust property, but is far from the end of the story.

(iii) The Counter Narrative: The Heperu *Claim*

In fact, there has been integration of the common law and equity through recognition of strict recipient liabilities, although not quite as envisaged by the revolutionary narrative. Recent Australian authorities recognise at least two common law recipient liabilities that protect equitable rights from third-party interference. The first—exemplifying the counter narrative of modern equity—comes from a series of decisions in New South Wales[56] building upon the House of Lords case *Lipkin Gorman v Karpnale Ltd*.[57] The fullest exposition of this liability is given by Allsop P in *Heperu Pty Ltd v Belle* in the NSW Court of Appeal, and the following discussion will refer to it as 'the *Heperu* claim'.[58] In *Heperu*, a fiduciary misappropriated the appellants' funds and paid them into his wife's bank account. He subsequently transferred the funds to a second account also in his wife's name. Some withdrawals from the account were made for mortgage repayments. A persisting property claim

[52] See, eg, P Birks, 'Misdirected Funds: Restitution from the Recipient' [1989] *Lloyd's Maritime and Commercial Law Quarterly* 296; P Birks, 'Misdirected Funds' (1989) 105 *LQR* 352; P Birks, *Restitution—The Future* (Sydney, Federation Press, 1992); A Burrows, *The Law of Restitution*, 3rd edn (Oxford, Oxford University Press, 2011) 424–31.

[53] Such as the claim in *Re Diplock* [1948] 1 Ch 465.

[54] See, eg, Lord Nicholls, 'Knowing Receipt: The Need for A New Landmark' in Cornish et al, above n 17, 231; P Birks, 'Receipt' in P Birks and A Pretto (eds), *Breach of Trust* (Oxford, Hart Publishing, 2002) 213. The technique of deconstructing equitable doctrines so as to clarify a doctrine's taxonomical home and render its elements more precise is common in the revolutionary narrative. See, eg, Birks and Chin, above n 25 (undue influence); S Worthington, *Equity* (Oxford, Oxford University Press, 2003) 227–32 (estoppel).

[55] *Akindele*, above n 47; *Farah*, above n 16.

[56] *Heperu Pty Ltd v Belle* [2009] NSWCA 252, (2009) 76 NSWLR 230; *Break Fast Investments Pty Ltd v Perikles Giannopoulos (No 5)* [2011] NSWSC 1508; *Sze Tu v Lowe* [2014] NSWCA 462, (2014) 89 NSWLR 317; *Fistar*, above n 23. See also *Ford v Perpetual Trustees Victoria Ltd* [2009] NSWCA 186 (2009) 75 NSWLR 42.

[57] *Lipkin Gorman v Karpnale Ltd* [1991] 2 AC 548.

[58] *Heperu*, above n 56.

was not pleaded. Nor was a knowing receipt claim available, as the wife, a volunteer, was found to have no knowledge or notice of her husband's fraud.

The claim recognised in *Heperu* and subsequent cases is a common law claim for money had and received against the recipient, D, for personal benefit of trust property or its traceable proceeds who retains that property, the rationale for which is unconscionable retention of benefit. It is said to be unconscionable for D to retain the benefit of the traceable trust property once on notice of the claimant, C's, claim, unless the bona fide purchase defence applies. In essence, D is required to account for the property.[59] This is a common law ancillary liability that protects equitable rights: the claim is to the value of equitable property, identified through equitable means, but enforced by the common law. It represents an integration of the common law and equity par excellence in which the common law/equitable appellation becomes unhelpful as a description of the cause of action.

The courts have aligned the *Heperu* claim with the equitable persisting property claim as its personal liability companion.[60] Broadly speaking, C traces the trust property to D's hands and either claims the value of the retained property under the *Heperu* claim or the property itself pursuant to the persisting property claim. Where D no longer holds the property, or where remedies other than restitution or specific relief are desired, a knowing receipt claim is available if it can be shown that D was at fault at the time of receipt. There are still questions concerning the *Heperu* claim, including whether an indefeasibility of title defence applies[61] and whether a change of position defence is available,[62] but they are beyond the scope of this chapter.

(iv) The Revolutionary Narrative: Great Investments Ltd v Warner

The second Australian development in relation to ancillary recipient liabilities is that the Full Federal Court, in *Great Investments Ltd v Warner*, has recognised the strict liability of a recipient of company assets transferred by an agent (on the facts, a director) without authority and not pursuant to a contract.[63] A proprietary remedy was awarded.[64]

The Court cited three cases as direct authority for the principle that strict liability applies to the recipient of an unauthorised benefit received from a company

[59] *Fistar*, above n 23, [31].

[60] In *Sze Tu v Lowe*, above n 56, Gleeson JA (with whom Meagher and Barrett JJA agreed) went further in appearing to elide the persisting property claim with the personal *Heperu* claim: see, eg, [144]–[145]. *Fistar*, above n 23, makes it clear that they are distinct claims.

[61] It appears to have been assumed incorrectly that because indefeasibility is a defence to the persisting property claim it must also be a defence to the personal *Heperu* claim: see, eg, *Heperu*, above n 56, [167]; *Break Fast*, above n 56, [96]–[102]; *Sze Tu v Lowe*, above n 56, [241]–[243]. cf *Fistar*, above n 23, [82].

[62] In *Heperu*, change of position concerns were subsumed into the determination of liability: D is only liable for the value of the retained trust property or its traceable proceeds. This does not protect an innocent recipient who retains traceable trust property but who changed position in reliance on its receipt. A recent case has accepted the possibility of a change of position defence: *Fistar*, above n 23, [83]. See also E Bant and M Bryan, 'Defences, Bars and Discretionary Factors' in E Bant and M Bryan (eds), *Principles of Proprietary Remedies* (Sydney, Lawbook Co, 2013) 184, 187.

[63] *Great Investments Ltd v Warner* [2016] FCAFC 85, (2016) 243 FCR 516.

[64] ibid [76]: 'orders to be made in equity to effect a conveyance of the rights that arise by registration and the bond certificates' to the claimant.

other than by way of a contract.[65] With respect, neither of the two modern cases (decisions of the English Court of Appeal in 2007 and of the Federal Court of Australia in 2015, respectively) provides a reasoned explanation of the law, supported by authority. Rather, each presents the matter as one of self-evident principle. In the latter case, for example, Beach J held:

> [the respondent director] caused [the applicant company] to pay out moneys for no proper purpose and in breach of the duties he owed to [the company]. [The company] suffered detriment by reason of this conduct while [the director] benefited from it. It would be unjust for [the director] to retain the benefit of those moneys. [The company] is entitled to restitution.[66]

It is not clear why this is not a straightforward instance of breach of fiduciary duty for which the director is liable in equity. An alternative explanation is that it is an instance of money had and received 'in respect of the monies improperly received by a fiduciary'.[67] With respect, the language of 'detriment', 'benefit' and 'injustice' does not add clarity or assist in understanding the nature of this claim: surely the director would still be subject to strict liability even if, for some unusual reason, there was no detriment and/or no benefit?

The 1740 Chancery decision of Hardwicke LC in *Harrison v Harrison*, also relied upon in *Great Investments*, is more difficult to interpret.[68] The Federal Court takes it to be authority for the strict liability of the recipient of company stock transferred in 'error', with no need to prove knowledge on the recipient's part. However, there are two inconsistent reports of the case. The fuller report (reported as *Harrison v Pryce*), by Barnardiston, states the facts as being that the South Sea Company transferred on its books stock belonging to one Edward Harrison to a second Edward Harrison. The reporter ascribes the stock transfer to 'Fraud', whereas the Federal Court in *Great Investments* describes it as an 'error'. The second Harrison then transferred the stock to his broker, who sold it for him. The widow of the first Harrison was held entitled either to have the specific stock in question purchased for her or to have the proceeds of the broker's sale paid to her. Confusingly, the language of trover and conversion is used; however, the Federal Court explained that the Lord Chancellor was arguing by analogy to the common law claims. The Lord Chancellor did not have to decide whether the South Sea Company might be liable to the widow if the second Harrison did not have sufficient assets to meet her claim; however, he 'seemed inclined to think that' it might be liable on the basis of being a trustee of the stock for the first Harrison.

The correctness of the report in Barnardiston was doubted by Best CJ in the 1824 Common Pleas case of *Davis v Bank of England*, who preferred the much shorter

[65] *Harrison v Harrison* (1740) Barn 324, 27 ER 664, also reported as *Harrison v Pryce* (1740) 2 Atk 121, 26 ER 476; *Blue Station Ltd v Kamyab* [2007] EWCA Civ 1073: successful claim by company against director for restitution of payment to which the director was not entitled and which could not be shown to have discharged a company debt; *Prestige Lifting Services Pty Ltd v Williams* [2015] FCA 1063, (2015) 333 ALR 674.

[66] *Prestige Lifting Services*, ibid, [270].

[67] *Roxborough*, above n 14, [66]. See also above n 39.

[68] *Harrison v Harrison* (1740) 2 Atk 121, 26 ER 476; *Harrison v Pryce* (1740) Barn 324, 27 ER 664.

report of *Harrison v Harrison* by Atkyns. Atkyns reports the case as one of breach of trust (presumably by the company) for which the trustee was strictly liable.[69] But this does not explain the second Harrison's liability. Best CJ went further and described the facts as being that the second Harrison 'fraudulently procured' the stock to be put in his name and hence was liable for specific restoration of the stock or payment of the proceeds of sale. Overall, the reports are unclear as to the trigger and rationale for Harrison's liability.

The point of this digression is to suggest that the authorities relied upon in *Great Investments* in direct support of the propounded claim are weak. Nevertheless, the lack of direct authority does not mean that the claim is unfounded; indeed, the Court in *Great Investments* went on to situate the claim within private law as a whole, finding that it '[reflected] a consistent and coherent pattern across the law'.[70] The Court concluded that there was:

> substantial authority that supports strict liability, subject to defences, for the receipt by a respondent of a company asset transferred without authority ... The difference between whether the personal claims are described as 'equitable' or as 'common law claims' is not a difference of principle because although the claim for money had and received is a common law claim, it has equitable roots.[71]

In other words, according to the Federal Court, a strict liability claim represents the integration of the common law and equity based upon commonality of principle. The Court went on to note, perhaps inconsistently with this, that an equitable characterisation of the claim would be necessary where proprietary relief was sought (as it was in this case).[72]

The *Great Investments* decision is consistent with the revolutionary narrative. For example, the Court referred to cases and commentary supporting an unjust enrichment rationale for the personal strict liability claim and for the persisting property claim.[73] A more subtle, but important, indicator of the revolutionary narrative is that the Court referred to the acceptance in Australia of *Lipkin Gorman*, citing *Heperu*, but, contrary to *Heperu*, appeared to favour Lord Goff's judgment rather than Lord Templeman's.[74] Significantly, Lord Goff had translated the eighteenth-century, equitable, conscience-based rationale for the action for money had and received ('the third party cannot in conscience retain the money') into contemporary parlance ('or, as we say nowadays') of unjust enrichment: 'for the third party to retain the money would result in his unjust enrichment at the expense of the owner of the money'.[75] In so doing, he adopted the Birksian unjust enrichment framework for determining the claim. By contrast with the Federal Court, the NSW Court of Appeal in *Heperu*

[69] *Davis v Bank of England* (1824) 2 Bing 393, 406–407, 130 ER 357, 363–63.
[70] *Great Investments*, above n 63, [63].
[71] ibid [68].
[72] ibid [70]–[76].
[73] ibid [59], [69].
[74] ibid [64].
[75] *Lipkin Gorman*, above n 57, 572. The Court in *Great Investments* also cited with approval Lord Nicholls's reference in *Criterion Properties plc v Stratford UK Properties LLC* [2004] 1 WLR 1846, [4] to a strict liability personal 'unjust enrichment' claim; however, it is far from obvious that Lord Nicholls's judgment would be followed by the High Court.

favoured Lord Templeman's judgment in *Lipkin Gorman*, retained the language of unconscionable retention of benefit and did not use the Birksian unjust enrichment framework.

(v) Has Either Narrative Prevailed?

What can be concluded from these developments in terms of the integration of the common law and equity? Clearly, the proponents of the revolutionary narrative should claim considerable credit. The fact that the Australian courts now acknowledge that strict personal recipient liabilities at common law coexist with equitable knowing receipt and the persisting property claim is surely due to ongoing academic discussion of the need for such claims and the precedents for them.[76]

However, it may prove difficult to reconcile these two lines of Australian authority: why should the formulation and elements of the *Heperu* claim and the *Great Investments* claim differ, perhaps markedly, when both concern the personal liability of a recipient of property that is subject to equitable rights and obligations? Does the pairing of the *Heperu* claim with the persisting property claim (and consequent requirement that D retain the subject property) justify the differences? How could that be, given that a proprietary remedy was given in *Great Investments* over the company's traceable property?[77] The *Heperu* claim is inconsistent with the revolutionary narrative: it is not an unjust enrichment claim in the Birksian sense, it requires D to retain the trust property, its rationale is conscience-based and change of position questions appear to be subsumed, partially if not wholly, into the determination of liability.[78] Conversely, the *Great Investments* claim unashamedly embodies the revolutionary narrative.

There are also questions concerning the relationship of the *Heperu* claim and the *Great Investments* claim to other ancillary liabilities pertaining to receipt of equitable property and to the persisting property claim. The current Australian law, in which a growing number of claims concerning recipients of misappropriated property are recognised, is clearly at odds with the taxonomical approach of the revolutionary narrative. This observation is suggested by a NSW Court of Appeal decision concerning the *Heperu* claim, *Fistar v Riverwood Legion and Community Club Ltd*.[79] In this case, D argued that recognition of the *Heperu* claim would outflank equity's knowing receipt claim and so should not be allowed.[80] In rejecting this argument, Leeming JA, with whom Bathurst CJ and Sackville AJA agreed, emphasised that it was in the nature of the common law that causes of action would develop on a pragmatic, ad hoc and gap-filling basis, with little or no reference to a 'regularly ordered taxonomy of causes of action'.[81] Whether or not the resulting complexity was desirable, it was

[76] The scholarship of Professor Bryan is notable in this respect. See, eg, M Bryan, 'The Liability of the Recipient: Restitution at Common Law or Wrongdoing in Equity' in S Degeling and J Edelman (eds), *Equity in Commercial Law* (Sydney, Lawbook Co, 2005) 327.

[77] *Great Investments*, above n 63, [76].

[78] See, eg, *Heperu*, above n 56, [150], [158], [161].

[79] *Fistar*, above n 23.

[80] ibid [23]–[24].

[81] ibid [50].

clear that there are 'many overlapping claims against recipients of stolen property'.[82] All this resonates more with the counter narrative of modern equity and against the 'cleaner' taxonomical approach of the revolutionary narrative. Nonetheless, the relationship of the various common law and equitable claims concerning receipt of property protected by equity requires further clarification before we can be comfortable with the complexity of this area of law and before it can be said that either narrative has prevailed.

V. CONSCIENCE

A. Introduction

The second strand to the revolutionary narrative of modern equity concerns the allegedly obfuscatory and dangerous—in that it is contrary to the rule of law—nature of the concept of 'conscience' in equity. Birks's intemperate criticisms in this regard provoked a heated response, but that was all some time ago.[83] The issue has become topical again, due to superior court decisions in Australia and England in which conscience-based reasoning has been prominent.[84] A recent contribution to the debate regarding conscience concludes: 'Ultimately, and fundamentally, the true role of conscience in contemporary Equity reflects a battle over the nature of private law.'[85] Clearly, the issue provokes strong feelings.

The use of conscience-based reasoning offends the revolutionary narrative's desire for clarity and simplicity in the exposition of the law. Judges are criticised for using 'conscience' in a conclusory, rhetorical and/or superfluous fashion, for example, which does not assist in understanding why a particular decision was reached.[86] But one needs to be careful before assuming that this is always the case; what is viewed as rhetorical flourish by one reader may to another be seen as shorthand for the equitable norms at play.[87] Conscience-based language is also criticised for not having a self-evident meaning. 'Unconscionable is not a word in everyday use by non-lawyers', as Lord Nicholls observed in *Royal Brunei Airlines Sdn Bhd v Tan* when reformulating the liability threshold for equitable accessory liability.[88] But even if this is so, why should it matter in a legal context?[89] General concepts

[82] ibid [36]; see also [53].

[83] Birks, above n 5, 16–17. Birks equated 'conscience' in its legal sense with Heydrich's reference to his personal conscience to justify his actions as head of the Gestapo.

[84] See, eg, *Kakavas v Crown Melbourne Limited* [2013] HCA 25, (2013) 250 CLR 392 ('*Kakavas*'); *AFSL*, above n 22; *Pitt v Holt* [2013] UKSC 26, [2013] 2 AC 108.

[85] G Virgo, 'Whose Conscience? Unconscionability in the Common Law of Obligations' in A Robertson and M Tilbury (eds), *Divergences in Private Law* (Oxford, Hart Publishing, 2016) 293, 320. See also R Havelock, 'Conscience and Unconscionability in Modern Equity' (2015) 9 *Journal of Equity* 1.

[86] See, eg, DR Klinck, 'The Unexamined "Conscience" of Contemporary Canadian Equity' (2001) 46 *McGill Law Journal* 571.

[87] See Harding, above n 2, 286, referring to the expressive function of conscience.

[88] *Royal Brunei Airlines Sdn Bhd v Tan* [1995] 2 AC 378, 392.

[89] Nor is this point self-evident: unconscionability language is creeping into the Australian vernacular, perhaps because of the popular ABC television programme, *The Checkout*, and its promotion of the Australian Consumer Law unconscionability provisions.

are used in all areas of law even though their meaning may not immediately be obvious to non-lawyers.[90] This does not mean that 'conscience' is not useful so long as its legal meaning in specific contexts is unpacked (as Lord Nicholls went on to acknowledge).[91] As will now be discussed, conscience and its synonyms are used in two main senses in the law.

B. The Two Roles of Conscience

Broadly speaking, 'conscience' as now used in judge-made law has two, related roles. First, conscience—and its synonyms of 'equitable fraud', 'inequitable', 'against equity and good conscience' and the like[92]—is sometimes stated as the rationale for a doctrine as a whole.[93] Secondly, it can be used as a determinant of liability in a particular case (a tool of legal reasoning). In the latter role, it may be present as a discrete element or as the standard against which other elements individually or in combination are measured.[94] The language of conscience for either role is not limited as a matter of principle or as a matter of history to equitable doctrines, although it is more common in that context.[95]

(i) Conscience as a Doctrinal Rationale: The Heperu *Claim*

When conscience is given as the rationale for a doctrine, it is being used as a shorthand expression for, or judicial distillation of, one or more judicial norms that underpin the case law. Pomeroy's description of this sense of conscience remains compelling:

> a metaphorical term, designating the common standard of civil right and expediency combined, based upon general principles and limited by established doctrines, to which the court appeals, and by which it tests the conduct and rights of suitors,—a juridical and not a personal conscience.[96]

[90] See Dietrich, above n 5, 567.

[91] *Royal Brunei Airlines*, above n 88, 392. Lord Nicholls's preference for 'dishonesty' over 'conscience' as more clearly denoting the threshold for equitable accessory liability proved to be no more certain in the short term. cf *Twinsectra Ltd v Yardley* [2002] UKHL 12, [2002] 2 AC 164; *Barlow Clowes International Ltd (in liq) v Eurotrust International Ltd* [2005] UKPC 37, [2006] 1 WLR 1476.

[92] The range of terms denoting conscience-based rationales for equitable intervention suggests that meaningful conclusions cannot be drawn from a word search of 'conscience' or 'unconscionable' in the English Reports. cf Havelock, above n 85, 12–15.

[93] cf Finn's description of 'an organising idea informing specific equitable rules and doctrines which do not in terms refer to, or require, an explicit finding of unconscionable conduct': P Finn, 'Unconscionable Conduct' (1994) 8 *Journal of Contract Law* 37, 38. See also Dietrich's description of 'general concepts as informing ideas or principles': J Dietrich, 'Giving Content to General Concepts' (2005) 29 *Melbourne University Law Review* 218, 222–23.

[94] Conscience in this role determines liability 'through the "filters" of specific doctrines and their elements, whilst at the same time imposing standards of conduct'. See Dietrich, ibid, 222–26.

[95] See, eg, *Baltic Shipping*, above n 17, 376. See also JD Davies, 'The Re-awakening of Equity's Conscience: Achievements and Problems' in S Goldstein (ed), *Equity and Contemporary Legal Developments* (Jerusalem, Harry and Michael Sacher Institute for Legislative and Comparative Law, Hebrew University of Jerusalem, 1992) 46, 71.

[96] SW Symons and JN Pomeroy, *A Treatise on Equity Jurisprudence*, 5th edn (San Francisco, Bancroft-Whitney, 1941) vol 1, §57, quoted in *Kakavas*, above n 84, [15].

It thus seems misguided to search for precision in meaning when considering this role for conscience; conscience in Pomeroy's exposition is a 'metaphorical' term. Conscience and its synonyms are simply pointers as to why equity intervenes in certain scenarios. This image of conscience as a fluid metaphor for the judicial norms underpinning doctrine resonates with the language of the counter narrative.

Critically, the content of conscience as a doctrinal rationale may well vary in relation to different doctrines: the norm or norms at play in relation to one legal doctrine will not necessarily replicate those involved in another.[97] In particular, it does not always relate to the personal conscience of D during the occurrence of the facts in issue.[98] Unconscionable insistence on legal rights may occur at the time of hearing and may be characterised as such without there being personal fault by D. This also suggests that a common criticism of conscience-based reasoning, namely, that *whose* conscience is in question varies, is misguided: sometimes the court is focusing upon a defendant's state of mind in order to determine what is in good conscience, but not always. This understanding of conscience as a doctrinal rationale can be illustrated by reference to the *Heperu* claim for money had and received.

As explained in section IV above, conscience is the rationale given for the *Heperu* claim. That this is a principled use of conscience reasoning becomes clear if an analogy is drawn to the cases on ancillary liability pursuant to equity's vitiating doctrines. A pervasive norm in equitable vitiating doctrines (for which the standard remedy is rescission of a transaction) is that it is wrong for a third party to a fraud to retain the benefit of that fraud (pursuant to the vitiated transaction) even if he or she was innocent at the time of the receipt of the benefit:

> The truth is that, in all cases of this kind, where a fraud has been committed, and a third person is concerned, who was ignorant of the fraud, and from whom no consideration moves, such third person is innocent of the fraud only so long as he does not insist on deriving any benefit from it; but when once he seeks to derive any benefit from it he becomes a party to the fraud.[99]

For example, this norm applies to the innocent recipient of a gift tainted by the undue influence of another person over the donor and it justifies the remedy of rescission. The principled rationale[100] for the strict liability imposed on the innocent recipient was expressed by courts from at least the early nineteenth century in the language of 'conscience'.[101] Three factors combine to make retention of a gift tainted by another's undue influence against conscience: the absence of consideration; the taint of undue influence; and the in-built change of position protection provided by the remedy of rescission.[102]

With one proviso, this conception of conscience also explains the unconscionable retention of benefit rationale of the *Heperu* claim for money had and received.

[97] *Tanwar Enterprises Pty Limited v Cauchi* [2003] HCA 57, (2003) 217 CLR 315, [20].

[98] ibid [25].

[99] *Scholefield v Templer* (1859) Johns 154, 162, 70 ER 377, 381. See also P Ridge, 'Third Party Volunteers and Undue Influence' (2014) 130 *LQR* 112, 120.

[100] There are also supporting, pragmatic rationales: see Ridge, ibid.

[101] See, eg, *Huguenin v Baseley* (1807) 14 Ves Jun 273, 290, 33 ER 526, 532.

[102] Ridge, above n 99.

The proviso relates to the need for a change of position defence to the *Heperu* claim to be explicitly recognised. The remedy for the *Heperu* claim is restitution of the monetary value of the property retained by D, rather than rescission of a transaction. Unlike rescission, restitution does not offer the same in-built protection against an indirect change of position by D, who retains the trust property. Thus, if the conscience rationale of the *Heperu* claim is to be fully persuasive, a change of position defence must be recognised.[103]

(ii) Conscience as a Determinant of Liability

The second role for conscience in judicial reasoning is as a determinant of liability. In this sense, conscience may constitute the overall threshold, or a discrete element, of liability. An example of the former usage occurs in the English law on assignment of choses in action. One way in which an imperfect gift of shares may be regarded as fully constituted is 'if it would be unconscionable, in the eyes of equity, vis-à-vis the donee to [change his or her mind]'. The question turns on 'the court's evaluation of all the relevant considerations'.[104] An example of the latter usage occurs in the English formulation of equitable recipient liability. Conscience is the standard by which D's mental state is assessed: was D's knowledge of the primary wrong in all the circumstances 'such as to make it unconscionable for [D] to retain the benefit of the receipt?'[105]

Whether as an overall threshold or as a discrete doctrinal element, both usages of conscience introduce a measure of indeterminacy into the court's decision making because they generally require a holistic and contextual inquiry into the facts. For this reason, their appropriateness in various doctrinal contexts can be a controversial and complex question on which (judicial) minds may differ.[106] Relatedly, both usages of conscience are also accompanied by a particular judicial method. This method is the subject of the next section.

VI. JUDICIAL METHOD

The third strand of the two narratives of modern equity concerns judicial method. Must liability be determined by the application of discrete elements, each satisfied to a fixed standard, or may liability be determined by balancing the requisite elements in a holistic, contextual inquiry into the facts? Equity's judicial method is sometimes, but by no means always, characterised by the latter approach: a holistic determination of liability by reference to 'basal principle'[107] (generally, 'conscience') and

[103] This appears likely to be the case. See above n 62.
[104] *Pennington v Waine* [2002] EWCA Civ 227, [2002] 1 WLR 2075, [64] (Arden LJ).
[105] *Akindele*, above n 47, 455.
[106] See, eg, the dichotomy between the English and Australian law concerning beneficiaries' access to trust documents discussed in: G Dal Pont, 'Beneficiaries and Trust Information' (2014) 39 *Australian Bar Review* 46.
[107] Finn, above n 14, 518.

elements of indeterminate weight. I will adopt the phrase 'judgment in the round' to describe this method.[108] The revolutionary narrative is strongly opposed to judgment in the round, whereas the counter narrative supports its availability. Judgment in the round has been endorsed as a legitimate form of judicial reasoning by a long line of distinguished senior judges, including, most recently, the members of the High Court in *Australian Financial Services and Leasing Pty Ltd v Hills Industries Ltd*.[109]

Judgment in the round is particularly appropriate when the law is in a state of flux. Doctrines become settled over time, but eventually a re-evaluation may be required—because, for example, the social or legal context in which the doctrine operates has altered. When this happens, effective doctrinal change may best be achieved by reformulating a doctrine in broad, holistic terms that respond to its rationale and objectives and that require judgment in the round. A reworking and embedding of the reformulated elements by subsequent courts will ensue so that, over time, a less indeterminate doctrinal inquiry may emerge. Judgment in the round may then no longer be required.[110] This may happen, for example, in relation to the equitable doctrine concerning mistaken gifts. Lord Walker's judgment in *Pitt v Holt* (an outstanding example of judgment in the round) marked a point of doctrinal reformulation for the equitable doctrine triggered by major changes in the common law requirements for restitution of a mistaken payment.[111] Over time, the reformulated elements of the equitable doctrine—'a distinct mistake ..., its degree of centrality to the transaction in question and the seriousness of its consequences'—will be given content by the courts and the basal principle, 'whether it would be unconscionable, or unjust, to leave the mistake uncorrected', will become correspondingly clearer in its application.[112] However, the basal principle need not become redundant; it may still be the ultimate reference point for determining liability in borderline cases.

Equity's accessory liability and recipient liability provide further illustrations of the utility of judgment in the round in times of change. Revived interest in these ancillary liabilities during the later twentieth century, accompanied by unsatisfactory formulaic applications of the nineteenth-century precedents, meant that the law was ripe for reform. A doctrinal re-evaluation was required. Given the unsuitability of the fixed rules at that time, doctrinal reformulation in terms of guiding criteria requiring judgment in the round was natural and this is what occurred in relation to accessory liability in the Privy Council—there was a rejection of formulaic elements in favour of a basal principle of dishonesty in relation to D's conduct and mental state.[113] The English Court of Appeal also reformulated the law of recipient

[108] The term is adapted from Lord Walker's judgments in *Gillett v Holt* [2001] Ch 210, 225 and *Pitt v Holt*, above n 84, [128]. It involves 'an inherently evaluative and fact-specific inquiry, rather than the application of formal rules': M Harding and R Hickey, 'Equity and the Value of Gifts' (2014) 8 *Journal of Equity* 1, 23.

[109] *AFSL*, above n 22. cf *Patel v Mirza* [2016] UKSC 42, [2016] 3 WLR 399, [263], [265] (Lord Sumption JSC).

[110] See Hon Sir A Mason, 'Themes and Prospects' in P Finn (ed), *Essays in Equity* (Sydney, Lawbook Co, 1985) 242, 244.

[111] *Pitt v Holt*, above n 84.

[112] ibid [128].

[113] *Royal Brunei Airlines*, above n 88.

liability, and a test of unconscionability with respect to D's requisite mental state was introduced.[114] Whether a similar approach might be taken in Australia is an open question.[115]

Thus, the appropriateness of judgment in the round may depend upon where, in its evolutionary cycle, a particular doctrine is situated. It is of most use when an area of law is undergoing substantial change. It is also useful when the essence of the doctrinal inquiry cannot be distilled into a set of rules: the nature and subject matter of the doctrine may mean that it can never fully be bedded down. That is, judgment in the round will always be required.[116] An observation of French CJ is apposite:

> There are many areas of the common law and of statute law which require the case-by-case application of broadly stated legal rules and standards and the judicial development of guiding criteria of liability within them. Such criteria may be inspired, may rise, and may be modified or displaced by the fruitful incremental interaction of advocacy, judicial reasoning, and academic suggestion and critique. Rarely, however, do they yield all-encompassing rules for the application of a foundation standard or norm.[117]

It should also be noted that judgment in the round is just as much a feature of the common law's judicial method, although equity appears to attract more criticism in this regard (perhaps because of the additional perceived indeterminacy of 'conscience'). One good example of how the issue transcends jurisdictional boundaries is in relation to the question whether private law claims tainted by illegal purposes should be enforced. The High Court of Australia has applied judgment in the round in this context to claims in trust, contract, tort and restitution with no evident difficulty or injustice.[118] A slim majority of the UK Supreme Court in *Patel v Mirza* also endorsed a judgment in the round methodology (in relation to illegality tainting a common law claim for restitution).[119]

Judgment in the round is criticised as allowing a judge to indulge in a subjective and normative assessment of the facts.[120] It is illogical, however, to think that the exercise of normative judgment can ever be completely eliminated from the determination of liability. Nor should it be: judging is a creative process by which social norms are transposed into the law by means of the existing law,[121] albeit at an incremental and generally imperceptible pace that is restrained by institutional checks and balances (such as the avenue of appeal).[122] Formulation of doctrine according to basal principle and elements of indeterminate weight allows for 'an element of value judgment in a borderline case'.[123] One restraint on subjectivity is transparency

[114] *Akindele*, above n 47.

[115] See further P Ridge, 'The Hallmarks of Australian Equity' in T Bonyhady (ed), *Finn's Law and Australian Justice* (Sydney, Federation Press, 2016).

[116] *AFSL*, above n 22, [23] (French CJ).

[117] ibid.

[118] *Nelson v Nelson* (1995) 184 CLR 538; *Fitzgerald v FJ Leonhardt Pty Ltd* (1997) 189 CLR 215; *Miller v Miller* [2011] HCA 9, (2011) 242 CLR 446; *Equuscorp Pty Ltd v Haxton* [2012] HCA 7, (2012) 246 CLR 498.

[119] *Patel v Mirza*, above n 109.

[120] See, eg, *Patel v Mirza*, ibid, [263] (Lord Sumption JSC).

[121] See Harding and Hickey, above n 108, 24.

[122] See Harding, above n 2, 290 concerning the checks and balances on judicial decision making.

[123] *Commonwealth v Verwayen* (1990) 170 CLR 394, 441 (Deane J).

in judicial decision making, but this is impeded where normative choices are hidden behind a façade of linguistic certainty.[124] At its best, judgment in the round (including associated conscience-based reasoning) is a transparent means by which normative judgment occurs.

The elimination of unrestrained and completely subjective decision making—judgment at *large*, so to speak—is a legitimate aspiration. Peter Birks, in a famous article, painted a dystopian picture of a society in which judgment at large, which he equated with equity's judicial method, was permitted.[125] Judgment in the *round*, however, is quite a different matter to judgment at large because it is constrained by the doctrinal content and framework, as well as being subject to institutional checks and balances. But perhaps it comes down to the degree of trust one has in the judiciary. Birks's critique was highly distrustful of the judiciary, and the checks and balances upon it. This can be contrasted with the counter narrative, which has been articulated as follows: 'Recognising that a judge has a normative discretion—albeit one which is constrained by principle—is the sign of a mature jurisprudence which does not assume that judges will act capriciously or arbitrarily.'[126]

VII. CONCLUSION

How successful has the revolutionary narrative been: does there remain something distinctive about modern equitable principle and method that gives relevance and meaning to the appellation of 'equitable'? My answer, which is rather less confident than when I began this inquiry, is still in the affirmative. The common heritage of equitable doctrines means that equity as a body of law is likely to display common genetic features in terms of its activating legal norms, terminology and methods. Knowing that a doctrine has equitable origins—and explicating those origins—helps us to understand its rationale and modus operandi. It may well be that, following such explication, we conclude that there is no further point in emphasising those equitable origins. Or, conversely, the equitable features of a doctrine may remain significant. The *Heperu* claim is an example. Labelling that claim as belonging to either the common law or equity does not tell us much about its nature or substance (or even historical provenance). It is a common law claim that embodies equitable norms and, probably, a distinctively equitable method. It confounds any simplistic distinction. Nonetheless, recognition that its features are equitable is essential to understanding its rationale and its operation.

The discussion in this chapter suggests that the essence of the two narratives is not about collapsing a perceived common law/equity divide. Indeed, it is possible to airbrush 'equity' and 'common law' almost entirely from the discussion. The three

[124] Such as the *Baden* five-point scale of knowledge used in Australian accessory and recipient liability: *Baden v Société Générale pour Favoriser le Développement du Commerce et de l'Industrie en France SA* [1993] 1 WLR 509, 575–76. cf *Grimaldi*, above n 51, [260]: the scale 'tends to invite the use of formulae to solve problems'.

[125] Birks, above n 5.

[126] B Kremer, 'Restitution and Unconscientiousness: Another View' (2003) 119 *LQR* 188, 191–92.

strands of the two narratives reflect different visions of judge-made law, specifically its organisation, formulation and method. These visions tend to be associated with either the common law or with equity, whereas in fact they are present in both. Furthermore, although the discussion in this chapter tends to favour the counter narrative, it is important to acknowledge the importance of the revolutionary narrative. The presence of two narratives in tension with one another is not necessarily undesirable: both seek a coherent and defensible legal order and both express legitimate concerns. They come to the fore in evolving areas of law that are not amenable to simple explanation. Understanding that competing narratives of the law are at play may assist in reaching principled outcomes. For that reason, it seems desirable for courts to give transparent and respectful attention to the concerns of both narratives and to where the balance between them is to be struck.

13

Concurrent Liability: A Spluttering Revolution

PAUL S DAVIES*

I. INTRODUCTION

CONCURRENCE IS A difficult issue. No matter what taxonomy is adopted when dividing the law up into discrete areas for exposition,[1] it seems inevitable that there will be disputes which can be analysed as falling within one or more categories. The approach of English law to this issue has evolved over time. In *Henderson v Merrett Syndicates Ltd* in 1994, Lord Goff said that 'it is a remarkable fact that there was little consideration of the problem of concurrent remedies in our academic literature until the second half of the 20th century, though in recent years the subject has attracted considerable attention'.[2] The focus of analysis has tended to be upon the relationship between claims in tort and contract. The initial approach of the law was to insist that the claim be brought in contract, not tort.[3] There was then a 'revolution' which departed from such jurisprudence, and held that the claimant had a free choice to bring his claim either in contract or in tort.[4] This remains orthodoxy, but increasingly there appears to be some doubt cast upon the desirability of an entirely free choice. One member of the Court of Appeal has said that the House of Lords took a 'wrong turning' in *Henderson v Merrett*.[5] Indeed, it has recently been recognised that a claim in tort may be limited by contractual rules of remoteness where the tortious duties exist in parallel to contractual duties.[6] This might undermine some of the advantages enjoyed by a claimant in having a free choice between concurrent causes of action, and lead to the conclusion that the contractual rules trump their tortious counterparts.

* I am grateful for comments from those present at Obligations VIII, and also to Clare McKay and Janet O'Sullivan for comments on an earlier draft. The usual disclaimers apply.

[1] See recently D Sheehan and TT Arvind, 'Private Law Theory and Taxonomy: Reframing the Debate' [2015] *Legal Studies* 480.

[2] [1995] 2 AC 145, 185.

[3] See, eg, *Groom v Crocker* [1939] 1 KB 194.

[4] *Midland Bank Trust Co Ltd v Hett, Stubbs & Kemp* [1979] Ch 348; *Henderson v Merrett*, above n 2.

[5] R Jackson, 'Concurrent Liability: Where Have Things Gone Wrong?' (2015) 23 *Tort Law Review* 3.

[6] eg *Wellesley Partners LLP v Withers LLP* [2015] EWCA Civ 1146, [2016] Ch 529.

The focus of this chapter concerns the professional negligence context, which provides a wealth of material to consider. For obvious reasons, claimants might be able to frame their claim either as one for breach of contract or the tort of negligence, and the contract/tort divide will be discussed first. This is the area which has generated the most analysis in the context of concurrence. But the analysis of concurrence needs to be expanded:[7] it is suggested that there is some hint that 'contractual rules' will prevail not only where tortious claims are brought, but also where the rival claim is for breach of trust.[8] For example, in *AIB Group (UK) Plc v Mark Redler & Co*, Lord Toulson thought that 'in circumstances such as those in *Target Holdings*[9] the extent of equitable compensation should be the same as if damages for breach of contract were sought at common law',[10] and in *Thanakharn Kasikhorn Thai Chamkat (Mahachon) v Akai Holdings Ltd*, Lord Neuberger, sitting as a non-permanent judge of the Hong Kong Court of Final Appeal, commented that

> even if the principles ... had suggested that Akai was entitled to equitable compensation in an amount greater than it should recover by way of common law damages, I would have been very sympathetic to the notion that the equitable remedy would have to be refashioned so as to equate the amount of such compensation with the common law damages.[11]

Where the contractual obligation and trust obligation are 'twinned'[12] and cover the same facts, it appears that although the claimant might formally be able to choose to bring a claim in breach of trust rather than in breach of contract, the advantage in doing so will often be eliminated if the contractual rules apply. However, the problematic rules regarding limitation of actions, which are in serious need of reform, might continue to provide a reason for claimants to continue to frame their claim as one in tort or breach of trust rather than breach of contract, for example.

It is suggested that the general trend of the law at the moment is to move away from allowing the claimant freely to choose how to label his or her claim in order to obtain all the advantages that flow from that characterisation. Generally, the contractual rules seem to have primary importance, at least where concurrent claims are 'twinned' in resting upon the same facts and basis. Different considerations might be relevant where a separate claim exists independently of a contractual relationship—such as a claim in unjust enrichment[13] or for breach of fiduciary duty,[14] or even a

[7] See also A Burrows, *Understanding the Law of Obligations: Essays on Contract, Tort and Restitution* (Oxford, Hart Publishing, 1998) ch 2, which includes unjust enrichment within the debate on concurrency.

[8] See also the speeches of Lord Browne-Wilkinson in *Henderson v Merrett*, above n 2, *White v Jones* [1995] 2 AC 207 and *Target Holdings Ltd v Redferns* [1996] AC 421.

[9] ibid.

[10] *AIB Group (UK) Plc v Mark Redler & Co* [2014] UKSC 58, [2015] AC 1503, [71].

[11] [2010] HKCFA 64, [155]. See also, eg, *Canson Enterprises Ltd v Boughton & Co* [1991] 3 SCR 534, 585–87 (La Forest J).

[12] JA Weir, 'Prescription, Classification and Concurrence of Obligation' (1962) 36 *Tulane Law Review* 556.

[13] See, eg, Burrows, above n 7, ch 2.

[14] See, eg, J Getzler, 'Am I my Beneficiary's Keeper? Fusion and Loss-Based Fiduciary Remedies' in S Degeling and J Edelman (eds), *Equity in Commercial Law* (Sydney, Lawbook Co, 2005).

claim for confiscation of the proceeds of crime[15]—but these tend not to arise in the professional negligence context and, for reasons of space, will not be considered further here.

II. CONTRACT VERSUS TORT

The focus here is on breach of a contractual duty to take care. This might overlap with a tortious duty to take care on the basis of an 'assumption of responsibility'.[16] Considering the piecemeal way in which the common law tends to develop, it is understandable how contract law might evolve without careful examination of what occurs in tort law, and vice versa. But this can lead to divergences which have very significant effects when the duty of care exists both in contract and in tort. Such divergences tend to focus on the type of loss that can be recovered, and the quantum of such an award. There is also the practically important issue of limitation, which might not apply in the same way in contract and tort. These areas will all be considered once the evolution of English law in this area has been outlined.

A. First Steps: Contract Trumps Tort

In Roman law, the law of contract and the law of delict were separate domains. Difficult issues of concurrence therefore did not arise. By the start of the twentieth century, however, it was clear that English law had to face the tricky issue of concurrence. The first intuition of the English courts was to exclude the possibility of concurrent liability. A leading case that clearly established this proposition was *Groom v Crocker*.[17] A claimant argued that his solicitor had acted wrongfully in settling an insurance dispute by stating that the claimant was negligent when it was known that he was not. The claimant sought relief both in contract and in tort, and also damages for libel. The libel claim is, for present purposes, distinct and can be separated: the interests protected by libel are clearly very different from those protected by a (contractual or tortious) duty of care. The Court of Appeal held that the solicitor had committed a breach of his contractual duty in admitting negligence by the claimant, and further insisted that the mutual rights and duties of a solicitor and his client are regulated by contract and contract alone: the solicitor could not be liable in tort to the claimant.

[15] Claims by the state to recover the proceeds of crime may trump competing private law claims: see, eg, P Davies, 'Bribery in Equity' in P Davies and J Penner (eds), *Equity, Trusts and Commerce* (Oxford, Hart Publishing, 2017).

[16] *Hedley Byrne & Co Ltd v Heller & Partners Ltd* [1964] AC 465. This chapter is concerned with situations where the 'assumption of responsibility' exists because of the voluntary relationship between the parties. As a result, circumstances where the tortious duty exists entirely independently of any contract are not considered: see, eg, the libel claim in *Groom v Crocker*, above n 3, discussed immediately below.

[17] Above n 3.

In *Groom v Crocker*, the claimant sought to frame his claim in tort in order to be able to sue for mental suffering and loss of reputation. The Court of Appeal expressed sympathy for the claimant and thought that such loss should perhaps be recoverable,[18] but nonetheless considered that the contractual rules governed the claim exclusively. Sir Wilfrid Greene MR commented that

> the cause of action is in contract and not in tort ... The relationship of solicitor and client is a contractual one ... It was by virtue of that relationship that the duty arose, and it had no existence apart from that relationship.[19]

Scott LJ was similarly clear that 'the mutual rights and duties of the two are regulated entirely by the contract of employment' unless fraud was established.[20]

This decision of the Court of Appeal was very influential. It was regularly followed, even after the important decision of the House of Lords in *Hedley Byrne v Heller*.[21] Indeed, the Privy Council offered strong support for the principle that the contractual rules should take precedence in *Tai Hing Cotton Mill Ltd v Liu Chong Hing Bank Ltd*.[22] Lord Scarman insisted that '[a]s between contracting parties the duties in contract and tort should be coextensive',[23] and that no greater liability should be imposed on a contracting party breaching a duty of care simply because the claim was framed in tort rather than contract:[24]

> Their Lordships do not believe that there is anything to the advantage of the law's development in searching for a liability in tort where the parties are in a contractual relationship. This is particularly so in a commercial relationship. Though it is possible as a matter of legal semantics to conduct an analysis of the rights and duties inherent in some contractual relationships including that of banker and customer either as a matter of contract law when the question will be what, if any, terms are to be implied or as a matter of tort law when the task will be to identify a duty arising from the proximity and character of the relationship between the parties, their Lordships believe it to be correct in principle and necessary for the avoidance of confusion in the law to adhere to the contractual analysis: on principle because it is a relationship in which the parties have, subject to a few exceptions, the right to determine their obligations to each other, and for the avoidance of confusion because different consequences do follow according to whether liability arises from contract or tort, e.g. in the limitation of action.

This clearly favours an approach which prioritises the voluntarily assumed obligations under a contract rather than the rights provided by the general law of tort. Since the parties are in a position to bargain with one another and modify their duties and responsibilities, the bargain should be respected above any rights afforded by the law of tort 'for free'.

[18] eg *Groom v Crocker*, ibid, 206 (Greene MR), 225 (Scott LJ). The scope of recovery for mental distress in contract has since been broadened: see, eg, *Farley v Skinner (No 2)* [2001] UKHL 49, [2002] 2 AC 732.

[19] *Groom v Crocker*, ibid, 205.

[20] ibid 222. See also MacKinnon LJ at 229.

[21] See, eg, *Bagot v Stevens Scanlan & Co Ltd* [1966] 1 QB 197 (Diplock LJ).

[22] [1986] AC 80.

[23] ibid 86.

[24] ibid 107.

B. Asserting Concurrent Liability

The division between contract and tort was blurred a little by the decision of the House of Lords in *Hedley Byrne*. It is not the purpose of this chapter to analyse that decision in detail.[25] But it is important to note that the potential overlap between contract and tort greatly increased since their Lordships recognised (albeit strictly *obiter*) the possibility of recovering pure economic loss in tort if the defendant had undertaken an 'assumption of responsibility' towards the claimant. Indeed, since it was possible to recover in tort even when there was no contract, this appeared to strengthen the argument that the claimant should still be able to recover in tort in situations where there was a contract: why should the claimant be worse off if he provided consideration to the defendant and created a contract?

Of course, in *Hedley Byrne* itself it was clear that there was no contract and so there was no issue of concurrence.[26] As a result, that decision did not make it clear whether both the contractual and tortious claims could be pursued in parallel. For some time, there was strong authority in favour of maintaining the approach in *Groom v Crocker*.[27] But this was in tension with the view that it would be artificial to restrict the tortious claim by reference to external considerations; in other words, there should be no reason not to allow the principle of 'assumption of responsibility' to enjoy its natural scope, regardless of whether there exists a contract between the parties. Thus, a defendant might have undertaken an 'assumption of responsibility' even where there was a contract in place. Indeed, the contract itself would be strong evidence that there was an 'assumption of responsibility'.

The 'revolution' against *Groom v Crocker* was perhaps commenced by Lord Denning in the Court of Appeal,[28] but was really driven forwards by a detailed and bold decision of Oliver J in *Midland Bank Trust Co Ltd v Hett Stubbs & Kemp*.[29] Despite only sitting at first instance, Oliver J felt able to point to conflicting authority which entitled him to make a choice whether to recognise concurrent liability. The judge felt compelled by the decision in *Hedley Byrne* to allow a claim in the tort of negligence to proceed even where there was a contract between the parties. In the *Midland Bank* case, a solicitor failed to register an option. This was a negligent breach of the solicitor's professional duty, and the client argued that the solicitor could therefore be sued either for breach of a contractual duty of care or in the tort of negligence (following *Hedley Byrne*). This was important for the purpose of limitation: in contract, time began to run at the point of breach, but in tort, time only began to run when damage was suffered.[30] Oliver J held that the tortious claim could succeed and that the claim was not time-barred.

[25] See further K Barker, R Grantham and W Swain (eds), *The Law of Misstatements: 50 Years On from Hedley Byrne v Heller* (Oxford, Hart Publishing, 2015).

[26] Beyond, perhaps, an argument that because there was no contract there could not be any duty in tort. But that was clearly rejected by the decision of the House of Lords.

[27] eg *Bagot*, above n 21; *Tai Hing Cotton Mill*, above n 22.

[28] See, eg, *Esso Petroleum Co Ltd v Mardon* [1976] QB 801.

[29] [1979] Ch 384.

[30] See further section I.C.v below.

Oliver J undertook a detailed historical analysis, and concluded that the origins of the 'contract trumps' approach were ambiguous and in some respects unconvincing.[31] Although the judge accepted that decisions of the Court of Appeal such as *Groom v Crocker* were prima facie binding upon him, he considered that the ratio of that case 'could not stand alongside that overriding decision of the House of Lords' in *Hedley Byrne*.[32] This was largely because the principle of *Hedley Byrne* liability was

> a perfectly general one and it is difficult to see why it should be excluded by the fact that the relationship of dependence and reliance between the parties is a contractual one rather than one gratuitously assumed, in the absence, of course, of contractual terms excluding or restricting the general duties which the law implies.[33]

Oliver J thought that the focus should really be upon what the relationship between claimant and defendant was, rather than whether that relationship arose voluntarily or gratuitously.[34]

Indeed, Oliver J pointed out a potential anomaly which would arise from maintaining the *Groom v Crocker* line of jurisprudence:

> The solicitor who gratuitously assumes to advise a relative and does it negligently remains liable to suit at any time within six years of damage occurring. The solicitor who charges a substantial fee to a client who retains his services in the normal way escapes any liability at all if the damage does not occur or is not discovered until six years has elapsed from the date on which the negligent advice is given.[35]

This would be odd: it would be unsatisfactory for a person who pays for advice not to be as well protected as a person who receives advice for free, when the breach of duty by the defendant is the same. This is emphasised in situations where both the contractual duty and the tortious duty arise from the same promise.[36] Yet the different limitation periods, for instance, can make the choice whether to frame the claim in contract or tort crucial. It is understandable why judges feel some sort of inclination to allow the claim in tort to proceed in order for claims not to be time-barred before claimants even have the opportunity to discover that there has been a breach. However, the limitation rules are in many respects unsatisfactory, and such decisions might really point to a need to reform the limitation rules that apply to claims for breach of contract.[37]

In any event, *Midland Bank* was a closely reasoned and influential judgment[38]—though by itself, the 'revolution' against *Groom v Crocker* would probably not have been successful. After all, Oliver J was merely a puisne judge, and the Privy Council in *Tai Hing* gave wholehearted support to *Groom v Crocker*. It was only through

[31] *Midland Bank*, above n 29, 406–408.
[32] ibid, 411.
[33] ibid.
[34] See also, eg, Lord Devlin in *Hedley Byrne*, above n 16.
[35] *Midland Bank*, above n 29, 417–18.
[36] cf R Stevens, *Torts and Rights* (Oxford, Oxford University Press, 2007) 199–204.
[37] See section I.C.v below.
[38] In *Wellesley*, above n 6, [148] Roth J described it as 'seminal'.

the decision of the House of Lords in *Henderson v Merrett* that *Groom v Crocker* was authoritatively departed from. This is perhaps the pinnacle decision favouring concurrent liability.[39]

The claimants were underwriting members—known as 'Names'—at Lloyd's. They sued their underwriting agents for giving them negligent advice. 'Direct Names' were in a contractual relationship with those agents, whereas 'Indirect Names' were not. In both instances, the Names sought to bring claims in tort. As regards Direct Names, a difficulty arose as to whether the claimants could sue in tort when a contract had been agreed between them and the defendants. The House of Lords clearly held that the duty to take care in providing advice existed concurrently in both contract and tort. This was again crucial for the purposes of limitation: the contractual claims would have been out of time (since time began to run upon the giving of the negligent advice), but the tortious claims would not be time-barred (since time only began to run when damage was suffered some years later due to huge payouts by insurers). As regards the Indirect Names, their Lordships held that the fact that a contract had not been agreed between the parties did not exclude any direct responsibility through a claim in tort.

Lord Goff gave the leading speech.[40] His Lordship strongly endorsed the approach taken by Oliver J in the *Midland Bank* case,[41] and considered that the logic underpinning *Hedley Byrne* inevitably led to the conclusion that concurrent liability in contract and tort was unobjectionable.[42] Lord Goff undertook some comparative analysis and noted that 'no perceptible harm has come to the German system from admitting concurrent claims'.[43] In a similar manner to Oliver J in the *Midland Bank* case, Lord Goff pointed out the 'startling possibility that a client who has had the benefit of gratuitous advice from his solicitor may in this respect be better off than a client who has paid a fee' if concurrent liability were not recognised.[44]

Lord Goff recognised that there were significant practical advantages that a claimant might enjoy by framing his claim in tort rather than contract. Limitation was perhaps the 'foremost',[45] but further considerations such as remoteness, contribution and the ability to obtain leave to serve out of the jurisdiction were also relevant. His Lordship then went on to say that:[46]

> It can of course be argued that the principle established in respect of concurrent liability in contract and tort should not be tailored to mitigate the adventitious effects of rules of law such as these, and that one way of solving such problems would no doubt be 'to rephrase such incidental rules as have to remain in terms of the nature of the harm suffered rather than the nature of the liability asserted' (see Tony Weir, XI *Int Encycl Comp L* ch 12,

[39] In *Wellesley*, ibid [148], Roth J said that *Henderson v Merrett* 'conclusively determined' the issue.

[40] Lord Browne-Wilkinson was the only other member of the panel to give a reasoned speech: see, eg, the text to n 53 below.

[41] *Henderson v Merrett*, above n 2, 188.

[42] ibid 187.

[43] ibid 184.

[44] ibid 185.

[45] ibid 185.

[46] ibid 185–86.

para 72). But this is perhaps crying for the moon; and with the law in its present form, practical considerations of this kind cannot sensibly be ignored.

At the time of *Henderson v Merrett*, perhaps such ideas were 'crying for the moon'. Whether this remains true today might, however, be doubted, and will be considered in the next section. In any event, Lord Goff was clearly not persuaded by any 'temptation of elegance'[47] in dealing with such cases exclusively in the law of contract, and thought that the common law was not prone to such logical and elegant development.[48] His Lordship approved the following passage by Le Dain J, delivering the judgment of the Supreme Court of Canada in *Central Trust Co v Rafuse*:[49]

> A concurrent or alternative liability in tort will not be admitted if its effect would be to permit the plaintiff to circumvent or escape a contractual exclusion or limitation of liability for the act or omission that would constitute the tort. Subject to this qualification, where concurrent liability in tort and contract exists the plaintiff has the right to assert the cause of action that appears to be the most advantageous to him in respect of any particular legal consequence.

This is a very claimant-friendly approach. Lord Goff felt that this also reflected the trend in other jurisdictions.[50] The law of tort was the general law which was not usurped by the existence of a contract.[51] He later said that:

> the common law is not antipathetic to concurrent liability, and that there is no sound basis for a rule which automatically restricts the claimant to either a tortious or a contractual remedy. The result may be untidy: but, given that the tortious duty is imposed by the general law, and the contractual duty is attributable to the will of the parties, I do not find it objectionable that the claimant may be entitled to take advantage of the remedy which is most advantageous to him, subject only to ascertaining whether the tortious duty is so inconsistent with the applicable contract that, in accordance with ordinary principle, the parties must be taken to have agreed that the tortious remedy is to be limited or excluded.

Lord Goff did recognise that the tortious claim should not be able to 'short-circuit' a chain of contracts,[52] but was clear that this was not an issue in *Henderson v Merrett* since the tort claims were founded upon the same duty as the contract claims.

Lord Browne-Wilkinson gave a short concurring speech. He focused upon the duty of care owed by fiduciaries, but clearly approved the decisive shift in favour of concurrent liability:[53]

> If the common law is not to become again manacled by 'clanking chains' (this time represented by causes, rather than forms, of action), it is in my judgment important not to exclude concepts of concurrent liability which the courts of equity have over the years

[47] ibid 186.

[48] See also Sir Thomas Bingham MR in the Court of Appeal in *Henderson v Merrett* [1994] CLC 55, 63.

[49] (1986) 31 DLR (4th) 481, 522.

[50] eg *Henderson v Merrett*, above n 2, 191–92.

[51] ibid, 193.

[52] ibid, 195; *Simaan General Contracting Co v Pilkington Glass Ltd (No 2)* [1988] QB 758. Compare the problematic decision of the House of Lords in *Junior Books Ltd v Veitchi Co Ltd* [1983] 1 AC 520, doubted in *Robinson v PE Jones (Contractors) Ltd* [2011] EWCA Civ 9, [2012] QB 44.

[53] *Henderson v Merrett*, above n 2, 206.

handled without difficulty. I can see no good reason for holding that the existence of a contractual right is in all circumstances inconsistent with the co-existence of another tortious right, provided that it is understood that the agreement of the parties evidenced by the contract can modify and shape the tortious duties which, in the absence of contract, would be applicable.

C. The Beginnings of a Counter Revolution?

The language of both Lord Goff and Lord Browne-Wilkinson in *Henderson v Merrett* was very forthright. That decision represents the high-point of concurrent liability, affording the claimant the freedom to choose how to frame his claim when the duties in contract and tort are coextensive. However, *Henderson v Merrett* has been criticised as a 'wrong turning',[54] and it seems that some of the fears of Lord Goff may have been overstated. In particular, it no longer appears (even if at one point the contrary were true) to be 'crying for the moon' when hoping for the reform of 'incidental rules'. For instance, there has been some shift towards the contract rules being applied even where the claim is framed in tort. Such developments will be analysed in this sub-section.

(i) Remoteness

Remoteness is a tricky topic in both contract and tort separately, and is perhaps especially difficult where the claims in contract and tort overlap. In *Henderson v Merrett*, the House of Lords was content to allow claimants to choose to frame a claim in tort in order to take advantage of more favourable rules on remoteness. A major reason why the tortious rules are generally preferred by claimants is that the type of loss only has to be foreseeable at the time of the tort,[55] rather than at the time at which the contract was concluded.[56]

Where the tortious duty arises out of an assumption of responsibility and exists concurrently with an identical contractual duty, it seems unduly generous to permit the claimant to rely upon the more favourable rules that have been developed in the tortious sphere. This explains why many commentators called for the contractual rules to apply to a claim brought in tort where there was a concurrent claim in contract.[57] The contractual rules are narrower because the parties have the opportunity to make each other aware of particular losses that might be suffered in the event of breach.[58] This can be contrasted with the paradigm tort case involving personal

[54] See Jackson, above n 5, in which the author also criticised the use made by Lord Goff of comparative law.

[55] *Overseas Tankship (UK) Ltd v Morts Dock & Engineering Co (The Wagon Mound)* [1961] AC 388.

[56] *Hadley v Baxendale* (1854) 9 Exch 341.

[57] H McGregor, *McGregor on Damages*, 19th edn (London, Sweet & Maxwell, 2014) [22-009]; A Burrows, *Remedies for Torts and Breach of Contract*, 3rd edn (Oxford, Oxford University Press, 2004) 88–94; A Burrows, 'Comparing Compensatory Damages in Contract and Tort: Some Problematic Issues' in S Degeling, J Edelman and J Goudkamp, *Torts in Commercial Law* (Sydney, Thompson Reuters, 2011) 3–7.

[58] *The Heron II* [1969] 1 AC 350, 385–86 (Lord Reid).

injury where the parties have no pre-existing relationship at all. However, the rationale for a narrower approach applies wherever the parties have an opportunity to disclose particular risks, even if the claim is framed in tort rather than contract. Yet, as recently as 2014, the Court of Appeal doubted the suggestion that where a duty of care arises in contract as well as tort the contractual rules necessarily trump the tortious rules.[59] This might be viewed as consistent with the liberal approach to concurrent liability put forward in *Henderson v Merrett*, but has since been doubted by the Court of Appeal in *Wellesley Partners LLP v Withers LLP*.[60]

Wellesley Partners LLP (Wellesley) claimed damages against its solicitors, Withers, for negligence in the drafting of a partnership agreement. Wellesley was a business specialising in head hunting in the area of investment banking. In order to expand, Wellesley entered into an agreement with a new investor, and consequently required a new partnership agreement to be drawn up. Unfortunately, Withers had negligently drafted the agreement so that an option for the investor to withdraw half its capital contribution could be exercised *within* the first 41 months of the agreement, rather than *after* 42 months, which is what had been intended. The courts found that this was a breach of Withers's duty of care. Wellesley sought to rely upon the more advantageous rules of remoteness in tort law—it appears to have been accepted that the 'reasonable contemplation' test in contract is more restrictive than the 'reasonable foreseeability' test in tort[61]—and so framed its claim accordingly.[62] At first instance, Nugee J felt constrained by the weight of previous authority to apply the tortious rules, since *Henderson v Merrett* afforded the claimant freedom to choose how to frame its claim. However, the judge did say:[63]

> It seems odd, and to my mind distinctly unsatisfactory, that the law should give two different answers to the question 'for what losses is a solicitor liable if he fails to take due care in carrying out a client's instructions?' depending on how the claim is framed. A rational system of law would only give one answer to that question.

The Court of Appeal unanimously agreed with the trial judge's concerns, and went on to hold that the contractual rules of remoteness should in fact apply. Their Lordships insisted that although *Henderson v Merrett* meant that the claim could be run in both contract and tort, that did not determine what rules of remoteness should apply to the tortious claim. As Floyd LJ put it:[64]

> What was in issue before their lordships in *Henderson v Merrett* was not the test for remoteness of damage in cases of concurrent liability, but whether there was in fact a concurrent cause of action in tort at all. Whilst the existence of the separate cause of action in tort is thus not open to challenge in this court, it is nevertheless open to us to consider the rule or rules for remoteness in the case of concurrent liability.

[59] *Yapp v Foreign and Commonwealth Office* [2014] EWCA Civ 1512, [2015] IRLR 112, [119] (Underhill LJ).

[60] Above n 6.

[61] ibid [74].

[62] Ultimately, though, the Court of Appeal (disagreeing with the trial judge) concluded that the loss was not too remote in contract law anyway, so the point was somewhat moot.

[63] [2014] EWHC 556 (Ch), [2014] PNLR 22, [212].

[64] *Wellesley*, above n 6, [66].

Indeed, his Lordship went on to note that:[65]

> In a case such as the present (although not in all cases) the responsibility is assumed under a contract. It would be anomalous, to say the least, if the party pursuing the remedy in tort in these circumstances were able to assert that the other party has assumed a responsibility for a wider range of damage than he would be taken to have assumed under the contract.
>
> …
>
> Nevertheless, I am persuaded that where, as in the present case, contractual and tortious duties to take care in carrying out instructions exist side by side, the test for recoverability of damage for economic loss should be the same, and should be the contractual one. The basis for the formulation of the remoteness test adopted in contract is that the parties have the opportunity to draw special circumstances to each other's attention at the time of formation of the contract. Whether or not one calls it an implied term of the contract, there exists the opportunity for consensus between the parties, as to the type of damage (both in terms of its likelihood and type) for which it will be able to hold the other responsible. The parties are assumed to be contracting on the basis that liability will be confined to damage of the kind which is in their reasonable contemplation. It makes no sense at all for the existence of the concurrent duty in tort to upset this consensus, particularly given that the tortious duty arises out of the same assumption of responsibility as exists under the contract.

Roth J explicitly agreed that

> the rationale for maintaining a broader principle of remoteness of damage for liability in tort than in contract … does not apply to a case of parallel liability, where the duty of care in tort rests on an assumption of responsibility arising from the contract.[66]

Longmore LJ emphasised that, in these sort of cases

> It cannot, moreover, be right that a claimant can opt to recover a contractual measure of damages but then opt to apply the tortious rules of remoteness; measure of damage and remoteness of damage must be assessed by reference to one system or the other, not by a sort of 'pick and mix'.[67]

Rules relating to the measure of damages and remoteness of damages should be consistent with one another.[68]

The decision in *Wellesley* is welcome. There is no reason to depart from the contractual rules when the parties are not strangers but able to make one another aware of special risks at the time of entering into their relationship. After all, even if the claim sounds in tort alone, a party might still add a disclaimer and thereby avoid liability for known risks.[69] The careful reasoning in *Wellesley* is convincing and highlights that the 'incidental rules' can be developed by judges. This does not appear to be 'crying for the moon'. The tortious claim should not be considered in isolation, divorced from the 'parallel liability' in contract.[70]

[65] ibid, [68], [80]. See also Roth J, [157].
[66] ibid [151].
[67] ibid [186].
[68] ibid [187].
[69] This was the case in *Hedley Byrne* itself, above n 16.
[70] There does remain a difficult question regarding the date on which foreseeability is assessed within long-term relationships, such as where a solicitor acts for his client long after signing the retainer but

It should be noted that the decision in *Wellesley* raises a theoretical difficulty concerning the rules of remoteness more generally, and this has become particularly acute since the decision of the House of Lords in *The Achilleas*.[71] In that case, Lord Hoffmann[72] held that the contractual rules of remoteness give effect to an allocation of risk implicitly made by the parties to the contract, and are not justified by reference to an externally imposed set of rules.[73] If correct, this explanation creates a deep division between contract and tort: because no agreement is necessary to a claim in tort, the rules of remoteness in tort law must necessarily be externally imposed by the courts. However, as the Court of Appeal noted in *Wellesley*, the status of Lord Hoffmann's views regarding 'assumption of responsibility' in contract law is not yet entirely clear,[74] and it is suggested that the better view is that the default rules of remoteness are invariably imposed by the law.[75] It is unrealistic to think that the parties meaningfully provided for rules concerning the remoteness of damages in their agreement.[76] Such an approach makes it easier to understand how contract and tort can be assimilated in this area.[77]

One related issue concerned the relationship with the complicated concept of 'scope of duty', which was relied upon by Lord Hoffmann in *SAAMCO*.[78] The 'scope of duty' analysis is best considered to be distinct from causation and remoteness.[79] *SAAMCO* itself was a case of concurrent liability, and the notion of 'scope of duty' applied equally to claims in contract and tort. It is impossible to evade this notion simply by relabelling the claim.[80] It is suggested that the inclination of the judgment in *SAAMCO* seems correct, albeit very difficult to apply.[81] The basic idea was surely that the negligent valuer should not be liable for a crash in the market about which he assumed no responsibility, and the client should not be able to escape a bad

at a time when unusual losses were foreseeable: see M Balen, 'Concurrent Liability and Remoteness in Long-term Relationships' [2016] *Lloyd's Maritime and Commercial Law Quarterly* 186, 188–89. It is suggested that the relevant date should remain the date on which the contract was entered into, provided that the solicitor was in fact committed to act: see also A Tettenborn, 'Professional Liability and Remoteness: Contract v Tort' (2016) 32 *Journal of Professional Negligence* 68, 70.

[71] *Transfield Shipping Inc v Mercator Shipping Inc (The Achilleas)* [2008] UKHL 48, [2009] 1 AC 61.

[72] Supported by Lord Hope and also Lord Walker.

[73] cf *Hadley v Baxendale*, above n 56. See also L Hoffmann, 'The Achilleas: Custom and Practice or Foreseeability?' (2010) *Edinburgh Law Review* 47.

[74] eg *Wellesley*, above n 6, [71] (Floyd LJ), [156] (Roth J).

[75] A Burrows, 'Lord Hoffmann and Remoteness in Contract' in P Davies and J Pila (eds), *The Jurisprudence of Lord Hoffmann* (Oxford, Hart Publishing, 2015).

[76] A Robertson, 'The Basis of the Remoteness Rule in Contract' [2008] *Legal Studies* 172.

[77] Indeed, *Hadley v Baxendale* concerned the tort of a common carrier's duty to deliver within a reasonable time, and was not in fact limited to the contractual sphere: see J Edelman, '*Hadley v Baxendale*' (paper presented to Obligations VIII, Revolutions in Private Law, Cambridge, July 2016).

[78] *South Australia Asset Management Corpn v York Montague Ltd* [1997] AC 191.

[79] *Nykredit Mortgage Bank Plc v Edward Erdman Group Ltd* [1997] 1 WLR 1627, 1638–39 (Lord Hoffmann); *Wellesley*, above n 6, [153] (Roth J) and [213] (Nugee J at first instance). See too, recently, *BPE Solicitors v Hughes-Holland (in substitution for Gabriel)* [2017] UKSC 21, [2017] 2 WLR 1029 . See also M Stiggelbout, 'Contractual Remoteness, "Scope of Duty" and Intention' [2012] *Lloyd's Maritime and Commercial Law Quarterly* 97.

[80] cf *Sentinel International Ltd v Cordes* [2008] UKPC 60, [50] (Lord Walker).

[81] See, eg, *Aneco Reinsurance Underwriting Ltd (In Liquidation) v Johnson & Higgins Ltd* [2001] UKHL 51, [2001] 2 All ER (Comm) 929. cf *BPE Solicitors v Hughes-Holland (in substitution for Gabriel)* [2017] UKSC 21, [2017] 2 WLR 1029.

bargain by recovering from the valuer losses suffered due to the crash in the market. This should apply equally to both the contractual and tortious claims.[82]

None of this analysis doubts the correctness of the result in *Henderson v Merrett*. The claimant should be no worse off because he has entered into a contract and provided consideration than if he only has a cause of action in tort. But there are (at least) two ways to ensure that the claimant is no worse off. One is to allow the tortious claim the freedom to apply unaffected by the existence of the contract. Another is to modify the tortious rules concerning remoteness so that they align with the contractual rules, meaning that there is no advantage to framing a claim as one in either 'contract' or 'tort'.[83] The latter is favoured in decisions such as *Wellesley* and *SAAMCO*, and seems the most logical.

(ii) Type of Loss

Another 'incidental rule' that could be tweaked in order to bring contract and tort into alignment concerns the type of loss that is recoverable. It is easier to recover for mental distress in tort than in contract.[84] However, relatively recent developments in contract law mean that damages for non-pecuniary loss are now recoverable in a wider range of circumstances. In *Farley v Skinner*,[85] a surveyor wrongly and negligently advised the buyer of a house that it was not unduly affected by aircraft noise, whereas in fact the property was subject to intolerable noise from aircraft which were in a holding pattern waiting to land at Gatwick airport. The surveyor was liable in breach of contract to pay £10,000 damages for the buyer's discomfort and inconvenience. The House of Lords held that non-pecuniary loss could be recoverable if a major or important part of the contract is to give pleasure, relaxation or peace of mind. This broadens the scope of recovery. So, too, does the alternative basis of the decision, which is that the award relates to the physical inconvenience caused by the breach of contract.[86] Damages for physical inconvenience resulting from breach—such as having to walk five miles home on a wet night—have long been recoverable.[87] But the scope of 'physical inconvenience' was broadened in *Farley v Skinner* to cover sensory discomfort. Such developments are welcome and the law should continue to evolve in this area:[88] at the very least, where a parallel

[82] cf D McLauchlan, 'Negligent Valuer Liability: The Paradox Remains?' (1997) 113 *LQR* 421. See also *How Engineering Services Ltd v Southern Insulation (Medway) Ltd* [2010] EWHC 1878 (TCC), [2010] BLR 537 (Akenhead J).

[83] Indeed, it may now be that the 'contract rules' of remoteness should apply to claims brought in tort on the basis of an 'assumption of responsibility' under *Hedley Byrne*: see, eg, Tettenborn, above n 70. cf A Taylor, 'Whither Remoteness? *Wellesley Partners LLP v Withers LLP*' (2016) 79 *MLR* 678.

[84] See, eg, *Groom v Crocker*, above n 3. cf *Cook v Swinfen* [1967] 1 WLR 457.

[85] Above n 18.

[86] This decision builds on *Watts v Morrow* [1991] 1 WLR 1421, where Bingham LJ highlighted that there are two categories of case where damages for 'mental distress' may be awarded: where the object of the contract was to provide pleasure or peace of mind, and where mental suffering was directly caused by physical inconvenience caused by the breach.

[87] *Hobbs v L & S W Rly Co* (1875) LR 19 QB 111 (contract to carry family from Wimbledon to Hampton Court; the train terminated at Esher, which meant that the family had to walk home).

[88] See also A Burrows, *Remedies*, above n 57, 332–33.

liability in tort and contract exists, the approach taken to (non-remote) mental distress damages should be the same regardless of how the claim is framed.

(iii) Contributory Negligence

It is now clear that in some cases contributory negligence will be a defence to breach of contract. In *Forsikringsaktieselskapet Vesta v Butcher*,[89] Hobhouse J—whose judgment was subsequently endorsed on appeal—held that there are three relevant categories of case. Category One arises where a defendant is in breach of a strict contractual duty. Category Two is where the defendant is in breach of a contractual duty of care. Category Three concerns situations where the defendant is in breach of a contractual duty of care and would also be liable in the tort of negligence. Contributory negligence is a defence only to Category Three. This is apparently because the defendant should not be deprived of the defence of contributory negligence simply because the claimant chooses to frame his claim in contract rather than tort; this has since been supported by the Court of Appeal.[90]

Whilst this approach does mean that the contractual and tortious rules on contributory negligence are assimilated in instances of concurrent liability, it has a somewhat odd effect. It means that there is an incentive for the *defendant* to argue that he did not just breach a strict contractual duty, but was also at fault and committed a tort. This is bizarre: surely it should be for the claimant to establish that a tort has been made out, and a defendant should not be in a better position if he is at fault than if he is not at fault? There are two directions that the law could take in order to be consistent. The first would be to allow contributory negligence to operate as a defence to all claims in breach of contract. This would have the advantage of ensuring 'fairness' by taking into account a claimant's faulty conduct. Such an approach might derive some support from the fact that contributory negligence applies to some strict liability torts, so why not to strict liability in contract as well?[91] The other route the law could travel is to abolish contributory negligence from the law of contract entirely. This would help to preserve certainty as to the remedies which might be awarded,[92] but it might lead to difficulties in situations of concurrence, given the current state of tort law doctrine.[93] If there is not to be any significant difference between contract and tort in instances of parallel liability, on balance it would seem preferable for contributory negligence to operate as a defence regardless of how the claim is framed.

[89] [1988] 2 All ER 43, CA.

[90] See, eg, *UCB Bank plc v Hepherd Winstanley and Pugh* [1999] Lloyd's Rep PN 963.

[91] See, eg, Law Commission, *Contributory Negligence as a Defence in Contract* (Law Com No 114, 1990). Compare Law Commission, *Contributory Negligence as a Defence in Contract* (Law Com No 219, 1993).

[92] See, eg, *Barclays Bank Ltd v Fairclough Building Ltd* [1994] 3 WLR 1057.

[93] cf R Stevens, 'Should Contributory Fault be Analogue or Digital?' in A Dyson, J Goudkamp and F Wilmot-Smith (eds), *Defences in Tort* (Oxford, Hart Publishing, 2015) esp 261–63. Compare J O'Sullivan, 'Contributory Negligence and Strict Contractual Obligations Revisited' in A Dyson, J Goudkamp and F Wilmot-Smith (eds), *Defences in Contract* (Oxford, Hart Publishing, 2016).

(iv) Choice of Law

If *Henderson v Merrett* were followed wholeheartedly, this could have a significant impact upon the rules of private international law. In particular, it would entitle a claimant to choose to frame his or her claim in contract or tort in order to ensure that the dispute was governed by the laws of a more favourable jurisdiction. It is entirely conceivable that this was one of the 'incidental benefits' envisaged by Lord Goff in *Henderson v Merrett*.

However, such a liberal approach to concurrence has been convincingly criticised from the perspective of the conflict of laws. For example, Briggs has called such concurrence 'objectionable' since, even though 'there may be only one duty and one alleged breach of it, the claimant is currently taken to have several bites at the choice of law cherry'.[94] This undermines certainty and seems substantively unfair. Of course, *Henderson v Merrett* itself did not involve any issue of private international law, which may be considered to raise distinct concerns. Nevertheless, those concerns indicate that the free accumulation of causes of action can have negative effects. Briggs has sensibly suggested that if accumulation is permitted, the choice of law rules should be harmonised such that the choice of law rules for contract should apply, whether a breach of contract is pleaded or not, if a claim is brought for concurrent liability in tort. In effect, the contract rules trump their tortious counterparts.

(v) Limitation

It is suggested that the rules on limitation are the most difficult of the 'incidental rules' to develop. This is because of the Limitation Act 1980 and how it has been interpreted. Time begins to run for breach of contract from the date of breach, regardless of whether or not the breach was discoverable, whereas in tort law the limitation rules are more sensible and time can begin to run from a later date.[95] Courts naturally have a tendency not to want claims to be time-barred before a claimant could even have discovered the existence of a cause of action, and this has driven some judges to favour a broad principle of concurrent liability. Indeed, *Henderson v Merrett* itself is a high-profile example of this. It would have been unsatisfactory for the claims to be time-barred because there was a contract in place when the claims would not have been so barred had there not been a contract. The claimant should not be worse off as a result of providing consideration.

This highlights that the law on limitation periods is in a very unsatisfactory state. Yet it would seem that the limitation tail is nevertheless able at times to wag the substantive dog concerning the law on concurrent liability.[96] Limitation should be another 'incidental rule' that could be reformed. The major obstacle is the legislation itself, which requires statutory (rather than judicial) reform. The Law Commission

[94] A Briggs, 'Choice of Choice of Law?' [2003] *Lloyd's Maritime and Commercial Law Quarterly* 12, 15.

[95] See, eg, s 14; see also Lord Walker, 'Pure Economic Loss—The Problem of Timing' (2012) 20 *Tort Law Journal* 77.

[96] See, eg, J O'Sullivan, 'The Meaning of "Damage" in Pure Financial Loss Cases: Contract and Tort Collide' [2012] *Journal of Professional Negligence* 248, 261–64.

has recommended that a similar regime apply to both contract and tort,[97] and those proposals should be adopted. It is to be hoped that the accelerated legislative procedure available for Law Commission projects on technical areas of the law might yet be exploited in order to achieve this. If successful, this would eliminate a major reason for preferring a claim to proceed in tort rather than contract, and would place the law on a more logical and coherent footing.

D. Conclusions

In general, revolutionaries are more likely to make excessive demands than mild, moderate requests. If they ask for the moon on a stick, this is not in the expectation that they will actually obtain the moon on a stick, but is simply an opening gambit. Ultimately, they will be prepared to accept a little less and still be happy with the results. It might be thought that, in order to break free from *Groom v Crocker*, the courts swung too far in favour of allowing the claimant virtually untrammelled freedom to choose whatever rules seemed favourable to him. Some correction to such revolutionary fervour may now be required, and by altering the 'incidental rules' a compromise might be reached. Although it is logical for rules to apply according to their natural scope, and to focus on whether the elements of a particular cause of action are satisfied, regard should still be had to the voluntary and consensual nature of a contractual bargain. As a result, the tort rules might legitimately be influenced by the existence of a concurrent claim in contract.

III. CONTRACT VERSUS TRUSTS

Traditional orthodoxy draws a clear distinction between claims for breach of contract and breach of trust. As Lord Millett has explained, extrajudicially:[98]

> Lord Diplock has said that a contracting party is under a primary obligation to perform his contract and a secondary obligation to pay damages if he does not. It is tempting, but wrong, to assume that a trustee is likewise under a primary obligation to perform the trust and a secondary obligation to pay equitable compensation if he does not. The primary obligation of a trustee is to account for his stewardship. The primary remedy of the beneficiary—any beneficiary no matter how limited his interest—is to have the account taken, to surcharge and falsify the account, and to require the trustee to restore to the trust estate any deficiency which may appear when the account is taken. The liability is strict. The account must be taken down to the date on which it is rendered. That is why there is no question of 'stopping the clock'.

On Lord Millett's view, a contracting party is (generally) able to breach his or her contract and walk away from the relationship by paying damages. But a trustee will be held to a higher standard and be expected to act as a 'good man'. As a result, a

[97] Law Commission, *Limitation of Actions* (Law Com No 270, 2001).
[98] P Millett, 'Equity's Place in the Law of Commerce' (1998) 114 *LQR* 214, 255.

trustee cannot simply walk away from being a trustee, and the court will not turn first to damages as an adequate remedy. Rather, performance of the trust obligations is sought, and the trustee's primary obligations are to be enforced specifically or through a money substitute.

However, it is doubtful whether this approach still represents the law in England and Wales.[99] The courts appear to have shifted to a model under which the trustee simply has to compensate the beneficiary for loss caused by a breach of duty. This was first recognised by the House of Lords in *Target Holdings*.[100] Lord Browne-Wilkinson gave the only reasoned speech, and concluded that it would be inappropriate for a trustee who wrongly misapplies trust monies to be liable for anything beyond the loss caused by his breach of duty. This echoes his Lordship's comments in other House of Lords cases at around the same time—such as *Henderson v Merrett*[101] and *White v Jones*[102]—where he expressed the view that it does not generally matter how the duty arises since the remedies available will be the same.

The result in *Target Holdings* might be explained on a number of bases,[103] but the recent Supreme Court decision in *AIB v Redler* appears to make it clear that the focus should be on loss caused by a breach of duty.[104] In that case, solicitors (Redler) were retained to act for a bank (AIB) on the remortgage of a family home. AIB advanced £3.3 million to Redler on the basis that it would obtain a fully enforceable first charge over the property and that all existing charges would be redeemed on or before completion. The letter of instruction incorporated the following term: 'You [Redler] must hold the loan on trust for us [AIB] until completion. If completion is delayed, you must return it to us when and how we tell you.' Unfortunately, Redler negligently failed to redeem the first charge, which already existed over the property. Having failed to resolve this error without involving the bank, Redler eventually told the bank of the breach of duty, and ultimately AIB's charge was registered as a second charge. By paying away the mortgage monies without obtaining a first legal charge over the property, Redler acted in breach of trust. AIB argued that completion had not yet occurred, so Redler remained under a duty to hold the mortgage advance on trust for AIB; AIB therefore sought £3.3 million in order to reconstitute the trust fund. Redler, on the other hand, argued that its liability should be limited to the difference in value of the bank's security caused by Redler's failure to pay off the entirety of the Barclays charge, which was only around £300,000. Redler's argument succeeded at every level. A unanimous Supreme Court insisted that a causal link between Redler's breach of duty and AIB's loss needed to be established, regardless of whether the claim was brought at common law or in equity.

[99] For further consideration of the approach in other jurisdictions, see P Davies, 'Compensatory Remedies for Breach of Trust' [2016] *Canadian Journal of Comparative and Contemporary Law* 65, 79–83.
[100] Above n 8.
[101] Above n 2, 185.
[102] Above n 8.
[103] See, eg, Millett, above n 98; J Edelman, 'Money Awards for the Cost of Performance' (2010) 4 *Journal of Equity* 122; M Conaglen, 'Explaining *Target Holdings* v *Redferns*' (2010) 4 *Journal of Equity* 288.
[104] Above n 10.

The reasoning in the Supreme Court is difficult.[105] On a traditional approach, the case might have been dealt with as involving falsification upon taking an account: the disbursement of the £3.3 million would have been 'falsified', or disallowed, and the beneficiary entitled to demand that the trustee make good the trust fund by restoring that sum of money. But that approach was clearly rejected by the Supreme Court, which insisted upon a causal link between the breach of trust and the beneficiary's loss.[106] However, it would appear that the traditional approach survives in Australia. Edelman J has said that

> When payment was sought following an account in common form there was a direct analogy with an order for specific performance or payment of a liquidated debt which was due. In each case it is no answer for the defendant to allege that the plaintiff had suffered no loss.[107]

This helps to explain why the appeal was allowed in *Youyang Pty Ltd v Minter Ellison Morris Fletcher.*[108] A company paid over monies to solicitors for the purposes of an investment. Part of those monies were to be paid away by the solicitors in return for a bearer deposit certificate which would provide security for the investment. Upon receipt of that certificate, the solicitors would then pay the rest of the money to an investment company for investment in speculative market activities. In breach of trust, the solicitors paid the money away without receiving the bearer certificate. The Court of Appeal had held that the beneficiary's claim should fail since 'the acceptance of the defective deposit certificate was a breach of trust which nevertheless did not cause any loss of Youyang's funds'.[109] The High Court of Australia, on the other hand, insisted that it was 'not to the point' that the conduct of third parties would have caused the loss anyway 'because the loss of the trust funds occurred as soon as the trustee wrongly disbursed them'.[110]

It is suggested that the approach of the UK Supreme Court in *AIB v Redler* is very different from that of the High Court of Australia in *Youyang*. It is perhaps possible that the Supreme Court was simply using the language of equitable compensation to short-circuit the accounting process,[111] but that is not at all clear. It is more likely that the focus in England has decisively shifted towards the loss suffered as a result of a breach of trust, although it is not yet certain what the content of the rules on causation, remoteness, mitigation and so on really are.[112]

Nevertheless, it may well be significant that Lord Toulson cited with approval an article by Professor Hayton.[113] Hayton argued that 'where a bare trust is mere

[105] P Davies, 'Remedies for Breach of Trust' (2015) 78 *MLR* 672; P Watts, 'Agents' Disbursal of Funds in Breach of Instructions' (2016) 1 *Lloyd's Maritime and Commercial Law Quarterly* 118.

[106] See, eg, *AIB v Redler*, above n 10, [64] (Lord Toulson).

[107] L Smith, 'The Measurement of Compensation Claims against Trustees and Fiduciaries' in E Bant and M Harding (eds), *Exploring Private Law* (Cambridge, Cambridge University Press, 2013) 371–72, referring to *Agricultural Land Management Ltd* v *Jackson (No 2)* [2014] WASC 102, [337].

[108] [2003] HCA 15, 212 CLR 484.

[109] ibid [29].

[110] ibid [63].

[111] R Nolan, 'Invoking the Administrative Jurisdiction: The Enforcement of Modern Trust Structures' in P Davies and J Penner (eds), *Equity, Trust and Commerce* (Oxford, Hart Publishing, 2017) 157–59.

[112] Davies, above n 99, 94–110.

[113] *AIB v Redler*, above n 10, [71], citing D Hayton, 'Unique Rules for the Unique Institution, the Trust' in Degeling and Edelman, above n 14.

incidental machinery in the furtherance of a contractual agreement it seems that there are sufficient policy reasons to oust traditional trust law principles as to consequential losses'.[114] Such a bare trust was at issue in both *Target Holdings* and *AIB v Redler*. This meant that claims for breach of contract and breach of trust could have been pursued concurrently. It is therefore possible to conceive of *Target Holdings* and *AIB v Redler* as being instances where the 'incidental rules' regarding compensation for breach of trust were modified in order to be consistent with their contractual counterparts. This might also help to provide certain limits upon Lord Toulson's observation that 'in circumstances such as those in *Target Holdings* the extent of equitable compensation should be the same as if damages for breach of contract were sought at common law'.[115] Perhaps this is because what is really going on in cases involving bare, commercial trusts is that the parties primarily create a contractual arrangement, and are not necessarily concerned with setting up a full-blown trust. This might explain why the contractual rules dominate the principles of recovery. However, it is apparent that any line between 'traditional' and 'commercial' trusts can be very difficult to draw,[116] and it seems likely that the contractual rules will greatly influence equitable compensation for breach of trust more generally.

Lord Toulson's approach has, unsurprisingly, been applied by the lower courts. Indeed, since Lord Toulson concluded that 'in a practical sense both [falsification and surcharge] are reparative compensation',[117] recent judgments have tended to accept that a claim for breach of trust adds little to a claim for breach of a contractual or tortious duty of care. This is also consistent with the views previously expressed by Lord Browne-Wilkinson.[118] Nevertheless, it appears to represent a departure from the traditional approach, under which the duty of care owed in equity was recognised to be distinct from that at common law.[119] This was largely based upon the idea that '[t]he mixture of vulnerability and difficulty of monitoring and control is the key policy reason why the law requires parties in that status [of trusteeship] to act differently, to take a more strict responsibility for the affairs of another'.[120] Yet this now seems to have given way to the contention that 'contract trumps'.[121]

[114] D Hayton, 'Unique Rules for the Unique Institution, the Trust' in Degeling and Edelman, ibid, 305. See also *Akai Holdings Ltd*, above n 11.

[115] *AIB v Redler*, above n 10, [71]. Of course, this leaves open the question of whether the 'traditional approach' might apply to 'traditional trusts', but early indications suggest that this is unlikely, and that the shift in approach which culminated in *AIB v Redler* means that a court will invariably seek to assess compensation for loss following a breach of trust: see, eg, *Brudenell-Bruce v Moore & Cotton* [2014] EWHC 3679 (Ch), [2015] WTLR 373 (Newey J). See also *Akai Holdings Ltd*, above n 11, [155] (Lord Neuberger NPJ); *Canson*, above n 11, 585–87 (La Forest J).

[116] Davies, above n 105, 687–88.

[117] *AIB v Redler*, above n 10, [54].

[118] In cases such as *Henderson v Merrett*, *Target Holdings* and *White v Jones*.

[119] For further discussion see, eg, Getzler, above n 14, 266–72; JD Heydon, 'The Negligent Fiduciary' (1995) 111 *LQR* 1.

[120] Getzler, ibid, 272.

[121] Claims for breach of trust may still be preferred by claimants to claims in contract or tort because, in the context of misapplied funds, liability is strict and the claimant does not need to prove negligence. Rather, it is incumbent on the trustee to prove that he was not negligent in order to have a chance of escaping liability under s 61 of the Trustee Act 1925. See further P Davies, 'Section 61 of the Trustee Act 1925: *deus ex machina*?' [2015] *The Conveyancer and Property Lawyer* 379.

This can be discerned from a number of recent decisions. For example, *Brudenell-Bruce v Moore & Cotton*[122] concerned the estate of the Earl of Cardigan. Lord Cardigan is the beneficiary of a bare trust administered by professional trustees. Lord Cardigan claimed that the trustees failed to maintain the Stable Block of Tottenham House, the seat of the Cardigan family. On the facts, the judge rejected the claim that the trustees had acted in breach of trust, but nevertheless went on to consider what the appropriate remedy would have been had there been a breach of trust. The beneficiary argued that the full cost of repair should be awarded, since even if

> it is going to cost £5 million to restore the Stable Block but fully restored it is only going to be worth £4 million, that is just the price that the trustees pay for allowing this collapse to have occurred in the first place.[123]

Newey J rejected that argument. The judge could

> see no reason why the Courts should be more willing to award compensation based on cost of reinstatement in circumstances such as those in the present case than they would be to measure damages in that way for breach of contract or a tort.[124]

Relying upon common law decisions such as *Ruxley Electronics and Construction Ltd v Forsyth*[125] and *In Southampton Container Terminals Ltd v Schiffahrtsgesellschaft 'Hansa Australia' GmbH (The 'Maersk Colombo')*,[126] Newey J concluded that the full cost of cure measure should not be awarded since that would be unreasonable.

Other examples can be given. For instance, in *Agouman v Leigh Day*,[127] a case of professional negligence brought against a firm of solicitors, Andrew Smith J recognised the importance of *Wellesley* regarding concurrent claims in contract and tort, and then went on to say that 'the claim in trust adds nothing'.[128] In *Daniel v Tee*, Richard Spearman QC, sitting as a Deputy High Court Judge, said that 'where claims for negligence, breach of contract and breach of trust arise out of the same facts, the level of compensation recoverable under each head of claim may be held to be the same'.[129] A similar view was taken by Foskett J in another case of professional negligence, *Various Claimants v Giambrone and Law*. The judge was initially reluctant even to deal with the claim for breach of trust, since he thought it added nothing to the claim.[130] However, he was persuaded to add a supplemental judgment to deal with the matter,[131] although he maintained that the claim for breach of trust added nothing, given the existence of liability in contract and tort. Interestingly, Foskett J thought that the claim for compensation for breach of trust would only be worth pursuing if it were 'the sole basis of a claim against the firm',[132] and thus not

[122] Above n 115.
[123] ibid [147].
[124] ibid [152].
[125] [1995] UKHL 8, [1996] AC 344.
[126] [2001] EWCA Civ 717, [2001] 2 Lloyd's Rep 275.
[127] [2016] EWHC 1324.
[128] ibid [134].
[129] [2016] EWHC 1538, [2016] 4 WLR 115, [55].
[130] [2015] EWHC 3315, [11].
[131] [2015] EWHC 1946, Appendix 3.
[132] ibid [1].

arising in the context of concurrent liability. Yet on returning to this issue, the judge also said that

> it was not necessary to demonstrate that an individual Claimant would not have proceeded with a purchase where breach of trust was relied upon, whereas that would be necessary if breach of contract or breach of a tortious duty was the cause of action relied upon.[133]

This is perhaps surprising, and represents something of a break from the trend of applying the contractual rules regardless of how the claim is framed. It does not sit easily with the decision of the Supreme Court in *AIB v Redler*, and at the time of writing the decision of Foskett J is under appeal.[134]

IV. CONCLUSIONS

Concurrent liability raises difficult questions, and the approach of English courts has evolved over time. The leading decision remains *Henderson v Merrett*, which affords parties the freedom to choose how to frame their claim. But it appears that the courts are retreating from the proposition that parties should be able to take all the benefits that might flow from suing in tort rather than contract, for example.[135] Although recognising that claims for breach of contract, tort and breach of trust may be brought concurrently, courts have been able to modify the 'incidental rules' such that parties derive little advantage from doing so. Moreover, it appears that the contractual rules now take priority. This might reflect McMeel's observation that '[w]hat really matters is that in the hierarchy of normative force English law accords primacy to contract because it records the intentions of the parties themselves, which is the whole purpose of the facilitative enterprise of private law'.[136] The real sticking point in developing the 'incidental rules' in a manner which would ensure consistency in instances of concurrent liability concerns the rules on limitation. This is because judges cannot develop the common law in this area, but have to apply the difficult provisions of the Limitation Act 1980. It is to be hoped that the law on limitation will soon be reformed along the lines proposed by the Law Commission.[137]

[133] [2015] EWHC 3315, [17].

[134] The decision of the Court of Appeal was handed down just before this book went to press: [2017] EWCA Civ 1193. The appeal was dismissed. Jackson LJ considered equitable compensation fully in the wake of *AIB*, and commented (at [63]) that '[t]his is a case where equitable compensation and contractual damages run in tandem'.

[135] P Cane, 'Contract, Tort and the Lloyd's Debâcle' in F Rose (ed), *Consensus ad Idem: Essays on the Law of Contract in Honour of Guenter Treitel* (Oxford, Sweet & Maxwell, 1996) 119.

[136] G McMeel, 'Unjust Enrichment, Discharge for Breach, and the Primacy of Contract' in A Burrows and A Rodger (eds), *Mapping the Law: Essays in Memory of Peter Birks* (Oxford, Oxford University Press, 2006) 230–31.

[137] See *Henderson v Merrett*, above n 2, 205 (Lord Browne-Wilkinson).

14

The Illegality Revolution

GRAHAM VIRGO

I. INTRODUCTION

THE IMPACT OF illegality on the law of obligations has proved to be controversial throughout the common law world, but especially in England. The illegality defence there has had a bad reputation, being described as 'notoriously knotty territory',[1] and extra-judicially by Lord Sumption as 'an area in which there are few propositions, however contradictory or counter-intuitive, that cannot be supported by respectable authorities at the highest levels'.[2] The operation of illegality as a defence to claims in contract, tort and unjust enrichment has been the subject of a significant number of cases in the English courts over a relatively short period. Recent decisions of the Supreme Court illustrate a fundamental disagreement amongst the judiciary about the nature of the defence and, even more significantly, about the nature of judging. In one camp are those judges who treat the defence as a rule founded on public policy which applies automatically if certain conditions are met. In the other camp are those judges who treat the defence as founded on justice to secure a fair result following careful consideration of the factual context of the case.

This disagreement about the nature of the defence has now been resolved by *Patel v Mirza*,[3] where a nine-Justice panel of the Supreme Court decided by six to three in favour of adopting a structured discretionary approach. This is an apparently simple case, where the respondent sought restitution of money paid to the appellant pursuant to an illegal contract to invest it following the receipt of inside information which was not forthcoming. However, whilst all the Justices agreed that restitution should be awarded despite the taint of illegality, the judgments display very different responses to illegality. This is without doubt a significant decision, but whether it is revolutionary or evolutionary requires careful analysis of the disparate doctrines which constitute the defence and its exceptions, and an assessment of whether the approach of the majority unacceptably departs from these doctrines. The decision has potentially wider significance, since it reveals a great deal about the nature of

[1] *Parkingeye Ltd v Somerfield Stores Ltd* [2012] EWCA Civ 1338, [2013] QB 840, [28] (Sir Robin Jacob).

[2] J Sumption, 'Reflections on the Law of Illegality' [2012] *Restitution Law Review* 1.

[3] *Patel v Mirza* [2016] UKSC 42, [2017] AC 467.

judging in the twenty-first century. It is this which might prove to be the most revolutionary aspect of the case, with its preference for discretion over rule, which may have significant implications for the development of other parts of the law of obligations.

II. THE CENTRAL CONTROVERSY: RULE VERSUS DISCRETION

Confusion about the operation of the illegality defence runs throughout the law of obligations.[4] The defence is traditionally formulated as a rule, which applies automatically if certain conditions are met. It applies in the form of the maxim *ex turpi causa non oritur actio* ('No action can arise from a base cause'),[5] meaning that the courts will not assist a claimant to obtain a remedy where the action is founded on illegal conduct. It is influenced by external considerations of public policy rather than securing justice between the parties.[6] As Lord Goff said in *Tinsley v Milligan*:

> [I]t is a principle of policy, whose application is indiscriminate and so can lead to unfair consequences as between the parties to litigation. Moreover the principle allows no room for the exercise of any discretion by the court in favour of one party or the other.[7]

In *Les Laboratoires Servier v Apotex Inc*, Lord Sumption emphasised that the defence was not based 'on the perceived balance of merits between the parties to any particular dispute',[8] thus placing it squarely within the external relationship between the court and the claimant,[9] rather than the internal relationship between the claimant and the defendant. It follows that the illegality defence has been considered to operate as a rule of public policy to defeat a claim and not a matter for judicial decision as to what is considered to be fair and just.

However, this treatment of the illegality defence has not been recognised consistently by the Supreme Court. In *Les Laboratoires Servier v Apotex Inc*,[10] although the Supreme Court held that a claim for damages should succeed on the ground that the illegality defence was not engaged through the infringement of a patent under Canadian law, the Justices' judgments reflected a fundamental division of approach.[11] The Court of Appeal had approached the defence on the basis that 'it required in each case … an intense analysis of the particular facts and of the proper application of the various policy considerations underlying the illegality principle so

[4] For tort see G Virgo, 'Illegality's Role in the Law of Tort' in M Dyson (ed), *Unravelling Tort and Crime* (Cambridge, Cambridge University Press, 2014) ch 7. For unjust enrichment see G Virgo, 'The Defence of Illegality in Unjust Enrichment' in A Dyson, J Goudkamp and F Wilmot-Smith (eds), *Defences in Unjust Enrichment* (Oxford, Hart Publishing, 2016) ch 8.

[5] *Holman v Johnson* (1775) 1 Cowp 341, 343 (Lord Mansfield). See also *Muckleston v Brown* (1801) 6 Ves Jun 52, 69 (Lord Eldon LC).

[6] *Hounga v Allen* [2014] UKSC 47, [2014] ICR 847, [42] (Lord Wilson), [55] (Lord Hughes); *Les Laboratoires Servier v Apotex Inc* [2014] UKSC 55, [2015] AC 430, [13] (Lord Sumption).

[7] *Tinsley v Milligan* [1994] 1 AC 340, 355.

[8] *Les Laboratoires Servier v Apotex*, above n 6, [13].

[9] See *Hounga v Allen*, above n 6, [56] (Lord Hughes).

[10] Above n 6.

[11] Described by Lord Sumption as a 'long-standing schism': *Patel v Mirza*, above n 3, [226].

as to produce a just and proportionate response to the illegality'.[12] This approach was specifically rejected by Lord Sumption, with whom Lords Neuberger and Clarke agreed. Lord Sumption emphasised that the defence was grounded on general rules of law and was not a mere discretionary power, involving fact-based evaluations of the effect of the rules in individual cases.[13] He considered the only key issues to be whether the relevant conduct involved sufficient turpitude and whether this was sufficiently related to the claim.[14]

This strict approach to illegality can be contrasted with that of Lord Toulson in the same case, who refused to criticise the approach of the Court of Appeal and who considered that, when determining whether the illegality defence should apply, 'it is right to proceed carefully on a case by case basis, considering the policies which underlie the broad principle'.[15] This is also the approach that was adopted by a differently constituted Supreme Court in the earlier decision of *Hounga v Allen*.[16] That court held that a claim in tort for race discrimination,[17] following wrongful dismissal from employment, succeeded even though the claimant was an illegal migrant who knew that it was illegal to work in the UK. This had been sufficient for the Court of Appeal to dismiss her claim, but the Supreme Court considered that the illegality defence was not engaged, explicitly for policy reasons. Crucially, Lord Wilson said, in the judgment of the majority, that it was necessary, first, to ask 'What is the aspect of public policy which founds the defence?' and, secondly, whether there was 'another aspect of public policy to which application of the defence would run counter?'[18] Lord Hughes, with whose judgment Lord Carnwath agreed, emphasised that in assessing what public policy requires, it is necessary to have regard to various factors, including the gravity of the illegality and the claimant's knowledge of it.[19]

In *Bilta (UK) Ltd v Nazir (No 2)*,[20] which concerned whether the wrongful activity of the respondents' directors was to be attributed to the respondent so as to give rise to an illegality defence, the disagreement between the Justices was reinforced, with Lord Sumption again emphasising the rule-based interpretation and Lords Toulson and Hodge the policy-based, context-dependent interpretation of the defence. Lord Neuberger,[21] with whom Lords Clarke, Carnwath and Mance agreed, identified the disagreement, but refused to resolve it, preferring the matter to be considered as

[12] *Les Laboratoires Servier v Apotex Inc* [2012] EWCA Civ 593, [2013] Bus LR 80, [75] (Etherton LJ).

[13] *Les Laboratoires Servier v Apotex*, above n 6, [13] and [22]. See also the judgment of Lord Mance.

[14] ibid [22].

[15] ibid [57]. See also *Gray v Thames Trains Ltd* [2009] UKHL 33, [2009] 1 AC 1339, [30] (Lord Hoffmann); *Stone and Rolls Ltd v Moore Stephens* [2009] UKHL 39, [2009] 1 AC 1391, [25] (Lord Phillips).

[16] *Hounga v Allen*, above n 6. The decision of the majority in *Hounga* was considered to provide 'the best guidance on the relevant analytical framework' by Sales LJ in *Best v The Chief Land Registrar* [2015] EWCA Civ 17, [2016] QB 23, [51]. See also *McCracken v Smith* [2015] EWCA Civ 380, [43] (Richards LJ).

[17] Contrary to the Race Relations Act 1976 (UK), s 4(2)(c). See now the Equality Act 2010 (UK), s 39(2)(c).

[18] *Hounga v Allen*, above n 6, [42], with whom Baroness Hale and Lord Kerr agreed.

[19] ibid [55].

[20] *Bilta (UK) Ltd v Nazir (No 2)* [2015] UKSC 23, [2016] AC 1.

[21] ibid [14].

soon as appropriately possible and preferably by a panel of nine Justices. That is what happened in *Patel v Mirza*. Lord Neuberger in *Bilta* summarised the spectrum of views as 'epitomising the familiar tension between the need for principle, clarity and certainty in the law with the equally important desire to achieve a fair and appropriate result in each case',[22] or, in other words, the operation of a rule versus judicial discretion.

This tension appears to arise from the perceived injustice caused by the absolute application of the illegality rule and that, in certain cases, such as where the illegality is minor or the defendant is more responsible than the claimant for participation in the illegal transaction, a claim tainted[23] by illegality should nonetheless be recognised by the courts. For instance, where the effect of rendering the claim unenforceable is wholly out of proportion to the illegal behaviour, 'most people's moral instincts'[24] would be that the defence should not apply. It is for this reason that the judiciary has sought to temper the strict rule to secure justice. For a few years in the 1980s, this was achieved through the reformulation of the illegality defence by reference to the public conscience test, whereby the defence would only succeed if the public conscience would be affronted if relief was granted. This test originated in *Thackwell v Barclays Bank plc*,[25] where an action for conversion failed by virtue of the illegality defence, but only after the court had considered all the circumstances of the case, including the nature of the illegality, to determine whether by granting a remedy to the claimant it would be seen to be indirectly assisting or encouraging his criminal act. A remedy was eventually denied because the claimant had been a knowing party to a fraudulent transaction. The public conscience test was, however, rejected by the House of Lords in *Tinsley v Milligan*,[26] on the grounds that it was inconsistent with previous authority and that it would replace a principled system of rules with a discretionary balancing operation.[27]

The rejection of the public conscience test was surely correct. The application of the test resulted in inconsistent decisions,[28] often turning on judicial outrage arising from the facts of the case.[29] Justice, as opposed to substantive fairness, is dependent on a high degree of predictability, which is lacking under the public conscience test. However, despite the rejection of that test, the preference for the adoption of a discretionary approach amongst some of the Justices in the Supreme Court indicates a clear judicial desire to temper the rigidity of the *ex turpi causa* rule to avoid unjust results. The *ex turpi causa* rule was, however, never absolute; it has always been qualified by various doctrines to limit its operation.

[22] ibid [13].

[23] AFH Loke, 'Tainting Illegality' (2014) *Legal Studies* 560.

[24] Sumption, above n 2, 2.

[25] [1986] 1 All ER 676. See also *Saunders v Edwards* [1987] 1 WLR 1116; *Howard v Shirlstar Container Transport Ltd* [1990] 1 WLR 1292; *Euro-Diam Ltd v Bathurst* [1990] 1 QB 1.

[26] [1994] AC 340. See also *Vellino v Chief Constable of Manchester* [2001] EWCA Civ 1249, [2002] 1 WLR 218, [60] (Sedley LJ); *Stone and Rolls Ltd v Moore Stephens (a firm)* [2009] UKHL 39, [2009] 1 AC 1370, [97] (Lord Scott).

[27] *Tinsley v Milligan*, ibid, 358–61 (Lord Goff), 363–64 and 369 (Lord Browne-Wilkinson).

[28] ibid 363 (Lord Goff).

[29] *Hewison v Meridian Shipping Services Pte Ltd* [2002] EWCA Civ 1821, [2003] ICR 766, 788–89 (Ward LJ).

A. No Reliance on Illegality

The illegality defence has typically been formulated in terms of the claimant being prevented from relying on the illegality to establish the claim;[30] it follows that a claim might succeed where its elements can be established without needing to rely on the illegality.[31] For example, in *Tinsley v Milligan*,[32] a majority of the House of Lords recognised that Milligan could vindicate her equitable proprietary right under a resulting trust even though she had participated in an illegal transaction, since, having contributed to the purchase of a property which had been put into Tinsley's sole name, the presumption of resulting trust was engaged without needing to plead the illegality. If, however, the claimant needed to refer to illegality to make good the claim, it would be defeated by the illegality defence.[33] Consequently, where money has been paid to the defendant pursuant to a contract which is void for illegality, the claimant will not be able to recover it if he or she has to rely on the illegality to establish the claim. Since the claimant needs to establish that the contract is no longer operative before a claim in unjust enrichment can be brought,[34] typically it will be necessary to plead the illegality to show that the contract is void,[35] save if another reason for invalidity of the contract can be established or another mechanism for avoiding the taint of illegality can be identified.

Whether a claim can be established without the claimant needing to rely on the illegality turns on chance. The Law Commission[36] concluded that such a principle 'produces complex and arbitrary results'.[37] For example, the result in *Tinsley v Milligan* would have been different had the presumption of advancement applied, for then Milligan would have needed to plead the illegal agreement to rebut the presumption. Further, the illegality defence applies even if illegality has not been pleaded, since it may be raised by the judge, suggesting that the no reliance principle is even more arbitrary. The validity of the no reliance principle has consequently been doubted. In *Stone and Rolls Ltd v Moore Stephens*,[38] Lord Phillips said:

> I do not believe ... that it is right to proceed on the basis that the reliance test can automatically be applied as a rule of thumb. It is necessary to give consideration to the policy underlying *ex turpi causa* in order to decide whether this defence is bound to defeat [the claimant's] claim.

The reliance principle should be rejected by virtue of its arbitrariness and formalism, since it does not take into account the seriousness of the illegality or the responsibility of the parties for the illegal conduct.

[30] See Lord Mansfield in *Holman v Johnson*, above n 5, 343; *Stone and Rolls Ltd v Moore Stephens (a firm)*, above n 15, [86] (Lord Phillips).

[31] See *Bowmakers Ltd v Barnet Instruments Ltd* [1945] KB 65.

[32] Above n 7, 376 (Lord Browne-Wilkinson).

[33] *Patel v Mirza* [2014] EWCA Civ 1047, [2015] Ch 271, [20] (Rimer LJ); [102] (Vos LJ).

[34] *Guinness plc v Saunders* [1990] 2 AC 663, 697–98 (Lord Goff); *Sandher v Pearson* [2013] EWCA Civ 1822.

[35] *Berg v Sadler and Moore* [1937] 2 KB 158, 163 (Lord Wright MR); *Patel v Mirza*, above n 33, [21] (Rimer LJ).

[36] Law Commission, *The Illegality Defence* (Law Com No 320, 2010).

[37] ibid 2.

[38] *Stone and Rolls Ltd v Moore Stephens*, above n 15, [25].

B. Withdrawal from an Illegal Transaction

Where the claimant has effectively withdrawn from an illegal transaction before any part of it has been performed, he or she will no longer be tainted by the illegality and a remedy can be awarded. This withdrawal principle, sometimes known as the *locus poenitentiae*, has long been recognised as a reason why a claim should succeed despite the taint of illegality.[39] Whilst the principle originally required proof of repentance by the claimant,[40] over time this requirement has been dropped,[41] it being sufficient that the claimant sought a remedy before any part of the illegal transaction had been carried into effect or the claimant had attempted to carry it into effect,[42] even though the only reason for withdrawal is that it is impossible to carry out the agreement as originally envisaged for reasons outside the control of the claimant, such as because the transaction had been frustrated;[43] withdrawal does not require any voluntary change of mind on the part of the claimant.

The operation of this radically reinterpreted withdrawal principle is illustrated by *Tribe v Tribe*.[44] The claimant feared that he would be forced to sell his shares in the family business to meet potential liabilities to creditors. Consequently, he transferred the shares to his son. The son never paid for the shares and was never intended to do so. This transfer of shares was an illegal transaction because the claimant's purpose was to defraud his creditors. No creditors were deceived, however, because alternative arrangements were made which prevented the liabilities from arising. Once the risk that the assets would be taken had passed, the claimant requested his son to return the shares to him, but he refused to do so. Since the equitable presumption of advancement applies in respect of transfers of property from a father to his son, it was presumed that the claimant had given the shares to his son. To rebut this presumption, the claimant needed to show that his purpose was not to transfer the shares absolutely, but that the son would hold the shares until the threat from his creditors had passed. This, however, was an illegal purpose which could not rebut the presumption of advancement. Despite this, the Court of Appeal held that the father had withdrawn from the illegal transaction. Consequently, he ceased to be tainted by the illegality and so was able to plead his true intention in transferring the shares to his son to show that he had never intended to give the shares to him absolutely. The withdrawal principle was considered applicable because, first, no part of the illegal purpose had been carried into effect. This was established because, on the assumption that the claimant's purpose was to deceive creditors, there had been no such deception. If, of course, the purpose was instead characterised as creating the appearance that he did not own any shares, this purpose had been achieved. If the

[39] See *Taylor v Bowers* (1876) 1 QBD 291; *Tribe v Tribe* [1996] Ch 107. See R Merkin, 'Restitution by Withdrawal from Illegal Contracts' (1981) 97 *LQR* 420.

[40] *Bigos v Bousted* [1951] 1 All ER 92.

[41] *Tribe v Tribe*, above n 39, 135 (Millett LJ).

[42] As occurred in *Alexander v Rayson* [1936] 1 KB 169; *Berg v Sadler and Moore*, above n 35; *Harry Parker Ltd v Mason* [1940] 2 KB 590; *Collier v Collier* [2002] EWCA Civ 1095.

[43] As recognized by the Court of Appeal in *Patel v Mirza*, above n 33.

[44] [1996] Ch 107.

illegal purpose had been carried into effect, even if only partly, the claim would have failed.[45] Secondly, the claimant had withdrawn from the illegal transaction by seeking restitution, even though he had only done so once it had become clear that the purpose of the illegal transaction would never be fulfilled and there was no evidence of contrition.

C. The Parties are not *In Pari Delicto*

In *Holman v Johnson*,[46] Lord Mansfield recognised the *in pari delicto est conditio defendentis* principle ('in the case of mutual fault, the position of the defendant is the stronger one'), which enables the court to determine whether the claimant is less responsible for the illegality than the defendant, for then, as between the two of them, the just result is that the claimant should not be denied relief, since the parties are not *in pari delicto*. In contrast, where the claimant is more responsible for the illegality or the parties are considered to be equally responsible, the *in pari delicto* principle applies and the claim will fail. The operation of this principle is illustrated by *Mohamed v Alaga and Co*,[47] where the claimant sued the defendant firm of solicitors for work done in preparing and presenting asylum claims. A contract between the claimant and the defendant concerning payment to the claimant for the introduction of clients to the defendant was illegal, as it was an unlawful fee-sharing agreement, but the claimant's restitutionary claim succeeded as regards the professional work he had legitimately done, because he was less responsible for the illegality than the defendant firm of solicitors, which was assumed to know the rules of the profession.[48]

That the illegality defence was always intended to be applied flexibly by virtue of the comparative responsibility of the parties for the illegality is reflected by *Holman v Johnson* itself,[49] which concerned an action to recover the price of tea supplied by the claimant to the defendant pursuant to a contract made in Dunkirk, which the defendant intended to smuggle into England. The claimant was aware of the defendant's intention, but was not part of the smuggling scheme. The defendant having failed to pay for the tea, the claimant sued for the price. The claim succeeded because knowledge of the smuggling was held not to be sufficient to bar the claim and because the claimant had not committed any crime. It would have been different if the price would only have become due once the tea had landed in England, but the claimant's interest was considered to be at an end once the tea had been delivered in Dunkirk. In later cases, the seller's claim failed where he both knew of the defendant's illegal purpose and assisted the defendant in fulfilling it. So, for example, in *Clugas v Penaluna*,[50] the claimant assisted in smuggling by packing the brandy and

[45] *Collier v Collier*, above n 42.
[46] Above n 5, 343.
[47] *Mohamed v Alaga and Co* [2000] 1 WLR 1815.
[48] cf *Awwad v Geraght and Co* [2001] QB 570, where the claimant was a partner in the firm of solicitors.
[49] See also *Vita Food Products Inc v Unus Shipping Co Ltd* [1939] AC 277, 293 (Lord Wright).
[50] *Clugas v Penaluna* (1791) 4 Term Rep 466.

gin which was to be smuggled into England from Guernsey. Buller J distinguished *Holman v Johnson* on the ground that 'if he takes part [in the transaction] it taints the whole of it'.[51]

D. The Policy Behind the Illegality

In Australia, the operation of the illegality defence is determined by reference to the policy of the law by virtue of which the relevant transaction was found to have been illegal.[52] The significance of this is illustrated by *Equuscorp Pty Ltd v Haxton*.[53] Money had been advanced under loan agreements which were made in furtherance of an illegal purpose to obtain tax deductions through an investment scheme. The claimant sought restitution of the money that had been transferred to the defendant, but it was held that the illegality which rendered the loan agreements unenforceable also denied the restitutionary claim, by reference to the scope and purpose of the statute which rendered the transaction illegal, particularly the purpose of protecting the class of persons from whom the claimant sought restitution. This has also been recognised in England. In *Best v The Chief Land Registrar*,[54] it was recognised that it was possible to acquire property rights by adverse possession as a squatter, even though squatting in residential property was a crime,[55] because it was considered that Parliament had not intended the criminalisation of squatting to have collateral adverse effects on adverse possession.

E. Close Connection or Inextricable Link

A further mechanism to limit the operation of the illegality defence is whether there is a sufficiently close connection or inextricable link between the claim and the illegality such that the court cannot permit the claim to succeed without appearing to condone the illegal conduct.[56] This was recognised by the Supreme Court in *Les Laboratoires Servier v Apotex*,[57] in holding that the turpitude must be sufficiently related to the claim. The validity of this close connection test is, however, controversial, since it will often be unclear when it is satisfied. Indeed, this might even be considered to be a generic test for disapplying the illegality defence, which will be met if any of the other mechanisms are established. So, for example, where the illegal purpose has totally failed or where the claimant is less responsible than the

[51] ibid 468. See also *Bernard v Reese* (1794) 1 Espinasse 91; *Waymell v Reed* (1794) 5 Term Rep 599, 600 (Lord Kenyon CJ).

[52] *Nelson v Nelson* (1995) 184 CLR 538.

[53] *Equuscorp Pty Ltd v Haxton* [2012] HCA 7, (2012) 246 CLR 498. See also *Miller v Miller* [2011] HCA 9, (2011) 242 CLR 446.

[54] Above n 16.

[55] Contrary to the Legal Aid, Sentencing and Punishment of Offenders Act 2012 (UK), s 144.

[56] *Cross v Kirby* [2000] EWCA Civ 426, [76] (Beldam LJ).

[57] Above n 6, [22] (Lord Sumption). See also *Best v The Chief Land Registrar*, above n 16, [61] (Sales LJ).

defendant for the illegal transaction, it could be concluded that the illegality is not sufficiently connected to the claim.

III. *PATEL v MIRZA*

It is against this background of illegality operating as a rule defeating the claim, but subject to a variety of moderating mechanisms, that the Supreme Court in *Patel v Mirza* had to determine how the illegality defence should be interpreted and applied.

Patel, the respondent, had transferred £620,000 to Mirza, the appellant, who was a City trader and who had suggested the scheme, so that Mirza could use the money to bet on share price movements in Royal Bank of Scotland shares based on inside information. Such insider dealing is a crime under Part V of the Criminal Justice Act 1993. The inside information was not forthcoming and so the agreement was not carried out. The respondent sought restitution of the money paid on the ground that the appellant had been unjustly enriched at his expense, the ground of restitution being that the basis for the transfer had failed totally since no investment had been made. Because the parties had committed a conspiracy to commit insider dealing,[58] and so were tainted by illegality, the appellant refused to make restitution.

The key issue in *Patel v Mirza* was simple and turned on the restitutionary nature of the claim in unjust enrichment: should a defendant who has been unjustly enriched at the expense of the claimant be able to retain the value of that unjust enrichment because the claimant has been tainted by illegality, even though the defendant has been tainted by the same illegality?

The trial judge had dismissed the restitutionary claim on the basis that the illegality barred the court from granting any remedy. This was rejected by the Court of Appeal. The majority did so on the ground that the respondent had sufficiently withdrawn from the illegal transaction, even though he had not repented of the illegality or had acted voluntarily, but simply because the scheme had been frustrated once the information had not been provided. Gloster LJ agreed that the illegality defence was not engaged, but she considered that this was because the illegality was collateral and not an essential ingredient of the restitutionary claim since it was not necessary for the respondent to rely on the illegality to establish the claim; he only needed to show that the money had been paid for a purpose which had failed and this did not require any reference to the terms of the contract, including the agreement to exploit inside information.[59] The majority disagreed with this latter point, concluding that the respondent had relied on the agreement and its frustration in his pleadings, but also that he needed to rely on the illegality to establish that the agreement was no longer operating. Consequently, he could not keep 'the illegal cat secure in the bag'.[60] This did not, however, defeat the claim, because his withdrawal, arising from the frustration of the agreement, removed the taint of illegality.

[58] Contrary to the Criminal Law Act 1977 (UK), s 1.
[59] *Patel v Mirza*, above n 33, [78]–[93].
[60] ibid [22] (Rimer LJ).

In the Supreme Court, the nine Justices unanimously held that the respondent should recover the money he had paid to the appellant. The logic of restitution prevailed, despite the taint of illegality arising from the conspiracy to commit insider dealing, such that all the Justices recognised that it was appropriate to restore the status quo by requiring restitution rather than to allow the appellant to profit from his participation in the illegal transaction. As Lord Sumption recognised,[61] 'an order for restitution would not give effect to the illegal act or to any right derived from it'.

It follows that there is very little role for the defence of illegality in the law of restitution, since the courts will usually be willing to unwind the transaction because the claimant will not profit from it. Illegality will, however, be much more significant within the law of contract, since the courts will typically not enforce an illegal transaction. The role of illegality in the law of tort is more controversial, but it is likely that it, too, will not have a significant impact where the claimant is compensated for harm suffered because, again, this does not involve profiting from the illegality but involves restoration of the status quo to the extent that money can do this.

Whilst there was agreement amongst the Justices as to the result, there was disagreement as to whether the defence should be certain and principled or flexible and context-dependent. On this issue, the Justices split six to three, with the majority preferring a 'range of factors' approach to that of a strict rule, and so appear to have opted for a discretionary approach to respond to illegality. This was reflected in the leading judgment of Lord Toulson, with whom Lady Hale and Lords Kerr, Wilson and Hodge agreed, and Lord Neuberger, who, whilst adopting a distinct approach, ultimately recognised that advocated by Lord Toulson. The ratio of the case is as follows:[62]

> one cannot judge whether allowing a claim which is in some way tainted by illegality would be contrary to the public interest, because it would be harmful to the integrity of the legal system, without a) considering the underlying purpose of the prohibition which has been transgressed, b) considering conversely any other relevant public policies which may be rendered ineffective or less effective by denial of the claim, and c) keeping in mind the possibility of overkill unless the law is applied with a due sense of proportionality. We are, after all, in the area of public policy. That trio of necessary considerations can be found in the case law.

Clarification, or possibly obfuscation, of the operation of this trio of considerations was provided by Lords Toulson and Kerr. In the light of their comments, it appears that the trio of considerations will operate in the following way.

(1) It is necessary to consider the reasons why the conduct was made illegal, although no guidance was given as to how this should be achieved and why it is relevant to the operation of the defence. Further, Lord Kerr interpreted this test to mean 'the reasons that a claimant's conduct should operate to bar him or her from a remedy which would otherwise be available',[63] which is significantly different from examining the purpose behind the illegality.

[61] *Patel v Mirza*, above n 3, [268].
[62] ibid [101] (Lord Toulson). See also [120].
[63] ibid [124].

(2) It is then necessary to consider the policies which would be affected by denying the claim, but again it is unclear what these policies might be and how they might be identified.

(3) Various factors were identified to assess the question of proportionality of denying relief, although Lord Toulson emphasised that this was not a closed list because of the infinite possible variety of cases involving illegality. The identified factors included the seriousness of the conduct, its centrality to any contract and whether there was a marked disparity in the parties' respective culpability. The significance of these factors was considered to be reflected in the decision in *Parkingeye Ltd v Somerfield Stores Ltd*,[64] where a remedy for breach of contract was awarded despite the taint of illegality. This result was commended in *Patel v Mirza* on the grounds that denying a remedy for breach of contract would have been disproportionate since the claimant had not set out to break the contract; the illegality was collateral to the contract; and denying the claim would have given the defendant a very substantial unjust reward. Despite this suggestion as to how proportionality will be assessed, it nevertheless requires a quantitative assessment against some objective guide, and no such guide was identified.

The operation of the 'trio of considerations' was acknowledged to involve the exercise of judicial discretion. Lord Kerr considered it to be a 'structured approach to a hitherto intractable problem [that would] promote rather than detract from consistency in the law'.[65] For Lords Sumption, Clarke and Mance, however, this approach was rejected for reasons of uncertainty, with Lord Mance describing it as 'highly unspecific' and 'non-legal',[66] and Lord Clarke suggesting that it came close to reviving the public conscience test.[67] Lord Sumption considered the majority's test to be:[68]

> far too vague and potentially far too wide to serve as the basis on which a person may be denied his legal rights. It converts a legal principle into an exercise of judicial discretion, in the process exhibiting all the vices of 'complexity, uncertainty, arbitrariness and lack of transparency' which Lord Toulson attributes to the present law.

Lord Toulson defended the 'trio of considerations' approach with three arguments. First, he considered the law already to be doctrinally riven with uncertainties. Secondly, he emphasised that uncertainty did not appear to be a problem in other jurisdictions which have adopted a relatively flexible approach to the illegality defence. Thirdly, he considered that the absence of certainty was not a relevant consideration when dealing with people who were contemplating unlawful activity. A similar view was expressed by Lord Kerr, who said: 'Certainty or predictability of outcome may be a laudable aim for those who seek the law's resolution of genuine, honest disputes. It is not a premium to which those engaged in disreputable conduct can claim automatic entitlement.'[69]

[64] *Parkingeye v Somerfield Stores*, above n 1.
[65] *Patel v Mirza*, above n 3, [123].
[66] ibid [206].
[67] ibid [219].
[68] ibid [265].
[69] ibid [137].

Lord Toulson did not consider that the framework he was proposing would mean that:[70]

> the court is free to decide a case in an undisciplined way. The public interest is best served by a principled and transparent assessment of the considerations identified, rather than by the application of a formal approach capable of producing results which may appear arbitrary, unjust or disproportionate.

The effect of applying the 'trio of considerations' to the facts of the case was that the respondent's participation in the illegality did not bar the claim for restitution. This would appear to be the typical result once the elements of an unjust enrichment claim have been satisfied,[71] although Lord Toulson acknowledged that there might be rare cases where the circumstances of the illegality were such that the court should refuse its assistance to the claimant.[72]

Lord Neuberger adopted a more nuanced approach. He identified a 'Rule' within the law of unjust enrichment by virtue of which the claimant is entitled to the return of money paid despite the taint of illegality, even where the contemplated illegal activity has been performed in whole or in part. He considered this Rule to be applicable to any contract where the illegality would prevent the court from being able to order specific performance or award damages for breach.[73] Although Lord Neuberger considered that the Rule would establish a 'degree of clarity and certainty',[74] he went on to adopt Lord Toulson's 'trio of considerations' to determine how the illegality defence should operate. He considered this to be a structured approach which was not akin to the exercise of judicial discretion and which provided the best guidance that could be offered. Significantly, he said:[75]

> Once a judge is required to take into account a significant number of relevant factors, and the question of how much weight to give each of them is a matter for the judge, the difference between judgment and discretion is, I think, in practice pretty slight.

But does this not collapse discretion into arbitrary decision making such that all his good work in developing the Rule and focusing on the need for certainty and clarity is dissipated? Lord Sumption's analysis of the majority's approach is surely correct. Whilst the 'trio of considerations' purports to be principled, there is a significant danger that it will not provide the guidance to judicial decision making that is required, as evident from subsequent decisions.[76] It is, for example, unclear how the considerations were applied on the facts of *Patel v Mirza* itself. The majority did

[70] ibid [120].

[71] See also *Harlequin Property (SUG) Ltd v Wilkins Kennedy (a firm)* [2016] EWHC 3188 (TC), [11] (Coulson J). Likewise the causation test which used to apply in tort claims, whereby illegality would defeat the claim if the damage was caused by the claimant's illegal act (as in *Joyce v O'Brien* [2013] EWCA Civ 546, [2014] 1 WLR 70), appears to be incompatible with the trio of considerations test.

[72] *Patel v Mirza*, above n 3, [116].

[73] ibid [159].

[74] ibid [157].

[75] ibid [173].

[76] See, eg, *Hague Plant Ltd v Hartley* [2016] EWHC 2663 (Ch); *Cenac v Schafer* [2016] UKPC 25; *Tchenguiz v Grant Thornton UK LLP* [2016] EWHC 3727; *Ronelp Marine Ltd v STX Offshore and Shipbuilding Co* [2016] EWHC 2228 (Ch); *Henderson v Dorset Healthcare University NHS Foundation Trust* [2016] EWHC 3275 (QB), [2017] 1 WLR 2673.

not identify reasons why insider dealing was made a crime, or explain why this was relevant to the determination of how the defence applied. No policies were identified which would have been affected had the claim been denied, nor was the question of proportionality considered explicitly.

Lords Clarke, Mance and Sumption, on the other hand, adopted a narrow but much more focused approach to illegality. For Lord Mance, it was important for the court to recognise:[77]

> a limited approach to the effect of illegality, focused on the need to avoid inconsistency in the law, without depriving claimants of the opportunity to obtain damages for wrongs or to put themselves in the position in which they should have been.

It is the approach adopted by Lord Sumption, however, which draws out the difference between the minority and the majority most significantly. He said:[78]

> When the law of illegality is looked at as a whole, it is apparent that although governed by rules of law, a considerable measure of flexibility is inherent in those rules. In particular, they are qualified by principled exceptions for (i) cases in which the parties to the illegal act are not on the same legal footing and (ii) cases in which an overriding statutory policy requires that the claimant should have a remedy notwithstanding his participation in the illegal act.

This is a much more attractive approach to the interpretation of the defence. It is essentially a rule-based approach, the effect of which is to deny the claim where the claimant has been tainted by illegality, but acknowledges that this is subject to 'principled exceptions', both of which have been previously recognised, namely that the parties are not *in pari delicto* or that the award of a remedy is consistent with the policy of the statute. This is surely the preferable approach because the judge is making a decision with reference to clearly identified principles. The 'trio of considerations' of Lord Toulson might be analysed in similar terms as being grounded on principles, but analysis of the three considerations reveals that they are too vague to provide the judge with the guidance required to resolve these difficult issues. For how is it possible to identify in a principled way the policies which militate against or in favour of awarding a remedy and determining whether the denial of relief is disproportionate? These three considerations will readily collapse into one and take English law perilously close to resurrecting the public conscience test[79] and the uncertainty in the law which inexorably followed.

The two factors identified by Lord Sumption certainly support the award of restitution on the facts of the case. First, the appellant can be characterised as being more responsible for the illegality than the respondent. The trial judge had found that the respondent had not acted dishonestly: it was the appellant who suggested the scheme to the respondent, and there was no evidence that the respondent had ever had dealings in stocks and shares, or that he knew that what was being proposed

[77] *Patel v Mirza*, above n 3, [192].

[78] ibid [264].

[79] ibid [219] (Lord Clarke). Strauss considers that the public conscience test, or something very like it, has been restored as a result of the decision: N Strauss, 'The Diminishing Power of the Defendant: Illegality after *Patel v Mirza*' [2016] *Restitution Law Review* 144, 163.

was unlawful. Whilst ignorance of law should not be a relevant consideration, for reasons of consistency with other parts of the law, the position of the appellant in a financial institution and the fact that he approached the respondent to participate in the transaction are relevant factors to be borne in mind when considering where the responsibilities for the illegality lie. If the balance of responsibility lies with the appellant, this is a strong reason why the transaction should be unwound and restitution awarded.

Secondly, awarding restitution would not undermine the policy behind making the transaction illegal in the first place. There is no inconsistency in allowing the respondent to recover his money after the insider-trading scheme had been abandoned; it would in no sense be condoning such schemes. The Criminal Justice Act 1993, which criminalises insider trading, does not provide that the respondent should lose his rights to the return of his money, nor would the award of restitution mean that the respondent would profit from his wrongdoing, whereas denying restitution would mean that the appellant did profit from his participation in the transaction. The key policy should be to encourage the unwinding of such transactions so that the parties are restored to their original position. Significantly, if the transaction is unwound, receipt of the £620,000 would not be subject to confiscation under the Proceeds of Crime Act 2002 because, since restitution operates to turn back time, the money will no longer be the proceeds of crime in the hands of the respondent. Further, the Supreme Court has previously recognised that restoring money to the victim does prevent a confiscation order from being made.[80] If, however, the appellant was allowed to keep the money, it may be forfeited under the Proceeds of Crime Act as the proceeds of crime. So, awarding restitution is also consistent with the policy underpinning the proceeds of crime legislation, namely that it should not be possible to profit from crime, but making restitution to the respondent does not result in his obtaining a profit.

Despite the disagreement amongst the Justices about the context-based or rule-based approach to the defence of illegality, it is significant that they all recognised the strength of the argument that, where both parties are tainted by the illegality and the claimant seeks restitution by virtue of the defendant's unjust enrichment, a restitutionary remedy will typically be awarded regardless of the illegality, since it is better to restore the parties to their original position rather than to allow the defendant to profit by retention of the enrichment. Unfortunately, Lords Sumption, Clarke and Mance analysed this restitutionary claim using the language of rescission. This, however, involves an abuse of language: rescission is a remedy which operates to set aside a valid contract, but where a contract has been tainted by illegality it is void, so there is nothing to rescind. Presumably what the Justices meant was to use the language of *restitutio in integrum* to describe the strength of the restitutionary response. Significantly, a number of the Justices emphasised the importance of an illegal transaction being void, since this means that there can never be a valid basis for the defendant's receipt of the enrichment. This was expressed most clearly in the judgment of Lord Neuberger, who justified 'the Rule', that the claimant is entitled

[80] *R v Waya* [2012] UKSC 51, [2013] 1 AC 294, [28] (Lord Walker and Hughes LJ).

to the return of the money which he has paid even where the contemplated illegal activity had been performed in whole or in part, on the ground that 'the law should not regard an inherently criminal act as effective consideration'.[81] It would follow, therefore, that if Mirza had invested some of the £620,000 in shares, Patel would still have been able to recover all of the money simply because the transaction was void for illegality.

Lords Neuberger and Sumption took the logic of 'the Rule' in support of restitution as far as they could and did not seem especially concerned about the seriousness of the illegality when determining whether restitution should be awarded. They both accepted that if, for example, the claimant had paid money to the defendant to murder a third party, the claimant should be able to obtain restitution of the money even if the murder was committed, because there could never have been any valid consideration for such an illegal transaction.[82] Lord Toulson and those concurring with his judgment would presumably baulk at such a conclusion, which they might well consider to be disproportionate in the light of the very serious nature of the illegality. Indeed, Lord Toulson suggested that there will be some circumstances where the nature of the illegality should defeat the claim, such as drug trafficking.[83]

IV. *PATEL v MIRZA*: REVOLUTION OR EVOLUTION?

In considering whether the decision of the Supreme Court in *Patel v Mirza* can be considered to be revolutionary or only evolutionary, it is vital to assess its impact on previously recognised legal doctrine and also how it has been received and applied subsequently.

A. Impact on Legal Doctrine

Whilst the judgments in the Supreme Court do not indicate that the old doctrines of *ex turpi causa* and *in pari delicto* have gone, at the very least such language seems inconsistent with the new approach embodied in the 'trio of considerations', an approach which does not start from any assumption that illegality operates as a defence to a claim but, rather, focuses on a variety of factors to assess whether illegality should have any impact on the claim. Consequently, such language should be avoided in future. Some of the old doctrines do, however, appear consistent with the trio of considerations. So, for example, it will continue to be important to determine whether one party is more responsible for the illegal transaction than the other, since the respective culpability of the parties was expressly identified as being relevant to determining what response is proportionate. Further, consideration of the underlying purpose of any statute which renders conduct illegal continues to be relevant.

[81] *Patel v Mirza*, above n 3, [176].
[82] ibid [176] (Lord Neuberger), [254] (Lord Sumption).
[83] ibid [10].

It appears, however, that two of the other mechanisms for controlling the illegality defence are no longer relevant, namely the reliance and withdrawal principles.

The majority recognised that the 'no-reliance' principle should be rejected.[84] This is primarily because of its perceived procedural nature and its arbitrary consequences. It follows that a claim will not be defeated simply because the claimant needs to establish the illegality of the transaction in order to make the claim. Even so, the majority considered that *Tinsley v Milligan*[85] would have been decided the same way, but without the artifice of considering whether or not it was necessary to rely on the illegality to establish the claim. Rather, the majority would have required the nature of the illegality to be considered explicitly, but would have concluded that it would have been disproportionate to have prevented Miss Milligan from enforcing her equitable proprietary interest which had arisen under a resulting trust, because this would have resulted in Miss Tinsley being unjustly enriched.[86]

The continued operation of the withdrawal principle is doubtful following *Patel v Mirza*. Lord Toulson did not consider that this doctrine was relevant on the facts of the case, so he did not examine it. Although the doctrine was not expressly recognised as being relevant to the trio of considerations, the fact that the claimant has voluntarily withdrawn from the illegal transaction will, presumably, be relevant to the assessment of proportionality and so the doctrine will probably be subsumed into the third of the relevant considerations.

Lords Neuberger and Sumption did consider the withdrawal doctrine still to be relevant and they reanalysed it. They rejected the previous connotations of repentance and the need for voluntary withdrawal from the transaction. Instead, they considered that the doctrine appears to be simply that, because the basis for an illegal transaction will always fail as a matter of law (since the basis is unlawful), restitution should generally be available in the normal way. This converts the withdrawal principle into a ground of restitution to establish that the receipt of an enrichment is unjust. It follows that *Tribe v Tribe* would presumably be decided in the same way, with restitution being awarded because no part of the illegal purpose had been satisfied, save if the application of the trio of considerations would defeat the claim.

B. Judicial Reception of the Decision

Judgments handed down after *Patel v Mirza* indicate a lukewarm response to the decision, and at times confusion. Whilst it has been acknowledged that the test recognised in *Patel v Mirza* is broader and wider-ranging than the old law[87] and that it has altered the terms of the debate by introducing a fact sensitive inquiry,[88] the application of that test appears not to have resulted in any significantly different result from the operation of the old *ex turpi causa* doctrine subject to its

[84] Confirmed by Lewison LJ in *Cenac v Schafer*, above n 76, [20]; *Tchenguiz v Grant Thornton UK LLP*, above n 76 (Comm), [41] (Knowles J).

[85] Above n 7.

[86] *Patel v Mirza*, above n 3, [110] (Lord Toulson) and [136] (Lord Clarke).

[87] *Cenac v Schafer*, above n 76, [20] (Lewison LJ).

[88] *Hague Plant Ltd v Hartley*, above n 76, [221] (Norris J).

various exceptions.[89] Consequently, it continues to remain important to determine whether the transaction is sufficiently tainted by the illegality. So, for example, in *Tchnguiz v Grant Thornton UK LLP*,[90] *Patel v Mirza* was not considered to be relevant when determining the validity of a settlement agreement because, even though the settlement related to claims involving conspiracy, this was not considered to be sufficient to taint the agreement.

The impact of *Patel v Mirza* is probably summarised most accurately by Norris J in *Ronelp Marine Ltd v STX Offshore and Shipbuilding Co*,[91] in which he stated that the case renders the law of illegality relatively clear and certain where a claimant paid money to the defendant to carry out an illegal activity which is not proceeded with, but in other areas the 'application of the law is uncertain to an exceptional degree'. The uncertainty of the law is reflected best of all in *Henderson v Dorset Healthcare University NHS Foundation Trust*,[92] which concerned a claim in the tort of negligence brought by a claimant who had murdered her mother, but who had successfully pleaded diminished responsibility at her trial and who sought damages against the defendant for failing to respond appropriately to her mental collapse. Whilst the judge referred to *Patel v Mirza*, he emphasised that he did not consider the case to supply a complete answer to illegality cases. Whilst making reference to elements of the trio of considerations, namely whether it would be disproportionate to deny recovery on public policy grounds, he clearly did not find their application to be straightforward, and relied instead on previous decisions[93] which had not been expressly criticised in *Patel v Mirza* and which he considered to involve a sound application of a flexible policy-based approach, even though such an approach was not explicitly endorsed in those cases. Indeed, in determining that the claim should fail by virtue of the claimant's illegality, particularly by virtue of her personal responsibility for the crime, the judge placed much greater reliance on the safety of precedent than the trio of considerations, going so far as to say that 'the doctrine of precedent retains its value in an ordered, hierarchical system and the application of an appropriate degree of judicial discipline in the instant case leads to only one conclusion'.[94]

In the light of these decisions, *Patel v Mirza* certainly appears not to be revolutionary in its impact and even its contribution to the evolution of the law of illegality might be in doubt.

V. SYNTHESIS

What will the impact of *Patel v Mirza* actually be?[95] There were three distinct routes which might have been followed by the Supreme Court. The first was the purely

[89] See *Cenac v Schafer*, above n 76, [20] (Lewison LJ).

[90] Above n 76.

[91] *Ronelp Marine Ltd v STX Offshore and Shipbuilding Co* [2016] EWHC 2228, [36]–[37].

[92] Above n 76.

[93] Notably *Clunis v Camden and Islington Health Authority* [1998] QB 978 and *Gray v Thames Trains Ltd*, above n 15.

[94] *Henderson v Dorset Healthcare University NHS Foundation Trust* above n 76, [93].

[95] Goudkamp has perhaps prematurely described it as 'pivotal': J Goudkamp, 'The End of an Era? Illegality in Private Law in the Supreme Court' (2017) 133 *LQR* 14.

public policy route, where illegality is treated as an absolute defence, and is constrained only by the adoption of a restricted definition of illegality and by the need to consider whether the illegality is sufficiently connected with the claim. Such an approach has no regard to the justice of the case as between the parties or countervailing policy considerations. The second route focuses on the public policies which underpin the illegality defence, but seeks to ascertain whether the operation of the defence can be justified in respect of any of those policies. The legitimacy of this approach turns on the validity and acceptance of the underlying policies. There is a danger of this collapsing from a principled exercise of judicial discretion into the exercise of arbitrary choice, potentially even returning to the old public conscience test. The third route adopts a middle way between the other two. It recognises the public policy dimension of the illegality defence as a starting point for its application, but then moderates this by reference both to how illegality is defined and to various recognised mechanisms which can be analysed as involving both countervailing policy considerations and the need to consider the justice of the case as between the parties.

The majority in the Supreme Court chose the second of these three routes. This decision was intended to resolve the controversy about the nature of the illegality defence for good, but the subsequent response to the decision at trial level and in the Privy Council, and the uncertainties arising from the application of the principles identified by the Supreme Court, suggest that this may not be the end of the matter. In fact, and despite the clear differences of approach between the majority and the minority, it might still be possible to find a route through the complexity of the law which respects the approach of both sides. That is the third route, which acknowledges both the public policy and justice dimensions of the illegality defence.

This third route requires an initial acknowledgment that a transaction tainted by illegality should not succeed, for reasons of public policy. Even this initial statement requires careful consideration in terms of determining what is meant by illegality and by the notion of tainting of the claim. The former question did not arise in *Patel v Mirza* because of the clear criminality of what the parties had agreed. Whilst criminal conduct is clearly treated as illegal, the defence of illegality has been recognised as being even wider. In *Safeway Stores v Twigger*,[96] Flaux J described illegal conduct as being 'morally reprehensible'. This has been held to encompass civilly unlawful conduct, which is quasi-criminal in form, such as price-fixing contrary to the Competition Act 1998;[97] lawful but immoral conduct; and even civil wrongdoing, such as the infringement of a patent[98] or the tort of deceit.[99]

Once the defence can be considered to have been engaged, it is necessary to determine whether it should be applied on the facts of the case. It is at this point that the trio of considerations could be relevant. As presently formulated, they are too vague to be of particular use to the judge. Lord Sumption was willing to recognise two moderating principles, namely the responsibility of the parties and the policy

[96] *Safeway Stores v Twigger* [2010] EWHC 11 (Comm), [2012] 2 Lloyd's Rep 39, [26].
[97] ibid.
[98] *Les Laboratoires Servier v Apotex*, above n 6.
[99] *Parkingeye v Somerfield Stores*, above n 1.

underlying the illegality. Other moderating principles should be recognised as well, with particular regard to the trio of considerations. The first two of these are particularly difficult to unpack and apply, but they could usefully be collapsed into a requirement to determine the policy that underpins the treatment of the conduct as illegal. Other factors should also be relevant to the operation of the defence, including the seriousness of the conduct, its centrality to the transaction that underpins the claim and the relative responsibilities of the parties. In other words, the factors which relate to the question of proportionality should be identified explicitly and the judge should be required to consider them. Consideration of the question whether denying the defence is disproportionate might include consideration of whether the claimant had repented of his or her involvement in the illegal transaction, so returning the withdrawal principle to its origins.

This approach to the defence of illegality allows the concerns of the majority and the minority to be respected. It depends on there being very careful consideration of the facts of the case and the context in which the dispute occurred, but with the benefit of clear principles which assist the judge in making his or her decision. It would follow that the defence of illegality should continue to be recognised as a rule denying the claim unless there is a good reason why the defence should not apply. That reason could be summarised under the general principle that it will not apply where it would operate disproportionately. Although Lord Sumption did recognise that the operation of the defence should not depend on 'a value judgment about the significance of the illegality or the consequences for the parties of barring the claim'[100] and that it was not based on achieving proportionality between the claimant's misconduct and his or her loss, a concept which he considered to derive from public law and not to be relevant to the law of obligations, that is precisely how the defence should operate.

Revolutions in the law can take many forms, ranging from seismic shifts to subtle changes the real impact of which can only be detected many years later. Sometimes, a decision which is anticipated as being revolutionary may turn out to be full of sound and fury but signifying nothing. It is unlikely that *Patel v Mirza* will be revolutionary on the seismic scale, such is the level of uncertainty arising from its interpretation and application. It is far more likely that it will be significant in facilitating the continued evolution of the defence of illegality. At the heart of the defence of illegality is a conflict between two responses, identified most clearly by Bingham LJ in *Saunders v Edwards*:[101]

> Where issues of illegality are raised, the courts have (as it seems to me) to steer a middle course between two unacceptable positions. On the one hand it is unacceptable that any court of law should aid or lend its authority to a party seeking to pursue or enforce an object or agreement which the law prohibits. On the other hand, it is unacceptable that the court should, on the first indication of unlawfulness affecting any aspect of a transaction, draw up its skirts and refuse all assistance to the plaintiff, no matter how serious his loss nor how disproportionate his loss to the unlawfulness of his conduct.

[100] *Patel v Mirza*, above n 3, [18].
[101] Above n 25.

If *Patel v Mirza* is to have the positive impact that is required, there is still a need to steer a middle course between the Scylla and Charybdis of rule and discretion. That middle way can be identified, and still be broadly consistent with the approach of the majority, by recognising a rule and being willing to moderate it with reference to recognised principles, albeit under the heading of proportionality. In so doing, it will be possible to ensure that the delicate equilibrium of protecting public policy yet securing justice is achieved. Being able to achieve that in this notoriously complex and controversial part of the common law would be truly revolutionary.

15

The Revolutionary Trajectory of EU Contract Law towards Post-national Law

HUGH COLLINS

I. A REVOLUTIONARY COCKTAIL FOR THE *ANCIEN RÉGIME*

AT BOTTOM, a revolution requires a significant change in the sources of law. In accordance with the theory of HLA Hart in his book *The Concept of Law*,[1] a revolution therefore requires change in the rule of recognition. The rule of recognition is a rule in each legal system which determines which other rules should be counted as parts of the same legal system and as valid law. One element of the rule of recognition in most countries, for instance, will be a rule that statutes enacted according to the proper procedures, such as majority votes in Parliament, will count as law until they are repealed by a similar process. Following Hart's analysis, the rule of recognition is ultimately determined by officials of the legal system, usually the most senior judges, who in practice will decide which sources or rules they will regard as binding law. As long as the secondary rule of recognition remains the same, the legal system has a continuous existence and a single identity even though the primary rules that determine rights and obligations are constantly changing. When the rule of recognition is altered, however, that moment may be described as a revolution, for the legal system will be renewed with a fresh identity described by a new conception of the sources of valid law.

On this jurisprudential view, therefore, for a revolution to occur, there is no need for those social upheavals popularly associated with the word 'revolution', such as a military coup, a violent overthrow of a dictator or emperor by the masses, or the beheading of a monarch. A revolution in Hart's sense can be engineered rather quietly by the judges, perhaps without most people being aware of what is happening. For instance, that is what happened when the UK joined the European Community (now the European Union (EU)). Following an expression of will by Parliament in the European Communities Act 1972, not itself capable of changing the rule of recognition, the judges accepted a new rule of recognition in which laws enacted

[1] HLA Hart, *The Concept of Law* (Oxford, Clarendon Press, 1961).

by the European Community would henceforth be regarded as applicable law in the UK, with the potential to override or dispense with national law. Perhaps it was because this revolution occurred quietly, even surreptitiously, that it took nearly half a century for the counter-revolutionary forces to contest this change in the rule of recognition.

Hart's theory of revolutions has its critics. From a semantic point of view, it does seem to be an over-inclusive theory, in that Hart seems to suggest that even minor changes in the rule of recognition count as 'revolutions'. It can also prove inaccurate, as John Finnis pointed out,[2] because after a change in the rule of recognition, many rules seem to continue as valid law, even though they would not count as law under the new rule of recognition and have not been re-enacted. For instance, after any repeal of the European Communities Act 1972, it is possible that EU Regulations might continue as valid laws on departure from the EU even if not re-enacted under the new rule of recognition. Furthermore, as AWB Simpson insisted,[3] in a legal system where most law is judge-made law, it will be extremely hard to distinguish between a supposed secondary rule of recognition and the primary rules of law, such as contract and tort, since both kinds of rules are essentially no more than the customary rules accepted by the judges as law. So, Hart's elegant distinction between primary and secondary rules tends to break down in practice in common law systems.

Whilst conceding the soundness of those criticisms, it will be contended nevertheless that EU contract law displays many signs of a revolutionary trajectory in Hart's sense. The key signs of this revolution consist of the recognition of new sources of law by the Court of Justice of the EU (CJEU). This chapter is not concerned with the evolution of the broader legal framework of the EU, where it is evident that the combination of Treaty changes and judgments of the CJEU have strengthened and expanded the law-making capacities of EU institutions. My narrow focus is on what is perhaps misleadingly called EU contract law, and how subtle changes in the methods by which CJEU has sought to articulate this part of the law have involved unacknowledged transformations in the rule of recognition with respect to the sources of EU contract law.

In outline, my narrative is that, in the pursuit of its objective of the completion of the single market, the EU has enacted a number of directives, which collectively have been described as constituting EU contract law.[4] Because these laws adopt a novel, highly instrumental paradigm or conception of law-making in respect of contracts, they provoke irritated and sometimes uncomprehending reactions from the established systems of national contract law. In response to these reactions, the CJEU and to some extent national courts have sought solutions to the proper integration of EU contract law into national contract law systems by revising conceptions of the sources of EU contract law. Such revisions to the sources of EU contract law

[2] JM Finnis, 'Revolutions and the Continuity of Legal Systems' in AWB Simpson (ed), *Oxford Essays in Jurisprudence*, 2nd series (Oxford, Oxford University Press, 1973).

[3] AWB Simpson, 'The Common Law and Legal Theory' in Simpson, ibid.

[4] See, eg, L Miller, *The Emergence of EU Contract Law* (Oxford, Oxford University Press, 2011); S Weatherill, *Contract Law of the Internal Market* (Cambridge, Intersentia, 2016).

necessarily entail what in Hart's terminology amount to a change in the rule of recognition. My claim is that this adjustment to the sources of contract law represents, at least for the UK, a profound reorientation of the legal system towards both a rights-based and a post-national conception of the sources of contract law. If this interpretation is correct, it can be fairly said that EU contract law provides an incendiary revolutionary cocktail for the *ancien regime* of private contract law. In the long run, even if the UK no longer accepts the applicability of new EU contract law after Brexit, much of the existing body of law will probably be preserved as domestic law. The interpretation of this law and connected aspects of the common law of contract may well be influenced by these significant revisions to the sources of EU contract law. To understand the causes and nature of this revolution in the sources of contract law, we need first to examine the character of the EU directives concerning contracts and transactions.

II. TECHNO-LAW

The name 'EU contract law' has been applied to a variety of phenomena, not all of which can easily be classified as law, especially when writers refer more loosely to European (rather than EU) contract law. However, the core focus of studies of EU contract law concerns EU directives that address various kinds of contracts, particularly, but not exclusively, consumer purchases of goods and services, and contracts of employment.[5] Membership of this group of directives labelled as EU contract law may be contested at the edges, but certainly there is a recognised core of directives concerned with everyday transactions, such as buying goods in the shopping mall or on the internet, as well as more complex transactions, such as package holidays, consumer credit agreements or mobile phone packages. EU contract law is, however, not really deserving of the name 'contract law', if contract law is understood strictly as the legal rules that regulate contracts or determine rights and obligations between the parties to a contract.

In general, EU contract law regulates the law of contract, not the contracts themselves. The EU directives usually set minimum standards or goals that the national contract laws of the Member States are supposed to implement properly and for which suitable remedies should be made available in order to ensure their effectiveness. EU contract law is therefore mostly a meta-law: it does not usually regulate contracts directly, but rather regulates national contract laws that regulate contracts. The directives are not private law but public law, because directives are addressed at governments, not private individuals. Of course, that description is only the pure theory of how EU law is supposed to work. The CJEU has shown itself to be adept at finding ways of making EU law tantamount to being directly effective in its horizontal application between private parties. In particular, since national contract law is supposed to conform to the standards set in directives, the meaning of any

[5] Occasionally EU regulations and even the Treaties also provide sources of contract law, such as the rules on anti-competitive agreements, as interpreted in Case C-453/99 *Courage v Creham* [2001] ECR I-6314.

provision in a Directive, as determined by the CJEU, should also be the meaning of the implementing national contract law.

This European contract law may usefully be described as techno-law. This label is intended to mean more than the fact that the law contained in directives is developed and proposed by civil servants in Brussels, with often only peripheral participation in the European Parliament and typically hardly any consideration in national parliaments and representative institutions. Habermas has challenged the democratic deficit of the EU from the perspective of someone who is nevertheless an enthusiast about the idea of a European Union. He believes (surely correctly) that only such transnational and, indeed, post-national bodies have a hope of combating the potential deleterious effects on ordinary people in Europe of that phenomenon known as globalisation.[6] However, he regrets how EU law has become in practice a method used by technocrats to pursue policy goals set by institutions that are remote from the deliberative discourses of democratic institutions. Whilst agreeing with that general line of argument, which is similar to the critique voiced in the *Manifesto on Social Justice in European Contract Law*,[7] I want to describe EU contract law as techno-law in a more precise sense. There are three features of techno-law that need to be highlighted in this context: its high degree of instrumentalism, its applicable scope defined in terms of functional entities instead of persons and its incompleteness.

A. Instrumentalism

To understand the instrumental quality of techno-law, it is necessary to compare it to the character of traditional national private law systems. In my view, traditional systems of contract law combine a broad range of instrumental goals with a concern to ensure justice between the parties to the dispute.[8] Those instrumental goals include support for market transactions for the sake of general welfare and the economic benefits achieved through contractual arrangements such as credit, investment and insurance. The traditional law of contract also protects market transactions against various potential abuses of the institution of contracts, such as the manipulation of preferences by coercion and fraud. At the same time, however, traditional contract law protects the rights or interests of the parties to contracts: their freedom is protected against imposed contracts and their expectations of performance are protected from disappointment and betrayal by the judicial ordering of remedies of corrective justice, such as the payment of compensation to the injured party to cover losses resulting from breach of contract. In this way, national contract law has traditionally been concerned with both the question of what would be fair and just between the contracting parties and the broader issue of what would be in the public interest, which in this context is usually understood as the promotion of trade through freely chosen contractual undertakings. My claim is that the techno-law

[6] J Habermas, *The Lure of Technocracy* (Cambridge, Polity Press, 2015).

[7] Study Group on Social Justice in European Private Law, 'Social Justice in European Contract Law: A Manifesto' (2004) 10 *European Law Journal* 653.

[8] In more detail see H Collins, *Regulating Contracts* (Oxford, Oxford University Press, 1999) 31ff.

that we find in European contract law strikes a different balance from that traditional private law configuration.

In essence, this techno-law focuses on a relatively narrow set of policy objectives, and those objectives are emphasised almost to the exclusion of the traditional private law's concerns regarding corrective justice between the parties and doctrinal coherence.[9] The contrast I seek to draw between traditional private law and EU techno-law is well illustrated by the Unfair Commercial Practices Directive.[10] The purpose of this Directive is to forbid certain kinds of sales techniques used by businesses towards consumers that may be described as misleading, aggressive or unfair. This law fits into the general objective of completing the EU internal market, because the widespread presence of such marketing practices would certainly discourage consumers from purchasing goods and services, especially if this involved unfamiliar practices in cross-border trade. Although this Directive effectively sets the outer limits of marketing practices that may be used by traders, there must be doubt about whether it is an instance of EU contract law at all, because it confers no rights whatsoever on consumers who are damaged by being the victims of unfair commercial practices. The Directive states laconically in Article 3(2) that it 'is without prejudice to contract law and, in particular, to the rules on the validity, formation or effect of a contract'. It is left to national contract law to find ways to relieve consumers from unwanted or extortionate deals and to award compensation in suitable cases. The aim of the Directive is to cleanse the single market of unfair practices, not to protect the interests of those who suffer at the hands of rogue traders. Although the complete absence of concern for remedying the losses suffered by victims of unfair commercial practices makes this Directive seem different from some of the others that might be more readily included under the rubric of European contract law, in my view it is merely an extreme example of a pattern of regulatory orientation in these directives.

Their focus is on addressing actual or perceived obstacles to cross-border trade in the single market. Having identified the obstacle, the task is to dismantle it by issuing a prohibition. The prohibition can be aimed at unfair commercial practices, unfair terms in contracts, or defective goods and services. Having stated what is to be prohibited, it usually suffices to instruct the Member States to implement the prohibition effectively. In the case of the unfair terms in consumer contracts Directive,[11] the purpose of the law is described in the Preamble as the prevention of unfair competition between Member States and the removal of a deterrent to

[9] cf R Michaels, 'Of Islands and the Ocean: The Two Rationalities of European Private Law' in R Brownsword, HW Micklitz, L Niglia and S Weatherill (eds), *The Foundations of European Private Law* (Oxford, Hart Publishing, 2011) 139; H Collins, 'The Hybrid Quality of European Private Law' in Brownsword et al, ibid, 453; CU Schmid, 'The Instrumentalist Conception of the Acquis Communautaire in Consumer Law and its Implications on a European Contract Law Code' (2005) *1 European Review of Contract Law* 210.

[10] Directive 2005/29/EC concerning unfair business-to-consumer commercial practices of 11 May 2005 [2005] OJ L149/22. The same point can be made about other directives, such as the duty placed on investment service providers to act honestly, fairly and professionally in accordance with the best interests of the client under Art 19 of Directive 2004/39/EC on markets in financial instruments [2004] OJ L145/1.

[11] Directive 93/13/EEC on unfair terms in consumer contracts [1993] OJ L95/29.

consumers from engaging in cross-border shopping. The main provision on remedies is Article 7.1 which states that: 'Member States shall ensure that, in the interests of consumers and of competitors, adequate and effective means exist to prevent the continued use of unfair terms in contracts concluded with consumers by sellers or suppliers.' This provision does not require any remedy to be available to the individual consumer; it is about market cleansing. Perhaps for the first time in EU contract law, this directive exhibits a hint of a private law character, because it also provides in Article 6.1 that national law should ensure that unfair terms should not be binding on the consumer, though this remedial proposal of unenforceability is still as much about market cleansing as it is concerned with individual consumer protection.[12] Thus, the Directive remains oriented towards its purpose of the removal of barriers to trade and devotes scant attention to the regulation of the competing interests of the parties.

My interpretation distinguishes techno-law from what Max Weber referred to as social law.[13] What Weber had in mind was laws such as consumer law, landlord and tenant law, and employment law, which in a contractual context modify the established liberal or libertarian framework of contract law to place mandatory constraints on bargaining processes and outcomes in the terms of contracts. Social law, on this view, creates a new balance of interests, in which those of the weaker parties to contracts receive better protection, with a view to achieving social justice or a fairer distributive outcome than would be achieved by an unbridled market. According to my thesis, techno-law differs from this kind of social law. It is true that both kinds of law are designed by reference to a goal—social justice in the case of social law and completion of the internal market in the case of techno-law—but techno-law differs because it is not concerned with rebalancing the interests of the parties; rather, it is exclusively concerned with the goal of ensuring that the market functions efficiently. EU consumer law directives, such as the Consumer Rights Directive,[14] increasingly require full harmonisation, not minimum standards, even though in some countries that will require a diminution of consumer protection, because only uniform laws satisfy the functional needs of the single market,[15] whereas minimum standards can satisfy the goal of social justice. In some instances, no doubt, the functionality of the market will be enhanced by some kind of rebalancing of the interests of the parties, as in the case of consumer protection against rogue traders. However, that task will be pursued by techno-law, not for the sake of some conception of social justice, but solely in support of the aim of a better functioning single market.[16]

[12] H Collins, 'The Hybrid Quality of European Private Law' in Brownsword et al, above n 9, 453, 455.

[13] M Weber, *Economy and Society*, G Roth and C Wittich eds, vol II (Berkeley, University of California Press, 1978) 886, 894.

[14] Consumer Rights Directive 2011/83/EU [2011] OJ L304/64.

[15] O Cherednychenko, 'Private Law Discourse and Scholarship in the Wake of the Europeanisation of Private Law' in J Devenney and M Kenny (eds), *The Transformation of European Private Law* (Cambridge, Cambridge University Press, 2013) 148, 152, giving as an example Case C-386/00 *Axa Royale Belge SA v Georges Ochoa Strategie Finance SPRL* [2002] ECR I-2209.

[16] HW Micklitz, 'The Visible Hand of European Regulatory Private Law: The Transformation of European Private Law from Autonomy to Functionalism in Competition and Regulation' (2009) 28 *Yearbook of European Law* 3.

Insofar as justice considerations influence techno-law, they are mainly concerned with access to markets, not the distributive outcome of those markets.[17]

Whilst traditional private law may embrace instrumental goals such as protection of the weaker party, the distinguishing characteristic of techno-law is its focus on a single goal—the promotion of the single market—at the expense of all others. Furthermore, the dimension of traditional private law systems of balancing the interests and rights of the parties to the transaction by providing a system of corrective remedies typically plays a subsidiary role in the EU directives, and in some it may be omitted altogether.

B. Functions

As a second crucial point of differentiation, unlike private law in national legal systems, techno-law is not concerned with people and their interests as ends in themselves, but rather with functioning economic entities in the market and the market itself. Its laws are not addressed to persons, but at traders, consumers, financial intermediaries, commercial agents, employers, undertakings and workers. EU contract law regards parties to contracts not as people or natural persons with independent interests, but rather as market functionaries—we only exist in EU contract law to play our roles in the internal market. In the jargon of the Commission, the directives regulate 'B2C', or business to consumer, transactions, never 'P2P', or person to person, transactions. As Gareth Davies once remarked, 'there is no space for the citizen or the person in the adjudication of economic law'.[18]

Within this scheme of market regulation, we all have parts to play or functions to perform. Consumers have to be confident to satisfy their preferences through transactions and especially to be willing to engage in cross-border purchases. Consumers must also be average, neither gullible nor especially sophisticated,[19] for the market is constructed to function well for the standardised consumer, not real people, with all their weaknesses to advertisers' seductive copy and irrational hopefulness.[20] Similarly, for the sake of any efficient transnational labour market, workers must be free to roam to find jobs across national borders. This open market should reduce levels of unemployment and increase prosperity, two key ambitions of the EU. This free movement of workers must be secured by deregulation of national measures

[17] HW Micklitz, 'Introduction' in HW Micklitz, *The Many Concepts of Social Justice in European Private Law* (Cheltenham, Edward Elgar, 2011) 3, 34–44; HW Micklitz, 'The (Un)-Systematics of (Private) Law as an Element of European Culture' in G Hellringer and K Purnhagen (eds), *Towards a European Legal Culture* (Baden Baden, Nomos, 2014) 81, 97–99.

[18] G Davies, 'The Consumer, the Citizen, and the Human Being' in D Leczykiewitz and S Weatherill (eds), *The Images of the Consumer in EU Law* (Oxford, Hart Publishing, 2016) 325, 327.

[19] See, eg, Case C-110/14 *Costea v SC Volksbank România SA* [2015] OJ C354—lawyer benefits as a consumer when entering a loan agreement with a bank.

[20] See, eg, Case C-470/93 *Verein gegen Unwesen in Handel under Gewerbe Koln eV v Mars GmbH* [1995] ECR I-1923. For consideration of some adjustments to recognise vulnerable consumers see N Reich, 'Vulnerable Consumers in EU Law' in D Leczykiewitz and S Weatherill (eds), *The Images of the Consumer in EU Law* (Oxford, Hart Publishing, 2016) 139.

that obstruct access to jobs, whilst at the same time protecting the workers in the host nation from so-called social dumping produced by employers posting cheap labour across borders. Workers seem to be granted rights by directives such as anti-discrimination laws[21] and the Posted Workers Directive,[22] not so much to protect them from exploitation as to ensure the smooth operation of competitive labour and capital markets.

An inherent quality of techno-law is that its instrumentality, aimed exclusively at the single market, necessarily deprives us of our personality as legal subjects and transforms us into cogs in a machine. It is as if the Marxist dream of a utopian society without law had become true and that contract law is withering away and is being replaced by 'the administration of things'.[23]

C. Incompleteness

Finally, we need to note especially that techno-law is always incomplete. In the absence of any comprehensive system of contract law at the European level, techno-law presupposes the existence and effectiveness of comprehensive national systems of contract law, together with their rules of civil procedure and civil justice. Even relatively complete directives tend to leave remedial issues to national law.

For instance, the Directive on Consumer Sales and Guarantees clearly foresees a potential remedy in damages for supply of non-conforming goods, when it states in Article 3.1 that 'the seller shall be liable to the consumer for any lack of conformity which exists at the time the goods were delivered'.[24] But the Directive leaves the issue of awards of damages and their quantification up in the air. Why is the remedy apparently so unimportant to the EU legislator? Having claimed in paragraph 2 of the Preamble to the Directive that a minimum protection of fair rules for consumers is implied by the very idea of free movement of goods, paragraph 6 then asserts that the main problems experienced by consumers 'concern the non-conformity of goods with the contract', so the Directive will only address that issue 'without however impinging on provisions and principles of national law relating to contractual and noncontractual liability'. Despite not apparently engaging with national contract law, it is evident that the Directive must presuppose and rely upon national private law systems not only for some elementary ingredients in the law, such as definitions of sales, goods and rules governing interpretations of the meaning of the terms of contracts, but also for principles governing what sorts of remedies might

[21] Directive 2006/54 of 5 July 2006 on the implementation of the principle of equal opportunities and equal treatment of men and women in matters of employment and occupation (recast) (Recast Sex Directive) [2006] OJ L373/37; Directive 2000/43/EC of 29 June 2000 implementing the principle of equal treatment between persons irrespective of racial or ethnic origin (Racial Discrimination Directive) [2000] OJ L180/22; Directive 2000/78/ EC of November 2000 establishing a general framework for equal treatment in employment and occupation (Framework Directive) [2000] OJ L303/16.

[22] Directive 96/71/EC concerning the posting of workers [1997] OJ L18/1.

[23] F Engels, *Anti-Dühring* (Peking, Foreign Languages Press, 1976) part III, ch 2; V Lenin, *The State and Revolution* (Peking, Foreign Languages Press, 1976) chs I and V.

[24] Directive 1999/44/EC of 25 May 1999 on certain aspects of the sale of consumer goods and associated guarantees [1999] OJ L171/12 7. 7.

be appropriate between the parties. Yet, only at one point does the Directive engage with details regarding remedies, in its insistence on a right of the consumer to return or repair of non-conforming goods—which specificity may be explained as fitting into the objective of cleansing the market of non-conforming goods. There is no further guidance on questions that may arise, such as a need to credit a trader for any benefits received by the consumer from enjoyment of the goods prior to their return.

III. THE IMPACT OF TECHNO-LAW

What EU law requires from national legal systems is to implement this techno-law faithfully and effectively. Insofar as the techno-law appears to require an adjustment of national contract law, that adjustment is bound to prove difficult for national legal systems. The silence of techno-law with respect to issues of corrective justice between the parties, together with its narrow policy focus, will inevitably cause puzzlement and irritation as it is integrated into national contract law. Whilst legislatures may simply place a copy of a directive into national legislation without troubling too much about how it affects the remainder of private law, national courts are likely to be reluctant to insert techno-law into national private law systems without seeking to find a way of integrating it into a coherent interpretation of the law that balances the interests of the parties and takes into account a wide range of policy considerations.

Consider, for instance, how the Unfair Commercial Practices Directive might be integrated into the law of contract concerned with the vitiation of consent by fraud, duress and related legal doctrines. The problem will arise that a court decides that a trader has committed an unfair commercial practice, but that the victim lacks an adequate remedy in national private law because the existing doctrines, such as misrepresentation and undue influence, may not match exactly the broad standard of the Directive concerning professional diligence or one of the prohibited examples of unfair commercial practices. When confronted with such a problem, one option for the court is to develop national private law to respond to this lacuna, a process which in effect would use the Directive to justify an evolution of national private law, even though the Directive expressly denies that it can have any such effect on contract law. An alternative course of action is to refuse to adjust private law to address the lacuna, leaving the law in a somewhat incoherent state because the victim of a criminal offence would not benefit from even the possibility of a compensatory remedy. My perception is that, on the whole, the national courts of the Member States try to avoid the incoherence of the second course of action by using techno-law instead as a justification for adjustments to national private law, which in turn produces a more elaborate version of techno-law once it has been implemented in the national law.

A national court has a third course of action available: it can make a reference to the Court of Justice, asking for an interpretation of the relevant EU directive. In reality, it seems to me that often the national court is asking the more complex question of how it should fit the techno-law into its existing body of contract law. Accordingly, the CJEU cannot ignore entirely the traditional private law conception of contract law that it is supposed to protect the interests of both parties. The interpretation of techno-law on a reference to the Court of Justice is likely therefore to reinsert into the directive, and thence national law, the kind of balancing mechanism between the parties to the dispute that one would expect to be applied in a private law dispute by a national court. In other words, the CJEU has to find an interpretation of the directive, if possible, that rewrites it so that it makes sense within national systems of contract law that rest on corrective justice principles.

For instance, in accordance with Article 3(3) of the Consumer Sales Directive, the consumer has the right to replacement or repair of non-conforming goods 'free of charge'. The seller can refuse to replace or repair the goods if the remedy is impossible or involves unreasonable costs in comparison to the other remedy.[25] A series of references from German courts have questioned whether such a rule is fair in circumstances such as *Quelle*, where the consumer had used a stove for a period and was not prepared to pay for that beneficial use when it was replaced, or in *Wittmer*, where the seller argued for the right to refuse replacement because the cost of installing new floor tiles would be disproportionate in comparison with the minor significance of the defect.[26] In these cases, as it happens, the CJEU insisted on maximum consumer protection and the full enforcement of the right to completely free replacement and rejected the more equitable proposals of the seller. My point is that the CJEU could not avoid creating new private law rules, even if in these cases it clung rigidly to the literal text of the directive, as it often does.[27]

In other cases, the CJEU has rejected the literal meaning of a directive in order to secure an outcome that balances the interests of the parties to the contract. The Acquired Rights Directive, concerning the continuity of contracts of employment following a sale of a business to a new owner, has provided a fertile source of examples of the reinsertion of private law reasoning into techno-law.[28] In one case, the Court candidly observed that

> although in accordance with the objective of the Directive the interests of the employees concerned by the transfer must be protected, those of the transferee, who must be in a position to make the adjustments and changes necessary to carry on his operations, cannot be disregarded.[29]

[25] See ibid Art 3.3 on certain aspects of the sale of consumer goods and associated guarantees: 'In the first place, the consumer may require the seller to repair the goods or he may require the seller to replace them, in either case free of charge, unless this is impossible or disproportionate. A remedy shall be deemed to be disproportionate if it imposes costs on the seller which, in comparison with the alternative remedy, are unreasonable, taking into account: the value the goods would have if there were no lack of conformity; the significance of the lack of conformity, and; whether the alternative remedy could be completed without significant inconvenience to the consumer.'

[26] Case C-404/06 *Quelle AG v Bundesverband der Verbraucherzentralen und Verbraucherverbände* [2008] ECR I-02685; discussed by K Lilleholt, 'Case:CJEU—Quelle' (2010) 6 *European Review of Contract Law* 192; Joined Cases C-65/09 *Gebrüder Weber GmbH v Jürgen Wittmer* and C-87/09 *Ingrid Putz v Medianess Electronics GmbH* [2011] ECR I-05257.

[27] H Schepel, 'The Enforcement of EC Law in Contractual Relations: Case Studies in How Not to "Constitutionalize" Private Law' (2004) 12 *European Review of Private Law* 661.

[28] Directive 2001/23/EC on the safeguarding of employees' rights in the event of transfers of undertakings [2001] OJ L82/16.

[29] Case C-499/04 *Werhof v Freeway Traffic Systems Gmbh* [2006] ECR I-2397; cf MF Starke, 'Fundamental Rights Before the Court of Justice of the European Union: A Social, Market-Functional or Pluralistic Paradigm?' in H Collins (ed), *European Contract Law and the Charter of Fundamental Rights*

Although the Directive does not speak about the protection of the interests of the employer, the Court feels obliged to interpret this techno-law by assimilating it into traditional conceptions of private law that balance the interests of the parties, even if that means to some extent defeating the purpose of the Directive. The effect of this interpretation is to rewrite the mandatory law to create exceptions based upon a traditional private law approach of balancing the interests of the parties. A similar step was taken in respect of a consumer's right of withdrawal from a contract concluded at a distance, where the Court permitted the national court to impose a charge on the consumer for the use of the defective computer for eight months before the contract was cancelled in accordance with the right of withdrawal.[30] The irritating qualities of the instrumentalist and functional techno-law are suppressed by adding to the normative content of the Directive, either by expanding its influence or by narrowing its application, so that national courts can develop a coherent private law system. My argument is that, in so doing, the CJEU necessarily adopts a revolutionary stance.

The problem for the CJEU is that it lacks a body of European contract law on which to draw in order to flesh out or confine the implications of a directive, and it also lacks any clear Treaty competence to create such a body of European contract law.[31] The CJEU cannot make the kind of argument that would be available to a national court, such as a concern to reconcile the techno-law with another important rule or principle in the civil code or the precedents of the common law. It cannot make that argument because there is no EU civil code. The Draft Common Frame of Reference,[32] if it had moved beyond the draft stage, might have provided a solution for the CJEU in offering a source of contract law.[33] However, the Draft Common Frame of Reference had to be shelved, because it clearly amounted to a considerable expansion of the competences of the EU that lacked significant political support—and that left the CJEU without the necessary source of private law principles by which to adjust techno-law to the requirements of national private law systems.

Instead, the CJEU has had to turn to two new sources of contract law. The first is the Charter of Fundamental Rights of the European Union.[34] These fundamental

(Cambridge, Intersentia, 2017) 93, 102. Other examples in connection with the Acquired Rights Directive include: Case C-132/91 *Katsakis v Konstantinidis* [1993] IRLR 179 (the automatic transfer of contracts of employment in the Directive did not destroy the employee's (private law) right to refuse to transfer) and Case C-426/11 *Alemo-Herron v Parkwood Leisure Ltd* [2014] 1 CMLR 21, [2013] ICR 1116 (refusal to make collectively agreed terms binding on the transferee for the sake of freedom of contract).

[30] Case C-489/07 *Pia Messner v Firma Stefan Krüger* [2009] ECR I-07315, interpreting Directive 97/7/EC on the protection of consumers in respect of distance contracts [1997] OJ L144/19.

[31] C Joerges, 'Disintegrative Effects of Legislative Harmonisation: A Complex Issue and a Small Example' in M Bussani and U Mattei (eds), *Making European Law, Essays on the 'Common Core' Project* (Trento, Universita delgi studi di Trento, 2000) 103; cf O Gerstenberg, 'Integrity-Anxiety and the European Constitutionalization of Private Law' in K Nuotio (ed), *Europe in Search of Meaning and Purpose* (Helsinki, Forum Iuris, 2004) 107; H Collins, *The European Civil Code: The Way Forward* (Cambridge, Cambridge University Press, 2008) 51–61.

[32] C von Bar (ed), *Principles, Definitions and Model Rules of European Private Law: Draft Common Frame of Reference* (Oxford, Oxford University Press, 2010).

[33] European Commission, 'Green Paper on Policy Options for Progress towards a European Contract Law for Consumers and Businesses', COM (2010) 348 final.

[34] See [2012] OJ C326/02 for a consolidated version of the Treaties.

rights now have the legal status of a Treaty,[35] so the Court can legitimately claim that it must uphold those freedoms and principles in its interpretation of directives. Thus, Charter rights can be manipulated to provide sources of law that may be employed by the Court to patch holes in directives so that they can be reconciled with the principles and goals of national private law systems. A second novel source of contract law, perhaps only used now when the Charter rights run out, is an assertion of the existence of common EU principles of private law based upon the legal traditions of the Member States. This *ius commune* functions rather like a common law of contract, as an unwritten source of law. The content of this customary law is usually discovered by using the techniques of comparative law.

In my examination of these two new sources of European contract law in the next two sections, the contention will be that they represent revolutions in the technical sense that they are new sources of contract law being recognised by the CJEU. Such a development of new sources might not be regarded as especially remarkable for the reason mentioned earlier, that in practice probably every rule of recognition undergoes minor changes at frequent intervals. However, in the case of the EU, such changes, though perhaps just as common as they are in national legal systems, may not be quite as easily dismissed as minor evolutionary developments, since the powers or competences of the EU are supposed to be fixed by the Treaties.[36] This claim highlights the fundamental character of the changes in the rule of recognition presupposed by these two new sources of law. The first change involving the Charter of Fundamental Rights seems to require an adjustment in our conception of the rule of law itself. The second change implies the radical notion of a post-national private law. Together, these changes in the sources of law may provide the necessary ingredients for a kind of Kantian cosmopolitan law.

IV. FROM RULE-BOOK TO RIGHTS-BASED CONCEPTION OF THE RULE OF LAW

In the opening essay of his book *A Matter of Principle*, Ronald Dworkin advances the thesis that there are two possible conceptions of the rule of law.[37] He draws a distinction between the rule-book version of the rule of law and a rights-based version of it. He draws this distinction for the purpose of arguing that judges are not necessarily engaging in inappropriate political activity when being activist and not following the rules of law strictly according to the literal meaning, provided that they are upholding the rights of individuals. Whatever the merits of that broader argument about the appropriate role of judges, what is crucial for my purpose is to appreciate the dichotomy between a rule-based conception of the rule of law and a rights-based version, for it is the switch from the former to the latter that I shall argue represents a revolutionary moment in European contract law.

[35] Treaty on European Union [2012] OJ C326, Art 6.
[36] ibid Art 5.
[37] R Dworkin, *A Matter of Principle* (Oxford, Clarendon Press, 1986) 9.

According to Dworkin, the rule-book conception of the rule of law

> insists that, so far as is possible, the power of the state should never be exercised against individual citizens except in accordance with rules explicitly set out in a public rule book available to all. The government as well as ordinary citizens must play by these public rules until they are changed, in accordance with further rules about how they are to be changed, which are also set out in the rule book.[38]

The rule-book conception of the rule of law is obviously indebted to the work of HLA Hart, and in its expression of the importance of freedom from arbitrary power it is plainly closely affiliated to what has become known as the republican conception of liberty.[39]

In Dworkin's second conception of the rule of law, the rights conception that he favours, citizens are regarded as having moral and political rights, which must be respected by positive law. Courts must therefore uphold those rights so far as is practicable. 'The rule of law on this conception is the ideal of rule by an accurate public conception of individual rights.'[40] Dworkin clarifies that, under this rights conception of the rule of law, judges should in general follow the positive rules of law that have been laid down in advance, for otherwise they would be likely to be acting unfairly, unjustly and in a way that defeats existing rights. The rights conception of the rule of law requires judges to enforce the law according to its plain meaning, because those transparent rules usually express an accurate public conception of individual rights. However, there will be cases, known as hard cases, where it will be necessary to depart from the existing rules of law, even though those rules contain prima facie evidence of what rights people have, in order to uphold the true rights of citizens properly and accurately. In his subsequent book, *Law's Empire*,[41] Dworkin explains how a hypothetical and super-human judge known as Hercules should carry out this task of ensuring that he always reaches the right answer by producing in his interpretation of the law an accurate conception of the rights of citizens.

It is my contention here that EU contract law is increasingly demanding a shift in the conception of the rule of law accepted by national courts when they apply contract law from the rule-book conception to the rights conception. That development was far from evident in the early days of the European community and the single market. The ECJ committed itself regularly to a rule-book conception of the rule of law, though it insisted that EU rules had a hierarchical relationship to national law, so that in cases of conflict EU law always overrode national law. That doctrine of supremacy of EU law made sense within the framework of techno-law and the task of completing the internal market by the dismantling of obstructions to trade presented by national law. Since about 2000 and the declaration at Nice of the Charter of Fundamental Rights, however, we have been witnessing a shift in how the EU institutions present their allegiance to the rule of law. Although compliance with

[38] ibid 11.

[39] P Pettit, *Republicanism: A Theory of Freedom and Government* (Oxford, Oxford University Press, 1997); Q Skinner, 'Freedom as the Absence of Arbitrary Power' in C Laborde and J Maynor (eds), *Republicanism and Political Theory* (Oxford, Blackwell, 2008).

[40] Dworkin, above n 37, 11.

[41] R Dworkin, *Law's Empire* (London, Fontana, 1986).

the complexities of the Treaty provisions is still held up as a major legitimating tool for EU institutional actions, now, increasingly, justifications for the positions of EU institutions are discovered in Charter Rights and more broadly through conformity with the European Convention of Human Rights.

Judges use Charter Rights in connection with EU contract law for two main purposes: legitimation and enhanced functionalism. These broad claims about the function of the Charter in this context of EU law cannot be properly substantiated in the space available here. Instead, I will merely try to explain these concepts, illustrate their application with some well-known cases and link them to a rights-based conception of the rule of law.

A. Legitimation

The first function of reliance upon Charter rights in EU contract law is to provide legitimacy for its market-oriented regulation. My earlier criticism that techno-law treats persons predominantly as functions and instruments rather than ends in themselves can now be met by the riposte that techno-law must always comply with the fundamental rights of EU citizens, as articulated in the Charter of Fundamental Rights and the constitutional traditions of the Member States. The implicit claim is that, provided EU laws comply with Charter rights, no one should be able to criticise them for their wholly instrumental orientation. Dan Wielsch presents a similar argument in slightly different terms, but the point is much the same. He argues that the EU's promotion of 'market rationality', by which he means the construction of the internal market throughout Europe, requires the EU to 'constitutionalise the very institution it has set free'.[42] His account presents this legitimating function of the insertion of Charter rights into EU contract law rather more as a logical necessity or even a dialectical development, which parallels a similar structure that was developed within national legal systems though in a different historical sequence, whereas my account tends to emphasise the pragmatic need of EU elites to justify the expanded sphere of the supremacy of EU law.

With regard to this first purpose to which the Charter is put in EU contract law, namely that the Charter serves to legitimate techno-law, let me illustrate it with a reading of *Alemo-Herron v Parkside Leisure*.[43] The techno-law here is a rule that when a business is sold to a new owner the existing employees keep their jobs and contracts of employment. The Acquired Rights Directive was originally introduced in the 1970s to try to create a level playing field in capital markets, because whilst France and Germany already had such a rule, the UK did not, and this was thought to give the UK an unfair competitive advantage in attracting inward capital investment.[44]

[42] D Wielsch, 'Responsible Contracting—The Requirement of EU Fundamental Rights on Private Law Regimes' in H Collins, *European Contract Law and the Charter of Fundamental Rights* (Cambridge, Intersentia, 2017) 257; D Wielsch, 'The Function of Fundamental Rights in EU Private Law—Perspectives from a Common European Sales Law' (2014) 10 *European Review of Contract Law* 365.

[43] *Alemo-Herron*, above n 29.

[44] H Collins, 'Justifying European Employment Law' in S Grundmann, W Kerber and S Weatherill (eds), *Party Autonomy and the Role of Information in the Internal Market* (Berlin, Walter de Gruyter, 2001) 205.

In the *Alemo-Herron* case, the terms of the workers' contracts, which they were entitled to keep after the transfer of the undertaking to a new owner, provided that their wages would be set by a collective agreement from time to time between a union and a group of public authorities. Following the transfer of the undertaking to a new private owner, the new owner realised that it was apparently bound to pay wage increases set by the public sector collective agreement to which it was not and could not be a party. This outcome was an especially nasty surprise for the transferee because it had probably been intending to reduce wage costs, which in England have typically run at about a 30 per cent reduction in wage costs on transfer to the private sector. No doubt sympathising with the employer's plight, the UK Supreme Court referred the case to the CJEU, which upheld the transferee employer's right to ignore the terms set by the new public sector collective agreement. The CJEU did so on the ground that binding the employer to the terms set by a collective agreement to which it could not be a party was an interference with the employer's freedom of contract, a freedom protected within the freedom to conduct a business in Article 16 of the Charter. Again, there is a strand in the reasoning that resists the validity of techno-law because it does not balance the interests of the parties, but now the Charter provides a legitimating tool for achieving that goal and rewriting the Acquired Rights Directive.

In *Alemo-Herron*, EU techno-law in the form of the Directive is found by the CJEU to have failed to respect the interests of a business, the transferee employer. This failure represents a typical problem of EU contract law, because its narrow instrumental focus typically rules out the normal approach in private law to try to balance the competing interests of both parties to a contract. The reference to a Charter right is brought into the legal reasoning of the CJEU in order to legitimate its rewriting of the techno-law to bring it closer to the normal balancing of interests that one might expect in national private law systems. The Charter right prevents the logic of the techno-law from being taken to its logical conclusion. In so doing, it legitimates the underlying directive and its regulation of capital markets. In applying the Charter, of course, the court overrides the interests of the workforce, who would presumably rather keep their higher wages set by the public sector collective agreement. However, the interests of the workforce are swept aside in the application of the truncated proportionality test. It seems likely, nevertheless, that the decision was the correct result in the sense that it complied with the purpose of the techno-law by ensuring that there is a level playing field in the capital market and that the UK is not disadvantaged by its peculiar unregulated arrangements with respect to collective bargaining.

What is most pertinent for my argument about the revolutionary moment of EU contract law is to notice how the CJEU decided this issue. The CJEU followed precisely the route that Dworkin proposed in his Herculean model of legal reasoning. Although the plain meaning of the law was reasonably clear and defensible as a purpose of techno-law, in accordance with the rights-based conception of the rule of law, Dworkin insists that judges must provide an accurate interpretation of the rights of the parties. In this case, the CJEU found that the Acquired Rights Directive failed to respect sufficiently the transferee employer's right to conduct a business freely. Accordingly, applying the rights-based conception of the rule of law, the Court interpreted the law to protect the employer's freedom of contract.

B. Enhanced Functionalism

The second purpose of invoking the EU Charter of Fundamental Rights in cases concerning EU contract law appears to be to find means for making the techno-law more effective by demanding that national obstructions to the implementation of EU should be struck down, not, as previously, simply on the ground of the supremacy of EU law, but now because the Charter rights must be upheld.

This second purpose of judicial invocations of Charter rights to decide contract cases can be illustrated by another group of well-known cases concerning the application of the Directive on Unfair Terms in Consumer Contracts to consumer credit transactions, in which consumers' homes were at risk for failure to repay instalments on a loan by the due dates. In such cases, the CJEU has often had to consider whether procedural obstacles in national law that appear to prevent a consumer from receiving the full protection of the Directive can be overcome by a more expansive interpretation of EU law. The Charter right to an effective remedy in Article 47 appears to provide a general instrument for arguing that, to the extent that national law makes it virtually impossible for the intended effects of the techno-law to be achieved, the national law has to be modified. Where the failure of a national court to provide an adequate or fair opportunity to argue for the invalidity of a term in a credit agreement also has the effect of depriving a person of his or her home, the right to respect for private life under the European Convention of Human Rights can be invoked as a further reason for ensuring that national procedures should be amended to comply with the high standard of consumer protection in the Directive. In *Kušionová v SMART Capital*, the CJEU stated: 'Under EU law, the right to accommodation is a fundamental right guaranteed under Article 7 of the Charter that the referring court must take into account when implementing [a directive].'[45] The Directive on Unfair Terms in Consumer Contracts only sets minimum standards, and says nothing about civil procedure and very little about remedies. The invocation of Charter rights during references regarding the meaning of the Directive permits the CJEU to claim that, for the sake of making the Directive effective, it must expand its scope to include elements of civil procedure at least to the extent of making sure that the procedure does not effectively deny the protection afforded by the Directive. This consumer protection directive therefore receives a boost by the expansion of its effectiveness as a result of arguments about fundamental rights.

Again, we can detect a rights-based conception of the rule of law in operation in such decisions. The CJEU is willing to trespass into the fields of civil procedure and remedies, hitherto reserved for national law, in order to ensure that its view of the scope of a consumer's rights under EU law is fully respected. To justify this activist approach, it invokes the fundamental rights of the consumer as laid out in the Charter of Fundamental Rights. Those rights are then said to require an interpretation of the Directive which fits uncomfortably with the plain text of the Directive and the division of competences in the Treaties. It is unclear whether the interpretation presented in these cases fits with the original purpose of the Directive, but perhaps

[45] Case C-34/13 *Kušionová v SMART Capital a.s.* (2014) ECLI:EU:C:2014:2189, [65].

the Court has felt the need to adapt it and apply it in the field of consumer credit in response to the chaos in the financial markets starting in 2008.[46]

C. The Implications of a Rights-Based Conception of the Rule of Law

The rights-based conception of the rule of law seems to be replacing the rather formalist rule-book conception that dominated EU legal reasoning for so long. No doubt the formalism of the rule-book approach meets other needs, such as giving apparent respect for the division of competences between EU law and national law established in the Treaties whilst preserving the assertion of the superiority of EU law. The shift to the rights-based conception of the rule of law has also been engendered by a search for ways in which to legitimise the EU institutions without attempting any more radical democratic arrangements for governance. My argument is that, as well as perhaps conferring legitimacy on EU institutions, the Charter rights have been employed more surreptitiously by the CJEU for the purpose of ensuring the better effectiveness and maximum scope for the techno-law that constructs and regulates the single market.

This rights-based conception of the rule of law is, of course, not unfamiliar in national legal systems. What is striking about this EU approach to a rights-based conception of the rule of law is the way it is not governed by the normal 'state-action' doctrine, which says it is the institutions of the state that must comply with fundamental rights, not private individuals. Although the EU can avoid a clash with this 'state-action' doctrine by denying that it ever gives Charter rights direct horizontal effect, this denial must be unconvincing. The project of creating a single market is necessarily about regulating relations between private individuals as well as regulating how states control their borders and their markets. Once the Charter rights become applicable to the interpretation of directives, they must have effects on private individuals, such as consumers and businesses. It is true that the effects can be described as indirect, for in theory all that the CJEU provides is an interpretation of the meaning of a directive, though in practice its interpretation will govern the relationship between the private parties. In *Alemo-Herron*, the employer was given a green light to abandon the collective agreement and to impose its own terms; in *Kušionová v SMART Capital*, the consumer had to be afforded more procedural opportunities to challenge the unfairness of the terms of the credit agreement, the likely effects of which would be to block foreclosure and repossession, at least for the time being. The Charter rights are therefore re-regulating the legal rights between the parties to the contract. This use of fundamental rights in private law may not occur frequently in most national legal systems, but it is becoming routine in the CJEU as it revises the rule of recognition towards a rights-based conception of the rule of law.

This use of fundamental rights is therefore revolutionary in a technical sense, for it will require courts, when deciding issues in contract law with a European origin, not

[46] J Rutgers, 'The Right to Housing (Article 7 of the Charter) and Unfair Terms in General Conditions' in Collins, above n 42, 125.

only to look at the rules in the national code, interpreted in the light of the underlying directive, but also to reflect, in a Herculean manner, whether the outcome that is apparently mandated by the rules in fact provides an accurate interpretation of the rights of the parties when viewed in the full context of the legal system, including the EU Charter of Fundamental Rights.

V. REAL TRANSNATIONAL LAW

Any EU law, including EU contract law, is in a sense transnational law. The EU is a transnational body, so the laws that it produces are transnational by virtue of their institutional source. We have noted, however, that in another sense EU contract law is essentially national, for the directives that constitute EU contract law cannot, in principle, have any direct legal effect on private parties until they have been implemented by national law. Given that it is national contract laws which courts must actually follow, albeit interpreted in the light of the underling directive, we could insist that in an important sense contract law still remains national law. This paradoxical feature of EU contract law, that is both transnational and national, can be expressed in the (unenlightening) terminology of the construction of a multi-level system of contract law.[47]

Here, I want to suggest that EU contract law has been received as transnational law in a different and more profound way than has so far been acknowledged in this chapter. To the extent that this treatment of EU contract law as transnational law has been accepted by senior judges in the national legal orders, this development may also be regarded as a revolution in the technical sense of a change in the rule of recognition.

For this revolution to occur, EU contract law has to be regarded or invented as part of a transnational body of a general law of contract. Lawyers must imagine that behind the details of the EU directives they will find such things as 'European principles of contract law' or more broadly 'European principles of private law'. Such principles may also be described as *ius commune*. This mindset that imagines the existence of such principles is particularly popular amongst professors of comparative law, but it is spread far more widely in university law schools, and even to some extent in senior national courts.[48] The CJEU sometimes encourages such a mindset

[47] H Collins, *The European Civil Code: The Way Forward* (Cambridge, Cambridge University Press, 2008) ch 7; cf C Joerges, 'European Challenges to Private Law: On False Dichotomies, True Conflicts and the Need for a New Constitutional Perspective' (1998) 18(2) *Legal Studies* 146.

[48] MW Hesselink, 'The General Principles of Civil Law: Their Nature, Roles and Legitimacy' in D Leczykiewicz and S Weatherill (eds), *The Involvement of EU Law in Private Law Relationships* (Oxford, Hart Publishing, 2012) 131; S Weatherill, 'Case Note: "The Principles of Civil Law" as a Basis for Interpreting the Legislative Acquis' (2010) *European Review of Contract Law* 75; C Mak, 'Hedgehogs in Luxembourg? A Dworkinian Reading of the CJEU's Case Law on Principles of Private Law and Some Doubts of the Fox' (2012) 20 *European Review of Private Law* 323; C Semmelmann, 'Legal Principles in EU Law as an Expression of a European Legal Culture between Unity and Diversity' in G Helleringer and K Purnhagen (eds), *Towards a European Legal Culture* (Baden Baden, Nomos, 2014) 303.

by its references to general principles of law.[49] The content of these principles is variously regarded as a kind of synthesis of existing national legal systems, perhaps best articulated by the 'Lando Principles',[50] or an elaboration of presuppositions behind existing EU directives. In my view, the latter account is improbable, given what I have called the techno-law aspect of EU directives and how they constitute a different kind of law from private law.[51] The former approach also encounters major problems since national systems of contract law differ significantly, so it is hard to discover or construct a synthesis. After all, it is those differences that are relied upon by the EU Commission as the main justification for the need for a harmonising directive as opposed to relying upon private international law. But let us assume that it might be possible to produce a plausible comprehensive statement of the general principles of European contract law and examine the mindset that treats those principles as a source of law.

In the *Simone Leitner* case, the question was whether damages could be awarded against a travel agent for a family's loss of enjoyment of a holiday owing to food poisoning. Under the relevant Package Travel Directive,[52] compensation could be awarded for the damage resulting from improper performance of the contract. Under the applicable Austrian law, compensation could be awarded for pain and suffering, but not for loss of enjoyment. The Court of Justice ruled that compensation for loss of enjoyment was required by the Directive apparently on the ground advanced by the Commission that most legal systems of the Member States recognised the principle of compensation for loss of enjoyment in such cases. Here, the Court of Justice relied on comparative law to find a common principle of European contract law in order to supplement the terse Directive. It imagined that behind the Directive lay a principle of European contract law that could be used to place a more precise interpretation on the Directive's statement that the consumer should be compensated for the loss of an enjoyable holiday.

The reason why such a mindset represents a revolution in the sense of a change in the rule of recognition is that it mandates a change in the way in which courts should interpret and develop the law of contract.[53] In a case such as *Simone Leitner*, it seems that in interpreting the Directive and the implementing national law, the Austrian court should have paid attention to the general principles of European contract law. To discover those general principles, it would need to treat the synthesis of

[49] See, eg, Case C-277/05 *Société thermal d'Eugénie-les-Bains v Ministère de l'Economie, des Finances et de l'Industrie* [2007] ECR I-06145, [24]; Case C-412/06 *Annelore Hamilton v Volksbank Filder eG* [2008] ECR I-02383, [42]; *Pia Messner v Firma Stefan Krüger*, above n 30, [26].

[50] O Lando and H Beale (eds), *Principles of European Contract Law, Parts I and II* (The Hague, Kluwer, 2000); O Lando, E Clive, A Prum and R Zimmermann (eds), *Principles of European Contract Law Part III* (The Hague, Kluwer, 2003).

[51] H Collins, 'The Alchemy of Deriving General Principles of Contract Law from European Legislation: In Search of the Philosopher's Stone' (2006) 2 *European Review of Contract Law* 213.

[52] Directive 90/314 on package travel, package holidays and package tours [1990] OJ L158/59, Art 5(2).

[53] H Collins, 'Governance Implications for the European Union of the Changing Character of Private Law' in F Cafaggi and H Muir-Watt (eds), *Making European Private Law: Governance Design* (Cheltenham, Edward Elgar, 2008) 269.

decisions of the national courts of Member States as determinative of their content. Of course, courts often look at what other judges have done in similar situations, in order to discover whether clever solutions have already been worked out elsewhere. What I am suggesting is a different use of foreign judgments, however, for in the mindset I am describing, a court feels under an obligation to consult these foreign sources because they must be regarded as at least persuasive legal authority, since they may express what could be termed the relevant general principles of European contract law.[54] If most or all other European legal systems would take a different approach to a problem, a court might feel under pressure to reconsider its own national law. In other words, the rule of recognition must have changed if national courts now regard it as necessary to align their decisions on interpretations of the law of contract with the principles of European contract law.

Furthermore, the mindset of transnational private law suggests that national courts must pay attention to the guidance to be derived from the interpretations placed by foreign courts on any national contract law that implements an EU directive. For example, a German civil court might regard it as necessary and appropriate to discover and probably copy what French and UK courts have viewed as the correct interpretation of a detailed implication of a directive. The interpretations by foreign courts are not strictly binding under EU law, for under the Treaties it is only judgments of the CJEU that are binding on Member States. Even so, it will clearly undermine the purpose of techno-laws that seek to harmonise or unify contract law if national courts each place their own different interpretations on laws that implement EU directives. Whilst it is inevitable that 'unifying law ends up making new differences' between national contract laws, as Teubner said,[55] national courts can reduce the problem by at least acknowledging from the perspective of techno-law the potential advantages of uniform interpretations and applications in concrete situations. It would indeed be odd if a term in a standard form contract that was regarded as unfair to the consumer and unenforceable in Germany could be enforced before the British courts. True, odd things happen sometimes,[56] but by treating the decision of the foreign court as persuasive authority in the sense of creating a presumption in favour of a particular interpretation, the deviations in interpretations should be minimised. That process of judicial harmonisation by interpretation appears to involve a change in the rule of recognition by elevating the decisions of foreign courts on a particular matter to the status of prima facie binding precedents, which is a status that they never enjoyed in the past.

[54] H Collins, 'The Voice of the Community in Private Law Discourse' (1997) 3 *European Law Journal* 407.

[55] G Teubner, 'Legal Irritants: Good Faith in British Law or How Unifying Law Ends Up in New Divergences' (1998) 61 *MLR* 11.

[56] Compare *Office of Fair Trading v Abbey National plc* [2009] UKSC 6 with the German decisions Bundesgerichtshof [German Federal Court of Justice], XI ZR 5/97, 21 October 1997 reported in (1998) NJW 309 and Bundesgerichtshof, XI ZR 154/04, 8 October 2005 reported in (2005) NJW 1645, as discussed in M Schillig, 'European Contract Law-Making and Development: Lessons from the Unfair Contract Terms Directive's Price Term Exemption' in J Devenney and M Kenny (eds), *The Transformation of European Private Law* (Cambridge, Cambridge University Press, 2013) 256, 267–71.

This belief in European contract law as real transnational law, in the sense that the source of contract law is ultimately to be discovered in a transnational common law rather than national law, is not a belief that has wholeheartedly been accepted by judges in Europe so far, though no doubt attitudes vary between countries and between individuals. To the extent that this belief in the existence in a real European transnational contract law becomes ever more popular, however, it demands another shift in the rule of recognition, for the principles of the *ius commune* (or however it is described) must logically be regarded as the ultimate source of European contract law.

VI. POST-NATIONAL LAW

In this chapter, I have suggested a narrative that explains how the directives that comprise the bulk of what is known as EU contract law have provoked reactions from national courts as they seek to incorporate this narrowly instrumentalised law into their existing systems of contract law. When national courts refer a case to the CJEU on the ground that some aspect of EU law requires a definitive interpretation, I have suggested that in fact what is often happening is that the national court is asking how best to integrate the EU directive into its national private law system, bearing in mind the latter's diversity of policy considerations and attachment to corrective justice principles between the parties. In the absence of a more general framework of contract law on which to rely, the CJEU has sought to discover solutions to this problem of reconciling EU legislation with national contract law by treating the Charter, and the fundamental rights expressed therein, as one source of contract law. An alternative strategy employed by the CJEU has been to assert the existence of a common law of contract, shared by Member States, from which unwritten principles may be derived.

Whilst these devices have provided the CJEU with some assistance in offering solutions to national courts, my contention has been that these new sources of EU contract law, found in the Charter of Fundamental Rights and general unwritten principles, represent a profound change in the rule of recognition for EU Member States. To discover the content of contract law where it is affected by EU Treaties or legislation, a national court must not only have regard to the applicable directive, but must also interpret that legislation in accordance with fundamental rights and general principles of law.

It has also been argued that these two new sources of contract law should not be regarded as minor changes in the sources of law. The reference to the Charter of Fundamental Rights implies a shift away from a formalist rule-book conception of the rule of law towards a more substantive rights-based rule of law. In other words, to discover the content of EU contract law, it is not sufficient to discover the meaning of the relevant legislation; rather, it is necessary to ensure that any interpretation conforms to an accurate interpretation of the moral and political rights of citizens contained in the Charter. The reference to fundamental principles of European contract law implies that the CJEU no longer regards national contract law as the most basic source of contract law, but rather is developing a post-national law that represents some kind of synthesis of the traditional private law systems of European countries.

Putting these two developments together, it seems accurate to claim that a revolution has taken place in the sense of a change in the rule of recognition. When viewed in combination, these changes in the rule of recognition appear to embrace the idea of a post-national law or a cosmopolitan law, which is really transnational because new norms and principles can be generated at a transnational level without the requirement for further authorisation by national law or positive EU law. Moreover, this post-national law seems to embrace elements of the idea of Kantian cosmopolitan law in the way that private law and the law of contract are regarded as framed by and legitimated by fundamental rights that are shared by all.[57]

[57] I Kant, *Toward Perpetual Peace and Other Writings on Politics, Peace, and History*, P Kleingeld ed, DL Colclasure trans (New Haven, Yale University Press, 2006).

Index

www.ingramcontent.com/pod-product-compliance
Ingram Content Group UK Ltd.
Pitfield, Milton Keynes, MK11 3LW, UK
UKHW050943290926
15470UKWH00005B/1613

9 781509 913244